# REAL LIFE *at the* WHITE HOUSE

## TWO HUNDRED YEARS OF DAILY LIFE AT
## AMERICA'S MOST FAMOUS RESIDENCE

# REAL LIFE *at the* WHITE HOUSE

## TWO HUNDRED YEARS OF DAILY LIFE AT AMERICA'S MOST FAMOUS RESIDENCE

John Whitcomb and
Claire Whitcomb

ROUTLEDGE *New York London*

PUBLISHED IN 2000 BY

Routledge
29 West 35th Street
New York, NY 10001

Published in Great Britain by
Routledge
11 New Fetter Lane
London EC4P 4EE

Routledge is an imprint of the Taylor & Francis Group.

*Cataloging-in-Publication Data is available from the Library of Congress.*

Title page and chapter opening photograph: south view of the White House, showing awning (Library of Congress). Title page photo of George Bush: detail of photograph that appears on page 445 (Corbis).

*For Jesse and Carrie Klein*

# Contents

# Introduction

"HONEY," Ronald Reagan said to his wife, Nancy, when he heard tourists downstairs at the White House, "I'm still living over the store." In the United States being president comes with an unstated requirement: the person who holds the office must live "over the store" in a house that is part national monument, part office, and last but not least, part home.

Beginning with John Adams, who endured still-wet plaster and an outdoor privy, each president has had to wrestle with the issue of livability. Rarely does a first family enter enamored of the decor of its predecessors. Tastes vary, and styles change. In a regular house redecoration might take place once or twice in a generation. At the White House change is constant, occurring every four to eight years as new residents arrive. In the course of two centuries, the White House has surely been redecorated and remodeled more frequently than any similarly historic house.

Often refurbishment has been a necessity, not a luxury, since the White House, first and foremost a public building, absorbs an enormous amount of wear. As wallpaper has frayed and carpets thinned, the White House, officially known as either the President's House or the Executive Mansion until Theodore Roosevelt formalized its name in 1901, has been termed everything from "Public Shabby House," as it was in John Tyler's time, to "national disgrace," the words of Nixon curator Clement Conger. But it also has been a showcase for the new and the best, acquiring a telephone long before there was anyone besides the Treasury Department to talk to, and being wired for electricity when turning off the switches still yielded shocks (Benjamin Harrison refused to turn off the lights, delegating the task to servants). In terms of design, the quest to be au courant has meant that decor has shifted from the French style admired by James Monroe to the Steamboat Gothic brought in by Ulysses S. Grant, from the high-society redecoration executed by Louis Comfort Tiffany for Chester A. Arthur to the neoclassical 1902 remodeling of Charles McKim, Theodore Roosevelt's architect.

In the twentieth century, the design pendulum has swung less widely, as presidents have primarily focused on making the house more "authentic," introducing American antiques and undoing the too-European beaux arts look of McKim. From Coolidge's time on, museum experts, architects, and design authorities have offered advice on decor, a process that was formalized when Jacqueline Kennedy established the Fine Arts Commission, chaired by Henry F. du Pont, founder of Winterthur Museum, the leading repository of early American decorative arts. She also established the Office of the Curator in 1961, bringing museum standards to the care of White House art and antiques. But over the last eighty years, the concept of what is appropriately American has changed. For instance the Blue Room, redone in 1972 to critical acclaim, was considered inaccurate and lackluster when its wallpaper and rug finally wore out twenty years later. Both the Clintons and the Nixons had the same goal—to bring back the house's design heyday, the twenty-five years that stretched from John Adams's arrival in 1800 to James Monroe's departure in 1825—but by 1994 the Nixon colors were not considered blue enough, the carpet was thought to be incorrect, the abundance of Duncan Phyfe furniture distracted from the historic Monroe Bellangé suite, and change became an academic necessity.

In addition to the obvious fascination with how forty different residents have altered one building, a chronicle of White House life offers an over-the-shoulder view of the presidency. Upstairs at the White House we see James Garfield wrestling with his children just before he departs for the train station where an assassin awaits. Downstairs we see Ulysses S. Grant, smoking, playing billiards, and exchanging war stories with old friends. What could characterize Herbert Hoover's standoffishness better than his insistence that the White House servants never be seen, even though that meant they had to take refuge in closets when three bells sounded his imminent arrival? What could illustrate Richard Nixon's introversion better than his habit of bowling game after solitary game, dressed in a shirt and tie, in the White House's lone bowling lane?

By looking at a president's domestic life we also see the impact of a first lady on his political success. Dolley Madison, with her talent for entertaining, courted favor among congressmen, which was important since at the time congressional leaders determined their party's presidential nomination. Sarah Polk served as her husband's secretary and adviser and boldly announced that she had little interest in housekeeping. Grace Coolidge's abundant charm did much to smooth matters for her taciturn husband, who preferred to eat in silence, even at state dinners. And of course Hillary Clinton, like her role model Eleanor Roosevelt, was deeply enmeshed in the affairs of state, breaking tradition and taking an office in the West Wing near her husband's.

In surveying the different cast of characters who have shared the same quarters, it is also possible to watch the changing pressures of the presidency. The amiable war hero William Henry Harrison was able to stroll downtown, market basket on his arm. Grace

Coolidge shopped at Garfinkels department store, where a salesgirl asked if people told her she looked like Mrs. Coolidge. Even Harry Truman set out for brisk 6 A.M. walks with his Secret Service agents until an assassination attempt curtailed his movements. From that time to the present, each successive president has slowly been surrounded by more and more security and longer and longer motorcades, essentially confining him to a small oasis of privacy: the private quarters on the second and third floors. But only Grover Cleveland, protective of his new bride and later his young daughters, was bold enough to purchase a suburban home and treat the White House as a place for work and official entertaining.

Designed "for the ages" as George Washington insisted it be, the White House was the grandest home in America until 1870, so grand that in Thomas Jefferson's time it was decried as "a great stone house, big enough for two emperors, one pope, and the grand lama." In the early years keeping up such a sizable establishment left many a president—Jefferson and Monroe, for instance—debt-ridden. The chief executive's $25,000 salary had to cover the requisite servants, their food, and the costs associated with dinners and receptions, including the traditional New Year's Day and Fourth of July open houses attended by hundreds and sometimes thousands. Though presidential budgets for entertaining were gradually established after the Civil War, even Franklin Roosevelt found it difficult to make ends meet and had to draw upon family resources to cover his White House expenses.

Though funds for decorating and furnishing are now primarily raised from private sources (a policy begun in the Kennedy administration), moneys were initially provided by Congress, at its discretion. If the legislative branch was feuding with the executive branch, presidents like John Tyler and Andrew Johnson found themselves having to make do with worn tattered curtains and upholstery, reminders of the thousands of guests who visited them each year. But when a spurt of decorating has been financed, presidents have had to live and often work while the house is refurbished around them. As a public building, the White House has no down time. When the Blue Room and State Dining Room were redone in 1994, January was chosen because it is the quietest time, after the influx of Christmas tourists and the giddy round of Christmas parties.

John Adams was the first to live with hammering and papering, which continued through Thomas Jefferson's term. James Madison continued the sprucing up, and just as the rooms finally approached an appropriate level of distinction, the British invaded Washington and left the White House a smoldering shell, nothing more than four fire-blackened stone walls. In a burst of flames, furnishings, plants, and artifacts, some dating back to George Washington's time, were lost.

James Hoban, the original architect of the White House, was brought in to supervise its reconstruction. When Monroe was able to move in the October after his 1817 inauguration, he faced the same situation Adams had: barely dry plaster and the pernicious smell of paint. Later Chester A. Arthur, Theodore Roosevelt, Calvin Coolidge, and Harry Truman all had to vacate the presidential home while major work took place.

But even when the house has been in tip-top shape, as it was when George Bush took office, all presidents have faced a compromised lifestyle because of the public nature of the home. From the beginning, the White House has been perceived as the people's house, and it was thought that any of its landlords had the right to come in for a look or confront the president with a problem. In the nineteenth century the East

Room and sometimes the state rooms were open to the public. Access was so casual that in Van Buren's day a drunk wandered in and slept on the sofa. Charles Dickens recorded how he walked up to the White House when Tyler was president and "thrice rang the bell, which nobody answered." So he walked in.

Normally a doorman screened undesirables, but visitors and job seekers were welcome. Until the assassination of James A. Garfield by a disgruntled office seeker prompted the institution of the civil service, the bulk of government jobs, everything from postman to ambassador, required presidential patronage. And so the job-hungry lined the stairway to the presidential offices on the second floor, leading William Henry Harrison to complain that he could not attend to "the necessary functions of nature." On one occasion he could not even find an empty room to hold a cabinet meeting and became so engulfed by frantic office seekers who insisted that he receive their papers that finally in desperation he gave in to them.

With the demands of the presidency increasing, especially during and after the Civil War, office space vied with living space on the second floor. Benjamin Harrison's wife Caroline, whose family numbered eleven, proposed an elaborate expansion of the White House, but she crossed Congress and the plan was vetoed. Two presidents later, when Theodore Roosevelt took office, Congress finally agreed that the time had come to stop shoehorning the presidency into the White House.

In 1902 Roosevelt brought in the fashionable New York architect Charles McKim, of McKim, Mead & White, who roamed the rooms, sketchbook in hand, and essentially rethought the White House. McKim was determined to "restore" George Washington's vision even though there were no original sketches to rely upon. He undid years of Victorian tinkering, including the elaborate redecoration by Louis Comfort Tiffany. He tore down the glass conservatories that had grown up on the roofs of the wings and the grounds adjacent to the White House and added what is now the West Wing as a home for the president's office and the business portion of his life. To meet the increased entertaining needs of the president, McKim expanded the State Dining Room by knocking out a wall. He moved stairways and added bathrooms but not closets—Edith Roosevelt thought they would compromise the scale of the family rooms. The actual Oval Office was not installed until Taft's time and it wasn't moved into its current corner position until Franklin Roosevelt's administration.

Unfortunately, the removal of the State Dining Room wall caused stress on the roof, which by 1923 started sagging. Cracks appeared in the second-floor rooms, and Calvin Coolidge was advised that the roof and the third-floor attic area needed to be totally rebuilt. For twenty years, this renovation was applauded because the garreted attic was expanded to make proper guest rooms. But the architects' overzealous addition of a 180-ton concrete-and-steel third floor left the White House tottering by 1949. Harry S. Truman moved out for four years while the building was entirely gutted and refitted with steel beams.

Redecorated with reproduction furniture from B. Altman, the New York department store, the White House remained a repository of middlebrow taste until Jacqueline Kennedy, wife of John F. Kennedy, moved in 1961. Her initial response to her government-required home was to burst into tears. But upon reflection, she determined it should be a museum-quality showcase of American decorative arts. Jackie Kennedy helped found the White House Historical Association, part guardian angel, part fund-raiser for the house. And she stimulated legislation that made presidential furnishings "inalienable and the property of the White House." Thus a president could no longer lose a barrel of White House china in a poker bet, as Warren G. Harding did, or send furnishings off to auction, as was routine in the nineteenth century.

Despite its two hundred years, the White House is perhaps more beautiful than ever. Millions of dollars of private money have filled it with rare art and antiques, with oriental rugs and historic wallpaper. Curator Rex Scouten and his skilled staff care for the house as if it were the Metropolitan Museum of Art. But is it a home? Raisa Gorbachev, wife of the Soviet premier, gave her view when given a tour by Nancy Reagan: "It's an official house. I would say that humanly speaking a human being would like to live in a regular home. This is a museum." Indeed the house is certified as a museum, so designated in 1988 by the American Association of Museums. But the family quarters, which include nine bedrooms, a family room, a presidential study, a formal dining room, and a tiny eat-in kitchen, create an oasis of privacy within a heavily guarded house.

Gone are the days when Calvin Coolidge could go to his Secret Service agent's hotel and rouse him for a walk. But a comment from Coolidge still characterizes the White House. Returning from a walk, a senator facetiously asked Coolidge, "I wonder who lives there?"

"Nobody," the president replied. "They just come and go."

# George Washington

## 1789–1797

## *The Foundation Is Laid*

THE MOST FAMOUS BUILDING that George Washington never slept in is the White House. He died in 1799, a year before the plaster dried and John Adams took up residence in a raw and muddy city. But Washington certainly slept in the White House in his imagination, because the building firmly reflects his vision of what a presidential home should be: a stately stone structure, rich in architectural embellishments; a design similar to an English country seat, built on as palatial a scale as politics would allow.

Other people—Secretary of State Thomas Jefferson chief among them—had differing ideas about what befitted the residence of a democratic leader. Jefferson lobbied for a temple-like brick building set in a small city with a plan similar to Williamsburg. New York and Philadelphia not only conceived their own mansions with the oval rooms Washington favored but went ahead and built them, hoping that the federal government's new home wouldn't be built within the ten-year deadline—1790 to 1800—that Congress allotted.

But Washington felt strongly that the hundred-square-mile tract of orchards, forests, and tobacco farms—land ceded by Virginia and Maryland that was neither north nor south—was the best place for the capital. He made the White House his project.

If anyone should know what was required of a presidential mansion, it was the man who lived in a redbrick mansion on Philadelphia's Cherry Street, the mansion rented to

1

the government by Robert Morris. The house, considered grand, was actually cramped when it had to accommodate the president, his wife, their two grandchildren, twenty servants, clerks, and guests who packed the president's weekly drawing rooms and levees. Washington complained that anyone coming to see him on business would have to climb "two pairs of stairs and pass by the public rooms." It was a situation he didn't want to recur.

At the beginning of his first term Washington said, "I walk on untrodden ground. There is scarcely any part of my conduct which may not hereafter be drawn into precedent." He had to decide how one of the first leaders of a democracy should live, having no role models save kings and dictators. At first Washington democratically kept his door open, welcoming any citizen who might wander by, but quickly learned the impracticality of the situation. "From the time I had done breakfast and thence till dinner and afterwards till bedtime," he wrote, "I could not get relieved from the ceremony of one visit before I had to attend to another."

His solution was announced three days after his 1789 inauguration in the *New York Federal Gazette of the United States:* "We are informed that the President has assigned every Tuesday and Friday, between the hours of 2 and 3 for receiving visits; that visits of compliment on other days and particularly Sunday, will not be agreeable to him. It seems to be a prevailing opinion that so much of the President's time will be engaged by various and important business imposed on him by the Constitution that he will find himself constrained to omit returning visits, or accepting invitations to entertainments."

Though officials wanting to see the president could make an appointment at any time, the restriction of "visits of compliment" to an hour a week provoked a round of public complaints. In response, Washington wrote to his friend James Madison, as well as to John Adams, his vice president, Secretary of the Treasury Alexander Hamilton, and Chief Justice John Jay asking them their opinions on "a line of conduct most eligible to be pursued by the President of the United States." His questions included: Was it sufficient to receive the public once a week? Would even that just invite "impertinent applications"? Would it be all right if he simply left to have tea with a friend?

The schedule was expanded to include Friday-night teas known as drawing rooms. They were held at 8 P.M. and hostessed by Martha Washington, dressed in white muslin and seated beside Abigail Adams, wife of the vice president. Tea, cake, and candied fruit were served, and sociability was the order of the day. In contrast, the one-hour levee, held at 2 P.M. in New York and later at 3 P.M. in Philadelphia, was male-only and pure pomp.

The term *levee*, borrowed from the courts of Europe, comes from the French "to rise," and the American interpretation was literal. George Washington stood, back to the fireplace, in an oval room barren of chairs and greeted gentlemen bearing an invitation or letter of introduction. The event was stiff, formal, and intermittently silent. After being announced, each guest would walk toward the president, who stood, one hand on his dress sword, the other on his feathered cockade hat. Handshaking thus deterred, the guest would bow and silently take a place on the perimeter of the room. After fifteen minutes, the doors were shut to bar further arrivals and Washington proceeded from one man to the next, bowing and making small talk. When he'd finished his rounds, he returned to his place, and the guests went up one by one, repeated their bows, and silently departed.

From a contemporary point of view, the whole affair seems slightly ridiculous, since little of substance could be accomplished. But Washington understood the ceremonial needs of a new country. His levees were well attended by politicians and businessmen, except on one snowy afternoon close to the Christmas holiday when he dressed in his black velvet suit, put on his silver knee and shoe buckles, and strapped on his dress sword only to find no guests had arrived.

Nonetheless Washington favored the levee. He'd replaced the square corners of two rooms in his Philadelphia house with bowed walls so that they'd be more suitable to receiving guests in a circle. And though he did not design the floor plan of the White House himself, it is no coincidence that oval rooms were included on both the first and second floor—today the Blue Room and the Yellow Oval Room. In addition a third oval room was built in the basement underneath the other two oval rooms. Once a furnace room, this is today the Diplomatic Reception Room. Nor is it a surprise that the White House includes the East Room, a large room for hosting crowds very like the one Washington added on to Mount Vernon.

Ultimately the White House was designed by architect James Hoban, using a Dublin estate called Leinster House as inspiration. But Hoban, a competent builder astute about changing political winds, was not Washington's first choice as presidential architect.

When Congress passed the Residence Act of 1790, putting the president in charge of establishing the capital, Washington turned to Major Pierre Charles L'Enfant to lay out the new city and design its buildings as one piece. Weaned on the grandeur of Versailles, L'Enfant had come to America in 1777 to fight in the Revolutionary War. He knew Washington and had painted his portrait at Valley Forge. L'Enfant's peacetime specialty was pageantry. He'd organized elaborate public fetes and parades in New York City and had redesigned the Federal Hall to evoke the senate of Rome.

In a country with few talented architects, L'Enfant was the natural choice to design the new capital, and he knew it. In 1789, before the federal district was even approved, he wrote Washington, saying, "I now presume to sollicit [sic] the favor of being Employed in this business." The president complied readily. Though the planning of the city was technically the domain of three federal commissioners—gentlemen who met monthly and worked without salary—L'Enfant viewed Washington's favor as license to do what he pleased. In the spring of 1791 he traveled to the proposed capital, sited a ridge for a palace, and planned a European-style city of grand vistas and broad avenues radiating from central points. By the winter of the same year, he'd supervised the digging of cellars for a palace five times the size of the house that ended up being built. Roads were staked through fields. And then after the turn of the new year, in February 1792, he was fired.

No one regretted this more than his faithful patron, Washington. The president had worked closely with L'Enfant on his plans and seconded his vision of a house for the ages, one large enough to anticipate governmental needs yet unknown. In March and then June of 1791 Washington traveled to the new federal city and walked with L'Enfant, pacing out his dreams. Dissatisfied with the site the designer had chosen for the White House, Washington shifted it to its current spot, higher on the ridge to the west. L'Enfant, temperamental on a grand scale, kept the president happy but approached the commissioners and virtually everyone else with arrogance. His interest was perfection, not speed, even though speed was a political necessity. The newly centralized government needed a home, and if L'Enfant couldn't build it quickly, New York and Philadelphia would be more than happy to provide a seat of power.

When Washington finally fired L'Enfant, no one was more thrilled than Jefferson, who saw a fresh chance for his small brick city. He convinced the president to hold a competition for the design of the president's house and capitol, and on March 14, 1792, advertisements were printed offering a prize of "500 dollars or a medal of that value" for winning designs. Despite Washington's insistence that the presidential dwelling be built of stone, Jefferson called for brick. His specifications were adroitly ignored by the winner.

James Hoban, an Irish immigrant responsible for some of Charleston's fine public buildings, had attracted Washington's interest when the president had made a tour of the South in 1791. But a year later his name had been forgotten. Inquiries were made and in June 1792, a month before the competition deadline, Hoban met with the president in Philadelphia and then at the president's bidding went south to contemplate the site L'Enfant had chosen. In July, Washington followed suit, traveling to Georgetown to review the nine competition entries, which included a Palladian-style Villa Rotunda attributed to Jefferson.

Hoban accepted his prize medal, and Washington, a gentleman architect who had significantly remodeled Mount Vernon, immediately began tinkering with the winning design. He requested that the size be increased by 20 percent and that carvings and architectural details be added. While he was still in Georgetown, the president went with Hoban to the site of the gaping foundation of the White House and made sure the

*The carvings over the north door were ordered by George Washington. Over the years their beauty was muted by over forty coats of paint but during the Bush and Clinton administrations, the layers of paint have been carefully stripped off and the carvings repainted.* (LIBRARY OF CONGRESS)

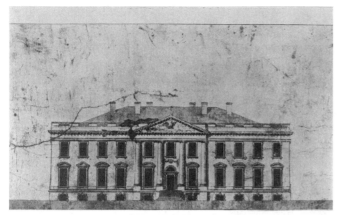

*Architect James Hoban was recruited by George Washington to enter a design contest for the new President's House. He used Dublin's Leinster House as inspiration and his original 1792 design, shown here, included a raised basement. This was eliminated due to rising costs.* (LIBRARY OF CONGRESS)

front door of the revised palace would remain exactly where L'Enfant intended it. Some months later, on October 13, 1792, the cornerstone was laid amid speeches and ceremony. Washington stayed in Philadelphia. His anchoring had already been done.

Hoban had planned a house of three stories, but the need to compromise quickly arose. The increased size and orders for embellishments led to rising costs. Rather than compromise the dimensions of the house, Washington agreed to eliminate the first story, reducing the White House to a size that is familiar today. The commissioners assured him that in the future an extra floor could be added, and indeed in the Coolidge administration the attic space was converted into a proper third story.

To further cut costs the commissioners decided to use solid stone on the bottom floor only. For the rest of the house they used brick faced with stone. Pale gray with tints of red, Aquia Creek freestone is a porous rock and needs to be sealed with lime wash or paint, a procedure that continues today.

Construction hit snags. In a city that was urban in name only, skilled laborers were scarce, especially since slave labor kept wages in the South low. Hoban advertised in Scotland for stonecutters, and slaves were hired out to help with the work. Slowly the walls rose, Ionic capitals were carved, and the roof was framed. Washington observed the progress now and then, stopping by on his travels from Philadelphia to Mount Vernon.

By the end of Washington's term in 1797, the house, which would be the largest in the United States for the next seventy years, was touted by Jefferson's Republican party as a folly. With the Capitol still unfinished, Congress threatened to set up shop in the president's house or use it to house the Supreme Court. The commissioners worried that workmen should be shifted to the Capitol. Washington quickly vetoed the plan, insisting that the President's House be completed as well. "I require it," he wrote in no uncertain terms.

On March 4, 1797, his long years of public service finally over, Washington and his family headed to Mount Vernon one last time. They stopped in what is now known as Washington, District of Columbia, and viewed the White House. The sky was visible through the roof. The floors were laid of wood instead of the more expensive marble that Washington had wanted. The yard was littered with construction supplies and workers' shanties. People called it the President's House, but the mansion was as much Washington's as the city that bore his name.

In 1788 the Constitution gave Congress the authority to establish a hundred-square-mile district for the capital in whatever states ceded the land. Sectional squabbling kept the new city's location in limbo until July 1790, when President George Washington won the support for a site on the Potomac River by agreeing to pay the states' war debts, a move that benefited the North and convinced it to let the capital go south of Philadelphia.

Maryland ceded land along the upper bank of the Potomac, Virginia land along the lower bank. The latter tract, which included the port city of Alexandria, was returned to Virginia in 1846. The Potomac and its tributary, the Anacostia, were edged by marshes, fields, and woods. Washington knew the area well. In 1785 he'd become involved in a company that built the Chesapeake and Ohio Canal.

As soon as Congress, meeting in New York, passed the Residence Act of 1790 transferring the seat of government to Philadelphia and then, in 1800, to the District of Columbia, the residents of the planned Federal City were transformed from a meandering assortment of farmers to avid land speculators. On March 30, 1791, George Washington wrote in his diary that "whilst they were contending for the shadow they might lose the substance."

He had a particular problem with one of the richest men in the area, David Burnes, whose property was located between the hill chosen for the Capitol and the rise selected for the President's House. In a letter, Washington referred to him as "the obstinate Mr. Burnes," and finally wrote him, "I have been authorized to select the location of the National Capital. I have selected your farm as part of it, and the government will take it at all events. I trust you will, under the circumstances, enter into an amicable arrangement."

With a series of skillful negotiations, Washington and the commissioners he appointed to oversee the federal city succeeded in acquiring 4,000 acres—about six square miles, a tract larger than Boston and roughly the size of Philadelphia—within the federal district. To lay out the city, the president called on Major Pierre Charles L'Enfant, who presented a magnificent plan of radiating avenues that the *Maryland Journal* heralded as an "inconceivable improvement over all other cities in the world" on September 30, 1791.

But few who came to Washington, D.C., when the government officially took up residence in November 1800 would have termed the city an improvement at all. The capital had 366 houses, 109 of them built of brick, and a population of 3,000, including several lawyers, three or four physicians, and about six pastors. There were 501 heads of household, 19 of whom were landowners who had made agreements with Washington.

To the west of the President's House lay Georgetown, connected by a mile-long rutted road. It had 5,000 inhabitants in 1800 and was deemed by Abigail Adams to be "the dirtyest Hole I ever saw." To the east of the President's House, Pennsylvania Avenue ran through what had been David Burnes's cornfield. It was "nearly the whole distance a deep morass, covered with alder bushes," wrote Congressman John Cotton of Connecticut.

Roads in general were scarce, and those that did exist were filled with holes and stumps. Travel at night was risky, especially because Congress refused to pay for such improvements as streetlights. "I took a hack after dinner to visit Nath'l Maxwell," wrote one New Yorker to his wife, "and . . . I considered my life in danger. The distance on straight lines does not exceed half a mile, but I had to ride up and down very steep hills, with frightful gullies on almost every side."

Amusements were few. A theater opened in August 1800 but closed the next month. Housing was scarce, and congressmen boarded two to a bed, except for the Speaker of the House, who had a bedroom to himself. Representative Richard Griswold of Connecticut wrote his wife, left behind as was the custom, that the city was "both melancholy and ludicrous."

The federal bureaucracy consisted of 131 employees. The chamber of the House of Representatives was used as a church, with ministers of different religions preaching from the desk of the Speaker. The Episcopalians set up shop in a tobacco house converted "in the plainest and rudest manner," according to Margaret Bayard Smith. A small group of Scottish Presbyterians worshiped in a corridor of the Treasury.

On the grounds of what is now Lafayette Park across from the White House a cherry orchard stood, uninterrupted by Pennsylvania Avenue, which didn't cut through until 1822. The Mall was a common for pasturing cows. The north side of Pennsylvania Avenue from Sixth to Thirteenth Streets was known as a good spot for fishing.

Despite the rawness of the town, the city was one of optimism. By the end of 1801 the number of finished houses had increased by nearly 40 percent in a single year. Patriotic praises were sung. "No town in the Union has advanced so rapidly," proclaimed the *Intelligencer.*

# John Adams

## 1797–1801

## *The Great Castle*

On October 13, 1800, John Adams, unaware that he would be unseated by the next month's elections, left his home in Quincy, Massachusetts. He'd summered there, safe from the yellow fever and pestilence of Philadelphia, a "bake-oven" that the government abandoned with the first heat wave. But Adams wasn't returning to the impressive brick mansion inhabited by George Washington in Philadelphia. He was heading south across rutted and torturous roads to an even less health-inducing place: a boggy swamp on the Potomac, the new, unfinished Federal City.

On July 17, 1790, Congress had decreed that the seat of government would move from New York to Philadelphia and then a decade later to Washington, D.C. Even with ten years' notice, construction was running late. At the President's House, only half of the thirty-six rooms had been plastered; wallpaper, chosen by the commissioners of the District of Columbia, had been hung only in the main rooms. In a last-minute attempt to cure some of the plaster, fires in the fireplaces burned round the clock.

George Washington had been greatly interested in the progress of the building, but Adams all but ignored it for the first three years of his term. Then as the time neared to crate the presidential furnishings and ship them from Philadelphia to Washington, he began to correspond with the commissioners. They assured him all would be ready for his autumn arrival. Adams decided to see for himself. When he left Philadelphia for Quincy, he and his secretary, Abigail's nephew William Shaw, made a quick detour to

Washington, traveling with two footmen and a new coachman. At the district line, an assemblage escorted them to Union Tavern in Alexandria. At Georgetown, a ceremony ensued. The next day they crossed Rock Creek Bridge and found a city very much under construction. Streets were unpaved, private houses scarce, but one wing of the Capitol neared completion, and the President's House appeared to Adams to have "a sufficient number of rooms" underway. The two stayed at Tunnicliff's City Hotel, suffered a round of entertainments, hastened to visit Martha Washington at Mount Vernon, and hurried north to join Abigail, who had preceded them to Quincy.

Now as Adams's return neared, the crated furniture and china were hastily unpacked and scattered round the house. The finished effect was far from successful. The new President's House, grander by far than the old, had rooms of such magnificent scale that only Gilbert Stuart's heroic painting of Washington—the lone work of art still in the house—looked at home.

The commissioners knew the date of Adams's departure from Quincy, but not that of his arrival. Guessing that the combination of roads and weather would put him in Washington on November 3, they inspected the President's House on the morning of the first. That afternoon, the Adams's coach and four, accompanied only by his servant John Briesler on horseback, rumbled down Pennsylvania Avenue. Throughout most of his journey, Adams had been greeted with such fanfare that he began to entertain hopes of a second presidential term. At the White House, however, all was quiet. Unanticipated, he entered the echoing rooms like an ordinary citizen. As his baggage was unpacked, word of his arrival spread, and callers arrived. After supper he took his candle, climbed the only finished stairway, a winding stair for the servants, and went to sleep.

The next day he wrote Abigail of his need for her: "The building is in a state to be habitable and now we wish for your company." He perhaps thought better of describing the condition the house was in, saying only that she would "form the best idea of it" when she saw it. He closed the letter with this now-famous petition: "I pray heaven to bestow the best of blessings on this house and all that shall hereafter inhabit it. May none but honest and wise men ever rule under this roof." Franklin Delano Roosevelt had the words inscribed on a plaque that was mounted on the fireplace mantel on the west wall of the State Dining Room.

As Adams penned his letter, Abigail was already on her way south. She left Quincy a week after her husband, stopping in New York to visit her son Charles for what would be the last time. Ruined by alcohol and financial speculation, he had been declining for some time, but now Abigail found him penniless, stricken with a consumptive cough, liver infection, and dropsy. He was twenty-nine and would not live out the month. The news of his death coincided with that of Adams's defeat in the November elections and cast an unshakable gloom over the White House.

Departing New York, Abigail took Charles's four-year-old daughter, Susanna, and continued to Philadelphia, where the two stayed at the old President's House, now a hotel. Then they braved the 150-mile trip to Abigail's "unseen abode." She traveled by carriage with ten horses and an entourage of nine. After Baltimore her party saw nothing but woods. The coachman took a wrong turn, causing them to become lost in woods so dense a man had to sit on the roof of the carriage, chopping away at branches. "Fortunately," Abigail would later write, "a straggling black came with us, and we engaged him as a guide to extricate us from our difficulties but woods are all you see until you reach the city which is so only in name." Washington's population at this time was about three thousand.

Exhausted by the trip, Abigail was glad to reach her new home but not overjoyed by the conditions that greeted her. The grounds of the President's House were littered with workmen's sheds, ditches, construction equipment, and piles of debris. The north and south porticoes had not yet been built. Abigail took her little granddaughter by the hand, and together they climbed a temporary wooden stair on the south facade that led to the inside of the house.

Abigail soon discovered that among the clothes and furnishings that had been shipped by boat, "many things were stolen, many things were broken." The high-ceilinged rooms were cold and drafty. "Shiver, shiver," she wrote. "Surrounded with forests, can you believe that wood is not to be had, because people cannot be found to cut and cart it." She suffered from feverish chills and rheumatism. The house required twelve stoked fireplaces to alleviate the damp and the cold. Her able servant Briesler purchased nine cords of wood and two hundred bushels of coal, expensive though it was. Proper grates were another matter. "We have indeed come into a new country," Abigail wrote.

When President Adams had visited in June, he'd stated two requirements: a vegetable garden and a system of bells to ring servants. The garden had duly been planted in the northeast corner, but as Abigail discovered, "To assist us in this great castle . . . bells are wholly wanting." In most proper houses, including the Adams home in Quincy, a cord could be pulled and a bell rung in the basement or kitchen to summon the necessary servant. The White House was cavernous and understaffed, and it remained so. In Philadelphia Abigail had thirty servants, and she estimated it would take a like number to run the White House and stables. Because Congress did not provide money for help, she brought only four servants with her to Washington. In addition John Briesler, who had been with the family in London and France, served as steward. His wife, Esther, acted as housekeeper.

As the Adamses set up house, construction continued. The back staircase was built, plastering and painting proceeded, leaks and cracks were repaired. But the constant flow of workmen was only one of the many inconveniences. The President's House lacked a well—it would arrive along with a wine cellar during Jefferson's administration. In the meantime, servants had to carry water from Franklin Park, nearly a half a mile away. For meat, animals were driven to the grounds and slaughtered on the premises. "We have not the least fence, yard, or other convenience without, and the great audience-room I make a drying room of, to hang up the clothes in," wrote Abigail. The "audience-room," later more democratically called the East Room, was a raw space, littered with tools, supplies, and construction debris. Washington had envisioned it as a space for formal entertaining, but the only use it saw in Adams's time was as a drying room.

The slow, inefficient, haphazard methods of southern construction bothered Abigail's New England soul. It was a different tempo of life. She deplored what she called "the want of punctuality." She believed that if the capital had been constructed in New England, "very many of the inconveniences would have been removed."

Abigail delved into the role of First Lady with determination, even though her chore of calling on ladies who left cards was far more difficult in spread-out Washington with its rutted, muddy streets than it had been in Philadelphia. "Yesterday I returned fifteen calls," she wrote—a time-consuming accomplishment. She marketed and returned calls in Georgetown—"the dirtyest Hole I ever saw."

Abigail had been apprehensive about following Martha Washington in the role of First Lady—she felt she lacked Martha's "patience, prudence, and discretion." But her deep love of politics—and her intimate intellectual partnership with her husband—made her perfect for the role. Abigail kept up on all the twists and turns of government, in addition to running a complicated household and managing the Quincy properties single-handedly. Plagued by insomnia, she was often up at five to read, pray, plan menus, and write the voluminous letters that kept her close to those she loved.

In Philadelphia the House and Senate called on the president at the beginning of a session, and so in November they braved the rain and the mud to cross the temporary wooden bridge that led to the north entrance of the President's House. Refreshments were prepared and served by the Brieslers, who were dressed in ordinary clothes, unlike Washington's servants in livery. Derogatory comments reached Abigail. Since the start of the administration, the cost of keeping up with Washington had worried Adams. "I expect to be obliged to resign in six months," he wrote when he first took office, fearful that his money would run out buying furniture and giving levees. When he first occupied the presidential mansion in Philadelphia, he was faced with replenishing a house with only a few pieces of run-down "public furniture" purchased courtesy of Congress. "There is not a chair fit to sit in. . . . The beds and bedding are in a woeful pickle. But somehow he and Abigail managed to find the $500 necessary to provide two hundred pounds of cake and two quarter casks of wine, plus quantities of rum, for parties such as a Fourth of July entertainment for members of Congress and various officials.

Although Abigail's letters from Washington, D.C., were full of the many problems she faced, she understood she was living in a house "built for the ages to come." She reveled in its "grand and superb scale" and the magnificent views of the Potomac. In a letter to her daughter Abigail she cautioned her not to repeat any criticisms, but when people "ask how I like it say that I wrote you the situation is beautiful."

As the president and first lady were settling into their new home, the election of 1800 unfolded. The electors of several states met on December 4. Though initial votes were in his favor, Adams's fate grew grimmer as the days passed. By December 23 it was clear that Jefferson and Burr had tied for the presidency, with seventy-three votes each. Adams, who had defeated Jefferson by just three votes in 1796, garnered only sixty-five.

A foreshortened tenure made the White House's inconveniences less important. Abigail said, "I could content myself almost anywhere three months." But defeat did little for Adams's spirits. The son of a Massachusetts farmer living in a small saltbox house, he had become one of the colony's preeminent lawyers and a leader of the Revolution in the Continental Congress. He had served as the first minister to Great Britain and signed the Treaty of Paris in 1783 that ended the Revolutionary War. With adoration and very little political tumult, he'd been elected as the first vice president, an

*John Adams became the second President and, in November 1800, the first to live in the still unfinished President's House, then the largest house in America. The capital had only about 400 structures and First Lady Abigail became lost in the woods trying to reach home.* (LIBRARY OF CONGRESS)

honor he deemed "the most insignificant office ever invented." He felt he deserved the presidency—along with the second term bestowed Washington. But the political seas were turbulent.

Though Adams and his fellow candidates kept to themselves and avoided the unseemly appearance of wanting an office, the papers boiled with vituperative sentiments. Once Benjamin Franklin Bache's *Aurora* went so far as to describe the president as "old, querulous, bald, blind, crippled, toothless Adams." The charges held an element of truth—Adams was sixty-four when he retired from the presidency. Dubbed "His Rotundity," he was five feet six inches, portly, and lacking in teeth. In politics, Adams was honest, blunt, and often tactless. Privately, in his diary, he called himself "puffy, vain, conceited." But in defeat he was simply wounded.

He had lived, he wrote, "a life of long journeys and distant voyages, in one or another of which I have been monthly and yearly engaged for two and forty years." He worried about embarking upon "a routine of domestic life," and wrote "something I must do or ennui will rain upon me in buckets." Abigail wrote to their son, Thomas, "I wish your father's circumstances were not so limited and circumscribed, as they must be, because he cannot indulge himself in those improvements upon his farm, which his inclination leads him to, and which would serve to amuse him, and contribute to his health."

Adams suffered a host of maladies—colds, headaches, heartburn, palsy. Writing was difficult and speaking even more so, due to a virtual absence of teeth (he refused to wear the crude dentures available). "My constitution is a glass bubble," he would complain. In times of crisis, his body always rallied, but the day-to-day toil wore him down.

"I am old, old, very old," he wrote upon turning sixty-four, "and I shall never be very well—certainly [not] while in this office, for the drudgery is too much for my years and strength."

Though heavyhearted about his March 4 eviction, Adams held the traditional New Year's Day reception in the style Washington had developed. He stood stiffly in full dress with a black velvet suit, silk stockings, silver knee and shoe buckles, and a white vest. His hair was powdered, he wore gloves, and he did not shake hands but bowed as Washington had done.

Adams had never been one for social engagements. He felt that there were "few people in this world with whom I can converse. I can treat all with decency and civility, and converse with them, when necessary, on points of business. But I am never happy in their company." But those who called John Adams "His Pomposity" would not have done so if they could have seen him playing with his grandson at home. Abigail wrote that every day after dinner the boy "sets his grandpapa to draw him about in a chair . . . to the derangement of my carpet and the amusement of his grandpapa." A messenger with urgent dispatches for the president passed a partly opened door and heard what sounded like a horse whinny. Upon looking in, he saw the portly president crawling on his hands and knees, tied to an overturned chair by a rope, and John Adams Smith in the chair waving a buggy whip and yelling "Giddap."

Abigail had planned to leave the White House before the spring thaw, when the roads would become even more difficult. She packed and dawdled, putting off her departure as the cliffhanger issue of Jefferson and Burr was being decided. Since the electoral college had produced a tie, the fate of the presidency lay with the House of Representatives. On February 11 the balloting began. Vote after vote the tie remained unbroken. Congressmen sent for pillows and blankets or napped at their desks. At 4 A.M. the tie remained. By morning the twenty-eight ballots were taken. On the thirty-sixth ballot, taken five days later on February 16, Jefferson finally was declared the victor.

Abigail finally pried herself away from the frenzy of rumor and intrigue. By February 13 she and her niece had reached Baltimore, "beat and banged," even though Louisa Smith, appalled by the "horrid" roads and "shocking wilderness," had pleaded to turn back. The two traveled with the usual array of coachman and servants, but without the assistance of a gentleman. This unnerved Louisa, but Abigail took pride in the fact that she was "accustomed to get through many a trying scene and combat many difficulties alone." When the two arrived in Philadelphia, the jubilant ringing of church bells accompanied news of Jefferson's victory. Abigail considered it an ironical celebration for "an infidel."

The president she left behind—brooding and depressed—spent his last days in the press of business, diligently appointing Federalists to offices. John Marshall, no friend of Jefferson's, agreed to become chief justice of the Supreme Court. The Republican papers charged Adams with devoting the wee hours of his administration to packing the courts with partisan appointees—"The Duke of Braintree's Midnight Judges." (Quincy was also known as Braintree.) Adams certainly spent time packing, but this last night, his attention turned to his possessions. He wanted to vacate the White House as quickly as possible. Barely on speaking terms with his vice president, Adams had no desire to participate in Jefferson's inauguration—and certainly, at this juncture in history, custom did not require it. Thus under cover of night, a convoy of wagons was loaded outside the White House. At 4 A.M., before inauguration day officially dawned, Adams mounted his coach and rode away from the house he had blessed. Sixteen months earlier he'd written to Abigail of his fear that going to Washington would bring the "certainty of leaving it on the fourth of March, with five hundred fifty or six hundred miles to ride through the mud." Adams's journey toward twenty-five years of retirement had begun.

# 3

# Thomas Jefferson

## 1801–1809

## *The Leveling Principles of Democracy*

FROM MARCH 4 to March 19, the fifteen days following John Adams's predawn flight from Washington, the President's House stood empty. Nary a servant stirred a fire, nary a messenger raced out the door. Never again in its history, save when it smoldered in ruins after the British attack in the War of 1812, would the seat of government be totally uninhabited. But Thomas Jefferson had little interest in hastening to his new home. The election of 1800 had routed the pro-central government of Adams and Washington, along with what critics called their monarchical pretenses. A new era had dawned, one of simplicity, democracy, and Republicanism, and Jefferson and his fellow Republicans thought of the house as a Federalist folly, "big enough for two emperors, one pope, and the grand lama in the bargain."

So for fifteen days after the inauguration, the president remained ensconced among the people at Conrad and McMunn's boardinghouse, two hundred steps from the Capitol. In November 1800 Jefferson, then Adams's vice president, had come to Washington with the rest of the Federal government. He lodged at one of the best houses in the city, the home of wealthy Thomas Law, recently turned over to Conrad and McMunn to ease the housing shortage. At this "commodious and handsome house," as one of his contemporaries described it, Jefferson awaited the outcome of the tumultuous election, learning that he was the victor only two weeks before inauguration day. On March 4, he dressed in simple clothes—"plain cloth," an English traveler wrote—and walked to the Capitol, eschewing the coach and horses with silver-mounted harnesses that Adams had left him. Riflemen paraded; cannon roared. In the Senate Chamber, the new president gave his inaugural address in a voice so weak that only those in the front rows could hear him. Accompanied by friends and congressmen, he walked back to Conrad's and that night dined at the common table in the company of thirty or so fellow boarders. Some felt he was carrying his belief in the "leveling principles of democracy" a little far by insisting on taking his regular seat at the foot of the table.

With a private bedroom and drawing room in which to receive visitors, Jefferson's accommodations may have offered more comforts than the unfinished, unstaffed, underfurnished, leaky President's House. During his first week in office, he inspected his future lodgings thoroughly, wrote up a list of changes, and then on March 19 moved in, accompanied by Joseph Rabin, his longtime French steward, a housekeeper, and three servants. Two weeks later Congress recessed, and he quickly left for Monticello. Ultimately he would have about twelve servants, including slaves from Monticello.

An inveterate remodeler—Monticello was unfinished even at his death—Jefferson had numerous ideas for the President's House. Some were practical—digging a well, erecting a post-and-rail fence, and tearing down a wooden outhouse, an eyesore that stood next to the mansion. In its place he installed two water closets on the bedroom floor. As at Monticello, tin reservoirs in the attic stored the rainwater that flushed the bowls. Just west of the house he ordered a wine cellar dug. Sixteen feet deep and lined with clay bricks, it housed racks of wine cooled by sawdust-packed ice set beneath the floor.

Other changes involved rethinking the house's function. In Adams's time, guests entered through the oval drawing room, now the Blue Room. But such a floor plan turned one of the most beautiful rooms in the house into little more than a lobby. Jefferson ordered the just-finished south stairs torn down and new ones built to the north, where visitors could assemble in a large rectangular hall. Funds were short, and for most of Jefferson's tenure this northern stairway, offering a glimpse of the kitchen below, was a very basic wooden affair.

In a pointed move, Jefferson turned Adams's levee room, today the State Dining Room, into his library and immediately abolished weekly levees, despite the protests of the ladies, who stormed the President's House at the customary time, begging for a continuance of tradition. Unmoved, Jefferson issued a new set of rules detailing social protocol in an effort to maintain "the principle of equality, or of *pêlemêle,* and prevent the growth of precedence out of courtesy." The customary party and ball marking the president's birthday were banished; the only celebrations sanctioned were New Year's Day and the Fourth of July, when the White House would be open to all who cared to call. On those occasions Jefferson initiated the democratic custom of shaking hands, doing away with the formal bows of Adams and Washington. He insisted on being addressed as "Mr. Jefferson," not "Mr. President," and was unusually accessible. He did not go visiting but received calls most mornings, whether from a congressman or a Pennsylvania delegation bearing a 1,235 pound mammoth cheese inscribed "The greatest cheese in America for the greatest man in America." (Strict about declining gifts, Jefferson insisted on paying $200, or 50 percent more than market price, for the cheese.)

The idea of opening the President's House to all citizens made sense in a new city in a new country. Newspaperman Samuel Harrison Smith described Jefferson's first Fourth of July party in a July 5, 1801, letter to his sister: "About 12 o'clock yesterday, the citizens of Washington and Geo.Town waited upon the President to make their devoirs. . . . We found about 20 persons present in a room where sat Mr. J. surrounded by the five Cherokee chiefs. After a conversation of a few minutes, he invited his company into the usual dining room, whose four large sideboards were covered with refreshments, such as cakes of various kinds, wine, punch, &c. . . . The company soon increased to near a hundred, including all the public officers and most of the respectable citizens, and strangers of distinction. . . . Mr. Jefferson mingled promiscuously with all the citizens." Clearly, everyone who was anyone could fit into the president's drawing and dining rooms.

As the years progressed, the Fourth of July celebration drew travelers from far and wide, turning the south grounds, normally a grazing ground for the presidential cows, into something of a state fair. Tents rose, booths were set up. Vendors purveyed food, drinks, rugs, and baskets. Cock- and dogfights were staged. Troops marched past the President's House, while Jefferson, "his grey locks waving in the air," stood with his cabinet, watching from the high steps. Then everyone was invited inside, where "confectionary, wines, punch, lemonade, etc." were there for the taking.

In abandoning levees, Jefferson in no way abandoned entertainment. President John F. Kennedy once described a group of twelve Nobel Prize winners as "the most extraordinary collection of talent, of human knowledge, that has ever been gathered together at the White House with the possible exception of when Thomas Jefferson dined alone." But Jefferson seldom, if ever, did. An epicure of the first degree, he loved nothing better than lingering over fine food served with six or eight incomparable wines, which he ordered by the barrel from Spain, France, Italy, and Portugal. He considered wine essential to health and drank one to four glasses a day. His wine bill was enormous—$10,855.90 in the course of his two terms. Indeed his annual expenses generally exceeded his $25,000 salary, contributing to the buildup of debt that would ultimately force the sale of Monticello after his death.

In Washington, few left his table without awe. English-born Louisa Adams, wife of John Quincy, described a November 1803 dinner: "The entertainment was handsome. French servants in livery, a French butler, a French cuisine, and a buffet full of choice wine: had he a tolerable fire on one of the bitterest days I ever experienced, we might have fancied ourselves in Europe."

"He dined at four o'clock, and they generally sat and talked until night," reported Jefferson's manager from Monticello, Edmund Bacon. "It used to worry me to sit so long; and I finally quit when I got through eating, and went off and left them."

"He has company every day," wrote Margaret Bayard Smith, wife of newspaperman Samuel Harrison Smith and a fixture of Washington society, "but his table is seldom laid for more than twelve. This prevents all form and makes the conversation general and unreserved. . . . When he had any persons dining with him, with whom he wished to enjoy a free and unrestricted flow of conversation, the number of persons at the table never exceed [sic] four, and by each individual was placed a *dumb-waiter*, containing everything necessary for the progress of dinner from the beginning to end."

Jefferson also was able to minimize the presence of servants by fitting his dining room with revolving doors that held dishes. Food from the kitchen could be placed on the outside, the section of the door turned, and waiters inside the dining room could carry it to the table, which was oval in shape to promote conversation.

When Congress was in session, the president focused his entertaining on the political, with all-male dinners (since congressmen routinely came to Washington without their wives, ladies were at something of a premium in society). For state dinners or occasions when a hostess was required, Dolley Madison acted as first lady. The Madisons stayed with Jefferson for several weeks in May 1801 and quickly felt quite at home. In 1803 Dolley took a visitor on a tour of the President's House, stopping at Jefferson's chamber, where, the visitor recalled, "in her usual sprightly and droll manner, she opened the President's wardrobe and showed his odd but useful contrivance for hanging up jackets and breeches on a machine like a turnstile."

During the season of 1802–3 Jefferson's daughters, Maria Eppes and Martha Randolph, stayed with him and served as official hostesses, the only time both were able to visit him. Jefferson once said, "The happiest moments of my life have been the few which I have passed at home in the bosom of my family." In what he called the "blessed interim" of congressional recess, he fled Washington whenever he could. He considered it "a trying experiment" for him to have to spend "the bilious months" on the tidewater: "Grumble who will, nothing should induce me to do it." In his first term he spent more than a quarter of his time—thirteen months—at Monticello, roughly the same amount of time John Adams had spent at Quincy. Messengers kept him in touch with important matters, mail was answered swiftly, and visitors crowded the unfinished homestead, even though guest rooms were scarce, given the fact that Martha and Maria usually moved their families to Monticello whenever their father was home.

Washington, being only three days' journey from Monticello, at first seemed to provide the possibility that his daughters could join their father during the government's working months. But pregnancies and the children's measles foiled plans during the first season Jefferson was in office. The sisters came for the second season, but the third found both homebound and pregnant. Martha, the more robust of the two, gave birth in the autumn of 1803, Maria in February 1804. Like her mother, Maria was frail. Childbirth left her so weak that Jefferson ordered his slaves to make a litter and carry her four miles up to Monticello. By the time Congress adjourned and he arrived home on April 4, 1804, he found her "so weak as barely to be able to stand, her stomach so disordered as to reject almost everything she took into it, a constant small fever, & an imposthume [abscess] rising in her breast." She did not live out the month. Jefferson, stunned by grief, refused to go into mourning, a custom for which he had little patience. Upon his return to Washington, he entertained and received as usual.

When Martha and Maria paid their earlier visit to Washington, they had left their husbands home. In March 1803 the situation was reversed. Both of Jefferson's sons-in-law, newly elected to Congress, came to Washington and stayed at the President's House. In the autumn of 1805 Martha accompanied her husband, bringing their six children, aged two to fourteen years. Aware of her social position as the president's daughter, she wrote to Dolley Madison, asking her to obtain some necessary items of fashion: a wig, a set of combs, and a "bonnet and shawl and white lace veil, for paying morning visits." But Martha's ability to go visiting and serve as her father's hostess was

*This 1807 drawing, signed by Benjamin Latrobe, shows the first major change in the design of the White House: the addition of the North and South porticos. Latrobe's design has been attributed to Thomas Jefferson* (LIBRARY OF CONGRESS)

curtailed by pregnancy: on January 28, 1806, she gave birth to James Madison Randolph, the first child born in the White House.

Save for the absences of his family, President's House suited Jefferson. On June 4, 1801, he wrote his son-in-law, Thomas Mann Randolph, "We find this a very agreeable country residence, good society and enough of it, and free from the heat, the stench, and the bustle of a close built town." He had lived in Paris, New York, and Philadelphia and understood the pleasures of civilization, but the almost rural landscape of Washington afforded him the opportunity to slip off on solitary expeditions into the nearby hills—"Not a plant from the lowliest weed to the loftiest tree escaped his notice," wrote Margaret Bayard Smith.

A compulsive recorder, Jefferson kept eight years' worth of neat charts documenting the earliest and latest appearance of twenty-nine vegetables on the Washington market. Broccoli—an unusual vegetable in his day—was available from April 7 to April 20 one spring. He asked foreign consuls to send back rare seeds, which he distributed, as Margaret Bayard Smith wrote, "among the market-gardeners in the City (for at that time there was abundant space, not only for gardens, but little farms, within the City bounds), not sending them but giving himself and accompanying his gifts with the information necessary for their proper culture and management, and afterwards occasionally calling to watch the progress of their growth. . . . For their further encouragement, the President ordered his steward to give the highest prices for the earliest and best products of these gardens." Jefferson's marketing was done daily, and his food bill was remarkable—often fifty dollars a day in an era when a whole turkey cost seventy-five cents.

Patrick Henry charged Jefferson with being "a man unfaithful to his native victuals." Jefferson was definitely guilty of being an unabashed gourmet. In addition to his French chef he brought two slaves from Monticello, Edy and Fanny, to learn French cooking. He introduced little-known delicacies from abroad—waffles from Holland, macaroni from Italy, anchovies from France. He is credited with introducing ice cream into the United States. He wrote the recipe out in eighteen detailed steps and liked the finished product served in little balls wrapped in shells of warm pastry. But Jefferson did not entirely disdain his "native victuals." In Washington he had a Virginia cook, Annette, who knew how to make batter cakes the way he liked them. She turned out fried apples, hot breads, and bacon and eggs that would please any southerner.

Jefferson ate two meals a day, breakfast and four o'clock dinner, and consumed little animal meat. He rose at dawn—"The sun has not caught me in bed in fifty years," he wrote in 1825 just before he died. At the President's House he worked and received in the morning. In the afternoon he found time for playing his violin—he was a talented musician and owned an extensive collection of sheet music. He kept carpentry and gardening tools in his office worktable drawers and devotedly tended the roses, geraniums, and plants that grew by the windows. Among his flora hung a mockingbird in a cage. When Jefferson was alone, the bird flew about freely, often sitting on his shoulder. He let it eat a cherry or other pieces of fruit from his lips; at night it hopped up the stairs after the president.

At one o'clock he liked to go out for a horseback ride, often covering seven or eight miles on Wildair, his favorite horse. Usually he rode alone. If he met passersby, he'd stop to talk. Few knew his identity. On one such occasion, a man made the mistake of launching a tirade against the president. Jefferson calmly inquired whether it was fair to repeat such stories about a man he had never met. Then he invited his new acquaintance to the President's House. Though taken aback by the realization that he'd come face to face with the president, the man accepted the invitation and fell under Jefferson's spell.

In November 1803 Anthony Merry, envoy extraordinary and minister plenipotentiary of His Britannic Majesty and specialist in pomp, arrived in Washington with a newly acquired rich wife and a staggering number of servants and luggage. He was horrified by Washington, pronouncing it "a thousand times worse than the worst parts of Spain." Dressed in full diplomatic splendor, he came to the White House to present his credentials, assuming he had an appointment. Madison, the secretary of state, met him and escorted him toward the president's office. The two encountered Jefferson, apparently by chance, in a hall. Merry made a short speech, and then prepared to leave. Because of the narrowness of the vestibule he was "obliged to back out."

Jefferson, he wrote home, wore his "usual morning-attire." He had been "actually standing in slippers down at the heels, and both pantaloons, coat, and underclothes, indicative of utter slovenliness and indifference to appearances, and in a state of negligence actually studied." His hair was loose, not tied neatly in a queue. "I could not doubt," Merry continued, "that the whole scene was prepared and intended as an insult not to me personally, but to the sovereign I represented."

The next evening insult turned to injury. Jefferson gave a dinner at the President's House and rather than escorting Mrs. Merry to the table, he gave his arm to his hostess, Dolley Madison. Floundering and embarrassed, the Merrys had to scramble for seating. At a subsequent party at the Madisons, they again suffered the "absolute omission of all distinction." Aggrieved, the Britannic envoy complained to the crown, but Washington society continued to offer nothing but snubs. Sir Augustus Foster, a member of the British diplomatic corps, wrote in his memoir that "the most vulgar of the democratic party took their cue from the style adopted at the great house, and in one way or other, either by remarking on her dress or diamonds, or treading on her gown, worried Mrs. Merry to such a degree that I have sometimes seen her on coming home burst into tears at having to live at such a place."

Though Jefferson certainly favored the French over the British, his casual treatment of Merry was, in the strictest sense, business as usual. The French and Spanish ministers had long been used to Jefferson's rules of etiquette, which specifically stated, "When brought together in society, all are perfectly equal, whether foreign or domestic, titled or untitled, in or out of office." Peder Pederson, chargé d'affaires of Denmark, was the only other foreign minister to have arrived after Jefferson took office; he had faced a similarly egalitarian reception at the President's House.

Not that this appeased Merry. The envoy extraordinary was the first full-fledged minister to be sent by Britain, and Pederson, according to Merry, was only a "minister of the third order." Furthermore, anyone who lived in Washington knew that Jefferson could dress to the nines. Contemporary accounts describe him as "fit to figure on a Watteau fan," with "a white coat, scarlet breeches and vest, and white silk hose." He pulled out all stops for dinner, but debonair attire didn't suit his temperament—or politics. Morning, the time of day Merry made the mistake of calling, found him wearing an air of negligent simplicity. On first sighting Senator William Plumer thought him a servant; another morning he found him more smartly attired than usual: "Though his coat was old and thread bare, his scarlet vest, his corduroy small cloths, and his white linen cotton hose, were new and clean—but his linnen was much soiled, and his slippers old. His hair was cropt and powdered."

For most visitors, the powdering of hair and status of slippers meant little. In 1802 Dr. Samuel Lathrop Mitchill, a congressman from New York, wrote that Jefferson "is more deeply versed in human nature and human learning than almost the whole tribe of his opponents and revilers." The president had mastered French, Spanish, Latin, and Greek and compiled vocabularies of the native American tribes. He had one of the finest collections of sculpture and painting in America. He was a lawyer, agronomist, archaeologist, musician, and inventor of such things as the plow moldboard, which he perfected during a vacation from the presidency in 1805. He wrote all his own letters, drew up his own state papers. He invented what he called a polygraph—a wooden instrument that followed his pen strokes with a second pen, creating an exact copy of each letter. At the President's House, he could be seen on all fours studying mastodon bones sent to him by Meriwether Lewis and William Clark. When the noted scientist Alexander Von Humbolt visited America, Jefferson asked him over to discuss mastodon teeth.

Few appreciated Jefferson's passion for botany and natural history better than young Meriwether Lewis. On February 23, 1801, Jefferson asked Lewis, a family friend, to work as his secretary, "not only to aid in the private concerns of the household, but also to contribute to the mass of information which it is interesting for the administration to acquire. Your knowledge of the Western country, of the army and of all its interests & relations has rendered it desireable . . . that you should be engaged in that office." The salary was low—$500 the first year, $600 the second—and personally paid by Jefferson. Lewis accepted with delight.

Carpenters were called in to frame off two rooms in the big, unfinished East Room as an office and a bedchamber for the new secretary, who arrived from Detroit with a string of mud-spattered packhorses. Initially Lewis faced the task of vetting the existing army, which Jefferson, a believer in government "rigorously frugal and simple," wanted to cut in half. An experienced officer, Lewis knew which men should stay and who should be fired. But after putting his check marks on the officer's roster, his job became one with little challenge to it. He copied routine documents, delivered messages to Congress, and in his free time hunted along Pennsylvania Avenue and some nearby areas, supplying the White House kitchen with game. "Excellent snipe shooting and even partridge shooting was to be had on either side of the main avenue," a British diplomat noted.

But Jefferson had bigger things in mind for his secretary. As his only companion in the White House, Lewis dined with the president and sampled the range of ideas volleyed about among the distinguished guests. He studied the maps lining Jefferson's office walls, traveled with the president to Monticello, and read from his geography books, the most extensive available on North America. Quietly, from the start, Lewis was being primed for the contribution he would so ably make to history.

In January 1803 Jefferson sent Congress a secret request for $2,500 to fund a westward expedition. Though it could be viewed as nothing but provocative by Spain, France, and England, all of whom owned parts of the western territories, Congress approved the moneys with dispatch, taking note of Jefferson's veiled reference to wresting the lucrative fur trade from the British.

In preparation for the journey, Jefferson taught Lewis to use the sextant and other instruments on the lawn of the President's House and sent him off to study with leading scientists in Philadelphia. Lewis left Washington on July 5, 1803, just as the news of the Louisiana Purchase was coming in. Now he would not be trespassing on much of the land through which he needed to travel.

Jefferson had not intended to purchase a major part of a continent—he had only hoped to secure the right of American goods to be transshipped through New Orleans or perhaps to buy the city itself. Napoleon's offer to sell all of the Louisiana Territory had taken the American commissioners by surprise. Jefferson had strongly opposed the attempts of Hamilton and the Federalists to strengthen the government's powers under the Constitution. Now he was confronted with what was clearly an unconstitutional act according to everything he had said or believed. He admitted he "stretched the Constitution until it cracked."

Jefferson's instructions to Lewis were to urge the Native American chiefs he encountered in this new United States possession to visit the president—their new "Great Father" in Washington—at the expense of the United States. In 1805 Jefferson wrote his daughter that forty-five chiefs from six different nations were "forwarded" by Lewis. Though some never made the journey, Pawnee, Osage, and Iowa arrived in due course, bringing presents and receiving gifts in return, putting on dances on the lawn of the President's House.

One of the most memorable visits occurred in July 1804, when a delegation of Osages came from Missouri at Lewis's behest. Questions of etiquette arose immediately. What should these "savages" wear to the President's House? Jefferson favored native dress for the warriors but left the matter of habiliment for the squaws to the wife of the Secretary of War. She was lobbied by some Washington matrons to deck them out in the finest silks and satins, by others to permit their woodland dress. Ultimately she decided on a "middle course," according to Margaret Bayard Smith—"short gowns and petticoats . . . of showy, large figured chintz, without any trinkets or ornaments."

Jefferson made it a habit to try to elicit surprise from American Indians faced, for the first time, with the wonders of civilization. But he claimed to have succeeded only once. During the Osages' visit, wine arrived at the table packed in ice. Bewildered, an elder chief grasped the ice. It was passed around amid cries of astonishment. "We now believe," the chief said, "that what our brothers told us when they came back from the great cities was all true, though at the time we thought they were telling us lies when they told us of all the strange things they saw. . . . Ice in the middle of summer! We now can believe anything."

As curiosities arrived from Lewis and Clark, Jefferson put them on view at the President's House, turning it into a museum for the people. In 1807 an added attraction arrived: "a pair of Grisly Bears—mail and femail" purchased by Zebulon Pike from the Indians on his expedition. Pike's men carried the young cubs "in their laps on Horse back." They became "extremely Docile," Pike wrote, and followed the men about camp like dogs. Jefferson placed them in a cage on the lawn; later they were donated to Charles Willson Peale for his Philadelphia museum; after one escaped and scared his family, he had them stuffed and put on exhibit.

As Jefferson's second term neared its close, the city he saw around him was a different one than the raw semiwilderness that had greeted him in 1800. Rows of Lombardy poplars had been planted, at his insistence, on Pennsylvania Avenue. Streets were still mired in mud, but curbs and sidewalks were being built. And the Capitol had made great progress. Since funds were short and the city's needs vast, Jefferson kept his requests for the President's House simple—fixing the roof, building the interior stair, finishing the plastering—until 1803, when an appropriation enabled him to begin addressing a vexing problem: what do to about storage and servants' quarters.

In the early 1800s, most large-scale private homes were surrounded by a complex of outbuildings—stables for horses, barns for cattle, smokehouses, storage houses, and so on. But the President's House was just a house—the biggest in America at the time—set on spacious, unlandscaped grounds. Horses were stabled at 14th and G Streets; leftover worker's huts served as ad hoc storehouses. Jefferson borrowed an idea from Monticello and designed wings with flat roofs and open-air colonnades, set into the slope of the land, the forerunners of today's East and West Wings. Completed March 1808, they provided space for an icehouse, wine cellar, henhouse, stables, servants' rooms, and servants' privy. Benjamin Latrobe, the architect Jefferson had hired in 1803 to assist in the completion of the city's public projects, complained about the wings' neoclassical style, saying, "I am cramped in this design by his prejudices in favor of the architecture of the old french books, out of which he fishes everything,—but it is a small sacrifice to my personal attachment to him to humor him."

Even before Jefferson's wings were completed, he had begun sending things home to Monticello. He longed for retirement openly, eagerly. In December 1807 he wrote a friend, "The ensuing year will be the longest of my life." The politics of the times were thicker than ever. His embargo against European powers kept the country out of war but destroyed 80 percent of the trade, leaving New England reeling and angry. The remainder of his presidency, Jefferson said, offered "nothing but unceasing drudgery, and the daily loss of friends." Two days before the inauguration of his friend and hand-picked successor, James Madison, Jefferson wrote, "Never did a prisoner, released from his chains, feel such relief as I shall on shaking off the shackles of power. Nature intended me for the tranquil pursuits of science, by rendering them my supreme delight. But the enormities of the times in which I have lived, have forced me to take part in resisting them, and to commit myself on the boisterous ocean of political passions." Jefferson had authored the Declaration of Independence, served as minister to France, secretary of state, vice president, and president. It was time to return to his grandchildren and his gardens. The seas had finally calmed.

# James Madison

## 1809–1817

## *Conflagration*

SOMETIME AROUND NOON on August 24, 1814, Dolley Madison stood on the roof of the White House and surveyed the surrounding countryside through a spyglass. The War of 1812 had been proceeding desultorily for nearly two years. But now the British were closing in on Washington. Citizens were fleeing in droves. At the White House only the first lady and a handful of servants remained. "Since sunrise," Mrs. Madison wrote to her sister that day, "I have been turning my spy glass in every direction and watching with unwearied anxiety, hoping to discover the approach of my dear husband and his friends."

Instead, she saw American soldiers darting through the woods—apparently in retreat. Cannon fire within earshot, a rider charged up, saying the president bid her leave. Dolley hastily relinquished her post.

Within hours, British forces arrived, matches in hand. By morning, America's grandest mansion was a smoldering ruin. An observer of the day later wrote, "In the [President's House], not an inch, but its crack'd and blacken'd walls remained."

Those walls were no doubt as familiar to James and Dolley Madison as those of their own home. Madison was Thomas Jefferson's hand-picked successor and had worked in the White House, serving as secretary of state. Dolley had presided over social affairs, acting as the widowed president's first lady and hostess.

But the Madisons' view of presidential life differed from the Republican simplicity practiced for the last eight years. While Jefferson had walked to his inaugural, Madison rode in an impressive carriage drawn by four horses and attended by a Negro coachman and Negro footmen. Afterward, with Jefferson still living in the White House, the Madisons held an elegant open house at their home overlooking the Potomac, on High Street in Georgetown. Jefferson was among the visitors, a surprise to everyone given that he was expected to be at the White House receiving well-wishers. Margaret Bayard Smith attended with husband Samuel Harrison Smith, the editor of the *National Intelligencer*. She described the scene:

> To-day after the inauguration, we all went to Mrs. Madison's. The street was full of carriages and people, and we had to wait near half an hour, before we could get in,—the house was completely filled, parlours, entry, drawing room and bed room. Near the door of the drawing room Mr. and Mrs. Madison stood to receive their company. She looked extremely beautiful, was drest in a plain cambrick dress with very long train, plain round the neck without any handkerchief, and beautiful bonnet of purple velvet, and white satin with white plumes. She was all dignity, grace and affability.

That night, the first inaugural ball was held at Long's Hotel—where the Library of Congress now stands. Four thousand of Washington's elite paid for the privilege to attend. Only those who met with the approval of the ball managers could get tickets. Jefferson was among the first to arrive. "Am I too early?" he asked. "You must tell me how to behave, for it is more than forty years since I have been to a ball." Apparently he had no intention of missing his friend and protégé's day in the sun. Mrs. Smith wrote of Jefferson that day, "His countenance beamed with a benevolent joy. I do believe father never loved son more than he loves Mr. Madison." John Quincy Adams, on the other hand, didn't think much of the ball. He wrote, "The crowd was excessive, the heat oppressive, and the entertainment bad."

When the Madisons arrived, forty-one-year-old Dolley, who would soon be setting the style for fashionable Washington, had changed gowns and donned a turban. As the evening wore on, the crowd of celebrants reached ridiculous proportions. Mrs. Smith records, "It was scarcely possible to elbow your way from one side to another, and poor Mrs. Madison was almost pressed to death. . . . As the upper sashes of the windows could not be let down, the glass was broken, to ventilate the room, the air of which had become oppressive."

The first couple were in no hurry to evict their friend from the White House, and it was two weeks before Jefferson finished packing his substantial belongings and they finally moved in. They were left with a rather sparsely furnished mansion. Much of the furniture and decorative items had been Jefferson's own, and after eight years of Jefferson's almost constant dinner parties, table linen, china, glassware, and cutlery needed to be replaced. Dolley, to whom Madison had always left household matters, invited congressmen to the White House to see the condition of the rooms for themselves. Congress quickly appropriated $12,000 for repairs and $14,000 for furnishings.

The Madisons, with architect Benjamin Latrobe, had begun planning changes to the interior of the White House before they even moved in, so work began immediately.

Jefferson's office was refurbished as the State Dining Room, which it remains today. Dolley also set about redoing her parlor (the present Red Room) and the oval drawing room (the present Blue Room). Rejecting the French court finery popular among Americans at the time as inappropriate for the republic, Latrobe opted for a neoclassical "Grecian" style that was all the rage in London and thus, ironically, very British in flavor. But his taste did not always prevail. "The curtains! Oh the terrible velvet curtains!" Latrobe wrote of Dolley's selection for the oval drawing room. "Their effect will ruin me entirely so brilliant will they be." These "terrible" curtains would be among the few nonessentials Dolley would see fit to save as she fled the White House five years later.

With the seas patrolled by British ships, Latrobe could not rely on imports and had to content himself with shopping in Baltimore, Philadelphia, and New York. Among his expenditures: $2,150 for three mirrors, $556.15 for new china, $28 for a guitar, and $458 for a piano that Dolley particularly wanted. The first purchase also included $220.90 for "knives, forks, bottle-stands, waiters, and Andirons."

The oval drawing room was not complete until December, but the dining room and parlor were ready by the end of May. And so Dolley formally announced that her first "drawing-room" would be held Wednesday, May 31, at 8 P.M., with receptions to be held every Wednesday evening thereafter when the first lady was in town. She issued no invitations, but anyone associated with the Madisons, in official life or not, or who had a letter of introduction from someone who did would be admitted. These gatherings of as many as two hundred typically started in the early evening and lasted until around nine. Dolley insisted that each lady curtsy to the president on arrival. Dinner, served at 4 P.M., consisted of many French dishes, the finest wines, and elaborate service. Following the main courses, a variety of desserts appeared—cakes, ice cream, macaroons, and preserves. These were then taken away, to be replaced by almonds, pecans, and various fruits. The weekly reception became a fixture of social and political life in the capital city:

> Many people . . . made appointments to meet each other there; there young men and young women were introduced to each other and fell in love under Mrs. Madison's kindly encouragement; marriages were made and political combinations arranged in corner conversations; people of musical accomplishments sang and played their best, because of Mrs. Madison's appreciation; people of wit made their best jokes, because she loved to laugh; ladies wore their best gowns, because she liked fine clothes; in short, there were golden hours at the first "drawing-rooms" in "the palace."

As for diplomatic receptions, delegations of Native Americans from the West continued to be commonplace. Jefferson had cheerfully received many, but Madison was not sympathetic to American Indians. His home was close to the Blue Ridge Mountains, and when he was young raids were feared. Once when Madison was hosting a tribal delegation, Dolley, about to retire for the night, saw in her mirror an American Indian in war paint. He had hidden behind her door. Calmly she got up and rang a bell in the next room. When the servant came, the warrior was persuaded to leave.

The success of these and myriad other events at the Madison White House was largely due to the vivacious first lady. Dolley Payne Todd met James Madison in May

1794, after Madison asked a mutual friend, Aaron Burr, to arrange an introduction. Dolley, then one of the most eligible young women in Philadelphia, wrote a friend, "The great little Madison has asked . . . to see me this evening." The wealthy, forty-three-year-old Virginia congressman was diminutive—less than five feet six inches and barely one hundred pounds—shy, and balding. But he was indeed great: Madison had earned esteem and fame at the Constitutional Convention of 1787 when his "Virginia Plan," a blueprint for a new, stronger national government, evolved into the Constitution of the United States.

Twenty-six years old, Quaker, and widowed less than a year, Dolley had lost her first husband, John Todd, and their younger son in a single day during a yellow fever epidemic in Philadelphia. To marry again so soon, and to marry a non-Quaker and a slave owner, no less, would mean expulsion from her sect. Dolley treasured the Quaker faith and its ideals, but she had always chafed under its asceticism. By August 1794 Dolley and James were engaged, and in September they were married. She called him "my darling little husband"; he called her "the greatest blessing of my life." Indeed Dolley's ability to charm was a boon to Madison's career, and it is difficult to see how he could have had a successful presidency or even become president without his wife. Nominations for president were controlled by Congress during this period, and Madison relied on his wife to court influence. While animated and genial among close associates, he was not one for party patter and at receptions was likely to be off in a corner talking politics. One guest remarked that he had "an abstract air and a pale countenance with but little flow of courtesy."

Dolley, on the other hand, put people at ease, combining, as Margaret Bayard Smith wrote, "all the elegance and polish of fashion" with "the unadulterated simplicity, frankness, warmth, and friendliness of her native character." Washington Irving met Dolley at a White House reception and found her "a fine, portly, buxom dame, who has a smile and a pleasant word for everybody."

At Dolley's drawing rooms, opposing political factions came together in an informal, civil atmosphere that smoothed over the hostilities engendered by the approaching war with Britain. While not unaware of her usefulness, and not above manipulating the social scene to further her husband's interests, the first lady largely avoided politics and did not share in her husband's political decisions. "Politics is the business of men," she declared. "I don't care what office they hold or who supports them. I only care about people."

One reason for Dolley's popularity was that she didn't put on airs. At a White House reception she offered one of the rising powers of the House of Representatives, Henry Clay, a pinch of snuff from the ornate lava snuffbox she was never without—as evidenced by her tobacco-stained fingers. "Mr. Clay, this is for the rough work," she explained, pulling out a bandanna handkerchief from her pocket. "And this," she said, "is my polisher," showing him the fine lace handkerchief she used to remove the last of the snuff from her nose. "You are aware that she snuffs," said Mrs. William Winston Seaton, "but in her hands the snuff-box seems only a gracious implement with which to charm."

By day, the first lady still wore a gray, straight-cut Quaker dress while doing chores such as marketing or skimming the cream off the milk. But she had a passion for flamboyant evening dress that was anything but Quaker. Her signature item was the turban—she even napped in one—and turbans became the rage in Washington. Dolley

*The charming and fashionable Dolley Madison made the White House the centerpiece of Washington society, easing her husband's political path. Congress readily appropriated money for redecorating but only her red velvet curtains, packed and taken in her carriage, survived the fire of 1814.* (LIBRARY OF CONGRESS)

wore daring styles featuring décolletage, false hair, and hats with soaring ostrich feathers (the better to spot her short figure at a party). She "rouged," a topic of much whispering about town, and she favored heavy doses of perfume. Her gowns were purchased in Paris—the president was startled but didn't complain when he saw the $2,000 duty he had to pay on "a valuable collection of clothes" picked out for her in Paris by a friend. Dolley found that "the dresses and every other article indeed are beautiful." Unfortunately the shoes were a size too small, but "the flowers, trimmings and ornaments were enchanting."

Madison, on the other hand, was described by a contemporary as always looking like a man on his way to a funeral. Fifty-eight when he took office, he was "but a withered little apple-John" to Washington Irving. Dressed in black, his hair powdered, Madison clung to knee britches, silver shoe buckles, and extra-high hats that made him appear taller. His diminutive size gave him an air of fragility, and indeed he was far from robust. As a youth he was too sickly to join the Revolutionary War army, and as an adult his diaries are filled with his health problems. He was well enough throughout most of his presidency, but in June 1813 barely survived a bout of malaria, which Dolley nursed him through at the White House.

Dolley ran the household with two dozen servants (twice Jefferson's bare-bones staff), including slaves from Montpelier, Madison's five-thousand-acre Virginia plantation, and hands hired locally. For her dinner parties, she hired additional slaves for 35 cents each from nearby plantations so as to provide one waiter for each dinner guest. She also relied a great deal on Jean-Pierre "French John" Sioussat. Born in Paris in 1781, Sioussat was educated, had witnessed the execution of Louis XVI, and had been in the French navy. He escaped the navy by jumping ship and swimming ashore in New York. He found employment with the British minister in Washington, Anthony Merry, who caused such a contretemps during Jefferson's term. When Merry returned to England, Sioussat was hired as White House steward (although Madison gave him the title "master of ceremonies"). Dolley entrusted him with managing her personal affairs, and he was devoted to her, if prone to indulging in too much wine. They became very close and remained so until Dolley's death.

But Sioussat could not manage the household's most vexing problem, Dolley's son, Payne Todd. When Madison and Dolley married, Payne was only two and sleeping in the same bed with his mother. Madison protested the arrangement, but Dolley always indulged her son. Payne eventually became Madison's personal secretary. He was pleasant and personable but irresponsible. Madison attached him to a mission to St. Petersburg, hoping the experience would help mature the young man. Instead, Payne enjoyed Europe so much he spent the next several years there, mostly in Paris, living it up and gambling. When Madison died in 1836, a sealed file, kept secret from Dolley, was found showing the huge debts Payne had run up and Madison had paid, including getting him out of debtors' prison.

Beyond the domestic realm, Madison confronted the same problems Jefferson had: how to deal with warring European powers that disregarded America's rights on the high seas. British impressment of sailors and confiscation of U.S. ships fanned a growing public indignation, and clashes in the West between British forces and American frontiersmen finally led to the outbreak of hostilities. Madison reluctantly agreed to a declaration of war against Great Britain. For the first two years the war went badly, and Madison's popularity fell. Washington seethed with rumors and unrest. Dolley began sleeping with a saber beside her bed—she and her husband used separate bedrooms, as the insomniac Madison got up frequently to read or write. He always had a candle burning in his bedchamber.

In April 1814 Britain's clash with France came to an end with the collapse of the French Empire, and Britain turned its full attention to the nagging problem of its former colony. On August 21, 1814, Rear Admiral Sir George Cockburn landed a force north of Washington and headed toward what British newspapers still called "the proud seat of that nest of traitors." Madison stationed one hundred militiamen around the White House as a guard. Dolley was urged to leave but refused—despite British boasts of exhibiting her in the streets of London as a prisoner of war. "I am determined to stay with my husband," she said. Madison rode off to the battlefront on August 23, leaving Dolley responsible for the White House. By the following day, she had only French John, a fifteen-year-old mulatto assistant named Paul Jennings, a gardener, a coachman, and Sukey, her maid from Montpelier. "My friends and acquaintances are all gone," she wrote in a letter to her sister Lucy—as were the one hundred militiamen, who had fled along with the populace.

Madison had told his wife to "be ready at a moment's warning" to escape in her carriage. Mindful of inducing further panic in the streets, she kept up the mansion's ordinary routines and prepared her escape discreetly. She packed two small trunks—all that could fit in a carriage—with state papers bundled in linen bags and a change of clothes. "Our private property must be sacrificed," she said. All her personal possessions, the beautiful imported gowns, turbans, and shoes, would be lost. By August 24, capture of the White House seemed imminent, and French John urged the laying of a train of powder as a fuse from the front gate to the mansion's door to blow up the British if they entered. Dolley refused. As she wrote to her sister, "To the last proposition I positively object, without being able, however, to make him understand why all advantages in war may not be taken."

On the afternoon of the twenty-fourth, Dolley climbed the roof of the White House and searched expectantly, spyglass to eye, for her husband. The president had intended to return from the battlefront around three, and to bring cabinet members, their wives, and some officers back for dinner. Dolley had charged French John with roasting the meat and decanting the wine for thirty guests. All of Washington seemed to have left or was leaving, but she believed Madison and his staff would need food. She agreed to leave only when James Smith, a free Negro Madison had sent from the front, galloped up at about 3 P.M., waving his hat: "Clear out! Clear out! General Armstrong has ordered a retreat!"

Dolley swept up a seemingly random collection of additional items to be quickly packed into her carriage and saved: the silver; some books; a small clock; and the velvet curtains, already packed and stored for the summer, that were so deplored by Latrobe. The last thing she insisted upon taking was the Gilbert Stuart portrait of George Washington hanging in the State Dining Room. As the portrait was screwed to the wall, French John broke the frame to get it down. Two passersby from New York, Robert de Peyster and Jacob Barker, had dropped in to offer their help. They promised to see to the safety of the canvas, still on its stretcher, and any other valuables and papers they could carry, if the first lady would be on her way. She agreed.

Dolley finished the letter to Lucy, writing, "Now dear sister, I must leave this house, or the retreating army will make me a prisoner in it, by filling up the road I am directed to take." She was gone by three-thirty.

When the president and a few of his staff finally reached the White House at about 4 P.M., only French John and the two New Yorkers, who had secured a cart, remained to greet him. He had some of the wine but declined a meal. (Madison was something of a wine connoisseur—as secretary of state he had spent a good part of his $5,000-a-year salary on cases of Madeira, and as president he stocked a good supply of Madeira, port, and French champagne.)

His drink finished, Madison rode off as skies darkened and a storm brewed, crossing the Potomac River on a ferry. De Peyster and Barker took to the streets with their cart. French John banked the fires in the kitchen, locked the White House doors, and with Dolley's macaw in a cage set off for the neutral territory of the nearby Octagon House, where French minister Louis Sérurier was quartered.

Admiral Cockburn arrived about 7:30 P.M. and was surprised to find the table set for dinner. One of his men later recalled "a dinner table spread. . . . Several kinds of wine in handsome cut-glass decanters were cooling on the sideboard; plateholders stood by the fire-place, filled with dishes and plates; knives, forks, and spoons, were arranged for immediate use; everything in short was ready for the entertainment of a ceremonious party." The British officers proceeded to make a party of it, enjoying the meal with

Cockburn toasting "Jemmy's" health. Cockburn did not permit looting—in any case, in the hours since Dolley's departure certain of Washington's remaining citizenry had already seen to that. But he did sanction a few souvenirs. For himself: an old hat to remember Madison by, and a chair cushion, which he declared would help him remember Mrs. Madison's seat. Then he ordered the furniture pushed into piles and the windows smashed. Margaret Bayard Smith recorded one witness's account of what happened next:

> [Mrs. William Thorton, wife of the architect of the Capitol] described to us the manner in which they conflagrated the President's H. and other buildings,—50 men, sailors and marines, were marched by an officer, silently thro' the avenue, each carrying a long pole to which was fixed a ball about the circumference of a large plate,—when arrived at the building, each man was station'd at a window, with his pole and machine of wild-fire against it, at the word of command, at the same instant the windows were broken and this wild-fire thrown in, so that an instantaneous conflagration took place and the whole building was wrapt in flames and smoke. The spectators stood in awful silence, the city was light and the heavens redden'd with the blaze!

A hurricane with violent winds and rains blew in the next day, hastening the British departure and putting out the fires. A British officer recorded: "A hurricane fell on the city which unroofed houses and upset our three-pounder guns. It upset me too. It fairly lifted me out of the saddle and the horse which I had been riding I never saw again." The storm passed, but Dolley's exodus was still fraught with difficulty. Traveling with her maid Sukey and an occasional attachment of guards, she encountered so much hostility from those who blamed their hardships on her husband that she gave up her carriage and disguised herself as a countrywoman. After thirty-six hours of missed connections and hardships brought on by the storm, she and her husband met at Wiley's Tavern in Virginia. But the president immediately pressed on to be with the troops. He was on horseback most of the four days of traveling, as much as twenty hours in one day.

News of the British retreat came on August 27. Dolley received word from Madison that she should return to the capital, and she rode there with navy clerk Edward Duvall and a group of dragoons. At the Potomac River they found that the long wooden bridge had been destroyed, and that they could not get back across at the ferry. The only barge was carrying munitions. The first lady revealed her identity to the colonel in charge and was allowed to cross.

The destruction of the capital represented a low point for the Madisons and for the country, the symbolic impact even worse than the reality. The White House had been reduced to a charred, roofless shell. The outer walls surrounded little more than a heap of ashes and rubble. French John and a party of laborers dug up some pots and skillets, the kitchen range, and some hardware, but apparently not much else could be salvaged. The Capitol building was the other grand casualty: "Those beautiful pillars in that Representatives Hall were crack'd and broken, the roof, that noble dome, painted and carved with such beauty and skill, lay in ashes in the cellars beneath smouldering ruins, were yet smoking," wrote Margaret Bayard Smith.

*When the British set fire to the White House in 1814, the flames were quickly put out by the drenching rain of a hurricane. Nonetheless, the building was entirely gutted. All that stood were the stone walls. Before rebuilding could begin, much of the original stonework had to be torn down because the intense heat and rapid cooling had damaged the remaining stone.* (LIBRARY OF CONGRESS)

With their home and belongings lost to fire, Madison did not know "where we are in the first instance to hide our heads." Mrs. Smith said, "Mrs. M. seemed much depressed. She could scarcely speak without tears." The Madisons found temporary shelter in Washington with Dolley's sister Anna and her husband, Richard Cutts. Though Madison ordered the immediate rebuilding of the White House just as it had been, it would not be finished before he left office. The couple soon moved with the few possessions they had left into the Octagon House. This private home, built in 1800, had been designed somewhat in the shape of an octagon to fit the angle formed by New York Avenue and 18th Street—one of the pie-shaped lots resulting from city architect Pierre L'Enfant's circles. The French minister had been staying in it during the city's occupation by the British, who honored his position as neutral and did not burn it. After a year in these comparatively cramped quarters, the Madisons would move into a block of houses at Pennsylvania Avenue and 19th Street, where the president would finish out his term.

In early November, Dolley resumed the Wednesday-night drawing rooms at the Octagon House. Her ability to regroup must have chagrined those who frowned upon her particular brand of hospitality. The *Washington City Gazette* editorialized on September 19, 1814, "The destruction of the President's house cannot be said to be a great loss in one point of view, as we hope it will put an end to drawing rooms and levees; the resort of the idle, and the encouragers of spies and traitors." The entertaining, however, was necessarily on a much smaller scale and, befitting the mood of the country, more subdued. And with many blaming her husband for the fumbled war, Dolley's invitations were for the first time regularly refused. Worse, some guests simply failed to show up.

But on February 4 came the electrifying news of General Andrew Jackson's overwhelming victory against the British at New Orleans on January 8, 1815. The mood swung to joy and jubilation. Nine days later word reached the Octagon House that a peace treaty had been signed two months earlier on Christmas Eve in Ghent, Belgium. Jackson's victory had been unnecessary, but it brought the war to a more decisive and satisfying end, lifting the humiliation of a burned capital. America seemed to have won its independence from Britain for a second time.

While Madison and his cabinet reviewed the terms of the treaty upstairs, Dolley dispensed hospitality downstairs to those who had come to call after hearing the news. Madison pronounced the treaty acceptable, and a call went downstairs to celebrate. Many got drunk, French John among them. Across the city, bells rang, bands played, houses were lit from top to bottom, and citizens poured into the streets to gather around bonfires and march down the avenues.

The Senate ratified the treaty unanimously on February 17, 1815. The Federalists, who had so heatedly opposed "Mr. Madison's war," fell out of favor in the afterglow of victory. Madison left office on an upswing in popularity and goodwill that launched successor James Monroe's term as "the Era of Good Feeling."

When Madison finished his second term in 1817, he and Dolley retired, blissfully, to idyllic Montpelier. One guest to the estate thought that the aging couple "looked like Adam and Eve in Paradise." Since Payne Todd was so irresponsible, Madison left the estate to Dolley when he died in 1836. She could never refuse her son anything, however, and paying his debts forced her to sell Montpelier and drove her into a genteel poverty. (When he died, three years after his mother, relatives had to pay the funeral expenses.) Richard Cutts offered Dolley free use of a house he had inherited on Lafayette Square, only a block from the White House. Daniel Webster lived next door and assumed a protective role. Paul Jennings, her one-time slave, was now working for Webster. Jennings, in his old age, recalled, "When I was a servant to Mr. Webster, he often sent me to her with a market basket of provisions, and told me whenever I saw anything in the house that I thought she was in need of to take it to her."

Now almost seventy years old, Dolley continued to lead an active social life and always had a place of honor at White House social functions. Congress even took the unprecedented step of allowing her a seat on the floor rather than in the public gallery. It became a tradition to walk across Pennsylvania Avenue to call on Dolley Madison after the president's New Year's open house, and for each newly inaugurated president to pay her homage and receive her blessing. Zachary Taylor would be the last so blessed.

As an aging Dolley's health failed, people visited, helped her financially, and listened again and again to the story of how she saved the George Washington portrait, which today hangs in the East Room. So beloved was the legendary first lady that she would receive a full state funeral. She died at eighty-one on July 12, 1849, in her bed at Lafayette Square. Every church bell in Washington tolled.

## The Rebuilding of the White House, 1814–1817

In the burned-out aftermath of the British invasion of Washington in August 1814, all that remained of the White House was its four charred walls. Humiliated and discouraged, Americans talked of building a new capital farther west, in a more secure, more central location. Cincinnati was a likely candidate.

But with news of the Treaty of Ghent and, more importantly, General Andrew Jackson's stunning defeat of the British at New Orleans on January 8, 1815, a bill appropriating $500,000 for the reconstruction of the capital buildings was hurried through Congress. It was approved on February 15—two days before the peace treaty was ratified by the senate.

James Hoban, the architect of the original President's House, was called back to Washington to perform the task again. Though others wanted to tinker with his original design, President Madison was adamant that the house be built exactly as it had been. "In carrying into execution the law for rebuilding the public edifices," he wrote on May 23, "it will best comport with its object & its provisions not to deviate from the models destroyed."

Though the walls of the White House stood, much of the stone had cracked when the intense heat of the August 24 fire suddenly gave way to the cooling rain of that night's storm. With no protection from the elements during the winter of 1814–1815, the empty shell had deteriorated even further. The brick interior lining on the upper floor was crumbling. Hoban realized that much of the walls would have to be torn down. This he reported to Colonel Samuel Lane, commissioner of public buildings, who became worried that Congress might well reconsider its decision to rebuild the house.

Hoban then devised a monumental sleight of hand. For a year he occupied himself with accumulating materials, hiring workers and foremen, and directing the stonecutters and carvers, who began their work almost immediately. New stone and supplies were stacked around the White House. Only when Congress recessed in April 1816 were huge sections of the shell hastily demolished and new stone put in place. Commissioner Lane continued to emphasize "rebuilding" and "repairing," choosing his words carefully in public. In truth, only the basement level could be said to have survived nearly intact.

To avoid giving Madison's successor an excuse to scrap the White House, Hoban and Lane hurried the project along. As many as thirty-two stonemasons worked twelve-hour days to restore the walls. The roof was in place by the winter of 1816–17, so the interior work could continue through the cold months. By James Monroe's inauguration on March 4, 1817, the flooring was being laid.

Monroe saw the rebuilt White House as the symbol of a reborn nation free of the political divisions of its first quarter century, and he wanted to move in as soon as possible. "Great exertions are indispensably necessary," he told the builders, and set a deadline of eight months after his inauguration for moving in. He intended to present himself at the White House when Congress reconvened in the fall of 1817. By June, the ceilings were being plastered and the door and window jambs put in place. Almost two hundred men worked long hours through the heat of a Washington summer. The exterior was finished with white lead paint, covering the new stone and the black scars of the fire on the old. Those scars would appear again in the course of a 1990 restoration.

When Monroe returned from a tour of New England in October, work had progressed a great deal, but the mansion was barely habitable. The president moved in anyway. Only a few rooms on the second floor were available to him, and much of the main floor was makeshift. Monroe was determined to hold the traditional open house on New Year's Day, 1818, wet paint and all. From noon to three that day some three thousand guests came to greet the new president and see the rebuilt house. Apparently it passed muster. "It was gratifying," wrote the *National Intelligencer,* "to be able once more to salute the President of the United States with the compliments of the season in his appropriate residence."

The house was finished in just under three years—a very short time given that a decade had been allotted for building the original. Innovations in construction helped get the job done, as did a structural shortcut: Hoban substituted timber for brick in some of the key interior walls. The ill effects of this expediency would surface more than 130 years later, when the White House required a virtual demolition and second rebuilding during the Truman administration.

# 5

# James Monroe
## 1817–1825

## *Good Feelings and Gold Spoons*

As James Monroe took the oath of office on March 4, 1817, he seemed a throwback to the days of the Revolution. Styles had changed, but he wore what he had always worn: an old-fashioned wig, black coat, black knee breeches, black silk stockings, and shoes with silver buckles. Yet he was well suited to the times, silver buckles and all. Having bested the British in the War of 1812, the upstart republic, brimming with confidence, was coming into its own. A leader who evoked proud memories of the War of Independence fit the mood, and the fifth president was seemingly made to order.

Monroe had fought alongside George Washington, and he even resembled the revered founding father. At fifty-nine, his bearing was erect. He was robust, almost six feet tall, his long, gray hair tied with a black ribbon. He carried a sword and still wore the cockade of the Revolution in his hat. He believed a leader needed to be reserved, and he was dignified and formal, as Washington had been. Also like Washington, Monroe felt he represented not just one party or region but the whole country. With the Federalist party in shambles after their opposition to the War of 1812, the latest Virginia Republican heir to the presidency was elected with almost no opposition. In 1820 he would be reelected with only one dissenting electoral vote.

When Monroe took office, a new White House was still under construction following the British burning of the capital three years earlier. The reborn edifice was the perfect backdrop for the return to pride and unity over which Monroe endeavored to preside.

Like his predecessors, he would attempt to position the building, and its goings-on, as a symbol, this time of a nation unified as it had not been since George Washington's reign.

Like many Americans, Monroe came from ordinary beginnings. Born in 1759, he was the son of a "gentleman carpenter." He grew up in a two-story wood-frame house in a region of Virginia known for its lavish plantation estates. His father was able to send him to the College of William and Mary in Williamsburg, but at eighteen Monroe abandoned his education to join the Revolutionary War army. He crossed the Delaware River with George Washington that icy Christmas night, and was with the general at Valley Forge. He led a charge at the battle of Trenton, in which he took a rifle ball in the shoulder that severed an artery; it would have killed him if not for a surgeon who was there by chance.

Monroe returned to Virginia to study law under then-governor Thomas Jefferson. Jefferson's mentorship, along with Monroe's war record, probably influenced Monroe's election to the Virginia House of Delegates in 1783. A year later he was a congressman. In 1786 he married Elizabeth Kortright, daughter of a wealthy New York merchant and a reigning belle. Thereafter he held a series of political jobs, including senator from Virginia, minister to France (where he was so well liked that in 1794 he became the only foreign representative allowed to sit in the French legislature), three terms as governor of Virginia, and finally, in 1811, his eye on the presidency, secretary of state to James Madison.

Monroe was almost universally characterized as a capable man of mediocre intellect and exceptional integrity. "He is not a brilliant man," as one colleague wrote, "[but] he is a man of great good sense, of the most austere honor, the purest patriotism and the most universally admitted integrity." The great Jefferson's assessment: "He is a man whose soul might be turned wrong side outwards without discovering a blemish." Monroe was also a good organizer. This he put to use at once in bringing the White House—now officially called the "Executive Mansion"—to order.

Monroe took a keen and abiding interest in every detail of the reconstruction and furnishing of his new residence. Eager to begin his ceremonial role—and eager to leave his temporary row-house quarters—he set a deadline of eight months after his inauguration for moving in. He immediately ordered weekly progress reports from Commissioner of Public Buildings Samuel Lane. After a few weeks, he demanded that the workmen be divided into specialized teams, "to promote dispatch," and pressed the builders to aggressively seek out the materials and workers they needed. "You ought to be especially forward in procuring all the materials, requisite for every part of the work. As great exertions are indispensably necessary . . . it would be particularly to be regretted if the want of labourers or of materials should retard the progress for a single day."

While he awaited the completion of the White House, Monroe began a tour of all thirteen states. He left in May 1817, purportedly to inspect facilities such as shipyards, but also to get away from the Washington heat and humidity. Intentionally or not, his national appearances reinforced the concept of unity. Crowds turned out everywhere, even in the old Federalist stronghold of New England. In reporting his visit, the pro-Federalist newspaper the *Columbia Centinel* used the phrase "Era of Good Feelings," which quickly became associated with the Monroe presidency. The optimism engendered by the nation's rapid westward expansion, a rising nationalistic spirit, and Monroe's links to the Revolution all created a climate of harmony.

When Monroe returned from his tour in late September, much of the White House was far from finished. But like John Adams before him, he braved drying paint and plaster and moved in. Secretary of State John Quincy Adams wrote in his diary on September 20, "He is now in the President's House which is so far restored from the effects of the British visit in 1814, that it is now for the first time habitable. But he is apprehensive of the effects of the fresh painting and plastering and very desirous of visiting his family at his seat in Virginia. He is, therefore, going again to leave the city in two or three days, but said his absence would only be for a short time."

Monroe had a privilege unprecedented in history. He was able to furnish the White House from scratch, since every stick inherited from Washington and previous presidents had been reduced to ashes in the fire. This was a task Monroe took to with pleasure. Throughout his two terms he would tinker with the mansion for years, inside and out, as funds allowed. Congress voted $50,000 altogether for furnishings, and the house was gradually appointed in high Parisian style.

Having been minister to France, Monroe was steeped in Parisian culture and favored all things French—food, wine, literature, manners, and decoration. In private or with their daughters the Monroes even spoke French. But ordering furniture abroad was a time-consuming matter. Items had to be commissioned, crafted, and then shipped, a process that took many months. As an interim measure, Monroe filled the White House with his own furniture and china—most of it French, with many Louis Seize pieces—even though the contents of the home he had occupied as secretary of state hardly filled the mansion. Since the pieces were being used in the public rooms, not just the family quarters, Monroe sold the lot to the government at its independently appraised value, $9,071.22. The complexities of this expeditious transaction, handled by his commissioner of public buildings, Samuel Lane, would come back to haunt him.

Monroe charged an American firm at the port of Le Havre, France, Russell and La Farge, with making his purchases. He specified in his February 12, 1818, order that every item be chosen with an eye to its fitness for the president's house. All must be not only elegant but durable, so they might be "handed down through a long series of service." He requested mahogany furniture, but unbeknownst to him, gilded furniture had come into vogue. "Mahogany is not generally admitted in the furniture of a Saloon, even at private gentlemen's houses," wrote Russell and La Farge. The agents took it upon themselves to outfit the oval drawing room (today's Blue Room) with a more costly, but suitably gilded, thirty-eight-piece Empire-style suite from renowned Paris cabinetmaker Pierre-Antoine Bellangé.

Other acquisitions included bronze candelabra, porcelain vases, a custom-decorated gilded porcelain table service and dessert service, carved and gilded lamps and sconces, and a set of gold-plated spoons. A circular, green velvet Aubusson rug custom-made for the Oval Room by Roger and Sollandrouze of Paris featured the arms of the United States of America. Monroe's greatest bargain was the centerpiece that still adorns the State Dining Room table: an elaborate mirror plateau, or *surtout de table,* thirteen and a half feet long and two feet wide, with matching candelabra and fruit baskets. He paid 6,000 francs for it, but the French craftsman said that he "lost by it near 2,000 francs."

*Monroe ordered much fine furniture and decorative accessories from Paris, including this discreetly clad Minerva, one of the few French clocks without "nudities." It remains at the White House.* (LIBRARY OF CONGRESS)

Today it is a priceless heirloom, as are the Hannibal clock and the Minerva clock. The clocks had been hard to find, because Monroe insisted that they be discreetly ornamented, and the French clock makers were resolute: it was "impossible to secure pendulums without nudities."

The decorating budget soon spiraled. The change to gilded furniture had required that everything else be upgraded accordingly. Also, as Russell and La Farge dealt with the artisans of Paris, they began to suspect that prices went up on mention of the president's "palace" in Washington. Monroe began to receive increasingly apologetic messages from Le Havre: "The furniture for the large Oval Room, is much higher than the prices limited. It must be ascribed to the gilt-wood and crimson silk trimmings, fringes, etc., which is 50 per cent dearer than other colors. . . . The christal and gilt bronze lustre is of superior workmanship . . . and if it was to be made again would cost 5,000 francs." More encouragingly, "The plate has been manufactured by Fauconnier, an excellent artist, and honest man. The tureens will, we hope, be found of the highest finish." The bills presented to Congress exceeded expectations, but in the end the furnishings were so undeniably impressive that few saw fit to complain. A Monroe supporter had argued before Congress that some items would last "twenty years or more." Ironically in just that time period—the administration of Martin Van Buren—Monroe's gold spoons would be fodder for accusations of an imperial presidential lifestyle.

As Monroe's furnishings went out of style, later presidents sent it off to auction, the Bellangé suite going under the gavel in Buchanan's administration in 1860. But in recent years diligent first ladies, Jacqueline Kennedy and Pat Nixon chief among them, were able to retrieve the pieces or have copies made. Today nearly all of the Bellangé suite resides in the Blue Room once again.

By New Year's Day, 1818, the White House was presentable enough to hold the traditional open house. Some three thousand people turned out on an auspiciously sunny day to see the new president and first lady in their grand residence, baptizing it with muddy boots. The stylish first lady, who bought all her clothes in Paris, wore a gown reportedly costing $1,500. "The charming weather of yesterday," reported the *National Intelligencer*, "contributed to enliven the reciprocal salutations of kindness and good wishes which are customary at every return of New Year's Day. . . .The President's House, for the first time since its reaerification, was thrown open for the general reception of visitors. It was thronged from 12 to 3 o'clock. . . .

Yet it would be a year and a half before the house could be called reasonably complete. Work had halted for the New Year's reception, and furniture and curtains installed only to be removed again when plastering, painting, wallpapering, hammering, and sawing resumed in February. Rooms were thus filled and emptied, sometimes for a single evening, every time the president held an event.

Despite the elegant quarters, the Monroes' social forays were not received with the "good feelings" that marked the administration's political policies. The Monroes were reclusive, partly because Elizabeth was perpetually ailing during the White House years. The specifics went unmentioned, although it is speculated today that she may have had epilepsy. Shortly after leaving the White House she suffered a violent seizure, fell into a fireplace, and was severely burned.

When the social season opened in 1817, Margaret Bayard Smith wrote, "Few persons are admitted to the great house and not a single lady has yet seen Mrs. Monroe, Mrs. Cutts [Dolley Madison's sister] excepted, and a committee from the Orphan Asylum. . . . Altho' they have lived 7 years in W. both Mr. and Mrs. Monroe are perfect strangers not only to me but all the citizens."

Elizabeth immediately antagonized the women of Washington by announcing that neither she nor her daughters would return or make social calls. Though precedent for the lack of calls had been set by the Washingtons, Dolley Madison had worn herself out catering to society, and Elizabeth or a substitute was expected to follow suit. She was accused of having acquired royal airs abroad, and her receptions were boycotted. Mrs. William Seaton, wife of the editor of the *National Intelligencer*, related in a letter, "The drawing-room of the President was opened last night to a beggarly row of empty chairs. Only five females attended, three of whom were foreigners." The boycott weakened, but Elizabeth remained aloof from society.

The drawing rooms, featuring refreshments and the Marine Band, were held every other Wednesday in the Oval Room. All who came were admitted provided they were dressed properly. A newspaper article described the resulting crowd: "The secretaries, senators, foreign ministers, consuls, auditors, accountants, officers of the army and navy of every grade, farmers, merchants, parsons, priests, lawyers, judges, auctioneers and nothingarians—all with their wives and some with their gawky offspring, crowd to the President's house every Wednesday evening; some in shoes, most in boots and many in spurs; some snuffing, others chewing, and many longing for their cigars and whiskey-punch left at home; some with powdered heads, some frizzled and oiled, whose heads a comb has never touched, and which are half-hid by dirty collars as stiff as pasteboard."

In 1825, just after John Quincy Adams was elected, a visitor to Washington described meeting the first lady at one such reception: "Mrs. Monroe's manner is very gracious and she is a regal-looking lady. Her dress was superb black velvet; neck and arms bare and beautifully formed; her hair in puffs and dressed high on the head and ornamented with white ostrich plumes; around her neck an elegant pearl necklace. Though no longer young, she is still a very handsome woman." She continued with the house: "The rooms were warmed by great fires of hickory wood in the large open fireplaces, and with the handsome brass andirons and fenders quite remind me of our grand old wood fires in Virginia. Wine was handed about in wine glasses on large silver salvers by colored waiters, dressed in dark livery, gilt buttons, etc."

Elizabeth, forty-nine when she entered the White House, retained her beauty, inspiring much discussion about whether she "painted." "Mrs. Monroe is an extremely handsome woman of fine complexion and great color," wrote one congressman to his presumably curious wife. "I observed the blood mantle in her cheeks several times, which satisfies me that it was not artificial. I believe that she is a very fine woman."

When she was absent from receptions—Elizabeth frequently left the White House to visit relatives—she sent daughter Eliza in her place. Eliza, the eldest of two daughters, lived at the White House with husband George Hay. Educated in Paris with the daughters of royalty, Eliza was unimpressed by foreign ministers and caused one of many social stirs when she refused to call on the diplomats' wives unless they called on her first. Secretary of State Adams, forced to juggle the controversy, labeled her an "obstinate little firebrand."

Eliza managed to draw her younger sister, Maria, into her feuding when Maria married. Born in France sixteen years after her sister, Maria was twelve when her father was elected president. In 1820, at sixteen, she married cousin Samuel Gouverneur in the first White House wedding. Eliza alienated society once again by declaring that the wedding would, in "the New York style," exclude all but close friends and relatives—even cabinet members. The ceremony took place in the Oval Room, where bride and groom exchanged vows while standing on the letters "U.S." in the Aubusson carpet. The couple lived in the White House, and later moved to New York City, where Monroe would move to live with them shortly before he died.

Elizabeth and her daughters were frequently absent from the mainstay of presidential entertaining, the dinner party. Since etiquette required a hostess in order for women to attend, these events were even more formal and stiff than they might have been. "On Wednesday I dined with the President," a congressman related to his wife. "It was a grave and serious party, conducted with much pomp and ceremony and seemed to be understood by all as a mere form. The President and Mrs. Monroe have

*Since all the furniture in the White House had been burnt when the British set fire to the White House, Monroe brought his own personal furnishings, including this desk bought while on duty in France. Later he used it for the signing of the Monroe Doctrine. After retiring Monroe took it with him. First Lady Lou Henry Hoover discovered it in the Monroe Law Office Museum in Fredricksburg, Va., and had a copy made for the White House.* (LIBRARY OF CONGRESS)

spent so much of their lives at the various courts of the European continent that sometimes people seem to think that they make their entertainments a little frigid." Another congressman wrote similarly to his spouse of a different dinner: "All bore the appearance of great solemnity. Not a whisper broke on the ear to interrupt the silence of the place, and every one looked as if the next moment was to be his last!"

James Fenimore Cooper described a White House dinner that did include Mrs. Monroe and other women:

The table was large and rather handsome. The service was china, as is uniformly the case, plate being exceedingly rare if used at all. There was, however, a rich plateau, and a great abundance of the smaller articles of table-plate. The cloth, napkins, etc., etc., were fine and beautiful. The dinner was served in the French style and a little Americanized. The dishes were handed around, though some of the guests, appearing to prefer their own customs, coolly helped themselves to what they found at hand. Of the attendants there were a good many. Mrs. Monroe arose at the end of the dessert, and withdrew, attended by two or three of the more gallant of the company. No sooner was his wife's back turned than the President reseated himself, inviting his guests to imitate the action. After allowing his guests sufficient time to renew, in a few glasses, he arose himself, giving the hint to his company that it was time to rejoin the ladies. In the drawing room, coffee was served, and every one left the house before nine."

One dinner with the British and French ministers was not quite so successful. Sir Charles Vaughan was sitting across from the Count de Sérvier, who bit his thumb every time the Englishman spoke. "Do you bite your thumb at me, sir?" Vaughan demanded. "I do," came the reply. The two jumped up and left the room together, drawing their swords, with Monroe after them. The president had to pull out his own dress sword to force the two combatants to uncross theirs. He then ordered his guests out of the house.

In another incident Monroe was attacked by his secretary of the treasury, William Crawford. Crawford had come to him with patronage recommendations, which Monroe objected to. John Quincy Adams recorded the incident in his diary: "Mr. Crawford at last rose in much irritation, gathered the papers together, and said petulantly, 'Well, if you will not appoint the persons well qualified for the places, tell me whom you will appoint, that I may get rid of the importunities.' " Monroe told Crawford that it was none of his business whom he might appoint and that his language was improper. Both were now aroused to anger. Crawford advanced, his cane raised, and called the president a "damned infernal old scoundrel." Monroe moved toward the fireplace and picked up the fire tongs, assumed a defensive posture, and let loose some verbal abuse of his own. At this Crawford recovered his senses and hastily left.

Monroe made efforts to keep out the rabble. He did not allow the public to walk around the mansion unattended, as had the previous administration. Most visitors were restricted to the entrance hall. In addition Monroe employed guards, though not in uniform, and installed iron fencing to keep people out. Nonetheless the public did gain entry, and at a crowded drawing room following John Quincy Adams's election, General Scott was "robbed of his pocket-book containing 800 dolls," according to one contemporary account, "and much mirth occasioned by the idea of pick-pockets at the Presidents Drawing room."

By and large Monroe's presidency was uneventful, in that he governed without organized opposition. It was an easy time to be popular. Even the Panic of 1819, a severe recession, failed to tarnish the president. In 1820 he was reelected with only one dissenting electoral vote, and his inaugural was seemingly characterized by unequivocal optimism. "Altogether, the scene was truly striking and grand," wrote Judge Joseph Story. "There was a simple dignity about it which excited very pleasing sensations. The fine collection of beautiful and interesting women, dressed with great elegance, the presence of so many men of talents, character and public services, civil and military— the majestic stretch of the hall itself, the recollection of our free and happy situation, all combined to produce a most profound feeling of interest. I do not know that I ever was more impressed by a public spectacle." After the ceremony at the Capitol, hundreds adjourned to the White House to offer their congratulations. The judge continued: "All the world was there, hackney coaches, private carriages, foreign ministers and their suites, were immediately in motion, and the very ground seemed beaten to a powder or paste under the trampling of horses and the rolling of wheels. The scene lasted until three o'clock, and then all things resumed their wonted tranquility."

Monroe's popularity was not merely circumstantial. He did successfully manage the affairs of the nation, particularly its foreign policy. Most notably, on December 2, 1823, he set forth the Monroe Doctrine, a bold assertion that the American continents "are henceforth not to be considered as subjects for future colonization by any European powers."

Finally, toward the end of Monroe's second term, the Era of Good Feelings began to evaporate, and partisan politics resumed. After eight years of relative serenity, Monroe was to conclude his presidency with a scandal. When he sold his own furniture to the government for the initial furnishing of the empty White House in 1817, he placed what would become a convoluted financial transaction in the hands of Samuel Lane, commissioner of public buildings and the person in charge of the congressional fund for furnishing the White House. Lane, unbeknownst to Monroe, mishandled the accounts. After Lane died in 1822, an audit showed $20,000 in public funds unaccounted for, and Monroe appeared suspect.

A legislative inquiry ensued. At one point Congressman John Cocke of Tennessee suggested that Monroe appear before the investigating committee to explain himself, and Monroe indignantly refused, terming Cocke a scoundrel. Monroe would eventually seek to diffuse the issue by offering to buy his furniture back and by inviting Congress to examine every transaction of his life in which the public might have a financial interest. John Quincy Adams described the unprecedented personal exposure as "almost as incongruous to the station of a President of the United States as it would be to a blooming virgin to exhibit herself naked before a multitude." But it worked. The inquiry petered out, and the nation ceased to buzz with rumors of presidential malfeasance. And Monroe, in the end, left furniture in the White House.

Monroe's finances were shaky throughout his life. The eight-hundred-acre Virginia plantation he purchased in 1789, not far from his mentor's Monticello home, was soil-poor and never did well. At Highland, as he called it (subsequent owners renamed it Ash Lawn), Monroe built a one-story wood-frame house so modest that historians would later question whether it was his. In 1806 Monroe's uncle, Judge Joseph Jones, died, leaving him some money and substantial lands in Loudon County, Virginia, northwest of Washington. The cottage on that estate became the Monroes' primary home outside Washington. As his second term began, the president finally built a fine brick mansion on the property. Oak Hill, designed by Jefferson and built by James Hoban, was, befitting of Monroe's office, sumptuous—all carved wood, marble mantelpieces, high ceilings, and formality. It was also costly, and would contribute to Monroe's later bankruptcy.

Monroe could not live on his $25,000 salary as president. Like his predecessors, he had to pay all White House expenses, including staff. The mansion required a great deal of labor just to operate day-to-day. Monroe used slaves, although, like Washington and Jefferson, he did not favor the institution. (He was a member of the American Colonization Society, and in 1821 helped acquire land in Africa—specifically Liberia—for the settlement of freed slaves. The country's capital, Monrovia, is named after him.) Additional slaves were hired for important social functions; they would work for over a week just to make the needed candles.

As Monroe's debts mounted near the end of his second term, he tried scaling down White House social affairs. His circumstances were aggravated by the Panic of 1819 and the subsequent drop in land prices. By 1822 he was $35,000 in debt. When he retired to Oak Hill in 1825, he was $75,000 in debt. He spent the rest of his life trying to get Congress to pay him for expenses he said he incurred during his diplomatic missions to Europe (the usual procedure was to pay expenses as they arose and expect Congress to reimburse them later). In 1826 Congress voted $29,513 for back expenses, but Monroe was adamant that this was far short of what was due him. By the end of his life he was nearly destitute. News of his financial plight stirred popular sympathy, and Congress would vote him an additional $30,000 shortly before he died.

Elizabeth died in September 1830, and Monroe's own health began to fail. Two months later he moved to New York City to live with his daughter Maria in her town house. It would be his last home. The following spring he put Oak Hill up for sale. "It is very distressing to me to sell my property in Loudon," Monroe wrote to James Madison, "for besides parting with all I have in [Virginia], I indulged a hope, if I could retain it, that I might be able occasionally to visit it, and meet my friends. . . . I deeply regret that there is no prospect of our ever meeting again." Madison replied, "The pain I feel . . . amounts to a pang which I cannot well express." Monroe died on July 4, 1831— the third of the first five presidents to die on the "glorious Fourth."

# 6

# John Quincy Adams
## 1825–1829

## *A Dull and Stately Prison*

WHEN JOHN QUINCY ADAMS moved into the White House in 1825, the mansion was still a work in progress. There was no running water. Cows, sheep, and horses were stabled beneath the dining room, which made for unpleasant odors in warm weather. The East Room was undecorated. The north portico had yet to be built, and a dozen sheds leaned against the building—shelter for the horses nearby Treasury and State Department employees rode to work. The house was at the edge of the nascent capital city, only two blocks from open country, and hogs and livestock wandered loose on the grounds.

"I believe it would be difficult to find such an assortment of rags and rubbish even in an Alms House," First Lady Louisa Adams complained when she took up residence at what she called a "half-finished barn . . . this great palace." Yet the White House would see few improvements during the Adams administration. The era of unity over which Monroe had presided was disintegrating into one of rabidly partisan politics. To spite him, Adams's adversaries withheld or cut normal appropriations for refurbishing the White House and didn't reverse course until Andrew Jackson took office.

The presidency should have been a crowning achievement for fifty-seven-year-old John Quincy Adams. The son of John Adams, a founding father, signer of the Declaration of Independence, and second president of the United States, he began his sixty-year public career at age fourteen, as private secretary to Francis Dana, a diplomat to the Russian court in St. Petersburg. He himself would go on to a brilliant career as a diplomat. In 1801, after a series of assignments abroad, Adams returned from Europe with his new wife, Louisa Catherine Johnson, whom he'd met and married in England. He served as a Massachusetts senator from 1803 to 1808. In 1809 he returned to Europe as the first American minister to Russia. He was called to Belgium in 1814 to negotiate the Treaty of Ghent, which ended the War of 1812. When an ambassadorial post in London ended in 1817, he returned to America and quickly distinguished himself as one of the most effective secretaries of state in U.S. history, under James Monroe, with whom he would formulate the Monroe Doctrine in 1823.

In 1820, at age fifty-three, the peripatetic Adams finally bought something resembling a permanent home, a three-story town house on Washington's F Street. The elegant home had belonged to James and Dolley Madison when Madison was secretary of state, and served as a stylish setting for the entertaining required of a man with designs on the presidency. Adams and his wife had a stormy relationship, but during her husband's eight years as secretary of state, Louisa was an industrious partner. She turned the F Street house into a prime social center in a city where, as a Philadelphian described it in 1823, "amusement is a business, a need, to which almost every body is given up from 5 o'clock till bed time."

The most famous and most political of the Adamses' parties was the elaborate nine-hundred-guest ball thrown on January 8, 1824, to celebrate the anniversary of the Battle of New Orleans. Guest of honor General Andrew Jackson, the hero of New Orleans, was Adams's most troublesome opponent in the presidential race. The party, a smashing success, was calculated less to honor Jackson than to elevate Adams's reputation as a patriot and thereby boost his candidacy.

Adams's mother, Abigail, had written to Louisa that she would rather see her son "thrown as a log on the fire than see him president of the United States." The remark was prescient: his election was more disappointment than victory, and his presidency was miserable from day one. Jackson received by far the most popular votes and the most electoral votes, but failed to attain a majority since Henry Clay, William Crawford, and Adams were also in the race. It was left to the House of Representatives to decide among the top three candidates. There Clay threw his support to Adams, providing the decisive votes.

Margaret Bayard Smith, wife of the *National Intelligencer* editor, described Adams's reaction: "When the news of his election was communicated to Mr. Adams by the Committee and during their address, the sweat rolled down his face—he shook from head to foot and was so agitated that he could scarcely stand or speak. He told the gentlemen he would avail himself of the precedent set by Mr. Jefferson and give them his answer in writing. One of the Committee told me from his hesitation, his manner and first words, he really thought he was going to decline." Whatever Adams's feelings at that moment, he clearly recorded his chagrin in his diary, writing that his election was not "in a manner satisfactory to pride or to just desire; not by the unequivocal suffrages of a majority of the people." His father, at least, was proud. When John Adams learned that his favorite son had become president, he wrote to him, "The multitude of my thoughts and the intensity of my feelings are too much for a mind like mine in its ninetieth year."

Adams quickly appointed Henry Clay secretary of state, which infuriated Jackson and his supporters. Clay later admitted that accepting was the stupidest move of his career. The politically inept move may not have been a deal, but it looked like one, and it gave the Jackson forces a rallying cry. They immediately began making plans to get Jackson elected in 1828 and to make the intervening years as difficult as possible for John Quincy Adams.

The modern two-party system was rapidly evolving, but Adams tried to stand above partisan politics. The new president's ethical standards would not allow him to put allies in office to build up a political base, and in making appointments he refused to dismiss "able and faithful opponents to promote my own partisans." He was alone in his high standards, however. Adams discovered that the Jacksonian Democrats united to defeat virtually every measure he put forth. His domestic program, including the establishment of a national university and projects in science and the arts, went nowhere. Even Clay admitted that some of the president's recommendations were "entirely hopeless." In his first annual message Adams urged a national astronomical observatory. His cabinet had warned him against it, but Adams was stubborn. He was a student of astronomy and had even mounted a telescope on the roof of the White House. Congress ridiculed and ignored his proposals. Adams was devastated. He said, "I shall be as I have been— a solitary."

His adversaries not only refused to accept his legislative program but, worse, actively attacked him. His years of service abroad became fodder for accusations—the deadly old standbys—that he was "monarchical" and "kingly." In 1826, a secondhand billiard table that he had acquired for $61—which included $5 for the cues and $6 for the billiard balls—was trumped up into a scandal. Adams had learned the game in Europe and played occasionally. Even the revered George Washington had played billiards. Still, the game evoked images of ill-lit, smoky rooms, liquor, gambling, and other, darker, evils. The purchase was made from his own funds and, in an unlucky bit of overzealousness, included on a long and detailed inventory of White House furnishings the meticulous Adams had submitted to Congress. The puritanical New Englander who read his Bible cover to cover every year was called "a corrupter of the youth of the nation" and charged with squandering public money on "gaming tables and gambling furniture." Protests that he had paid for the items personally were ignored, and believing a president should be above such squabbles, Adams failed to defend himself further.

Massachusetts senator Elijah Mills described the combative atmosphere at the Capitol in a letter to his wife on February 8, 1826: "[The president] meets with a most formidable and virulent opposition, especially in the Senate, and it is no small task, I assure you, to overcome it. The session is getting to be more stormy and unpleasant than any I have known since I have been in the Senate, and I fear will be growing more and more so."

The president's remote, unbending personality, intimated by a high, shrill voice and thin, habitually compressed lips, was no help. He had many of the same characteristics—good and bad—as his father. With what he himself called his "reserved, cold, austere and forbidding manners," he managed to antagonize most people. He suffered fools badly. He was honest, even blunt—a dangerous thing in a politician. As Albert Gallatin, minister to Britain at the time, observed, Adams "wants to a deplorable degree that most essential quality, a sound and correct judgment." He was also demanding, setting high standards for others but also for himself. His self-discipline could be harsh: he took ice-cold baths, rubbing his body with a horsehair mitten. He was politically out of touch with the people but didn't care. He felt awkward among common people; he often traveled by public stage and steamship, but avoided talking to his fellow passengers.

Like his political career, Adams's marriage was at a low point during the White House years. "Our union has not been without its trials," he once admitted. Louisa Catherine Johnson, the only foreign-born first lady, was born in England and raised there and in France. Her mother was English, her father a wealthy American merchant who would lose his fortune just as Louisa married. Her relationship with the twenty-eight-year-old American diplomat she met in 1795 was contentious from the start. Immediately after their engagement, Adams left London for several diplomatic missions of unknown duration, telling his distressed fiancée that she must accept such "untoward Events" as tests of "character." She felt his letters were "severe," "cold," and "peremptory." As she came to realize that Adams welcomed deprivations as tests of his own character, she protested that his "boasted philosophy" was "a *dreadful* thing." Nevertheless, they were married after only a year-long engagement, on July 26, 1797, in London.

In 1801, following a four-year mission in Berlin, the couple sailed to America with their three-month-old son, named for the late George Washington. Having lived all her life in handsome European style, Louisa was struck by the crudeness of her husband's family home in Quincy and everything else in her new country. "Had I stepped into Noah's Ark, I do not think I could have been more utterly astonished," she said.

Eight years later President James Madison offered to make Adams the first American minister to Russia. Adams not only accepted without consulting his wife, but did

*The son of the second President, Adams began his brilliant career as a diplomat and finished it serving seventeen years as "Old Man Eloquent" of the House of Representatives. But his four years in the White House were the most miserable of his life.* (LIBRARY OF CONGRESS)

not tell her until they were about to board the ship that their two oldest boys would be left behind in Boston. She would not see them again for six years. "Can ambition repay such sacrifices?!" she wrote in her diary, "Never!"

When he was president, Adams vacationed away from the White House annually from August to October, spending a few months in his Quincy home. Louisa refused to accompany him. She stayed in the White House or visited friends. Their infrequent letters were stilted: Adams addressed his wife as "Mrs. Louisa C. Adams," and she addressed him as "The President."

Louisa was attractive, played the piano and harp (her harp is now in the Smithsonian Institution), sang well, wrote stories, plays, and poems, and was agreeable enough with guests. But she had suffered through several miscarriages and the loss of a year-old daughter. By the time she entered the White House at forty-nine, she was plagued by migraine headaches, depression, and fainting spells that brought everyone rushing to her side. She often wrote, bitterly, of the way society cast off women once their youthful beauty was gone and their childbearing duties finished. She seemed to wallow in self-pity, writing to son Charles in 1828, "I take pleasure in the idea that I am gradually sinking into that state which leads to a happier and better world."

The first lady found her evenings long and lonely, as Adams often nodded off to sleep over his reading. She described the mansion as "that dull and stately prison in which the sounds of mirth are seldom heard. . . . There is something in this great, unsocial house which depresses my spirits beyond expression, . . . [and it is] impossible for me to feel at home or to fancy that I have a home anywhere." She sought compensating outlets, such as reading, sketching, and cultivating silkworms. She had several hundred silkworms and gathered their silk herself. She started gorging herself on chocolate candy. At times she retreated to her room, often for days. "I am now always cross and unpleasant to myself and everybody else," she acknowledged.

Louisa did dutifully plan the requisite entertainments, including the weekly receptions, though for the most part without the flair she mustered as the wife of the secretary of state. Adams too had little enthusiasm for these obligatory events. He had to stand for hours while waiters passed trays laden with coffee, tea, wine, cakes, jellies, and ice cream. In his diary he noted that the affairs were becoming "more and more insupportable to me." Louisa also planned frequent dinners for thirty or more guests, but was often absent from these events. Her husband tended to be a dull host. The well-read Adams could discuss a wide range of subjects with his intellectual equals—he once wrote that he "talked too much at dinner"—but he was incapable of small talk. He also conceded in his diary that he could not "altogether avoid a dogmatical and peremptory tone and manners." As one visitor described, guests seated next to the president had "a hard time of it."

One of the couple's worst disagreements during the White House years was financial. When his father died in 1826, Adams inherited the family home in Quincy, with its 300 acres. He could have sold the property and presumably come out ahead, but he could not bear to part with the "Old House." He had to pay $12,000 into his father's estate to keep the farm, and went heavily into debt. Louisa had demanded that he sell it. She viewed the Adams homestead as "a large unprofitable landed estate," and in any case did not like Quincy, especially in winter. "I cannot endure the thought," Adams replied. Louisa refused to take possession of the house until 1830.

Adams was committed to his family, but as hard on his children as he was on himself. Louisa tried to be forgiving, but she was often overruled. Adams once refused their son John permission to come home from Harvard for Christmas because he ranked only forty-fifth in a class of eighty-five. "I take no satisfaction in seeing you," Adams wrote his son. "I could feel nothing but sorrow and shame in your presence."

George Washington Adams, their eldest son, bore the brunt of his father's pressure to succeed. He was also the least able to cope with it. George was brilliant but unstable. He became a lawyer but fell into debt, had a child by a servant girl, and began a downward spiral. Adams wrote urging him to avoid alcohol, tobacco, and other vices but got no response. The president had "troubled thoughts, the most oppressive of which regard my son George." At the end of his presidency, Adams ordered George to come to Washington to escort Louisa home to Quincy. Facing his stern father unsettled him, but George boarded a ship. He was en route to Washington when he evidently jumped overboard in the middle of the night and drowned. He was twenty-eight years old. His parents learned of his suicide in April 1829, shortly after vacating the White House, from a newspaper story. Louisa would always maintain that her son had been sacrificed to the political ambitions of her husband.

Life at the White House was further strained by the three orphaned children of Louisa's sister, Nancy Johnson Hellen. The three became permanent members of the Adams household in 1818, and all three caused problems. One boy got involved with a White House chambermaid Louisa described as "a bold and cunning minx" and ended up marrying her. The second son would die a drunk at twenty-four. The daughter, Mary, became engaged to George, who frequently visited Washington, then switched her affections to John, who served as his father's secretary. Louisa favored the second match; Adams refused his permission. Adams finally gave in, and John and Mary were wed in the Oval Room on February 25, 1828. Adams's first grandchild was born on December 2 of that year, the second child to be born in the White House.

The President and first lady even disagreed about what was one of the crowning events of his presidency: a visit from the legendary Marquis de Lafayette, who came to stay at the White House in the summer of 1825 just prior to his return to France. Lafayette, a French general and statesman whose enthusiasm for the American Revolution had led him to fight alongside George Washington, was the last living important general of the War of Independence. In 1824 he was invited to cross the ocean as a guest of the United States. When he arrived in New York, the whole city turned out to welcome him. He dressed in his continental uniform, and the crowds went wild. He spent a year visiting all twenty-four states. Congress gave him $200,000 and an entire township of land. He was showered with gifts—from Indian tomahawks to furniture to a live alligator—that amounted to several tons of cargo. Congress arranged for a warship, the USS *Brandywine,* to take his largesse back to France. Meanwhile everything was stored in the East Room of the White House—including the alligator.

When Adams invited Lafayette and his entourage to stay at the White House, Louisa was not pleased. "I admire the old gentleman but no admiration can stand family discomfort," she said, ". . . since we are obliged to turn out of our beds to make room for him and his suite." The sixteen maids and other staff employed by the White House could not attend to so many guests, and Louisa was forced to hire additional staff just for the general's stay. On September 6, 1825, Lafayette's sixty-eighth birthday, Adams gave a farewell White House dinner for him. In making their speeches, the president and the general became quite emotional. Lafayette threw himself into his friend's arms, and both men were in tears. When Lafayette left the next day, a general holiday was proclaimed in Washington.

If President Adams was austere and aloof as charged, he was also accessible to a fault. The White House door was always open during the day, with Adams receiving visitors from shortly after breakfast to five in the afternoon. Any citizen could walk into the mansion and get in line on the stair, even to simply shake the president's hand. These visitors consumed his days, which forced him to write state papers at night. "I can scarcely conceive a more harassing, wearying, teasing condition of existence," he said.

The daily visitations were not entirely uneventful. Adams once had a long conversation with a "wretched looking man" who declared himself a messenger "from God Almighty" and claimed he was St. Peter. After listening to some "wild incoherent" talk, Adams asked the man who he was before he became St. Peter. The man replied, "Peter McDermot, an Irishman." On another occasion, an Eleazar Parraly barged in unannounced and interrupted the president's meeting with Secretary of State Henry Clay. When Adams discovered that the traveler was a dentist, he excused Clay and, since there were no dentists in Washington, "took the opportunity to have a decayed tooth drawn." The dentist obliged and refused payment.

Adams even granted an audience to a man who had publicly threatened to kill him. Dr. George P. Todson had been court-martialed and removed from his position as assistant surgeon in the army. Adams had already declined requests to reverse the verdict. Subsequently, Todson had, in the words of his attorney, "come to the most cool and inflexible determination" to murder Adams. The attorney warned the president, but on December 16, 1826, Adams not only let Todson in but denied his request again, face to face. After more visits over several months, Adams was able to get Todson an assignment on the frontier and never saw him again.

The methodical Adams also had his personal routines, which tended to be rigidly scheduled. In a diary entry on April 30, 1825, he wrote, "I usually rise between five and six—that is, at this time of year, from an hour and a half and two hours before the sun. I walk by the light of the moon or stars or none, about four miles, usually returning home in time to see the sun rise from the eastern chamber of the house. I then make my fire, and read three chapters of the Bible with Scott's and Hewlett's Commentaries. Read papers until nine." He also read Greek and Roman classics in the original languages, but seemingly less for pleasure than for the sake of setting higher and higher demands on himself. In fact his main enjoyment seemed to be in reaching the goals he set for himself. Toward the end of his term he lengthened his morning walk, pushing himself to do more. Much of the weekend was reserved for church. He would often attend twice on Sunday, morning and evening, mostly Unitarian and Presbyterian services but occasionally Catholic or others. He once went to three services in one day and returned to the White House that evening to find himself locked out and the porter gone off with the key.

In the summer Adams varied his exercise routine by taking a morning swim in the Potomac. At sixty the president could swim across the river where it was about a mile wide. His favorite outdoors companion was White House steward Antoine Giusta, a deserter from Napoleon's army. The two met when Adams was in Belgium in 1814, and Adams hired him as his valet. When Adams was stationed in London, Giusta married Louisa's maid, Mary. The couple had run the Adams households, including the White House, ever since. Adams could not afford to keep them after he left office, so they opened a successful oyster and coffee house in Washington. At that time Adams was in need of money, so he borrowed from the obliging Giusta and soon owed him as much as $5,000.

Giusta was with Adams the day the president nearly drowned in the Potomac. Early on the morning of June 13, 1825, the two walked from the White House to their favorite spot, near a big sycamore tree. They decided to paddle an old, leaky canoe to the opposite shore and then swim back. Midriver a squall came up, and the canoe began filling with water. There was nothing to bail with, and the canoe sank. Giusta was naked, and Adams had taken off his shoes, coat, and vest, but his remaining clothes impeded him. "My principal difficulty was in the loose sleeves of my shirt," he recorded. The sleeves filled with water and were like weights on his arms. He was gasping for air by the time he reached the far shore.

It was decided that Giusta would wear Adams's wet clothes and walk back across Long Bridge to get a carriage and fresh clothes for the president. Meanwhile, a messenger appeared at the White House with the exaggerated news that the president had drowned—not a surprise to the first lady, who had long predicted just such an accident. But Adams was happily wading and swimming, or just waiting for Giusta, "sitting naked basking on the bank." When Giusta came back with a carriage, the two returned "half dressed" to the White House. Louisa termed the affair "altogether ridiculous" and urged her husband to give up his morning swims. Adams paid her no heed—he was back in the river a few days later.

Shortly before Adams died at age eighty, he yielded to "an irresistible impulse" to visit the spot by the sycamore tree. He swam for half an hour, drying himself off with his shirt.

Adams developed another early-morning activity: gardening. Two years into his term he knew he would probably not be reelected, and the more depressed he became over his political future and his family relationships, the more he found satisfaction in his gardening. In his diary, his bitterness leaves when he writes about his garden. He would even skip his morning walks in favor of the "attractions of the garden." He read books on botany and became quite knowledgeable. He rode horseback through the woods surrounding the White House searching for acorns, seeds, vines, and shoots, and asked U.S. consuls abroad to send him seeds.

Adams began his cultivation virtually from scratch. The White House grounds, as described during the Monroe era, were barren and muddy. Chunks of masonry and Ionic pilaster caps littered the ground. Jefferson's mass plantings seem not to have survived the mansion's reconstruction. The effect, architect Charles Bulfinch wrote, was "such as no gentleman of moderate property would permit as his own residence." In 1818 Bulfinch had been employed by James Monroe to complete the Capitol, and had also produced drawings for the landscaping of the White House grounds. Many of Adams's improvements, and later Jackson's, were probably inspired by Bulfinch's plan.

The grounds were graded and filled, and the president went to work with his gardener, John Ousley, who would remain head White House gardener for many years, living with his family in the East Wing. Adams embarked on a nationalistic planting program that made the White House garden a museum of American plants, especially trees: walnut, persimmon, willow, catalpa, honey locust, oak, tulip, and chestnut. An expanse to the right of the south entrance gate became the main ornamental garden, Adams's pride and joy. "In this small garden of less than two acres," he wrote in the summer of 1827, "there are forest and fruit-trees, shrubs, hedges, esculent vegetables, kitchen and medicinal herbs, hot-house plants, flowers and weeds to the amount, I conjecture, of at least one thousand." Within a year, he had planted seven hundred trees. An elm he planted as a seedling lasted a century and a half. He sometimes worked in the vegetable garden, an old straw hat on his bald head, planting seedlings in cold frames. The White House had always had a vegetable and herb garden, and storing and preserving produce was a major annual undertaking. From the herb patch he plucked "leaves of balm and hyssop, marjoram, mint, rue, sage, tansy, tarragam, and wormwood."

Adams carefully observed the results of his gardening experiments. In early June of 1827 he wrote, "This morning, after planting in my eastern seed-bed eighteen whole red-cherries and visiting the southern bed, where the casual poppies are now all (six) in flower, the mustard and anthemis in full bloom, the altheas still coming up and the wild cherries apparently stationary, I remarked that the strawberries are ceasing, and the currents, red and black, becoming ripe."

Gardening was something he was able to be philosophical about: "A planter must make up his mind to endure many disappointments." The disappointments of his political and personal lives, however, were more difficult to bear. With two years still to serve, Adams became depressed. "My own career is closed. My hopes such as are left to me, are centered in my children." He turned inward to self-discipline, work, and reading classics such as Milton and Cicero. He complained a good deal about his health—skin problems, indigestion, insomnia, cramps, and constipation, all of which may well have been, at least in part, psychosomatic. Louisa wrote to son George that Adams, nearing the end of his term, had "almost total loss of appetite and general weakness and languor."

By now the president was suffering from bouts of depression. When he realized he would not be reelected, he felt "a sluggish carelessness of life, an imaginary wish that it were terminated." He would be the second president—the first being his father—to be cast from office after just one term. The ugly election of 1828 was hard on both candidates. Adams, an inveterate diarist, leaves a telling gap between August and December of that year, but his letters of the time record his astonishment with the foul tactics. After his trouncing by Jackson, Adams tried perhaps too hard to mask his humiliation, as Margaret Bayard Smith observed in a December 20, 1828, letter:

You ask how the administration folks look since their defeat. . . . Mr. and Mrs. Adams have gone a little too far in this *assumed* gaiety at the last drawing room they laid aside the manners which until now they have always worn and came out in a brilliant masquerade dress of social, gay, frank, cordial manners. What a change from the silent, repulsive, haughty reserve by which they had hitherto been distinguished. The great audience chamber, never before opened, and now not finished was thrown open for *dancing*, a thing unheard of before at a drawing-room! The band of musick increased the hilarity of the scene. . . . As one of the opposition members observed, "The Administration mean to march out with fly-ing colours and all the honors of war."

On January 1, 1829, as his last two months in office began, Adams noted in his diary, "The year begins in gloom." The outgoing president sent word to Jackson that he would be willing to vacate the White House early, so that Jackson might hold his March 4 inaugural reception there. Jackson initially declined, then reconsidered. Adams rented a house on Meridian Hill, two miles away from the White House and from the center of the city. In the days before Jackson's inauguration, he moved his wife and possessions to the rented house, sending with them "the offensive billiard table." Adams stayed on in the White House to check his garden. He walked to the Capitol to sign last-minute bills, especially new appointments, before the Jackson forces took over. Then he too rode off to Meridian Hill, skipping Jackson's inaugural the next day. A notice appeared in the March 3 *National Intelligencer:*

> The citizens of Columbia and others, friends of Mr. Adams, who might be dis-posed, conformable to the usage heretofore, to pay him a visit, after the Inaugura-tion of the President elect, on Wednesday the 4th inst., are requested by Mr. Adams to dispense with that formality which the distance of his residence from the Capitol would render inconvenient to them. He thanks them for all the kind-ness which they have constantly extended to him, and prays to them to accept the assurance of his best wishes for their health and happiness.

Adams, now sixty-three, seemed to have reached the anticlimactic end of his politi-cal life. "From indolence and despondency and indiscretion may I specially be pre-served," he wrote prayerfully in his diary a few days later. But he was despondent. "My whole life has been a succession of disappointments," he wrote after he left office. "I can scarcely recollect a single instance of success to anything that I ever undertook. . . . I have no plausible motive for wanting to live."

Yet he would soon return to the fray with a seventeen-year career in the House of Representatives, where he would be admired as "Old Man Eloquent." In part he accepted for need of the congressman's salary: $8 a day. His 900-acre farm wasn't espe-cially profitable, and his finances were tenuous and would continue to be. As a repre-sentative, he walked to congressional sessions to save the 25-cent hack fare. Even so he was also forced to borrow money, including, once, $10 from a niece to get to Washing-ton from Quincy. But he distinguished himself in the legislature, in particular by fight-ing every attempt to extend slavery.

"More than sixty years of incessant active intercourse with the world has made polit-ical movement to me as much a necessary of life as atmospheric air," he wrote in a March 23, 1841, diary entry. "This is the weakness of my nature, which I have intellect enough to perceive, but not energy to control. And thus while a remnant of physical power is left to me to write and speak, the world will retire from me before I shall retire from the world."

And so it did. On February 21, 1848, Adams collapsed over his desk on the floor of the House of Representatives. He died two days later on the sofa in the office of the Speaker. He never made it home. His last words were, "This is the end of earth. I am content." Louisa died four years later, on May 15, 1852.

# Andrew Jackson

## 1829–1837

## *The People's Choice*

A FRONTIERSMAN and war hero, Andrew Jackson was ushered into the White House by the common man, newly enfranchised by the elimination in many states of property requirements for voters. "The People's President" belonged to everyone, and now so did the White House—as was evident from the day of Old Hickory's boisterous inauguration.

"I have never seen such a crowd before," Daniel Webster said of the mass of humanity that overran the capital for Jackson's March 4, 1829, inauguration. "Persons have come five hundred miles to see General Jackson, and they really seem to think that the country has been rescued from some dreadful danger." The federal city had been packed for days. Every bed in Washington was spoken for, and the overflow of well-wishers slept on billiard tables and floors. On the streets, all things hickory were de rigueur: horsemen boasted hickory bridles and hickory stirrups, and women wore hickory-nut necklaces.

The president-elect was staying at Gadsby's Tavern. On March 4, he walked to the Capitol, his pace slowed by the crowds. Still in mourning for his wife, Rachel, he dressed plainly, all in black, and was hatless. Nevertheless, at six foot one, with a shock of straight, snow-white hair and an almost regal bearing, he stood out. He had to duck into the back of the Capitol and enter through the basement. When the hero stepped up to make his speech, the sun suddenly burst through the clouds that had hung over the city all morning. "The shout that rent the air, still resounds in my ears," Margaret Bayard Smith, wife of the *National Intelligencer* editor, wrote a week later. Jackson, not an orator, gave an inaugural address that was inaudible to most of the vast audience, but it hardly mattered.

The new president's first challenge was to make his way to the White House. Mrs. Smith described the scene:

> It was with difficulty he made his way through the Capitol and down the hill to the gateway that opens on the avenue. Here for a moment he was stopped. The living mass was impenetrable. After a while a passage was opened, and he mounted his horse which had been provided for his return . . . then such a cortege as followed him! Country men, farmers, gentlemen, mounted and dismounted, boys, women and children, black and white. Carriages, wagons and carts all pursuing him to the President's house. . . . In about an hour, the pavement was clear enough for us to walk. . . . we set off to the President's house, but in nearer approach found an entrance impossible, the yard and avenue was compact with living matter.

The reception was an unprecedented free-for-all, a near riot. One guest, writing to then New York governor Martin Van Buren, called it "a regular Saturnalia." It was attended, wrote Supreme Court Justice Joseph Story, by "immense crowds of all sorts of people, from the highest and most polished, down to the most vulgar and gross in the nation. I never saw such a mixture. The reign of KING MOB seemed triumphant. I was glad to escape from the scene as soon as possible." The "king" himself was forced to escape. He received his admirers in the Oval Room for a time, but so many people pressed into the room that he was forced to the rear wall, where he gasped for air. Despite his reputation for toughness, the sixty-one-year-old president was actually quite frail. His secretary and nephew, Jack Donelson, and others locked arms to form a protective cordon around him. Slowly they eased him out one of the big windows, carried him down the steps, into a coach, and into his bed at Gadsby's Tavern. Meanwhile, refreshments were set up on the lawn in an attempt to draw people out of the house.

Mrs. Smith and friends, when they found they could not get in, went home, rested, and tried again around four or five. They found

> a rabble, a mob, of boys, negros, women, children, scrambling, fighting, romping. What a pity, what a pity! No arrangement had been made no police officers placed on duty and the whole house had been inundated by the rabble mob. . . . Cut glass and china to the amount of several thousand dollars had been broken in the struggle to get the refreshments, punch and other articles had been carried out in tubs and buckets, but had it been in hogsheads it would have been insufficient, ice-creams, and cake and lemonade, for 20,000 people, for it is said that number were there, tho' I think the estimate exaggerated. Ladies fainted, men were seen with bloody noses. . . .It is mortifying to see men with boots heavy with mud, standing on the damask-satin-covered chairs and sofas. Ladies and gentlemen only had been expected at this levee, not the people en masse. But it was the People's day, and the People's President and the People would rule.

Jackson would stay at Gadsby's for a week while the White House was cleaned up. The *Washington City Chronicle* wrote the next day, "We regret to say that the President's hospitality on this occasion was in some measure misapplied."

The man who inspired this celebratory melee was born in 1767 in a log cabin somewhere along the North Carolina/South Carolina frontier. At thirteen, he became a militiaman in the Revolution and barely survived it (neither of his brothers did). As a wild teenager, he dissipated an inheritance from a grandfather in Ireland, but went on to make a fortune in Tennessee as a lawyer and speculator in land and slaves. Land was the currency of the frontier, and Jackson collected legal fees at the rate of an acre for every 10 cents of his services. He was elected to the House of Representatives in 1796. Around that time he was described as a "tall, lanky, uncouth-looking, personage . . . queue down his back tied with an eel skin." After one session he was appointed, in 1797, to the Senate. After one session there, he resigned to attend to his personal affairs in Tennessee. Six months later the legislature elected him to the state supreme court. He was already well known, and his courtroom escapades and a bloodless duel with the governor of Tennessee only made him more popular.

But in 1804 Jackson's finances collapsed as his land speculations went bad. He accepted worthless bank notes in exchange for land, and incurred debt backed by those notes. He also acquired an animosity toward banks that would drive one of his most important policy battles as president. His bankruptcy forced him to sell virtually everything and he moved with wife Rachel from their comfortable home to a log house on a farm just south of Nashville dubbed the Hermitage. The couple lived there for sixteen years, receiving scores of distinguished visitors, including President Monroe and Jefferson Davis.

As Jackson recovered his financial footing, he began raising and breeding racehorses, developing one of the finest stables in the country. Horse racing was at the time America's most popular spectator sport. His best stallion, Truxton, became the most famous horse of the day and earned his master a fortune. During one of his periodic financial downturns, Jackson, who liked to gamble heavily, bet on Truxton in a race against a horse named Greyhound. He put up land, supplies from the store he owned, slaves, and what money he had. Truxton won, and Jackson's fortune was restored. By 1819 he was building a brick mansion at the Hermitage that would ultimately be as fine as that of any aristocratic president before him.

After the battle of New Orleans in 1815, Jackson became a war hero of presidential proportions. "[He has] slain the Indians and flogged the British," said one supporter, "and . . . therefore is the wisest and greatest man in the nation." But when queried about the job in 1821, Jackson responded, "Do they think I am such a damned fool: No sir; I know what I am fit for. I can command a body of men in a rough way; but I am not fit to be President."

But few men have been able to resist the siren call of the presidency. Jackson lost— barely—to John Quincy Adams in the election of 1824, which was decided in the House of Representatives. But he came back to trounce Adams in 1828. The victory was bittersweet. Jackson was in mourning for his beloved wife, who had become a central figure in one of the nastiest campaigns in American political history. The trauma may well have caused her death.

*On January 8, 1824, Louisa Adams organized a ball to celebrate the anniversary of Andrew Jackson's spectacular victory over the British at New Orleans in 1815 and to promote her husband's chance for his party's nomination for the presidency. It was one of Washington's historic social successes—about 1,000 attended. Adams went on to defeat Jackson and they became bitter enemies.* (LIBRARY OF CONGRESS)

Jackson married Rachel, née Donelson, in Tennessee in 1791. She was twenty-four and, they both thought, divorced from Lewis Robards, whom she'd married at seventeen. It turned out, however, that Robards had not secured a divorce, only permission from the state legislature to sue for divorce. This became clear to Jackson two years after his marriage when news, which crossed the frontier with difficulty, arrived saying that Rachel's divorce was final. He was forced to go through a humiliating second marriage ceremony. This legalized the marriage but also publicly acknowledged that Jackson had wed a married woman.

Both before and after the event the couple had a happy union. Rachel was intensely religious, and Jackson, himself a regular churchgoer (as president he rented a pew for $32.50 a year at the First Presbyterian Church), regarded her almost as a saint. "Aunt Rachel," as she was known throughout the Nashville area, lived her Christianity, caring for strangers in need and taking in stray children, at least ten of whom became full-time members of the family for some period. Attractive when young, Rachel put on weight over the years, becoming obese and acquiring a heart condition that was not helped by her fondness for smoking corncob pipes and even occasional cigars. One observer described the two demonstrating a frontier dance at a New Orleans ball: "The general a long, haggard man, with limbs like a skeleton, and Madame le Ge'ne'rale, a short fat dumpling, bobbing opposite each other like half-drunken Indians, to the wild melody of 'Possum up de Gum Tree,' and endeavoring to make a spring into the air. . . . Very remarkable."

Now, after thirty-five years, the 1828 campaign dredged up the circumstances of their marriage. Jackson's enemies called Rachel "a convicted adulteress" and a "profligate woman," and mocked her rough-hewn frontier character. They claimed that Jackson had "torn from a husband the wife of his bosom." Jackson tried to insulate his wife from the assault, but she came across a pamphlet that revealed the insults, began sobbing, took to her bed, and declined as the campaign proceeded. "Enemyes of the Genl have dipt their arrows in wormwood & gall and sped them at me," she wrote. When she heard that her husband had been elected, she said, "Well, for Mr. Jackson's sake, I am glad; for my part, I never wished it. . . . I would rather be doorkeeper in the house of God than live in that palace in Washington." She got her wish. Rachel died on December 22, 1828. Ten thousand people attended her funeral at the Hermitage. Jackson's emotional words were: "In the presence of this dear saint, I can and do forgive all my enemies. But those vile wretches who have slandered her must look to God for mercy."

One of those Jackson would not forgive was John Quincy Adams. The president had, characteristically, stayed above the campaign mudslinging, but Jackson thought he could have prevented it. But partisanship was the order of the day. Jackson's supporters had leveled equally vile accusations, saying that Adams had lived in sin before his marriage, and as a diplomat in Russia had been a pimp for the czar.

The partisanship was so extreme that even though Congress recognized that the White House was desperately in need of refurbishment, no work was authorized until Adams was gone from the premises. As soon as Jackson arrived, construction on the long-postponed north portico commenced almost immediately, in the early spring of 1829. Based on the original drawing for the White House, the dominating, many-columned portico functioned as a porte cochere, ending beyond the steps to cover the driveway. Then, in 1833, President Jackson ordered that the two pairs of stone gate piers at the Pennsylvania Avenue entrance be moved farther apart. He apparently found the carriage circle too tight. Today they remain where he placed them.

As a horse lover, Jackson set upon expanding the White House stables. He brought his own racehorses and jockeys with him to Washington and entered his horses in local events under the name of his secretary, Jack Donelson. Jackson frequently attended races at the National Jockey Club and other tracks to watch his horses run—especially fillies Emily, Lady Nashville, and Bolivia. The expanded stables also made it possible to move the animals out of a secondary stable under the White House dining room, which had been plagued by foul odors. It also created some badly needed space in the basement work area, there being nowhere to hang the laundry to dry except in the hallway.

Household chores were made easier in 1831 when a spring at Franklin Square was purchased and pipes laid to bring running water to the White House for the first time. Major hotels already offered this convenience, especially for bathing, but most Americans still hauled water by the bucket. The springwater flowed into a large pond and from there could be hand-pumped to the basement level for washing dishes. To bathe, the household would for a time continue to depend on hot water carried up two stories to a portable tub. Around late 1833, a bathing room with a hot bath, a cold bath, and a shower bath was established in the East Wing.

Inside, the large, oft-criticized East Room, eighty feet long and forty feet wide, was finally decorated for the first time. Of the $50,000 Congress allotted for the White House interior, a fifth went to finishing and furnishing the East Room. It was outfitted with wood paneling, decorative wooden beams, three large cut-glass chandeliers, each with eighteen oil lamps, and, for $1,058.25, a Brussels carpet in fawn, blue, and yellow with a red border. Bronzed and gilded tables had tops of "Italian black and gold slab." Drapes in blue and yellow moreen complemented lemon yellow walls, and blue damask satin upholstery was used throughout for the twenty-four armchairs and four sofas. Also for the East Room: twenty spittoons at $12.50 each. Jackson purchased a splendid silver service from the Russian minister for $4,308, a set of crystal with nine sizes of wine glasses, a new dinner service of blue French china for $1,500, and a matching dessert set for $1,000—costly items his second vice president and successor Martin Van Buren would have been vilified for using.

Despite all the improvements, the actress Fanny Kemble in 1833 described the White House as "comfortless." It was true that the big rooms were hard to heat with fireplaces. Even Jackson said of the finished East Room, "Hell itself couldn't warm that corner."

Altogether Jackson spent about $45,000 on furniture, silverware, and furnishing. It was more than John Quincy Adams had spent, but there was little criticism. A newspaper reporter sent from New York approved of the addition of chairs, saying, "They won't be kept standing upon their legs as they do before kings and emperors, as practiced by Mr. Clay's President, till they are so tired as scarcely to know whether they have legs to stand upon."

On the grounds, Jackson picked up where Adams, a passionate gardener, had left off; he too developed an interest in the garden, if not a hands-on one. The south grounds down to the river were uncultivated, or "desolate," as Fanny Kemble so graciously put it. White House cattle grazed there and provided milk for the White House kitchen. But in the summer of 1833, as many as sixty-five men labored over both the north and south grounds. The south side was graded, and garden paths laid out and spread with gravel. The next spring, the most extensive landscaping yet seen at the White House commenced: ornamental planting, vegetable gardening, and the building of trellises, benches, fences, and a hothouse.

Jackson believed in an elegant lifestyle and entertained lavishly. There were dinner guests nearly every night. On a daily basis the household seems to have favored American country fare, but Jackson did not hesitate to pull out all the stops.

Consider the mansion readied for guests, as recalled by Jessie Benton, daughter of Missouri senator Thomas Hart Benton: "The great wood-fires in every room, the immense number of wax lights softly burning, the stands of camilias. . . . After going through all this silent waiting fairyland, we were taken to the State Dining Room, where there was a gorgeous supper table shaped like a horseshoe, and covered with every good and glittering thing French skill could devise, and at either end was a monster salmon in waves of meat jelly." Or the even more elaborate dinner described by John R. Montgomery, a guest from Lancaster, Pennsylvania:

> The first course was soup in the french style; then beef bouille, next wild turkey boned and dressed with brains; after that fish; then chicken cold and dressed white, interlaid with slices of tongue and garnished with dressed salled; then canvass back ducks and celery; afterwards partridges with dressed breads and last pheasants and old Virginia ham. The dishes were placed in succession on the table, so as to give full effect to the appearance and then removed and carved on a side table by the servants. The first dessert was jelly and small tarts in the turkish style, then blanche mode and kisses and dried fruits in them. Then preserves of various kinds, after them ice cream and lastly grapes and oranges.
>
> The wines on the table were Sherry and Port to drink with soups and the first course of meats. When the wild turkey and fish were served, Madeira was handed out and while the wild fowl was eaten. Champagne was constantly poured out by the servants; after these were gone through with, Claret was substituted to be taken with the dessert and old Cherry was put on to drink with the fruits. As soon as all had taken what their appetites could possibly endure, we left the table and returned to the drawing room.

It took three hours to serve all this sumptuous food, set down in the State Dining Room beneath a large chandelier lit with thirty-two candles. Jackson's uniformed slaves, brought from the Hermitage, provided clean plates with each course. Though he was known in his youth for wild drinking and carousing, Jackson sipped only a glass or two of wine and ate sparingly. He actually preferred his old army meal of plain rice.

Tall, erect, and wearing the trademark long coat that covered his painfully thin 140-pound frame, Jackson cut a splendid figure in public. But he was unwell for all of his eight years in office and at times near death. He ranks as the sickliest of the presidents. He had an enormous tolerance for pain, having survived imprisonment and smallpox in the War of Independence, and in the Creek campaign of 1813, hunger so extreme he existed on acorns. For many years he suffered acutely from dysentery and took large amounts of the standard remedy of the time, calomel, which contained mercury and may have given him poisoning—as indicated by the bloody diarrhea he had throughout his presidential years.

Jackson's health problems were compounded by his unique health beliefs and his self-medication. He claimed that a cough medicine called "matchless Sanative" made a "new man" out of him. It was fruit flavored and contained a large percentage of alcohol. He was also devoted to coffee and tobacco. He told one doctor in Philadelphia, "Now, Doctor, I can do anything you think proper to order, and bear as much as most men. There are only two things I can't give up: one is coffee, and the other is tobacco." He chewed tobacco, spit, and had a large collection of pipes, many sent to him as gifts. He told his friend from the Creek campaign days, Sam Dale, "I still smoke the corn cob, Sam. It's the sweetest and best pipe."

It seemed a miracle that Jackson survived his myriad infirmities during his eight years in office. "I try to live my life as if death might come at any moment," he once said. In his first year as president, Jackson was in an acute phase of the chronic infections that afflicted him. He coughed up what he termed "great quantities of slime." His bronchial system was affected, and his legs and feet began to swell. By the end of his second term, even when he wasn't bedridden, his legs and feet were so swollen he could only stand for short periods. He had severe diarrhea. His headaches were so painful they blurred his vision. His teeth were badly decayed, and he had trouble eating. The previous year he had fallen and torn apart ligaments in his left shoulder that did not heal well.

Some of his health problems were related to the bullets lodged in his body. The most famous of Jackson's innumerable duels was fought in 1806 against a crack shot, a lawyer named Charles Dickinson, who had insulted Rachel. Jackson took Dickinson's shot at eight paces. The bullet lodged a little more than an inch away from his heart, but an incredulous Dickinson saw Jackson still standing. The rules required that he stand for his opponent's shot. Jackson shot him dead. The victor walked away with blood trickling down into his boots, two ribs broken, and a lung punctured. Doctors of the day could not operate to remove a bullet so close to the heart, so there it stayed. The putrid abscesses that formed around it erupted periodically, causing fever, chest pains, shortness of breath, and the coughing up of blood and pus, all of which Jackson endured for the rest of his life.

In a gun-and-knife brawl in downtown Nashville with brothers Thomas and Jesse Benton in 1813, Jackson's shoulder and upper arm were shattered by a bullet. Doctors ordered that the arm be amputated, but Jackson refused. Surgery to remove the bullet was considered too dangerous because of the earlier bullet near the heart. Two decades later, a Philadelphia surgeon, Dr. Harris, was visiting the White House and told Jackson he thought he could remove the bullet in his arm. Jackson invited him to try, right then and there. Jackson held onto his cane while Harris made the incision, and the bullet fell to the floor. Thomas Benton was now a senator and a friend. Jackson sent him the bullet. After all, he said, it was Benton's property. "Yes, I had a fight with Jackson," Benton admitted. "A fellow was hardly in the fashion then who hadn't." But when it came to keeping the bullet, he demurred, saying that Jackson had "acquired clear title to it in common law by twenty years peaceable possession." Parted from Benton's bullet, Jackson's health improved—relatively speaking. He was still in poor shape.

His health curtailed an 1833 tour through New England. Jackson had been greeted enthusiastically at every stop. Harvard awarded him an honorary Doctor of Laws. (Harvard graduate John Quincy Adams refused to attend the ceremony, calling his successor "a barbarian who could not write a sentence of English grammar and hardly spell his own name.") But the intermittent hemorrhaging in his lungs resumed, and in Concord, New Hampshire, he collapsed. He seemed to be dying and was returned to the White House by steamer. Acutely ill for several days, the president lay in bed, apparently beyond hope. Through it all he refused to stop dosing himself with calomel and a cure-all of the time, lead acetate, which he used externally and took internally, probably compounding the lead poisoning from the bullets. He had doctors bleed him, and he bled himself. He survived the attack, but it was not the last. Near the end of his second term a doctor persuaded him to treat the hemorrhaging with a warm plaster of dried beetles.

Given the president's riotous 1829 inauguration, it stood to reason that his second inauguration in March 1833 would entail all manner of celebration. Due to his ill health, however, it was not held outside—a simple ceremony in the chamber of the House of Representatives sufficed. Nor was there any reception at the White House. Two inaugural balls went on without him.

In October 1833 Jackson wrote that he often felt feverish at night, and blamed the canal behind the White House, which was more or less an open sewer. "Incessant labour with the prevalance of billious disease occasioned by the unholesome miasma from the vegetable deposit thrown up by digging the canal thro the swamp . . . that has rendered our city very sickly, has vissited me for the last ten days." Jackson would not be the last president to complain about the canal.

Jackson usually managed to at least make an appearance at the traditional drawing rooms, which in any event were so large that some people never saw the president even when he stood tall and stately in the center of the room. An invitation was not required, and anyone might appear in the long receiving lines. Often there were Native Americans present, painted and jeweled. Davy Crockett was a frequent visitor.

As hostess Jackson relied on Rachel's niece, Emily Donelson, who had married Rachel's nephew, Andrew Jackson Donelson. The two came to live at the White House. Though only twenty-one, Emily became a successful White House hostess. She wrote to a friend that she intended to make the White House a "model American home" that women might emulate. She did a fair job managing the household and its eighteen servants, though, busy with childbearing—she had four children in the White House—the requisite social calls, and the traditional drawing rooms, she often deferred to steward Antoine Giusta. Giusta and his wife, servants to the Adamses, had stayed on when Jackson moved in, but not without conflict. The Giustas often visited their former employers on Sunday, which angered Jackson, who questioned their loyalty.

Andrew Jackson Jr., another nephew of Rachel's who was adopted by the Jacksons at birth in 1809, also lived in the White House for a time. He and wife Sarah Yorke had two children there. Other members of the household included Major Lewis and Mary Eastin, Emily's young cousin. In addition, visitors from Tennessee, most of them Rachel's relatives, came to stay for months at a time.

Between the various couples and their children, and an array of young friends and relatives, the White House was a lively family home. Jackson probably did more baby-sitting and had more children of all ages running about than any other president. He fretted over mumps, measles, and teething as if the children were his own. Andrew and Sarah named their daughter after Rachel, and she became a joy to him. Jackson often walked the floor at night with his "dear little Rachel" in his arms. Secretary of State Martin Van Buren once arrived at the White House for a conference and found Emily Donelson's baby, Mary Rachel, asleep in the president's arms.

At family meals, the children were always served first: "They have better appetites and less patience." Jackson said they were "the only friends I have who never pester me with their advice." In December 1835 he invited more than one hundred of his friends and official family to bring their children to "a frolic in the East Room."

A visitor to the White House described a typical family evening:

> There was light from the chandelier, and a blazing fire in the grate; four or five ladies sewing around it. . . . Five or six children were playing about regardless of documents or work-baskets. At the farther end of the room sat the President in his arm-chair, wearing a long loose coat and smoking a reed pipe, with a bowl of red clay; combining the dignity of a patriarch, monarch, and Indian chief. Just behind was Edward Livingston, the Secretary of State, reading him a dispatch from the French Minister for Foreign Affairs. The ladies glanced admiringly now and then at the President, who listens, waving his pipe towards the children when they become too boisterous.

Even with an abundance of family, Jackson felt Rachel's absence keenly. He wore a cameo with an image of her on a cord around his neck, which at night he removed and placed by his bed. He began each day by gazing at her image before slipping the cord over his head. In her memory, he planted two magnolia trees along the south side of the White House.

Just as Jackson thrived on domestic activity, he lived for the good fight. "I was born for the storm," he said. "Calm does not suit me." His first term was consumed by the scandal that became known as the "Petticoat War," which Jack Donelson said did more "to paralyze his energies than 4 years of regular and simple operations" of the government, not to mention complicate White House entertaining.

The nexus of the battle was Peggy O'Neale Timberlake Eaton, a friend of Jackson's and wife of his dear friend and secretary of war, John Henry Eaton. Jackson first met Peggy when he and Eaton, then a Tennessee senator, were guests at her father's Washington hostelry. He liked her, calling her his "little friend Peg." Peggy was married to John Timberlake, an often absent sailor, but Eaton and Peggy became close friends. Later, when Timberlake died at sea of tuberculosis, rumors began circulating that he had killed himself because of his wife's extramarital involvement with Eaton. The two were in an embarrassing situation, but Eaton was in love with Peggy. He sought Jackson's advice, which was, "Well, your marrying her will disprove these charges and restore Peggy's good name." They married on the New Year's Day before Jackson's inauguration.

When Jackson took office, he immediately chose his campaign manager, Eaton, to serve as secretary of war. Peggy—"Pothouse Peg" to some Washington ladies—had been reared in the morally loose world of the tavern, and Washington society was mortified.

The wives of other cabinet members and of Vice President John C. Calhoun refused to receive the secretary of war's wife or to come to White House receptions when she was present. Reminded of the vicious gossip his dear Rachel had endured, Jackson stood firm, even when a group of clergymen denounced Peggy as "a disgrace to virtuous womanhood." "An indignity to Major Eaton is an indignity to me," Jackson said. "Eaton is the last man on earth I ought or would abandon. . . . I would sooner abandon life."

The issue gradually assumed crisis proportions, involving most of the top levels of government. Jackson was so angry when Dutch minister Bangeman Hugeness's wife left a White House dinner attended by Peggy that he forced the minister to return to Holland. Cabinet members were ordered to receive Peggy or call on her, but their wives rebelled. To Jackson's dismay, Emily Donelson also refused to receive Peggy. When he ordered her to, she was so angered that she packed and left, with her children, for Tennessee. She did not return for two years, after Eaton had left Washington to serve as governor of Florida. In September 1829 Jackson finally called a cabinet meeting and summoned two ministers, the Reverend Ezra Ely and the Reverend John N. Campbell, to hear their charges "having to do with the private lives of Secretary and Mrs. Eaton." Jackson laid out his own evidence and delivered the verdict that Peggy was "chaste as a virgin."

Martin Van Buren made the most of the affair. Van Buren, who had resigned as governor of New York to become Jackson's first secretary of state, championed Mrs. Eaton and gave dinners in her honor. He once told Peggy Eaton, "General Jackson is the greatest man that ever lived—the only man among them without a fault. But don't tell him what I said, I would not have him know it for all the world." When she did tell Jackson, he had tears in his eyes and said, "Ah, that man loves me." Needless to say Jackson's second vice president and hand-picked successor was Van Buren.

In addition to fighting the Eaton contretemps, Jackson waged other political wars. He set about destroying the congressionally sanctioned Bank of the United States and forcing South Carolina to accept protective tariffs, despite its threat to secede. Though he remained overwhelmingly popular, he gained numerous enemies. In the course of his two terms he received more than five hundred threatening letters—this in an era when mail was infrequent.

One who chose not to write was Robert B. Randolph, a former navy lieutenant who had been discharged for embezzlement. On May 6, 1833, the president was sitting in the cabin of a steamboat, smoking his pipe and reading his paper, his chair wedged between a table and a berth. Randolph entered and approached Jackson, who extended a welcoming hand. Instead of taking his hand, Randolph punched him in the face. Others present came to the president's aid, but after a scuffle, the attacker escaped. Jackson had blood on his face but said he was not injured, except that "in endeavoring to rise, I have wounded my side, which now pains me more than it did." Randolph had been recognized by a bystander, who offered to find him and kill him, but Jackson declined the offer: "I want no man to stand between me and my assailants, and none to take revenge on my account. Had I been prepared for this cowardly villain's approach, I can assure you all, that he would never have the temerity to undertake such a thing again."

On another occasion, Jackson narrowly escaped an attempt on his life. On January 31, 1835, he was walking through the rotunda of the Capitol supported by his cane and the arm of Levi Woodbury, secretary of the navy. A well-dressed young man waited until the president was within several feet, then pulled out a pistol and fired at him point-blank. The report reverberated loudly against the echoing walls of the rotunda, but only the cap had fired, not the main charge. Jackson never flinched but went at the shooter with his cane raised. The assailant immediately drew a second pistol, also already cocked, and this too misfired, the sound like a firecracker in the rotunda. Congressmen present, including Davy Crockett, subdued the man, a Richard Lawrence. A court declared him not guilty because he "was under the influence of insanity." Lawrence had declared that he was the legitimate heir to the British throne and that Jackson was thwarting him. The pistols were subsequently tested, and invariably they fired properly. The only explanation for the misfires was that the day of the attack had been humid. Someone calculated the odds of the consecutive misfirings as 1 in 125,000.

Despite such threats, there was virtually no security at the White House. One foreign visitor recorded his surprise at walking up to the front door of the mansion, finding no guards, knocking, and being ushered by a porter into a parlor, where Jackson interrupted what he was doing to chat for a few moments. The front door was locked at night, but this did not prevent an incident in which a robber entered and climbed the stairs to Jackson's bedroom. Jackson awoke, and servants were able to capture the intruder and lock him up in the stables, only to have him escape by climbing out a high window.

*Common people surged into the White House to greet Old Hickory, their hero, in the rowdiest inaugural reception ever. The frail President was pushed to the rear wall by the crush of people to such an extent that friends had to lock arms around him for protection and finally escort him out a window and back to his rooms at Gadsby's Tavern.* (LIBRARY OF CONGRESS)

Detractors and murderous ill-wishers aside, Jackson remained the much-loved hero of the common man. He was unassuming, friendly, and easy to talk to. He was available to anyone who walked into the White House to see him and was unfailingly courteous and patient. Admirers often asked for a lock of his hair, and sometimes he obliged them; he learned to save snippings of his hair when he got it cut.

Jackson was showered with gifts. Farmers in Pennsylvania sent him whiskey, and those in New York sent him beef. The sultan of Morocco gave him a Numidian lion, which Jackson sold off at auction for $3,500 to benefit a local orphanage. The "Democratic-Republican Citizens of New York City" gave him a beautiful phaeton (a light, four-wheeled, horse-drawn vehicle). Made from the wood of the famous frigate *Constitution,* known as "Old Ironsides," it had crimson satin cushions and silver trimmings. He also received a sulky made entirely of hickory wood, except for the wheels. He left it for his successor, Van Buren.

But his most famous gift was a gigantic cheese draped with Jackson slogans, bestowed in 1835 by the dairymen of Oswego County, New York, who had been supplying the White House with cheese since Jackson's election. At 1,400 pounds, four feet in diameter, and two feet thick, it arrived in a cart pulled by twenty-four gray horses. Jackson let it age for two years in the White House vestibule, then announced that on Washington's birthday, 1837, his last big reception before leaving office the next month, he would hold a cheese tasting. The public was invited.

Shops and offices closed early, and a throng descended on the White House. The marshal of the city and his deputies screened people at the front door, but what a contemporary called "rag-a-muffins of the city" got into the gardens, climbed to the terrace, and entered through the East Room windows to mix with congressmen, officers in dress uniform, and elaborately arrayed diplomats. The rooms overflowed with people, until the hall, the doorway, every possible space, were filled. Jackson, looking "thin, pale and emaciated" to at least one guest, left after a short time, and Van Buren, the president-elect, took over the handshaking. The cheese was demolished in two hours; the White House floors and carpets were likewise demolished, and the mansion reeked of cheddar for months.

Jackson's public success—he was as popular at his exit from office as at his entrance—belied growing personal failures. At the end of his presidency, the cotton crop at his Tennessee plantation failed two years in a row. He had also left the Hermitage in the wrong hands. Jackson had sent his adopted son, Andrew Jackson Jr., to Tennessee to manage the estate, which he did so ineptly that he virtually bankrupted his father. Meanwhile, Andrew Jr. lived well, and was unfaithful to wife Sarah. "I find my funds nearly exhausted," Jackson said a year before leaving office, yet he never blamed his son. As always, he would bounce back, but he left the White House with only $90 in his pocket.

Jackson in turn would leave the country in dire financial straits, though this would not be apparent until he had left Washington and was on his way home to Tennessee. After destroying the Bank of the United States, Jackson signed the Distribution Act, which divided future surpluses among the states. Unfortunately, the attendant removal of fiscal controls would help bring on the Panic of 1837 and a nationwide depression, which doomed the presidency of his successor, Martin Van Buren.

Jackson was eager to turn over the reins of government to Van Buren even before his term ended. In late 1836 Emily Donelson had died of tuberculosis, and Jackson was grief-stricken as well as ill. "I am counting the days of my captivity here," he wrote, "& every one that passes, console myself that it is shortened 24 hours." His health had worsened even further. "My bowels are become quite torpid and I have grown weary of taking medicine so frequently," he said. "I postponed it too long, having passed over three days without a passage." He dosed himself with "Dr. Rush's Thunderbolt" and then had nausea and severe diarrhea. He had very bad headaches. Around the time of his last annual message he suffered from violent coughing and hemorrhaging. The doctors bled him: "I lost in less than 48 hours, by the lance & otherwise upwards of 70 ozs. of blood." His dropsy was now far advanced, his lower body so swollen he could hardly stand. Through it all he refused to stop chewing tobacco or puffing on his pipe.

After the inauguration, Van Buren urged Jackson to stay an extra three days at the White House, then insisted that the surgeon general accompany him to Nashville. Old Hickory was now seventy, and the doctors feared he would not survive the trip. But Jackson held up for eight more years, feisty to the end. He told one of his doctors that the great regret of his presidency was that he had not hanged John C. Calhoun as a traitor.

The Old Warrior died on June 8, 1845. On his deathbed, Jackson awoke to find his slaves weeping. "I hope to see you all in Heaven," he told them, "both white and black, both white and black." He was buried beside Rachel, in their garden at the Hermitage.

# 8

# Martin Van Buren

## 1837–1841

## *Felled by a Gold Spoon*

"LET US ENTER his palace, and survey its spacious courts, its gorgeous banqueting halls, its sumptuous drawing rooms, its glittering and dazzling saloons, with all their magnificent and sumptuous array of gold and silver, crimson and orange, blue and violet," said an obscure member of the House of Representatives from Pennsylvania, Charles Ogle, launching into what is now the famous "Gold Spoon Speech." The election of 1840 was in full swing, and Martin Van Buren, anointed by Andrew Jackson, was up for a second term. Ogle went on to describe the White House as "a PALACE as splendid as that of the Caesars, and as richly adorned as the proudest Asiatic mansion," and claimed that Van Buren dined on exquisite china with gold spoons and silver plate.

The gold spoons were real—they had been bought by Monroe twenty years before. Subsequent presidents had used them, but facts meant little. The country was going through the worst financial panic in its history. No one had seen it coming. One of Jackson's last acts as president had been to make the final payment on the national debt, and Van Buren in his inaugural speech bragged about "human prosperity surely not elsewhere to be found. . . . Every patriot has reason to be satisfied." But Jackson's destruction of the Bank of the United States had left the country with few fiscal controls; the private banks that suddenly got rich when federal deposits were transferred to the states made too many bad loans. In Jackson's last year in office, New York real estate values doubled; just weeks after Van Buren's inauguration, the bottom dropped out of the market. The Panic of 1837 was on. Banks, factories, and railroads failed. In some towns, crowds rioted for bread. Van Buren responded to the crisis by creating a new monolith, the "independent treasury," which did help stabilize the economy by the close of 1838—not soon enough to save his presidency.

The hard times were so severe that the slightest whiff of ostentation could, and did, set off a feeding frenzy. Ogle's outlandish performance began on April 14 and continued for three days, filling thirty-two pages of the *Congressional Record*. Politics was the entertainment of the day, and the Capitol galleries were soon packed with spectators come to join the fun. The speech became so popular that it was printed as a pamphlet.

Ogle entertained his listeners by pulling out bills, vouchers, and other documents, most of which pre-dated Van Buren, and reading from them. He used a bill for finger bowls in describing Van Buren dipping his "pretty tapering soft, white lily fingers" in "Fanny Kemble Green finger cups," referring to an actress of the day. He described Van Buren lolling about in a bath, spraying his whiskers with "French Triple Distillé Savon Daveline Mons Sens." Ogle claimed the president ate "fircandaus de veau" instead of "fried meat and gravy, or hog and hominy," which the representative said he himself preferred. He conjured up a Louis XV bed in which the president slept, and gold-framed mirrors "as big as a barn door" in which he gazed at "his plain Republican self."

There was almost no way for Van Buren to counter such preposterous charges. Representative Levi Lincoln rose in the midst of the speech to point out how poorly furnished parts of the White House were. Many of the rooms were so dumpy, he said, that a gentleman would not lodge his servant in them. One room had only an old pine table in the corner and "an old worn-out sofa worth five dollars."

Van Buren did not come from aristocratic lineage. An old-line Dutch New Yorker, he was born to a father who owned a farm and a tavern overflowing with eight children, six slaves, and paying guests. His first language was Dutch; all his life he would say "conthiderable" for "considerable." Working as a bartender, he learned how to listen, and how to get along with the tavern's diverse patrons. This unlikely training ground served him well. Even during the election of 1840, he made very few enemies—no small accomplishment for a politician. John Quincy Adams, though not an admirer, nicknamed him *l'ami de tout le monde,* "the friend of all the world."

By his mid-twenties, Van Buren was a powerful state political leader, successful lawyer, and land speculator. In 1807 he married a Dutch woman he had known since childhood, Hannah Hoes. They had four sons, but Hannah contracted tuberculosis and died in 1819. We can only speculate as to the nature of their relationship: Van Buren never mentions her in his autobiography. The boys lived with friends and relatives, for the most part; Van Buren would never make a true family home.

At the White House, his lifestyle was fairly modest relative to that of his predecessors—including Jackson—but he was stereotyped as a dandy. When he first met Andrew Jackson, he was wearing a snuff-colored coat, mauve trousers, a large lace-tipped cravat, yellow gloves, and morocco shoes. By the time he became president, his hair had turned white except for his elaborate red sideburns, and he wore it combed it back in unruly, curly waves. Five feet six inches tall, he held himself rigidly erect, so that he seemed taller than he was. He could not abide the unkempt crowds that overran the executive mansion under Jackson, and his entertainments became exclusive. He had a taste for bourgeois elegance and rode in a fine carriage pulled by matched horses, with a footman and grooms.

Yet, in going about the requisite sprucing up of the White House, Van Buren was mindful of the taxpayers. He got rid of worn-out furniture by selling it at auction, rais-

*Martin Van Buren was an elegant dresser given to lace-tipped cravats and yellow gloves. He suffered unfair political attacks ridiculing him as effete and his White House lifestyle as sumptuous although he lived no more elaborately than Jackson did before him.* (LIBRARY OF CONGRESS)

ing $6,000. He used a $27,000 appropriation from Congress for little more than new china, rugs, and general refurbishing—all badly needed after the surging crowds of the Jackson years. As one disappointed visitor to the Van Buren White House commented, "We have seen the private dwellings of many merchants in Boston, New York, Philadelphia and Baltimore, the fitting up of which must have cost a much larger sum."

Without a wife to whom he could delegate the task, Van Buren managed the redecorating personally. The mansion had been through French and British phases, the rigid formality of diplomats, and the studied informality of the Democrats. Now, as far as the budget would allow, Van Buren brought to it the bourgeois vigor and showiness of 1830s New York. Monroe's Green Room was repapered in silver, and the yellow East Room in silver with a gilt border. The oval saloon, first red, then green under Jackson, was changed to blue, thus becoming the Blue Room we know today. Very little new furniture was bought. Instead, Van Buren had the old scrubbed down, revarnished, and otherwise cleaned.

When Van Buren moved in, the White House was still heated solely by fireplaces at a time when the most affluent were beginning to take central heating for granted. (Monroe did not rebuild the limited system Madison installed before the British burned the mansion.) In 1837 Van Buren ordered a central heating system. It did not heat the entire White House, but included the state rooms and some bedrooms. A fireman, hired to manage the furnace and keep it fed with wood, was on duty twenty-four hours a day, with summers off.

The new president's staffing of the mansion was also modest relative to his predecessors. He kept Jackson's steward, Joseph Boulanger, to whom eight or ten servants reported. The doorman was the only paid government worker inside the house; the wages of all the other workers came out of the president's $25,000 salary. He was also expected to feed them all at least one meal a day, including the doorman. Outside the house the government paid for the gardeners at $1 a day, plus day and night watchmen. One way Van Buren was able to control costs was to put his son Abraham, his private secretary, on the government payroll as a second auditor in the treasury department. This common procedure allowed presidents to ease the burden of clerical costs before Congress decided, just before the Civil War, to pay for a presidential assistant.

Van Buren, as secretary of state and then as vice president, had been a regular visitor to the White House in the Jackson years and had disapproved of the lack of guards. Despite threats to Jackson's life, anyone could walk in. President Van Buren hired guards at his own expense and stationed them at the doors to keep out "improper persons"—though he didn't use the term "guard" or have anyone in uniform who looked like a guard. Even so, access was not terribly difficult. A drunk once managed to spend the night on a sofa in the East Room. Van Buren also denied tourists access to all but the East Room; the parlors were closed off.

In all his long political career Van Buren had always taken rented quarters. His four sons—Abraham, John, Martin Jr., and Smith—had lived at school or with relatives since their mother's death, but he was close to them, and they spent as much time as possible at the mansion. Van Buren's wife had been dead almost twenty years, and he had turned away a succession of ladies interested in taking her place, so he had no hostess during his first two years in office. Thus the White House was almost exclusively a male place, and Van Buren seemed somewhat lonely, although he was always courteous and an engaging conversationalist. One guest noticed that he "seems to take little plea-sure in society."

Dolley Madison noticed as well, and apparently decided to do something about it. After James Madison died, the former first lady had moved to nearby Lafayette Square and, beloved as ever, was a regular part of White House life. Now she invited her cousin, Angelica Singleton, the daughter of a rich South Carolina planter and a relation to some of the most powerful families of the South, to visit. Angelica met the president and two of his sons, Abraham and Martin Jr., at a White House dinner. By summer she was engaged to the eldest, Abraham, and in November 1838 they were married. She made her first appearance as White House hostess, at age twenty-two, on New Year's Day of 1839.

At the close of the social season, the newlyweds were off to Europe, in part on a goodwill mission during which Abraham might assure the British that America's econ-omy was on the mend. In Europe they were treated as American royalty, and Angelica was a great success. She soaked up the manners of the French and English courts; not-ing that Queen Victoria did not shake hands at her receptions, she did not see why America's acting first lady should. Back at the White House, with Dolley Madison's encouragement, Angelica decided to bring some of the practices of the foreign courts to the receptions. In imitation of Queen Victoria, she had a low dais built and arranged herself, princesslike in a white dress with a train, flowers in her hair, and bouquet in hand, in a tableau, so as to create a "living picture." Soon, she completed the picture with the addition of several other young ladies dressed in white. The president, mean-while, shook hands at the door. The tableaux were criticized and ridiculed in the press and by the Whigs, and didn't last long. Still, the theatrics contributed to the president's increasingly aristocratic image.

The tableaux would have been curtailed in any case. Angelica had returned from Europe pregnant and soon went into seclusion until her daughter, Rebecca, was born. She had a difficult time with the birth and suffered a period of ill health. Rebecca was never a well child and died in the fall. Van Buren's last months in the White House were somber.

Without Angelica to serve as hostess until 1839, Van Buren initially limited his White House entertaining to small, intimate dinners, served to both friends and enemies. Cal-houn and Clay, among other Jackson nemeses, were frequent guests. "Mr. Van Buren gave charming little dinners, always in the more homelike family dining-room," said one who often dined with the president. "The regular receptions, both day and evenings, were for ceremonious visits; but on any evening the family of the President was to be found at home—with needlework and books and intimate friends—in short, living as other people do."

In addition to being without a hostess, Van Buren probably limited his receptions in order to save money. On top of being responsible for most of the cost of running the White House, the president was expected to entertain congressmen, diplomats, and visiting travelers if they had the proper introductions. He had dinner guests every day, and likely at least one party a week. A dinner for thirty was not unusual, and at times they were so large that the State Dining Room was abandoned for the East Room. His sons were popular in society and gave parties of their own. Thus, like his predecessors, Van Buren found that his $25,000 salary barely paid the bills. His taste for the good life compounded matters. Further, Angelica was accustomed to being waited on by numerous servants. She apparently required a small army on a daily basis and of course when traveling, probably made up of her own slaves from South Carolina.

Financial concerns aside, Van Buren simply did not like public receptions. Unlike his amiable political patron, Jackson, he was not comfortable in the midst of crowds of ordinary people. He did not open the White House to the public until New Year's Day 1838, almost a year into his term, and finally held the first of his infrequent public drawing rooms in March of that year. When he received a giant cheese as a gift (though only about half the size of Jackson's), he had the cheese placed in a local store, where pieces were sold off to benefit a local charity. He tried discontinuing refreshments at his receptions, but only succeeded in annoying his guests.

Of all the public receptions, Van Buren disliked the Fourth of July celebration the most. In 1839, for the first time in U.S. history, the president did not put on the hallowed Independence Day reception. Instead, he went to New York, where he appeared in a showy parade, yet again providing fodder for his critics.

If Van Buren tended to neglect the social aspects of the presidency, he did not neglect its work. He spent more time in Washington than any president before him, being the first to routinely remain in Washington year-round. No president had ever had so much business to attend to. While his predecessors took long summer vacations, Van Buren closed the White House, packing away curtains and rugs and covering furniture, and retreated part-time to a rented suburban mansion known as Woodley. The mansion, which still stands in the vicinity of Washington Cathedral, was about three miles outside the city. Every morning the president rode on horseback to the White House to work in his office, returning to Woodley in midafternoon. Though he had to pay for the house, the summer arrangement probably saved him money because the smaller house was easier to maintain, and he could get away with living more privately and entertaining less.

The Gold Spoon Speech was only the beginning of the false characterizations that contributed to Van Buren's defeat by General William Henry Harrison, the long-term governor of Indiana Territory and a war hero. The Whigs promoted Harrison as "The Log-Cabin Candidate," and the public loved it. As in the 1828 campaign—which Van Buren himself helped orchestrate—it was the common man against the arrogant aristocrat. The Whigs had beaten the Democrats at their own game. Never mind that it was Van Buren who was the common tavernkeeper's son, and that Harrison, a Virginia blue blood whose "log cabin" was a seventeen-room mansion, was the American equivalent of nobility.

The president was seemingly unruffled by the absurdity of it all. But the nation was fully absorbed, as the audience for these campaign shenanigans was larger than ever. The election of 1840, even more than that of 1828, marked a true upswell of democracy. More citizens voted than had ever voted before, about 2.5 million—a million more than in 1828.

Van Buren, his usual urbane self, took his defeat gracefully. He not only attended Harrison's inaugural but was one of the first to shake his successor's hand. His unfailing courtesy finally won him the admiration of the press. From a friend's home, he watched the ruckus of the log cabin voters celebrating in the streets.

As he left the White House, Van Buren was fifty-eight years old and still in his prime. He had been one of the healthiest presidents, and would escape serious illness until he was over seventy years old. Despite the expenses of the presidency, he still reckoned his net worth at $75,906, which yielded an income of about $6,000 a year (his salary as vice president had been only $5,000 a year). For the first time in his life he purchased a home, taking special pleasure in the fact that his 200-acre Hudson River estate had belonged to the very aristocrats who snubbed his tavernkeeper father. The old Van Ness mansion, a stately Georgian structure southeast of the village he grew up in, was renamed Lindenwald for the many linden trees in the surrounding woods. Van Buren's youngest son, Smith, would later move in to keep him company in his old age.

Van Buren remained active in politics and tried, without success, to return to the White House. He narrowly lost the Democratic nomination in 1844. In 1848 he won the Free Soil party's nomination and, opposing any expansion of slavery, took about 10 percent of the vote. But he claimed that his years as a gentleman farmer were his happiest. "You have no idea of the interest I take in farming or the satisfaction I derive from it," he wrote to Andrew Jackson. "The Whigs would hardly believe that a much larger portion of my time is taken up with [improving my] quantity and . . . quality of manure than in forming political plans." He devoted his final years to his autobiography, and died on July 24, 1862.

# 9

# William Henry Harrison

## March 4–April 4, 1841

## *Mourning*

NEWLY ELECTED PRESIDENT General William Henry Harrison, hero of the Battle of the Thames in the War of 1812, left his seventeen-room "log cabin" in North Bend on the Ohio River and headed to Washington, arriving on the day before his sixty-eighth birthday, February 8, 1841. Born in 1773, he was the last president to begin life a British subject. Full of foreboding, his wife, Anna Symmes, stayed behind in North Bend. "I wish that my husband's friends had left him where he is happy and contented in retirement," she said after his election. At sixty-five, she was not in good health. Her doctors wanted her to wait until spring to make the trip to Washington; as it turned out, she would never have to go.

Harrison was accompanied by daughter-in-law Jane Irwin Harrison, the widow of William Henry Jr., who had died an alcoholic at thirty-five, and her son. Jane would serve as White House hostess. Also traveling with him were a niece from Richmond, Mrs. Thomas Taylor, and Mrs. Harrison Findlay and her two daughters.

Harrison arrived exhausted but in good spirits. One observer who had thought him "very feeble" three months before said he seemed "different-looking now . . . instead of being bowed with age, and shivering with cold, he walked with an elastic step." Van Buren invited his successor to the White House for dinner the next evening and afterward commented that he was "the most extraordinary man I ever saw. He does not seem to realize the vast importance of his elevation. He talks and thinks with such ease and vivacity. He is as tickled with the Presidency as is a young woman with a new bonnet."

Like Andrew Jackson, Harrison had run as a man of the people, and changes in the voting system had enabled 2.5 million people—a million more than in the 1828 election—to cast their ballots. They turned out for Harrison because, in contrast to the supposedly aristocratic Van Buren, he was a simple man. A detractor characterized him by saying, "Give him a barrel of hard cider and settle a pension of two thousand a year on him and, my word for it, he will sit the remainder of his days in a log cabin . . . and study moral philosophy." Rather than be insulted, the Whigs rallied around a log cabin and hard cider banner, even though Harrison's home, which admittedly began as a log cabin, was so elegant riverboats slowed to let passengers get a good glimpse, and his tastes ran to cognac, not cider.

Harrison's military claim to fame came when he defeated the British at the Battle of the Thames. But "Tems" had no ring to it, so instead the Whigs played up his somewhat clouded 1811 victory over the Native Americans at Tippecanoe Creek. When John Tyler came on board as "Old Tip's" running mate, the two were "Tippecanoe and Tyler too," one of the most famous slogans in American politics.

As the inauguration approached, crowds of Whig adherents and office seekers descended on Washington in a flood reminiscent of Andrew Jackson's election. Hotels put beds in the dining rooms, parlors, and halls. "Half a dozen in one room and three in a bed are common arrangements," wrote a New York newspaper correspondent. At the National Hotel on Pennsylvania Avenue, Harrison found he could get little rest or peace. Someone was always kicking on his door, and the halls were never quiet. Turning down Van Buren's offer to vacate the White House early, he decided to visit his family home at Berkeley, one of the grandest of the grand plantations of tidewater Virginia. A brick mansion on the James River, it boasted acres of rose gardens and well-tended lawns.

He returned to Washington in the last week of February and moved in with the mayor, William Seaton, venturing out for strolls down Pennsylvania Avenue. He walked unattended, talking and joking with those he met. The pickpockets had a field day with the crowds. The *Washington Globe* commented, "No sooner had he put his foot on the Avenue than the robbing commenced."

Harrison penned a lengthy inaugural address filled with the classical references he loved. Daniel Webster was assigned the task of reading through it. Mrs. Seaton, the mayor's wife, found him working late and noted he appeared haggard. An exhausted Webster explained that he had just "killed seventeen Roman proconsuls dead as smelts every one of them." Even with Webster's deletions the speech was far too long: 8,500 words and an hour and forty-five minutes, the longest inauguration speech on record.

March 4, 1841, blustered with a biting north wind, one of the coldest inaugural days in history. The Whigs of Baltimore had given Harrison a fine coach, but he persisted in his plan to ride his favorite horse, Old Whitey. He wore neither overcoat nor gloves, and was waving his hat. He delivered his interminable speech to an estimated fifty thousand wrapped up in heavy coats and shawls. The crowd was said to be the largest since the inauguration of George Washington.

Harrison's lips were blue, but he insisted on riding Old Whitey back to the White House. He was accompanied by floats, militia companies, and a log cabin covered with

Whig banners and filled with Whig supporters. The exposure to the cold would leave him with a chest cold and cough, but he would recover within a week. At the White House he lay down for half an hour while someone rubbed his temples with alcohol. At 3 P.M. he began receiving the many who jammed the White House, declining, as announced in the papers, to shake hands. That night he attended two parties plus the inaugural ball. Many commented on his energy and stamina.

Both would be tried. Even before his inauguration Harrison recognized his biggest problem: Senator Henry Clay. Clay had virtually created the Whig party and was the commanding figure within it. He actually turned down Harrison's offer to be secretary of state because he felt he was more powerful controlling the Whigs in Congress. Clay had expected to get the presidential nomination but accepted Harrison, believing he could dominate him. Initially, Harrison played along. In a letter accepting the Whig nomination, Harrison described himself as "retired and unpretending. . . . Some folks are silly enough as to have formed a plan to make a President of the United States out of this Clerk and Clodhopper." But actually Harrison had doggedly sought and won public office for much of his life, serving in the House of Representatives, the Ohio senate, and the United States Senate, and as minister to Colombia. "[His] thirst for lucrative office is positively rabid," John Quincy Adams said.

Harrison was willing to be a figurehead, up to a point. He liked the crowds, the applause, and the telling and retelling of his war experiences. He agreed to accept only one term, vowed never to interfere with the legislative branch, and promised not to initiate any legislation. But he had his pride, and was soon at loggerheads with Clay.

When Clay tried to push his own candidates for appointments, the general listened politely for a while, then snapped, "Mr. Clay, you forget that I am president." Clay asked for a special session to be called to address the nation's ongoing financial crisis. He penned his request in arrogant tones, even including a draft proclamation. Harrison wrote back: "You use the privilege of a friend to lecture me and I take the same liberty with you. You are too impetuous." Clay left for Kentucky in a rage. Harrison was upset too—this was not what he wanted from his presidency.

Secretary of State Daniel Webster, who also wanted Harrison to march to his orders, was another source of trouble. Harrison wanted a wartime friend, John Chambers, to be governor of Iowa Territory. Webster wanted James Wilson for the position and got the cabinet to agree with him. Harrison called a cabinet meeting and asked Webster to read aloud a proclamation he had written for him. Webster read, "William Henry Harrison, President of the United States . . ." Harrison then rose and forcefully announced: "And 'President of the United States' tells you, gentlemen, that by God, John Chambers will be governor of Iowa."

Both Webster and Clay continued to vex Harrison. "They will drive me mad," he said. Most of their conflicts were over patronage. Now that the Whigs had finally come to power, they wanted their rewards in jobs, and Webster and Clay demanded that all Democratic employees be replaced with loyal Whigs. Harrison was besieged. The marshal of Washington, General Alexander Hunter, came to the White House and found the president surrounded by office seekers and trying in vain to get into a cabinet meeting. Hunter tried to disperse the crowd but couldn't. Harrison pleaded with them, saying that he had important public business to attend to. Finally, to halt their pestering, he accepted their petitions, which filled his arms and pockets. Harrison complained that he was so set upon by office seekers that he could not attend to "the natural functions of nature."

Such pressures forced Harrison to abandon some of his preferred routines. He was always an early riser and liked to walk to market, a basket under his arm. "General Harrison at first did his own marketing," a friend said, "but only for a few days, for the worry of office and the importunities of office-seekers seriously interfered with his domestic activities, and drove him solely to depend on his steward." Early on, however, the president did find time to personally buy a cow—the latest in a long line of White House cows—to supply the household with milk. Another purchase, perhaps his last, was a Bible. He liked to read the Bible in the evening and hadn't found one in the White House. As a young man he had read the Bible as a duty, he said, but "it has become a pleasure." He did not permit the presidency to impinge on his religious commitments. An Episcopalian, he attended Sunday morning services at St. John's, across the square from the White House, and afternoon services at a Presbyterian church. He refused to discuss politics on Sunday.

Harrison undertook the entertaining required of every president, and he managed to hold a number of dinner parties during his month at the White House. On a Saturday evening two weeks after the inauguration, Henry Gilpin attended a dinner at the mansion and observed that Harrison seemed ill at ease with his new role: "Before dinner the poor old man was bursting and fidgetting about—running out three or four times into the dining room. . . . The dinner was scarcely over before the old man began with giving toasts, and talking incessantly across the table." The tone changed after dinner, as the guests drank and talked. "The party became quite jovial, and when it broke up certainly had nothing of the gravity of the palace about it." Another of that evening's guests wrote to friend Martin Van Buren that the dinner was "a regular hard cider affair . . . [with] plenty of drinking and a great deal of noise, of which the General contributed his full share and a little more."

Although Harrison appeared hale and hearty, and Whig campaign literature portrayed him that way, his constitution had always been weak, and he was naturally growing frail with age. Indigestion was a recurring problem. Disruptions in his routine of regular exercise and his upsetting clashes with Henry Clay took their toll. On March 26 the president called a doctor and told him he had not felt well for several days. He complained of fatigue, mental anxiety, and coughing and sniffling. The doctor gave him no medicine but prescribed rest: no work, bed rest, no excitement. That evening Harrison had a get-together with wartime friends. The next day he went for a walk in the morning, and was sitting in a cabinet meeting in the afternoon when he was stricken with chills. He was put to bed. Harrison's physician, Dr. Thomas Miller, felt he was too old to be bled but applied hot cups to his skin, which caused painful blistering but was presumed to draw the "bilious pleurisy" from the patient.

The next day Harrison had a high fever. Additional doctors came and went over the next week, some applying remedies considered out of date by many physicians of the day. They purged him by bleeding, and gave him castor oil and calomel and a powerful emetic, ipecac, which irritated his chronic colitis. The result was vomiting and diarrhea, which left him so weak and debilitated that they dosed him with opium, camphor, and shots of brandy. Harrison now had constant diarrhea and hepatitis.

When the president did not attend either of his churches on Sunday, the public was alerted to a possible problem. The first mention of the president's illness in the press did not come until March 31, when a report quoted an attending physician as saying the president was greatly improved.

He was not. As Harrison slipped into semiconsciousness, the great and near-great trooped into his bedroom: cabinet members, the mayor of Washington, the marshal of the District of Columbia, the clerk of the Supreme Court. At times he would recognize his visitors, at times not. Semiconscious, he was heard to say, "These applications, will they never cease?"

On his last day he realized his fate: "I am ill, very ill, much more so than they think me." On April 4, 1841, the ninth president died.

Funeral arrangements befitting the high office had to be devised, and quickly. Harrison's body lay in state in the East Room, which was darkened, with its mirrors and chandeliers all draped in black. The outside of the White House was also draped in black, as were taverns, banks, public buildings, and homes.

Early on the morning of April 7, the crowd outside the White House filled Lafayette Park. The windowed coffin was set up in the entrance hall of the White House, outside the glass screen, so citizens could pay their respects. There was a funeral ceremony in the East Room, attended by invitation only. Among the mourners were John Tyler, suddenly president, and heads of departments, judges, clergy, foreign ministers, senators, and congressmen. The ceremony was simple, but dramatic in its gravity and novelty. A reporter for the *National Intelligencer* wrote,

> The great East Room of the President's House—that room in which I had seen a thousand gay and joyful faces glowing in the light of ponderous chandeliers, radiating the light of a hundred burners, was now the scene of death! Those brilliant fountains of light were hid in dark robes of mourning. . . . In short, this magnificent room, in every part of it spoke in the appropriate language of silent grief, announcing to all—Death is here! . . . Silence, deep and undisturbed, even by a whisper, pervaded the entire assembly. The solemn event which they were now gazing upon fixed every eye and hushed every tongue.

The body was placed in a funeral car drawn by eight horses. Old Whitey followed behind, saddled but riderless. The largest procession the capital had yet seen headed toward a public vault in the Congressional Cemetery. In June his body would be moved, with great ceremony, to North Bend. Soldiers fired a last salute, and the door of the tomb was shut.

Anna Harrison lived another twenty-three years, sustained in part by $25,000 from the government, the first pension ever for a president's widow. She died on February 25, 1864. Her husband's father had signed the Declaration of Independence. Her grandson would grow up to be the twenty-third president of the United States.

# 10

# John Tyler

## 1841–1845

## *Courtship*

WHEN JOHN TYLER took up residence at the White House in April 1841, the state rooms were still hung in black in mourning of President William Henry Harrison. Tyler, dubbed "His Accidency" by the ever-wry John Quincy Adams, had quite unexpectedly become the first vice president to replace a sitting president. The Whigs had chosen Harrison for his relative malleability, but left his running mate "wholly unquestioned about his opinions." Tyler wasted no time in defying the Whig party leadership, and Congress responded by refusing to spend a dime on the home of its renegade president, even though the White House's deplorable condition had earned it the nickname "Public Shabby House."

Tyler, used to a bit more luxury than his run-down public quarters, was born in 1790 at Greenaway, his family's 1,200-acre plantation on the James River in tidewater Virginia. He absorbed a states' rights creed—and a love for fiddle playing—from his father, a judge and onetime governor. He became a successful lawyer, and went on to serve in both houses of the Virginia legislature, as governor of Virginia, and in both houses of Congress. Always independent and highly principled—or perhaps, as some said, simply obstinate—Tyler twice resigned from Congress rather than compromise his beliefs. "Whether I sink or swim on the tide of popular favor," he said, "is a matter to me of inferior consideration."

Tyler was a background figure during the campaign and expected to stay that way when he became vice president. On inauguration day, huge crowds swarmed the Capitol grounds to see the hero of the battle of Tippecanoe Creek, while "Tyler too" slipped unnoticed from Brown's Hotel and into the Senate chamber to take his oath. Afterward, he left the city for the comfort of his home in Williamsburg and what he assumed would be the four years of peaceful obscurity typical of his office. When the seemingly hardy President Harrison took to his bed on March 27, even Tyler was not aware of the illness until the *National Intelligencer* reported, on March 31, that the general was "much improved." Four days later, Harrison was dead. Fletcher Webster, chief clerk of the State Department and son of Secretary of State Daniel Webster, galloped off to Virginia. He rode all night and by 5 A.M. on April 5 was pounding on Tyler's door to inform him that he was the new president of the United States. Tyler had breakfast, arranged with a friend to borrow enough money for the trip, and set out for Washington, arriving early the next morning.

The 230-mile trip, on a special train from Richmond, allowed Tyler plenty of time to consider his unique situation. Although the Constitution had anticipated the scenario, its wording could be interpreted in two ways: Tyler was either a president with full powers, or a vice president acting as president. "In case of the removal of the president from office," it reads, "or of his death, resignation, or inability to discharge the duties of said office, the same shall devolve on the Vice President." Did "same" mean the office or just the duties? Southerner Tyler was well known as a strict constructionist with regards to the Constitution. Yet his first and perhaps most significant decision, made without hesitation, was that he was, unequivocally, the president of the United States. So certain was he that he argued he did not need to take the oath of office. Friends talked him into taking it anyway, to reinforce his position in the public mind. At noon on April 6, the day he arrived in Washington, he was sworn in at Brown's Hotel by William Cranch, a chief justice of the circuit court of the District of Columbia. Only fifty-three hours had passed since Harrison's death. The funeral took place the next day, in the East Room of the White House.

Harrison had been the oldest president, and now Tyler, at fifty-one, was the youngest, which was no help to his credibility. A week after Harrison's funeral, he moved into the White House and began asserting his authority. Henry Clay had said "Vice-President" Tyler was a "flash in the pan," someone to hold down the job until Clay himself could take it over in 1844, and Congress tried but failed to give him the title of "Acting President." But when Tyler received letters addressed to "Acting President Tyler" and "Vice President acting as President," he returned them, unopened, marked "Addressee Unknown." Tyler began to shore up his position by making himself and his White House highly visible. That meant plenty of dinners, teas, and receptions.

With Tyler's wife, Letitia, largely confined to bed since a stroke in 1839, son Robert's wife, Priscilla, became the official White House hostess. The daughter of renowned tragedian Thomas A. Cooper, Priscilla had taken the stage herself, often opposite her father. Before her marriage, she had played in most of the major cities of the United States. Upon being cast as White House hostess, she sought the advice of Tyler's close friend, former first lady Dolley Madison, still the grande dame of Washington society.

Among her questions was whether she must return all calls made to her, a matter of contention among society in years past. Dolley's answer was, "By all means." So three hours a day, three days a week, Priscilla reluctantly went "driving from one street to another in this city of magnificent distances." But Priscilla enjoyed the other aspects of her role as hostess: "Here am I . . . actually living in, and—what is more—presiding at, the White House! . . . I am considered 'charmante' by the Frenchmen, 'lovely' by the Americans, and 'really quite nice, you know,' by the English."

During the social season Priscilla was obliged to run two formal dinner parties each week, typically one of twenty guests and the other of about forty. Once a month there was a public reception, requiring no invitations but attended only by society. And there were the traditional large receptions on New Year's and the Fourth of July. On New Year's Day she stood in the Blue Room for three hours shaking hands. "Such big fists as some of these people have," she said, "and such hearty handshakes they gave my poor little hand." The schedule was trying at times. Halfway through the dessert course of one formal cabinet dinner in 1843, Priscilla fainted in exhaustion. She was four months pregnant and had not only made all the dinner arrangements but had been tending to her sick infant daughter. Daniel Webster came to her assistance, as did her helpful husband, who doused her and the secretary with a pitcher of ice water. Priscilla wrote that it ruined her "lovely new dress, and I am afraid, produced a decided coolness between myself and the Secretary of State. I had to be taken to my room, and poor Mr. Webster had to be shaken off, dried and brushed."

The real coolness was between the president, his cabinet, and nearly everyone else around him. Tyler recognized that he was "surrounded by Clay-men, Webster-men, anti-Masons, original Harrisonians, old Whigs and new Whigs," yet he decided to keep Harrison's hostile cabinet intact for the sake of continuity. At his first cabinet meeting, the new president was informed by Daniel Webster that Harrison had always been guided by the will of the cabinet majority. Tyler thought Webster displayed "adamantine cheek" and informed him, "I, as president, shall be responsible for my administration."

His administration was challenged almost immediately. The autocratic Henry Clay pushed through Congress a fiscal bill to reestablish the Bank of the United States, dismantled by Democrat Andrew Jackson in 1833. He knew the states' rights president wouldn't like it. "Tyler dare not resist," he said. "I will drive him before me." The bill was a major legislative effort for the Whigs, but Tyler, just four months into office, did resist. He vetoed it. Clay paid a visit to the White House to confront him. Tyler, as a courtly Virginian, was polite and gentlemanly to a fault, but Clay breached his limits, and finally he blew up: "Go you now, then, Mr. Clay, to your end of the avenue, where stands the Capitol, and there perform your duty to the country as you shall think proper. So help me God, I shall do mine at this end of it as I shall think proper."

That evening, August 16, 1841, a group of opposition Democrats called on Tyler at the White House to congratulate him on his "patriotic and courageous action." Hours later a drunken mob of Whig demonstrators, angry and armed, gathered at the north entrance gate beating drums and blowing bugles, screaming, cursing, and throwing stones. Shots were fired. The household was thoroughly terrorized. The next night the mob came again but settled for burning Tyler in effigy on the street in front of the mansion. Tyler received assassination threats, and there was talk of impeachment. He was expelled from the Whig party—a presidential first—in a removal ceremony held outside the Capitol. In practical terms, the Whig-elected president was now a member of the Democratic opposition, though his alliance with any party was tenuous. One month later, on September 11, six of seven cabinet members submitted their resignations one by one. Only Secretary of State Webster remained—though by 1843 he too would be gone. Tyler filled the posts with difficulty, as Congress, which now attacked him almost daily, repeatedly rejected his nominations.

Tyler continued to receive bomb and other threats. Once an unmarked package feared to contain a bomb was discovered in the entrance hall. Neither Tyler nor the servants would go near it. Martin Renehan, the Irish doorman, was called. "The divil himself puts into the heads of his children to manufacture infernal machines," Renehan warned, "and who knows but that powder and balls, and percussion dust, have been arranged with a view to blow you up for vetoing the Bank bill!" Renehan rashly attacked the wooden box with a meat cleaver while Tyler dashed behind a marble column. Renehan chopped at the box until it revealed its contents: a model of an iron stove. For fear of being ridiculed in the press, Tyler warned the doorman not to say anything. "If you do they'll have me caricatured," he said.

Questions of White House security had been raised for years, with various presidents since Jefferson taking informal measures. But in the 1840s, increasing numbers of assassinations in a restive Europe were making headlines, and the threat of violence seemed more real than ever. So despite its malice, Congress in 1842 passed Tyler's bill establishing the first permanent White House security force. The four-man force was empowered by Congress to make arrests, but the men were not uniformed and were referred to as "doormen" to avoid any obvious militaristic associations. The guards became an important part of daily life in the household, carrying messages, meeting guests at the train station, receiving all callers in the entrance hall, and mingling with the crowds at receptions, occasionally ejecting suspicious characters.

The cooperative granting of the guards was an anomaly. Congress took every opportunity to spite the president, denying, among other things, the usual funds for the upkeep of the executive mansion. When Martin Van Buren took office in 1837, he had decorated elegantly but superficially, working within a tight budget. By 1841 the walls needed painting, the furnishings were grimy, padding was popping out of chair seats, and hundreds of spiders made webs in high corners. A newspaper reporter wrote that the White House was "a contemptible disgrace to the nation," and that many of the chairs of the East Room "would be kicked out of a brothel." Charles Dickens, visiting America and its president, noted that the tobacco chewers "bestowed their favors . . . abundantly on the carpet." The white pillars at the north entrance were spattered with tobacco juice.

Congress had allotted Harrison just $6,000 for new furnishings, with the restriction that they be "of American manufacture so far as may be practicable and expedient, to be expended under the direction of the President." The money was now in Tyler's hands, and it was all he would get. His effort to secure an additional $20,000 appropriation was in vain. So the Tylers made do by bringing some items from his family home in Williamsburg and purchasing desks and other furniture for the upstairs office, a testament to the growing amount of paperwork attached to the presidency.

Tyler certainly could not afford to put his own money into the mansion. Like many southern plantation owners, he was in debt and chronically short of cash. At the White

House he lived in a kind of genteel poverty. Like those before him, he was forced to pay for basic maintenance, much of the staff, and the constant entertaining, and found that his salary fell short. An additional expense was his large family—he had eight children by Letitia, and after the presidency would have seven more by his second wife. Children ranging in age from eleven to twenty-six "flock" to the White House, as Tyler put it. But Tyler welcomed them. "My children are my principal treasure," he once said.

To save on expenses, he brought his own slaves to the mansion. He rode in an old carriage, recently discarded by the secretary of the navy, and dressed his waiters in second-hand uniforms. He began ordering food in wholesale lots from New York. "I am heartily tired," he said, "of the grocers here who exact extravagant prices for everything."

Ever the courteous, smiling, dignified gentleman, Tyler never discussed his financial problems. Nor did he discuss his concern for his wife, who was slowing dying in an upstairs bedroom. A shy and unassuming woman, Letitia had participated little in her husband's public life even before her crippling stroke. At the White House, her health only declined; she received few visitors and returned no calls. She appeared at a public event only once, for the marriage of her daughter Elizabeth to William Waller in September 1842. She died shortly thereafter on September 10, at age fifty-two, and there was another funeral in the East Room. All social events, with the exception of the politically important monthly public receptions, were canceled for a time. "Nothing," wrote Priscilla, "can exceed the loneliness of this large and gloomy mansion, hung with black, its walls echoing with sighs."

All that would change when Tyler, on June 26, 1844, married a woman half his age less than two years after Letitia's death. The woman who induced Tyler to become the first president to marry while in office was Julia Gardiner. Daughter of a wealthy former New York State senator, she was known as the "Rose of Long Island" after an apparel firm used the line with her likeness in an advertisement—to the shock and dismay of her social class. She was widely admired for her beauty. She had dark, oval eyes and wore her black hair parted down the middle and pulled back in tight buns. Her family lived in East Hampton and owned nearby Gardiners Island. To the beautiful, flirtatious, high-spirited Julia, East Hampton was isolated and dull. So her father brought her and her sister, Margaret, to Washington in January 1842 for the social season to give them some excitement, and perhaps find them husbands.

Of course Julia visited the White House, which was the center of Washington social life. She enthusiastically wrote her mother of the "thousand compliments" paid her by the president. Tyler's compliments were so forward, she wrote, that people nearby "looked and listened in perfect amazement." Years later she would recall how on that night both she and her sister noted "the silvery sweetness of his voice . . . the incomparable grace of his bearing and the elegant ease of his conversation." Letitia died that September, and the president went into mourning. The Gardiner daughters returned to the boredom of East Hampton.

The following year the Gardiner family returned to Washington for the 1842–43 social season, staying at Mrs. Peyton's boardinghouse. A servant was sent out to deliver their cards to various homes, including the White House. President Tyler was still mourning for Letitia, but his son and secretary, John Jr., soon called at Mrs. Peyton's. John was married, though separated from his wife, drank a great deal, and performed

*John Tyler's wife, Letitia, died in the White House in September, 1843 and a few months later the President met and then married Julia Gardiner. She was half his age and immediately enlivened the White House social life. She successfully introduced a daring new dance—the waltz—that Tyler had previously banned.* (LIBRARY OF CONGRESS)

so poorly as presidential secretary that in 1844 his father would relieve him of the position. But Julia found him "distingué" and "quite handsome," and his conversation "interestingly sentimental." She said he "laid quite a siege to my heart." He wrote her poetry and sent her candy from the White House kitchen.

The president invited the Gardiners to dinner at the White House on Christmas Eve 1842. And on New Year's, when the family arrived late at St. James Episcopal Church and found nowhere to sit, Tyler rose and generously offered them space in his personal pew. Julia, ill, was not there, but the next day she attended a public reception at the White House, where Tyler flattered her by reaching past others in the crowd to shake her hand. By the next month, with his mourning period over, Tyler had "quite a flirtation" with Julia at a small White House gathering, according to Margaret. He tried to kiss Julia's hand, but she snatched it away and "flew down the stairs with the President after her around the chairs and tables until at last he caught her. It was truly amazing."

The president was smitten. He joined the bevy of suitors that kept Julia and her sister out late several nights a week, and proceeded rapidly with the affair. He had courted Letitia very differently. Then, he was engaged for five years and did not even kiss the hand of his betrothed until three weeks before the wedding. Now, lonely following Letitia's years of illness, he wasted no time. The Sunday following the flirtatious chase at the White House, he made his interest public by walking the Gardiners home from church, and the rumors and gossip began. On February 22, 1843, at a Washington's Birthday ball at the White House, Julia promenaded with him. She was dressed in white tarlatan and a Greek cap with a dangling tassel. She was dancing when Tyler cut in with, "I must claim Miss Gardiner's company for a while." He took her by the arm, led her to a more private room, and proposed. Julia would write, "I had never thought of love so I said, 'No, no, no,' and shook my head with each word, which flung the tassel of my Greek cap into his face with every move. It amused me very much to see his expression as he tried to make love to me and the tassel brushed his face." Julia was five feet two inches tall and Tyler was a slight-framed six feet. The president was undeterred. A few days later Julia and Margaret visited the White House for tea, and, as Margaret recounted, she and Julia "raced from one end of the house to the other, upstairs and down, and he after us. Waltzed and danced in the famous East Room, played the piano, ransacked every room."

Julia had not dared to tell her father of the budding romance for fear she would be blamed "for allowing the President to have reached the proposing point." But the affair was now secret to no one, and when both father and mother realized the situation, they were pleased. They delayed their return to East Hampton until an informal understanding was reached. East Hampton was awash in rumors that one of their own might soon become first lady. That summer, Tyler's love letters were tracked by the locals at the post office, read aloud in the Gardiner household, and even sent to Julia's brother in New York. Tyler called Julia "the most beautiful woman of the age," and wrote her poems and love songs. Reminded by a friend that at fifty-three he might be too old to be marrying a vivacious twenty-three-year-old, he simply said, "Pooh. Why, my dear sir, I am just full in my prime."

When the Gardiners returned to Washington in February 1844, a marriage date had yet to be set, but the arrangements would be hurried along by tragedy. On February 28, some 350 distinguished guests boarded the navy's newest ship, the steam frigate *Princeton,* at the invitation of the president's friend Captain Robert Stockton. They cruised down the Potomac to witness the firing of a huge new gun called the Peacemaker. The president, members of the cabinet, Dolley Madison, and the Gardiner family were among those on board. The Peacemaker was fired twice to cheers. The guests had gone below deck and were being entertained and served food and drink when Captain Stockton was persuaded to fire again. He and a number of guests returned to the deck. Tyler started up but paused to hear William Waller, his son-in-law, finish a song. When the gun was fired, the breech exploded, sending out large fragments of metal. Eight men lay dead, Julia's father among them. When Julia learned this, she fainted. The *Princeton* returned to the navy yard, and Tyler carried Julia ashore in his arms.

The dead lay in state in the East Room, and yet another funeral was held there before the bodies were moved in a long, sad procession to the Congressional Cemetery. But the grief-stricken Julia soon told Tyler that she was ready to set the date for their marriage. "After I lost my father," she would say, "I felt differently toward the President." Tyler—frugally reusing an envelope—wrote to Mrs. Gardiner, declaring that Julia had given him permission "to ask your approbation of my addresses to her," and adding hopefully that his "position in society" would be sufficiently known to her. Mrs. Gardiner, however, was not that easily impressed by the president's position. The Gardiners were considerably more wealthy than the Tylers. In her reply she asked for assurances that Julia would have all "the necessary comforts and elegancies of life." So assured, she gave her consent.

The wedding was set, secretly, for June 26, 1844, a date some would find surprisingly close to Letitia's death less than two years ago, not to mention the elaborate funeral of Julia's father, just four months past. The president arrived at Howard's Hotel in New York late the night before and had the hotel owner lock up his servants for the night so there would be no leaks to the press. The newspapers were caught completely by surprise. One Washington paper had reported that Tyler was going to New York for "repose." Tyler's daughters were stunned, as well. His eldest, Mary, five years older than her new stepmother, had received a letter from her father just three weeks before in which he said he had "nothing to write about which would be of any interest to you." The church ceremony was brief and quiet. Julia wore a simple white dress of lisse with a gauze veil hanging from a circle of white flowers, but no jewelry as she was still in mourning for her father.

The newlyweds spent a few days at the White House before continuing on to Virginia. Julia enjoyed being the center of attention, noting the crowds that came to "gaze at the President's bride." A distinguished group gathered in the Blue Room for a wedding reception, described by Julia as "very brilliant—brilliant to my heart's content." Secretary of State John C. Calhoun helped her cut the cake. Tyler tried to get some work done, but this was his honeymoon. Julia's sister warned her not to "spend so much time kissing," as the president had more important things to do. And her mother admonished her, "Reserve your caressing for private leisure and be sure you let no one see it unless you wish to be laughed at."

In Virginia the couple made a short stopover at Fortress Monroe, where they were put up in a newly renovated cottage. Julia thrived on the attentions of the officers who called, on the naval guns saluting her, and on the parades in her honor. "True love in a cottage," she wrote, "and quite a contrast to my dirty establishment at Washington." To her mother she wrote, "The P bids me to tell you that the honeymoon is likely to last forever for he finds himself falling in love with me every day." From Fortress Monroe they traveled upriver to Tyler's plantation, which he called Sherwood Forest. The main house was ninety feet long, but Tyler was going further into debt to extend it to an incredible three hundred feet. The house, reputed to be the longest frame structure in the country, is still home to Tyler's descendants. He rounded up the slaves to introduce them to their new "missus" and asked, "Well, how do you like her looks?" Though she was from New York, Julia accepted slavery easily, the more so at Sherwood, which was free of whips and chains. Before 1827, when slavery was abolished in New York, slaves worked her family's 3,300-acre farm on Gardiners Island.

Upon their return to the White House, Julia set about changing things at once. "I have commenced my auspicious reign," she wrote her mother, "and am in quiet possession of the Presidential Mansion." Some called her "Lady Presidentress," or "Mrs. Presidentress," which were much to her liking. As the social season approached, she announced her intention "to do something in the way of entertaining that shall be the admiration and the talk of Washington." Gardiner money paid for some of the elaborate entertainments, and even some sprucing up of the neglected mansion. Julia overhauled the somewhat stuffy Tyler as well. He had considered the waltz, which some thought daringly suggestive, "rather vulgar," and had forbidden his daughters to dance it. But Julia introduced it to the White House and had her husband dancing in no time. And when she heard that the polka was popular among the young people in New York, she introduced that too. Perhaps the only thing Julia toned down was her dress. Being in mourning, she eschewed fashionable blues, pinks, and crimsons and wore black during the day and white in the evening. The diamond star that she normally wore, hung from a band of pearls, on her forehead was replaced by black jet.

For the grand receptions, the young first lady enlisted a variety of sisters, cousins, and in-laws as her "maids of honor" and resurrected the low, court-inspired dais introduced to such controversy by Angelica Van Buren five years before. So elevated, she and her maids sat in regal splendor, Julia wearing a crownlike flowered headdress. That New Year's Day, 1845, over two thousand visited the White House. It was the general public's first chance to meet the much-talked-about first couple. After the handshaking was finished, Margaret Gardiner related, "the President and Julia made two circuits around the East Room followed by her maids of honor, the crowd gaping and pushing to see the show." And at a public reception on January 21, Julia decided the president should move out of the center of the Blue Room, where he was surrounded by the jostling, pushing crowd, to a side wall where guests could be ushered past him in an orderly manner. She then arranged herself and her maids where they could see, as Margaret reported, "a crowd of admiring faces."

One thing Julia did not change was her flirtatiousness. At a dinner she sat next to John C. Calhoun and later reported to her husband that he "actually repeated verses to me. We had together a pleasant flirtation." Tyler's response was, "Upon my word, I must look out for a new secretary of state if Calhoun is to stop writing dispatches and go to repeating verses."

The newspapers overflowed with reports on the presidential couple and the new merriment at the White House. Priscilla, who had moved out of the mansion when her father-in-law married, was heartbroken. "My dear Father," she wrote Tyler from Philadelphia, ". . . Reading in the various papers of the profusion of plum cake and champagne consumed at the Executive Mansion in the last day or two—as I can't participate in your happiness by being with you, I would at least like some of the crumbs that fall from your table; so I wish you would order [John] Wilkins to have me a nice black cake made and iced in first-rate style, . . . I suppose you have read with delight all the paragraphs in the various newspapers complimentary to your 'fair young bride.' . . . I am afraid I am already forgotten."

Julia's reign would last only eight months, however. Tyler loved politics and wanted a second term, but no party wanted him. He considered forming his own party, or running as an independent in hopes of throwing the election into the House. At the Democratic convention a month before his marriage, Tyler was hardly considered for the nomination. A dark horse emerged to succeed him, James K. Polk of Tennessee, and Tyler gave up on continuing his presidency.

In the face of this grave disappointment, Julia found sufficient excuse for one last "grand affair": the vote of Tammany Hall, the powerful Democratic party organization of New York County, instructing its congressmen to vote in favor of the annexation of Texas. Tyler felt strongly about bringing Texas into the Union—it would "crown my public life," he said—and the question had dominated the last part of his term. Votes in the Senate to approve an annexation treaty fell far short of the needed two-thirds majority. Julia took up the issue as her own, and set about charming recalcitrant senators. Tyler ultimately abandoned his strict constructionist principles and opted, successfully, to acquire Texas by a joint resolution of Congress, which would require only a majority vote.

The party was set for Wednesday, February 18, and weeks of detailed preparation began. Over two thousand invitations were sent out, and over three thousand people attended. "We were as thick as sheep in a pen," Julia's sister said. The East Room was lit with over six hundred candles. Champagne flowed. Julia, her sister wrote, was dazzling in a "white satin headdress hat embroidered with silver and ostrich feathers and her set of diamonds." Tyler was led to quip, "They cannot say now that I am a President without a party."

Tyler's last few days at the White House were busy. On March 1, just three days before the end of Tyler's term, Congress at last passed the joint resolution to annex Texas. Even with last-minute concessions and compromises, and lobbying by both Julia and the president, a switch of one vote in the Senate would have killed it. After signing the resolution, Tyler gave the pen to Julia. She wrote her mother saying that she would always wear around her neck "the gold pen with which the President signed my annexation bill." On March 3, Florida became the twenty-seventh state, and Tyler's veto of a maritime bill was overridden—the first-ever congressional override of a presidential veto.

After Polk's election, Tyler had graciously welcomed the president-elect with a White House party, and had moved out of the mansion early to facilitate the transition. He planned to leave Washington on a 9 A.M. boat, but he arrived late and, rudely experiencing his sudden lack of clout, found the boat had left. He and Julia returned to their hotel and departed that evening instead.

At Sherwood Forest, the Tylers lived an idyllic southern plantation life. Tyler rode out to his fields each day, a floppy Panama hat on his head, and Julia bore him seven children, who he delighted in rocking by the fire. His last child, Mary, was born in 1860, when Tyler was seventy: her father was born when Washington was president, and she died during Truman's administration. Tyler's golden years were tarnished by the growing threat of civil war, which would draw him back into public life. He was an adamant moderate who urged his fellow southerners to accept the territorial restriction of slavery. When the Peace Convention he headed in February 1861 failed, however, he finally voted for secession and accepted a seat in the Confederate Congress. In April, war broke out. In late January 1862, Union forces would overrun Sherwood Forest. But Tyler, who died on January 18, would not be alive to see it.

# James Knox Polk

## 1845–1849

## *Attention to Detail*

WHEN JAMES K. POLK and his wife, Sarah, crossed the threshold of the White House on March 4, about nineteen hours after the Tylers' departure, they walked into a house down on its heels. To spite John Tyler, Congress had withheld funding for furnishing and maintenance, and the mansion was worn and dirty. The legislators made up for it by giving the incoming administration $14,900, but Polk, who favored limited government and hoped to cut costs across the board, declared he would spend only half of it.

At forty-nine, Polk, the youngest president up to that time, took the role of public servant seriously. "No President who performs his duty faithfully can have any leisure," he said, and would drive himself with tragic determination like no president before or since. Polk was short, thin, and angular, with habitually compressed lips and long, graying hair combed straight back. He dressed in unfashionably long coats, the pockets of which often bulged with letters. Charles Wilkes, a famous naval explorer of the time, said Polk reminded him of a "penny postman" who had "little to converse about" besides politics. Polk indeed had few interests outside politics and almost no sense of humor.

Even hearing the news of his election left him poker-faced. Counting votes took a long time in 1844, and Polk, a dark-horse Democratic candidate, was not expected to win. Initial reports of his defeat brought friends to his doorstep of his home in Columbia, Tennessee, to offer their condolences. Polk knew they should be offering congratu-

94

lations because the Cincinnati postmaster, who'd heard updated results, scrawled the news on a mail packet headed for Nashville. The Nashville postmaster, a friend of Polk's, in turn rushed a secret note to the new president, thirty miles away. But straight-arrow Polk refused to share these glad tidings and sent his friends away thinking he'd been defeated.

"Who is James K. Polk?" the opposition asked in the election, but once in Washington, the new president had no intention of being ignored. He set about turning the White House into a showplace with a complete redecoration, readied in time for the New Year's Day reception in 1846. He purchased some of the most elegant china to ever grace the White House—scalloped plates, rimmed with gold and, on the dessert plates, flowers worthy of a botanical artist.

Polk entertained extensively, reinstating the weekly drawing rooms, not held since the Madison administration. As the country entered the Mexican War in 1846, party-giving accelerated, as it was now particularly crucial for the president to keep abreast of public opinion and maintain political ties. Drawing rooms were held twice a week, Tuesdays and Fridays; anyone properly dressed could drop in, and attendance averaged two hundred when Congress was in session. Other gatherings occupied an additional two or three nights a week.

During the war years, 1846 to 1848, many uniformed men attended every White House reception. Volunteer companies, state militias, and regular army companies headed west often stopped at the White House, where Polk reviewed them on horseback, and soldiers camped in nearby Lafayette Park attracted crowds of spectators. During the 1848 Fourth of July reception, the president was called to his office to receive a messenger who had arrived, unexpectedly, with the Treaty of Guadalupe Hidalgo, approved in May by Mexico and the United States negotiator. Polk signed the document immediately, adding more than five hundred thousand miles of territory to the United States, which now stretched to the Pacific Ocean. Recent reports of vast quantities of gold in California—harbingers of the gold rush—made the achievement all the more exciting, and the 1848 social season was celebratory and dense with military heroes.

A frequent honored guest was Dolley Madison, now in her late seventies and living in a genteel poverty across the street from the White House. The Polks always invited the former first lady to their receptions and took special care of her. The president personally helped her out of the rickety carriage in which she traveled the one block from her home to the White House, and Sarah would even give Dolley her place at the dinner table.

Unavoidably during the war White House events were politically charged, and elegant Sarah Polk was instrumental at smoothing away friction. She was a very different type of first lady than some of the frail, reclusive women who preceded her. Daughter of wealthy planters, Sarah entered the White House at forty-two and was called "fine looking" and "handsome." One White House visitor, a John S. Jenkins, was impressed by her "unfailing courtesy" and "ease of manner," and found her "dignified but unaffected." In a day of rabid partisanship, she remained on good terms with her husband's rivals, even obstreperous Henry Clay. Massachusetts senator Charles Sumner, a Whig, said her "sweetness of manner won me entirely." Men enjoyed her company, and at times she declined to accompany the ladies to the drawing room after dinner, preferring to discuss politics. "She was always in the parlor with Mr. Polk," one contemporary recalled. In mixed company her habit of engaging in repartee with the men led more retiring ladies to pronounce her too bold.

She liked being the center of attention. Parisian friends sent her the latest fashions, elaborate, often low-cut gowns in silk, grosgrain silk, or cotton mull with full skirts and even trains. She once spent over $600 on a single gown. For the grandest occasions she might wear an ostrich-plumed headdress, or a turban à la her friend Dolley Madison, whose company she often enjoyed while riding about town in an open carriage.

Sarah, who was childless, to her sorrow, made no bones about her lack of interest in domestic matters. During the election campaign a voter threatening to switch to Clay argued that Clay's wife was a better housekeeper. Sarah's feisty reply: "If I get to the White House I expect to live on $25,000 a year and I will neither keep house nor make butter." For years she had served as her husband's private secretary and confidante, and at the White House she continued the role. She was the one person Polk could completely trust and was usually by his side. Anyone who wished to speak to the president might well have to do so in the presence of the first lady.

Yet she did concern herself with domestic matters. To lessen the wartime tensions at White House events, she tried to vary the routine by always having music. There was of course no dancing. Sarah was a devout Presbyterian. "Would you dance in so public a place as this? I would not," she replied when some of the younger ladies pleaded with her to hold a dance. "To dance in these rooms would be undignified, and it would be respectful neither to the house nor to the office. How indecorous it would seem for dancing to be going on in one apartment, while in another we were conversing with dignitaries of the republic or ministers of the gospel." She decided "a juggler or sleight of hand performer" would be acceptable, to "exhibit before a select company." The president was called from his work to enjoy the performance, and he found the show "innocent in itself," but his time "unprofitably spent."

At smaller gatherings, Sarah invited guests to gather around the piano in the Red Room to sing hymns. Anyone who called on her on the Sabbath would be asked to join her at church. In addition to banishing dancing, she prohibited the playing of cards, and—in step with the growing temperance movement—the drinking of hard liquor. (Her husband, also deeply religious, had no such compunctions. When he ran for state representative, he supplied the voters in just one district with twenty-three gallons of liquor. It was a common practice, if not a Presbyterian one.) The dearth of liquor sorely disappointed Washingtonians, accustomed as they were to finding a variety of strong whiskey punches at the White House. However, Sarah had no objections to wine during formal dinners, and brandy after. This was no help to the strained household budget: whiskey was cheap; wine, champagne, and brandy were not. The first social season's wine bill alone was over $300.

The ever-growing numbers of guests made it even more likely that Polk, whose physical presence was far from imposing, would go unnoticed when he entered the room. Sarah is credited with solving the problem by enlisting the Marine Band to announce the president's arrival with an old Scottish anthem, "Hail to the Chief." The custom persists to this day. For dinners, she introduced a march designed to induce guests to fall in line and proceed in an orderly fashion from the reception room to their seats in the State Dining Room.

To make sure dinners were the height of elegance, Sarah hired a French chef who sometimes served up 150 different courses, each served with fresh plates. Everything was conducted in the French manner with elaborate service and a free flow of wine. But the Polks ate little at these affairs, preferring plain foods. When, on leaving the White House, they were honored with a lavish repast, Polk was less than appreciative. "It was, I suppose, a sumptuous breakfast," he said. "All the dishes were prepared in the French style of cooking, and to one unaccustomed to it [it] was difficult to tell of what they were composed. . . . I could see nothing before me that I had been accustomed to." So he discreetly asked a servant to please bring him "a piece of cornbread and boiled ham."

In the realm of decoration, Sarah sanctioned the addition of gaslight made possible by a new gas line run from the Capitol to the White House. But she preferred the warm glow of candles and drew the line at the conversion of her favorite chandelier, the one in the Blue Room. Society thought her unduly old-fashioned, until the next grand reception: when the gas company shut down at 9 P.M., the Blue Room alone was invitingly lit.

The president attended the traditional, and politically important, receptions resignedly and had little patience with what he considered a waste of time. New foreign ministers were customarily required to go through a ceremony of presenting their credentials to the president. These tedious rituals were frequent enough that in one instance, Polk replied to a diplomat who had addressed him at length in French without waiting for a translation; he did not understand the speech, but he had heard it all before. On another occasion the Russian minister, Baron Alexandre de Bodisco, arrived in full dress regalia to announce such significant events as the death of the czar's niece. "These matters of ceremony are so ridiculous," Polk said, "that I could scarcely preserve my gravity."

Like his predecessors, Polk developed a strategy for avoiding a sore hand and arm. When a man approached, hand extended, he said, he "took advantage of him by being a little quicker than he was and seizing him by the tip of the fingers, giving him a hearty shake, and thus preventing him from getting a full grip on me."

Inevitably with such multitudes, unsavory characters occasionally slipped by the guards. At one reception a man entered with a loaf of bread under each arm and a bottle of wine in each hand. Suddenly he went berserk, running through the rooms waving a knife. He broke into Sarah's parlor—probably the Blue Room—terrifying her and her lady guests before he was brought under control.

One diplomatic duty Polk actually seemed to enjoy was receiving Native Americans. In June 1846 a group of approximately fifty Comanches—chiefs, braves, and women—listened to a short piano recital and then were shown through the White House. "Large mirrors in the parlors attracted their attention more than anything else," Polk noted in his diary. "When they saw themselves full length, they seemed to be greatly delighted." One chief confessed to the president that before his visit he thought the Comanches could defeat anyone, but he now knew that white men were more plentiful "than the stars." Polk gave the chiefs silver medals "as a token of friendship" and said they were "well pleased." A group of Winnebagos visited in the fall of 1846, and Polk declared them "the finest looking men of any tribe who has visited me." The Indians presented him with a long, richly ornamented peace pipe and invited him to smoke it with them. Undeterred by any religious scruples, he did.

Such satisfying diversions were few and far between for the workaholic president, who once worked on a message to Congress from six in the evening until seven the next morning. "The Presidency is not a bed of roses. . . . I am the hardest working man in this country," he said. Polk was in fact more involved in the day-to-day running of the government than any president before him. "I prefer," he said, "to supervise the whole operation of government than entrust the public business to subordinates." That included his cabinet, of which he said, "I have conducted the government without their aid. Indeed, I have become so familiar with their duties and workings of the government, not only upon general principles but on most of its minute details, that I find but little difficulty in doing this. It is only occasionally that a great measure or a new question arises upon which I need the aid and advice of my Cabinet."

His attention to detail was legendary. He once picked out a passage in a diplomatic letter he was given to sign and told Secretary of State James Buchanan, also noted for meticulousness, that it did not conform to standard usage. Buchanan insisted it was correct, and they bet a basket of champagne over it. Polk was right, but declined the champagne.

Compounding matters, the government provided the president no clerical assistance. Polk did, however, hire his twenty-nine-year-old nephew, Joseph Knox Walker, as his private secretary. Walker and his wife, Augusta, occupied two White House rooms. Four of their children, two of whom were born in the White House, lived with them.

Given his unwillingness to delegate, Polk's schedule was unrelenting. He rose at dawn and after a short walk and an early breakfast worked through the day and on into the night, stopping only for dinner and another walk or horseback ride. On mornings following an evening reception, he would often rise even earlier to make up the lost time. Polk insisted on reading each of the hundreds of letters he received, and made himself available to the public four mornings a week. Visits from numerous citizens who expected to be received at the White House could easily occupy the entire morning.

Many of those lined up to see him sought appointment to office, and Polk lamented, "Will the pressures for office never cease! . . . The idea seems to prevail with many persons that the President is from his position compelled to contribute to every loafer who applies. . . . I am ready to Exclaim God deliver me from dispensing the patronage of government." He was particularly besieged during the Mexican War, when applicants for military commissions—often incompetents who were friends or relatives of congressmen—flocked to his office. He came to view office seekers as "the very scum of society" and joked that he should get "one of Colt's revolving pistols to clear out my office of the office seekers." Within one hour of receiving a telegram informing him that the army paymaster had died of cholera, he had received applications for the position. And when the marshal of the District of Columbia fell ill, Polk complained that he received "a half a dozen applications for his place, if he should die."

Yet the president felt duty-bound to listen to the stories of his visitors, many of whom were obviously unqualified. "It is a great and useless consumption of my time," he complained, "and yet I do not see how I am to avoid it without being rude or insulting, which is not my nature to be." He listened patiently, then turned them down, except, he said, "in a few cases where I am satisfied that the persons applying are . . . in great distress."

The flow of office seekers and others was managed, if not stemmed, by steward Henry Bowman. Polk did not take kindly to interruptions, even by friends. Ensconced in his north entrance office, Bowman registered everyone who came to call on the president, playing an official role in presidential business as had no steward before. If the president, once informed by a servant, agreed to see the caller, Bowman ushered the visitor to the upstairs office and announced him. Polk ordered Bowman not to admit any visitors to the White House on Sunday, but sometimes a crisis forced an exception. And, while expressing regret, he occasionally held cabinet meetings on Sunday.

With so many callers and with so much public business going on, the mansion's residents felt little privacy. Joanna Rucker, a niece of Sarah's from Tennessee, was once startled by a strange man who burst into the upstairs oval parlor, where she sat writing. "He pretended to miss his way in going from the President's office and came down in the private part of the hall into the parlor," she wrote. "The house belongs to the government and everyone feels at home and they sometimes stalk into our bedroom and say they are looking at the house."

If Polk was bothered by the lack of privacy, he was unwilling to compromise his work ethic by seeking it outside the White House. During his first year in office, he left the District of Columbia only once, for a one-day trip to George Washington's home at Mount Vernon. He and Sarah were the first White House couple to spend their summers in the mansion. In four years, Polk was absent from the capital for a total of just six weeks. He even tried to prevent his cabinet members from vacationing, and complained when his overworked nephew took two weeks off from his secretarial duties (Sarah covered for him).

Finally exhausted, Polk took a boat to Fort Monroe in Virginia to rest. At Norfolk a delegation of admirers boarded the boat and insisted the president attend a celebration in his honor. The crowds were large, and Polk described the day as "one of the hottest . . . I ever felt." He was compelled to march in a parade, attend a formal dinner, shake endless hands, and endure numerous speeches. He attempted to avoid some of the functions, but preparations had already been made and people were waiting. By the time the celebration wound down, he said he was "almost overcome with excessive heat." He was soaked through with perspiration and developed chills. All that night and the next day he was severely ill, and recovered only slowly from the good intentions of his supporters.

Polk was working himself to death. He would die less than four months after he left office, at just fifty-three, making his life the shortest of all the presidents. Despite his generally weak constitution and chronic diarrhea, he was reasonably healthy as his term commenced. But as it wore on he suffered increasingly from malaria (common in the capital), dysentery, shortness of breath, and fatigue. He was not unaware of his fragility. As early as his fiftieth birthday, November 2, 1845, he wrote in his diary of "the reflection that I had lived fifty years, and that before fifty years would expire, I would be sleeping with the generations which have gone before me. I thought of the vanity of this world's honours, how little they would proft me a century hence, and that it was time for me to be 'putting my House in order.' " And again on November 2, 1848: "I will soon go the way of all earth. I pray God to prepare me to meet the great event." In that election year, extending his reign was out of the question. "They have been four years of incessant labor and anxiety and of great responsibility," he said. "I am heartily rejoiced that my term is so near its close."

Regardless, when Polk was nominated in 1844 he had agreed that he would serve only one term. He entered the White House sharply focused, with four major goals: to establish an independent treasury (a precursor of the Federal Reserve); lower the tariff; favorably settle the Oregon territory boundary dispute with Britain; and acquire the New Mexico and California territories. He accomplished them all, a rare feat for a one-term president.

The Polks moved out of the White House to the Willard Hotel on Saturday, March 3. Because March 4, the traditional inauguration date, was a Sunday, Zachary Taylor was not sworn in until the fifth. Polk was true to form right to the last. He went to the Capitol on Saturday and signed papers until 2 A.M. On Sunday he returned to the Willard and fell into bed next to Sarah with his clothes on, exhausted. He was wakened at 6 A.M. to sign more bills. "I disposed of all the business on my table down to the minutest detail," he said, "and at the close of the day left a clean table for my successor."

For their retirement, the couple had bought a home in Nashville, which Sarah had spent the last year remodeling and refurbishing and was not quite finished. The relieved ex-president and his wife now took a long, leisurely trip back to Tennessee by way of New Orleans. On the way, Polk suffered a recurrence of the intestinal disorder that so frequently afflicted him, and he arrived in Nashville weak and tired. Nevertheless, he set about managing the completion of their house. He became seriously ill on June 2, and died June 15, 1849. Sarah died at eighty-seven, and was buried beside her long-dead husband. Shortly thereafter, in 1891, the home of the strangely unremembered eleventh president was demolished to make way for "Polk Apartments."

# 12

# Zachary Taylor

## 1849–July 9, 1850

## *Tragedy*

THE MEXICAN WAR produced a new hero and a new president, Zachary Taylor. A general as unconcerned about his dress as about hardships he had been nicknamed "Old Rough and Ready" during the fierce Seminole War (1835–1842). Thick-bodied at five feet eight inches tall and about two hundred pounds, he had long, gangly arms, a mahogany-colored face, and very short bowlegs—he needed help mounting a horse. He wore loose-legged pantaloons, long, full shirts, and a broad-brimmed hat of woven palmetto leaves, which, along with his civilian bearing, caused him to be mistaken for a rube farmer. Even as president he would dress for comfort—typically in a black broadcloth suit, with a silk hat pushed back on his head—rather than style.

When he arrived in Washington for his inauguration, Taylor was rough and perhaps not quite ready. His education was rudimentary, his inaugural address one of the shortest in history, and his delivery poor. Polk, who thought Taylor a "well-meaning old man," "narrow-minded," "bigoted," and "exceedingly ignorant of public affairs," noted that the new president read "in a very low voice and very badly as to his pronunciation and manner." But no matter. The *National Intelligencer* reported that "followed by a vast concourse of people, the President entered the Mansion . . . and there received . . . the salutes of some thousands of persons, passing in a long array in front of him."

That night, Taylor and Vice President Fillmore drove from the White House through the snow to three inaugural balls, the last of which was at City Hall. *New York*

*Tribune* founder and editor Horace Greeley said the event was distinguished by "the largest ballroom, the largest company, the most painful and dangerous pressure . . . I ever witnessed; from four to five thousand persons were present, each one of whom seemed to think that he or she was alone entitled to be there; but it was nevertheless a grand affair." The dining hall was set up for half the number of revelers, and an Englishman who witnessed the free-for-all wrote that he "saw knots of men like so many vultures, pulling and hauling" at stripped turkey skeletons, leaving the impression that some of the men "doubtless had . . . nothing to keep body and soul together." Given the crush, the cloakrooms had become disaster areas, and people had no choice but to leave in any coat that fit. Abraham Lincoln, for one, went home at four in the morning without his hat. Taylor left the scene for the White House around one o'clock.

Such pomp and ceremony, not to mention chaos, held no interest for the pious first lady. Taylor had married Margaret "Peggy" Smith in 1810. Now at sixty, she was graying but slender and erect, and was often described as "stately." A loyal, deeply religious woman, she had been uncomplaining over the course of his forty-year military career, joining her husband at his remote stations, living in log cabins or tents, and learning how to protect herself with a gun—a frontier necessity. But after the privations of army life, losing two of six children in childbirth, and welcoming Taylor home from a battle that left bullet holes in his uniform, she had been ready to settle down and enjoy her family. She had prayed nightly for her husband's defeat, viewing his nomination as a "plot to deprive me of his society, and shorten his life by unnecessary care and responsibility."

Initially, her husband agreed. When first questioned about running for president, the man who crushed Mexican commander Antonio López de Santa Anna's army said, "Such an idea never entered my head. Nor is it likely to enter the head of any sane person." As the pressure built for Taylor to run in 1848, he said over and over that he was not a candidate. "I want quiet & should have it at my time of life," the sixty-two-year-old hero wrote. "I do not care a fig about the office." Yet, he concluded, "I suppose I must serve if elected."

Still, the Whigs nominated Taylor at their convention in Baltimore. Taylor was at home in Louisiana when he heard the news from friends. The official notification, however, was mailed without prepaying the postage, not unusual in those days. Taylor had been getting a lot of postage-due mail and had told the postmaster he would not accept any more. So the document languished in the dead-letter office until a second, postage-paid announcement was sent. During the campaign, the party touted their hero's military record and personal virtues, and those were persuasive enough to win the election. When an oblivious fellow passenger on a steamship asked the reluctant president-elect if he had favored Taylor in the election, he replied, "I did not vote for him—partly because his wife was opposed to sending 'Old Zach' to Washington, where she is obliged to go with him."

Her husband might feel the call of duty, but Peggy had no intention of serving as White House helpmate. Besides, her health was failing. She was soon forced to retreat to her upstairs room, rarely leaving it except to attend St. John's Church, which she did daily, or to join the family at meals. She was content with knitting, the company of her grandchildren, and being the center of family attention. So her youngest daughter, Mary Elizabeth, universally known as "Betty," took over her mother's social duties. She made an ideal White House hostess. "Miss Betty," twenty-five, was attractive, well educated for the time, spoke French, and was well acquainted with the ways of society via much time spent in New Orleans.

Just before Taylor's election, Betty had married Colonel William Bliss. The Taylors were overjoyed—Betty was her father's pet, and Bliss was like a son to him. In the army Bliss had served Taylor well as adjutant general. While Taylor could get along in Indian sign language, he had difficulties with ordinary pronunciation and spelling, and Bliss's rewriting of his military dispatches in good, colorful language helped the general become a kind of folk hero. At the White House, Bliss became Taylor's secretary and principal assistant, kept his accounts, and managed the house as well. Taylor's son Richard also lived in the White House, and also served as a secretary to the president. Educated in Scotland and France and graduated from Yale, he joined the Confederate army when the Civil War broke out in 1861. When the war ended, he was the last general to lay down his arms. Taylor's military aide, Joseph Eaton, also lived at the White House.

Another family member of sorts was Taylor's aging warhorse, Old Whitey. The bullets and cannon fire of Mexican War battles had not fazed him, and he had endeared himself to Taylor. After the war, Old Whitey had been returned to New Orleans by ship and for a while grazed on the lawn of Taylor's Baton Rouge home. When Taylor was elected, he wanted Old Whitey with him in Washington, and shipped the horse north by steamboat. Old Whitey was grayish white, shaggy-maned, and knock-kneed. He contentedly cropped the grass of the White House lawn—unless a military band went by. Then his head came up, and he pushed his way into the line of march. He was a favorite of tourists, and lost most of the hairs on his tail to souvenir hunters.

This tight family circle admitted few outsiders. Senator Jefferson Davis, a Mississippi Democrat, was an exception—much to the consternation of Taylor's Whig friends. As a young officer in Taylor's command, Davis had courted the general's daughter Sarah. Taylor opposed the marriage and forbade Davis to enter his home. The two almost came to a duel. Nevertheless, Sarah and Davis married. Her parents did not attend the wedding. Davis took her home to his plantation in Mississippi, and three months later they both came down with a malarial fever. Only Davis survived. Taylor and his onetime son-in-law eventually forgot their differences and became friends. Davis visited frequently, often joining the family for meals. Meanwhile, his second wife, Varina, pleased Taylor by bringing interesting ladies to call on Margaret.

The first lady's condition was blamed by some on the supposedly unhealthy vapors thought to emanate, in summer especially, from the swampy lowlands south of the White House. With cholera a deadly threat to the city from May to November, the grounds seemed almost menacing. Some believed that James Polk had shortened his life by insisting on spending summers at the White House. Plans were put forth for a series of landscaped terraces that, above all, would help drain the area.

Inside the White House, thanks to Polk's thorough redecoration, there was little need for new furniture, reupholstering, and the like, but the exterior of the house needed painting again, and the roof leaked. During Polk's administration, gas had replaced candles for most lighting. Taylor now ordered the system expanded, bringing more light to the offices and family quarters. The gas bills, paid by the government, were surprisingly high. An investigation found that some of the hotels along Pennsylvania Avenue had secretly tapped into the gas line that ran between the Capitol and the White House and were enjoying free gaslight.

*As a general in the Mexican War Taylor won spectacular victories but his casual dress once led him to be mistaken for a farmer. His legs were so short he had to be helped up onto a horse. At the White House he liked to sit with his short legs up on a desk and spit tobacco juice at a cuspidor—he was known as a sure shot.* (LIBRARY OF CONGRESS)

Taylor apparently made no innovations at the White House, simply continuing many of the practices instituted by the Polks, including weekly drawing rooms. He upheld the ban on hard liquor, but there were dances and young people's parties. In an effort to cut expenses, no food or drink was served at the drawing rooms. Mrs. Taylor's health was a handy excuse for fewer dinner parties, often no-frills stag ones at that. There were usually two official dinners a week, and on warm Saturday evenings the Marine Band played on the south portico as the public wandered through the lawns and graveled walks, a custom begun by Tyler. Everyone from senators to shopkeepers attended. Even in October, one visitor wrote, "The surpassing splendor of the President's garden . . . elicits high admiration from every visitor. Dahlias, roses in many varieties, and indeed every description of flower and shrubbery, appears in gayest attire." Taylor often strolled the lawn among the public, ready to shake hands with anyone who introduced himself. Guards at these and other events attempted to screen out pickpockets and prostitutes—and even free blacks—with limited success. At the New Year's reception in 1850, a number of men lost their pocketbooks and a lady her gold watch as pickpockets worked the crowd.

While Polk tightly controlled the comings and goings of visitors to his office, Taylor kept his upstairs office wide open. He worked in the southeast corner room, which had a flat-topped table for a desk and a wood-fired Franklin stove. Business callers or strangers who walked in off the street simply to shake his hand were likely to find him sitting with his short legs up on the table, a sawdust-filled box within easy range. Taylor neither drank nor smoked, but he did chew tobacco, and as a spitter he was known as a sure shot. One visitor observed that "he never missed once" or ever "put my person in jeopardy." But if there was no spittoon in sight, the president, like the many White House visitors who chewed tobacco, used the carpet.

Taylor, whom people tended to address as "general," was accessible after hours as well. As the *Washington Whig* reported, "[The President] mingles with the crowd in the most familiar manner. He has no personal attendants . . . to stand between him and the people." He often strolled down to the market stalls and engaged farmers in conversation. And there was nothing to stop people, especially office seekers, from accosting him at the White House in the evening. A southern Democratic newspaper described the routine: "At eight o'clock P.M. . . . office seekers go . . . to his room, where himself and lady, and Col. Bliss and lady receive company. . . . They 'sit it out' till the ladies retire, then open their battery upon the President. . . . Last night he was unable to . . . go to bed, till from 12 to 2 o'clock. Such treatment is more than flesh . . . can bear. [President Taylor] has determined that those who perseveringly annoy him shall not be selected for office."

Yet Taylor was virtually always polite and friendly even to his more annoying visitors. It was this amiability, and his easygoing, frank, and unassuming manners—rather than his leadership—that secured his popularity. Taylor had his opinions, but he was a weak politician at a time when political differences were splitting the nation in two. America was obsessed with the question of extending slavery to the western territories acquired by Polk in the Mexican War. In the fall of 1849 California applied to be admitted to the Union as a free state, and the South was so incensed that civil war seemed imminent. Taylor wanted California admitted without concessions to the South, and opposed what became the Compromise of 1850, devised by Daniel Webster and Henry Clay, which admitted California as a free state in exchange for more a stringent fugitive slave law. Because of the debates, Taylor decided he should remain in Washington during the summer of 1850.

In general Taylor's health was good; as a young man, he was known for an iron constitution. His weaknesses were limited to a susceptibility to intestinal disorders and an imbalance in his eye muscles that could produce double vision. He tended to squint. He had glasses for reading but seemed to misplace them constantly. But at sixty-four he was old for the time and tended to be a worrier. Friends began to comment that he looked ill.

With a summer heat wave came rumors that the deadly Asiatic cholera plaguing the country had reached Washington. The previous summer, Asiatic cholera had taken many lives in the capital. In 1850 Washington's forty thousand residents were spared that fate—the death rate did not rise sharply—but the less serious ailment known as "cholera morbus" was rampant. Water and sewer systems were primitive. Many people fell ill with gastrointestinal problems, and all were warned against eating fruit, vegetables that were not well cooked, or any meat that was not first quality. Some residents left the city, and there was talk of Congress adjourning.

On the Fourth of July, 1850, Taylor attended ceremonies at the partially completed Washington Monument. The day was hot and the speeches long, and Taylor also walked around in the sun afterward. On his return to the White House he was both hungry and thirsty. Accounts vary as to what he consumed. The most common relates that he drank a large amount of ice water, and then washed down a great number of cherries with ice milk. He had also had water at the ceremony. (Despite warnings, he was known to drink whatever water was available and was fond of raw fruit and vegetables.) A few hours later he developed severe stomach cramps. He refused all medicines except for some brandy. He worsened steadily, suffering fever, diarrhea, and vomiting. By July 6 he was growing dehydrated despite taking fluids. Dr. Alexander D. Wotherspoon, a military surgeon, diagnosed acute gastroenteritis due to milk or water. He administered calomel and opium, which he believed had "a good effect."

Convinced he would die, Taylor became depressed. "God knows I have tried to do my honest duty. But I have made mistakes," he brooded. "My motives have been misconstrued and my feelings have been outraged." By Monday, July 8, there were four physicians in attendance, including Dr. Wood, a son-in-law summoned from Baltimore, and Dr. Thomas Miller, longtime doctor to the presidents despite accusations that he had bled William Henry Harrison to death a decade before. Taylor ate ice continually, but his stomach was rejecting fluids. He became distressed and incoherent. Colonel Bliss had begun posting bulletins every two hours, and at 11 P.M. reported, "The President is laboring under a bilious remittent fever, following . . . severe cholera morbus; and is considered . . . seriously ill." The gates of the White House were closed and guards stationed there.

The next day, July 9, Senator Daniel Webster interrupted the Senate debate to announce, "The President of the United States is dying, and may not survive the day." The House and the Senate adjourned. That evening Taylor's frightened family, Jefferson Davis, and his doctors gathered around him. At about 10 P.M. the president spoke: "The storm, in passing, has swept away the trunk. . . . I'm about to die. I expect my summons very soon. I have tried to discharge my duties faithfully; I regret nothing, but I am sorry I am about to leave my friends." He died a half hour later. The tolling of bells in the night brought the news to all of Washington.

Margaret Taylor was distraught. She endured, much as Mary Lincoln would fifteen years later, the sounds of pounding carrying through the White House as carpenters constructed the catafalque, a stand that would hold her husband's coffin. On July 12 the body was placed in the East Room, and the public converged there to pay respects. It was observed that many left with "a leaf, a flower, a withered branch . . . consecrated by . . . having once rested on the bier of ZACHARY TAYLOR." Margaret moved out of the White House the next day, the day of the funeral, and did not attend the afternoon service. She never spoke of the White House again.

In October Taylor's body would receive a permanent burial near Beargrass Creek in Kentucky, but now a procession of over one hundred carriages wound past a reported one hundred thousand spectators to the Congressional Cemetery two miles away. Old Whitey, curried for once, riderless and carrying boots reversed in the stirrups, ambled behind the coffin.

---

## SOUVENIR HUNTERS

It wasn't anything new that Zachary Taylor's famous warhorse, Old Whitey, lost the better part of his tail. Souvenir hunters plagued the White House almost from the beginning. British admiral Sir George Cockburn, about to set the building on fire in 1814, helped himself to one of Dolley Madison's yellow seat cushions. Andrew Jackson anticipated the wishes of his fans, saving snippings of his hair for them, but other presidents have not received the lust for mementos quite so amiably.

- After Abraham Lincoln's second inaugural, presidential friend Noah Brooks wrote, "Some of the aesthetic pilferers have even cut out small bits of the gorgeous carpet, leaving scars on the floor as large as a man's hand. Others, on larger game intent, have actually cut off a yard or two from the lower end of some of the crimson satin window hangings."
- Rutherford B. Hayes's son, Birchard, reported, "After every public reception a man had to go the rounds with a basket of crystal pendants to replace those taken from the chandeliers. They cut pieces off the bottoms of curtains, and carried off everything in sight."
- The Clevelands' baby Ruth—a child so popular the candy bar was named after her—was surrounded by tourists when her nurse took her out on the White House lawn. One visitor even tried to snip a lock of hair as a souvenir.
- Caroline Harrison was distressed by the condition of the White House when she moved in, especially the evidence of souvenir hunters who came equipped with pocket knives.
- William Taft had the Secret Service watch out for guests who might take mementos at state dinners. The agents were trained to say such things as, "Let me dispose of that table napkin for you," or "Let me put that spoon down for you."
- On a naval cruise to Hawaii, Franklin Roosevelt thought Fala, his Scottie dog, was shedding. It turned out the crew had been snipping fur for souvenirs.
- Franklin Roosevelt's housekeeper, Henrietta Nesbitt, reported, "I hate to say it, but so many pieces of silver were missing after teas and other affairs that I stopped having the spoons and things monogrammed." She sent twelve-inch trays to the executive office with cheese, crackers, and drinks. "They just didn't

come back," she said. Once so many spoons vanished during a large tea party that she decided to forgo spoons altogether the next time.

- Grace Coolidge discovered that in the East Room "the little tassels of the finishing braid on the edges of the brocaded hangings at the windows had been pulled off as high as the hand could reach." Once at a tea for cabinet wives in the second floor library, she noticed a lady slipping a napkin into her purse: " 'You may as well bring it right out, for I saw you put it in,' I said. With that she drew forth the little Madeira square and held it up in astonishment. She had thought it was one of her husband's handkerchiefs, which she had brought because she had a slight cold, but it was a White House napkin and—it was full of holes!"

- When he was about to leave office, Lyndon Johnson beat the souvenir hunters to the punch. He collected all the presidential china and silverware on Air Force One. Some was for his planned presidential library, the rest for his Texas ranch.

- Nancy Reagan found the china service so depleted that she couldn't effectively entertain crowds. "Although the great majority of guests behave themselves," she said, "there's always somebody who just can't leave the White House without taking home a souvenir." Among the somebodies was Reagan's daughter Maureen, who rounded up "more matchbooks than I knew what to do with" when she stayed at the White House.

# 13

# Millard Fillmore

## July 1850–March 4, 1853

## *The Last Whig*

THE POUNDING on Vice President Millard Fillmore's hotel door late the night of July 9, 1850, was not a surprise. Zachary Taylor had succumbed to a mild form of summer cholera, and Fillmore had visited the president earlier that day. It was clear that Taylor was dying and Fillmore had decided to stay at the Willard Hotel rather than return to his residence in Georgetown. Still, the news unsettled Fillmore, and he passed the rest of the night sleeplessly. The next day at noon he took the oath of office before a joint session of Congress. The ceremony was simple; he made no speech. He attended Taylor's funeral in the shrouded East Room and then left the White House for his hotel around the corner.

Had Taylor not taken sick on July 4 and had the press of business been different, Fillmore would have quitted disease-plagued Washington for the healthier airs of the Jersey shore, where Abigail was passing the summer. But the Senate was locked in one of the most heated struggles in its history—whether to allow slavery in new territories—and it had been Fillmore's duty as vice president to preside over it. With his sudden elevation to president, his chances of leaving vanished. But rather than live in the White House, Fillmore commuted from his rented Georgetown quarters. The *Baltimore Patriot* explained, "President Fillmore, by advice of his physician, has taken apartments in Georgetown in consequence of the unhealthy condition of the White House."

Abigail remained at the seashore, and Fillmore joined her there for about a week in September, after handling the initial problems of his transition to chief executive. Among other things, Taylor's cabinet, which paid Fillmore little heed, resigned between July 20 and July 22. Fillmore happily made new appointments that included Daniel Webster as secretary of state. On September 9 the Fillmores returned to Washington, but did not so much as set foot in the family rooms at the White House until the end of the month.

On the very day of his return, Fillmore signed and supported the Compromise of 1850, which checked the expansion of slavery into new territories while strengthening the Fugitive Slave Act. Taylor had died in the midst of the battle over the compromise, which he opposed as making too many concessions to the South. "God knows I detest slavery," Fillmore said, ". . . but we must endure it." The compromise satisfied neither North nor South, however, and its signing set off a firestorm. The president sent troops to quell riots in several northern cities, and to intimidate secessionist radicals holding conventions in the South. The furor gradually died down, but the Whig party was now hopelessly divided.

In the midst of all this the new president, assured that the risk of cholera had faded, finally assumed his proper residence. The White House could not have been a cheerful place to come to. The mourning period for President Taylor continued, and the furniture in the state rooms was still draped in black, the mirrors masked, and the chandeliers wrapped. When it came time for the unwrapping, the black crepe and silk were stored away, but not for very long. Less than a year after assuming the presidency, Fillmore suffered the loss of his patron, Senator Henry Clay, who died on June 29, 1851. He ordered the White House dressed in mourning.

Fillmore was interested in modernizing the White House. He insisted on a bigger furnace and more heating ducts and a modern stove for the White House kitchen. The cooks were still using kettles and pots in open fireplaces, just as in colonial times. Fillmore ordered a hotel-size iron stove, but the bewildered cook became frustrated with the pulleys and drafts. The president couldn't figure it out either, and had to go to the Patent Office for instructions and then help the cook with the first meal.

Fillmore also installed the first permanent bathtub with running water. The zinc-lined tub got hot water from a newly installed hot water furnace. This was truly a luxury in the Washington of the 1850s. Some people still considered bathing unsanitary, and Fillmore was unusual in that he liked to bathe regularly and used exotic toiletries like "Corinthian Oil of Cream" and a concentrated "extract of eglantine."

Abigail's innovation was the establishment of the White House's first permanent library, a reflection of a marriage rooted in learning. Fillmore, born in a one-room log cabin in Locke, New York, grew up with only three books in the house—a Bible, a hymn book, and an almanac. Apprenticed to a clothmaker, Fillmore was seventeen before he saw a dictionary or a map. But once he got hold of a dictionary, he tried to memorize words from it while he worked. "While attending the carding machines," he recalled, "I used to place the dictionary on the desk—by which I passed every two minutes . . . and . . . I could have a moment . . . to look at a word." When an academy opened in nearby New Hope, he enrolled and became a favorite pupil of his tall, auburn-haired teacher, Abigail Powers, whom he married in 1826.

The Fillmores had four thousand books in their home in Buffalo, New York, so Abigail was astonished to find that no reading material awaited them at the White House. Previous presidents had treated books like clothes—items that were brought and then taken away. Abigail succeeded in getting Congress to appropriate $2000 to fill the upstairs Oval Room with classics of literature, history, travel, and law, along with a few modern novels. Shelves were made and the room fitted out with a piano. Today the library remains, though it is located on the lower floor of the East Wing.

A few years before her husband assumed the presidency, Abigail had injured an ankle in a fall, making it very difficult for her to stand in reception lines for long periods. Her eighteen-year-old daughter, Mary Abigail, often made social calls on her behalf and substituted for her at public appearances. Yet Mary also was plagued by bronchial ailments and spent much of her time in the family quarters reading and playing the piano. She could also play the guitar and harp and performed at White House social events. Shortly after Fillmore left the White House, she died of cholera at age twenty-two.

When the Fillmores did entertain, there was no dancing or card playing. The president was also against liquor, gambling, and smoking, though the long, formal dinners did include wine. (After taking office he ordered an inventory of the wine cellar and found there were 642 bottles of wine in thirty-two varieties plus 198 quarts and 58 pints of champagne.)

Fillmore dressed meticulously; as president, he wore a black suit with a starched white shirt at White House receptions, held in the Blue Room. Deep-voiced, he spoke softly and deliberately. He had presence. At six feet tall, with blue eyes, a ruddy com-

*When Millard Fillmore was introduced to the British court in 1855, Queen Victoria called him the handsomest man she had ever met. He updated the White House kitchen with a hotel-sized iron stove that the cook couldn't figure out how to use. Fillmore went to the Patent Office and obtained instructions.*
(LIBRARY OF CONGRESS)

plexion, and thick wavy hair gone white by the time he took office, Fillmore was considered handsome. When he was introduced to Queen Victoria during a trip to London in 1855, she said he was the handsomest man she had ever met.

As president, Fillmore was known for his integrity and his logical, practical mind. He was civil and polite, though he tended to be stolid. He believed in strict rules, both for himself and those around him. He was aware of every employee and his or her responsibilities. He was a hard worker who kept his smooth-running office open seven days a week. Meetings with callers were brief, formal, and proper, and visitors who did not conduct themselves properly were escorted out by the doorman. Fillmore hired R. G. Campbell as his private secretary but soon replaced him with his son, Millard Powers Fillmore, who handled the mail that with the development of railroads and lower postal rates had climbed to one hundred letters a day.

Fillmore was in the frustrating position of being a stopgap president. His two-and-one-half year tenure precluded the completion of any long-term projects. He tried to bring about an elegant landscaping of the White House and indeed had hired Andrew Jackson Downing, the most famous landscape architect of the day, to draw up plans. Downing proposed a complete overhaul whose extensive lawns and groves of trees would sweep away most existing landscaping and tame the tidal marshes, often polluted, that were a breeding ground for mosquitoes and thought to be the source of many an illness in the mansion. Work began in the spring of 1851, but the following July Downing died on his way to Washington when the Hudson River steamer *Henry Clay* burned on July 28, 1852. Work on his grand plan ceased, never to be revived.

In 1853 Fillmore launched another plan that was completed, albeit when Franklin Pierce became president. He decided to send a fleet of ships to Japan under the command of Commodore Matthew C. Perry to demand a treaty that would pry open that isolated empire to western commerce. Fillmore worked closely with Perry to plan his trip, meeting with him at the White House or the Baltimore or Annapolis shipyards where Perry's flagship, the *Mississippi,* was docked. It was Fillmore's last important order of business.

In February 1853 Democrat Franklin Pierce arrived in Washington. Fillmore graciously honored him with a dinner at the White House and enjoyed a series of dinners and receptions held for him and the president-elect. A day before the inauguration, the Fillmores vacated the White House, taking rooms at the Willard Hotel. The thirteenth president was fifty-two years old and not ready to retire. Apparently he was already thinking about reclaiming his office in 1856, because he planned a swing through the South before returning home to Buffalo.

Inauguration day was raw, with wet snow and a cold wind. As Abigail stood on the Capitol portico, behind the ongoing ceremonies, her husband noticed that her face was drawn and her lips blue. Fillmore escorted Pierce back to the White House and the crowd of well-wishers who awaited him there, and then returned to the Willard Hotel. The next morning, Abigail was suffering from a severe cold. By evening she had a high temperature and rapidly developed pneumonia. She slowly worsened, and on March 30, 1853, died in her sleep.

Fillmore canceled his southern trip and journeyed to Buffalo in a private railway car, sitting next to Abigail's casket. His home seemed desolate. Fillmore, who had always lived modestly, now worried about the propriety of his six-room, two-story frame house, particularly with a neighboring house in disreputable condition. He believed a president—even an ex-president—ought to have a dignified home. This was not a matter of pride or entitlement: he would soon decline an honorary degree from Oxford because he didn't believe he had the attainments for it.

Fillmore had enough assets—about $75,000—to provide a comfortable income, but not enough to receive guests and live in the manner he felt befitted an ex-president. He considered going back to his law practice, taking only highly suitable cases. In 1856 he ran for president as a candidate for the anti-Catholic, anti-immigrant American Party. He thought the "Know-Nothing" party, as it was called, might serve as an alternative to the Southern-dominated Democrats and the antislavery Republicans. During his unsuccessful campaign, he warned his audiences against reopening the slavery debate. "We are treading on the brink of a volcano," he said. He carried one state, Maryland.

Two years later his financial problems were resolved when he married a wealthy widow from Albany, Caroline McIntosh. They bought an ornate Gothic mansion on Buffalo's Niagara Square, and Fillmore settled into a happy retirement of entertaining and civic projects until his death on March 8, 1874. "My own house is the most comfortable place I can find," he wrote friend Dorothea Dix, "and my wife and library . . . the most charming society."

# 14

# Franklin Pierce

## 1853–1857

## *Twice Forgotten*

DRESSED IN black, Franklin Pierce took the oath of office March 4, 1853, in the middle of a blinding snowstorm. His wife, Jane Appleton Pierce, was miles away in Baltimore, having gotten off the train because she was so distressed at the prospect of the presidency. Indeed she'd almost refused to board when the Pierces left their hometown of Concord, New Hampshire. Wild with grief over the recent death of their young son Bennie, Jane had recently uncovered her husband's duplicity. He'd told her he was nominated against his wishes, when indeed he'd allowed friends to submit his name to the convention.

Jane hated Washington and public life, having viewed it firsthand as her husband was elected to Congress and then the Senate as a representative from New Hampshire. In 1842 she convinced him to resign his Senate seat and return to Concord to practice law. But the Mexican War gave Pierce fame as a brigadier general, and the limelight beckoned. His chances for the Democratic nomination were remote, but the convention deadlocked, and as a pro-South northerner, Pierce became the compromise candidate.

When Jane heard the news, she and her husband were out for a carriage ride. A messenger came galloping up with the convention results. Jane promptly fainted. She was not the only unhappy member of the family. Before the election, the Pierces' eleven-year-old son, Bennie, wrote his mother, "I hope he won't be elected for I should not like to live in Washington and I know that you would not either."

His words would soon haunt the Pierces. They doted on Bennie, having lost two other children, one in infancy and one at the age of four to typhus. On January 6, 1853, two months after having won the presidency by a landslide, the family was on a train near Andover, Massachusetts, when a coupling broke and their car derailed, rolling down an embankment. Pierce climbed from the wreckage and found Bennie lying in the snow, his head crushed. The boy was the only fatality. Both parents were devoutly religious and in their grief sought God's purpose in the calamity, submitting themselves to a rigorous Calvinistic self-questioning. Jane concluded that Bennie was sacrificed in the furtherance of her husband's presidency; Pierce could now devote himself to that higher purpose without distraction.

And so Pierce took the oath of office by himself, as a snowstorm raged around him. He gave his address entirely from memory, his thoughts frequently morbid. "No heart but my own," he said, "can know the personal regret and bitter sorrow which I have been borne to a position so suitable for others." His deep mourning precluded inaugural balls. Now snow forced the cancellation of the customary parades.

Pierce returned to the White House where receptions were held. Afterward the house was in disarray, the carpets muddied, empty refreshment dishes abandoned everywhere. Jane's role would have been to oversee the transition from one administration to the next and give the servants instructions. Pierce could not find anyone to instruct—the servants were off he knew not where. Sidney Webster, the young lawyer who was to be Pierce's secretary and constant companion, located a single candle and led the way upstairs. Pierce's possessions, still in boxes, and those of Fillmore, still not shipped out, were all about. In the bedrooms, the furniture had been pushed aside and the beds stripped and taken apart. Pierce, kept awake the night before by a group of drunken revelers and a band that had serenaded him outside his hotel window, was exhausted. He slept on a mattress on the floor, wrapped in his coat to keep warm.

That first night was a harbinger of things to come. Stricken with grief and guilt following the death of his son and out of touch with antislavery sentiments, Pierce floundered. Vacillating and ineffective, he left a nation increasingly divided into North and South rudderless and drifting closer to civil war. By 1856 people wanted to forget him, and the Democratic slogan was "anybody but Pierce."

Jane would not come to the White House for several weeks. Upon arrival she immediately withdrew into a darkened upstairs room, staying there the better part of the first year, spending entire days sitting at her table as if in a trance. She ordered mourning bunting placed over the furniture of the state rooms. She wrote letters to her dead son asking his forgiveness, convinced she should have done more for him. She even called in well-known Washington mediums Margaret and Kate Fox in an attempt to communicate with Bennie. Many prominent people were taken in by the Foxes' strange rappings, which were later discovered to be caused by their toe joints. One of Jane's only excursions that first year was with Pierce's friend Nathaniel Hawthorne, the novelist, who while visiting the White House persuaded Jane to take a trip to Mount Vernon and George Washington's tomb.

Pierce, for his part, numbed his depression with drink. His alcoholism had begun in college and intensified when he moved to Washington, where hard-drinking congressmen whose wives were back home lived like bachelors in Washington boardinghouses. Pierce, whose own wife often escaped the city during those years by visiting relatives, liked this convivial environment, but one drink affected him far more than it did others. He brought his habit under control when he left Washington for small-town Concord, New Hampshire, which went dry in 1844. He swore off liquor and became chairman of his state temperance society. But now, at the White House, he sought solace in drink.

Always religious, Pierce continued to attend church regularly, usually at the 4½ Street church of the Reverend Byron Sunderland, and sometimes at the Presbyterian church on Ninth Street. Jane came with him when she felt able to, and urged her servants to attend services. Each morning the president read from *Thornton's Family Prayers* to Jane, any guests, and servants, and he said grace at meals. The Pierces' observance of the Sabbath was strict. No business was transacted at the White House on Sunday, not even the opening of mail.

Friends noticed the change in the once spontaneous and amiable Pierce. Between Bennie's death and Jane's collapse, he had lost all interest in the presidency. Less than six months into his term, he was exhausted and distracted. "I find myself so weary at the close of each day," he wrote sister-in-law Mary Aiken on August 26, 1856, "that it is difficult to overcome a disinclination for anything like labor in the evening." His health suffered too. Doctors blamed his chronic bronchitis on the dampness of the White House and his consumption of alcohol. The Potomac marshes south of the White House became a breeding ground for mosquitoes in warm weather, and in his first spring in office Pierce also endured a long siege of malarial fever. Mrs. Henry Clay would later write a friend, "A year before his inauguration I had seen him bound up the stairs with the elasticity and lightness of a schoolboy. He went out after four years a staid and grave man, on whom the stamp of care and illness was ineradicably impressed."

*Jane Pierce reluctantly followed her husband to Washington. She spent her first year upstairs in her room, writing long letters to her son, Bennie, who had recently been killed in a railway accident. The White House was not a happy place during the Pierce administration.* (LIBRARY OF CONGRESS)

Meanwhile, the capital brimmed with Pierce's supporters—he'd won a landslide victory, forfeiting only four states to General Winfield Scott. At the onset, he opened receptions from noon to 2 P.M. on Fridays. They overflowed, subjecting the public rooms to unusually heavy wear and tear. The crowds continued, with later New Year's and Fourth of July receptions and special events becoming so packed that the commissioner of public buildings installed a temporary wooden platform and steps outside one of the south windows of the East Room as an exit. And on a daily basis, tourists and business callers flooded the mansion. Restrictions to access, which had never been formal, diminished further, despite growing concerns about security. Anyone was admitted during the mansion's regular hours—excepting Negroes, who were barred from every "place of entertainment" in Washington at the time. Office seekers ensconced themselves on the stair to the left of the entrance hall, rather seedy-looking groups often made themselves at home in the East Room, and the mansion became correspondingly worn and dirty.

In response to public complaints about the condition of the house, the usually tight-fisted Congress granted $25,000 for upgrading and redecorating. Pierce insisted that a White House official, not the Interior Department via the commissioner of public buildings, be in charge of the funds. The responsibility initially fell to Pierce's overwhelmed secretary, Sidney Webster, but ultimately was assigned to an officer from the Army Corps of Engineers, Captain Thomas Jefferson Lee. The relationship between the White House and the corps proved satisfactory, and became institutionalized after the Civil War.

Work was well under way by summer. The *National Intelligencer* reported on June 25, 1853, "All the lower suite of rooms of the Presidential Mansion, with some in the second story, are in occupancy of the bricklayer, the plasterer, the carpenter, and the like, who are making considerable changes and effecting improvements and repairs."

The state rooms on the main floor were redecorated and the house outfitted with the best domestic technology the 1850s had to offer. Pierce installed a new bath in the dressing room off his bedroom; it was the mansion's first permanent bath above the basement level. A bathtub with hot and cold running water, one of the few in Washington, replaced portable tin tubs. The long-standing bathing procedure had been to line the tub with linen towels to prevent burns from the hot tin, then fill it with hot water from kettles warmed in the hearth or hauled from the coal-fired boilers in the bathing room on the first floor of the east wing.

The heating system was also upgraded—for the third time since Van Buren's administration—and a screen of glass and bronze added to the heavily used front entranceway helped repel the breezes from the north.

To upgrade the swampy south grounds, Congress appropriated another $12,000. The extensive plans commissioned by Fillmore had been lost when their designer, Andrew Jackson Downing, died, so Pierce approved gardener John Watt's plans to renovate the existing gardens. Watt repaired the trellises, pruned, and demolished the old greenhouse to make way for a modern one, completed in 1853. This incorporated a conservatory where the president could sun amid tubs of fruit trees and ferns, a private retreat.

The new conservatory and upgraded greenhouses helped provide the White House with an abundance of fresh flowers. Earlier administrations had relied on wax flowers in deference to the popular notion that fresh blooms gave off unhealthy vapors. But now the letters of politicians and their wives frequently commented on the beauty of the flower-laden White House dinner table. The wife of Alabama senator Clement C. Clay Jr. would recall the "remarkable bouquets," taken home as mementos, beside each plate at state dinners. "They were stiff and formal things, as big and round as a breakfast plate, and invariably composed of a half-dozen wired japonicas ornamented with a pretentious cape of marvellously wrought lace-paper."

The decorating and most other projects were complete by the fall of 1853, and a curious public got its first look on New Year's Day, 1854, at the traditional White House reception. Washington's *Daily Union* estimated that five thousand people "from every walk of life" toured the mansion between 11 A.M. and 2 P.M. The public also got its first real look at Mrs. Pierce, who finally emerged to stand by her husband at the reception.

The first lady's deep mourning ended, and she began attending state dinners and other functions. But she remained spiritless and isolated. She wore mourning garb, including a mourning veil during the day, through her entire White House stay. "Everything in that Mansion seems cold and cheerless," Charles Mason of the Patent Office wrote in 1854. "I have seen hundreds of log cabins which seemed to contain more happiness." Jane made few friends in Washington, relying on visits from New England relatives and friends, including nieces, nephews, and cousins from Boston and Andover, for entertainment. Jefferson Davis, Pierce's secretary of war and close friend, and his wife, Varina, brought some light to the house. Varina, who had been such a source of companionship to Margaret Taylor, attended almost every dinner party.

Pierce relieved Jane of all domestic duties by bringing in a New Hampshire hotel-keeper, William H. Snow, and his wife to handle the servants, hire caterers, and keep the accounts. They moved into the White House immediately. To juggle her social responsibilities he called in Mrs. Abby Means, a wealthy widow who had known Jane since childhood and could provide the first lady companionship as well. Even with this help, there were few large gatherings at the White House in Pierce's first year, though, starting four days after his inauguration, he held frequent smaller dinners. This was no doubt a financial help. Where other presidents left the White House in debt from lavish and constant entertaining, Pierce, always thrifty, saved almost half his $25,000 salary.

At evening receptions Pierce would lead a promenade around and around the East Room for about half an hour, smiling and nodding to guests, the men in formal black suits and the women their finest evening dresses. There was no dancing, drinking, or card playing in the Pierce White House. In warm weather the grounds were open to the public one night a week, with the Marine Band playing marches and popular songs from the south portico. The night had been Saturday since the custom was instituted by Tyler, but Jane changed the night to Wednesday because the noise intruded on her preparations for the Sabbath. Pierce often attended, mingling freely with the crowd. At one evening concert, a country man approached Pierce and said, "Mr. President, can't I go through your fine house? I've heard so much about it that I'd give a great deal to see it." Pierce answered, "Why my dear sir, that is not my house. It's the people's house! You shall certainly go through it if you wish." He then instructed one of the doormen to give the citizen a personal tour.

The president enjoyed such encounters. He was by nature an affable, gregarious man, and remained friendly despite the burden of Bennie's death. A well-recognized figure on Pennsylvania Avenue, he got out of the White House a good deal, leaving Jane upstairs with Mrs. Means to comfort her. He often attended concerts and called on friends, especially Varina and Jefferson Davis, at whose home he was welcome to drop in any time. Driving back to the White House one night, he accidentally ran down and injured an aged woman. He was arrested, but police dropped the charges when they realized who he was.

While he liked people, Pierce was wary. He had witnessed the assassination attempt against Andrew Jackson in 1835. Since that time, the admiring crowds that accosted presidents in the streets had grown ever larger, occasionally becoming disorderly in their enthusiasm. As the slavery issue became more volatile, so did security concerns. So Pierce, by choice, became the first president to have a full-time, government-funded bodyguard: Thomas O'Neil, who had been Pierce's orderly in the Mexican War, and who tended him in the midst of a battle when he was wounded. When Pierce was at the mansion, O'Neil kept watch in the entrance hall. The president never left the White House alone. Horseback riding was Pierce's main form of exercise, and he was often seen riding about the city on his prized gelding, Union, with O'Neil alongside.

In at least once instance, though, the president's guard wasn't there when Pierce needed him. Waiting for his carriage outside the Capitol one day in 1854, Pierce was accosted by a young man who shook hands with him and then offered him a drink. Pierce declined and was entering his carriage when the youth hit him with a hard-boiled egg. The attacker was arrested and taken into police custody, where he attempted suicide with a penknife. Pierce withdrew his complaint.

More troublesome than egg throwers were office seekers. Pierce was not averse to the spoils system: in his first several months in office, he made over seven hundred new appointments. But an estimated thirty thousand office seekers visited the White House in Pierce's first year alone. The red-carpeted stairway leading to his upstairs office was typically lined with hopefuls for whom there was no room in the hall above, where there was a waiting area with chairs around the perimeter, an oil cloth protecting the floor, and the usual spittoons.

Access to the president's office was relatively easy, but not without procedure, even with such large crowds. Callers reported to the doorkeeper, signed a register, and returned to the hall to wait with the multitudes. The doorkeeper gave the messenger a slip of paper with the caller's name, and the messenger took an unseen service stair to the second floor, traveled the length of the hall through the family quarters, finally arriving at the offices, where he presented secretary Webster with the name. Webster noted his approval or disapproval and the slip was returned to the doorman, who escorted accepted callers upstairs.

The offices comprised three rooms in the southeast portion of the second floor: the anteroom at the head of the stairs, the president's private office, which also served as a cabinet room, and a smaller office for his secretary and the files. All three were connected by doors, and also opened onto the corridor; the anteroom could overflow into the corridor when the waiting crowd was large, as it often was. The president's office had a long mahogany table, and Pierce worked at Andrew Jackson's stand-up desk, with its pigeonholes for papers. There was also a sofa with chairs on each end, plus a wash-stand. The president called Webster from the next room with a bell pull. When Webster's workload became too much, Benjamin B. French, a patent lawyer and perpetual office seeker, was finally employed as his assistant. The president's bodyguard was also recruited for office tasks. With the secretaries and the doorkeeper fully occupied, Pierce tended to use O'Neil as a messenger.

Despite his emotional distraction, Pierce was a hard worker. A detail person, he visited government departments on a regular basis to learn about day-to-day operations. He tried to tighten the management of government and increase accountability, introducing forms and procedures, banning public work from private houses and private business from public offices, and raising salaries in hopes of reducing employees' interest in padding their incomes dishonestly. He had larger ambitions as well. He investigated acquiring Hawaii, Alaska, Lower California, and Cuba. When he threatened to take Cuba by force if Spain would not sell the island, his administration was almost universally condemned, and his expansionist program quickly petered out.

The real blow to his administration came in the spring of 1854. The relative calm that had settled over the country in the wake of the Compromise of 1850 was shattered when Pierce and Senator Stephen A. Douglas pushed the Kansas-Nebraska Act through Congress. The act repealed the Missouri Compromise, lifting certain restrictions on slavery in the territories. The inhabitants of Kansas and Nebraska would vote to determine the fate of slavery within their boundaries. During the debates, which would define the Democratic and Republican parties as the principal forces in American politics from then on, the White House entry hall was more crowded with callers for the president than anyone could remember. After the vote, the reaction of northerners was ferocious. The administration was now bound by conflict.

A rare moment of glory occurred when Commodore Matthew C. Perry returned from Japan on April 23, 1855. Perry had won a trade treaty, and brought the president all manner of gifts from the Japanese, including swords, porcelain vases, silks, writing tables, figurines, and two birds. But what most delighted Pierce were several "very singular animals," as Varina Davis put it, that had arrived ahead of Perry. The day they arrived, Pierce appeared at the Jefferson Davis household exclaiming, "General, I have a dog for you!" The tiny dog was one of seven "sleeve dogs" among the gifts from the Japanese. Varina described it as "a little creature with a head like a bird with a blunt beak, eyes large and popped, and a body like a new-born puppy of the smallest kind . . . a coffee saucer made an ample scampering ground for him." The objects Perry brought back were put on public display at the White House. Huge numbers of people filed into the Blue Room to see the oriental oddities lined up on tables and the floor behind a rope barrier that kept visitors from handling them. The collection was moved to the larger East Room, but the crowds still proved unmanageable, and finally the entire exhibit was moved to the Patent Office.

In June 1856 Pierce, just fifty-two, badly wanted to be renominated for a second term. But that year in Kansas, two hundred people died in a battle between "pro-slave" and "free-soil" settlers. The country was boiling over. The Democrats, in a rare repudiation, abandoned their sitting president in favor of Pennsylvanian James Buchanan.

Pierce graciously moved out of the White House to the Willard Hotel a day before James Buchanan's March 4, 1857, inaugural. Arrangements were made for Pierce to ride with the president-elect to the Capitol, but the inaugural procession had made its way down Pennsylvania Avenue to the National Hotel, where Buchanan was staying, when someone on the arrangements committee realized they had neglected to stop at the Willard for Pierce. Bands, floats, and militia companies all waited for twenty minutes while a carriage was sent to the Willard to retrieve a president neglected on his last day, just as he had been on his first.

There was more injury to come. When the ex-president and his wife arrived in Concord, where a new house awaited them, their reception was distinctly cold. In the coming Civil War years, Pierce further cultivated the bitterness of his neighbors by persisting in his southern sentiments, criticizing the war and opposing Abraham Lincoln's Emancipation Proclamation. When Lincoln was assassinated, he had to defend his house against an angry mob.

Nathaniel Hawthorne was a frequent visitor to the Concord house, and wrote of Pierce in the years immediately following his presidency that "something . . . seemed to have passed away out of [him] without leaving a trace." Indeed, when asked what a president should do after leaving office, Pierce replied, "There's nothing left . . . but to get drunk." And so he did, the more so after Jane died of tuberculosis on December 2, 1863, followed by Hawthorne a few months later. Pierce died October 8, 1869. It would be another half century before New Hampshire honored her only native son president with a statue.

# 15

# James Buchanan

## 1857–1861

## *The Eve of Rebellion*

WHEN JAMES BUCHANAN turned over the presidency to Abraham Lincoln in 1861, he said to his successor, "If you are as happy, my dear sir, on entering this house as I am in leaving it and returning home, you are the happiest man in the country." Buchanan, sixty-nine, was tired. He had spent his entire political life maneuvering himself into the White House—serving in Congress, the Senate, as Jackson's minister to Russia, Polk's secretary of state, and Pierce's minister to England. In a less troubled era, his presidency might have been the happy ending to a long and distinguished career. But the nation was on the brink of civil war. Unwilling to take a stand, the president left office scorned by both sides. At the end of his life, their accusations still rang in his ears.

Domestically, however, the White House was an oasis of calm, unruffled by the growing sectional controversy. Buchanan entertained formally and brilliantly, providing safe haven for friends and enemies, all the while politely fending off the Washington widows determined to end his reign as the only bachelor president.

Though unmarried, Buchanan didn't lack for family. He had some twenty-two nieces and nephews and thirteen grandnieces and grandnephews. Of these, seven were orphans in his full care, and several were half-orphans he helped support. One orphaned nephew, James Buchanan "Buck" Henry, came to live at White House and serve as his uncle's private secretary. For a hostess Buchanan turned to his orphaned niece, Harriet Lane. The two were very close. She called him "Nunc" and inherited the bulk of his $300,000 estate.

At twenty-seven, Harriet was worldly and cultured. She'd been to London with Buchanan when he was Pierce's minister to England. There, she had many a beau and even caught the eye of Queen Victoria, who hoped she would marry and remain in England. Attractive and knowledgeable about formal entertaining, Harriet was determined to make the White House a social showplace, and luckily Buchanan did his part. His tastes were epicurean, and he insisted on the finest food, wine, and flowers. He didn't skimp. He asked a White House supplier not to deliver champagne in pints, explaining, "[They] are very inconvenient in this house as the article is not used in such small quantities." The White House, so quiet during the Pierces' grief-stricken years, was once again the focus of society. Its dinners, balls, and receptions were quickly hailed as the most socially brilliant since Tyler's.

Harriet faced a major obstacle in her desire to elevate the social tone of the White House. When he came to Washington, Buchanan also brought Miss Esther "Hetty" Parker, his efficient longtime housekeeper and general superintendent at Wheatland, his Lancaster, Pennsylvania, home. Initially, the president gave the two women a kind of joint command over the household operations. A domestic crisis ensued. Harriet threatened to pack up and leave if she were not the hostess in charge; Hetty continued to give orders as she had always done. Finally the president was forced to send Hetty back to Wheatland, even though she had long functioned as a member of the family. He invited her to visit the White House anytime, and she often did.

With Hetty out of the picture, Harriet was treated officially as first lady. Traditionally the president's secretary planned entertainments, but Harriet had an aptitude for it and took the job from Buck, her cousin. She sent out invitations with the help of friends, whom she invited to the White House for lunch or tea and several hours of conversation and writing. White House invitations were always delivered by a servant or office messenger, never by mail, and turned down so seldom that a response was necessary only if declining.

Ladies were instructed to wear formal evening attire. Men were required to wear black or imperial blue suits—no frock coats—with gloves in white or straw, and cravats in white only. Either boots or shoes were permitted, and in the summer, white trousers could be worn, but only with a black or dark blue coat. Harriet, who loved clothes, began appearing in low-cut gowns, and décolletage became all the rage. Formal receptions and balls called for trains.

Dinner parties had a set procedure, passed down largely intact from previous administrations. Guests were received in the Blue Room while the Marine Band played. When it struck up "Hail to the Chief," the president entered and led the guests down the transverse hall to the dining room for a French-style repast. The president's place was at the side rather than the head of the table, and Harriet sat directly across from him, with the rest of the guests taking their places by rank according to a seating chart held by the secretary. The gilded and mirrored plateau purchased by James Monroe still graced the dining table, its vases filled with fresh flowers.

After dinner, the women adjourned to a nearby parlor and toilet room for perhaps half an hour, leaving the men behind closed doors in the dining room, where chamber pots were available. The men and women reassembled briefly in the Red Room for conversation and coffee, cigars, and whiskey. The night ended when the president took his leave, and he did so reasonably early—at about ten or ten-thirty—in order to spend a few more hours behind his desk.

The two most heralded social events of the Buchanan White House occurred near the end of his term. In May 1860 Buchanan received the first Japanese ambassadors to this country, a delegation that included two royal princes and twelve nobles, objects of intense curiosity in the city. The Japanese insisted on calling Buchanan "Emperor" and "Your Majesty," and were shocked when he mixed with the crowd at a Marine Band concert on the south lawn.

The second event was even more highly anticipated. Many titled Europeans whom Buchanan had met during his diplomatic service visited the White House. The president was on good terms with Queen Victoria, and when he heard that her son was planning a trip to Canada, he wrote her to invite the prince to the White House. The arrival of Albert, Prince of Wales, in September 1860 caused a great stir of excitement, as he was the first British royal to visit America since the Revolution. Harriet was eager to throw a huge ball, but Nunc said, "No dancing in the White House." Harriet, though she loved the waltz and quadrille, knew him well enough to know she should drop the idea. Buchanan's sense of propriety also led him, in anticipation of Albert's arrival, to

*Buchanan's receptions were elaborate and he did not skimp on expenses although at this time presidents still had to pay all costs from their salary. He had known Queen Victoria while on diplomatic service in Europe and invited her son Albert, Prince of Wales, to stay at the White House. It was the social highlight of his term.* (LIBRARY OF CONGRESS)

order Harriet to remove her picture from the nineteen-year-old prince's bedroom and hang it in the library.

The future King Edward VII arrived with a large entourage, most of whom were put up by the British. But the royal party would stay in the White House, whose modest living accommodations were nearly filled even by Buchanan's small family. The president gave up his own bedroom to the royal party, only to find that not a single bed in the mansion was left free. He slept on a cot in the anteroom to his office. While there was no ball, a grand state dinner was held in Albert's honor. Then, Secretary of the Treasury Howell Cobb convinced Buchanan to allow a cruise to Mount Vernon on the Coast Guard cutter *Harriet Lane*. The group visited George Washington's tomb and returned to the ship to find that Cobb and his wife, renowned as entertainers, had ordered a banquet, flowers, and champagne. Soon enough the Marine Band was playing popular tunes, and people were waltzing. Afterward, Buchanan discovered that the Treasury had been billed for the refreshments. Secretary Cobb shortly saw fit to pick up the tab himself.

Harriet, delighted with her new status as first lady, was eager to make purchases for the White House, and Buchanan had to curtail a shopping trip to New York by carefully informing his niece of the modest balance of funds. Initially Congress appropriated $11,000 for upkeep. In June 1858 it voted an additional $12,000. Harriet was thrilled and began spending immediately, re-covering furnishings with a fashionable mix of patterns and textures, and purchasing new curtains and carpets.

By this time the forty-year-old Empire furnishings of the Monroe era were out of style. Buchanan sold off most of Paris cabinetmaker Pierre-Antoine Bellangé's gilded creations, some fifty pieces, many of which were later purchased and returned to the White House. In 1860 Harriet replaced these with a suite of monumental pieces in the Louis XV revival style, carved and gilded, from Gottlieb Vollmer, a German manufacturer in Philadelphia. The suite was upholstered in blue brocatelle, and was associated with the Blue Room for many years. A familiar piece from this set is still in the White House: the "circular divan," or "Ottoman sofa," which was placed in the center of the room so people could sit all around it.

On the grounds, the expansion of the nearby Treasury building necessitated relocating the stables and demolishing the old garden and greenhouse. The garden was not replanted, but the greenhouse was replaced by a conservatory, built on the roof of the West Wing, a private location accessible from the transverse hall on the main floor. Construction began in April 1857, and Buchanan was delighted with the results, despite cost overruns.

Buchanan was meticulous about money, keeping financial records to the penny. Once, on discovering he had paid three cents too little on a merchant's food bill, he forwarded the three cents. He had a fussy streak and could be quite inquisitive about personal matters. He once quizzed his secretary of the treasury, Howell Cobb, in some detail about his wife's finances. He inquired into the departmental details of his cabinet members to such an extent that they became secretive about discussing the operations of their departments. He also had a habit of opening Harriet's mail and passing it on with "opened by mistake" written across it. Harriet and Nunc had a spat about it, to no avail. Harriet finally got around the president by sending and receiving mail in a butter tub. The White House kitchen regularly received fresh butter in a locked kettle. Harriet got the key from the steward and made a duplicate, and she and her friend, Mrs. Sophia Pliff, kept up a private correspondence "via the kettle."

To his nephew-secretary, Buck Henry, Buchanan was a taskmaster. "As private secretary," Henry later recalled, "I had to be in my office . . . adjoining that of the President, whenever he was there, which was from eight in the morning until Luncheon at one o'clock, and from that time until five, when, with rare exceptions, he took an hour's walk." Halfway into his uncle's term, he quit and went to New York when Buchanan disputed his right to grow a mustache. Another cousin, James Buchanan II, replaced him.

Buchanan liked things just so. He arose promptly at 6:30 A.M. and dressed carefully, generally in a black suit with a high cloth collar and flowing white neckerchief. By 8 A.M. he had finished breakfast and was at his desk. He received visitors in the morning, and usually met with his cabinet after lunch. Cabinet meetings were called daily early in the administration, then at least three times a week, and again daily during Buchanan's last care-fraught months. His exercise consisted of a walk in the afternoons. He allotted exactly one hour to it, walking along Pennsylvania Avenue and in the residential section across from the White House, around Lafayette Park, often greeting friends along the way. At 7 P.M. he dined. In the evenings, even after a dinner party, Buchanan typically fired up his gas lamp and worked past midnight. He finally retired after reading his Bible.

A stickler for procedure, Buchanan and Buck Henry added to the official forms fashioned by Pierce for use throughout the government. Henry registered every document

*The unmarried Buchanan relied on his niece Harriet Lane as his hostess. Here she walks in a conservatory with a friend. Buchanan began a half-century of adding conservatories to the tops of the White House wings and along the grounds adjacent to the house.* (LIBRARY OF CONGRESS)

that came through the office. Many were forwarded to departments, but hundreds might require executive action on a given day, and temporary clerks were employed to handle the minor documents. Henry spent all morning sorting the president's mail, so that by afternoon, when Buchanan returned from lunch, he could present his boss with a neat file of papers, organized by subject, that required his attention.

The office routine continued even when Buchanan left the White House on July 5, 1857, for nearby Soldiers' Home, a retirement place for disabled soldiers founded in 1851. It was set on a large tract of land near Rock Creek Cemetery, just outside the District of Columbia in Maryland. Buchanan took advantage of the original stone farmhouse, vacant since it was too drafty for year-round living but perfect for a summer residence. He had it repaired and furnished with whatever the White House could spare. As commander in chief, he was not required to pay rent. Buchanan returned the subsequent summer of his presidency, and his successors made a tradition of it through the mid-1880s. He drove his coach into the city every day except Sunday to work at the White House, whose rooms were shrouded in their summer slipcovers.

Perhaps because of these summer accommodations, Buchanan was able to avoid the malarial fever Pierce had suffered. He was healthy throughout his term, except at the time of his inauguration, when he and others came down with "National Hotel disease." The illness, probably picked up from the water supply at the hotel where he awaited his inauguration, felled some thirty or so guests. It produced violent diarrhea, and the symptoms persisted for weeks. Occasionally it was fatal. Buchanan felt queasy the day of his inauguration and half an hour before the ceremony took brandy and a medication given to him by his doctor. He was ill for six weeks, sometimes bedridden.

Buchanan began the tradition of having a personal physician by inviting a doctor friend to live at the White House. He wrote a friend on December 20, 1860, "I have never enjoyed better health or a more tranquil spirit than during the past year. All our troubles have not cost me an hour's sleep or a single meal. . . . I weigh well and prayerfully what course I ought to adopt, and adhere to it steadily, leaving the rest to Providence." That very night, however, news that South Carolina had seceded reached Buchanan at a wedding reception. Cabinet members began to resign. By the new year federal property in the South was being taken over, and before January was out six more southern states seceded. Buchanan met with delegates from the border states, tears coming down his face, to no avail. He defended the southerners' reasons for seceding while denying that they had a right to secede. Yet, he said, the president had no authority to forcibly prevent it. In short, he didn't know what to do, and more or less did nothing. He wished only to maintain the status quo until his successor could take office. As his term neared the end, he wrote a friend, "I am now in my sixty-ninth year and am heartily tired of my position as president."

The new cabinet, heavy with Union men, met daily, sequestered for hours in Buchanan's office. A guest who attended a White House reception at this time remarked, "Probably a similar scene never occurred in the White House before. With very few exceptions, the party that elected Mr. Buchanan to the office he now holds was absent. . . . One of the officers of the White House remarked at the close of the levee that he never saw so many republicans there before."

Lincoln took office on March 4, 1861, and Buchanan gladly retreated to Wheatland. Lancaster welcomed him home as a hero with a thirty-four-gun salute, a brass band, a parade, and speeches. But he would have no peace in his retirement. He had pleased neither South nor North, and once the war began, both attacked him, blaming him both for not preventing the war and for not starting it sooner. He received a threat that his house would be burned down, and he was afraid to drive in to Lancaster in his carriage. Volunteers from the Masonic Lodge guarded Wheatland for months, until the high feelings settled. Congress took away his franking privileges, and the Senate tried to pass a resolution condemning him. Congressman Thaddeus Stevens, who would one day lead the impeachment charge against Andrew Johnson, called Buchanan "a bloated mass of political putridity."

At first the verbal attacks distressed him, but Buchanan recovered his composure and began supporting Lincoln publicly despite his disapproval of emancipation. He published a long defense of his actions in office, *Mr. Buchanan's Administration on the Eve of the Rebellion*, but it did little to stem the tide of criticism, or later, to advance his place in history. He died at Wheatland on June 1, 1868, at age seventy-seven, convinced that history would vindicate him.

# 16

# Abraham Lincoln

## 1861–April 14, 1865

# A "Whited Sepulcure"

WHEN ABRAHAM LINCOLN was elected in November 1860, senators and representatives from the South began resigning and leaving town. Washington was given over to an atmosphere of danger and unrest. Lincoln, traveling from Illinois to the capital, got as far as Baltimore before a plot to kill him was uncovered. Abandoning all scheduled fanfare, the president-elect boarded a special railroad car, where he climbed into an upper berth much too small for him, drew the curtain, and in the early morning hours of February 23, 1861, slipped into Washington unannounced.

On inauguration day, March 4, Lincoln made his way down Pennsylvania Avenue to the Capitol with more than the usual escort. Soldiers lined the streets, and riflemen were stationed on the roofs and at windows. John Wilkes Booth was among the spectators. James Buchanan, finally relieved of the burden of his office, escorted President Lincoln back to the White House, where they said a friendly good-bye and Lincoln began greeting visitors in the Blue Room. Later the president and first lady, Mary Todd Lincoln, would sit down to a dinner thoughtfully ordered by Harriet Lane, Buchanan's niece and White House hostess, before facing that night's inaugural balls.

The Lincoln family was unknown to Washington society but for rumors and gossip. They were thought to be crude frontier people, and opposition papers referred to Lincoln as an ape or baboon because of his long arms. Even Harriet Lane did not know what to expect, having heard that Mary was "awfully western, loud & unrefined." Now Washington would get a good look at the first couple.

For his campaign biography in 1859, Abraham Lincoln wrote this cursory description of himself: "I am, in height, six foot four inches, nearly; lean in flesh, weighing, on an average, one hundred and eighty pounds; dark complexion, with coarse black hair, and gray eyes—no other marks or brands recollected." His cousin, Dennis Hanks, offers a more vivid portrait: "Well, now, he looked like any other baby, at fust—like red cherry pulp squeezed dry. An' he didn't improve none as he growed older. Abe never was much for looks." Some considered Lincoln, with his gangly limbs and sunken eyes, downright ugly.

Mary Todd Lincoln thought otherwise. Intelligent and sophisticated, she came from a distinguished Kentucky family. Far from the unrefined westerner she was rumored to be, Mary had attended excellent schools and studied music and the arts, and spoke French fluently. She was as ambitious as her husband, telling a friend after her marriage in 1842, "He is to be President of the United States someday; if I had not thought so I never would have married him for you can see he is not pretty. But look at him. Doesn't he look as if he would make a magnificent President?"

The principal inaugural ball commenced at nine, with two to three thousand people attending. The Lincolns arrived around eleven. Mary entered the hall on the arm of Senator Stephen A. Douglas, Lincoln's political opponent and her former beau. The *New York World* described the new first lady as "superbly dressed in a blue silk trimmed with Alencon lace and a blue ostrich feather in her hair which was exceedingly becoming." Lincoln wore brand new white kid gloves. He left around midnight, while his wife stayed to dance until the early morning hours.

The Lincolns held their first White House reception on April 8, 1861. "Such a crush was, I imagine, never seen in the White House before on a similar or any other occasion," wrote Charles Francis Adams. W. H. L. Wallace wrote to his wife, "Mr. Lincoln wore kid gloves and worked away at shaking hands with the multitude, and with much the same air and movement as if he was mauling rails." The Marine Band signaled the end of the party by playing "Yankee Doodle." It was the last White House gathering in which North and South would mingle for some time to come. The hostilities broke out just a few days later, on April 12, 1861. When South Carolina seceded, federal troops had taken refuge at Fort Sumter, in the bay at Charleston. When they refused to surrender the fort, Confederate authorities finally opened fire. Lincoln responded by calling for seventy-five thousand volunteers.

The war was on, but entertaining at the White House continued. Lincoln assigned responsibility for dinners, the stuff of politics, and weekly receptions to his capable secretary, John Nicolay, bypassing his wife. Mary had the necessary background to handle White House social affairs, but not the judgment and mental stability. Proud and stubborn, she was given to fits of explosive, often irrational anger toward her husband, servants, or tradesmen. Anyone who thwarted her, or simply failed to say "good morning," risked open conflict and a lashing from her sharp tongue. Nicolay's job forced him to say no to Mary more often than anyone, and she hated him. White House servants who could not abide her outbursts quit. The president paid one girl an extra dollar a week to tolerate his wife without complaint. Those who initially praised the first lady eventually turned on her with remarks such as this one from a reception guest: "The weak-minded Mrs. Lincoln had her bosom on exhibition."

Her instability could come out in her jealousy of other women. Lincoln teased her at times. Once, just before a White House reception, he asked her, "Well, Mother, who will I talk with tonight—shall it be Mrs. D?" and proceeded to bait her with other choices. Mary answered, "I don't know as it is necessary that you should talk to anybody in particular. You know well enough, Mr. Lincoln, that I do not approve of your flirtations with silly women, just as if you were a beardless boy, fresh from school." But the problem escalated beyond private exchanges. Once, when the president was reviewing the troops at City Point, in Virginia, Mary saw him riding with the young, attractive wife of the base commander, General Edward Ord. Mary went into a screaming rage before the startled officers and their wives. Mrs. Ord retreated in dismay. When Julia Grant, General Ulysses S. Grant's wife, tried to calm the first lady, Mary turned on her: "I suppose you think you'll get to the White House yourself, don't you?"

Lincoln greeted his wife's tirades with almost unfailing calm and patience. One day back in Springfield, some workmen came to Lincoln to tell him Mary had ordered the single shade tree in their yard cut down. Lincoln responded, "For God's sake cut it down, clean to the roots!" When she interrupted a cabinet meeting with an angry torrent, he rose, picked her up, and carried her out of the office. When he returned, he locked the door and resumed the conversation as before. Yet Lincoln didn't always help matters. His manners were often crude, he was perpetually late for dinner, and he embarrassed Mary in front of her friends. During the campaign he'd insisted on milking the cow and, despite a maid, answering the door in his shirtsleeves to talk with reporters and admirers.

Mary's instability also revealed itself in her spending habits. She could be stingy, haggling over small change with tradesmen, but she could also be reckless. She reveled in the opportunity to redecorate the White House with government funds. From August to September of 1861, the mansion was crawling with workmen. The first lady ordered rooms repaired and repainted and went on extended shopping trips to Philadelphia and New York—eleven trips to New York alone. She bought furniture, carpets, drapes, china, glassware, gold and silver tableware, damask table linens, and more. Among her purchases at A. T. Stewart, the huge New York department store, on May 24, 1861, were 117 yards of crimson "Wilton" for the Red Room and a new "velvet," or cut-pile, carpet for the East Room. "Its ground was of pale green," Mary Clemmer Ames wrote, "and in effect looked as if ocean, in gleaming and transparent waves, were tossing roses at your feet." Her most famous purchase was a huge carved rosewood bed for the state bedroom. Known today as the Lincoln Bed, it is the one their son Willie later died in and was probably never Lincoln's bed. The bed and other furniture Mary bought are today in what is called the Lincoln Bedroom, which in Lincoln's time was his office.

In December 1861 Lincoln was informed that in just nine months his wife had overspent by $6,700 the $20,000 Congress appropriated for refurbishing. He was enraged. "It would stink in the nostrils of the American people," he seethed, "to have it said that the President of the United States had approved a bill over-running an appropriation of $20,000 for flub-dubs for this damned old house, when soldiers cannot have blankets." Lincoln at first insisted on paying the $6,700 himself, but in the end the excess was buried in other accounts.

Mary also spent a great deal on clothes. As she explained to Elizabeth Keckley, the mulatto ex-slave whose Washington dress shop she frequented, "I must dress in costly

*Mary Lincoln is wearing a heavy white silk dress with sixty velvet bows sewn into it by her seamstress and confidante Elizabeth Keckley. The First Lady is tightly laced in, but she thought she looked too heavy in the picture and ordered photographer Matthew Brady to destroy all copies. Brady did not obey.* (LIBRARY OF CONGRESS)

material. The people scrutinize every article that I wear with critical curiosity." Indeed her clothes were often front-page news. She wore magnificent ball gowns, tightly corseted, with low necklines. She liked décolletage and New York fashions, as Julia Grant would a few years later. Lincoln, like Grant, protested unsuccessfully. And she always wanted the very best. "Do have my bonnet got up in exquisite taste. It is a bonnet for grand occasions & I want it to be particularly stylish & rich," she wrote when she ordered a bonnet from New York, specifying a "long and beautiful" feather and "lace trimmings very rich & full." In four months she reportedly bought three hundred pairs of gloves. For Lincoln's second inaugural she spent $2,000 on a white silk and lace gown. For whatever reason, she also purchased $1,000 worth of black mourning clothes. Lincoln did not always appreciate Mary's costumes. Keckley recalled a scene in which the Lincolns prepared to descend the stair for a dinner party, Mary in a new gown with a long train. "Whew!" said Lincoln. "Our cat has a long tail tonight."

By the end of her husband's first term, Mary's debts for clothing were $10,000. She told Lizzie Keckley, who had become a good friend and her only confidante, "If he should be defeated, I do not know what would become of us. To me, to him, there is more at stake in this election than he dreams of. I have contracted large debts of which he knows nothing, and which he will be unable to pay if he is defeated." She wrote Alexander Stewart, head of the famous New York department store, asking him to delay settlement of her debt to him as "an especial favor to me." In the same letter, she ordered a $1,000 black camel's hair shawl. Her schemes for remedying her cash shortage were seldom feasible. When the steward left, she tried to have his salary turned over to her to spend on running the White House. And she once ordered the gardener to sell manure from the stables, resulting in more jokes than cash.

Mary's problems were exacerbated by the increased focus of reporters on the White House and the first family. No first lady had ever been so scrutinized, and Mary was not accustomed to being in the public eye. When she and her entourage embarked on a big shopping trip to Philadelphia and New York, in a private railway car provided by the Baltimore and Ohio Railroad, the press tried to cover her visits to A. T. Stewart and Lord & Taylor. When the first lady evaded them or refused to speak to them, they made up wild stories about her purchases or embellished what they could find out.

Also unusual was the fact that the Lincolns were raising a family. When her husband took office, Mary was only forty-two years old and still had young children: Robert, seventeen, Willie, ten, and Tad, seven. Robert was quite shy and serious. When Lincoln invited the famous midget Tom Thumb to the White House, Robert wouldn't come out of his room to meet him. And he was not amused by the antics of his father and younger brothers. When Tad was given an officer's commission by Secretary of War Edwin Stanton, the youngster ordered up some muskets and issued them to the servants and gardeners. He proceeded to drill them on the White House lawn and assigned them to guard duty, relieving the regular guard. His elder brother was upset by this and reported it to their father. To Robert's dismay, Lincoln just laughed.

Robert attended college at Harvard for most of his father's presidency, but the younger boys lived in the White House full-time. Tad and Willie explored the mansion from attic to cellar. In the attic they discovered the central mechanism for the bell system, figured out how to work it, and created havoc among the servants. They were tutored upstairs in the Oval Room, which the family used as a parlor. Tom Cross, one of the messengers, was assigned to look after them but apparently wasn't around all the time: Tad and his friend Halsey Taft once completely disappeared. Servants went searching for them, without success. Finally, after dark, the boys were returned by a gentleman in a carriage. They had gone to the Capitol, about a mile away, where they descended to the lower levels and got lost. Halsey said they "went down steps pretty near to China," and it was "awful dark." There were rats, too. A workman heard their calls for help.

Lincoln enjoyed his sons' antics, and neither parent wanted to discipline the boys. The president could often be found playing with them, rolling on the floor with them, or carrying Tad around the house on his back as the boy let out war whoops. Halsey's sister Julia once discovered her two younger brothers and the Lincoln boys on the floor holding the president down by his hands and feet. They urged Julia to sit on his stomach, but she thought it undignified and declined.

As promised, Lincoln bought the boys a couple of ponies when they got to the White House. They would ride through the streets of Washington on them with their father following on his own horse. When Willie developed a cold and a serious fever after riding his pony in the rain, the doctors were reassuring. Lincoln kept a vigil at his bedside night after night. But on February 20, 1862, Willie died, probably not from the pony ride but of typhoid fever contracted from the polluted White House water supply. The bedrooms now had sinks, and running water was piped to the mansion straight from the

*During the Civil War crowds gathered after important battles around the portico calling on Lincoln for a speech. Lincoln would appear at the window over the main doorway to speak to them. John Wilkes Booth was in the audience on April 11th, 1865, and vowed that it would be Lincoln's last speech. It was.* (LIBRARY OF CONGRESS)

Potomac. Lincoln walked down the hall to his secretary's office, where he broke down in sobs. Mary, screaming, was helped to her bed. Her tears drenched the sheets. Tad would also get typhoid, but he survived.

Mary was never the same again. She stayed in mourning for almost two years, gave away all Willie's toys except his pony, and could not bring herself to look at his picture. She never again entered Willie's bedroom, or the Green Room, where he was embalmed. Once, during one of her paroxysms of grief, Lincoln pointed out a White House window and said, "Mother, do you see that large building on the hill yonder? Try and control your grief, or it will drive you mad, and we will have to send you there." Lincoln's own grief was renewed when, one night two years after Willie's death, he saw flames coming from the White House stables. He raced to the scene only to learn that Willie's pony, along with the rest of the horses, had perished when it refused to come out of the stable.

Lincoln held up, but Mary's grief did seem to drive her closer to madness. She began having visions of Willie, and also of Eddie, their son who died in infancy, among others. "He comes to me every night," she told her half sister, Emilie Helm, "and stands at the foot of my bed with the same sweet, adorable smile he has always had; he does not always come alone; little Eddie is sometimes with him and twice he has come with our brother Alec. . . . You cannot dream of the comfort this gives me." In her grief she turned to spiritualists. She visited Mrs. Cranston Laurie in Georgetown, and believed that the medium communicated with Willie. Laurie also told her that all the members of the cabinet were her husband's enemies.

Lincoln did not entirely dismiss his wife's visions. Witches and wizards abounded on the frontier of his childhood. When his son Robert was bitten by a dog back in Illinois, he took him to the "curing rock." He himself had dreams and visions, which he interpreted and shared with others. At one cabinet meeting General Ulysses S. Grant reported that the President was waiting to hear from General William Sherman following a battle with General Joseph E. Johnston. Lincoln declared that good news was imminent: "I had a dream last night, and ever since this war began I have had the same dream just before every event of great importance." But he didn't take the seances Mary held in the Red Room seriously, though he attended some of them. When a popular spiritualist who called himself Lord Colchester convinced Mary some strange rappings were loving messages from Willie, Lincoln asked Dr. Joseph Henry, the head of the Smithsonian Institution, to investigate. Henry revealed that Colchester produced the tappings himself by flexing his muscles to operate an instrument strapped to his arm.

With Willie gone, Lincoln doted on his youngest son, with whom he'd always had a special bond. The boy's formal name was Thomas, but as a baby he had a large head and squirmed like a tadpole, so Lincoln nicknamed him Tad, and it stuck. He had a cleft palate and a lisp, and a warm, loving personality. Tad adored his father and would crawl into his bed and sleep with him. Lincoln went to the theater regularly, and often took Tad along. Once the actors pulled a surprise by dressing Tad up and putting him onstage with them. Lincoln recognized him and burst into laughter.

Tad was also untamable. At twelve he still could not read, but Lincoln would say, "Let him run." Tad established a guard post at the foot of the stair to the offices and exacted a toll from the hordes of office seekers—"five cents for the benefit of the Sanitary

Fund." One night he locked his father into the fenced-in Lafayette Park. Another time he stood in front of the White House waving the Confederate flag while his father was reviewing Union troops. He would interrupt cabinet meetings by rapping on the door in a secret code he learned at the War Department. No matter how important the meeting, Lincoln would let him in, explaining, "I promised never to go back on the code." Lincoln's patience with his son seemed endless, but the White House staff was less tolerant. The head gardener lost all the strawberries he had been forcing to ripeness for a state dinner when Tad helped himself to them. He flew into a rage and sought out the boy. When reminded that the culprit was madam's son, the gardener snarled, "The madam's a wildcat."

And then there were the goats. After Willie died, Tad lost interest in his pony, which seemed to remind him of his brother. Out for a carriage ride with his parents one day, he was intrigued by some goats. Lincoln had one of the household staff buy a pair of goats for $5 each and named them Nanny and Nanko. Tad and his father played with the goats for hours on the south grounds. The animals grew to know the sound of the president's voice and would come when he called them. Lincoln just laughed when Tad took Nanny and Nanko to bed with him. But Tad further enraged the gardener by turning them loose and chasing them through the White House flower beds, whooping and hollering all the while. He even harnessed the animals together one behind the other and hitched them to a turned-over chair to make a chariot, on which he tore screaming through the East Room, startling and upsetting some visiting Boston ladies. His father, meanwhile, was out of sight, so convulsed with laughter that he had to hold a napkin over his mouth. Finally, Mary and Tad went away on a trip, leaving Lincoln in charge of the goats. Nanny kept getting loose and wandering into the flower beds, so the president brought her inside, where she explored the halls. She curled up on Tad's bed, only to be chased out by Mrs. Cuthbert, the housekeeper. After that Nanny "disappeared." Lincoln wrote Mary, "This is the last we know of poor Nanny."

Lincoln's amused handling of the goats was typical of a White House style that was quintessentially his own. Lincoln was good-natured, easygoing, uncomplaining, and without pretension, and that didn't change just because he was in charge of the executive mansion. His friend Noah Brooks, correspondent for the *Daily Union* in Sacramento, California, had breakfast with him one day and noticed that the president was served a glass of milk, unusual at breakfast for somebody from the Midwest. Lincoln admitted, "Well, I do prefer coffee in the morning but they don't seem to have sent me in any." On another morning, Brooks passed the president standing by the White House fence looking down the street. "Good morning, good morning!" Lincoln said. "I am looking for a newsboy. When you get to that corner I wish you would start one up this way." The president once asked his Irish coachman to go out for a morning paper, and when the paper didn't arrive learned that the coachman thought it beneath his dignity to run errands. Lincoln fetched the paper himself. The next morning he ordered up his carriage and asked the coachman to take a member of the household staff out to get the five-cent *Morning Chronicle*. The chagrined coachman got the message.

To visitors, it could look as if no one was in charge at the White House. When Prince Napoleon, the nephew of Napoleon III, paid a call at the White House in August 1861, doorkeeper Edward McManus wasn't there, and Willie met him at the door. The prince noted in his diary, "One goes right in as if entering a café."

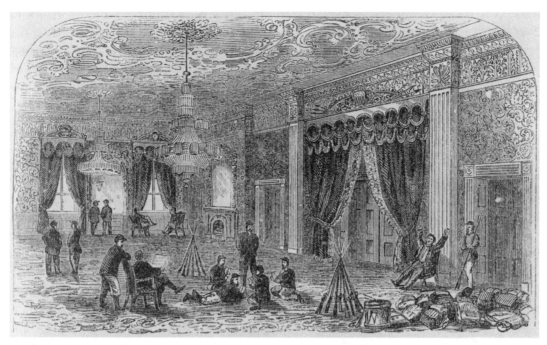

At the beginning of the Civil War, Washington was in danger of being captured by the South. To protect the White House, troops were stationed in the East Room. The White House survived the encampment, but the carpeting and accessories did not. (LIBRARY OF CONGRESS)

Despite Lincoln's displays of lightheartedness, he felt the human cost of the war acutely, as did Mary. He was appalled by the interminable lists of casualties, the hardships and deprivations. Both he and the and first lady visited the suffering wounded at city hospitals. Mary lost two half brothers she was very close to—both killed fighting for the South. Her half sister Emilie's husband, Ben Helm, of whom Lincoln too was fond, also fought and died for the South. In September 1863 Emilie took Helm's body to Atlanta for burial, then could not get back through Union lines to her home in Kentucky because she refused to take the Oath of Allegiance. Notified of this by the War Department, Lincoln wired, "Send her to me." There was a tearful reunion of sisters, which led to heartbreaking rumors that the first lady was aiding the Confederates, that she herself was a Confederate spy, and that Lincoln was harboring a spy.

The president faced additional tragedy with the death of Elmer Ellsworth. Ellsworth had worked as a clerk in Lincoln's Illinois law office, where Lincoln took a liking to him. Once elected, Lincoln invited him to live in the White House, where the young man shared a room with Robert. In May 1861 Ellsworth raised a regiment in New York, brought the men to Washington, and led them across the Potomac to drive the rebels out of Alexandria, Virginia. The rebels gave up easily. But when Ellsworth saw a Confederate flag flying from a hotel, he climbed the stairs and hauled it down, only to be shot dead in the hallway by the hotelkeeper. Lincoln, overwhelmed by the news, broke down in tears. He had the coffin brought to the East Room. A vision of Ellsworth's face haunted him for the rest of the war.

Though he worked hard and long, Lincoln remained accessible to the public despite the war. The White House was inundated by job seekers. Lincoln said getting rid of them was like "trying to shovel a bushel of fleas across a barn floor." He once received so many recommendations for two candidates vying for the job of postmaster in an Ohio town that he piled the letters on scales and gave the job to the man with the heaviest pile. When Lincoln contracted a mild case of smallpox, after his November 19, 1863, speech at Gettysburg, he returned to the White House and lay in bed feverish and aching all over, his skin broken out with the tell-tale red spots and blisters. "Now let the office seekers come," he said. "I have something to give them."

Once the fighting got under way Lincoln was also besieged by requests for special consideration, passes, and pardons. In just one year, thirty thousand court-martial cases came through his office. The Civil War became unusual among wars for its rarity of executions because Lincoln saw fit to save thousands of men from the death sentence. He frustrated the military by frequently granting pardons or lighter sentences for a variety of offenses. He could not, for example, abide the death penalty for sleeping on guard duty. "Some of my generals complain that I impair discipline and subordination," Lincoln said, "but it makes me feel rested after a hard day's work, if I can find some good excuse to save a man's life." One day Mrs. Nancy Bushrod, seeking her soldier husband's back pay, ducked under the arm of a guard and ran down the hall to the president's office. Stopped by another guard, the nearly hysterical woman created such a disturbance that Lincoln came to the door. "There is time for all who need me," he said. "Let the good woman come in." As Lincoln once explained, "If I have one vice, and I call it nothing else, it is not being able to say, 'No.' "

As the war ground on, Lincoln became careworn and gaunt. He was plagued by constipation and cared little about food. Mary might plan an elaborate family dinner only to have her husband ask for fruit salad, cheese, and crackers. His breakfast was usually an egg and coffee; his lunch, a biscuit, fruit, and milk. By his second term the already lean president had lost thirty pounds. His hands and feet were chronically cold, and he had insomnia. He wandered down the hall late at night to talk or read a book to his secretaries, John Nicolay and John Hay, who shared a room near the offices. On March 14, 1865, he was so exhausted he couldn't get out of bed. Horace Greeley, the influential founder and editor of the *New York Tribune,* said he "seemed unlikely to live." Modern analysis suggests he was in the early stages of congestive heart failure.

Lincoln was urged to close the White House and cut off the stream of visitors, but he would not. "[They] don't want much. . . . They get but little and I must see them," he said. Presidents "moving only in an official circle are apt to become mere official," he said, calling his "public opinion baths" "renovating and invigorating . . . no hours of my day are better employed." The public receptions were exhausting, with the president greeting hundreds personally. The war in no way discouraged attendance. At Lincoln's last New Year's Day reception, in 1865, people packed in so tightly that children and even ladies were lifted above the crowd to save them from being crushed. Some who were caught in the surge of the crowd screamed and fainted. In the calm before these receptions, Lizzie Keckley, who had become part of the White House family, would brush Lincoln's unruly hair. "Well, Madame Elizabeth, will you brush my bristles tonight?" the president would ask, and then sit in an easy chair while she arranged his hair. In the aftermath, the Lincolns would retreat to the upstairs parlor and Mary would rub and soak her husband's swollen, blistered hand.

Lincoln intended to sign the Emancipation Proclamation into law on New Year's Day, 1863. It would be one of most important events ever to take place in the White House. But after the traditional reception the president's hand was "swollen like a poisoned pup. . . . I have been shaking hands since nine o'clock this morning and my right arm is almost paralyzed." He was concerned that his signature be firm: "Now this signature is one that will be closely examined. If they find my hand trembled they will say, 'he had some complications.' But anyway, it must be done. . . . I never in my life felt more certain that I was doing right, than I do in signing this paper." He signed it, firmly, on the cabinet table.

Lincoln's exhaustion would have been concern enough for his doctors and family, but his life was threatened throughout his presidency. Washington, after all, was at that time still a very southern city with southern ways and largely southern sympathies. One apparent assassination attempt occurred in the summer of 1864. In the heat of summer the Lincolns left the White House for the higher, cooler, and healthier Soldiers' Home three miles outside the city. Eschewing a cavalry escort to and from the White House, Lincoln sometimes rode back to the Soldiers' Home alone at night. On one such night at about eleven, he had just reached the grounds of the Soldiers' Home when a bullet tore through his "eight-dollar plug-hat," as he called it. The shooter was never identified, and the incident was kept out of the press.

Lincoln, however, paid such dangers little heed. He was fatalistic: if he was going to be killed, nothing could prevent it. He kept written threats in a file marked "Assassinations." Ordinary citizens of Washington hesitated, for fear of crime, to walk the streets at night, yet Lincoln did, sometimes alone. There were no telegraph connections to the White House, so to get the latest news he would take the service stairs to the cellar and slip out the back of the mansion to the telegraph office in the nearby War Department. Sometimes he slept there, on a couch. Noah Brooks reminded Lincoln that walking there at night through areas of trees and bushes—where petty criminals and even assassins might lurk—was dangerous. Lincoln laughed and showed him the thick stick he was carrying. On election night in 1864, Ward Hill Lamon, U.S. marshal for the District of Columbia and an old friend of Lincoln's from Illinois, was particularly concerned for Lincoln's safety. He armed himself with pistols and bowie knives and camped in the hall outside the president's bedroom, only to discover that Lincoln had walked to the theater with two friends Lamon described as unable to defend themselves "against an assault from any able-bodied woman." Finally, in late 1864, as the war neared an end, four plainclothes bodyguards were hired to protect the president around the clock.

It was in this atmosphere of heightened danger that Lincoln's second inauguration took place on March 4, 1865. There was utter havoc at the White House reception the next night, as described by William H. Crook, one of Lincoln's bodyguards:

> The White House looked as if a regiment of rebel troops had been quartered there—with permission to forage. The crowds were enormous, and there were some rough people present. A fever of vandalism seemed to seize them. We had always found that some odds and ends had been carried away as souvenirs after

every public reception, but the damage created by this one was something monstrous. . . . A great piece of red brocade, a yard square almost, was cut from the window-hangings of the East Room, and another piece, not quite so large, from a curtain in the Green Room. Besides this, the flowers from the floral design in the lace curtains were cut out, evidently for an ornament for the top of pincushions or something of the sort. Some arrests were made, after the reception, of persons concerned in the disgraceful business. These things distressed the President greatly. I can hardly understand why, when he was so calm about things usually, these acts of rowdyism should have impressed him so painfully. It was the senseless violence of it that puzzled him. "Why should they do it?" he said to me. "How can they?"

Lincoln would be dead forty days later, and in hindsight, Crook speculated that the crowd somehow knew what was coming. "It seems some premonition that there would not be much more of Mr. Lincoln's administration must have come to them and made them lawless," he said. "They wanted to get mementos while they could." In the confusion following the president's assassination, the unsupervised state rooms would be further devastated. But if the public had a foreboding, they weren't alone. Shortly before his death Lincoln dreamed he heard distant sobs in the White House, and in his dream he wandered from room to room seeking the source. In the East Room he was startled to find a catafalque on which a corpse lay dressed in funeral vestments. Soldiers stood guard, mourners passed by. When Lincoln asked who had died, he was told it was the president, who had been assassinated.

When Richmond, Virginia, fell to Union forces on April 2, 1865, Lincoln took a steamer there and walked through the shattered city holding Tad by the hand. By the time he returned to Washington, the war was over: Robert E. Lee surrendered to Ulysses S. Grant on April 9, 1865. The capital city was in a festive mood. After great Union victories hundreds of people would gather on Pennsylvania Avenue to serenade the president, and he would go to the window over the north door to address them. A White House doorman would draw the curtain and hold high a candle so the president could be seen. Sometimes Tad would be at his father's feet to catch the pages of his speech as he dropped them. Following Grant's decisive victory, on April 11, Lincoln opened the White House gates to the crowd of celebrants who had converged on the mansion. John Wilkes Booth was among them. After Lincoln addressed the crowd, Booth said to his accomplice, David Herald, "That is the last speech he will ever make."

On April 14, Good Friday, Lincoln held a cabinet meeting from 11 A.M. to 2 P.M. Afterward, General Grant backed out of his commitment to see the play *Our American Cousin* at Ford's Theater with the Lincolns that night. Major Henry Rathbone, a member of Lincoln's staff, and Rathbone's cousin, Miss Clara Harris, were substituted. Around 3 P.M. Lincoln and Mary went for a ride, alone, in an open barouche. "Dear Husband," Mary remarked, "you almost startle me by your great cheerfulness." Lincoln answered, "And well I may feel so, Mary. I consider this day, the war, has come to a close. . . . We must both be more cheerful in the future—between the war & the loss of our darling Willie—we have both, been very miserable."

They arrived late at the theater. The play was stopped, and a band struck up "Hail to the Chief" as the president and his wife made their way to the presidential box, where

Lincoln as usual sat in his rocking chair. Booth left the theater barroom shortly before 10 P.M. and entered Lincoln's box unopposed. He fired his single-shot derringer into the president's head at close range. Lincoln's head fell forward, and Booth leaped from the presidential box, crossed the stage, and escaped on horseback down a back alley. The ensuing manhunt would last nearly two weeks and end with Booth's death. Dr. Charles Leale, a twenty-three-year-old surgeon who was in the audience below, made his way to the box and pronounced the wound fatal. Lincoln was carried to the Peterson boardinghouse across the street. He was too long for the bed. Lincoln died at 7:22 the next morning.

Mary, spattered with blood at the theater, had become so hysterical in the Peterson house that Secretary of War Edwin Stanton had her escorted back to the White House, where she took to her bed. Mary endured the all-night hammering of the carpenters downstairs in the East Room as they built the catafalque that held Lincoln's coffin. Over and over, she cried out that she heard gunshots in the house. She was prostrated with grief for over a month, not even attending the April 19 funeral. To Lizzie Keckley she said, "God, Elizabeth, what a change! I had an ambition to be Mrs. President, that ambition has been gratified, and now I must step down from the pedestal. My poor husband! Had he never been President, he might be living today. Alas! All is over with me!" It was six weeks before Mary roused herself to pack up and leave the White House. Other family members responded almost resignedly. Lincoln's stepmother, Sara, still living in a log cabin at seventy-six, said his assassination did not surprise her: "I knowed they kill him. I've been waiting for it." Tad would ask a White House visitor if his father was in heaven. "I have no doubt of it," he was told. "Then I'm glad he has gone," Tad said, "for he was never happy after he came here. This was not a good place for him."

Mary was left with an estate valued at $111,000, and furthermore received a government pension, yet she felt compelled to raise money. She even peddled her husband's monogrammed shirts in New York. She fled to Europe with Tad, who devotedly cared for her until he died, at seventeen, in 1871. Her erratic behavior led her son Robert to commit her to a private sanitarium in 1875 for a short time. Mary died on July 16, 1882, and was buried alongside her husband in Springfield. She looked back on her White House years only with sadness: "All the sorrows of my life occurred there & that Whited Sepulcure broke my heart."

---

CIVIL WAR WASHINGTON

Washington had been invaded once, during the War of 1812, and some fifty years later a second onslaught was feared possible. The city was a prime target for Confederate armies, and its residents lived under intermittent threat of attack. To protect the perimeter Union forces built a string of forty-eight forts and laid down a barricade of felled trees fifteen miles long and a mile and a half wide. For most of the war the city's only defense was raw militia troops and government clerks organized to fight in an emergency.

At times troops were quartered in both the Capitol and the White House, causing predictable damage. Foggy Bottom, a low area near the White House, was fitted with wagon sheds and corals in order to house thirty thousand army horses and mules. Coal and lumber yards intruded on the Mall as the city took on the trappings of war.

But even more threatening than Confederate armies was the spread of disease. By 1863, in the middle of the war, smallpox had reached plague proportions, and typhoid and dysentery were rampant. Many of the estimated fifty thousand Union soldiers in military hospitals in and around the capital died not from their wounds but from these illnesses. Central to the problem was Washington's explosive population growth, which overwhelmed its primitive sanitation system. In 1860 the capital's residents numbered sixty-one thousand. Three years later the population had tripled thanks to a rapidly expanding government bureaucracy and an influx of former slaves. An estimated forty thousand blacks freed by the Union armies poured into Washington, aided by an April 1862 act of Congress that freed slaves in the District of Columbia.

Most of these new residents lived without sanitation, in shacks in the city's seventy-seven miles of alleys. A young army wife wrote home to her mother, "What would you think if all the slops from sleeping rooms were thrown either into the gutters or alley. . . . I was never in such a place for smells." Butchers at Central Market regularly dumped poultry innards, rotted fish, and animal carcasses into the sluggish drainage canal that, on its way to the Potomac, flowed behind the White House, where Constitution Avenue is today. Consequently, the Executive Mansion—which was also adjacent to foul, mosquito-infested marshes—was no place to be in hot weather. Forced to remain there one summer, Lincoln's secretary, John Nicolay, wrote, "I am alone in the White pesthouse. The ghosts of twenty thousand drowned cats come in at night through the south windows."

The most notorious section of the city, a slum called "Murder Bay," was found along the canal. It contained army encampments, houses of prostitution, taverns, and gambling halls. But crime was rampant all over the city. The superintendent of the Metropolitan Police Board admitted that the police were overwhelmed and that without the help of thousands of soldiers on patrol the District would be uninhabitable. In one attempt to clear the streets of petty thieves, police rounded up a group of them, put placards on them that said "Pickpocket and Thief," and paraded them through the city.

Yet Lincoln was unwilling to relinquish the grand vision of a national city. From the White House he could see the Washington Monument, an unfinished stump. It had been raised by voluntary subscriptions, but its construction had been halted due to lack of funding. He would not let the Capitol, its dome likewise unfinished, meet the same fate. The president ordered the work to continue: "If people see the Capitol go on," he said, "they will know that the Union will go on."

# 17

# Andrew Johnson

## 1865–1869

## *Traitor to Patriot*

IN THE WAKE of Abraham Lincoln's assassination on April 14, 1865, Washington and the White House were in disarray. After the shot rang out at Ford's Theater, Leonard J. Farwell, a friend of Andrew Johnson's, did not linger. Mindful of rumored plots against top government officials, he ran the two and a half blocks to Johnson's Pennsylvania Avenue hotel to see to the vice president's safety. Johnson had declined an invitation to attend the theater that night, and was asleep at the Kirkwood House, his home away from his Tennessee home.

At the hotel, Farwell announced that the president had been shot and ordered guards put on the stairs as he ran to Johnson's second-floor room and pounded on the door. Johnson had gone to bed around nine-thirty. Groggy, he roused himself, put on his pants, and let Farwell in. Soon other friends arrived. Secretary of War Edwin Stanton put a guard on Johnson and surrounded the hotel with soldiers. It was later learned that Booth had assigned George Atzerodt to kill the vice president, and Atzerodt had taken a room directly above Johnson's. In it were found a pistol, cartridges, a large bowie knife, and a bankbook in Booth's name. Atzerodt, however, had lost his nerve, gotten drunk, and disappeared.

Against the advice of his alarmed friends, Johnson insisted at 2 A.M. on going to the boardinghouse across from Ford's where the president lay dying. Nothing could be done. Johnson's presence made Mary Lincoln and others uneasy, so he soon left. Lincoln was dead by morning, and Johnson took the oath of office in the parlor of the Kirkwood House.

Mary Lincoln, hysterical, retreated to the White House, where for weeks to come she secluded herself upstairs in mourning for her dead husband. The White House went into a kind of limbo for one of the few times in its history. Johnson urged Mrs. Lincoln to remain there as long as she wished, and temporarily conducted official business from an office in the Treasury Department. During this time the mansion was virtually unregulated. Upstairs, Lincoln's secretaries sifted through and packed his papers and books. "They are taking away Mr. Lincoln's private effects, to deposit wheresoever his family may abide," wrote one visitor a month after the assassination, "and the emptiness of the place, on this sunny Sunday, revives that feeling of desolation from which the land has scarce recovered." Downstairs, the public roamed unimpeded. Curtains, furniture, and lamps were ravaged or simply carried off. The East Room remained as it had been for Lincoln's funeral, and visitors picked apart the mourning vestments for souvenirs. By the time Commissioner of Public Buildings B. B. French took inventory after Mrs. Lincoln left in May, no lamps, vases, or other easily movable items remained, and most everything else was damaged. "All curtains badly cut—rest of furniture pretty badly used," he wrote. The bill for the replacement of stolen china and silver alone came to $22,000.

Johnson immediately moved out of his hotel and into a vacant house offered by Representative Samuel Hooper. His first morning as president began with the discovery that there was no food in the pantry. He had to send someone to the market for his breakfast. Johnson was alone in the house. His family was still in Tennessee, and, after the initial assassination scare, he had no bodyguards. Despite Lincoln's murder, the thinking was that only monarchs needed guards, not democratically elected presidents. Mrs. Lincoln did not vacate the White House for six weeks, leaving May 22. Finally, on June 9, the new president moved into the Executive Mansion.

No president has ever risen from deeper poverty than Andrew Johnson. He was born in 1808 in Raleigh, North Carolina. His father, a porter and handyman at an inn, died when Andy was three, and his mother struggled to survive as a seamstress and washerwoman. When he turned fourteen, in 1822, his mother apprenticed him to a tailor. She signed the agreement with an X. At seventeen he ran away, and the tailor advertised a reward of $10 for his return. Within a year he resigned himself to serving out his apprenticeship, but the tailor refused to take him back, leaving him an unemployable fugitive in North Carolina. So he led his mother, his new stepfather, and his brother west across the Great Smokies, carrying everything they owned in a two-wheeled cart pulled by a blind pony. At Greeneville, Tennessee, he opened a tailor shop. After he married Eliza McCardle on May 17, 1827, he rented a two-room cabin, each room twelve by twelve feet, and set up his tailor shop in the front room.

Johnson never spent even one day in school, making him the least educated president. But Eliza—who at sixteen married younger than any other first lady—had received a basic education. She read to her husband as he worked, and in the evenings taught him to read and write. He occasionally paid someone 50 cents a day to read to him while he worked. He especially liked to read newspapers and discuss politics, and his shop became the local political center. He found he was a good orator, and was made an alderman in 1828. He was elected mayor of Greeneville in 1832, and was soon in the statehouse. In 1843 he was elected to Congress, serving five terms. In 1853 he won the governorship of Tennessee, and by 1857 he had risen to the United States Senate. By then he had achieved a moderate wealth, but he never stopped denouncing the rich and defending the hardworking common people with whom he identified. "I have grappled with the gaunt and haggard monster called hunger," he often said.

Johnson owned slaves and defended slavery, but he opposed disunion, the only southern congressman to do so. In Tennessee he was burned in effigy, and Jefferson Davis, eventual president of the Confederacy, spoke for the South when he named Johnson a "southern traitor." The *New York Times,* on the other hand, called Johnson "the greatest man of the age." Lincoln wanted the Democrat on his ticket in 1864 to show that the Civil War was not a partisan Republican war.

Now the southern traitor was in the White House. President Johnson sent for his family in Tennessee in early August, and they had a joyful reunion in the mansion. The Johnson family was a dozen strong, and the upstairs living quarters were crowded. Along with Johnson and Eliza were their two sons, Robert and Andrew Jr.; daughter Martha and her husband David Patterson, United States senator from Tennessee, and their two children; and daughter Mary Stover, a widow, and her three children. They were a close-knit family; outsiders were seldom admitted.

The grandchildren had the run of the house and could burst in upon their grandfather any time and find an affectionate welcome. Johnson took them by carriage to Rock Creek Park, which still exists northwest of the White House, to play while he walked in the woods or skipped stones on the water. He enjoyed other people's children as well. On December 29, 1867, his sixtieth birthday, he held a grand party in the East Room for children of friends and diplomats. The East Room was brilliantly lit and decorated, and there was singing, dancing, and refreshments. Eliza emerged from her room to attend—one of only two appearances by her at a formal function. The other was for the visit of Queen Emma of the Sandwich Islands, now Hawaii.

Eliza was two years younger than her husband but was feeble and seemed older. She would outlive him by just a few months. In her middle years she had developed "slow consumption," or tuberculosis, and by the time she reached the White House she was a near invalid who needed help up the stairs. She had her choice of bedrooms and chose a small one next to the Prince of Wales Room, which the family used both as a bedroom and a sitting room. Despite her suffering she was sweet-tempered and pleasant. She was not immobile, but for tuberculosis doctors prescribed staying indoors and resting, so she spent most of her time in her room and took her meals there. She was content to knit, sew, and enjoy her grandchildren. The children were tutored at the White House, and after their lessons they ran to Eliza's room to visit their grandmother.

The Johnsons enjoyed a harmonious marriage. To please her husband, the first lady dressed in rich, expensive clothing, employing only the top dressmakers. Johnson was unfailingly tender and considerate to her. Eliza read a great deal, and from her several newspapers clipped articles about the president, putting good news in one pile and bad in another. She looked after him, checking his clothes—typically a conservative black frock coat and clean stiff collar—and ordering the menu for his meals. A staff aide described the Johnsons' relationship as "the nearest approach to the ideal married life that I have ever known."

*In the mid-1800s the South Lawn was like a public park. The Marine Band played and the public could stroll or picnic. Presidents like Andrew Johnson felt free to stroll and to mingle with the crowd.* (LIBRARY OF CONGRESS)

Eliza, besides being ill, was less than enthusiastic about her husband's new importance and life in the White House. "It is all very well for those who like it," she said, "but I don't like this public life at all." Martha and Mary took over their mother's social duties. Though they were not glamorous as hostesses—their conservative high-necked dresses with long sleeves seemed odd to fashionable Washington ladies—they did a commendable job. Martha, the elder daughter, had gone to some of the best Washington schools and had been a guest of the Polks in the White House. It was she who handled the household accounts and supervised a complete cleanup of the mansion.

Mindful of the criticisms garnered by the extravagant Mary Lincoln, Martha used the $30,000 appropriated for repairing and redecorating the White House economically, being careful not to overspend.

Extensive renovations took place between the summer of 1866 and spring of 1867. The recent public ravaging was not the only problem. The state dining room was moldering, as Mrs. Lincoln had closed it off in order to save money for other things, and the East Room was infested with lice from the troops that had been bivouacked there. Martha supervised the workmen as they restored the parlors, and she negotiated contracts with suppliers. The old, intricately patterned wallpapers were replaced by "French panels," gilt frames forming a series of rectangles that were papered inside to contrast with painted walls. Worn places in the carpeting were cut out, and the remainder pulled up and taken to the south lawn to be beaten, washed, and sun-dried. Carpets and oilcloths were pulled up and the wooden floors beneath washed with lye water. Martha then took on areas of the house that most first ladies never touched. She had the attic emptied, scrubbed, and whitewashed. In the basement, the servants' quarters and the kitchens were cleaned and whitewashed, and additional toilet facilities installed for the servants. The White House may never have been so thoroughly cleaned before.

She even confronted the rats that scurried across the floors and worktables in the basement. The White House had a long history of rat infestations, and Martha fought back with large doses of poison, cats, and traps, but it was a losing battle that would continue long after she was gone. Meanwhile, upstairs in her father's bedroom, mice had gotten into some packets of white flour he had received from a mill he owned back home in Greeneville. Unlike his daughter, Johnson had a fondness for animals that encompassed even rodents, and he had no plans to do battle with them. "The little fellows gave me their confidence," he said, and left them flour and water on the hearth.

Martha also faced structural problems. The East and West Wings of the house still functioned as extensions of the basement. The East Wing, after years of use by gardeners as a toolhouse, potting shed, and compost storehouse, was in such disrepair that in June 1866 Martha finally had it demolished. Repairs to the West Wing were curtailed when the wood-frame conservatory on its roof, built in Buchanan's day, was destroyed by fire. The West Wing roof was rebuilt, and then the conservatory. In the refurbished West Wing she also ordered a dairy built, which she took special interest in. She bought two Jersey cows, and a cow man brought pails of milk to the house daily. Martha was fond of cream and butter, and particular about how they were made. She ran the dairy herself, arriving each morning wearing a calico dress and a clean apron. Her dairy was reported to be one of the cleanest in Washington.

Martha's redecorating and cleaning were virtually complete in time for the 1867 New Year's reception. Since the late 1850s, most receptions, excepting on New Year's and the Fourth of July, had been by invitation only. Johnson, in keeping with his democratic ideals, reintroduced the levee, a true open house for all who wished to come. The levees were thronged, with lines so long that not everyone made it into the mansion before the doors closed. Martha took steps to save wear and tear on the newly decorated house. Most of the state room furniture was removed to the Red Room and the State Dining Room, which were locked, and protective runners were laid down over the carpets where callers crossed the Blue and Green Rooms. The East Room carpet was covered from wall to wall. Martha got rid of the temporary stair under the south windows, used as an exit for years, and devised a easier, ramplike exit to the driveway on the north, where the windowsills were closer to the ground.

At the same time, Martha had no qualms about curtailing the kind of unsupervised public access that had in the past resulted in general dilapidation and heavy losses to souvenir seekers. It helped that the extensive looting and damage to the mansion that followed Lincoln's assassination convinced Congress to pay a steward to look after its investment instead of relying on the president to do it. The first official White House steward was William Slade. He was bonded for $30,000 and held personally responsible for all government property in the mansion, including dishes and silverware. Also, though the public was permitted to tour the East Room Monday through Saturday from nine to three, as allowed by Lincoln, the room was watched over by detectives. It was still open to all—on occasion people even got married in the East Room, bringing along a minister and friends—but those who lounged all day or slept on the sofas were ejected, and anyone who tried to leave with a souvenir was likely to regret it.

Through these innovations and her ingenious work with modest funds, Martha had made the White House a place to be admired again. Both Martha and Mary were a great source of help and comfort to their father. His sons, Charles, Andrew Jr., and Robert, were not. All three were alcoholics. Charles, the eldest, died fighting the Confederates in Tennessee. Andrew Jr. lived in the White House while attending school in Georgetown. He later suffered from tuberculosis in addition to alcoholism and died at twenty-seven. Robert became a lawyer, and Johnson made him his private secretary, but he was an embarrassment, going on drunken sprees and entertaining prostitutes in the White House. He even set off a White House scandal when he became involved with Mrs. L. L. Cobb, a "pardon broker" paid to use her physical charms to gain pardons for former Confederates.

People seeking pardons began lining up at daybreak in front of the White House doors, which opened at 9 A.M. It could take weeks to finally see the president. A pardon would restore an ex-Confederate to citizenship and jobs, but the process was intentionally difficult. "Pardon brokers," generally women posing as a sister or mother, became adept at helping for a fee. Some said a pretty woman in tears could easily get a pardon from the president, while Johnson claimed he could spot a phony: "You can distinguish between them as quickly as you can distinguish from the pure waters of a river, the muddy torrent that flows into it from deep ravines of clayey soil." He granted almost two thousand pardons during his first three months in office. Robert, recognizing Mrs. Cobb's attractions, used his relationship with his father to help her in her work. The ensuing scandal compelled Johnson to get his son out of Washington. Secretary of the Navy Gideon Welles and Secretary of State William Seward put together a long, ostensibly diplomatic, mission to Africa for Robert, which Johnson paid for personally. Robert would die of alcoholism in 1869, at thirty-five.

Johnson himself was a moderate drinker, though he was often accused of being a drunkard. His public image suffered unfairly when he was sworn in as vice president in 1865. Johnson had been suffering from a fever and had not wanted to attend the ceremony, but Lincoln pressed him to do so. Beforehand, outside the stuffy Senate chamber, Johnson felt nauseous and had taken a couple of stiff shots of whiskey. He appeared before the crowd red-faced, watery-eyed, somewhat disheveled, and smelling of liquor. His speech was slurred, and he maundered on without any manuscript for more than twice his allotted time. When members of the audience began muttering, he denounced them. Senator Hannibal Hamlin, Lincoln's outgoing vice president, tugged on Johnson's coat so that he might stop. Johnson realized he had publicly disgraced himself. Lincoln came to his defense: "I have known Andy a great many years, and he ain't no drunkard." But to Johnson's enemies—and he had many—he would be referred to as "Andy the Sot."

Johnson's appearance and personality fueled rumors of heavy drinking. He was five feet ten inches tall and about 178 pounds, and his face was craggy with blotches and deep lines. He shunned Washington society, keeping to his close family. He was generally reserved, even cold, but could be combative. Far from a drunkard, however, Johnson was hardworking and methodical, if prone to spending undue time on bureaucratic details. When Johnson was still working out of the Treasury Building, Treasury secretary Hugh McCulloch noted that the new president "arrived at his office every morning before nine o'clock and rarely left before five. His room was open to everybody. His luncheon, when he had one, was a cup of tea and a cracker." At the White House Johnson rose before dawn and ate breakfast at eight, lunch at one, and dinner at seven. In the evening he often took his pet cat and a pot of coffee to the library to work some more. He liked to work standing up at a high desk in his office, a position that helped relieve the almost constant pain of kidney stones—possibly the source of his reticence and chronically grim expression. In 1857 he broke his right arm in a train accident, and thereafter he usually dictated letters, which was no doubt preferable because his grammar and spelling were not good.

Johnson used the same office Lincoln had, but his staff was permanently increased thanks to postwar administrative burdens. He employed six secretaries to Lincoln's two, and the room across the hall, where Lincoln's secretaries had slept, became another office. In another change, substantial numbers of official papers were stored at the White House for the first time, necessitating a rearrangement and reorganization of the offices to make room for cabinets, shelves, and drawers. The suite began to look like a modern office. And in 1866 a telegraph line was finally installed in the White House, at the southeast corner office.

Given his schedule, Johnson had few pastimes: checkers, perhaps, or watching baseball, which was becoming the national sport. A portion of the south grounds of the White House known as the White Lot was the site of many a game. The crowds of spectators grew, and in 1867 the lot was enclosed with a white fence and an admission of 25 cents charged.

All of Johnson's hard work could not overcome his antagonistic, and finally hysterical, relationship with Congress. Incensed by Johnson's magnanimous postwar policies toward the South—policies in line with Lincoln's leniency—the "Radical Republicans" controlling the House of Representatives attempted to impeach him four times, starting in 1866. No president had ever endured such violent, trumped-up attacks, and Johnson was not one to pacify his enemies. As a southerner and lifelong Democrat, Johnson had no power base with the Republicans, and in 1868 they finally succeeded in impeaching him. He was charged with violating the Tenure of Office Act, which said he could not fire his own cabinet member without Senate approval. Johnson had vetoed the act as unconstitutional (in 1926 the Supreme Court would so rule), but the Radicals passed it over his veto. Johnson nevertheless fired Secretary of War Stanton, a Radical

*Johnson used Lincoln's office, today the site of the Lincoln Bedroom, and like Lincoln he was available to anybody. Normally the office and the hall outside were jammed with callers. Office seekers and ex-Confederates seeking pardons began pushing inside at 9 A.M.* (LIBRARY OF CONGRESS)

sympathizer. But while the Republican House of Representatives impeached him, the Senate failed, by a single vote, to convict him and remove him from office.

The Senate trial was a political circus with little relationship to constitutional law. Supreme Court chief justice Salmon Chase presided, but the Senate voted to overrule many of his decisions. Thaddeus Stevens, who had led the attack in the House and presented the charges in the Senate, called Johnson an "alien enemy, a citizen of a foreign state, and therefore not now legally President." Johnson followed the proceedings closely from the White House, a mile away. He had wanted to attend, but his advisers, knowing his temper and impetuosity, convinced him otherwise. Johnson already had a record of making damaging comments when angered by taunting crowds. Instead he went about his duties and even spent time reading English literature and memorizing favorite passages. The climactic vote on May 16, 1868, came down to one uncommitted freshman Republican, Senator Edmund Ross of Kansas. "I almost literally looked down into my own grave," Ross said later. His vote saved Johnson and the presidency but ruined him politically, as he knew it would. When news of his acquittal reached Johnson, tears ran down his cheeks. He ordered whiskey, wine, food, and cigars for everyone in the room, and soon the White House and the streets were filling with people celebrating his vindication.

The president now threw open the doors of the White House even more generously than before, throwing all manner of dinners and parties. One of these was another children's party, which cost more than an average state dinner. "There has never been," wrote Colonel William H. Crook, the White House disbursement officer, "a children's party so wonderful. . . . The dancing was in the East Room. There were a great many square dances, and a few waltzes and polkas; but the fancy dances were the best. . . . There was the 'Highland Fling,' of course, and the 'sailors' hornpipe.' There was a Spanish dance, danced by small Miss Gaburri in a Spanish dress flashing with sequins. . . . At the end of the whole company, tots and big girls and boys, were lined up for the 'Virginia reel.' After that came 'refreshments'—the real 'party' most of the children thought."

The political environment remained hostile, and Johnson ran into more problems when he arranged the purchase of Alaska. Secretary of State Seward negotiated the treaty with the Russians and helped persuade senators to ratify it. But the anti-Johnson House refused to pay for the acquisition for over a year. The president frustrated them by taking possession of Alaska anyway, sending in American forces and raising the U.S. flag at Government House in the capital of Sitka with no objections from the Russians. The House fumed but finally passed the necessary appropriation in July 1868.

After the impeachment attempt failed, Johnson's popularity rose, and he sought another term, but neither party wanted him. Meanwhile General Ulysses S. Grant, hero of the Civil War, aligned himself with the Radical Republicans and was swept to

*Andrew Johnson was the only President who never had any schooling. He developed a passionate, stump-style of speechmaking but hecklers could get his violent temper to explode. Here he speaks at the North Portico on February 22, 1866.* (LIBRARY OF CONGRESS)

victory in 1868. Johnson graciously invited the president-elect to the White House, but Grant, who had previously gotten along well with Johnson, refused to come. In addition, Grant refused to ride to the March 4, 1869, inauguration ceremonies in the same carriage as Johnson or even speak to him. Johnson subsequently decided not to attend the ceremonies and left the White House not a minute sooner than the official end of his term, noon on March 4, 1869. As the clock struck twelve he descended to the north portico, shaking hands and saying good-bye. To Navy Secretary Welles he said, "I can already smell the sweet mountain air of Tennessee."

The Johnsons spent two weeks in Washington before heading for Greeneville's sweet mountain air. Eight years before, a banner reading "Andrew Johnson Traitor" had stretched across the main street. Now he received a festive welcome home, with a banner over the same street reading "Andrew Johnson Patriot." A quiet retirement was not for him—he could not stay out of politics. In March 1875 he returned to Congress as a senator from Tennessee, the only ex-president to enjoy that privilege. He made a dramatic, emotionally charged entrance to the scene of his impeachment trial. The galleries burst into applause, and he was greeted with flowers. He shook hands with old friends and enemies alike. Not long afterward, on July 31, 1875, he died. At his request he was buried in Greeneville, his body wrapped in an American flag, and beneath his head a well-worn copy of the Constitution.

# 18

# Ulysses S. Grant

## 1869–1877

# *A Bright and Beautiful Dream*

WHEN THE CIVIL WAR began in 1861, Ulysses Grant was a thirty-nine-year-old failure. He was clerking in a Galena, Illinois, leather-goods store owned by his father and run by his two younger brothers. By the time the war was over four years later, he would return to Galena a national hero showered with adulation and gifts, including a nicely furnished house. In three more years he would be president of the United States, and living in an even more nicely furnished house at 1600 Pennsylvania Avenue.

Born in 1822 in the trading town of Point Pleasant, Ohio, Grant grew up in relative comfort in Georgetown, where his father became a successful businessman. A timid, naive, almost effeminate youth who was made physically ill by the sight of bloody skins in his father's tannery, Ulysses was nicknamed "Useless." When his father got him an appointment to West Point, Grant told him, "But I won't go." Of course he went. Grant always obeyed. "I have no recollection of ever being punished at home, either by scolding or by the rod," he later wrote. The young cadet's full name was Hiram Ulysses Grant, but the army had him down as Ulysses Simpson—his mother's family name— and he did not object. Soon U. S. Grant became Uncle Sam, or just Sam. At West Point he was uninterested in all things military and earned many demerits, but set the record for high jumping a horse. It was as a cadet that he met his future wife, Julia Dent.

But during the Mexican War, Grant discovered the drama of combat. He himself was one of the "few men" who were, he wrote, "always aching for a fight when no enemy was near, [and] were as good as their word when the battle did come." He spent eleven years in the army and rose to captain, only to resign in disgrace in 1854 because of his drinking, which only became a problem when he was separated from his family on isolated West Coast posts. Over the next several years he tried a variety of occupations. He ran a Missouri farm given to Julia, whom he married in 1848, by her father, collected back rents for a real estate firm, and even sold firewood on the streets of St. Louis. In despair, he sought help from his father, who in 1860 gave him the clerking job in Galena for $800 a year.

The next year Grant left Galena to fight in the Civil War, and distinguished himself in battle early and often through innovation, pragmatism, and sheer fearlessness. He never lost his squeamishness for blood, yet he wasn't afraid to shed it. Critics called General Grant "the butcher," but Lincoln refused to dismiss his commander in chief. "I can't lose this man," the president said. "He fights." Grant became famous for demanding unconditional surrender—his initials were borrowed for the nickname "Unconditional Surrender" Grant. Yet when General Robert E. Lee surrendered to Grant on April 9, 1865, ending the war, Grant was exceptionally generous to his enemy.

Grant now found himself one of the most popular men in American history. But when he came up as a possible Republican presidential candidate, he said, "Being President would be highly unfortunate for myself, if not for the country." He had little incentive to seek the office. An act of Congress had revived the position of lieutenant general, vacant since George Washington, and Lincoln had nominated Grant to fill it. The post was a sinecure worth almost $25,000 a year, and Grant would have to give it up to take the temporary job of president at $50,000 a year. Also, Grant, a shy, private person who avoided controversy and found public life distasteful, was ill suited to politics. He could not bring himself to make a political speech. But few can resist the lure of the presidency, and Grant, in the end, did not. One likely reason he decided he could handle the job was that he believed, as had earlier presidents, in congressional superiority. Congress would run the country while he merely executed its legislation and managed the machinery of government.

Of course the nation elected its idol. Grant, just forty-six years old, would be the first president to complete two terms since Andrew Jackson. On inauguration day he managed to read his short speech. He was always brief. The new president went to the White House to greet the waiting well-wishers, but Julia returned to their house on I Street—another of the three houses bestowed upon her husband by a grateful public. They went together to the inaugural ball that night, but Grant did not dance. "I would rather storm a fort," he said. Nor were he and his wife eager to move from their elegant home into the White House. Julia even considered not moving in at all and using the mansion only for dinners and receptions and as an office, but public opinion dictated otherwise. So she began visiting the White House every day to supervise the changes she had ordered, and she began to appreciate it. "I love the dear old house," she would later say.

Grant married Julia, the sister of a West Point classmate, after a four-year engagement during which they only saw each other once because Grant was fighting in the Mexican War. She called him "Ulys." Julia was described as "plain," and her weight came to equal her husband's. She had been handicapped by badly crossed eyes ever since, as a girl, she was struck in the eye with an oar during a boating party. In order to see across a room, she had to turn her head sideways. To avoid bumping into furniture she developed a crablike, side-to-side walk. At the big receptions she normally stood in one place and was escorted on someone's arm when she had to move. Photographs almost always show her in profile. Near the end of Grant's first term as president she was packing to leave for New York for a corrective eye operation when her husband protested: "I met you and fell in love with you the way you are, and, anyway, I'm not such a handsome fellow myself." She didn't go.

Though self-conscious about her eyes, Julia was neither reticent nor retiring. When she looked the White House over she found much she didn't like. She had the hall carpets replaced, saying they were "much worn and so ugly I could not bear to look at them." Fourteen rooms got new wallpaper. The Blue Room was done over in blue, silver, and gold, with new upholstery in blue satin. A new "reflector" chandelier—a dazzling collection of glass prisms, etched glass, and frosted glass globes—replaced the gilded one that Sarah Polk had loved and refused to convert to gas. The Red Room was hung with a massive portrait of the Grant family that covered over half the wall. She also ordered the original grand staircase redone to create a wider stair with a more gradual descent for the formal entrance of couples. The change also created more room at the top of the stair on the second floor by the big lunette window, which Julia made into a family living area.

Later on, in 1873 and early 1874, the Gilded Age arrived at the White House when the East Room was redone in fashionable "New Grecian" style. The huge room was visually divided into three parts by massive freestanding Corinthian columns topped with beams that spanned the room. Walls were white, but all the relief work was gilded. Plain ceilings were embellished with a Grecian-themed fresco, planned around three vast, thirty-eight-burner gasoliers hung with thousands of faceted glass prisms.

As for the running of the household, Julia was chagrined to find the doormen and messengers lounging about, smoking and eating their lunches in the room off the front entrance. She promptly evicted them and made the room a waiting area for visitors. Doormen, much to their dismay, were outfitted in black dress suits and white gloves. The general's wife forbade loitering and ordered that breaks and meals be taken in the servants' quarters in the cellar. Visitors were subject to new rules as well. She held afternoon receptions for women and required that her guests wear bonnets. "Once in a while," she later recalled, "a lady . . . would impose upon my good nature by attending . . . without a bonnet. . . . This little maneuver was never repeated by the same person."

Julia's social duties also included "calling," a long-standing social custom by which the first lady honored a household. When Julia went out calling, Jerry Smith, a tall, handsome black man who had worked in the stables, accompanied her. Smith, dressed in dark blue livery with silver buttons, helped her out of the carriage, escorted her to the door, then waited to escort her back to the carriage, usually no more than fifteen minutes later. If the lady of the house was not in, or unprepared for callers and therefore not "at home," Smith ceremoniously presented Julia's engraved card, which he carried in a silver case. When pressed for time, as she often was, Julia sometimes sent Smith calling without her, and he would simply present her card. Even a card from the first lady was a flattering recognition.

In the realm of White House entertaining, the Grants had a few things to learn. Their dinners initially catered to the president's own tastes for plain, hearty food—

steaks, roasts, apple pie. He hired his army quartermaster as chef. Because of his aversion to blood, rare meat nauseated him—it had to be charred. He maintained he "could never eat anything that went on two legs," which eliminated all fowl. Julia didn't care for the quartermaster, and White House guests certainly were not accustomed to army-style food, charred or not. She hired restaurateur Valentino Melah, who had worked at the very fashionable Stetson Hotel in the resort town of Long Branch, New Jersey, to produce more sophisticated fare.

State dinners promptly became elaborate, three-hour affairs with up to twenty-nine courses. Each place was set with six wineglasses of varying sizes. The lush setting of the State Dining Room featured the spectacular gilt-bronze plateau purchased fifty years ago by Monroe, which Julia had refurbished and modified to accommodate contemporary floral decorations. Since the White House was once again in need of a china service with enough matching pieces to serve guests, Julia ordered 587 pieces. The scalloped plates were a fashionable "Grecian" earth color, with a gold eagle and shield on the rim, and a cluster of flowers on a white background in the center. The most noted of the Grants' state dinners was held on December 18, 1874, for the first reigning monarch to visit the United States, King Kalakaua of Hawaii. His retinue included a man who stood behind him at the table and examined each dish before placing it before the king.

Yet the Grant White House was very much a family home. The Grants enjoyed and indulged their children, Fred, Ulysses Jr., Nellie, and Jesse. The eldest, Fred, was seventeen when Grant was elected and was in college or away for most of the White House years, but the others lived at the mansion. Ulysses Jr., called "Buck," eventually became his father's personal secretary. Thirteen-year-old Ellen, called "Nellie," was the family's darling. Jesse was the youngest, only eight when his father took office. The three of them went off to school in a yellow wicker pony cart. The family ate nearly every meal together. Breakfast began promptly at eight-thirty, with husband and wife descending to the first-floor family dining room arm in arm for a hearty meal: Spanish mackerel, steak, bacon, fried apples, rolls, buckwheat cakes, and coffee. Grant usually finished first, but always waited to escort Julia back upstairs to the sitting room.

When dining en famille, Grant occasionally entertained the children by rolling the bread into little balls and tossing it at Jesse or Nellie. When he scored a hit, the victim was rewarded with a kiss on the cheek. Once at a formal dinner, the president forgot himself and rolled up a ball of bread and tossed it at Lady Thornton, wife of the British minister. Kisses were not exchanged, and all was forgiven.

The children received many gifts. A Mexican ambassador gave Jesse a parrot. An admirer sent a black Labrador. When it arrived, Grant summoned the White House steward. "Jesse has a new dog," he told him. "You may have noticed that his former pets have been peculiarly unfortunate. When this dog dies, every employee in the White House will be at once discharged." The dog lived for many years after the Grants left Washington.

Jesse's favorite gift was a small but powerful telescope he set up on the White House roof. He and his father became so interested in studying astronomical charts by lantern light that Julia would have to send up a messenger when it was time for Jesse to go to bed.

With all the mail coming into the White House, Jesse took up stamp collecting. He and his cousin, Baine Dent, saved five dollars, a large sum, and sent for a collection of foreign stamps advertised in the newspaper. They waited and waited and nothing arrived. Distraught, Jesse broached his father. "A matter of this importance requires consideration," Grant told him. "Suppose you come to the Cabinet meeting tomorrow and we will take the matter up there." Though the secretary of war and the secretary of state both volunteered to take action, the cabinet decided to turn the matter over to Officer Kelly, a member of the city police force who was assigned to the White House. Using White House stationery, Kelly wrote to the firm: "I am a Capitol Policeman. I can arrest anybody, anywhere, at any time for anything. I want you to send those stamps to Jesse Grant right at once." The stamps arrived in short order.

The extended family included Grant's father, Jesse, who lived in the White House from time to time, even though Grant's mother never visited, and Julia's father, Colonel Dent, who was a fixture during their first term. The colonel was colorful and loved verbal duels, and the sparks flew between the grandfathers. "You should take better care of that old gentleman, Julia," Dent said about Grandfather Grant. "He is feeble and deaf as a post, and yet you permit him to wander all over Washington alone. It is not safe; he should never be allowed out without an attendant." Grant, admittedly deaf, rallied and replied, telling little Jesse, "I hope I shall not live to become as old and infirm as your Grandfather Dent."

Jesse Grant was strongly opposed to slavery, but Colonel Dent was an unreconstructed Confederate rebel. He had owned slaves, and had given slaves to Julia, which Grant, the last slave-owning president, had used when he tried farming in Missouri. Julia did not officially exclude blacks from the White House, but years later she naively observed that no "colored people" came to call during the eight years she presided over the mansion.

The family and social highlight of Grant's administration was Nellie's wedding. Returning home by ship from a trip to Europe at age eighteen, Nellie met and fell in love with a twenty-three-year-old Englishman, Algernon Sartoris. The young man faced the formidable task of entering the office of the president of the United States and announcing to General Grant, "I want to marry your daughter." His reception was not warm. Neither parent favored the marriage, even though Colonel Dent had opposed their own union. The groom's parents were dubious, knowing their son was troubled. The Grants tried to persuade Nellie that she was too young, but she had her way, as she always did.

The White House wedding on May 21, 1874, was the subject of endless public fascination. An elaborate bower of flowers—some blooms were shipped from as far as Florida—was constructed in the East Room. It stood on a dais covered with a rug, a gift from the sultan of Turkey. A huge wedding bell of flowers hung overhead. On the day of the wedding, spectators hoping to catch a glimpse pressed to the fence around the grounds and climbed trees along the streets. Nellie, wearing a $2,000 gown, entered the room on the arm of her father, who, the *New York Herald* noted, "looked steadfastly at the floor." He was later found sobbing in Nellie's room. Nellie and her new husband went home to England, and the marriage would eventually end in divorce.

The attention paid Nellie's wedding was part and parcel of the new spotlight on the White House, which was a more public place than ever before. By the late 1860s national magazines and larger newspapers were emerging, and the country was beginning to take considerably more interest in the White House and the first family. In addition to

*The Grant children, Buck, Nellie, and Jesse, went off to school in a pony cart made of wicker and painted yellow. "Reb" and "Billy Button" provided the pony-power. In the evening the whole family gathered in the upstairs oval room and the children did their homework.* (LIBRARY OF CONGRESS)

news articles on the president, there were now articles on the children, Grant's horses, and the mansion itself. Julia was the first president's wife to give interviews. Local papers across the nation carried the details of clothes-conscious Washington's ball gowns. Emily Edison Briggs of the *Philadelphia Free Press*, writing under the name "Olivia," explained that while private parties were off-limits, the White House was not: "It is public. It belongs to the people. When we go to the White House we go to our own house. . . . Whoever goes to a levee at the Mansion becomes public property, and has no more right to complain because he has been caught in the net of a newspaper's correspondent than the fish who has swallowed the hook of an honest fisherman."

Privacy became an issue, for the family and its guests. The children had no private place to play. When Julia first tried walking with them on the south grounds, she realized that the grounds were open to the public. "Whenever we entered the grounds we were followed by a crowd of idle, curious loungers which was anything but pleasant," she complained. Her husband had the south grounds closed. Every window of the house but those to the north was fitted with shutters, both for security and to shield the interior from prying eyes. Even daytime entertainments were often lighted by gas, with shutters, blinds, or curtains drawn shut.

Grant led a relaxed, family-oriented life. He rose at seven to read the papers before the family breakfast, and took a short walk before starting his workday, typically only four hours, at ten. At noon he went downstairs for lunch with the family. By three he usually called it a day and descended to the basement to cut across the grounds to the stables for a visit with his horses. In the afternoons he sometimes went to the south grounds to watch the baseball games there, even taking a turn at bat or umpiring. Dinner was generally at five, again in the private dining room with the entire family. After dinner the family went upstairs to the Oval Room, where the children did their homework and then were sent off to bed. Grant and Julia returned downstairs to the Red Room, where they often received their friends on weekday nights. The atmosphere was informal—cigars, coffee, tea, brandy. Guests chatted or played parlor games. Grant was naturally taciturn, and Julia had learned to get him talking by starting a story that was familiar to him and intentionally telling it wrong. Grant would tell her she was wrong, and she would say, "Well, how was it then?" and he would tell it. When the president was not entertaining in the evening, he liked to stroll over to the home of Secretary of State Hamilton Fish, on Scott Square. Grant walked around Washington at any hour without a guard. Residents knew him, and he returned their greetings.

Second only to his family were his horses. Grant's fondness for animals developed when he was a small boy without close friends. He had a special knack for horses, and one of the first things he did as president was to have the stables rebuilt and enlarged, and a new walk laid down from the house to the stables. What Grant liked most, according to Colonel William H. Crook, Lincoln's bodyguard, who was now the disbursement officer, was "to sit on the edge of his seat in a light racing buggy, pull the brim of his slouch hat down over his eyes, lean forward until his arms and shoulders were just above the dashboard, and by speaking a few words to the magnificent trotting-horse in front of him, sweep past every other pair of heels that was kicking up the dust of a smooth road." Once he was zipping along on his way back to the White House when a policeman stopped him for speeding. When he recognized the president, he hesitated. "Officer, do your duty," Grant said. He was fined $20. Afterward he wrote to the police department commending the officer who had stopped him. On another occasion three of his horses got loose, and it cost him $6 to get them out of the pound.

After horses, billiards was Grant's favorite pastime. He had a billiard room built right on the main floor of the White House, adjoining the conservatory, where it was easily accessible from the State Dining Room. After dinner the men would retire there to play. If there was no company, wrote Colonel Crook, Grant spent hours there practicing by himself, "puffing clouds of smoke through half-closed lips, while he perfected himself in different shots and combinations." The president liked male company and camaraderie, especially with other former Civil War officers. He spent many evenings hashing over old campaigns, telling stories, and smoking cigars, with everyone forgoing rank and calling each other by last names.

In his last message to Congress, Grant could only say, "It was my fortune, or misfortune, to be called to the office of Chief Executive without any previous political training." General William Sherman, who was close to the president, said, "Grant's whole character was a mystery even to himself—a combination of strength and weaknesses not paralleled." At times Grant was alarmingly naive, made terrible decisions, and was too trusting of and loyal to those around him. Consequently, his administration has been called the most corrupt in U.S. history, though Grant himself was not party to the corruption. (He did not hesitate, however, to give jobs to dozens of relatives; one of them, an Oregon cattle driver, became minister to Guatemala.)

*Grant went to Mount McGregor in the Adirondacks to write his memoirs as he was dying of throat cancer. The hero of the Civil War was addicted to cigars and the adoring public sent him thousands of them.* (LIBRARY OF CONGRESS)

One of the people Grant trusted too easily was Orville Babcock. Grant had known Babcock during the Civil War and made him his private secretary. Babcock was loyal, nonthreatening—and shrewd. He seemed to read Grant's mind and always agreed at the right time. He was also involved in the notorious "Whiskey Ring," by which the nation's big brewers avoided taxes by paying off government officials such as Babcock. When Babcock, among others, was brought to trial in St. Louis, Grant declared his friend innocent despite clear evidence of his guilt. The president even wanted to take the unprecedented step of testifying on behalf of Babcock. He was talked out of it, but gave a deposition that got Babcock off the hook. When Babcock returned to Washington, Grant welcomed him back to his old job as his personal secretary. The vigorous protests of Secretary of State Hamilton Fish and others persuaded Grant to ask for Babcock's resignation. Even then, Grant expressed his "confidence" in Babcock's "integrity and great efficiency" and made him Lighthouse Inspector.

Despite flourishing corruption, powerful leaders continued to back Grant. As his second term drew to a close, the president, only fifty-four years old and in good health, seriously considered calls for him to run for a third term. For his own part, he later recalled, "I never wanted to get out of a place as much as I did to get out of the Presidency." Julia was another matter. Grant knew she loved life in the White House and badly wanted another four years. "It was quite the happiest period of my life," she wrote later. "It was like a bright and beautiful dream and we were immeasurably happy." But one Sunday afternoon cabinet members began arriving and gathering in Grant's office. Julia, curious, followed them in, asking, "Is there any news? Why is it you all happened to call today?" When they lit up cigars, she left the room. After the meeting she accosted her husband. "What is it? Tell me." He revealed that he had written a letter declining the nomination for a third term. Julia demanded to know why he had not shown it to her. Grant said it was already posted and beyond recall, and that if he had allowed her to see it first, he knew he would never have sent it. Julia told her husband she was "deeply injured."

As their train pulled away from the Washington station, she wept. "Oh, Ulys," she said, "I feel like a waif, a waif on the world's wide commons." For the next two years the couple did wander the world, but hardly as waifs. They traveled around the globe and were treated as royalty everywhere they went. Upon returning to America, Grant said, "I have no home but must establish one. I don't know where." In New York rich friends purchased a $100,000 brownstone. Then William K. Vanderbilt lent him $150,000 to invest in a stock brokerage firm to be run by his son Buck and Ferdinand Ward. "Grant and Ward" went bankrupt, Ward went to jail for illegal practices, and the ex-president was left virtually penniless. He gave Vanderbilt his war trophies and gifts from world leaders to cover his loan and began writing his memoirs.

In the spring of 1884 Grant was diagnosed with throat cancer, probably the result of the twenty cigars he had smoked every day since the Civil War. Doctors swabbed his throat with cocaine, but Grant lost his voice completely and had to stop dictating his memoirs. Yet he struggled on, finishing the book nine days before he died on July 23, 1885. *The Personal Memoirs of U. S. Grant* earned his family $450,000 in two years. It ranks high as a memoir and as a testament to Grant's courage and determination.

# 19

# Rutherford Birchard Hayes

## 1877–1881

## *Lemonade*

ON ELECTION NIGHT, November 1876, Democratic candidate Samuel J. Tilden went to bed convinced he had won the presidency, and Ohio governor Rutherford B. Hayes had gone to bed convinced he had lost it. But that night General Daniel E. Sickles, en route to his home from an after-theater supper, stopped at the nearly deserted Republican National Committee headquarters in New York City. The winner needed at least 185 electoral votes. Tilden appeared to have 203. His popular vote margin was more than 250,000. Realizing that if the results came in as expected, Tilden would win, the general wired four states, Florida, South Carolina, Louisiana, and Oregon, telling them, "With your state sure for Hayes, he is elected. Hold your state." So began a scramble. Votes were thrown out as fraudulent, threats were made, corruption was charged. Florida, South Carolina, and Louisiana submitted two sets of electoral votes to Congress, each certified as valid.

Had the race been fair and unfettered by corruption on both sides, Hayes felt he could win. But given the circumstances, he expected to lose, and he wrote to his son Rutherford at Cornell University that it was just as well—he had escaped the anxieties of high office. Then after learning that he might win after all, he tried to stay above the partisan fray while the dispute went to a congressional committee. "I shall keep cool," he said, "and endeavor to act as Washington would have acted under similar circumstances." The country and the Congress, however, were in turmoil. Hayes received threatening letters, and one night while he and his family sat down to dinner at their Columbus home, a bullet crashed through the window. Opposition newspapers fanned the flames by calling him "Rutherfraud B. Hayes." As the inauguration approached, he was urged to sneak into Washington early and unannounced, but he thought it only proper to wait until the election results were official. On March 1 the election was still undecided. He could delay no longer and boarded a train for the capital.

The next morning around dawn, near Harrisburg, Hayes was awakened and given a telegram confirming his victory. The congressional committee had split eight to seven for Hayes on every disputed electoral vote, leaving Hayes with 185 to Tilden's 184 votes.

President Ulysses S. Grant invited Hayes to stay at the White House until the inauguration, but Hayes, wary of the slightest appearance of impropriety, declined. He stayed at the home of a friend, Senator John Sherman. Though seemingly unruffled, Hayes was aware of the danger he might be in and deputized his twenty-one-year-old son Webb, who, armed with a revolver, served as a personal bodyguard.

Because Grant's term ended on a Sunday, Hayes's official swearing in was scheduled for noon on Monday, March 5. But Grant and his secretary of state, Hamilton Fish, decided this was no time to be without a president for twenty-four hours: there were rumblings of violence, rioting, even assassination, and rumors flew that Tilden would find some way to be sworn in on Sunday. They conceived a secret ceremony. Hayes later said, "I did not approve but I acquiesced." On Saturday, March 3, 1877, Hayes appeared at the White House for dinner. Before dinner was served, Grant and Fish led the president-elect out of the dining room. They took a circuitous route to the adjoining Red Room, which had been readied by Julia Grant with floral decorations, and where Chief Justice Morrison R. Waite was waiting for them. The only thing missing was a Bible. They proceeded without it. Hayes took the oath of office, and wrote it out by hand as well. The three men returned to dinner, keeping what they had done to themselves.

On Monday Hayes returned to the White House. He and Grant made their way to the Capitol in a horse-drawn carriage surrounded by six Secret Service agents, who scanned the crowds for assassins. Lincoln's death was not soon forgotten. The president and president-elect walked arm in arm to the inaugural platform, where Chief Justice Waite swore Hayes in again, this time with a Bible. The same carriage took the two men back to the White House, where Julia Grant had a lavish luncheon waiting. Afterward the president and First Lady Lucy Webb Hayes escorted the Grants to the steps of their carriage and bade them farewell.

That afternoon, there was a reception at the White House, and in the evening another at the Willard Hotel. In view of the election dispute, there was no inaugural ball or parade, but there was plenty of celebrating. Mary Clemmer Ames, a friend of Lucy's, wrote, "The city is one blaze of light tonight. For miles the torchlights stream, and the air is all ablaze with red lights and rockets. The mottoes in the windows, the finest flag and streamer flying from the housetops, are as clearly visible as at noonday." Hayes realized his possession of the White House was questionable. In order to ease the opposition to him, he stated publicly and unequivocally that he would serve only one term, and proceeded to carry out his duties with confidence.

As he took office, Hayes was fifty-four years old. He stood about five feet eight inches tall, though he appears taller in photographs, partly due to his fondness for Prince Albert coats. He had a high forehead, and dark blue eyes. His reddish beard, grown when he fought for the Union in the Civil War, had begun to turn gray. Hayes had a solemnity about him—Lucy said he was "always calm"—and could come across as stuffy. The press portrayed him as a man of grim austerity. His unsmiling face seemed to confirm this, but at home with his family, he was relaxed and informal. In the private quarters, he often dressed in worn clothes and his old army boots. He considered it his duty each morning to walk the central corridor—in robe and slippers, hair and beard uncombed—and call out to guests and children to wake up.

The Hayes White House, a warm, friendly, happy home, was always overflowing. The Hayeses had five surviving children. Three boys, Birchard, Webb, and Rutherford, known as "Rud," were born before the Civil War and were young adults by the time their father took office. But the post–Civil War children were young: Fanny was nine, and Scott just six. Lucy invited relatives for long stays—weeks and sometimes months—and even welcomed the daughters of friends. One such young guest was Helen Herron, the future Mrs. William Taft, who promptly fell in love with the White House and determined to come back as first lady.

Adding to the general hubbub were pets: Scott had two dogs and a goat that hauled him around the White House grounds, while Lucy kept a mockingbird and a Siamese cat sent to her from Bangkok by the U.S. consul, who told her it was the first Siamese cat ever sent to America.

The place was so full that when son Rud, who was away at college most of the time, returned to his family, he seldom had a bedroom to himself. "When all the others had been provided for, I curled up on whatever was left and then went to sleep," he recalled. He slept on cots, couches, billiard tables, and in bathtubs. "Even father had virtually no privacy," Rud said. "I have seen him retire to the bathroom, lock the door and prepare some important state paper."

The children were always in evidence. Fanny and Scott were tutored at the house, in a schoolroom improvised in the upstairs corridor. In the winter, the two might be seen sledding on the White House lawn. Fanny received two large dollhouses as gifts from Hayes's admirers and kept them in the upstairs hallway. One was an elaborate three-story Victorian home. Young Scott, according to White House disbursement officer Colonel W. H. Crook, got into "a good deal of trouble" romping about the halls. For Scott's seventh birthday party, a game of blind man's bluff was organized in the East Room. The boy especially enjoyed meeting the delegations of Native Americans that occasionally called on the president. Once a Sioux chief, Red Cloud, patted him on the head and referred to him as a "young brave."

Presiding over it all was Lucy Webb Hayes, whose happy spirit permeated the White House. A graduate of Wesleyan Female College—the first of the presidents' wives to receive a college degree—Lucy had a vibrant, magnetic personality and enjoyed meeting people. When Congress closed the Capitol grounds to the traditional Easter Monday egg roll on April 22, 1878 (the growing horde of children ruined the grass on the steep western lawn), she immediately shifted the event to the White House. Today it is still a celebrated tradition.

Forty-five when her husband took office, Lucy loved being "the first lady of the land"—she was the first "first lady" to be referred to as such in print. She complemented her husband well, and theirs was a fruitful and happy marriage. The couple even renewed their vows at the White House in celebration of their twenty-fifth wedding

*Rutherford B. Hayes liked wine but went along with his wife, "Lemonade" Lucy, when she decided to go beyond banning alcohol, as several other Presidents had done, and exclude wine at state dinners. Friends came to sing hymns with them upstairs at the White House on Sunday evening.* (LIBRARY OF CONGRESS)

anniversary, December 30, 1877. Close relatives and friends, some from the original wedding party, attended the reenactment in the Blue Room. The original minister, Dr. L. D. McCabe, conducted the ceremony again, while niece Laura Mitchell held Lucy's hand, just as she had when she was a little girl. Lucy's brother, Joseph Webb, said his sister was "merry as a girl" in her altered-to-fit twenty-five-year-old wedding dress.

Lucy was five feet four inches tall, and by the time she reached the White House she weighed about 160 pounds. She generally wore her hair parted in the middle and braided in the back with a comb or flower in it. She was very conservative—she had a nude painting called *Love and Life* taken down and put in storage—and so were her dresses. She avoided the décolletage preferred by Mary Lincoln and Julia Grant. The *National Republican* described the gown she wore at her second levee as "a rich garnet velvet dress, trimmed with silk and at her throat a bunch of pink roses nested among the folds of white crepe lisse." Lucy's gowns were also modest in cost, from $100 to $400, and while previous first ladies, such as Mary Lincoln, were censured for their expensive tastes, Mrs. Hayes was sometimes criticized for being cheap.

One of her principal enjoyments was music, especially folk and gospel songs. The family was deeply religious, and, in addition to gathering in the upstairs library to kneel in prayer and listen to a chapter from the Bible each morning, they gathered each evening to sing hymns. Lucy often invited musicians to the White House to perform, and the presidential family were known for their Sunday night "sings," held in the library. Lucy had a beautiful contralto voice, and Secretary of the Interior Carl Schurz, a widower, often played the piano. Vice president William A. Wheeler, also a widower, was a fine tenor, and often brought along *The Presbyterian Hymn and Tune Book*.

Unlike most first ladies, Lucy would have little opportunity to redecorate her new home. The hostile Congress refused even basic upkeep, and the White House was in dire need of attention. Even the plainclothes guards employed to watch over the public rooms could not keep up with the petty thefts by tourists and other visitors. Lucy searched the attic and cellar for usable furniture. Thanks to the souvenir hunters, workmen were patching and painting constantly, with Hayes paying for some of the work himself. Upstairs, new tubs with running water replaced the old copper tubs in the children's bathroom off the upstairs hall. Nothing, it seems, could be done about the rats that had always plagued the White House. Stanley Mathews, a friend from Hayes's college days, and his wife, Mary Ann, told stories of rats so numerous they scampered over the president's bed and even nibbled at his toes.

Despite the impossibility of redecorating, Lucy did make her mark on the White House. When she moved in, she decided the interiors of the house should evoke its history, beginning a trend toward preservation that continues to this day. She persuaded the Library of Congress to fund her efforts to expand the collection of presidential portraits hung in the East Room, and, in a first, began acquiring portraits of former first ladies.

As a hostess, Lucy initiated regular public receptions on Saturdays from 3 to 5 P.M. The guests were "all on an equal footing," reported the *National Republican*, "the ladies generally appearing in street costume and always retaining their bonnets." Lucy received the visitors in the Blue Room, assisted by several young, attractive belles. The big receptions during the winter social season were grand affairs. Guests entered through the Red Room and were led into the Blue Room, where they stood in a receiving line to greet the president and first lady before continuing through the Green Room into the East Room. Colonel Thomas L. Casey, in his role as commissioner of public buildings and grounds, introduced each guest to the president. Lucy generally stood at her husband's side, and shook so many hands that her white gloves lost their shape and color. Those on intimate terms with the first family could go "behind the lines"—that is, behind the receiving line, indicating family or VIP status—where Lucy's young belles waited to greet them. No one was ever turned away—the reception didn't end until the last caller was greeted.

At one reception Lady Thornton, wife of British minister Sir Edward Thornton, had to leave early and, wishing to do so unobtrusively, apologetically asked to be guided to a side door. Lucy put Lady Thornton in the hands of her son Rud. Normally the only door used by the president and his guests was the front door at the north entrance. Luckily, Rud had explored every inch of the mansion. "I recalled a door near the coal-bin, and led her through the dark, musty basement and let her out of this door," Rud later said. "She was very jolly and laughed heartily over the escapade. I have no doubt she often told of her experience, when attending dignified courts in Europe, as showing the simplicity of the life of the ruler of the young giant among nations."

White House entertainments under the Hayeses were set apart by their ban on all alcohol. Presidents Polk, Taylor, and Fillmore had banned hard liquor, but the Hayeses frowned upon wine as well, quite altering the character of state dinners. Many White House visitors, especially Europeans, were sorely tried, as they considered wine an essential part of a meal—especially an official affair, which could run to three hours. The White House was widely ridiculed. Even Secretary of State William Evarts joked of one dinner, "The water flowed like champagne." The Hayeses replaced the traditional after-dinner drinking session with a promenade along the paths of the plant-filled conservatories, gaslit for the evening. When the president and first lady returned to the foot of the grand staircase, they said their goodnights and ascended to the family quarters. The evening was over by ten.

An exception to the no-alcohol rule was made on August 19, 1877, when the Hayeses gave a formal dinner honoring the visiting Grand Duke Alexis of Russia. Evarts was concerned about the royal guest facing a "cold water" meal. The president's close friend Stanley Mathews warned him, "A dinner without wine would be an annoyance, if not an affront." Hayes relented on this occasion—and this occasion only. The State Dining Room was elegantly decorated with colorful floral arrangements and ropes of smilax (though one woman reporter commented on the shabbiness of the carpet), and at each of the thirty-six place settings were six wineglasses, apropos the many courses to come. The president and first lady abstained, but the temperance societies were nevertheless indignant over the event.

The temperance movement was gaining momentum nationwide, and from that quarter the first family was much praised for its ban. Hayes went along, even though he had always welcomed what he called a "schoppen" of beer with his friends in Cincinnati, and he continued to oppose Prohibition legislation. Lucy was the real teetotaler. The newly formed Woman's Christian Temperance Union (WCTU) adopted her as their own.

Quickly dubbed "Lemonade Lucy," the first lady had an uneasy relationship with the WCTU. The organization wanted to recognize her with a gift and proposed erecting a drinking fountain on the White House lawn. The president exercised his veto power, suggesting instead a memorial picture. Lucy agreed hesitantly; she disliked what she termed "notoriety" of any sort. To pay for the picture WCTU sent out a fund-raising letter, which, to Lucy's consternation, suggested that contributions could be as low as ten cents. To a wealthy woman, soliciting meager sums of money was demeaning. Lucy and the president were further embarrassed to learn that the organization was using the portrait as a gimmick to raise funds to finance temperance publications. "This begging is painful for me," Lucy said. Hayes requested that the WCTU halt the fund-raising with "as little publicity and friction as possible" once enough money was raised for the painting. In the end, the family liked Daniel Huntington's flattering portrait of Lucy, lovely in a wine-colored dress. As young Fanny said, "Mama's picture is perfectly splendid." The formal presentation of the portrait wasn't made until March 8, 1881, after the Hayeses had left the White House. The painting hangs in the White House today.

Unlike some temperance women, Lucy was not militant about her position. On one occasion, she and the president were guests at a shipboard dinner where claret punch was available in the lower cabin before, during, and after the meal. In what she intended as a private conversation, Lucy said, "I want people to enjoy themselves in the manner that is most pleasing to them." When the remark became public, the Lucy Hayes Temperance Society in Washington dropped her name.

Like Lucy, Hayes was affable and at ease in all levels of society, and even as president he enjoyed traveling incognito and talking informally with people from all walks of life. In 1879, as he traveled to Philadelphia by train, day coach, to spend Thanksgiving with the family of Methodist bishop Matthew Simpson, a clerk from a wholesale firm sat next to him. "I got much interesting information about his business and the trade generally," Hayes said.

New ideas fascinated the president, and he had wide-ranging interests. He liked everything from musicales to sports, travel to books—his Ohio home housed a collection of six thousand. When he learned that Thomas A. Edison was demonstrating his new phonograph at the Capitol, Hayes wanted to see it. At about 11 P.M. Edison received word that the president would be pleased to see him at the White House. Edison of course went, and Hayes was so excited by the phonograph that he sent word up to Lucy, who was already in bed, to come down. She and some of the other ladies in the house got dressed. The thirty-one-year-old genius didn't leave the White House until 3:30 A.M. Another new instrument that caught the president's attention was the telephone. He had tried it out on his travels to New England and ordered one installed in the White House. The phone hung on the wall of the telegraph room, near the offices, with a wire trailing out the window to the nearby Treasury Department, but it was hardly practical. Few people had phones, and there were no operators. But it was fun to sing songs over the phone. Once, a quartet of the Hayeses friends was singing "The Grave Digger" into the White House phone. Lucy wanted more volume, so one of the four, W. A. Widney, struck a high C, shattering the soundboard of the new telephone.

If the phone was more useful for entertainment than business, no matter: the business side of the White House was still a relatively small operation. A staff of nine helped Hayes run the government. Prior to the Civil War, the presidents paid their private secretaries out of their salaries. Oftentimes they filled the job with a family friend or a son. Now, it was a government-paid position. Hayes needed a strong adviser for the post, but several capable people turned him down, as they considered the position beneath them. He ended up with William K. Rogers, an old friend who was loyal, but often ill and not especially competent. He once turned away Mark Twain, a Hayes supporter, because he confused the writer with someone else. Hayes's son Webb eventually came to live at the White House and acted as a kind of unofficial secretary. The government also paid each of two executive clerks $2,000 a year to answer routine mail, screen visitors, and copy the president's letters and papers. Hayes did not like to dictate letters, and the typewriter was just coming into use, so he wrote everything out.

Though still small, the office staff now overflowed into the office waiting area at the east end of the upstairs hall, which had niches for people like the telegrapher. The children's bedrooms opened onto this hall, and they had to go through it to get to the water closet, although a partition separated the main bedroom area from the business offices. And the president could get from his office on the south side of the hall to the private living area without going through the hall by using a private door from the cabinet room to the upstairs Oval Room. To the extent that the offices encroached on the living space, the situation was relieved by the fact that Hayes, in a radical change from previous administrations, admitted office seekers by appointment only. The offices, historically overrun, became far less hectic and crowded.

In addition to the office staff, there were about twenty other government-paid workers in the White House, all directed by Colonel Thomas Casey, the commissioner of public buildings and grounds. These included a doorkeeper with four assistants, a messenger also with four assistants, two of whom were mounted, a watchman, a fireman, and kitchen help. In the stables was a coachman who earned $60 a month, and a hostler (a horse tender) at $30 a month. Cooks earned $30 a month, and the laundresses $20 to $30, but Hayes added an extra $5 of his own to all of their paychecks.

Also on the government payroll was a clock winder, Oscar L. Berger. There were clocks all over the house, including the famous, French-made Hannibal and Minerva clocks purchased by James Monroe. Some of the clocks could not be reached without a ladder, and many had heavy glass covers that had to be removed in order to wind them. Hayes paid for some of the White House servants entirely out of his own pocket because he believed they shouldn't be on the federal payroll.

The key person in the entire operation was the steward. He was held responsible for all government property, hired caterers and other extra help for the state dinners, and ordered all the food. The president was obligated to provide meals for all the household employees—about two thousand meals a month. Hayes was probably the wealthiest of the nineteenth-century presidents, having inherited the bulk of Uncle Sardis's estate in 1874. He felt no need to conserve his $50,000 salary and didn't skimp. He spent $8,000 to $9,000 a year on food for staff, family, official functions, and a certain amount of charity. Lucy was known to order the steward to send out wagons loaded with food for the poor. Grant had purchased food from the army commissary at cost, but Hayes refused to do this. Instead he had the steward order from the local markets, "like other men." But he thought steward John A. Simms was accepting too much in commissions from the vendors he did business with. In June 1879 Simms was replaced by William T. Crump, who had been an orderly for Hayes during the Civil War.

Hayes also brought his own domestic servants with him from Ohio, including Winnie Monroe and her daughter. Winnie, a cook and nurse, had lived in the Hayes home in Cincinnati for several years. At the White House, Hayes put her on the federal payroll at $30 a month and added $20 more from his own pocket. Winnie found life in the nation's capital to her liking. She referred to herself as "the fust culled lady in the lan'!" A large, pleasant woman, she was a good cook and good with the children. When Mr. and Mrs. Hayes went on an extended trip to the west coast, she took care of Fanny and

Scott. She tended to argue with her boss, Crump, and with her coworkers, which made problems for Lucy. When Hayes's term ended, Winnie returned to Ohio with the family, but she must have found it a letdown, because she returned to Washington and lived there on her own until she died. Hayes paid the funeral expenses of $70.

The largest single White House expense was the conservatories—Lucy loved flowers. The staff of ten, also directed by Colonel Casey, included a head gardener (Henry Pfister, a well-known Cincinnati florist), a fireman, a bouquet maker, and a lady with a horse and cart who delivered Lucy's floral gifts. Each day the first lady sent out as many as twenty bouquets accompanied by an engraved White House card. It was a pleasant substitute for calling in person. Lucy often visited the conservatories twice a day, morning and afternoon, to choose bouquets and to decide on the floral arrangements that decorated nearly every White House room.

The conservatories were on the roof of the West Wing and leaned against the upper west side of the house, so they were directly accessible from the main floor. To make them even more accessible, Hayes set up a billiard room in the basement carriage passage between the house and the West Wing and tore down the one his predecessor built off the State Dining Room, constructing a plant room in its place. Now, the series

*During the Hayes administration, White House servants included five doorkeepers, a watchman, a fireman, and five messengers, two of whom were mounted.* (LIBRARY OF CONGRESS)

of twelve conservatories could be entered directly from the dining room. The conservatories were particularly appreciated for their moist heat in winter, when the furnace-cooked air in the mansion was so dry that furniture came unglued and skin cracked. Yet the heating system barely affected some parts of the house. Hayes recorded in his diary on January 3, 1879, that the temperature in the vestibule of the main, or north, entrance was three degrees below zero.

The summer White House had other discomforts. In the hot months, the family was affected by the malaria that was chronic in the city. "No doubt I am somewhat affected by the Washington malaria," Hayes wrote in his diary. "Symptoms, slight headache at night—bad dreams, a tendency of the blood to the head—flushed face at times . . . not serious, but I shall be glad to get away next month." The Hayeses, in keeping with the tradition started by Buchanan, retreated to a government house at the Soldiers' Home, a retirement place for disabled soldiers located in Maryland, just outside the District of Columbia. The president and his son Webb would ride to the White House to work each day.

When Hayes could get home to Spiegel Grove, his twenty-five-acre estate, near Fremont, Ohio, the days typically revolved around the outdoors. Hayes loved hunting, fishing, swimming, and skating, and was a good shot with a rifle. "There is not enough exercise in this way of life," he complained of his White House years as a heavy diet slowly pushed his weight from 180 to 192 pounds. He did calisthenics each morning before breakfast, walked rapidly through the lower hall five or ten minutes before each meal, and generally went for a long walk later in the day. Lucy too enjoyed the outdoor life. While on a summer vacation at Saranac Lake, in northern New York State, with her daughter Fanny in 1878, she hooked a fifteen-pound trout, which she sent back to the White House for her husband's dinner.

The summer getaways were not respite enough for Hayes. To escape the pressures of office, he did more traveling than any president before him. The *Chicago Tribune* called him "Rutherford the Rover." Lucy said he was "scenery mad," although many of his shorter trips were to ceremonies or dedications. Hayes defended his trips: "You have no idea how much they are needed. Eight months of wearying worry over details is enough to kill a strong man. Every month a man in this place ought to shake off its oppression. Nothing does it better than a 'popular bath,' a 'junketing,' or a journey."

In September 1878 Hayes traveled as far west as Dakota Territory, but waited to take a full cross-country holiday until the end of his term. In part, as he had willingly agreed to serve only one term, he wanted to be out of the way while his friend James Garfield campaigned. He departed Washington August 26, and when he returned seventy-two days later, he had traveled ten thousand miles. He was the first president to visit the West Coast while in office. Lucy of course went with him, as did sons Rud and Birchard, niece Laura Mitchell, and valet Isaiah Lancaster. In all there were nineteen family and staff.

They traveled by train, stagecoach, army ambulance, ferryboat, tug, and ocean steamer. In Echo Canyon, Utah, Rud and Birchard rode on the cowcatcher at the front end of the locomotive, while their mother and father rode with the engineer in the cab. From northern California to Oregon they were in a stagecoach with army chief of staff general William Tecumseh Sherman up front riding shotgun beside the coachman. Most nights were spent on army posts or as guests of friends, but in the little mining town of Jacksonville they stayed at Madame de Robaum's boardinghouse. The next morning she astounded them by presenting an exorbitant bill—$100 for five overnight guests. One of the president's traveling companions, John Herron, gave Madame $25 and told her they didn't want to buy her boardinghouse. In New Mexico Territory they entered a dangerous area of Apache raiders and white outlaws where there was no railroad. They rode in horse-drawn army ambulances with a heavy military guard, camping overnight until they reached a railhead. They went on to Santa Fe, where they witnessed a colorful fiesta, and then took a train back home to Ohio in time to vote for Hayes's successor, James Garfield, on November 2.

With the Republican victory, the president felt vindicated in his policies. He was satisfied with his achievements and said he looked forward to the end of his term "as a schoolboy longs for the coming vacation. . . . I am tired of this life of bondage, responsibility, and toil." Lucy wholeheartedly agreed: "I am getting more and more anxious to get home . . . though I am sure no one ever had a happier time [at the White House] than I have had." Their last reception, in February 1880, brought out "the largest and gayest throng of the year," Hayes wrote in his diary. "Many could not get in, and left without reaching the door. Others got in and left without entering the Blue Room— going out through windows because they could not get out at the door."

In retirement Hayes lived at his Ohio estate, Spiegel Grove, and traveled to support many of the causes that interested him, such as education and prison reform. As always, he was active in the affairs of Civil War veterans. In these last years of his life he proclaimed, "The two happiest people in the country are here in Spiegel Grove." He died on January 17, 1893.

# 20

# James Garfield

## March 4–September 19, 1881

## *Death Watch*

ONE WEEK after his inauguration, James Garfield wrote his brother-in-law, "We envy you the restful quiet which does not yet live in this house." In the six months before his assassination, he would not have a chance to find that peace.

In the beginning, though, Garfield seemed blessed. The last of the log cabin presidents, he was a rags-to-riches icon in an era that venerated Horatio Alger's self-made man. Indeed Garfield's campaign biography, *From Canal Boy to President,* was written by Alger. Garfield was willing to make political hay out of his humble origins, but he never glossed over the hardships he endured. "I lament sorely that I was born to poverty," he wrote. "In the little great things of life . . . How sadly weak and inferior I feel. Let us never praise poverty."

Eighteen months after he was born, his father died, and his mother labored alone to eke out a living for herself and four children on their thirty-acre farm. At sixteen he left to make his fortune, finding employment as a lowly canal tow boy in Cleveland, Ohio. Through hard work and determined saving he graduated from Williams College, becoming a teacher, then president of Ohio's little Hiram College. In 1858 he married Lucretia "Crete" Rudolph. Garfield went on to be a Union general in the Civil War and then was elected to the United States House of Representatives for seventeen years. He prospered, but unlike Hayes he was far from wealthy. A grand house like the White House was certainly a step up.

Having withheld money for decorating and upkeep from Hayes, Congress welcomed Garfield with a $30,000 appropriation. Before making any changes, Garfield and Crete decided to research the history of the house. They consulted with A. R. Spofford, the librarian of Congress, who agreed to gather the relevant books and documents. The first lady traveled to New York to call on decorators and furniture warehouses, and invited several firms to send representatives to the White House.

Family life hummed along. Only fifty-two when he entered the White House, Garfield still had young children. His two eldest boys, Harry and Jim, had tutors and were preparing for college. Mollie, fourteen, took lessons on the grand piano and walked to Madam Burr's school. The youngest, nine-year-old Abram, invited his friends over to race bicycles in the big East Room with its smooth carpet, gouging the fine wainscoting. Eleven-year-old Irvin was more of a daredevil. He liked to coast down the grand staircase and through the marble corridor, then barrel into the East Room yelling for visitors and office seekers to get out of the way. High-wheeled bicycles, or velocipedes, were new at the time, and even the clerks practiced in the East Room when the first family was away. Garfield's mother also lived in the White House, and occasionally took her place in the receiving line, seated in a chair. When she grew tired, her son carried her upstairs to her room.

Garfield himself relaxed over the billiard table, but White House life had its cares—and its expenses. Though no longer poor, Garfield, unlike his rich predecessor, relied on his $50,000-a-year salary, which had to cover staff, food, and entertaining. Hayes had found that a single reception could cost as much as $2,400. The staff of fifty included ten gardeners, an assortment of cooks, bakers, and maids, and even a barber. The telephone was so new that few people owned one, so messengers were still a necessity. The White House had five, two of whom were mounted on horseback. The stables were another major expense. Garfield had never been able to afford a horse and carriage, and transportation was now essential. Fortunately Rutherford Hayes, who liked Garfield, loaned his own elegant $1,150 carriage.

Another cause for worry was the decision on whether to serve wine at the White House. In keeping with the burgeoning temperance movement, the Hayeses had banned all alcohol from the White House, and had been both praised and ridiculed for doing so. Garfield had no strong feelings either way. Frances Willard, leader of the Woman's Christian Temperance Union, was among those who tried to sway the president toward abstinence, and she wasted no time. Four days after Garfield's March 4, 1881, inauguration, she and fifty temperance women converged on the East Room, ostensibly for the presentation of a full-length portrait of "Lemonade Lucy" Hayes, and proceeded to harangue him with their views. Garfield nevertheless decided to resume serving wine only, but he was never to give a state dinner, and the bottles remained unopened.

But the real bane of Garfield's presidency was the office seekers who lined up at the White House to vie for jobs. From the first day he was overwhelmed by "the Spartan band of disciplined office hunters, who drew papers on me, as highwaymen draw pistols . . . with whom I had to wrestle like a Greek." The president was soon suffering from both insomnia and depression. "Four hours sleep only," he confided to his diary. "The crowd of callers commenced early and continued in great force." To his secretary he said, "These people would take my very brain, flesh and blood if they could. They are wholly without mercy." The two factions of his own party—called the Stalwarts and the Half Breeds—were eternally squabbling over appointments. Like several presidents before him, he began to wonder why he had wanted high office in the first place: "My God! What is there in this place that a man should ever want to get into it?"

While her gregarious husband enjoyed White House receptions, Crete, a shy woman, found them trying, not to mention exhausting. She once endured four days of back-to-back diplomatic, military, and public receptions, shaking hands for hours in the receiving line alongside her husband. She wrote after one of these, "Before the first hour was over, I was aching in every joint, and thought how can I last through the next long sixty minutes." She disliked the lack of privacy. A staff member recalled a visitor who "pushed himself in past the doors that marked the private domain of the family and took his afternoon siesta upon the most comfortable sofa he could find."

In early May, all the pleasures and discomforts of the White House were suddenly inconsequential. Crete became seriously ill. Her recurring headaches had been blamed on the sewer odors from the city's primitive sanitation system, which drifted over the malarial swamps south of the house and in through her bedroom window. Her bedroom was moved to the north side, but on April 25 she developed a fever that reached 104 degrees. In coming days, she was barely conscious, clumps of her hair fell out, and she was believed close to death. Garfield was beside himself.

With Crete he shared an intellectual kinship and religious faith—the two belonged to the Disciples of Christ sect. But the couple's closeness had been tested from the start. Crete was considered somewhat plain, and during their courtship Garfield, who had no trouble attracting women, admitted he felt no "delirium of passion" for her. He had affairs before and during his marriage, eventually making a promise to reform and keeping it. Now he paced the floor at night, and at times fell to his knees, praying and sobbing. As he kept his vigil, Crete gradually improved, and it was decided that she should go to the New Jersey seashore to convalesce.

On June 18 Garfield escorted his wife to the Washington train station. Unknown to him, Charles Guiteau, an office seeker who believed that "[the] world owes me a 'living,' " followed, pistol in his pocket. Guiteau failed to shoot, he said later, because "Mrs. Garfield looked so thin, and she clung so tenderly to the President's arm that I did not have the heart to fire upon him."

Guiteau's association with the president had begun with a courteous note: "What do you think of me for Consul General at Paris?" He got in line at the White House, and when ushered into the president's office presented Garfield with a copy of a campaign speech he'd written for Garfield and had printed. He wrote "Paris Consulship" on the cover, expecting Garfield to be impressed. He was polite and left without pressuring the president further. In the months preceding the shooting, Guiteau's almost daily letters were filed by clerks into what they called the "eccentric file," which was full of prophesied catastrophies, threats to blow up the White House, the ravings of a mad scientists named Frankenstein, and more. Guiteau also spent a good deal of time at the mansion, simply lounging for a few hours, sometimes using the White House stationery, which was easily accessible. At his trial he would later testify that he once attended a White House reception and managed to talk with Crete, whom he deemed "quite chatty and companionable." After being told that his application had been turned over to the State Department, he pestered Secretary of State James G. Blaine so much that

Blaine finally exploded: "Never speak to me again on the Paris consulship as long as you live."

Guiteau had become well known to the White House staff, and the ushers and doorkeepers—the closest thing to guards—were instructed to keep him out. On May 13 he had a row with one of the doorkeepers. White House disbursement officer Colonel W. H. Crook saw him coming out of the White House that day. He asked the doorkeeper, "What does that fellow want here today? I thought we got rid of him." "He came as usual," the doorkeeper answered, "and asked how the President was." Although the term "guard" had always been avoided at the White House, it was understood that the ushers and doorkeepers should keep out undesirables.

Garfield had rejected a proposal to station uniformed guards in the White House because he felt they would create the wrong image: the President's House was the people's house and should be open to them. Despite Lincoln's assassination, Garfield and the country persisted in the notion that guards were for European monarchies, not the Republic, with its democratically elected chief executive. Colonel Crook had served as a personal bodyguard for several presidents, but usually for ceremonial occasions only, and never in uniform. Garfield even walked the streets of Washington alone at night. He also shared the fatalistic thinking of many presidents, Lincoln and Kennedy included. "Assassination can no more be guarded against than can death by lightning," he said, "and it's best not to worry about either." Garfield's murder would finally shock America into action on civil service reform, by which government jobs would be filled competitively rather than by appointment.

But Guiteau was not merely a disappointed office seeker. He was a deeply disturbed and mentally unbalanced man whose life had been a long succession of failures and irrational acts. In his autobiography, published while he was in prison, he stated his long-held belief that he would become president: "My idea is that I shall be nominated and elected as Lincoln and Garfield were—that is, by an act of God." He convinced himself that he had been instrumental in Garfield's successful campaign and should be rewarded with a job. He was broke and desperate. And on the night of May 18, as he lay on his cot in a boardinghouse, an impression entered his mind, as he described it, "like a flash." If Garfield were "removed"—he avoided the word *killed*—"this whole thing would be solved and everything would go well." Other flashes convinced him that it was God's will. He managed to borrow enough money to buy a gun, and on June 6 paid $10 for the largest revolver in the display case, a .44 caliber British bulldog. He paid an extra dollar for a wooden handle, which he figured would be more appropriate for the gun's eventual display in a museum. The salesman helpfully showed Guiteau, who had never fired a gun, how to load the cartridges. Guiteau also inspected the jail where he anticipated—correctly—ending up, just to be sure it was adequate.

Now began almost a month of stalking the president. In addition to the day at the railway station, Guiteau passed over several opportunities to kill him. After following Garfield to church one Sunday, Guiteau, no marksman, determined that the angle was bad. It was a disappointment, as he felt there was "no more sacred place for removing him." He sometimes sat on a bench in Lafayette Square across from the White House, occasionally calling across to the gatekeeper to ask where the president was. One night he saw Garfield come out of the mansion alone. He followed him to Secretary of State Blaine's house on Fifteenth Street. Soon Blaine and Garfield came out and walked arm in arm through the park. Again Guiteau did nothing, later explaining only that the night was very hot and humid.

At Garfield's last cabinet meeting before he left to join Crete at the Jersey shore, he asked Secretary of War Robert Todd Lincoln to relate the premonitory dream his father had shortly before his assassination. Just before his own inauguration, Garfield had experienced a period of nightmares and was overcome with a sense of foreboding. But on the day of his departure, July 2, the president was exuberant. He found his young sons doing somersaults on their beds and amazed the boys by doing a handspring, then singing loudly with them. On his way out, he joyfully shook hands with the White House staff, which had lined up to see him off.

Guiteau of course knew that Garfield was leaving town, and that the time had come to act. He arrived at the train station well before the president and arranged for a hackman to hold a cab so that when his job was done, he could escape what would likely be a lynch mob. He promised the hackman an extra $2—which he didn't have—to wait, and told him he would be going to the Congressional Cemetery. From there he intended to run to the nearby jail and turn himself in. With his plan in order, he had his shoes shined and asked a newsstand attendant to hold a package for him. It contained a brief autobiography and instructions for depositing all his writings and his revolver in the State Department library. He expected authorities would quickly discover the package, and they did.

When Garfield entered the train station waiting room with Blaine, the assassin was ready. Garfield and Blaine were arm in arm, talking, when Guiteau approached from the rear, extended his arm straight out, and fired from only three feet away. Garfield's hat flew off, and he flung his arms upward. "My God! What is this?" he exclaimed. As he fell Guiteau fired a second shot. Guiteau calmly placed his weapon back in his pocket and headed for his cab. Before he could reach it, a policeman, Patrick Kearney, nabbed him and hurried him off to the nearby police station amid the anticipated cries of "Lynch him!" On the way, Guiteau tried to give his act an improbable political twist. "I am a Stalwart," he said, referring to the Republican faction. "Arthur is now President of the United States." A jury would later find Guiteau sane and order him hanged.

Garfield lay on the floor of the waiting room, pale and bathed in sweat, his breathing labored. One bullet had grazed his arm, and the other had entered his back just to the right of the spine. The matron of the ladies' waiting room cradled his head in her lap. Robert Todd Lincoln had come to see the president off, and so was on the scene for the shooting. "How many hours of sorrow I have passed in this town," said Todd, who had been by his father's side when he died in a boardinghouse outside Ford's Theater. (Chance would put Robert Lincoln at the scene of a third assassination, William McKinley's in 1901.)

Doctors materialized and immediately began a lengthy probing for the bullet with unwashed hands and instruments. They concluded that the slug had gone through an organ and that the president would not live out the day. Garfield evidently heard or sensed their verdict, for when one of the doctors tried to encourage him, he said, "I thank you doctor, but I am a dead man." Mattresses taken out of a Pullman car were laid on a baggage wagon, and Garfield was gently moved to an upstairs bedroom at the White House. Some two dozen doctors came and went, each probing for himself, each agreeing that it was hopeless. Dr. D. W. Bliss, who Garfield eventually put in charge in order to cut down the number of examinations, announced, "There is no hope for him. He probably will not live three hours and may die in half an hour. The bullet pierced the liver and it is a fatal wound." Bliss bristled when Dr. John H. Baxter, Garfield's family doctor, arrived on the scene. "Yes, I know your game," Bliss told him. "You wish to sneak up here and take the case out of my hands." Threatened with forceful eviction, Dr. Baxter left. Meanwhile, a private train hurried Crete back to Washington from the New Jersey shore. When she arrived the next day, Garfield's pulse and temperature were near normal, and Dr. Bliss now assured her that recovery was probable. More doctors arrived, and Garfield submitted to their examinations. One doctor, a leading surgeon from New York, ventured, "Ultimate recovery is beyond all reasonable doubt."

Over the first part of July, Garfield did appear to be mending. On July 13 Dr. Bliss informed the public that "gradual progress toward complete recovery is manifest and thusfar without serious complications." The team of doctors was still preoccupied with the missing bullet, though the president's improving condition would indicate that it had become encysted and was doing no further harm. The doctors' continued investigations, performed with unwashed hands and instruments on their unanesthetized patient, were another matter. American doctors had yet to accept antiseptic surgery, though its inventor, Joseph Lister, had lectured in the United States a few years before. One day Dr. Bliss thought he had found the bullet's path when his instrument suddenly slipped downward. He pushed it forward through some muscle tissue until it became stuck between the fragments of a rib, and he had a difficult time extracting it.

Garfield seems to have been uncomplaining, always thanking the doctors. Crete visited him regularly, but his doctors thought it best to ban all his male friends, including Blaine. By now, Garfield had been on his back for weeks, immobile except for the painful shifting of his body every hour or so to prevent bedsores, and he begged for the company of his friends. Instead, the doctors ordered screens put up around his bed and soldiers stationed at all the doors. His wound was dressed daily, and his feet were rubbed, as they became numb. He was given quinine to prevent malaria. He had trouble with solid food, so the doctors prescribed lime water, milk (from the White House cow), and oatmeal, which Garfield hated. They also tried rectal feeding. What Garfield really wanted was something he remembered fondly from his younger days: squirrel soup. The commandant of the Soldiers' Home, where presidents of the era often lived during the summer, rushed through a permit for Colonel Crook to shoot squirrels on the grounds of the mansion, but somehow Garfield never got his soup.

There was one more attempt to find the elusive bullet, this time employing the latest, noninvasive, technology. Alexander Graham Bell rigged up an electrical induction system that, connected to a telephone receiver, served as a rudimentary metal detector. In the presence of metal, the coiled detectors generated a faint humming sound in the receiver. Garfield was propped up in bed, and Bell stood behind him with the receiver as an assistant moved the coils over the president's body. Bell believed he heard a hum. Even Crete listened. But the surgeons, no doubt a bit skeptical, said it was too dangerous to operate at the place indicated. As an autopsy was to prove later, both Bell and the doctors were mistaken about the bullet's location.

Garfield's discomfort increased with the infamous Washington heat and humidity, not to mention the stench from the malarial flats beyond the south grounds. By now the entire city was plagued by fevers and loose bowels, and even the drinking water in

*Mortally wounded by an assassin and suffering in the heat and humidity of Washington, Garfield longed for the healing airs of the New Jersey shore. Finally his doctors agreed that he could be moved from the White House, a scene depicted here. The president was carefully placed in a carriage bound for the train station. Horsecar tracks on Pennsylvania Avenue were covered with sawdust so to smooth his ride to the station.* (CORBIS)

Garfield's room looked and tasted foul. All this was what he had been trying to escape by going to the seashore. The doctors didn't want the president moved, so engineers found an innovative, if elaborate, means of reducing the heat and humidity. They filled a large chest with six tons of ice. Fans pushed air over the ice, through a cast iron chamber filled with hanging strips of terry cloth, and on into the bedroom.

The daily medical bulletins remained cheerful, but Garfield was failing. As summer wore on, it became clear that the wound was not draining properly, and that secondary areas of infection were developing. Garfield's weight dropped from over 200 pounds to 130. Finally the medical team relented and granted the president's wish to escape to the New Jersey shore and its sea breezes. On September 6, in the midst of a heat wave, Garfield was transferred to a railway baggage wagon to begin the move to the seaside town of Elberon. Most states held a day of prayer, and the worried nation came to a virtual standstill. Rutted street intersections were covered with sawdust to smooth the ride, and rail tracks were extended to avoid cobblestones. All traffic was banned from streets being traveled by the president. To reduce smoke and soot, the train engine burned only anthracite coal. In the baggage car, seats were removed to make room for a bed on springs, which was set over boxes of ice. A pilot engine preceded the president's train to warn other trains to stop and to prevent them from sounding their whistles. The night before, hundreds of men had quickly laid a spur almost two miles long from the main rail line to the door of Francklyn Cottage, the twenty-two-room seaside home where Garfield would be staying. Hundreds of willing hands pushed the railway car the last few hundred feet.

A joyful Garfield rallied once more. The ever-helpful Dr. Bliss announced that the most miraculous cure in medical history was imminent, and set about drastically reducing the size of his staff. But Garfield soon relapsed, this time for good. He died September 19 of an aneurysm and blood poisoning.

Modern medicine could have saved Garfield. He died not of the wound, but from infection, no doubt from the numerous septic probings. One respected physician of the time wrote, "It is indeed humiliating to the historian to record such a mass of irretrievable blunders," and cited specifically "the repeated introduction of fingers, probes and catheters." A significant number of doctors concurred. Guiteau even denied he killed the president: "The doctors did that. I simply shot at him." In view of Garfield's death—and of the accusations of incompetence, perhaps—Congress slashed the fees charged by his doctors. Garfield might have died even without all the extra medical attention lavished on him as president, but his last days probably would have been less painful were he an ordinary citizen.

Fortunately for the country, the entire eighty-day episode took place during summer, when Congress was out of session. The government had little difficulty operating without a president—or an acting president. During the days of Garfield's lingering decline, the cabinet had been in full agreement that Vice President Chester Arthur should act as president, but Arthur refused. Among other things, Arthur had made no secret of his contempt for Garfield, and Guiteau's wild statement about making Arthur president had put him in a delicate position. In any case, Garfield's medical team felt that such action could be shocking to him and might even kill him.

The president's body was transferred to Washington, where it was placed in the Capitol rotunda. For two days some seventy thousand mourners filed by the coffin. Then he was returned to Cleveland, where a pavilion nearly one hundred feet high had been erected not far from the dock where, thirty-three years before, a young Garfield had been a canal boy. Capped by a huge angel on top of a gilt ball, the pavilion was draped in black and decked with flowers.

During Garfield's presidential campaign, the outgoing Rutherford Hayes wrote of him, "The truth is no man ever started so low that accomplished so much in all our history. Not Franklin or Lincoln even." After his death Murat Halsted wrote wistfully of seeing Garfield, hearty and smiling, at a private White House gathering: "He was well dressed, of splendid figure, his dome-like head supported by immense shoulders, and he looked the President indeed, and an embodiment of power. . . . It was a supreme hour and only an hour."

Grieving Americans contributed $225,000 to raise a richly decorated Romanesque turret in his memory. Yet Garfield became one of those little-known post–Civil War presidents indistinguishable from one another in the public mind, one of the "lost Americans," as described by novelist Thomas Wolfe, whose "gravely vacant and bewhiskered faces mixed, melted, swam together."

# 21

# Chester Alan Arthur

## 1881–1885

## *Tiffany Tastes*

WHEN CHARLES GUITEAU'S shot rang out, felling President James A. Garfield four months into his term, his cry that "Arthur is now president" created a very difficult situation for Vice President Chester Alan Arthur. No great friend of Garfield's, he'd fought his nomination and been asked to be vice president to heal political wounds. For three months, Garfield hung between life and death. The public grieved, distressed not only at what it might lose but what it might gain. One paper expressed the general sentiment when it called Arthur "about the last man who could be considered eligible" for the office. Even a leading Republican said, "Chet Arthur President of the United States! Good God!"

Arthur's qualifications were far from exceptional. A lieutenant of New York Republican party boss Senator Roscoe Conkling, Arthur owed what fame he possessed to his work as Collector of the Port of New York. Ulysses S. Grant appointed him to the position, the plum patronage job in the country, in 1871. It came with a yearly salary of $40,000 and responsibility for processing close to 75 percent of the national tariff revenue. Though generally perceived as honest himself, Arthur oversaw nearly one thousand employees who made "voluntary" contributions to the Republican party, aware that if the party fell out of power, they would probably lose their jobs. Reformers called for the establishment of a civil service to curtail corruption. When President Hayes removed Arthur from his post as Collector of the Port of New York in 1877, it was seen as a victory for political reform.

Had Garfield died immediately, the uproar against Arthur might well have prevented him from becoming president. As it was, Guiteau's trial soon revealed his lunacy—a persistent office seeker, he in fact envisioned himself as president—and Arthur held potential criticism at bay by keeping a low profile. During Garfield's illness, he sequestered himself in his four-story New York brownstone, at 123 Lexington Avenue, made no statements, and refused to go to Washington to take over the government although Garfield's cabinet had unanimously urged him to do so.

Late on the evening of September 19, 1881, Arthur heard through the open window of his brownstone the shouts of the newsboys: "President Garfield is dying!" He received a telegram from cabinet members confirming the president's death. Reporters rushed to Arthur's home for a statement. Alexander "Alec" Powell, Arthur's valet and personal assistant, answered the door and told them, "He is sitting alone in his room sobbing like a child, with his head on his desk and his face in his hands. I dare not disturb him." Just hours later, at 2:15 in the morning, Judge John R. Brady of the state supreme court was at Arthur's home administering the oath of office. The new president traveled to Washington and on September 22 was officially sworn in by Chief Justice Morrison Waite at a quiet Capitol—Congress was still out of session for the summer.

Without Garfield's tragedy, Arthur never would have reached the presidency. The "Gentleman Boss," as he was called, was aloof, fastidious, avoided the press, and preferred to work behind the scenes. He had little interest in political issues. What interested "Elegant Arthur," as many called him, was living well, and his administration would be characterized by its style and social life more than its policies. As one critical observer, Mrs. James G. Blaine, said, "Flowers, wine, and food and slow pacing with a lady on his arm . . . make up his book of life. The pages of that book are certainly not for the heading of the nation." So, as president, Arthur wasted no time in making his White House an appropriately fashionable residence.

During the Hayes years, the house had been badly neglected by a hostile Congress, and the Garfields never had the chance to improve upon it. Now Arthur inspected the mansion and pronounced it "a badly kept barracks." And if Congress refused to pay to fix it, he said, "I will go ahead and have it done and pay for it out of my own pocket. I will not live in a house like this." He went through every room marking items he wanted to auction off. Twenty-four wagon loads were carted off, including such attic treasures as Nellie Grant's birdcage, a pair of Lincoln's trousers, spittoons, rat traps, and "Lemonade Lucy" Hayes's sideboard, which a local saloon bought. On April 15, 1882, five thousand people turned out to bid on the White House wares, generating several thousand dollars.

While the renovations began, Arthur lived and worked at the home of Senator John P. Jones. He set up his personal office on the second floor, while the clerical staff took over the first floor. It was impossible to move all the records and equipment from the White House offices, so a steady stream of clerks and messengers went back and forth. Nearly every evening Arthur walked over to the White House to see how his changes were progressing. By December 7, he found his new home acceptable enough to move in.

There was much more work to be done, however. The initial renovations revealed that the eighty-year-old mansion had serious problems. The basement had always been wet, but now it was clear that the septic system's pipes had decayed, leaving the soil beneath the basement saturated with what Treasury Department engineer George E. Waring termed "foul matters." The wooden floorboards were rotting, and the servants' quarters were so dank as to cause illness. In the kitchen, whitewash was peeling off the walls in such quantities that it fell into pots of food cooking on the stove.

The Army Corps of Engineers submitted a plan to demolish the White House and rebuild it to look exactly as it had on the exterior, but with an interior devoted solely to offices. A new residence would be built nearby. Arthur pushed for this—apparently it was even his idea—but there was much opposition to destroying the historic building, and Congress never accepted the plan. Instead, the mansion underwent the most extensive repairs since its reconstruction following the War of 1812.

New septic fields were created; decayed pipes were ripped out of the walls and replaced. The first White House elevator was installed. Its interior was upholstered in tufted plush, and it had a seat. Powered by water stored in a large wooden tank on the roof, it never worked well, and the tank put a heavy strain on the roof. But Arthur's real interest was the decor, which he deemed not only shabby but provincial. Lucretia Garfield had begun redecorating, but her efforts were not at all up to the level of taste required by Arthur. He called in the fashionable New York decorator Louis Comfort Tiffany, son of his friend Charles Lewis Tiffany, fresh from his success in decorating the New York Armory. Tiffany's bill alone would be $15,000.

Tiffany subscribed to the Victorian view that no surface go undecorated—he stenciled nearly every inch of the East Room with intricate motifs and elaborate colors—but in his hands, rooms shimmered with color and pattern. Trained by George Inness, among the era's leading luminist painters, Tiffany was noted for his concern with the effects of light on the objects, materials, patterns, and colors. In the Red Room, for example, he chose deep purple-red for the walls and finished the ceiling with bronze and copper stars that caught the light. A reporter called the result an example of the decorator's "high art." In the Blue Room robin's-egg walls were topped with an eight-foot frieze of silver and ivory paper. But Tiffany's most famous addition was to the north entry. Since the 1830s a glass screen had been installed to lessen the blasts of cold that came with each opening and closing of the door. Now Tiffany replaced the ordinary glass with a jeweled stained-glass screen, a mosaic of red, white, and blue that was ten feet high and extended fifty feet across the foyer. It was a White House showpiece for two decades until tastes changed and the screen, thought to be gloomy, was sent to auction by Theodore Roosevelt.

White House visitors sometimes noticed Arthur's own touch, on a table in the hall: the portrait of a beautiful woman, which always had fresh roses beside it. It was Arthur's wife Ellen, who had died at the age of forty-two, shortly before Arthur became vice president. Ellen, whom Arthur called "Nell," had come from a fine Virginia family and, like her husband, enjoyed living in style. Five Irish immigrant servants helped her run their New York townhouse. But Arthur lived a political life—travel, late meetings, late dinners with friends—and badly neglected his wife. She contracted pneumonia while he was away on a trip, and he never saw her conscious again. Heartbroken, he kept her room in New York exactly as she had left it.

They had two children. Chester Alan Jr., seventeen when his father became president, was away at college in Princeton, New Jersey. Arthur warned him to stay out of politics, and he became a gentleman of leisure. Daughter Nell was ten when she moved into the White House with her father. She sometimes helped out at receptions, but she was too young to serve as the official hostess, and Arthur needed one. In his era, women could not attend social events without a hostess present. He persuaded Mrs. Mary McElroy, the youngest of his six sisters (he also had one brother), to live at the White House during the four months of the year that constituted the social season.

"When I went to it," Mary said of the White House, "I was absolutely unfamiliar with the customs and formalities." But she quickly endeared herself to Washington society. Mary had four children of her own, and she was assisted in her duties by her eldest daughter, May, and by Nell. The three stood together in the Blue Room to receive visitors, and Mary found that the effervescence of the young girls "soon did away with any stiffness there might have been." The receptions, as always, were heavily attended. At Arthur's last one the crush was so great that General Phil Sheridan had to climb in

*To redo the White House in fashionable style, Chester A. Arthur brought in Louis Comfort Tiffany. His transformation of the Red Room is seen here. The walls were a dark purply red and the ceiling finished with bronze and copper stars.* (CORBIS)

through a window with the help of two policemen. And the Marine Band, now under the direction of John Philip Sousa, got so caught up in the sea of humanity that it could no longer play. Sousa, commissioned by the Hayes administration on October 1, 1880, made the once-conservative band one of the most famous in the world.

Invitation-only events were often unusually large as well. Arthur frequently entertained fifty guests and had the state dining table expanded by adding rectangular tables at each end to make an **I** shape. Always making their way onto the guest list were husband-hunting widows and spinsters. But the president took special delight in small all-male dinner parties with intimate friends, their names concealed from the White House staff. The first room he redecorated to his tastes was the small private dining room on the main floor. He covered the walls in heavy gold paper and fixed the wood-burning fireplace. Arthur had a Victorian taste for fine food, wine, and cigars, and even these small parties were elaborately prepared by his French chef, George Cupplinger. "He wanted the best of everything, and he wanted it served in the best manner," said Colonel William H. Crook, a long-time White House staffer. A dinner for friends in March 1882 boasted fourteen courses accompanied by six wines. Served late in the evening, up to midnight, these meals were invariably accompanied not only by pleasant chatting and stories, but by excellent cigars and plenty of liquor.

Arthur also indulged a taste for fine clothes. His wardrobe was extensive. Colonel Crook said Arthur was "the first President, so far as I know, to have a valet, and one was needed, for Mr. Arthur dresses fashionably." Arthur ordered his clothes from his tailor in New York, who fit his six-foot two-inch, 225-pound frame with as many as twenty-five coats at one time. He was said to own eighty pairs of pants. He had suits for every occasion. The office called for a Prince Albert coat, always with a flower in the buttonhole, and a colored silk handkerchief. At lunch he wore a cutaway, and at dinner a tuxedo. For the large evening receptions he dressed to the nines with pearl-tinted gloves.

Former president Rutherford Hayes heard about Arthur's White House lifestyle, and said, "Nothing like it ever before in the Executive Mansion—liquor, snobbery, and worse." But when a temperance advocate appealed to Arthur to follow Hayes's lead and ban liquor in the White House, Arthur replied, "Madame, I may be President of the United States, but my private life is nobody's damned business." He meant it. Two days before he died, he would instruct a friend to burn all of his papers—leaving much of his private life obscure to historians.

Arthur enjoyed the social life of the White House but found the presidency wearisome. Public policy bored him. He procrastinated. It once took him a month to attend to a routine letter prepared for him by the State Department for transmission to a European court. Receiving callers to his office was especially onerous, even with the doormen screening them, taking visitors' cards at the door and routinely turning away undesirables and cranks. It didn't help that he could not truly leave the office. "You have no idea how depressing and fatiguing it is to live in the same house where you work," he said. He rarely appeared in his office before ten, and he left for lunch at noon, after which he would take a long pleasure drive. His dark green landau, with his coat of arms painted on the door, was drawn by a pair of mahogany bays. The curtains were gold lace, the lap robe otter fur, all monogrammed in gold thread with "C.A.A." When he finished his drive, he didn't always return to the office. From five until seven he rested, read, and dressed for dinner. For exercise he took long after-dinner walks, which often kept him out as late as two or three in the morning. He walked through the streets or the landscaped paths of the Mall, generally with friends, unguarded. Rarely did he get to bed before 2 A.M.

Yet he did leave a political legacy, one that came as a complete surprise. Presidents of the era typically appointed some eighty thousand people to government jobs, creating a spoils system by which the politicians of the ruling party could reward supporters. Civil service reform was seen as the key to breaking the stranglehold of the political machines, and finally Guiteau's assassination of President Garfield had rallied the needed support for it. Arthur himself had helped build the corrupt system and had benefited from it, but as president, Arthur broke with his former boss, Senator Conkling, and supported reform. The Pendleton Act, passed in 1883, put approximately fourteen thousand jobs under civil service—Conkling called it the "snivel service." Arthur not only signed it but appointed reformers to the Civil Service Commission to enforce it. His popularity grew with the public but not with the party bosses. As one former ally said, "He has done less for us than Garfield, or even Hayes." He had no real chance of getting the Republican nomination in 1884. Arthur would come in second, behind James G. Blaine, though far ahead of other also-rans.

In the meantime, as his term wore on, Arthur escaped his duties whenever he could, happily traveling to make dedication speeches. He was at the dedication ceremony for the Brooklyn Bridge. He was also the last president to use the presidential summer residence at the Soldiers' Home, which he decorated to his tastes, and spent warm evenings sitting on the porch smoking and drinking with friends.

Arthur also took several extended trips. On April 5, 1883, he embarked on a fishing trip to Florida, traveling in a private railway car with a parlor, dining car, and kitchen. The president had to pay his own travel expenses, but the railroads were generally happy to let him ride for free in a private car. He brought along his chef, who had packed the White House silverware, linens, and china. The trip's difficulties began when the railway car broke a coupling and was stranded for several hours in the countryside. The weather became hot and muggy, and Arthur grew exhausted and irritable. The party traveled by river steamer, buckboard, carriage, and train to reach a camp on the Kissimmee River. Arthur caught a ten-pound trout—he was an expert fisherman—and a member of the group shot an alligator. But the swarms of mosquitoes and other insects compelled them to return to St. Augustine, where Arthur realized he had become infected with malaria, probably at the Kissimmee camp. They stayed four days in St. Augustine. The weather was cooler, and Arthur could stroll practically unnoticed along the streets.

Later in the year, on August 18, 1883, he left on a month-long vacation to Yellowstone. From Chicago he traveled by train to Rawlings, Wyoming, then by a mule-pulled wagon train to Fort Wasakie on the Shoshone Indian reservation, and on horseback from there. He and his companions rode, camped, and fished for three weeks. At times, the high elevations were below freezing at night. In one day he and Senator George G. Vest caught 105 pounds of fish.

Arthur's lackadaisical approach to his presidency, and his indulgent lifestyle, can be understood at least in part to be a result of his health: he was dying of Bright's disease, a painful, progressive kidney ailment. It was a well-kept secret. Only a few intimates knew, and it was many years before historians understood the seriousness of his illness.

Symptoms—nausea, depression, indolence—can precede diagnosis by several years, but Arthur probably learned he had the disease during his second year in office, when he was ill much of the time and physically tired.

The malaria Arthur contracted in Florida was severe, and complicated his health problems from then on. While returning to Washington by ship after that trip, he awoke screaming in pain, and was feared to be dying. He revealed his disease to his doctor, whom he swore to secrecy. The doctor told reporters the president was suffering from overexposure to the sun and indigestion due to seasickness. But reports that the president was suffering from Bright's disease had surfaced in print the previous year. Arthur had declined comment, but a close friend denied the reports "on the authority of the President himself." Now the press was suspicious of this sudden attack. Arthur was irate that the episode had become public. On arriving in Washington he told a welcoming crowd, "I am feeling perfectly well, as well as ever, in fact. I have not been sick at all."

When he was diagnosed with Bright's, Arthur had been told that the only way to prolong his life was plenty of rest, a bland diet, and avoidance of alcohol. Such a drastic lifestyle change would have meant admitting—to both himself and the public—that he was ill, which he never brought himself to do. Though his health precluded a second term, he did little to discourage friends who supported him at the 1884 nominating convention. And when someone asked him about his plans once out of office, the fifty-six-year-old president said, "Well, there doesn't seem to be anything else for an ex-President to do but to go into the country and raise big pumpkins." More seriously, he said he would resume his law practice in New York.

It was a facade; he was not up to it physically. In his last six weeks as president Arthur's health was, in the estimation of a friend, "deplorable." Doctors visited him constantly. Yet the next year, just months before his death on November 18, 1886, he wrote, "My progress in recovering my health is slow and tedious, but I have strong hope that ere the summer is past I shall be as good as new."

# 22/24

# Grover Cleveland

1885–1889, 1893–1897

## *Love, Marriage, and a Baby Carriage*

"SOMETIMES I WAKE at night in the White House and rub my eyes and wonder if it is not all a dream," Grover Cleveland told a friend during his first year as president. Some might have felt themselves deposited at White House by a fairy godmother. Not Cleveland. He disliked crowds and speech making. He had come to despise the press and political shenanigans during the 1884 campaign, which had dredged up an old indiscretion. Back in 1874, an alcoholic widow in Buffalo, Maria Halpin, bore a son she claimed was Cleveland's. She had also been intimate with other men, all married, but Cleveland accepted the responsibility and took care of mother and child financially. Over time Halpin's alcoholism grew worse, and Cleveland eventually arranged for the child to be adopted. During the campaign, some Buffalo clergymen leaked exaggerated stories about Halpin and Cleveland. Cleveland would never forget the betrayal. "I have no home at home," he wrote to a friend. When the scandal broke in the newspapers, Cleveland never tried to deny it. He instructed supporters in answering reporters' questions: "Tell the truth." Cleveland won the presidency by a narrow margin, becoming the first Democrat to hold the office in nearly a quarter century.

A bachelor, he wandered the elegant rooms at a loss. Back in Buffalo, New York, where he'd been governor, he could eat sausages and drink beer at Schenkelberger's Restaurant. Here he was faced with French food sent up by his predecessor's French chef, George Cupplinger. "I must go to dinner," he once wrote a friend. "I wish it were to eat pickled herring, Swiss cheese and a chop of Louis' instead of the French stuff I shall find." Once, as he sat down to one of Cupplinger's meals, he detected a familiar odor from outside the window. He called William Sinclair, a mulatto servant he'd brought with him to the White House and given the $1,800-a-year position of steward:

"William, what is that smell?"

"I am very sorry, sir, but that is the smell of the servants' dinner."

"What is it—corned beef and cabbage?"

"Yes."

"Well, William, take this dinner down to the servants and bring their dinner to me."

Cleveland, in recounting the story, added that the corned beef and cabbage was "the best dinner I had had in months."

He fired Cupplinger and persuaded the cook he'd had at the governor's mansion in Albany, Eliza, to come to the White House. She obligingly sent him breakfast at eight— oatmeal, beefsteak, eggs or a chop, and coffee. For state dinners, he brought in a chef or caterer.

His bachelorhood posed another problem: he lacked that White House essential, a hostess. He invited his sister Rose, also unmarried, to fill the role. An avowed feminist with a career of her own as a college professor, lecturer, and author (while at the White House, she published *George Eliot's Poetry and Other Studies*), Rose was initially perceived as too forthright for her times—she had opinions and didn't hesitate to express them—but she won over society by dutifully making the requisite social calls, traveling about the capital in a carriage, and serving as hostess for her brother at receptions. In the evenings Rose continued her intellectual pursuits, writing in her upstairs office. Often her light in the northeast corner and her brother's at the other end of the hall were shining late at night.

Cleveland was a lifelong workaholic—he would even work on his wedding day. He typically rose at seven-thirty in the morning, had breakfast at eight, and worked into the night. Details absorbed him. When he moved into the White House he measured the amount of hay left over in the stable and sent his predecessor, Chester Arthur, a check in payment. He didn't like to delegate responsibility. During his tenure as sheriff of Erie County, New York, from 1871 to 1874, he personally hanged two men rather than push the job off on subordinates. His friend Samuel J. Tilden, who'd run against Hayes, called Cleveland "the kind of a man who would rather do something badly for himself than to have somebody else do it well." Consequently, the task of filling government posts was even more onerous than it had to be. At the time, only about 16,000 of 125,000 federal employees had been put under the civil service. Most of the remainder were appointed by the president, and Cleveland personally examined applications even for fourth-class postmasterships. "The dreadful, frightful, damnable office seeking hangs over me, surrounds me," he said. Examining pension bills was also painstaking. It was an era of budget surpluses and aging Civil War veterans, and Congress passed pension bills for individual veterans by the hundreds. The pensions were of course meant for deserving (Union) veterans, but they were used as political rewards for constituents. Cleveland stayed up until 2 A.M. night after night reading each one, and vetoed many.

His regular relaxations were few. Cleveland was five feet eleven inches tall, thick-necked, and badly overweight at 250 pounds. He disliked even walking. Bodily movement was, he said, "among the dreary and unsatisfying things in life." He occasionally

took a carriage ride, strolled through the White House conservatories to sniff the flowers, or played cribbage or billiards. But when he had time, his passions were hunting
and fishing, with regards to which he admitted he was "utterly incorrigible and shameless." During his two terms in office he spent so much time hunting and fishing that the
press criticized him, as religious leaders did when leisure occupied his Sundays. He was
an authority on both subjects and following his presidency wrote magazine articles on
them for the *Saturday Evening Post,* among others. He even shot rabbits: "plain, little,
everyday plebeian rabbits—sometimes appropriately called 'cotton tails.' I am not
ashamed of their pursuit." He called his favorite rifle "Death and Destruction."

A hunting trip was in order come Cleveland's first summer as president. He was
already tired of the "cursed constant grind" of the White House. "I fairly yearn to be let
alone," he said. He disappeared into the Adirondack forests of New York State with a
few friends and a guide, leaving no word as to where he was going or when he might be
back. At night he shot deer by "jacking" them—catching them in a spotlight so they
froze, becoming easy targets. But hunting was a bit strenuous for him, and on this trip
he was more inclined to fish, play cards, and drink whiskey. The newspapers decided
that the president was "lost" and sent a reporter into the woods to find him.

Little did the press know, the real story was brewing right under their noses. That
Cleveland was plotting an end to his loneliness surprised the public, but not his sister
Rose. The president had long been in love with Frances Folsom, the daughter of his
friend and Buffalo law partner, Oscar Folsom. Cleveland was twenty-seven when she
was born. Her parents named her Frank after a favorite uncle, and though she changed
her name to Frances, Cleveland would always call her Frank. He bought her first baby
carriage. She called him Uncle Cleve and used to climb up on his knee. When Frances
was eleven, her father was killed in a buggy accident, and Cleveland became her legal
guardian and administrator of Folsom's estate.

By the time Cleveland took office in March 1885, Frances was in her last year at
Wells College. In April, on vacation from school, Frances visited the White House with
her mother, Emma. The relationship between Frances and Cleveland was quite formal,
even distant. Cleveland later remembered of this visit, "It is true I did say some things
to her one night, when we were walking together in the East Room." Over the summer
there were more visits with the Folsoms. Some of Cleveland's friends assumed his
interest was in Emma, and they would not be the only ones to make that mistake.

Frances and her mother had planned a nine-month European trip for after gradua-
tion, so Cleveland proposed by letter in August, before they left. The engagement was
supposed to remain secret, but an affectionate bon voyage telegram to the ship was
copied by a telegraph operator and released to reporters, who concluded that the president was romancing Mrs. Folsom. "I don't see why the papers keep marrying me to old
ladies all the while," Cleveland remarked. Frances agreed by mail from Europe to a
June 2, 1886, wedding date, which would fall just six days after her return to America.
Meanwhile, Cleveland considered how he might prepare the White House for his
bride. He wrote to his elder sister, Mary Hoyt, "It has occurred to me that it would be
nice to have the little room adjoining mine . . . fixed up for a dressing room, etc., for
Frank, or a place where she could sit and stay during the day."

As Frances and her mother headed back across the Atlantic toward the port of New
York, the *New York Herald* speculated—of Mrs. Folsom—"WHAT IF IT PROVE TRUE?"

Cleveland sent his trusted secretary, Daniel Lamont, to New York, where Lamont hired a boat and met the ship in the harbor. He was able to escort the Folsoms to a Fifth Avenue hotel before the reporters caught on. Then the White House announced Cleveland's engagement to Frances. In the pandemonium that followed, a police guard had to be placed around the Folsoms' hotel. On Memorial Day, Cleveland traveled to New York to review the traditional parade from a reviewing stand only two blocks from the hotel. Frances came to the hotel balcony and waved a handkerchief; the president tipped his hat. One of the passing bands broke into Mendelssohn's "Wedding March," and another played a tune from the popular new Gilbert and Sullivan operetta *The Mikado,* whose lyrics included, "He's going to marry Yum-Yum!"

The wedding ceremony took place in the Blue Room before close family and friends—no reporters. The bride's gown was of heavy corded satin—the upstairs maid discovered that it could stand upright by itself—with a fifteen-foot train and a veil secured with real orange blossoms and seed pearls. The bride, age twenty-one, and the groom, forty-nine, descended the grand staircase together unescorted, with the Marine Band, under the direction of John Philip Sousa, playing the wedding march. Following the ceremony there was a promenade around the East Room, then dinner in the State Dining Room, whose table featured a large three-masted ship, christened the *Hymen,* made out of pansies and pink roses. After dinner the newlyweds left by way of the south portico. Thousands of people pressed up to the fences around the grounds for a glimpse. The couple were escorted to the train station by mounted police, where they boarded a private railway car for Deer Park, a resort in western Maryland, with the reporters in hot pursuit.

The new Mr. and Mrs. Cleveland stayed in a private cottage, and meals were brought in from the resort's hotel, but they had little actual privacy. The spying of the reporters, many with binoculars, was an affront to Cleveland's strong sense of dignity. From the cottage, he said, "I can see a group of them sitting on a bridge, which marks one of the limits, waiting for some movement to be made which will furnish an incident." They lifted the covers from the food dishes en route to the cottage so they could write about what the Clevelands were having for dinner, and recorded where their mail came from. Cleveland felt they were violating a sacred personal experience, perpetuating, he said in an angry letter to the *New York Post,* a "colossal impertinence." He managed to slip away for a little trout fishing with his bride, and showed her how to bait a hook, but reporters finally located them in the remote woods. In future, Frances left the fishing and hunting to her husband, and never tried to curb his appetite for them—but she did tone down the loud checked clothing he often wore.

Back at the White House, Cleveland told the new first lady, "You will find that you get along better in this job if you don't try anything new." Frances wasn't out to change things too much, but she was a breath of fresh air in the mansion, and every member of the household staff was an instant fan. When she arrived the morning of her wedding, Colonel W. H. Crook recalled, "She tripped up the steps, and swept through the great entrance like a radiant vision of young springtime, . . . from that instant every man and woman of them all was a devoted slave, and remained such." The youngest first lady in history, Frances, bright and witty, proved a success as a hostess. She established Saturday open houses for working women, which highlighted her husband's concern for the welfare of workers. Her political value was obvious to her husband and his aides, and

*Frances Cleveland was one of many First Ladies who chose the area by the big lunette window at the west end of the upstairs hall as a living room. But the Clevelands spent as little time as possible in the White House preferring homes they bought in rural parts of Washington.* (LIBRARY OF CONGRESS)

she was the first president's wife to be consciously groomed as a public figure. Watching Frances's performance in the reception line one afternoon, Cleveland commented proudly to Mrs. Folsom, "She'll do! She'll *do!*"

The White House did not pass muster so easily. A reporter calling on the president noted on his way up to the office that the stairs were covered with "an old piece of Brussels carpet which was good once, but which has been patched, sewed, and resewed. It would not bring 50 cents at an auction." As he sat in the waiting room he noticed the water cooler, which had "a tin slop bucket to catch the drippings" and a jelly tumbler for a drinking glass. He had also noticed as he entered through the north portico that he could look over a railing into the basement and watch the servants ironing the president's "nightshirts and other unmentionable garments." Other embarrassments were better hidden. Although President Arthur had auctioned off two dozen wagon loads of excess furnishings, the White House attic was still "a terrific mess of junk," according to staff member Robert Lincoln O'Brien, and the basement "a place of rubble and overturned ash cans."

The mansion was also infested with all manner of undesirable creatures. The infamous White House rats remained plentiful. Frances kept a canary in a cage by her window, and one day a servant came around just as a big rat that had forced its way into the cage was about to devour the bird. Spiders were even more abundant—one estimate put the building's population at one million. When the outside of the house was hosed down during a cleaning, a shower of spiders blanketed the ground. That evening, the white columns were black with them as they crawled back from whence they came. And then there were the cockroaches. One staff member said, "I didn't know there were so many species of cockroaches as I got acquainted with at my daily work." In winter, groups of mangy dogs slinked about the grounds when they weren't bedding down under the leaves that were raked into the fountains to protect their basins from the cold.

Yet the condition of the house probably didn't bother the Clevelands as much as the lack of privacy. Thanks to Frances's compelling presence, the press and the public suddenly became outright fascinated with White House doings. At her first Saturday reception, she and her husband stood in the receiving line for hours shaking an estimated nine thousand hands. The excitement was so great that a group of women, pushed by the crowd, careened into a stand of palms screening the Marine Band. As the nuptial excitement died down, the Clevelands tried to return to a more private life but were virtually stalked by the press. The couple might have improved their lot had they consented to occasional interviews. One group of reporters, faced with a deadline

*The famous Lincoln bed, shown here with Victorian drapings that have since been abandoned, was a good size for 250-pound, five foot, eleven inch Grover Cleveland. By his second term, a child's bed shared the room.* (CORBIS)

and no news, came up with a story that Mrs. Cleveland hated the bustle and had decided to abolish it. Rather than contest the reporters, Frances stopped wearing a bustle. But when the press, during the 1888 election year, reported that Cleveland physically abused his wife, Frances was compelled to comment publicly on her marriage, writing, "I can wish the women of our country no greater blessing than that their homes and lives may be as happy, and their husbands may be as kind, attentive, considerate and affectionate as mine."

Despite his indignation, Cleveland refused to curtail access to the mansion. "The White House belongs to the nation. The nation has a right to come in." So the couple purchased a home on twenty-three acres in a higher, more rural section of the District of Columbia, near where Washington Cathedral stands today. They turned it into a working hobby farm. The Clevelands had a vegetable garden, and Frances indulged her fondness for animals, keeping over twenty pets, including chickens, ducks, horses, cows, kittens, foxes, quail, dogs, and white rats. Her favorite was a mockingbird. Cleveland added acreage, enlarged the house by adding a two-story porch around two sides, and had the roof painted bright red. Frances called the place "Oak View"—it had views of surrounding forests and hills—but the reporters called it "Red Top," which was all they could see from their distant vantage point on the road. At last the couple had some semblance of privacy. They lived at Oak View nearly full-time May through December, and part-time during the winter social season, with the president commuting to his White House office.

Cleveland sold Oak View for a profit of almost $100,000 when he lost the election of 1888 to Benjamin Harrison—despite winning the popular vote—and moved back to New York. As Frances said good-bye to the White House servants on their last day in the mansion, March 4, 1889, she told Jerry Smith, "Now, Jerry, I want you to take good care of all the furniture and ornaments in the house, for I want to find everything just as it is when we come back again." Smith had been at the White House a long time and had never seen a defeated president come back. He ventured to ask Frances just when they might be returning. She told him, "We are coming back four years from today." And they would. Cleveland became the only president to serve two nonconsecutive terms.

In the meantime, though, the Clevelands moved into a four-story brownstone at 816 Madison Avenue in New York City. The ex-president joined a law firm based downtown on Broad Street. Occasionally Cleveland walked to his large, well-furnished office, but generally he rode the Sixth Avenue Elevated train. He selected his cases carefully and made sure he was free in the summer. The first of five children, Ruth, was born on October 3, 1891. The family bought a summer home in Massachusetts, on Buzzard's Bay, where Cleveland fished literally all day long. The cottage, which they called Gray Gables, was secluded but had a fine view of the water. Some of Cleveland's happiest days were spent at Gray Gables with his wife and children. But when Ruth died at age twelve from diphtheria, the place lost its charm, and he sold it.

Just as Frances had predicted, she and her husband returned to the White House on March 4, 1893, exactly four years after leaving it. Cleveland had won the popular vote for the third time in a row. Frances arrived through the south portico with two-year-old Ruth, while at about the same time her husband came through the north portico to be greeted by outgoing President Harrison. During this second term, privacy would be an

*Cleveland was the only President married in the White House. His baby, Ruth, born between Cleveland's two terms, was so popular that a candy bar was named for her. In his second term Frances gave birth to another daughter, Esther, the only presidential child born at the White House.* (LIBRARY OF CONGRESS)

even greater issue. Ruth was so popular a candy bar was named after her—the Baby Ruth. Frances looked out the White House window one day and saw to her horror that a group of adoring women, ignoring the protests of the nurse, had lifted Ruth from her carriage and begun patting her and passing her around. In response, Cleveland closed the White House grounds to the public. The press was soon reporting that the child was being hidden because she was deformed. The Clevelands ignored these stories and purchased another suburban home, Woodley. Privacy was even more essential because Frances arrived pregnant. Nonetheless Frances redecorated the White House, doing away with some of Tiffany's effects and repainting and papering the family quarters. She created a nursery for Ruth and Esther—the only child of a president to be born in the White House.

This time around, however, the Clevelands could less easily escape the pressures of the White House. The stock market crashed in 1893, and the government's supply of gold was almost exhausted, creating one of the worst financial crises in American history. To complicate matters, Vice President Adlai Stevenson opposed Cleveland's conservative gold standard views. The hard times that followed were characterized by labor unrest and violent strikes.

Then, in the midst of the national crisis came a personal one. On May 27, 1893, the president was brushing his teeth when he encountered a rough spot. A biopsy revealed cancer. An immediate operation was imperative, but any publicity was certain to further destabilize the country's already critical financial situation. Even Frances was not told of it beforehand. A hospital, Gray Gables, and the White House were all ruled out—reporters would get wind of it. Cleveland turned to a wealthy friend, Elias C. Benedict, who owned the yacht *Oneida,* on which Cleveland had been a guest. Operating equipment, tanks of compressed gas, and doctors were moved on board secretly. The operation itself was risky. Cleveland was now fifty-six years old, and the anesthetic, nitrous oxide (laughing gas), was dangerous to use for an extended operation, especially on a heavy person. Dr. Joseph Bryant, the president's personal physician, had performed only two of these difficult operations.

Cleveland left Washington on June 30 in a private railway car, then changed to a carriage, where he was kept hidden from sight. He was taken across the Hudson River to Manhattan and onto the *Oneida,* which steamed out into Long Island Sound for the operation. Part of the roof of his mouth had to be removed, and one of the doctors later wrote, "What a sigh of relief we surgeons breathed when the patient was once more safe in bed." But his recovery would be difficult. Cleveland became depressed. He told Attorney General Richard Olney, "My God, Olney, they nearly killed me!"

When the *Oneida* arrived in Buzzard's Bay, Cleveland was able to walk into Gray Gables. Frances, by now alerted and waiting to greet her husband, covered for him, telling reporters he'd had "an unusually bad attack of rheumatism," and "we have made him give up entirely to resting." He was not an easy patient. Frances caught him eating a peach—not part of his postoperative diet—and exclaimed, "Wouldn't you think a *child* would have more sense?" Dr. Bryant told reporters that the president was "suffering from rheumatism and somewhat from his teeth." Cleveland's attempts at speech were pitiful, and in three weeks he would have to address the Congress, which he had called into special session on account of the financial crisis. An expert dental surgeon set up a lab at Gray Gables and fashioned an artificial rubber jaw. By August 7 Cleveland was able to return to Washington and make a brief speech to Congress.

At the outset, a few reporters had heard rumors of a malignant growth and didn't believe the cover story, but decided to accept it. The rumors persisted, especially in the opposition press, and Secretary of War Daniel Lamont finally called a press conference in which he announced that the president was feeling better after having teeth extracted.

At the end of August a reporter for the *Philadelphia Press* revealed that a critical operation had been performed on the president, named the doctors, and questioned Cleveland's competence to remain in office. Cabinet members continued to deny everything, and the reporter's story was characterized as a hoax. One of Cleveland's doctors, John F. Erdmann, later said, "I did more lying during this period than in all my life put together." Other doctors avoided reporters or invoked medical ethics. It wasn't until twenty-four years later, long after Cleveland's death, that Dr. William Keen revealed the truth in the *Saturday Evening Post.*

Following his illness, Cleveland tired more easily. He was no longer able to do the prodigious amount of work he was accustomed to. He had also aged noticeably since his first term. His hair had thinned and turned white, and he had rheumatism and gout, which would become so painful that he would not be able to stand up to greet his successor, William McKinley. The Clevelands again bought a suburban home and spent as little time as possible in the White House. Meanwhile, Cleveland managed to outrage nearly everyone with his policies. He'd made his mark in politics as a reform mayor of Buffalo, earning the nickname "veto mayor." As governor and president, he continued to wield the veto to powerful effect, killing three times more bills than all previous presidents combined. He would also make plenty of new enemies, but as he once said, "What is the use of being elected or being reelected unless you stand for something?" In 1884 the Democrats proudly proclaimed, "We love him for the enemies he has made." But by 1896 Cleveland's bluntness had left him widely criticized by the public and renounced by his party.

The president looked around for a place to retire to. "I would like to buy a house . . . and in this house I want to be free from all sorts of social and other exactions that might interfere with the lazy rest I crave," he said. He ruled out his hometown of Buffalo—"the place I hate above all others"—which had so wounded him during the 1884 campaign. He chose the small college town of Princeton, New Jersey, but retirement was not all lazy rest. He wrote, and he became a trustee of Princeton University. He also became a parent three more times—his last child was born when he was sixty-six. Cleveland died on June 24, 1908. His last words were said to be, "I have tried so hard to do right." He left Frances an estate of $250,000. Five years later she married a Princeton professor of archaeology. She died October 29, 1947.

# 23

# Benjamin Harrison

## 1889–1893

## *No Room to Spare*

"NONE BUT knaves should ever enter the political arena," Benjamin Harrison was warned by his father, a two-term congressman. Harrison's great grandfather had signed the Declaration of Independence, and his grandfather, William Henry Harrison, "Old Tippecanoe," had been the ninth president of the United States. Politics was in his blood, but that didn't assure "Little Ben," as the Union troops called their five-foot-six-tall general, a winning streak.

Returning from the Civil War a brigadier general—he saw more personal combat than any of the Civil War presidents except Ulysses Grant—Harrison twice ran for governor of Indiana and lost. In 1881 he was elected to the Senate, but lost his reelection bid. He was no one's first choice for the presidency in 1888, but the front-runners became deadlocked, and the party bosses considered him "safe" and easy to control. On election night he polled ninety thousand fewer votes than Democrat incumbent Grover Cleveland, but with typical behind-the-scenes maneuvering, the party bosses secured the necessary electoral votes.

Ever earnest, Harrison declared, "Providence has given us the victory." Republican National Committee chairman Matt Quay quickly corrected him, saying "Providence hadn't a damn thing to do with it."

On Inauguration Day, March 4, 1889, there was a cold, driving rain, and Harrison wore chamois-skin underwear beneath his Prince Albert coat. His speech, though only half the length of his grandfather's, was much too long. After the ceremonies at the Capitol and reception at the White House, he and his wife, Caroline Scott Harrison, attended an inauguration ball in the Pension Office Hall along with some twelve thousand guests. There were two bands, including the Marine Band, under the direction of John Philip Sousa, and the president and first lady led the grand promenade. Back at the White House, they went straight to bed, exhausted.

Harrison had casually invited neighbors and friends from Indianapolis to drop in on him in the White House, and they started arriving the very next day, along with thousands of well-wishers come to attend a public reception. His Civil War regiment, Ben's Boys, provided volunteer guard service. By midafternoon the crush of visitors was so great that the doors of the White House had to be closed to restore order. By the time it was over, Harrison estimated that he had shaken the hands of eight thousand people.

Harrison, now fifty-five years old, had white hair and a full beard tended by a barber he brought from Indianapolis and put on the White House payroll as a messenger. Harrison was known for being dignified, methodical, brusque, and cold—some who knew him called him "a human iceberg." A senator who came to him pleading for patronage appointments and was greeted with silence said, "It's like talking to a hitching post." Further, many thought him, in the words of fellow Republican Theodore Roosevelt, a "psalm singing politician" who was "narrow-minded, prejudiced, [and] obstinate."

*By the late 1800s crowds attending White House social functions were so big—they numbered in the thousands—that a temporary wooden bridge out a window was normal procedure. Also it became routine during large receptions to shore up the floors from the basement.* (LIBRARY OF CONGRESS)

On the other hand, Harrison was an excellent public speaker and a master of detail. "I was born to be a drudge," he said. Without question he was on the side of the rich and big business at a time when business was looked up to. His own sixteen-room Indianapolis home of twenty years had more living area than the White House, despite being stuffed with massive furniture and cascading crystal chandeliers, his era's symbols of affluence. He even had a rowing machine and a weight-lifting set, but had nevertheless developed a definite paunch.

Harrison would find the White House less comfortable. "Very few people understand," Caroline lamented, "to what straits the President's family have been put for lack of accommodations." Four generations of Harrisons, as many as nine people at times, crowded into the five bedchambers available in the second-floor living quarters. These included Caroline's father, the ninety-year-old Reverend John Scott, and her niece Mary Dimmick, thirty years old and a widow. The Harrisons' two children, Mary and Russell, also stayed at the White House most of the time. Mary's own family consisted of her husband, J. Robert McKee, and two-year-old son, Ben. Russell and his wife, also named Mary, also had a two-year-old, Marthena.

There were only two full baths in the family quarters, one for the president and first lady and another, a so-called double bath with several tubs and lavatories, for everyone else—though the bedrooms had chamber sets and washstands with running water. Common space was also at a premium. Caroline turned the long central hall into a living room one hundred feet long and twenty-five feet wide, running from the glass partition dividing the private quarters from the office wing to the top of the grand staircase. Curtains on low rods separated the cavernous space into several smaller areas. It was roomy, yes, but it was also dark, drafty, and lacked privacy due to the grand staircase, which was sometimes used by the staff. Caroline decided to turn over parts of the state floor to the family and closed the state parlors, the dining room, and the transverse hall to visitors. That left only the entrance hall and the East Room open for public viewing. But she soon retreated upstairs when she discovered that privacy was impossible with the state rooms' grand windows and doors.

Caroline, proving herself a first lady to be reckoned with, took another tack. She proposed an expansion. Her design was inspired by George Washington's Mount Vernon home—apropos given that 1889 was the one hundredth anniversary of the founding father's inauguration. The proposal entailed expanding the building into a large quadrangle, described by the architect as a "series of salons, anterooms, corridors, rotundas, conservatories, and winter gardens." There would be plenty of room to separate living quarters from business activities, and for receptions and entertaining. The popular promenades could circle twelve hundred feet around the quadrangle, "thus avoiding the confusion of returning the same way." Caroline showed the plans to an enthusiastic Senator Leland Stanford. Stanford rallied the Senate's approval, but the House never even voted on the proposal—Speaker Thomas Reed had a score to settle with the president over a patronage dispute.

So the Harrisons worked with what they had, continuing to prop up the state room floors from below during large receptions and watching as overcrowding forced guests to exit out the East Room window via a temporary wooden bridge. The house might be run-down, but Caroline insisted it be clean. In Indianapolis, she'd kept house with only one or two servants. She had no fear of wielding a broom and saw to it that the house was cleaned from attic to basement.

The attic, consisting of a long hall with nine or ten small, deteriorating rooms off it, was overflowing. By the light of a kerosene lamp, Caroline culled the mess for anything of historical value—while an attendant occasionally shot a rat with his pistol, provoking screams from the first lady. She sent unwanted excess off to auction, then had the attic dusted and scrubbed down. The basement, home to servants and laundry and kitchen facilities, was worse. Not only were there more rats, but its notorious dampness had rotted the wooden floors and formed a green mold on the walls. When she had the kitchen floor taken up, she found layer upon layer of rotting floors underneath. She ordered a new floor of crushed brick layered over with cement.

Rats had infested the White House for decades, and were not confined to the attic and basement, as the Harrisons soon discovered. When the president found a rat on the side table in the family dining room, the family called in exterminators. In addition to traps and poison, they brought ferrets, which killed hundreds of rats.

The president and first lady also renovated their private bathroom with new white tile and a porcelain-lined marble tub. "It looks very clean and much improved," Harrison wrote Caroline, away at the seashore in New Jersey. And the tub, he said, would "tempt a duck to wash himself every day."

In the second half of Harrison's term, the White House was wired for electricity. Irwin "Ike" Hoover was assigned to oversee their installation in the White House, and was soon part of the permanent staff. He was employed at the mansion for a total of forty-two years, and eventually came to run it as chief usher. Electricity was only a supplement to gaslight—electricity was not entirely dependable—so the gas lamps and chandeliers were not replaced. The Harrisons liked the additional illumination, but refused to turn the switches on and off for fear of electrical shock, so they left the lights burning all night.

*Caroline Harrison tried to solve the problem of living in cramped quarters among expanding government offices by adding huge wings on the White House. Senator Leland Stanford said: "This is the kind of plan we want" and shepherded it through the Senate but the House did not agree.* (LIBRARY OF CONGRESS)

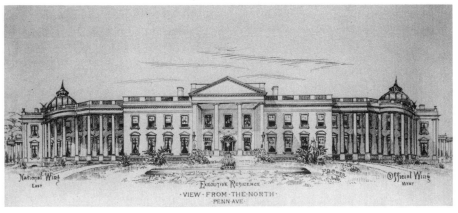

The wiring required tearing into the walls, providing Caroline with a perfect opportunity to repaint, rewallpaper, and otherwise redecorate. The urbane Chester Arthur's 1883 redecoration by the famed Louis Tiffany was by now showing wear. Over the summer of 1891, many of the state rooms were stripped back to white plaster, and by mid-September Tiffany's mix of complex patterns and colors had given way to the classical simplicity that was coming back into vogue.

Life in the Harrison White House was easy and informal among the close family group. Breakfast was at eight-thirty, followed by prayers led by the president or Caroline's father, Reverend Scott. Lunch was at one-thirty and dinner at six-thirty. The grandchildren were the center of family life. The president and first lady set aside the northwest corner room on the second floor as a nursery and brought in a German nurse. When Marthena got scarlet fever, the White House was quarantined and had to shut down for a few days. For little Ben's fourth birthday party, the president acted as host, handing out the ice cream and cake, and for Christmas he dressed up as Santa Claus and handed out presents to the children. At family meals, Ben, in his high chair, always sat next to the president. Once, Ben was crawling around the president's study when Harrison realized he was missing an important roll of papers. Ben was using them to stir the brown, liquid contents of a spittoon.

Many gifts came to the White House for the children, including a pony, a cart, and a goat. The goat, called "His Whiskers," pulled Ben around the front lawn in a cart. Once, Harrison saw from the north portico that His Whiskers, with Ben in tow, had escaped through the front gates and taken off down Pennsylvania Avenue. The stout president gave chase in his high silk hat and frock coat, waving his cane and calling for His Whiskers to stop. Ben, however, enjoyed the ride. His Whiskers had a habit of attacking Willis, the coachman, who told the president that either the goat went or he would. Harrison reached a compromise, moving His Whiskers from the main stable to a pen built under the south portico.

Ben, known to the press as "baby McKee," starred in reports written for a public that had become fascinated with human interest stories about the first family. When Mary walked the grounds with Ben, she would take him to the fence to greet people. He became, doorkeeper Tommy Pendel said, "one of the principal personages of the White House." But Ben was not the only one who lived in the public eye. While Cleveland, bitter over his stalking by the press, had hidden himself from the public, carefully orchestrating appearances, Harrison continued as if still back in Indianapolis. He took walks with friends, dressed in a plain black overcoat, brown kid gloves, a tall hat, and a black silk tie. He'd stop to chat or tip his hat to ladies. He often made brief, unannounced appearances in the East Room, chatting with tourists. Caroline did her own shopping around town, on foot. Once, in a milliner's shop on a side street, the saleslady was busy with another customer and did not recognize the first lady. Caroline quietly waited for a while, then gave up and left.

Caroline disliked being in the public eye. "If there is one thing above another I detest and have detested all my days, it is to be made a circus of, and that is what has come to me in my old age," complained the first lady, who was fifty-six when her husband took office. It annoyed her that tourists "spied" on her while she was out gardening, even photographing her bending over pulling weeds. She was particularly stung by early criticisms of her personal campaign to clean the White House. Her housekeeping

*Office seekers plagued Benjamin Harrison as they had his grandfather fifty years before. Here they wait on the second floor, limiting the privacy of the four generations of Harrisons who were crowded in the five bedrooms and one bath of the private quarters.* (LIBRARY OF CONGRESS)

struck Washington society as below her station, and the press occasionally made fun of her. Nearly in tears, she told staff member Colonel William H. Crook, "Oh, Colonel Crook, what have we done! What have we ever done that we should be held up to ridicule by newspapers, and the President be so cruelly attacked and even his little, helpless grandchildren made fun of, for the country to laugh at! If this is the penalty for being the President of the United States, I hope the Good Lord will deliver my husband from any further experience."

Nonetheless she performed her public role with aplomb. During the 1892 winter social season, the *Washington Post* wrote, "Mrs. Harrison has mastered the art of entertaining. She avoids crushes of guests when possible, for on such occasions . . . she is unable to give the personal attention to guests that she would like to." The reporter also spoke of "a friendliness of manner that is proof against criticism."

Which was not to say she enjoyed herself. Caroline was never comfortable in large groups, and the state dinners were ordeals for her. Standing for hours shaking hands at the big receptions hurt her back and neck, until she came up with the idea of holding a large bouquet of flowers. She also disliked the state dinners for their many courses of rich food. They gave both her and the president indigestion. The White House steward, Hugo Zieman, had hired a new French chef, Madame Petronard, who believed presidential food should be rich in sauces and pastry. A newspaper report said that the president had tried her dishes, and they "laid him out." Caroline could not convince her to cook plain food, and both the cook and the steward were fired. Zieman went to the press with a story that Harrison had dozed off holding a banana and that rats "pulled the banana from his hand and scampered away." Madame Petronard created a scene, threatened to sue for a season's wages, and had to be appropriately rewarded before she would leave quietly. She was replaced by Dolly Johnson, a black woman from Kentucky, who knew how to make the simple foods the Harrisons liked. She earned fifteen dollars a month as opposed to Madame Petronard's fifty dollars a month.

One of Caroline's social successes was to start day classes at the White House, inviting groups of twenty-five women to join each one. French class met in the Red Room, china painting in the conservatory. China painting was her hobby, and she taught that class herself. She also decorated objects such as candlesticks and milk pitchers. When it came time to buy a new set of china for the White House, she naturally designed it. She took her sketches, featuring very American goldenrod and sweet corn, to a designer who made the final drawings. She wanted it to be manufactured in the United States, but there was still no such high-quality capability here. So the china was actually made in Limoges, where she had her designs painted on French "blanks." And when in the course of her cleaning the first lady came across a closet full of odds and ends of china, she investigated their history and made plans to display them. So began the White House custom of collecting historical china.

Perhaps the biggest social event of the administration was the centenary celebration of George Washington's inauguration, which included a big banquet in the State Dining Room on April 28, 1889. The centennial created unusual public interest in the history of the presidency and the White House. The press churned out more articles on the White House than had been printed in the building's entire previous history. Harrison's own interest in history was piqued. He was particularly fond of the U.S. flag, and he decorated the East Room with presidential shields and flags. He also ordered all federal offices to display the flag daily, and had a flagpole put on the roof of the White House on which the flag was raised each morning and lowered at sundown.

Harrison had plenty of time for historical and other pursuits. He seldom worked more than half a day, and, as a Sabbatarian, never worked on Sunday. Still, the newspapers criticized him for taking a pleasure excursion down the Potomac on a Sunday. Weekday afternoons he went for a walk, weather permitting. Sometimes he was accompanied by a member of the Metropolitan Police, but he often walked alone or with his secretary, Elijah Halford. The staff noticed that he also liked to walk with Caroline's niece, Mary Dimmick. In bad weather he might play billiards or go for a carriage ride. He liked fine carriages, and bought a dark green Studebaker landau for $2,000 and a family carriage for $1,000. Sometimes he rode the Studebaker into Maryland or Virginia. If he was alone he liked to take his buggy and drive it himself, then stop, tie his horse to a tree, and take a pleasant stroll.

Harrison also enjoyed travel, and in 1891 he went on the longest trip of any president up to that time: to the West Coast and back, 9,232 miles in one month and three days (carefully avoiding travel on Sunday). The railroads gave him and his family a private five-car train with a luxurious double drawing room in blue plush. With reelection in mind, he made many speeches and shook many hands.

The president and first lady also got away from the White House each summer. They vacationed at Cape May, on the New Jersey seashore, in a twenty-room "cottage" given to them by Postmaster General John Wanamaker and some of his rich friends. When the newspapers got wind of the story, Harrison sent Wanamaker $10,000 in payment.

Whether walking around the capital or vacationing by the sea, the president usually went without bodyguards. There were plainclothes security guards at the White House, though. Once Harrison was sitting on the south portico when a drunk climbed over the iron fence and came up to talk to him. Harrison conversed with him while pulling the bell ring for help, but the man proved harmless. More seriously, a mentally unbalanced man once broke into the mansion. Threatening to kill Harrison, the man knocked down one of the two doorkeepers, who were unable to control him. Harrison heard glass shatter and went to help, pinning the man down and helping to tie him up.

As Harrison went into the last year of his term, he grew depressed. "I sometimes wonder that I am still alive," he said, and told Elijah Halford that the White House was his "jail." Then Caroline fell ill. Her health had long been frail, and conditions in the White House didn't help. Escaping sewer gases permeated the house on humid summer days, and hordes of mosquitoes came in the unscreened windows. The general dampness of the house and the dry, somewhat sooty air produced by the heating system in winter aggravated her colds. In the spring of 1892, she developed what was initially diagnosed as nervous prostration, then as tuberculosis. She became depressed, losing interest in everything. Harrison spent several hours each day with her but wrote that she "has not shown the improvement we had hoped." He took her to Loon Lake in the Adirondacks, but here she grew worse, developing pleurisy and enduring coughing spasms and a lung hemorrhage. By fall the prognosis was grim. On September 14 the press was informed of her condition for the first time. On September 20 she returned to the White House, and she died there October 25. The funeral was held in the East Room. Harrison returned to Indianapolis with the casket on October 28.

Only a week later Harrison lost his reelection bid to the man he had defeated four years earlier, Grover Cleveland. Because of Caroline's illness and death, Cleveland had refrained from campaigning against Harrison, but he won anyway. On election night, Harrison waited upstairs in the White House for the returns to come in, finally going to bed at 3 A.M., knowing he had lost. "For me there is no sting in it," Harrison said of his defeat. "Indeed after the heavy blow the death of my wife dealt me, I do not think I could have stood the strain a re-election would have brought."

He returned to Indianapolis to his law practice, bringing the goat His Whiskers with him. He wrote his son Russell, "My life now, and much more as I grow older, is and will be a lonely one and I cannot go on as now." Three years after Caroline died, Harrison, at sixty-two, married Caroline's niece, Mary Dimmick, now thirty-seven. His children were outraged and refused to attend the wedding, so Harrison cut them out of his will. He and Mary became parents when he was sixty-six. Four years later, he died on March 13, 1901.

## PONIES, SNAKES, RACCOONS, AND OTHER WHITE HOUSE PETS

Benjamin Harrison's goat, His Whiskers, joined a long line of White House pets. Here are some examples:

- Thomas Jefferson had a mockingbird that sat on his shoulder and took food from his lips as well as grizzly bear cubs sent to him by the explorer Zebulon Pike.
- Zachary Taylor's horse from the Mexican War, Old Whitey, grazed on the White House lawn and joined processions that marched to martial music.
- Franklin Pierce received sleeve dogs from the Orient, brought back by Commodore Matthew C. Perry. The dogs were so tiny they scampered around on a coffee saucer.
- Abraham Lincoln purchased two goats for his sons that he allowed upstairs in the bedrooms, where they created no small amount of turmoil. Outside they chased Willis, the coachman, over a fence.
- Grover Cleveland's household included canaries, a poodle, a monkey, and rabbits. At the home he purchased outside Washington, D.C., and used as a presidential refuge, he and his wife kept over twenty pets, including foxes, quail, and white rats.
- William McKinley would whistle the first part of "Yankee Doodle," and his pet parrot would complete the tune.
- William Howard Taft's cow, Pauline—the last White House cow—grazed on the lawn and provided milk.
- Theodore Roosevelt had a menagerie including the pony Algonquin, Emily Spinach the snake, a kangaroo rat, Eli, a blue macaw, and Loretta, a parrot.
- Warren G. Harding's Airedale, Laddie Boy, had his own chair at cabinet meetings.
- When Calvin Coolidge's kitten Tiger wandered off, Grace broadcast a radio appeal. A guard discovered him hiding in a munitions building near the Lincoln Memorial. Coolidge issued two collars—green for Tiger and red for his other cat, Blacky—each labeled "White House." Despite the collar, Tiger later ran off for good.
- Herbert Hoover's son, Allan, was supposed to keep his pet alligators in the bathtub at night but sometimes they ran loose.
- Eleanor Roosevelt had little love for her husband's famous Scottie, Fala. She had him banished from the dining room. The Secret Service's code name for the dog was "The Informer." When Roosevelt's train stopped, Fala had to be walked, and then it was no secret that the president was on board.
- John Kennedy received Pushinka, daughter of Russian space dog Strelka, as a gift from Soviet leader Nikita Khrushchev. The household included numerous hamsters, Robin, a canary, lovebirds Maypole and Bluebell, Tom Kitten, ducks, Charlie, a Welsh terrier, Clipper, a police dog, and Leprechaun and Macaroni, ponies.

- Lyndon Johnson's daughter Luci rescued Yuki, a pooch from a gas station, and the president gave him the run of the Oval Office. Johnson's beagles, Him and Her, became an international news story when Johnson picked Him up by the ears and the dog yelped—in front of a swarm of reporters and photographers. The chairman of the Canine Defense League in London was one of the few who defended Johnson's dog-handling technique.
- Chelsea Clinton's cat, Socks, became a celebrity who received much mail at the White House. All postcard replies were sent out signed with a paw print.

# William McKinley

## 1897–1901

## Better Than a Bishopric

"MOTHER" MCKINLEY, an agile eighty-seven years old, journeyed from Canton, Ohio, to Washington for her son's inauguration, waving to the crowds as she stepped off the train with an armful of roses. Life was turning out well, but not according to plan. "But, Mother," Abner McKinley, the president-elect's brother, was overheard saying, "this is better than a bishopric."

No doubt William McKinley would have made a good bishop. His dignity and integrity impressed others. He endlessly repeated platitudes about fundamental American principles. Genial, kindly, and good, he was a "mother's boy" in a day when this was meant as a compliment. His friend and political mentor, Mark Hanna, proclaimed him "a saint." Assassination earned him that stature nationally, but domestically he was a true saint to his wife, Ida Saxon McKinley.

Daughter of a wealthy Canton, Ohio banker, Ida Saxon was not raised to be a shrinking violet. Her father, recognizing her intelligence, sent her off on a grand tour to Europe and even let her work at his bank. When McKinley first met Ida at a picnic in 1857, she was vivacious and strikingly attractive. She knew how to dress well—her White House trousseau had cost $10,000, paid for with her own money. Her inheritance of $70,000 made her one of the wealthiest first ladies. At the White House Ida wore diamond earrings, rings, and necklaces and even had diamonds in her hair.

McKinley often said she was the prettiest girl he had ever seen. He closed one letter to her, "Your faithful Husband and always your lover."

But in the early years of their marriage, Ida had lost her mother and both of their young children. Deeply depressed, she took to sitting in a darkened room, moaning and rocking an imaginary baby in her arms. She believed her children's deaths were God's punishment. She began to have fits that would plague her until the day her husband died. The dreaded word *epilepsy* was never used. Ida was said to be "delicate," to have a "nervous condition," or "fainting spells." She needed McKinley at her side.

During the presidential election of 1896, McKinley ventured no farther than the white porch of their Canton home. There he touted the gold standard and entertained 750,000 people from thirty states while his opponent, William Jennings Bryan, logged eighteen thousand miles talking up silver-based currency. On inauguration night at the ball, McKinley was promenading with Ida, dressed in white satin and diamonds, when she suddenly fainted. McKinley calmly swept her into his arms and took her to the White House, leaving the crowds to wonder what they would.

Over the years McKinley had learned how to take care of his wife and did so with infinite patience. "The relationship between them was one of those rare and beautiful things that live only in tradition," said friend Jennie Hobart. He helped to feed her when necessary, and when the headaches came, he patted her, soothed her, and spent hours reading to her or just rubbing her head in a darkened room. Ida became completely dependent on him. She never called him by his given name but always "my precious love," "my dearest," or "Major," referring to his Civil War title. When he died, she sobbed, "I want to go too, I want to go too." But she endured another six years, oddly enough without seizures.

At the White House, Ida remained in her room most of the time. The affliction was poorly understood, and there were no drugs to help, which made Ida's seizures—involving convulsions, frothing at the mouth, incontinence, memory loss, and infantile behavior—particularly frightening. She also developed phlebitis in both legs, so that she needed help just to walk, and then came raging headaches so severe she had her hair cut off because she couldn't stand the weight. The headaches plagued her periodically all her life. Baffled doctors could only dose her with sedatives to get her through the days and barbiturates to get her through the nights.

At times she was so drugged she resembled a smiling mannequin. At other times she played cards or knitted and greeted friends, especially enjoying the visits of children. Cards were a favorite pastime, and she often played euchre with her husband in the evening. She did not like to lose, so her ever-considerate husband would "accidentally" drop cards or reveal his hand to her in order to let her win. When her hands weren't occupied by cards, her crochet needles flew. She knitted an estimated thirty-five hundred pairs of slippers at the White House. Her maid mounted the crocheted slippers on cork soles and laced them with satin ribbons, and they were given away to relatives and charities. Ida had a temper and a sharp tongue, as any woman who got the least bit cozy with her husband quickly discovered.

No matter how pressed by presidential business he was, McKinley found time to walk over to the living quarters several times a day to visit Ida. It was a long-standing habit. As governor of Ohio he would leave their Columbus hotel in the morning and cross over to the Capitol grounds, turn, remove his hat, and salute Ida's window. Then, each afternoon at 3 P.M., he would interrupt whatever he was doing to go to the window and wave his handkerchief to her.

McKinley's concerns about Ida were never far from his mind. While smoking cigars on the south portico with the president one evening, H. H. Kohlsaat listened as his old friend talked about his problems—Ida's health was particularly bad, events were pushing the country into a war with Spain, and he had had little sleep for weeks. Suddenly, Kohlsaat recalled, McKinley "broke down and cried like a boy of thirteen."

"Are my eyes very red?" McKinley asked when he calmed down. "Do they look as if I had been crying?"

"Yes," Kohlsaat said.

"But I must return to Mrs. McKinley at once. She is among strangers."

"When you open the door to the room," his friend advised, "blow your nose very hard and loud. It will force tears into your eyes, and they will think that is what makes your eyes red."

He did this, making "no small blast," Kohlsaat said, and it worked.

Many assumed that Ida, like so many invalid first ladies in the 1800s, would spend her White House years confined to the family quarters and leave the hostess duties to someone else. But Ida's will was strong and during the first winter social season she was beside her husband on every occasion.

Inevitably, seizures came. McKinley handled these incidents with utter calm. During formal dinner, he would cover her face with a napkin. The darkness of the napkin seemed to soothe her. When it was over, he resumed his dinner as if nothing had happened. William Howard Taft recalled that he was once in a conference with McKinley and had just asked for a pencil when Ida began to make "a peculiar hissing sound." McKinley matter-of-factly put a handkerchief over his wife's face with one hand and handed Taft a pencil with the other. Normally, attacks of this sort lasted only a minute or so, and McKinley would just continue as if nothing happened. When he saw a major attack coming, he got Ida out of the room in such a graceful way that others often didn't realize what was happening.

Ida often participated in the big public receptions, held three afternoons a week. Anyone who was reasonably presentable could come to the White House and shake the president's hand. McKinley stood at the East Room door in his frock coat, and Ida was usually seated next to him holding a bouquet of flowers to ward off handshaking, nodding to the callers as they passed. Unlike many presidents, McKinley actually enjoyed meeting the public this way. "They bring no problems with them, only good will. I feel better after the contact." He remembered names by fixing the face in his memory with an initial unflinching stare, an experience some of his visitors found disconcerting. He could shake eighteen hundred hands an hour while warding off fatigue with this technique: he would smile, grab the guest's right hand, and squeeze it quickly before his own got squeezed. By holding the caller's elbow with his left hand, he could pull him along and turn to smile at the next person in line.

For formal evening receptions, the president stationed himself in the Blue Room in front of a line of sofas meant to serve as a barrier. In the closed-off area behind the sofas, distinguished guests were seated. Captain Theodore A. Bingham, commissioner of public buildings and grounds, escorted out anyone who penetrated the line of sofas.

He stood in full dress uniform to the president's left and presented each guest to him. Everyone was expected to wear full evening dress. The Marine Band set up in the conservatory just off the main corridor. The preparations for these receptions were elaborate and could take several days. Captain Bingham directed it all, assisted by Henry Pfister, who was in charge of the greenhouses and gardens. Pfister and his staff of twelve rearranged the furniture and adorned the reception rooms with hundreds of potted plants and trees and thousands of flowers and smilax. A coarse woven fabric called "crash" was spread out over the floors to protect the carpet. On the night of a reception, Bingham also stationed a fireman in the attic.

At dinners, McKinley upset protocol in order to protect Ida. Traditionally, the president escorted the wife of the guest of honor to the dinner table and seated her on his right, while the guest of honor escorted the first lady to the opposite side of the table. Since McKinley needed to be near his wife in the event of a seizure, he seated her on his right. When dinner commenced, he consented to be served first, as protocol required, but he didn't like it. "All my married life Mrs. McKinley has been served first," he said, "but it is a custom and we cannot change it. We are governed by White House etiquette, handed down for generations." Often Ida turned down the elaborate meals in favor of a few crackers on a plate.

White House customs had held up better than the White House itself, however. The old mansion was ill equipped for many of these events, and had been for years. The State Dining Room held a maximum of only about fifty, and larger dinners required the use of the central hall. Dinners were held during the social season—while Congress was in session—normally December to March. Despite Tiffany's stained-glass screen, cold winds blew in through the north portico doors every time they were opened. Cushions were removed from chairs and sofas for the ladies to warm their feet on. The eight- to twelve-course dinners began at eight o'clock and were considered tedious affairs. The service was slow, as food had to be brought up from the kitchens in the basement. Mark Hanna, a Republican party boss and wealthy Ohio industrialist, would sit at the table with his watch in his hand remarking on how long the servants took.

But if dinners were uncomfortable and slow, the large receptions were potentially dangerous. The Army Corps of Engineers advised that any crowd larger than two thousand might be more than the old house could safely stand, yet crowds of three thousand or more were not unusual at receptions. People often jammed the rooms so tightly that it became impossible to lift an arm. Ladies found their dresses ruined, especially if they had trains, and some lost jewelry or fainted. The sagging floors were bolstered from the cellar below with wooden beams and bricks. Needless to say, the White House furnishings did not fare well, either.

The McKinleys had few complaints about the upstairs living quarters—five bedrooms plus two dressing rooms. The president's bedroom contained two brass beds, a table with an electric lamp plugged into the chandelier overhead, a couple of tufted easy chairs, two large wardrobes, a sofa, and two cheap wooden rocking chairs. They used the west end of the big central corridor as a parlor. First families usually chose the Oval Room as their parlor, but office space was increasingly tight, and the room was sometimes commandeered for meetings.

On the business side of the second floor, however, it was crowded. In the corner were tables and chairs reserved for the press, who McKinley handled deftly, unlike his reclusive and adversarial predecessor, Grover Cleveland. He did not give interviews or allow any direct quotes, but he had his secretary speak to reporters twice a day. The unwritten rule was that reporters could not direct questions to the president unless he spoke to them first. The corridor was lined with chairs usually filled with office seekers or petitioners of some kind. Callers waiting to see the president also pressed into the Cabinet Room, and any further overflow waited on chairs in the president's office. McKinley found working in front of an audience unsatisfactory, so he set up shop in the smaller Cabinet Room and turned the larger office into a waiting room. He pulled a swivel chair up to the cabinet conference table and set up his blotter and inkstand there. Six clerks and typists shared two rooms, one of which had a toilet concealed by a wooden partition. Appointments to official positions had to be signed on sheepskin, which could not be blotted dry and had to be spread out all over the furniture and the floor to dry. During the Spanish-American War, which brought numerous commissions

*The Spanish-American War greatly accelerated the need for communications and staff workers, but there was little space to house an expanded staff. Everyone agreed something had to be done but frail Ida McKinley said she would have no "hammering" while she was living in the White House.* (LIBRARY OF CONGRESS)

for army and navy officers, the problem was even worse. McKinley was heard to mutter, "Something ought to be done about this." The war meant office staff increased, doubling and then tripling. Fifteen phone lines ran out the window where before there had been only one, and twenty-five new telegraph lines were installed.

Clearly, the presidency was outgrowing the White House. Proposals to expand it or build a new structure had come and gone over the years, and several plans were put forward during McKinley's term as well, by the Army Corps of Engineers, among others. Each plan entailed drastically changing the shape of the historic building, and none of them went anywhere. The first lady weighed in by saying simply that she didn't want any "hammering." The only thing that was improved upon was the almost total lack of adequate facilities for storing hats and coats. Captain Bingham bought secondhand coat racks, boxes for hats, and velour curtains at 60 cents a yard and created temporary facilities in the entrance hall.

Bingham tried various schemes to hold down the size of the receptions to one thousand, but was singularly unsuccessful. He tried limiting the number of invitations by decreeing that no one person would be invited to more than one reception during the season, but only succeeded in outraging important people, many of whom protested loudly or demanded exceptions. He then got McKinley to agree to the one thousand limit, not realizing that McKinley would never agree to forcibly prevent anyone from entering.

Gate-crashing at the White House was a way of life. There was little social life in the capital, so the evening receptions were important to dignitaries and politicians, especially when they had out-of-town guests. If not invited, the bolder ones just pushed their way in. Captain Bingham tried hiring spotters to identify known gate-crashers, but he could only embarrass them. If they had enough nerve and persistence, he had to let them in. Bingham sent the president a memorandum complaining that "butchers, cabin, market and grocery clerks, and the scum of the city" were appearing at receptions. But McKinley did not want the White House to be known as elitist, and the memo backfired. He called off Bingham's attempts to limit attendance.

But Bingham persisted in his elitist attitudes. He sent a notice to the *Washington Evening Star* explaining that women should not attend evening receptions at the White House wearing bonnets because "the law of evening dress" required an "unbonnetted head." Similarly, men who showed themselves in anything but evening clothes "detracted from the fitness and harmony, to say nothing of the brilliancy, of the most important of all the social functions, a presidential levee." He was a stickler for protocol. He was even annoyed to see Ida painfully descending the stair while clinging to her husband's left arm—protocol called for the right. McKinley finally summoned Bingham for a heart-to-heart talk, saying, "I can stand anything around me but a fool."

The president not only ran the federal government, he oversaw the eighty or so employees who ran the White House. Indeed, it was in his interest to monitor the operation of the mansion, since he not only lived in it but personally paid a sizable portion of the expense of running it. He had to feed the domestic staff every day, and pay the salaries of his personal servants and the cook. He paid Clara Thorin, Ida's personal maid, $30 a month, and gave her and her husband a bedroom in the family quarters. McKinley put Clara's husband on the federal payroll as a doorkeeper, but evidently he did little. The president was also responsible for the stables, paying a head coachman $60 a month to run them. He also paid for a staff barber, but McKinley liked to shave himself. He was the first clean-shaven president since Andrew Johnson. While in the army he had learned to shave without a mirror and, using a straight razor, used his left hand for the left side and his right hand for the right side.

Before the Civil War, presidents also had to pay for their own private secretaries and so tended to use their sons or relatives. Not until James Buchanan's time did Congress create the position of "Private Secretary at the White House." Under McKinley it became "Secretary to the President." George B. Cortelyou started out as a clerk. He was also a good stenographer, and McKinley, thankful to find someone so capable, gave him more and more responsibility, and finally made him secretary. He grew close to McKinley personally, and became almost indispensable to him. He would later serve Theodore Roosevelt in the same capacity.

The key position in the operation of the White House was that of the steward, who was responsible for government property. He was bonded, as he took care of valuables such as silverware and was in charge of buying food and other household supplies. William Sinclair had served Cleveland in this position and—at the outgoing president's urging—McKinley kept him on at a government salary of $1,800 a year.

The civil service now protected such positions as clerks, messengers, doorkeepers, firemen, and watchmen, though the president could remove them from the White House and send them to some other government post. "Employees pass from one administration to another," McKinley noted. "Some have been here over thirty years." Thomas Pendel, a doorkeeper, remembered Abraham Lincoln. He had opened the door for him as he left for Ford's Theater. Proud of his association with Lincoln, he would tell visitors stories of his experiences, even offering a snip of his own hair as a souvenir. Jerry Smith started as a stable hand, but Julia Grant spiffed him up with a uniform and he escorted her to the doors of her hosts as she went calling. By McKinley's time he was known as "worthless Jerry," because he sometimes swept cigar butts or the remains of lunches into obscure corners, or tossed the contents of spittoons out the window. The latter precipitated a career crisis when he doused a guard, ruining his uniform. Jerry saved his job by appealing to the softhearted McKinley, explaining that he had been cleaning up the spit on the rug near the president's desk and had "squze [sic] a rag out the window." Ike Hoover, who would work at the White House for forty-two years, becoming a well-known chief usher, was at this time an electrician making $75 a month to take care of the new and not entirely safe electrical wiring.

Despite all the expenses he incurred in running the White House, McKinley's $50,000-a-year salary was ample, and he was even able to save a substantial portion and indulge his penchant for expensive clothing. He was particular about his clothes and his appearance, and never dressed casually. On one vacation, he was persuaded by staff members to go fishing, and he wore a frock coat and silk hat. When he got a bite and tried to reel it in, he wobbled the boat so badly that it sank. The water was shallow, and his frock coat, silk hat, and even his dignity were unaffected, but his shoes and pants were a mess. His suits were made by a New York tailor, to whom McKinley sent his measurements. He received callers in a black Prince Albert coat, boiled shirt, high collar, white vest, dark tie, and striped pants. He might change into a clean white vest several times a

*The McKinleys' bedroom was not the height of luxury. A cord dangled from the spidery chandelier to the electric lamp on the table; the rocking chairs were the kind that could be bought for $1.95 apiece. But the McKinleys were happy with the White House and Ida appreciated the fact that her husband's office was only down the hall, enabling her to summon him easily.* (LIBRARY OF CONGRESS)

day. Pince-nez glasses hung from a black silk ribbon. He needed glasses only for reading and was vain about being seen wearing them. He usually wore a red carnation in a buttonhole. Often he would remove it and pin it on the lapel of a guest or someone he had to deny a favor, telling him to give it to his wife with the president's best wishes.

Another indulgence was cigars, a habit he had learned to enjoy in the army and ever after was unable to break. He smoked a dozen or so a day, but never in Ida's presence or while being photographed. "We must not let the young men of this country see the President smoking," he said. His favorite was an imported Garcia, but cigars were not a major expense, for he received plenty of them as gifts. Sometimes he would bite a cigar in two and chew on half of it, as if it were chewing tobacco. He often enjoyed smoking a cigar while sitting on the south portico talking with friends.

His taste in food was less refined. A French chef from New York was hired to prepare the state dinners, but for private meals with Ida, McKinley hired a family cook at $40 a month to prepare plain food. Breakfast ran to fruit, coffee, eggs, hot breads, potatoes, and steak.

McKinley had gained weight during his years as a congressman, when long work hours allowed him little time for exercise. As president his workload and the need to be near Ida meant he got even less exercise, and he grew decidedly portly. In the summer of 1897 he tried the relatively new sport of golf, but found it required too much walking. He was a good horseman and enjoyed horseback riding, but as president gave it up. Automobiles were just coming into use, and he once tried riding in a steamer. McKinley sat in the backseat, held on with both hands, and almost lost his hat when the car reached eighteen miles an hour. He decided to stick with the horse and carriage. During the first part of his presidency he sometimes strolled the streets of Washington, slipping out without telling his guards. But the pressures of the job steadily increased, and ultimately he had to settle for an occasional drive with Ida on pleasant afternoons.

Early in his term, the atmosphere in the White House was placid and relaxed. The office staff had time to play baseball on the south lawn after lunch. McKinley cheerfully whistled the first part of "Yankee Doodle" to his pet parrot and listened to the parrot finish it. On Sundays the president went to church, always hoping to be treated as any other parishioner, and always finding that the congregation persisted in standing for him. Sunday evenings he would invite guests to the Blue Room to sing hymns with him.

In the summer, after Congress adjourned, he could return to Canton and sit on the porch, fanning himself with his hat and waving to passersby.

But the political heat was turned up in early 1898 as tensions mounted between the United States and Spain over Cuba. McKinley began working until after midnight, agonizing over difficult decisions. Circles began to appear under his eyes. "I have been through one war," he said; "I have seen the dead piled up and I do not want to see another." He proceeded in his usual cautious manner while the hawks in Congress and the yellow press screamed for war. Theodore Roosevelt, McKinley's assistant secretary of the navy and soon to be his second-term vice president, said the president had "no more backbone than a chocolate eclair."

The U.S. battleship *Maine* was sunk in Havana harbor on February 15, 1898, and on April 25, the United States declared war on Spain. Fortunately the United States defeated Spain in only three months, but difficult problems remained. The main one was what to do with the Philippine Islands. Public opinion was sharply divided. At the start of the war the president, like most Americans, was only dimly aware of the Spanish possession. He explained to one White House caller that the islands were "somewhere away around the other side of the world." Now the future of the islands was in his hands. "I walked the floor of the White House night after night until midnight," he said. "I went down on my knees and prayed Almighty God for light and guidance. . . . And then one night late it came to me this way . . . there was nothing left for us to do but to take all of them, and to educate the Filipinos, and uplift and civilize and Christianize them, and by God's grace do the very best we could by them, as our fellow men for whom Christ also died. And then I went to bed and slept soundly."

The war greatly increased McKinley's popularity. It was short and crowned with stunning victories and heroes, and it thrust America onto the world stage as a colonial power. It was, Secretary of State John Hay said, "a splendid little war." Buoyed by victory, and by feats of scientific and industrial progress, America entered the twentieth century full of optimism and reelected McKinley by a landslide in 1900.

Symbolic of that optimism was the Pan-American Exposition in Buffalo, New York, in 1901. Naturally, the president would attend, though the immense crowds would pose a security threat. During the Civil War, the Treasury Department created the Secret Service to catch counterfeiters, and that was still its main concern, though it did occasionally protect the president. George Cortelyou, McKinley's devoted secretary, worried constantly about the president's safety. He once sent an aide to check on the Secret Service guards, and one was found sleeping in a second floor bedroom. Mark Hanna, a close friend and supporter, worried too. He once said to McKinley of the public receptions, "What would happen, do you think, if some crank got in there with a revolver in his pants?"

But McKinley enjoyed having people around and disliked security measures. He dismissed his secretary's concerns with, "I have no enemies. Why should I fear?" He reopened the south grounds—what he called "the yard"—after Cleveland had closed them. They became a public park again, and people liked to picnic there. He also had Cleveland's sentry boxes removed. The north driveway became a thoroughfare for pedestrians. All rooms on the first floor of the White House were open to the public until 2 P.M. daily except the president's private dining room, which looked out on the north driveway.

As the president made plans to attend the exposition, Cortelyou was particularly worried by a proposed visit to the Temple of Music for a handshaking session. Twice Cortelyou had taken it off the schedule, and twice McKinley had put it back in. He would not give it up. "Why should I?" he said. "No one would wish to hurt me." Security was deemed tight at the exposition. McKinley and Ida were staying at the Milburn house, home of the exposition's director, and uniformed and plainclothes officers guarded it around the clock. When the McKinleys went out in their carriage, there were contingents of soldiers and police in front, on the sides, and in the rear. The president made a major speech to a large crowd on September 5. The next day he visited Niagara Falls with Ida, and headed for the handshaking session at the Temple of Music, scheduled for 4 P.M. Cortelyou had persuaded McKinley to limit it to ten minutes. It hardly seemed worth it for such a short time, Cortelyou then told the president. Only a small fraction of the crowd would get to meet him. "Well, they'll know I tried," McKinley answered.

The Temple of Music did not lack for security forces, which included soldiers in full dress, exposition police, Buffalo detectives, and the Secret Service. Ida had intended to join her husband, but the visit to the falls had tired her, and she decided to return to the Milburn house. McKinley handed her her bottle of smelling salts. "Good afternoon, Mrs. McKinley. I hope you enjoy your ride; good-bye." Waiting in line at the Temple of Music was Leon Czolgosz, a brooding, disturbed loner and anarchist. He had a .32-caliber Iver-Johnson revolver in his pocket. Once inside the building he slipped the gun into his hand and wrapped both in a bandage. At some point the head Secret Service agent, George Foster, looked him in the eye. Czolgosz calmly looked back. "I thought he was a mechanic out for the day to do the Exposition and wanted to shake hands with the President," Foster would say later.

Cortelyou, watch in hand, was waiting to signal the guards to cut off the flow of visitors. It was about eight minutes after four when McKinley reached for Czolgosz's hand. Foster actually had his hand on Czolgosz's shoulder and was ready to urge him along when two shots rang out. McKinley, shot in the stomach, fell back in the arms of a Secret Service agent. Czolgosz went down under a barrage of fists and rifle butts, his bandage on fire from the shots. McKinley said, "Be easy on him, boys!" And to Cortelyou: "My wife—be careful, Cortelyou, how you tell her—oh, be careful!" Czolgosz's last words before his death in the electric chair would be, "I am not sorry."

The president needed surgery immediately. Buffalo General Hospital, with its new operating room and X-ray machines, was twenty minutes away, but the president was taken to the exposition's emergency medical center. Outside, the 389-foot Electric Tower glowed in tribute to electric light, but the lights in the emergency center were inadequate, and gas lamps could not be lit because the ether used to anesthetize the president was highly flammable. Dr. Matthew D. Mann, an obstetrician and gynecologist, was called in to remove the bullet. He had not been told why he was called, and was not prepared for surgery. He was forced to use instruments from a fellow doctor's pocket case. Surgeon General Marion Rixey, McKinley's personal physician, managed to rig up an electric light and a reflector to help Dr. Mann see. Still, Dr. Mann said he was operating "at the bottom of a deep hole." The hour-long operation never produced the bullet. The holes in the stomach wall were closed and washed, and the surface wound closed, and the president was taken to Milburn House. Later, a complete set of surgical instruments was found in the anteroom.

Vice President Roosevelt and officials rushed to Buffalo. McKinley's temperature fell to 100 degrees, and he asked for a cigar—a sure sign he felt better. Dr. Charles McBurney from New York arrived on the scene and made himself official spokesman. He told the press that the operation on the president marked "the epoch of the century in surgery" and that the physicians had bolted the door against the "grim monster of death." He then left for Albany. The cabinet members left, and Roosevelt returned east and set out on a camping trip in the Adirondacks.

On Thursday evening, September 12, came a new report: "The President's condition is not quite so good." Gangrene had gradually spread along the track of the bullet. It was time to locate Theodore Roosevelt. A party was sent out into the woods, but he could not be found until late on the afternoon of the following day, September 13. That same day McKinley rallied and was given oxygen and a heart stimulant. Finally he said, "It is useless, gentlemen. I think we ought to have a prayer." He died at 2:15 A.M. Saturday, September 14, 1901. An hour before he breathed his last breath, Roosevelt set out over dark mountain roads, traveling thirty-five miles before reaching North Creek, where a train awaited him. He arrived in Buffalo on the afternoon of the fourteenth, immediately paid his respects to the dead president, and then took the oath of office at the home of his friend, Ansley Wilcox.

# 26

# Theodore Roosevelt

## 1901–1909

## *The Reign of Enthusiasm*

ON SEPTEMBER 20, 1901, Theodore Roosevelt returned from William McKinley's funeral in Canton, Ohio, to take up the presidency. His wife and six children were still in Oyster Bay, New York, at their home, Sagamore Hill. For two days, Roosevelt used the White House as an office, sleeping at the home of his sister, Bamie Cowles. He took up residency on September 22, 1901, and his family arrived five days later. The White House would remain officially in mourning until October 19, and entertaining would be prohibited until the new year, but the reign of enthusiasm had begun.

"No President has enjoyed himself as much as I have enjoyed myself," maintained Roosevelt, who at forty-two was the youngest president in history. *Frank Leslie's Weekly* proclaimed that the new president "does as much work as two presidents might be expected to do." An English visitor, John Morley, who spent two days at the White House, wrote, "I have seen two tremendous works of nature in America. One is Niagara Falls and the other is the President of the United States."

Roosevelt galloped through his duties. He once dictated a thirty-thousand-word critique of a book he had just read, then called for a fresh "shorthand man" to take some more thoughts. He regularly wore out strings of stenographers. His secretary's office had several clerks, four typists, and six stenographers plus six messengers, and he kept them all busy.

Not one to waste a minute of time, he held "Barber Chair Interviews" with Washington correspondents while he was being shaved, discussing issues ranging from the Panama Canal to conditions at Ellis Island, never allowing his words to be quoted directly. He called reporters by their first names and was a master at feeding them human interest stories, never allowing his words to be quoted directly. His barber had to be a master, too, for the president found it difficult to speak without jumping up, gesticulating, and pounding his fist into his other hand.

Roosevelt had a photographic memory, and seemed to retain everything he had ever read. "I remembered a book that I had read some time ago," he once said, "and as I talked the pages of the book came before my eyes." When Count Albert Apponyi of Hungary called at the White House, Roosevelt astonished him by reciting a long piece of Hungarian historical literature. Roosevelt had read it twenty years before. He could also recall facts and figures about a bill in Congress or names of people he met years ago.

He read voraciously, often a book a day. To compensate for his bad eyesight, he held books up to his nose and scanned the pages rapidly. When he read magazines, he tore out the finished page and tossed it on the floor. Roosevelt even kept a book by the main entrance downstairs so he could read while waiting for distinguished guests. His choices could not be classified as light, as the following note written on March 11, 1906, to Senator Henry Cabot Lodge's wife shows: "Dear Nannie: Can you have me to dinner either Wednesday or Friday? Would you be willing to have Bay and Bessie also? Then we could discuss the Hittite empire, Pithecanthropus, and the Magyar love songs, and the exact relations of the Alti of the Volsunga Saga to the Etzel of the Niebulungenlied, and both to Attila—with interludes by Cabot about the rate bill, Beveridge, and other matters of more vivid contemporary interest. Ever Yours, Theodore Roosevelt."

Among the many books Roosevelt published from his college days onward was one advocating "The Strenuous Life." It was a phrase he'd lived by ever since he was a sickly, asthmatic child. "I'll make my body," he told his father and at age twelve began a regimen of strenuous exercise and later boxing lessons. As a student at Harvard, Roosevelt, five feet eight inches tall and just 124 pounds, almost won the lightweight boxing championship. In 1880 he graduated Phi Beta Kappa and magna cum laude, but a doctor told him he was not likely to live out the decade. He had a weak heart and should avoid going up stairs too fast, the doctor said. Roosevelt replied, "Doctor, I'm going to do all the things you tell me not to do. If I've got to live the sort of life you have described, I don't care how short it is." Not long after, he climbed the Matterhorn.

At the White House, Roosevelt's wife, Edith Carow Roosevelt, had a tennis court installed on the grounds, and the president was known to have played as many as ninety-one games in one day. On June 10, 1908, aide Archie Butt hit the president hard on the head with a ball. When he began to apologize, Roosevelt cut him short: "If I hit you, Captain, I am not going to apologize, so just bang away at me as you like and say nothing in the fray." Once, when a game was stopped by rain, Roosevelt announced, "Just the day and time for a long walk and run. We will go!" The group set out for Rock Creek Park. On the way back, Roosevelt announced, "From here it is exactly four miles to the White House gate. We will now run every step of the way back!"

Roosevelt was famous for his "point-to-point" walks, in which one had to climb, swim, or wade through any obstacle—there was no bypassing anything. French Ambassador Jules Jusserand was once invited to go along with the president, and later described the experience: "I arrived at the White House punctually, in afternoon dress and silk hat as if we were to stroll in the Tuileries Garden. . . . To my surprise the President soon joined me in a tramping suit. . . . Two or three other gentlemen came and we started off at what seemed to me a breakneck pace. . . . On reaching the country, the President went pell-mell over the fields, following neither road nor path. . . . At last we came to the bank of a stream, rather wide and too deep to be forded . . . I saw the President unbutton his clothes." The ambassador recalled the president saying, "We had better strip, so as not to wet our things in the Creek." The ambassador did so but refused to remove his lavender kid gloves, as it "would be embarrassing if we should meet ladies."

An avid horseman, the indefatigable Roosevelt went riding at every opportunity—he preferred the horse and carriage to the automobile, just coming into use. One of his trips as president was a western tour that included 150 miles by horseback and 200 miles on foot. Edith, too, was a fine horseback rider. The couple liked to go by carriage to the fringes of the capital, then get on riding horses that would be waiting for them.

After receiving reports that many senior army officers in Washington were in poor physical condition, the president ordered a physical fitness test that included a ninety-mile horseback ride over three days. To prove its feasibility, he set out into the Virginia countryside with his personal physicians, Dr. Cary Grayson and Dr. Marion Rixey, at 3:30 A.M. in harsh winter weather. They encountered frozen, cut-up roads and had to ride along the embankments. En route they changed horses, and Roosevelt made a speech to a crowd surprised to have the president of the United States visiting them. They rode through a snowstorm and driving sleet. Roosevelt's glasses became so caked with ice he could see nothing, but he trusted the horse. They returned to the White House at eight-forty that evening, having covered ninety-eight miles. Edith treated them to juleps.

At the White House, he continued to set up challenges. He took up jujitsu, and wrote his son Kermit, "I am not the age and build, one would think, to be whirled lightly over an opponent's head and batted down on a mattress without damage, but they are so skillful that I have not been hurt at all." He also resumed boxing. It became an almost daily activity, and he invited well-known boxers to spar with him. But it was while sparring with Edith's cousin, Dan Taylor, that he received a blow to the eye that probably caused his eventual blindness in that eye—which was a well-guarded secret.

Roosevelt's favorite pastime was his six children: Alice, seventeen, Theodore Jr., fourteen, Kermit, twelve, Ethel, nine, Archie, seven, and Quentin, four. Worked stopped at 4 P.M. for what he called the "Children's Hour," usually reading and romping or a game of hide-and-seek where nothing in the White House was off limits. When he was off on his travels or the children away at school, he penned letters with little drawings that were so delightful that they were later published as a book.

Roosevelt's personal servant, Pinkney (on the federal payroll as a steward, although he performed none of the steward's duties), not only took care of Roosevelt but helped get the children to and from school. The older ones went to private schools, but when Quentin reached school age he attended Washington's Force Public School on Massachusetts Avenue. Edith called Quentin her "fine little bad boy." His inclinations were decidedly anarchic. He and his brother Archie followed the lamplighter around the White House grounds turning off the lights until a watchman caught them. When his father told him not to wreck the White House flower beds by walking through them on

*Nine-year-old Archie Roosevelt loved to ride his pony Algonquin on the White House grounds. Here the remains of the old conservatories as well as the new executive office buildings can be seen in the background.* (LIBRARY OF CONGRESS)

stilts—the gardener objected—Quentin said, "I don't see what good it does for you to be President. You can't do anything here."

Edith encapsulated her husband's attitude toward their children: "He thinks children should be given entire freedom for their own inclinations." Quentin's teacher once sent a note of complaint home to his parents about his conduct. By way of a reply, the president said that he didn't want to hear about his son "dancing when coming into the classroom" or "singing higher than other boys," but assured the teacher that if his son was found "defying your authority or committing any serious misdeeds let me know and I will whip him." Roosevelt's valet, James Amos, was allowed to paddle the children, but Roosevelt was not one to discipline that way.

When he discovered that Andrew Jackson's portrait, which hung in the second-floor hallway, had been hit by spitballs, he summoned Quentin and his friends, who were staying at the White House overnight. He escorted them to the scene of the crime. Actually the boys had climbed up and arranged the spitballs: one on each ear, three across the forehead, one on the nose, and one on each button of Jackson's coat. While the president was interrogating the boys—Quentin's "White House Gang"—an usher appeared with a message. "Later, later," Roosevelt said. "Tell him that I am dispensing justice." Quentin's friends were banned from the White House for a week.

The gang swore oaths that began, "By Buzzard," and Quentin, the leader, signed his name "Q." Quentin was quite fearless and very determined, and he and his cohorts explored parts of the White House never seen by any president, including the attic eaves. A favorite gang game involved Roosevelt baring his teeth, growling ferociously, and chasing the boys around the attic. Once, one of the boys turned off the lights, and the president's head hit a post with a solid whack, his eye just missing a projecting nail. One particularly interesting feature of the attic was a rectangular opening in the hall floor that allowed the gang to look down on the second-floor hall. Once, Edith was having tea there with an Italian diplomat who was wearing a monocle when Edith became aware of their spying. Her sudden, sharp cry, "Quentin!" caused the astonished diplomat to look up, and his monocle fell into his tea. The eyepiece entranced the boys, who later made their own from old watch crystals.

In another incident, the gang went to the roof after a snowstorm, rolled up a large snowball, and pushed it off onto the head of a White House police officer below. The president happened to be only a few feet away, about to enter his carriage. Shaking his fist, he called, "You! You! Come down from that roof at once!" And to his staff, "Go and catch them! Let not one escape! By George! Let not one escape! Bring them all to me!"

Quentin once interrupted a conference between his father and the attorney general by entering the room on roller skates and dumping a large king snake and two smaller snakes on the president's lap. He had gotten them "on approval" from a local animal store. Roosevelt calmly told him he had to wait his turn with the congressmen in the next room, and to take the snakes with him. The snakes might enliven their waiting time, Roosevelt said.

The Roosevelt White House menagerie also included cats, rabbits, guinea pigs, dogs, squirrels, birds, raccoons, a badger, and Kermit's kangaroo rat. Reformer and writer Jacob Riis was a guest at breakfast one morning when Kermit brought out the kangaroo rat. Riis recalled watching it hop across the table to the president, who fed it a lump of sugar. The badger, named Josiah, had been given to Roosevelt on a western trip, along with two bears, a lizard, a horned toad, and a horse. Roosevelt turned Josiah over to Archie, who would say, "He bites legs sometimes but he never bites faces." The most famous White House pet was Algonquin, a 350-pound calico pony. Quentin brought the pony up the White House elevator to Archie's bedroom to cheer him up when he was sick with both measles and whooping cough.

For all his antics, Quentin caused less trouble than Alice. "I can do one of two things," Roosevelt once said to Harvard classmate and writer Owen Wister when his eldest daughter interrupted their conversation; "I can be President of the United States or I can control Alice. I can not possibly do both."

When Alice was an infant, Roosevelt abandoned her to the care of his sister, Bamie. He lit out for the Dakota Territory after his first wife, Alice Hathaway Lee, and his mother both died on Valentine's Day 1884. He stayed away two years. Despite his spectacles and Harvard education, he won the respect of the cowhands of the Dakota Badlands by sharing their hardships and by displaying remarkable grit and courage. Roosevelt wrote in his diary only once about his wife's death: "When my heart's dearest died, the light went out of my life forever." He never mentioned his first wife again, not even in his autobiography. In 1886, at age three, Alice acquired a stepmother when Roosevelt married Edith Kermit Carow. She learned about her real mother only indirectly, and while she was never mistreated, she felt like an outsider among her half-siblings.

When Roosevelt took office, Alice initially refused to come to the White House for several months, as she felt she wasn't wanted. Once she moved in, she was every bit the rebellious teenager. At formal dinners she ate asparagus with her fingers—without removing her white gloves. She and her younger siblings would slide down the grand staircase on the largest trays they could find in the pantry. She had a macaw she called Eli Yale and a garter snake named Emily Spinach, which she would pull from her purse to startle White House guests. She informed her parents that she would need $50,000 for clothes. Edith, who believed in frugality, did not comply. When Alice needed drawers Edith bought muslin for Alice's maid to sew. "It is expensive to buy readymade," Edith explained. No matter—Alice could always get money from her grandparents, the wealthy Lees of Massachusetts. And she smoked cigarettes—something no proper lady of her day would think of doing. "Alice! You shall not smoke under my roof!" her father stormed. So she went to the White House roof to smoke, via an interior stair to the attic that let out onto a flat section of the roof.

Alice socialized with the Newport crowd—people whom her progressive father was publicly denouncing as "malefactors of great wealth"—including the family of railroad baron Edward Harriman. She bet at the racetrack, and the press photographed her collecting her winnings from a bookmaker, though the White House staff managed to suppress the pictures. She got another bawling out from her father. As she said, "I was in great disgrace." Alice and her socialite friend, Ellen Drexel Paul, raced their runabout from Newport to Boston in what the newspapers called record time. They were reported to have driven the car at speeds of twenty-five miles an hour in the open country between towns, but the shocking part was that they were unchaperoned.

All this and more made the gossip columns and the front pages, much to the distress of her parents. Edith was a very proper person who believed a lady's name should appear in the newspapers only at birth, death, and marriage. When her husband was assistant secretary of the navy, reporters asked him to give them a picture of his wife. "If I should," Roosevelt explained, "Mrs. Roosevelt would consider my act grounds for divorce."

Alice made her social debut in the White House on January 3, 1902. She was upset that Edith would not permit champagne and that the East Room had no hardwood floor for dancing. Worse, her guests had to dance on "crash," a coarse fabric laid down to protect the carpets during big events, which Alice described as the color of "the underbelly of a fish." The East Room was also crowded with padded seats, potted palms, and huge vases that the younger Roosevelt children liked to hide in and pop out of at unexpected moments. However, the room was beautifully lit, as always, by its three big chandeliers, each hung with 6,300 pieces of crystal.

Alice began dating Congressman Nicholas Longworth, and so did her friend Maggie Cassini. Once Alice got on the White House elevator on her way to meet Nick and Maggie, who were waiting downstairs, but the self-service elevator stalled between floors—the work of little brothers Archie and Quentin. Alice was not amused; she screamed. She was stuck for an hour, while her rival was with Nick.

But Alice got her man—after Maggie turned him down—and married him on February 17, 1906, in one of the grandest weddings in the history of the White House. The *Washington Post* devoted its entire front page and much of its first section to details about "Princess Alice" and her wedding. On the day of the wedding, crowds surged around the White House grounds from early morning on, but Alice slept late. "I wasn't excited," she would later claim. "I wasn't nervous. It was another big party and I had been to big parties." One thousand carefully selected guests wedged themselves into the East Room as Alice appeared, belatedly, on her father's arm. When the time came to leave the White House and say good-bye to the family, Edith told her stepdaughter, "I want you to know that I'm glad to see you go. You've never been anything but trouble."

Most of the family feared Edith, who even dominated Roosevelt. She had known him since she was two. When he went off to Harvard, it seemed understood that they would marry. But Roosevelt fell in love with Alice Lee. Edith attended the wedding and the reception. After Alice died and Roosevelt returned from his self-imposed exile in the Badlands, he resumed his relationship with Edith. She left the rearing of her stepdaughter to Theodore, but she usually knew what her children were doing and took care to see that they were reined in when necessary. She kept tabs on her husband, as well. When the president worked past 10:30 P.M. in his upstairs study, Edith could be heard to call her husband's name from the next room. And when he talked too much at dinner, he fell silent after one look from Edith. She also read several newspapers a day and marked articles for him to read. Roosevelt tended to be impulsive and reckless with money. Edith, neither impulsive nor reckless, was the stabilizing force he needed. "Whenever I go against her judgment, I regret it," he admitted.

Though in her early forties, Edith wanted another child. She got pregnant twice during the White House years, but miscarried both times, perhaps due in part to the stress of being first lady. Later she would admit, "I never realized the strain I was under until it was all over."

She was described by a contemporary account as "an indefatigable hostess," meeting the cabinet wives every Tuesday morning in the Green Room and entertaining lavishly. She ran a proper household with the coach and footman in livery, the waiters in tuxedo coats for afternoon receptions and evening dress for nighttime parties and dinners. Always, the waiters wore white gloves. To assist in her role as hostess, she hired the first White House social secretary, Isabelle Hagner, at a salary of $1,400 a year.

Roosevelt was under strain too, and Edith worried about him, although he would always claim to have enjoyed his presidency. To give him some serenity, Edith bought a cabin on five wooded acres in Virginia for $195. Called Pine Knot, it was about 125 miles from Washington and was just the kind of place Roosevelt loved—rustic, simple, and deep in the woods. That the two-story house had no plumbing, not even a well, and no electricity bothered the president not at all: "In the morning I fried bacon and eggs, while Mother boiled the kettle for tea and laid the table. Breakfast was most successful, and then Mother washed the dishes and did most of the work while I did odd jobs like emptying the slops etc." There was a nice front porch where Roosevelt could sit and read in a rocker. Favorite pastimes at Pine Knot were chopping down trees for firewood, and hunting. "I was on the turkey grounds before the faintest streak of dawn had appeared in the east," he wrote of a cold November morning in 1906, "and I worked as long as daylight lasted."

A 1902 Roosevelt hunting trip made headlines when the president refused to shoot a bear cub. The incident found its way into a newspaper cartoon and inspired a smart entrepreneur to create a new toy, the "teddy bear." Teddy was a name Theodore disliked, and anyone who used it to his face was likely to be dressed down as "impertinent."

While Roosevelt was a hunter, he was also a naturalist. His interest in nature and animals began at age seven, when he saw a dead seal in a market, which, he said, "filled me with every possible feeling of romance and adventure." Somehow he obtained the head of the seal and started what he immodestly called the "Roosevelt Museum of Natural History" in his bedroom. As president, he invited John Burroughs, America's foremost naturalist, to Pine Knot. Together they identified seventy-five species of birds, and Burroughs was taken back by the president's knowledge: "He knew them in the trees overhead as quickly as I did." He was not only an outstanding ornithologist but also a recognized authority on large American mammals. When the National Museum in Washington had a specimen for dissection that no one on the staff could identify, it was sent to the White House, where the president immediately identified it. One of his last

*In Theodore Roosevelt's term the conservatories had reached their maximum after fifty years of expansion. Architect Charles McKim insisted they be torn down to restore the architectural integrity of the original White House. Edith Roosevelt consented, even though she loved flowers.* (LIBRARY OF CONGRESS)

actions as president was to have two bison heads carved into the mantelpiece in the State Dining Room, while removing the lions' heads that were at the tops of the mantel's columns. He felt that bison better represented America.

Roosevelt used the presidency as a bully pulpit to awaken public support for preserving the national heritage. In 1903 hunters were decimating the birds on Pelican Island, off Florida, and President Roosevelt asked, "Is there any law that will prevent me from declaring Pelican Island a Federal Bird Reservation?" The answer was no. "Very well, then I so declare it." It was the first of fifty-one bird sanctuaries he so declared. He also set aside 125 million acres of national forest, 68 million acres of coal reserves, 2,500 power sites, and the first national monument, Devil's Tower, Wyoming. In taking these actions, he admitted, "I did broaden the use of executive power." Speaker of the House Joseph "Uncle Joe" Cannon put it differently, saying that Roosevelt had "no more use for the Constitution than a tomcat has for a marriage license."

Roosevelt had many injuries and close calls throughout his life, and the White House years were no exception. Climbing in Rock Creek Park with his son Archie, the president was about to reach the highest point when he slipped and fell. "Imagine my horror," Archie said, "when I saw him lose hold, slip and go tumbling down. I stood paralyzed with fear. However, he managed to miss all the sharp projections and fall into the water. With a laugh he clambered to the bank and started up once more, making it this time." While riding in 1904, his horse tripped on a loose plank on a bridge and somersaulted, throwing Roosevelt onto his head, which resulting in a large skinned area and a brush with meningitis. Less seriously, the jujitsu wrestling aggravated his rheumatism. As a result of parrying with single sticks with friend Leonard Wood, former commander of the Rough Riders, his wrists and knuckles swelled. He strained a leg boxing and worsened it when he jumped a fence on horseback and broke a blood vessel in his inner thigh. Roosevelt described the bruise as a "huge black and purple place . . . literally as big as two dinner plates."

He also had a number of accidents unrelated to his athletic pursuits. In 1908 he was thrown through a glass window while in a ship collision in the Gulf of Mexico, but apparently escaped without substantial injury. But his most serious accident as president

*White House life was dominated by the six Roosevelt children. They filched trays from the pantry and slid down the grand staircase on them or were chased through the dark attic by a ferociously growling President, the biggest boy of them all.* (LIBRARY OF CONGRESS)

occurred near Pittsfield, Massachusetts, on September 3, 1902, during a speaking tour of New England. (Roosevelt enjoyed meeting citizens around the country; in his first four years in office, he visited every state, traveling more than fifty thousand miles.) Roosevelt was traveling in an open landau with a driver, his secretary George Cortelyou, Secret Service agent William Craig, and Governor Murray Crane of Massachusetts. Passengers on an electric trolley spotted the president ahead, and urged the motorman to catch up with his carriage. At a curve the two collided. The trolley "struck the rear wheel of the carriage" and "ploughed through the front wheel," according to a local report. Everyone in the carriage was thrown violently from it. Only the governor was unharmed. Agent Craig was thrown into the path of the trolley, and was run over and killed. Cortelyou received a severe head wound. The president, who had been thrown forty feet, had cuts to his lip and face, and a bruised leg, all of which he termed "trivial." In half an hour he resumed his journey to Lennox, where he made a short speech.

But as the trip wore on, Roosevelt's leg began to swell painfully. At Indianapolis on September 23, he underwent an operation to drain the wound and prevent blood poisoning. He was put on a private train back to Washington, where he endured an enforced rest with his leg propped up on pillows. Four days after his return to the White House, the doctors were forced to drain the wound for a second time, as Roosevelt was getting no relief. For the first operation they had used a local anesthetic; this time they used only cocaine, despite having to scrape the shin bone. Roosevelt was in a wheelchair for weeks, and though he concealed this injury as well, ever after his leg ached when he was tired or when he jarred it. "The shock permanently damaged the bone," he later admitted, but he never showed his discomfort in public.

The greatest danger to Roosevelt's health, however, was his overeating. A friend referred to him as an "eager and valiant trencherman." Roosevelt preferred quantity to quality, consuming at least twice what an average person would. He ate as many as a dozen eggs for breakfast. His coffee cups were huge—"more in the nature of a bathtub," according to Teddy Jr.—and he took five to seven lumps of sugar. He would drink four large glasses of milk at a sitting. He was overweight despite all his exercising, and although he was unaware of it, already developing arteriosclerosis. He consumed little alcohol, though. At state dinners, he did not want to draw attention by abstaining, so he had his valet, Amos, fill his wineglasses with ice before the guests reached the table so as to dilute the alcohol.

The food produced by the White House kitchen was unremarkable, so Edith had banquets catered. Roosevelt insisted on champagne, saying that he wanted "only the best served in the White House." Catered dinners ran to $10 a plate including the wine, but Roosevelt didn't mind. He had, Edith said, a "horror of trying to save money out of his pay." Edith confided to son Archie that Roosevelt in fact saved none of his $50,000-a-year salary: it had all gone into keeping up the White House with cigars, champagne, and what the president called "only the best."

One occasion that called for the best was the state visit in 1902 of the brother of the German emperor, Prince Henry of Prussia. Roosevelt met him in the Red Room without a formal introduction because there was no American ranking high enough to perform this function. A formal dinner was scheduled for February 24, but questions of protocol were raised. Roosevelt wondered how they would walk in and asked, "Will the prince take Mrs. R. while I walk in solemn state by myself? How do we do it anyhow?"

The solution was to have a reception for the ladies first, followed by a stag dinner in the East Room. Thousands of tiny electric lights were hung in different shapes, such as anchors and stars. The table was set in a crescent shape, and an elaborate menu was printed on three pages of heavy cardboard tied with red, white, and blue ribbons.

Another important guest was Booker T. Washington. Soon after Roosevelt took office, he invited the educator to a quiet White House dinner to talk about furthering opportunities for African Americans. He failed to foresee the furor this would create. The *Macon Telegraph* said, "God set up the barrier between the races. No President of this or any other country can break it down." Another paper commented that now no southern woman with any self-respect would accept an invitation to the White House.

Edith brought distinguished people to the White House as well, though her choices were perhaps less controversial: historian Henry Adams, sculptor Augustus Saint-Gaudens, author Henry James, pianist Jan Paderewski, and a young cellist, Pablo Casals, who would return a half century later to play for another first lady, Jacqueline Kennedy.

Like the Kennedys, the Roosevelts had a keen sense of history and reverence for the house they lived in. One of the president's first acts was to make "White House" the official name of his new residence. The mansion had always been popularly referred to as the White House since it had always been covered with white wash or paint to preserve the porous Aquia Creek sandstone. But officially, it was known as the "President's House" until mid-century, when it became "Executive Mansion." Roosevelt noted that every state had an "executive mansion"—he had lived in one as governor of New York—so there were many executive mansions, but only one White House.

That very structure might have been lost to history had Roosevelt not taken office. Thomas Jefferson had rattled around in the huge house—then often called a palace—with his live-in secretary, Meriwether Lewis. A century later, the upstairs rooms had been taken over one by one for government offices, and formal events regularly exceeded the capacity of the state rooms, requiring exits through the windows and the propping up of floors. Many proposals to enlarge the White House or abandon it altogether had come and gone. This time, the Army Corps of Engineers had the ear of Congress, and their preference was to tear down the White House and start over. They had little interest in or even awareness of the architectural beauty of the house or its history or symbolism. Recent presidents had accepted or encouraged the Army Corps in their thinking. Not Theodore Roosevelt. He insisted the president live in the White House and Congress complied, appropriating the funds necessary to renovate the White House and move the business offices out of the second-floor living area and into an ostensibly temporary new office building on the West Wing. Construction began in 1902, and the Roosevelts retreated to their home in Oyster Bay, on New York's Long Island, for the summer, returning in early November after the bulk of the work was done.

As the house was torn apart, it was also emptied out. On January 21, 1903, twenty-eight wagon loads of furniture and fixtures were sold at public auction. Included were the decorative columns installed in the East Room by Ulysses Grant, and the famed Tiffany stained-glass screen from the north entrance, which went for $275. Edith disapproved of the custom of auctioning off or giving away china and glassware that was damaged or no longer in complete sets. Instead she ordered them broken and thrown into the Potomac River. In the finished White House she lined the East Corridor of the basement floor with examples of china dating back to George Washington.

Edith clashed with architect Charles McKim at times. The huge rosewood bed bought by Mary Lincoln and the elaborately carved wardrobe and table that today are the features of the Lincoln Bedroom were anathema to McKim, and he wanted to banish them to auction, but Edith overruled him. She not only liked carved Victorian furniture, but both she and the president appreciated the historical connection to Lincoln, aware that Willie Lincoln had died in the bed. As Edith went over the plans for the bedrooms, she generally eliminated the built-in closets. The new bathrooms distorted the balance of the rooms, and rather than make it worse by adding closets, she opted to keep using wardrobes.

Once the White House was redone, Edith also rescued the painting *Love and Life* by George Watts, which had once hung in the mansion. "Lemonade Lucy" Hayes had objected to the nude and taken it down, and it somehow made its way to the Corcoran Gallery. Edith now had it hung in the upstairs hall, where, she said, "it can't shock the multitude." In addition, she reclaimed a pier table of the Monroe era from the White House attic.

The work was completed in 1902, in time for the winter social season. The family had far more space and privacy, though noise still filtered upstairs. "Edie says it is like living over the store," Roosevelt reported. The rebuilt White House was now also far better able to handle large crowds, and Roosevelt was equal to the task. On New Year's Day 1907 he shook a record-breaking 8,150 hands.

Born in 1858 in New York City to a family that numbered among New York's elite "400," Roosevelt was accustomed to upper-class living and entertained well. Opponents attacked him for the grand banquets, the tennis court, the presidential yacht. It was true that White House entertaining had become more elaborate, but the president still paid for it out of his salary. "I pay the butcher, the baker, and the grocer at Washington just as I do at Oyster Bay," he said. He admitted that the tennis court cost the government $400, adding that it replaced the old White House greenhouses, which were much more expensive to operate (fresh flowers were now brought in daily from the city's government propagating gardens). He explained the yachts by arguing that the White House entourage could move more cheaply by boat.

Roosevelt was concerned about his income for most of his life. While he was a student at Harvard, his father died and left him a lifetime income of $8,000 a year, but he lost almost half of the inheritance in a ranch and cattle venture in the Badlands. When he needed money, he turned to writing. Altogether he wrote some forty books plus numerous articles on a wide variety of subjects for prestigious magazines. While still a college student he published a book called *Summer Birds*. He was a good taxidermist and at eighteen was listed in a national directory of biologists. Then, when he was courting Alice Lee, he began an extraordinary work, *The Naval War of 1812*. This required extensive and difficult research in England, France, and the United States and a knowledge of nautical terms, shipbuilding, and naval tactics—all subjects he knew very little about when he began. He finished the book at age twenty-three. It became a classic recognized by historians and used as a text at the Naval Academy. His four-volume *The Winning of the West*, begun in 1889, was not only praised by historians but became a best-seller, earning him healthy royalties.

Roosevelt loved the West and as president kept up with the frontiersmen he knew during his sojourn in the Dakotas. On a trip through Yellowstone he reminisced with

"Hell-Roaring Bill Jones"—after he was sobered up. Another friend, Jack Abernathy, a former army scout against the Sioux, was known for killing wolves with his bare hands, which he accomplished by shoving his fist into the wolf's mouth. The feat had been captured in a film, which Roosevelt wanted to screen in the East Room for guests. Edith vetoed the idea. For his final luncheon at the White House, Roosevelt wanted to invite everyone closest to him, including cabinet members and diplomats, but also the man he made marshal of the Oklahoma Territory, Jack Abernathy.

Roosevelt appointed one of his unpolished friends marshal of Arizona Territory, and found himself questioned by a Senator Hoar as to about how well he knew the man. Roosevelt said he knew him from his Rough Rider regiment.

"Do you know," the senator demanded, "that he has killed three men?"

"You don't mean it," Roosevelt said.

"It is a fact," the senator assured him.

Roosevelt appeared outraged, and said he would "read him the riot act. He told me he'd only killed two."

Though what the White House staff called "the cowboy bunch" was always welcome in Washington, not all received access to the White House. When Roosevelt found out that a particularly scruffy-looking friend had been turned away, he wrote that if it happened again, the man should just "shoot through the windows."

Presumably, the friend carried a gun, as did Roosevelt, wary after McKinley's assassination—the third presidential killing in thirty-seven years. "I go armed," he told a concerned Burroughs at Pine Knot, slapping his hand on his hip, "and they would have to be mighty quick to get the drop on me." When the president attended his twenty-fifth reunion at Harvard in 1905, college president Charles William Eliot escorted Roosevelt to his room. "The first thing he did," Eliot said, "was to pull off his coat, roll it up with his hands, and fling it across the bed so violently that it sent the pillow to the floor beyond. The next thing he did was to take a great pistol from his trousers pocket and slam it down on the dresser." The president carried his pistol around at the reunion, although, as Eliot noted sadly, it was against Massachusetts law to do so. "Very lawless," he commented. "A very lawless mind."

Secret Service agents from the Treasury Department were now officially assigned to guard the president, but Roosevelt did not like having them around. At times he simply dismissed them. He still went out alone at night to jog around the Washington Monument. At times a lone agent followed him at a discreet distance. In a letter to his daughter Ethel, Roosevelt described "marching" to church with a Secret Service agent, James Sloan, trailing about twenty-five yards behind. Suddenly Roosevelt saw two terriers attack a kitten. He "bounced forward" and after "some active work" with his umbrella drove off the dogs, while Sloan rescued the kitten. The president then went to the neighboring porches, asking people if they knew who owned the kitten. "Then I saw a very nice colored woman and a little colored girl looking out of the window of a small house," he wrote. He walked up and asked if they would like a kitten, and they said they did. "I felt I had gotten it a home and continued toward church."

On April 20, 1907, the *New York Times* reported an anarchist plot to assassinate Roosevelt. The Roosevelts were at isolated Pine Knot, and Edith lay awake, she recalled, "in terror-stricken panic." She arranged for two Secret Service agents, James Sloan and Frank Tyree, to come down from Washington, but she didn't tell her husband because "it would irritate him." The agents stayed in a nearby farmhouse and patrolled at night, staying out of sight during the day.

Roosevelt did face an assassination attempt, but it was not until October 14, 1912, four years after he had left the presidency and was challenging Taft's reelection. As he was leaving his hotel in Milwaukee to make a speech, John Schrank, a mentally unbalanced saloonkeeper, fired at him from close range. The bullet pierced through a speech folded in his pocket and was deflected by Roosevelt's metal eyeglass case. He had not expected to throw his hat into the arena after being elected by a landslide in 1904 and retiring in 1908. "Under no circumstances will I be a candidate for or accept another nomination," he declared, and set about getting his friend and close associate William Howard Taft nominated to succeed him.

Immediately following his friend's inauguration, Roosevelt, only fifty-one, escaped the political scene by embarking on an extended hunting trip to Africa, where he shot nine lions, five elephants, thirteen rhinoceroses, and seven hippopotamuses among a total of about three hundred killings. He came home to find that Taft was not the president he had expected him to be. In 1912 he made a bid against Taft for the Republican nomination, failed, and split the Republican party by running as a Progressive or Bull Moose candidate. He polled many more votes than Taft, but he had opened the door for his Democratic opponent, Woodrow Wilson.

Roosevelt returned to Sagamore Hill, his rambling, twenty-five room home in Oyster Bay. When World War I broke out, Wilson, whom he despised, denied him the chance to lead a regiment to France. Roosevelt died at Sagamore Hill on January 6, 1919, and was buried there. Edith lived until 1948, and is buried beside her husband. Roosevelt's home at Sagamore Hill and his birthplace in New York City are National Historic Sites, and his visage is carved into Mount Rushmore in South Dakota, overlooking his beloved Badlands.

When Theodore Roosevelt took office in 1901, he said, "The White House is the property of the nation, and so far as it is compatible with living therein should be kept as it originally was, for the same reasons that we keep Mount Vernon as it originally was. . . . It is a good thing to preserve such buildings as historic monuments, which keep alive our sense of continuity with the nation's past."

Theodore and Edith Roosevelt's views were sharply at variance with those of their predecessors. Chester Arthur had thought the White House in such bad condition it should be torn down. Benjamin Harrison's wife, Caroline, had the Army Corps of Engineers develop a plan to expand the house into a huge quadrangle for promenading. During William McKinley's term, Colonel Theodore Bingham of the Army Corps of Engineers developed his own plan for the White House. Bingham was in charge of all government construction in Washington, had powerful connections in Congress, and did not recognize civilian architects as professionals. In 1900, the centennial year of the White House, Colonel Bingham presented his vision of a White House enlarged by huge wings on each side complete with domes and large Ionic columns. Washington architect Glenn Brown called it "a mongrel" and said it was "out of harmony with and destroying the individuality of the old building."

Before anything could be done, McKinley was shot by an assassin on September 6, 1901, and his death brought the young, dynamic Theodore Roosevelt to the presidency. Perhaps more importantly as far as the future of the White House was concerned, it also brought a new first lady, Edith Carow Roosevelt. Both appreciated the historic White House, although, with six children, they were acutely aware of its inadequacies. The family quarters had only eight rooms and two bathrooms. The State Dining Room could seat only sixty, so presidents put the overflow in the front hall or used the East Room. During large receptions, the floors had to be propped up from the cellar below. The elevator stalled between floors and spit sparks. The Army Corps of Engineers reported, "The present mansion is old and dilapidated, its floors are sunken, its basement is coated with mold and infested with vermin, which is [sic] impossible to exterminate."

When a reporter questioned President Roosevelt about a plan to turn the White House into offices and build a new executive residence, he allowed himself to be quoted, something he seldom did, saying, "Mrs. Roosevelt and I are firmly of the opinion that the President should live nowhere else than in the historic White House." To Colonel Bingham's dismay, Edith Roosevelt turned not to him but to America's leading architect, Charles McKim of the firm McKim, Mead & White, for a solution. McKim walked through the mansion with Bingham and promptly told the first lady that only a complete overhaul would do. On June 28, 1902, Congress appropriated $475,445 to refurbish the White House and to relieve overcrowding by moving the business offices out of the second-floor family quarters to a new building in the West Wing. McKim shrewdly never referred to modernizing or refurbishing the White House, but always to "restoring" it to the way it was originally. Just what constituted "originally" was impossible to determine; Hoban's drawings had been lost. McKim liberally reinterpreted what he conceived to be the architect's intention, updating it in keeping with the current taste for the neoclassical.

When construction got underway in 1902, McKim described the scene: "The house is torn to pieces. . . . Bedlam let loose does not compare to it." The pace was frantic. Roosevelt had ordered that the work positively must be done for the first scheduled state dinner in December.

McKim's biggest problem was the glass conservatories that had been added on the wings gradually during the past half century. To McKim they were an eyesore. They violated the pure lines of the house and had to go. To Edith they were a joyous source of potted tropical plants for decorating at social affairs and provided an abundance of fresh flowers for the rooms and for gracious gifts. Only after McKim's assurances that the glasshouses would be relocated and the plants and flowers still available did she agree to "smash the glass houses," as her husband put it in typically emphatic fashion.

Another major construction problem was the enlargement of the dining room. McKim's solution was to rip out a load-bearing wall and extend the dining room north into the hall area. In place of the demolished wall, he anchored a large steel truss in the brick walls to support the ceiling. Two decades later, a sagging roof would be blamed on the strains created by this truss. Removing the dining room wall also required relocating the grand staircase in the area where the business stair had been. Since the offices were being moved out of the White House, the business stair was no longer needed. The change also brought more privacy to the family quarters, because the grand staircase no longer came up into the bedroom area.

McKim constructed a new public entrance in the East Wing, and the traditional north entry became a private one. This allowed the public to enter on the basement floor and take advantage of coat rooms and rest rooms before ascending to the state room level. McKim removed the Tiffany glass screen installed by President Arthur in the north entrance foyer and put in new columns. The columns they replaced were tossed into the Potomac.

The basement hall had been filled with work areas, laundries, and storage. McKim restored the beautiful groin ceilings and buried the heating pipes under the floor. Modern kitchens replaced the old ones, along with their fireplaces and layers of grease. The boiler room—an oval room beneath the Blue Room—became the Diplomatic Reception Room.

The upstairs offices in the White House had become busier and larger over the years, especially during the Spanish-American War. Telegraph lines were run in, twenty to thirty office workers were on duty, and hundreds of visitors came in daily. McKim knew that the solution was to get the offices out of the White House, but building new offices was a potentially touchy political problem. He decided to attach a new office structure to the West Wing. It was termed "temporary" to deflect any criticism about changes in the White House function, yet the appropriation from Congress contained the condition that the walls be thick enough to allow a second story to be built at a later time.

The biggest office, with a bow window, belonged to Roosevelt's secretary, George Cortelyou. In addition to another secretary's office and a cabinet room, there was, according to a period account "a telegraph and a telephone room; a large room for stenographers; a room for the press; a main hall to be fitted for a reception-room, and file rooms and closets in the basement." The Oval Office wouldn't come until Taft's time. Roosevelt worked in a room described as being "thirty feet square and almost destitute of ornament. It contains a fireplace, a big desk, a few books, an art nouveau lamp, a few vases of flowers, a tiny clock on the mantel, and on the walls a rather poor oil portrait of Lincoln, a photograph of a big bear, and a framed autograph copy of the late Senator Ingall's well-known sonnet on 'Opportunity.' There is a globe in one corner, and the divan, chairs and desk are all olive, the walls are covered with olive burlap, and the windows overlook the White House grounds toward the south, including the tennis court, and in the distance the Potomac, the Washington Monument and the Virginia hills. So severe is the room that very few business men have not its superior in decoration, if not simple comfort."

Roosevelt also kept an office upstairs in the White House, knowing that it was not politically wise to entirely separate work and home. He used it for important occasions such as signing bills or meeting distinguished guests.

On November 4, 1902, the Roosevelts were back in the White House, although the state rooms were still being worked on downstairs. All the painted wood-work was sanded between the layers of paint and the last coat rubbed with pumice powder to give the surface a hard, porcelainlike look. The oak parquet flooring was lightly bleached and waxed. The large East Room was painted a cream white, and without rugs and the Victorian clutter, it looked startling different. McKim wanted to establish traditional simplicity. The Red, Blue, and Green Rooms were kept in their traditional colors. The Blue Room, as the formal reception room, had copies of the famous furniture made in 1817 for James Monroe by Paris cabinetmaker Antoine Bellangé. The fireplaces in the entrance hall were removed and large mirrors added. The State Dining Room, by contrast, had carpeting and dark wooden paneling, rich green velvet draperies, and two ornate seventeenth-century Flemish tapestries. Large stuffed animal heads such as moose and elk were purchased from a New York decorator for $2,000 and mounted on the walls—Roosevelt was a hunter, after all. The dining room could now seat about 120, depending on the table arrangements. An architectural historian called it "a stately hall of Early English Renaissance." *Architectural Record* in April 1903 declared that a White House "all carried out in strict Colonial Style would be but a monotonous and insipid mansion."

With the renovation complete, President Roosevelt declared that the house, once "disfigured by incongruous additions," had been restored "to what was planned to be by Washington." Most people seemed pleased with McKim's changes, at least after they had time to grow accustomed to them. The few who didn't Roosevelt called "yahoos."

# William Howard Taft

## 1909–1913

## *Not Where He Wanted to Be*

WHEN WILLIAM HOWARD TAFT took office in 1909, it was the fulfillment of a lifelong dream—not his, but his wife's. The White House had loomed large in Helen Taft's imagination for decades. As a teenager, "Nellie" had been invited to live there for several months by President Hayes, a law partner and close friend of her father's. She even served as hostess when First Lady Lucy Hayes was away. "Nothing in my life," she would later recall, "reaches the climax of human bliss I felt when, as a girl of sixteen, I was entertained at the White House."

Nellie Taft knew what she wanted, and always had. As a young woman her determination and dominant personality were already apparent. At college she studied unusual subjects for a woman of the day, such as chemistry; she read law at her father's office; she preferred the conversations of men and avoided those of women. Her ambitions were clear as well. She would not, she confided to some girlfriends, marry a man who was not "destined to be president of the United States." When Taft married Nellie in 1886, he was employed as a collector of internal revenue—hardly a fit position for the husband of an aspiring first lady. Taft was soon appointed to the Ohio Superior Court, and in 1890 President Harrison offered him the post of solicitor general. Nellie, her eyes on Washington, urged him to take it.

In 1906 Taft, now secretary of war to Theodore Roosevelt, and Nellie were visiting the Roosevelts at the White House. The president, Taft's friend and political mentor,

236

took them aside and sat down in a chair as if in a trance. The Tafts heard a deep voice say: "I am the seventh son of a seventh daughter, and I have clairvoyant powers. I see a man weighing three hundred and fifty pounds. There is something hanging over his head. . . . At one time it looks like the presidency. Then again it looks like the chief justiceship."

"Make it the chief justiceship," Taft, the 350-pound man in question, urged.

"Make it the presidency," said Mrs. Taft.

William Taft was less politically ambitious than his wife, though in his way driven to succeed. Born into a prominent Ohio family, he was subject to the highest expectations. His father had been both secretary of war and attorney general under Grant. Both parents envisioned a similarly illustrious future for their son. Their pressure, and Taft's fear of disappointing them, took a toll. While a student at Yale, the affable Taft once flew into a rage and tore apart his room when some friends persisted in distracting him from his studies. Indeed, when he graduated second in his class at Yale, both mother and father were somewhat chagrined.

Taft's own dream was to serve on the Supreme Court, and later, as chief justice, he would prove well suited to that job. The demands and discord of politics, however, strained his natural character, which was genial, modest, often self-deprecatory, and noncompetitive. Taft was almost universally well liked. Theodore Roosevelt called him "the most lovable personality I have ever come in contact with." Taft's personality was a political asset only in that he won friends and allies easily. Asked in 1908 how it was that, at fifty-one, he'd already had so many important jobs, the often uncouth Taft replied, "I got my political pull, first, through my father's prominence: then through the fact that I was hail-fellow-well-met with all of the political people of the city convention-going type."

When Roosevelt handpicked Taft as his successor, he did not foresee that these traits, which made him suitably moldable, would also make Taft ineffectual as president. Even Taft's mother saw that he was not cut out for the job: "I do not want my son to be President, he is not my candidate," she had told reporters years before his election. "His is a judicial mind, and he loves the law." Taft himself knew this to be true and said more or less the same thing many times. But, true to form, he would try to do what was expected of him.

Taft dutifully pursued the political career that would eventually take him, and Nellie, to the White House. After a brief return to the law via an appointment to the Ohio Circuit Court, he accepted President McKinley's assignment to set up a civil government in the Philippines, then under martial law. In 1901, Taft was sworn in as governor, and his family of five moved into the vast Malacanan Palace in Manila. The post seemingly served as a rehearsal for life at the White House, and certainly foreshadowed Nellie's style as first lady. She took full advantage of the situation, quickly acquiring the trappings of prestige: a large retinue of servants, five carriages, thirteen horses, and a handful of exotic animals. She decorated the walls with native bolos, hats, spears, and so on, much of which she would bring to the White House, which was consequently nicknamed "Malacanan Palace." And she threw lavish parties, including a farewell Venetian fete, complete with barges festooned with flowers, when Taft finished his work as governor in 1903.

Soon enough, the Philippine rehearsal would yield to the real thing. Once appointed secretary of war, Taft was positioned for a short trip to the presidency thanks to the endorsement of the immensely popular Roosevelt. When Taft was sworn in, his wife was "inexpressibly happy." She thought the day glorious, and said outright, "It had always been my ambition to see Mr. Taft President of the United States." She broke all previous precedent by insisting she ride right up alongside her husband in the car as it came down Pennsylvania Avenue to the White House. The new president, however, looked glum. Conspicuously, he never bowed or waved.

Following the inaugural parade, Taft returned to the White House, threw himself into a big chair, stretched out, and naively announced: "I am President now, and tired of being kicked around." Unfortunately, the kicking around was just beginning. His daughter, Helen, would later say: "Those years in the White House were the only unhappy years of his entire life."

They were perhaps Nellie's happiest. She set about taking over the White House before she even moved in. However, her enthusiasm seems to have gotten the best of her, and she was quickly labeled bossy. When First Lady Edith Roosevelt invited her to inspect what was soon to be her new home, she heard Nellie whisper, none too softly, "I would have put that table over there." Mrs. Roosevelt ignored it, but surely the comment did not endear Nellie to her. Taft's relationship with Theodore and Edith Roosevelt was very warm until their falling-out during the election campaign of 1912, but Nellie's never was. Further friction resulted when Nellie began tinkering with the routine and staffing of the household, upsetting Mrs. Roosevelt by dismissing longtime servants. All the white ushers in frock coats became black servants in blue livery. "I decided to have, at all hours, footmen in livery at the White House door," Nellie wrote. Furthermore she ordered that all male employees be clean-shaven. The mutterings of revolt, especially among those with prized mustaches, were dismissed by the new first lady, who had her way. As she said, "Each new mistress of the house has absolute authority . . . and can do exactly as she pleases." She also made plans to replace the male steward with a female housekeeper who "could relieve me of the supervision of such details as no man . . . would ever recognize." Relatively small changes all, but injudiciously arranged while the Roosevelts still reigned so as to be effective the moment the Tafts crossed the threshold of the executive mansion. The seeming presumption irritated Roosevelt supporters already resentful of Taft.

Once ensconced in the White House, Nellie tackled the decor, to the extent that she could. Taft was Roosevelt's chosen successor, and just as there was little room to tamper with his politics, there was little room to tamper with the house he'd just had done over by prestigious New York architects McKim, Mead and White. Nellie adorned the upstairs living area with palm trees and pieces acquired in the Philippines: oriental and Japanese furniture, screens, floor mats, and tapestries. Her own library, in particular, was filled with "cunningly carved teakwood chairs and tables and cabinets, wonderful Eastern fabrics for curtains and brilliant splashes of gold dragons on rich backgrounds, a screen of soft wisteria bloom, and wall panels of the tender grays of Japanese art," according to *Good Housekeeping Magazine*. She turned one end of the wide second-story corridor into a sitting room "so screened off that among its soft-toned sepia rugs, its easy chairs and window draperies, it appears exactly like the living-room of any built-for-comfort home." It was here that Nellie kept her custom-made grand piano. The Eastern motif even showed up in Taft's wardrobe. He once wrote his older brother,

Horace: "It is a hot Sunday afternoon, and with drawers and a kimono, in the presence of Nellie, and looking like a Chinese idol, I am walking my room dictating to you."

The basement quarters underwent more substantive changes. Nellie established a second kitchen by reclaiming a small storeroom, and upgraded the twenty-six servants' quarters, replacing castoffs and wooden antebellum bedsteads with enamel iron beds. The basement also contained one of Nellie's favorite rooms: the flower room, in which all the blooms for the White House table and rooms were stored and prepared. She visited the basement daily to select every bouquet, including the vase of carnations she sent to her husband's desk each morning.

Despite her strivings to make the White House her own, Nellie Taft made her mark not within the mansion, but on the grounds of the surrounding city. In 1909, in the first public project by a first lady, she created Potomac Park and what became Potomac Drive, which was reminiscent of the tree-lined drives she enjoyed in Manila. It was she who saw to the planting of the renowned cherry trees whose flowering each spring is today as much a symbol of Washington as the White House itself. When Mayor Yukio Ozaki of Tokyo heard of her intention to plant cherry trees, he sent two thousand of them as a gift to the United States. They were shipped to the West Coast and crossed the country in three railroad cars, accompanied by a special agent sent along to assist in their planting.

Oddly enough, Taft himself made the most significant changes to the White House. Theodore Roosevelt had cleared the business offices out of the upstairs living area by moving them into a newly built "temporary" wing. Now, Taft ordered the wing doubled in size, dropped the word *temporary*, and created the first Oval Office in the midst of a row of offices. Some two decades later, Franklin Roosevelt would again greatly enlarge the West Wing and move the Oval Office to its present corner location. But in the Taft White House, the office had little of the aura of power and prestige that surrounds it today. Taft simply used it as a workstation, greeting important dignitaries in an office he kept upstairs in the White House proper. The walls of this denlike upstairs office were covered with framed photographs of his professional and personal lives: commissions on which he had served, cabinet meetings, rulers whose guest he had been, his father and mother in a Russian sleigh at St. Petersburg, and many pictures of his children.

Regardless of its location or use, the Oval Office had little chance of earning distinction with Taft occupying it. The president was at home neither in the White House, which he referred to as a "prison," nor with his power. "The White House," he said shortly after entering it, "is a bigger proposition than one imagines." Even his title did not sit well with him. When asked how he like his new position, President Taft said, "I hardly know yet. When I hear someone say Mr. President, I look around expecting to see Roosevelt." In the beginning of his term, whenever Taft mentioned "the president," he always meant Roosevelt. "You mean the ex-president," Nellie once reminded him. "I suppose I do, dear," replied Taft, "but he will always be the president to me, and I can never think of him as anything else." And when he read in the paper that the president had a conference with House Speaker Joseph "Uncle Joe" Cannon, Taft confessed, his first thought would be to wonder what they talked about.

Nellie might have taken to presidential decision making more readily than her husband. Politics interested her. When Taft held a stag dinner, she arranged to have her meal set up in an adjoining anteroom so she could hear. She began sitting in on White House conferences, and although she seldom said anything openly, she usually got what she wanted. Major Archibald Butt, Taft's military aide and right-hand man, once called on the president-elect and found him laughing. "I was Cabinet-making early this morning," Taft explained, "and I thought I had settled one place at least, and just as you were announced I told my wife. She simply wiped him off the face of the earth and I have to begin all over again. The personal side of politics has always been funny to me, but nothing has been quite as funny as to have a man's career wrecked by a jealous wife."

Nellie quickly interrupted: "Not jealous at all but I could not believe you to be serious when you mentioned that man's name. He is perfectly awful and his family are even worse. I won't even talk about it."

Taft had always craved affection and approval and had managed to get them by pleasing his parents, his wife, and Theodore Roosevelt. Now, any decision was sure to rile some segment of the public, the press, or the power structure. Taft became increasingly unhappy, insecure, and indecisive. He became known as "the Great Procrastinator," much irritating Republicans and Democrats alike. Not only did he put things off, he rashly promised more than was possible in order to please. He prolonged unimportant conversations with those he should have cut off, while annoying important callers by making them wait for days to see him. He spoke his mind freely, blurting out things he never should have said, trusting those he never should have trusted. Eventually, even Roosevelt derided Taft as a "floppy-souled creature" and a "puzzlewit."

At first the press was friendly, but Taft mishandled reporters, gave out little news, and bristled at criticism. One newspaper correspondent remarked, "In the first place the President never talks for publication. In the second place, when he does talk you must not quote him." Consequently, the press interviewed opponents or made up stories about him. Taft, becoming uncharacteristically irritable and less genial, only added to his troubles when he resorted to using intemperate language to condemn the press.

Among other things, Taft did not appreciate the press dwelling on the amount of time he spent on the golf course. Always devoted to his work, he'd never had time for leisurely pursuits and had never played the game before his election. Now, however, he devoted himself to escaping the White House and its pressures. Golf became something of an obsession, one that grew in proportion to his unease. "The beauty of golf to me is that you cannot play it if you permit yourself to think of anything else," Taft said to Major Butt. He also rationalized that the exercise would keep his weight down (it did not).

Theodore Roosevelt, always attuned to his public image, never played golf and advised Taft not to. He said the public viewed the sport as elitist—as it was during its early phase—and called it a "siss" game. But Taft became the first devoted presidential golfer and publicly supported the game, saying that it was "in the interest of good health and good manners," and that it "affords the chance to play the man and act the gentleman."

The press did not exaggerate Taft's time on the course. In a letter to Nellie, Taft wrote: "My time is pretty well filled up now, especially as I insist on taking the whole afternoon off for golf." When the press began to take notice, Taft resorted to sneaking out to play. On August 4, 1911, a ceremonial signing of the General Arbitration Treaty with Great Britain took place at the White House. It was raining, but Taft kept an eye on the weather. As soon as he saw a break, he called Archie Butt over and whispered, "I believe we can get in a game." With that he left the room, leaving Major Butt to usher the British ambassador out while explaining that the president had been called to his office on a matter of some importance. On another occasion, the assistant secretary of state urged the president to attend an important diplomatic meeting, and Taft responded, "I'll be damned if I will give up my golf game to see this fellow."

Taft was agile and a good dancer despite his weight, but his girth did inhibit his golf swing. To compensate he used heavy, extra-long clubs, a baseball grip, and a short, choppy swing. His score was generally mediocre, around 100—he once took nineteen strokes to get out of a sand trap—but he enjoyed the game and seldom responded to a bad stroke with anything worse than "Oh, me." At Hot Springs, Virginia, Butt recorded that the president "enjoyed his golf game this morning as if he had been a boy of ten."

Taft also escaped from his White House prison by traveling as often as possible. He covered an estimated 114,559 miles—the equivalent of thirty-eight trips from coast to coast—during his four-year term, an astounding distance given the transportation of the day. "I want to get in as much traveling as I can during these four years," he explained, "for after they are over I do not know when I will get another opportunity." He also set a presidential record for vacationing. Summers he would flee to his summer home in Beverly, Massachusetts, leaving instructions not to forward any mail. He spent

*Taft's weight ballooned up to 350 pounds and it took two men to pull him out of his bathtub. He ordered a new tub that was seven feet long, 41 inches wide, and weighed a ton. Here four workers demonstrate its size.* (**LIBRARY OF CONGRESS**)

mornings playing golf, afternoons dozing on the veranda, and evenings sailing on the presidential yacht, *Sylph*.

Almost any pretext would do for a trip, and Taft was likely to accept any invitation from almost any group. Sometimes he didn't even know the reason for the invitation. After traveling six hours to and six hours back from a Methodist chautauqua, he wrote Nellie: "I don't know why I went unless it was that there was a Yale man at the head of it." Taft once left Washington for New York and Connecticut simply to see a couple of plays. Archie Butt wrote, "The President enjoyed himself hugely. He refused to take a secretary with him and therefore attended to no business while away." On another trip, Butt recorded: "We are leaving at five for Worcester, Mass., for what purpose I am not certain. We are going to see 'Aunt Delia,' I know but for what else I have not the foggiest idea. The President takes these trips just as a dipsomaniac goes on his periodic sprees."

As soon as the railroads became a convenient form of travel, presidents began using them for extensive trips, generally justifying them by speech making along the way. Not surprisingly, Taft took readily to trains. On a cross-country trip in 1911, he was gone fifty-eight days, visiting twenty-eight states and making 380 speeches to an estimated 1.5 million people, and appearing before twice that many. After a single night back at the White House following this odyssey, he departed for a three-day trip to New Haven, Connecticut.

Taft also liked automobiles and, naturally, was the first president to make extensive use of them. He was the first president to ride in an automobile in his inaugural parade, and thereafter cars allowed him to flee the White House on the spur of the moment. Theodore Roosevelt had not used cars as president, much preferring the horse. But Taft got a $12,000 appropriation from Congress specifically for cars. He bought two Pierce Arrows, a zippy little Baker electric, which Nellie liked, and a big White Steamer, a black-lacquered seven-seater embellished with silver plate, made by the White Sewing Machine Company.

Traveling by automobile was still venturesome. On impulse Taft once decided to go to Baltimore. The trip there took two hours, plus the twenty minutes it took the chauffeur to fix a flat tire. Coming back, "We made the machine sing," Archie Butt said—so much so that the heat generated caused the car's woodwork to catch fire. Butt proudly recorded that the forty-mile trip took only one hour and forty-five minutes.

The White Steamer was Taft's favorite. The steam-powered car cost $4,000, and it was huge. The chauffeur turned it around by driving to one of Washington's many circles. Taft took up the whole backseat and would go off to sleep there, swaying back and forth. It was an open car, but photographers had a difficult time catching the president on film after he discovered, to his delight, that the car could be made to emit an obscuring cloud of steam.

The White Steamer truly did him proud on a particular day trip to Manassas, Virginia, for a speech to Civil War veterans. Reporters and senators accompanied the president in their gasoline-powered cars. Heavy rains had caused flooding along the route, and one carful of senators became stuck in water reaching nearly to the top of the wheels of their car. They were "frantic," and with the water still rising, they yelled for the president not to attempt a crossing. The ever-present and resourceful Archie Butt jumped out of the Steamer, pulled off his boots, and waded in to find the best spot to cross. He figured that the water would extinguish the pilot light but that there would be enough steam built up to get across. So he waved the chauffeur on. Taft beamed with pride as his "rickety old car" plowed majestically across, pushing a wall of water before it. As they passed the marooned senators, a delighted Taft called out, "Oh, you old standpatters!"

Besides allowing him to escape the White House and evade political pressures, traveling was for Taft an opportunity to abandon his weight-loss regimen. One of Taft's responses to pressure was to eat more. He had always been a big man, and his weight peaked at 350 during his unhappy presidency. Both Nellie and his doctor were after him to diet. His lack of control over even this vexed him. "I tell you, it's a sad state of affairs when a man can't even call his gizzard his own," he once said.

Taft once called for a snack on an evening train trip to Ohio only to be told there was no dining car. Greatly annoyed, Taft yelled to his secretary, Charles Norton, who tried to placate the president by reminding him they had just had a dinner in the White House and that arrangements had been made for breakfast in the morning.

"Where's the next stop, damnit?" Taft demanded. "The next stop where there is a diner?" The answer was Harrisburg. Glaring at Norton, Taft said, "I am president of the United States, and I want a diner attached to this train at Harrisburg. I want it well-stocked with food, including filet mignon. You see that I get a diner."

When Norton again tried to calm him, Taft roared: "What's the use of being president if you can't have a train with a diner on it!"

Taft alternately indulged and fought to keep his weight down. The housekeeper, a Mrs. Jaffray, noted that Taft had a twelve-ounce steak for breakfast "nearly every morning" to go along with "two oranges, several pieces of toast and butter, and a good deal of coffee, cream, and sugar." When Taft started on one of his periodic diets, he told her, "Please, Mrs. Jaffray, I wish you would give me only a six ounce steak instead of the man-sized one. It's a terrible sentence the doctor has imposed on me." And to no avail. Taft was so large that he could not tie his own shoes—that was a job for his valet. Worse, he sometimes got stuck in the White House bathtub. On these occasions, it took two men to haul him out. Finally he got a new tub, seven feet long, forty-one inches wide, and weighing one ton. (The tub is no longer there.)

Taft's weight undoubtedly contributed to his habit of nodding off to sleep almost anytime, anywhere. Nellie called the president her "Sleeping Beauty." Taft slept sitting up in his automobile, at cabinet meetings, and even once when in a face-to-face discussion with Speaker Cannon. Archie Butt sought to mitigate the problem by sitting next to Taft and coughing loudly when he sensed the president dozing off. At church he didn't think it proper to cough, so he prodded Taft with an elbow. Taft would awake "with such a start as to attract the attention of everybody around him." At one funeral, Butt had to give up his seat next to Taft to Chief Justice Edward White and watched, horrified, as Taft started nodding. Fearing a loud snore, Butt started toward him but then noticed that Justice White was asleep also and resolved to blame him if necessary.

Nellie had her own struggles with her health. Less than a month into her husband's term, what is now believed to have been a stroke curtailed her enjoyment of the realization of her White House dream. Her face became slightly disfigured, her speech slurred, and she had difficulty moving about. She referred to the "nervous disorder" as "a serious attack of illness," went into seclusion for over a year, wore a veil, and gradually recovered.

The public was never the wiser. As Butt said, "We have been able to keep the serious side of her illness entirely from the press."

Taft was always a devoted and considerate husband, but never more so than at this time. He read to her by the hour every day and helped her practice forming words to recover her speech. He would also bring flowers daily and with a smile announce, "I stole these for you." The smile and the comment referred to an incident that brings into high relief the tenor of life in the Taft White House. It began with Taft, the ubiquitous Archie Butt, and a reporter named Price crossing the south grounds toward the Washington Monument on a walk. Butt recorded the outing:

> We walked through the mist and rain, for it began to drizzle later, around the Monument, and the President expressed a desire to go up it. We found the keeper, but the fires were out and the elevator would not run. So we continued to amble on until we came to the flower beds in front of the Agricultural Department. Here a funny incident happened which I see is still unmentioned among the news of the day.
>
> The President thought he would like to pick some flowers himself for Mrs. Taft, and he went among the roses, I among the peonies (I think they were

*The Tafts are pictured on the South Portico with their three children. First Lady Helen (Nellie) had vowed to marry only a man destined to be President. She pushed her reluctant husband into the job where he spent the four unhappiest years of his life.* (LIBRARY OF CONGRESS)

peonies, for they had no odor and were large), while Price began to gather pansies. In a few minutes there was the greatest yelling I ever heard, from the watchman, who put us all under arrest.

At this point the watchman recognized the president of the United States, who was laughing.

"I am put here for a purpose," the watchman said solemnly, "and I have to obey my orders whether it is the President or not."

"Right you are," Taft said, obviously enjoying the situation. "Do you want me to go to the station house with you? But I must ask you to let off these other gentlemen as they were only acting under my orders."

The unfortunate watchman, abashed and speechless, was forced to concede. Taft reveled in the incident and in retelling it to Nellie.

Such was the informality with which Taft navigated his presidency, and his life at the White House. The mansion itself still had an open and informal air about it. The Tafts came and went more or less as they pleased, going to plays once or twice a week. They organized a dancing class and invited friends to dance to music played on a record player cranked by the president himself. Visitors too came and went with little formality. When the president was away, tourists were allowed to go into his office, sit down, and even bounce in his desk chair. Ira Smith, who spent a record fifty years sorting White House mail, once showed his girlfriend around the president's office. Seeing a vase of roses, on impulse he decided to present her with one. As he snatched it the vase tumbled over, spilling water onto a pile of army commissions that Taft had just signed. Some were ruined. Smith saved himself by getting duplicates made the next day and shoving them into a pile of papers to be signed.

Archie Butt and Taft often went horseback riding together and occasionally went walking. The Secret Service had been guarding presidents since McKinley's assassination, but they tended to be lax, and Taft often mischievously evaded them. In one instance, he started on a walk on the south grounds with Butt, then suddenly said, "I have not been on F Street or Pennsylvania Avenue since I was president. Let's take a try at it." They did, much to the dismay of the Secret Service agents—and their superior. But before long Taft was at it again, this time gaily Christmas shopping in the crowded stores along Pennsylvania Avenue. When he bought something, he would say, "Please charge that to me," and "Is my credit good?" Or, "Do you know where I live?" He was like a boy in a toy store.

Even Nellie shook off some of the expected White House formalities. It was the custom in the mansion that any family member who was late for breakfast would be escorted to the dining room by a servant and announced. Nellie put an end to that, being of no mind to bind her home life with stuffy restrictions. A magazine of the day made much of the fact that she also replaced the conventional crystal at the breakfast table with less formal, and less fragile, engraved silver cups.

The casual environment was extended to the garage, where a cow shared space with the elegant Steamer and the Pierce Arrows. Of the many gifts the Tafts received, a 1,500-pound Holstein named Pauline Wayne was the most famous. She arrived from Wisconsin in a railroad boxcar and was put out on the White House lawn to graze. Initially she enjoyed traditional stables, but those were eventually torn down following Taft's switch from horses to cars. A cow man assigned to her brought milk to the mansion twice a day. Nellie took a special interest in Pauline, whom she called "Mooly-mooly," and saw to it that she was taken care of. Pauline was the last of many White House cows dating back to the mansion's earliest days.

Mooly-mooly notwithstanding, Nellie never lost her taste for the glamour and privileges of the White House. In what was to be the most memorable event of her term as first lady, she planned an extravaganza for her silver wedding anniversary, June 19, 1911. She had given brilliant entertainments before, but never on this scale, which she said would require "all outdoors." She sent out some eight thousand invitations. The greenhouses were emptied of plants to decorate the interior of the White House. Workmen spent days installing thousands of lights in the trees and illuminating the fountains. Nellie called for more and more lights, which were borrowed from navy bases and rush-shipped. For the first time, the White House was totally illuminated with floodlights, shining on the United States flag on the roof. The flag blew straight out, in any weather, thanks to concealed fans.

*Thomas Jefferson began the tradition of an open house on New Year's Day and personally shaking hands with everyone. By 1911 when this line formed to greet President Taft, crowds reached 8,000.* (LIBRARY OF CONGRESS)

Gifts poured in by the carload. "Well, I never knew there was as much silver in the world," was Butt's dry comment. "It is hideous to see such profligacy," he added. Nellie, on the other hand, was ecstatic: "Silver was showered upon us until we were almost buried in silver." Much to her husband's consternation, for years afterward Nellie recycled pieces of her loot as wedding gifts by altering the monograms.

The success of the celebration depended on using both the house and the grounds, so fair weather was essential. Alarmingly, Professor Willis L. Moore, chief of the Weather Bureau, informed the Tafts, "There will be showers this afternoon and tonight. It is raining almost everywhere, even in the British Isles and Scandinavia." The same forecaster had predicted sun at Taft's inaugural, and there was heavy snow and seventy-mile-per-hour winds. Apropos that debacle, the evening of the party was remarkably clear and blue skied.

The gates to the grounds were opened at eight. A crowd of onlookers estimated at fifteen thousand gazed in awe at the spectacle from behind the iron fence surrounding the grounds. The Engineers Band and the Marine Band played continually. At nine the Tafts descended from the south portico to greet their guests, Nellie in a white satin dress embroidered with silver roses and carnations. At eleven the state dining room was thrown open for a buffet supper, which included a seventy-five-pound anniversary cake. Food was also served in the East Room and in small tents on the lawn. One band came in to provide music for dancing in the East Room and on the veranda. At midnight Nellie left the party for her bedroom on the second floor but, unable to sleep, watched from her window. At one in the morning the leader of the Engineers Band sent Taft a note asking if it was time to play "Home Sweet Home." Taft's answer was an unqualified no, and he mixed in with the company on the grounds. Finally, at two, the music stopped.

Taft, if more modest than Nellie, was himself no miser. He never skimped on White House expenses, explaining, "Never in my life have I been able to be as generous as I would wish, and always I have had to retrench in entertaining others from necessity. This is the first time in my life I have ever been in a position where I could let the innate feelings of hospitality have full scope, and I propose to indulge this weakness to the utmost for the next four years."

Taft felt he should have only good cigars and good wine at the White House. When it was suggested to him that he did not need to give out expensive cigars, except perhaps to certain favored people, he responded by having Butt order five thousand cigars from Cuba. The household food bill—an average month ran to $868.93—for state dinners and official receptions came out of Taft's own pocket, but that didn't dampen his generosity. Chief Usher Ike Hoover figured a quart of champagne for every four people at a party, and once it was iced, it was never returned to the vault. Any excess went to lucky White House employees. Not until Harding's time, a decade later, did Congress allot for such things. Fortunately for Taft, Congress did raise the president's salary from $50,000 to $75,000 a year, authorized $25,000 for travel, and agreed finally to pay the salaries of White House domestic help.

Taft might well have celebrated his departure from the White House with a Cuban cigar and a bottle of champagne. But by the election of 1912, in what he would call "the greatest tragedy of my life," his friendship with Theodore Roosevelt had grown rancorous and soon disintegrated completely. Taft had consistently said in private that he only wanted one term. However, the increasingly hostile Roosevelt had returned from an extended African hunt still young and ambitious, and his associates filled him with stories of Taft's failings and "disloyalty." When Roosevelt contested his renomination in 1912, Taft, indignant, fought back. "I'm a man of peace," he said, "and I don't want to fight." But he did, for as he also said, "Even a rat in a corner will fight." The personal battle was a Republican disaster. Taft got the party nomination, Roosevelt ran as a Progressive, or Bull Moose, and Democrat Woodrow Wilson won handily. Taft knew he would lose. Reflecting his bitterness, he said, "If I cannot win I hope Wilson will." He trailed both Wilson and the popular Roosevelt. Nellie tasted the bitter cup too. When Roosevelt contested the nomination, she reminded her husband, "I told you so four years ago and you did not believe me."

On her last day in the White House, Nellie Taft wandered about the upstairs living area aimlessly, sadly, delaying the final moment, while the staff waited to bid her farewell. Taft had gone to the Capitol for Wilson's inaugural. Finally, as noon and the end of the term neared, she put on her hat and furs and walked out to her waiting Pierce Arrow without a good-bye to anyone.

Taft told the new president, "I'm glad to be going. This is the loneliest place in the world." Wilson would come to understand this later.

# Woodrow Wilson

## 1913–1921

## *Love and War*

THE MORNING of his inauguration, March 4, 1913, president-elect Woodrow Wilson danced around his first wife, Ellen Axson Wilson, in their hotel room, chanting, "We're going to the White House today." When he took the oath of office that afternoon, the lifelong academic was the embodiment of dignity: fifty-two years old, he was a slender five feet eleven inches, with a high forehead and cheekbones, a long, thin nose, and a jaw that thrust forward. Ellen, overwhelmed by the crowds and the notoriety, covered her face with her hands and wept.

At the White House that night, the day ended as differently as it had begun. The president of just a few hours could not find the clothes he had brought with him, not even his pajamas. He noticed a panel of buttons, and not knowing what each one was for, pressed several. It was now close to midnight, but a doorkeeper appeared, and a search was undertaken for the president's trunk. By the time it was recovered, Woodrow Wilson was asleep in his underwear.

Thomas Woodrow Wilson was born in 1856 in Staunton, Virginia, but grew up in Augusta, Georgia. He was called "Tommy" until, as a young adult, he substituted the more dignified "Woodrow." The most highly educated president in history, he studied law at Princeton, the University of Virginia, and Johns Hopkins, where he received a Ph.D. in 1886. A noted scholar, he became president of Princeton in 1902. He finally entered politics in 1910, when he was elected governor of New Jersey on a reform

Democratic ticket. Two years later, he was running for president of the United States. It took the Democrats forty-six ballots to nominate him at their 1912 convention. He was a compromise candidate, and he won the election only because popular ex-president Theodore Roosevelt had entered the race and split the Republican vote.

"God ordained that I should be the next President of the United States," Wilson said when he was elected. The son of a well-known Presbyterian minister, he was deeply religious—some said self-righteous—and claimed that his life "would not be worth living if it were not for the driving power of religion." At the White House he read the Bible each day, said grace before meals, and prayed on his knees each morning and night. French Premier Georges Clemenceau said that talking to Wilson was "something like talking to Jesus Christ."

Before heading to Washington for his inauguration, Wilson went to the bank and, for the first time in his life, borrowed a large sum—$5,000—to meet the expenses of becoming president. He asked that the inaugural ceremonies not strain his resources, and for the first time in many years there was no inaugural ball. His new expenses included clothes fit for the leader of a nation and a diamond pendant for its first lady. Wilson was used to dressing casually, polishing his own shoes, and riding his bicycle to class (in a tall hat and striped trousers). He didn't own a car. Even with a wife and three daughters, he sometimes spent more on books than on the family's clothes. His White House valet, Arthur Brooks, who had served predecessor Howard Taft, was shocked to find that the new president had only a few suits, and that these were ready-made. With encouragement from Wilson's wife, Brooks convinced him to see a tailor. Brooks himself selected the fabrics and checked the fit. Wilson got trim wool suits for winter and white pants, a blazer, and a boater for summer.

With or without a dapper wardrobe, Wilson had presence. Before large crowds he was expansive, supremely self-confident, a gifted, moving orator. Face to face with strangers, however, even in small groups, the cerebral president was awkward and shy, even aloof. Newspaper editor William Allen White said Wilson's handshake felt like "a ten-cent pickled mackerel in brown paper—irresponsive and lifeless." For his few intimates he reserved the side of his personality that was warm, passionate, and boyishly silly. "Fortunately," Wilson once said, "I have a special gift for relaxation and being amused." He liked to entertain friends by imitating the dancers and singers he'd seen at the theater, or by relating funny stories. He could tell stories in Scottish or Irish dialects, dance a jig, do the cakewalk, imitate a drunk, or do impersonations. His youngest daughter, Eleanor, remembered hearing loud laughter coming from her father's cabinet meetings. He often played charades with the family. He had a nice tenor voice and liked to sing with his daughters. At Princeton he sang with the glee club. He was fond of detective stories, and also had a penchant for limericks. One of his favorites was: "There was a young monk of Siberia / Whose existence grew drearier and drearier / Till he burst from his cell / With a hell of a yell / And eloped with the Mother Superior."

Wilson often said he wished he had become a performer, and vaudeville was one of his passions. As president he attended Poli's Theatre so often that the manager reserved a box for him and cut a new doorway through the theater wall so his limousine could pull up and let the president out near a back stairway that led to his box. Wilson didn't know it, but balcony tickets were not sold to the general public but issued only to known persons. Reputedly Wilson attended the theater more than any other president, and during January and February of one year he went almost every night. His Secret Service guard, Colonel Edmund Starling, remembered taking the president backstage to meet the performers, "particularly the good-looking ladies."

As Wilson wrote Ellen in 1899, "I am particularly susceptible to feminine beauty and all feminine attractions. A pretty girl is my chief pleasure." His wife became the most influential person in his life. As he once said, "No man has ever been a success without having been surrounded by admiring females." During his courtship of Ellen, he expressed his love in some of the most ardent love letters ever written by a president. "I tremble with deep excitement . . . I never quivered so before with eager impatience and anticipation." And: "Are you prepared for the storm of love making with which you will be assailed?" Ellen devoted herself to hearth and home, supporting her husband's intellectual work. As her three daughters grew up, she returned to the study of art that had occupied her during her courtship. Starting in 1905 she summered at the artist colony in Old Lyme, Connecticut that produced such famous American Impressionists as Childe Hassam and Willard Metcalf. Her husband's increasing prominence made her loath to exhibit. Finally, in 1911 she entered a painting to be judged for an exhibition in New York City under the name of W. Wilson and won an award. She revealed her identity, and the gallery owner became her agent. Just before moving in to the White House in March 1913, she had a one-woman show of fifty landscapes in Philadelphia.

By the time they arrived at the White House, daughters Eleanor, Jessie, and Margaret were all in their mid-twenties. Wilson was always close to the girls, and they had many happy times together in the White House. But he didn't like the speculative news stories linking them romantically with various men. He threatened, "On the next offense, I shall do what any other indignant father would do. I will punch the man who prints it in the nose." Finally, he told the press, "I am a public character . . . but the ladies of my household are not public characters, because they are not servants of the government. I deeply resent the treatment they are receiving at the hands of the newspapers. . . . If this continues, I shall deal with you not as President, but man to man." It did not continue.

But the press had a proper story to report when Jessie, the middle daughter, married on November 25, 1913, in a ceremony replicating Alice Roosevelt Longworth's wedding. Eleanor, the youngest, followed suit in an intimate Blue Room ceremony on May 7, 1914. Earlier she'd told her father when he was selecting his cabinet, "Well, I don't really care who you choose, as long as you make that nice Mr. McAdoo Secretary of the Treasury." McAdoo proved so nice Eleanor married him. The eldest daughter, Margaret, remained unmarried during the White House years, serving as her father's hostess after her mother's death.

As first lady, Ellen's interests were in literature and art and in improving the conditions of the poor African Americans living in Washington's blighted alleys. She did some redecorating, but for the most part confined her efforts to the private quarters, which had hardly been touched since 1902. This included portions of the third, or attic, floor, for which Congress had appropriated $9,500 to convert to family use. Ellen disliked the dark colors chosen by the Roosevelts, and with an artist's eye for color had the dark green burlap on the walls of the long upstairs hall replaced with Japanese grass cloth dyed amber. New curtains and upholstery were a mix of chintzes, cretonne, and hand-woven

*In 1913 Wilson's first wife, artist Ellen Axson Wilson, replaced Edith Roosevelt's colonial garden with this formal rose garden, emphasizing vistas in the seventeenth-century Italian manner. Today this is the site of the current Rose Garden started by Jacqueline Kennedy.* (LIBRARY OF CONGRESS)

"craft" materials, and the bedroom furniture, modern French-style pieces that suggested antiques. Ellen was particularly happy with a bedroom set of glossy white imitation Louis XVI furniture.

But Ellen had little opportunity to enjoy her efforts. She began failing in the spring of 1913. She suffered from a variety of problems, none of which seemed serious at first. In March 1914 she slipped on a polished bedroom floor and was confined to bed. Then she had a breakdown. By June there was little hope. Just weeks before she died, she was finally diagnosed with Bright's disease, a painful and progressive kidney ailment. She died in the White House on August 6, 1914, but not before telling her husband to marry again. By now, war had broken out in Europe, and Wilson would come to feel Ellen's death had spared her from the subsequent chaos. "She was so radiant, so happy," he later said to one of his daughters. "We must be grateful for her sake that she did not see the world crash into ruin. It would have broken her heart."

Wilson was beside himself. At first he would not allow her body to be placed in a coffin. He kept it on a sofa in the bedroom, and he hardly moved from her. He admitted at the time that he was "not fit to be President," as he could no longer think straight and had "no heart" for what he was doing. Finally he allowed the funeral to proceed. Services were held in the East Room August 10 and her body returned to Georgia for burial.

The next nine months of grieving constituted one of the most difficult periods in Wilson's life. He was severely depressed, even expressing a wish to be assassinated. Then one day as he stood at the elevator, out walked Edith Galt, an attractive widow with a figure described as "Junoesque." Their meeting was apparently by chance, although Dr. Cary Grayson may well have had something to do with it. On her deathbed, Ellen had not only told Wilson to remarry but had asked Grayson to help him do it. The president's closest companion as well as his doctor, Grayson worried about Wilson's depressed state and understood his need for feminine support. Edith was in the White House for the first time in her life because Grayson had arranged for her to meet Helen Bones, Ellen's secretary and Wilson's first cousin, who lived in the family quarters. Helen took her turn with the Wilson daughters as official hostess, but after Ellen's death, she, like he, was lonely. Helen and Edith took a walk in Rock Creek Park, and the two went back to the White House for tea. Grayson and Wilson were playing golf but returned to the White House after only twelve holes. All four then had tea together in front of the lunette window in the second-floor hall.

When Edith later showed Mamie Eisenhower the spot near the White House elevator where she first met the president and her future husband, she recalled the adage, "Turn a corner and meet your fate." Indeed, after Ellen's death, but before she met Wilson, Edith had visited Washington's noted clairvoyant Madame Marcia, who told her she would be the next Mrs. Wilson. Helen later said that the day Wilson met Edith was the first time she had seen her cousin smile since his wife's death. Asked how long it took Wilson to become interested, she answered, "About ten minutes." Less than two months later, after dinner with guests in the State Dining Room, the president led Edith out to the south portico and proposed marriage. She did not commit herself then. Widowed seven years ago, Edith, now forty-two, had not expected to find love. Later that night she wrote her suitor, "I am a woman—and the thought that you have need of me—is sweet!" Wilson was aroused. He had a direct telephone line connected to her home, sent her an orchid every day, and wrote her nearly every day, sometimes more than once—long, passionate, handwritten letters delivered by a private messenger.

They began meeting often, while maintaining the niceties. Edith came to dinner at the White House or on the presidential yacht as Helen's guest. Afterward, Edith and Wilson would go to his study. His letters showed their growing intimacy: "As I lay between sleeping and waking you came and nestled close to me. I could feel your breath on my cheek, our lips touched, and there was all about me the sweet atmosphere that my Darling always carries with her." They went for walks in Rock Creek Park, with the president playfully leaping rock barriers. They went for rides together in the backseat of the White House limousine, the curtains and the divider drawn. On one such ride, in 1915, with the chauffeur and Secret Service agent in the front seat and Helen with them in the back, Edith put her hand in Wilson's and whispered that she was "ready to be mustered in as soon as can be."

There was one small obstacle. Wilson's advisers feared that such a swift remarriage would alienate voters in the 1916 election. McAdoo went to the president with a fabricated story that if the wedding were pursued, Mary Hulbert Peck would publish effusive letters Wilson had written to her while married to Ellen. Wilson was devastated, but he told Edith the whole story of his friendship with Mrs. Peck. She responded with a passionate pledge of her love and loyalty: "I will stand by you—not for duty, not for pity, not for honor—but for love." Years later Colonel Edmund A. House, another adviser, admitted to Edith that the story was a hoax—he and McAdoo had dreamed it up to prevent what they considered to be a politically damaging marriage.

In October 1915 the couple announced their engagement. Wilson called on Edith at her home on DuPont Circle in the evenings, driven in a limousine and escorted by Secret Service agent Edmund Starling. Sometimes late at night he chose to walk back to the White House. Starling recalled one such evening: "We walked briskly, and the President danced off the curbs and up them when we crossed the streets. If we had to wait for traffic—delivery trucks were about all we found abroad at that hour—he jigged a few steps, whistling an accompaniment for himself. There was a tune he had heard in vaudeville which he liked, and almost unconsciously it seemed, he would whistle it as he waited for a truck to pass us on the corner of N Street. He whistled softly, through his teeth, tapping out the rhythm with restless feet. 'Oh, you beautiful doll! You great big beautiful doll! Let me put my arms around you, I can hardly live without you . . .' "

They were married December 18 at Edith's home. Escaping from reporters, they were driven incognito to Alexandria, where a private train was waiting in the freight yards to take them to Hot Springs, Virginia, for a two-week honeymoon. The next morning, Starling went back to the sitting room on the train and found the president with his back to him, in top hat, tail coat, and gray morning trousers, hands in his pockets. Starling watched as the newlywed clicked his heels in the air, again whistling the tune, "Oh, you beautiful doll."

Edith easily adapted to the life of a first lady. "My first public appearance as the wife of the President," Edith later wrote, "was at a reception to the diplomatic corps. There were 3,328 guests. I wore a white gown brocaded in silver with long white tulle drapery, then known as 'angel sleeves.' It was thrilling, the first time, to greet all the cabinet in the Oval Room upstairs and then with the President precede them down the long stairway with the naval and military aides forming an escort, the Marine Band playing 'Hail to the Chief,' and the waiting mass of guests as we passed into the Blue Room." And the White House staff adapted easily to her. "Mrs. Wilson was what I would call a perfect wife," housekeeper Elizabeth Jaffray said.

The huge Lincoln Bed was moved into the president's bedroom, replacing the twin beds he and his first wife had used. The couple's routine was breakfast together alone (they ate all their meals together, but not always alone), then on to golf or to the study, where Edith blotted papers after her husband signed them. At 9 A.M. a stenographer came in, but Edith often stayed to listen. When Wilson left for the Oval Office in the West Wing—he was due there at eleven and was never late—she walked over with him through the rose garden, clinging to his arm and listening to his animated talk. He looked at his watch, kissed her, and then followed her with his eyes as she walked back along the path. At the other end she turned and waved to him. They were together most of the day. Edith never left Wilson alone with another woman. In the afternoon she sat quietly in his White House office while he got through his appointments, then they went motoring together. In the evening they might go to the theater, or play pool in the billiards room downstairs. Wilson found solitaire relaxing, and they sometimes played side by side. But if Wilson had to work late, she sat with him. He would look up with a smile and say, "You don't know how much easier it makes all this to have you here by me. Are you too tired to hear what I have written?"

Wilson shared everything with his wife and always wanted her advice. She screened his mail, and encoded and decoded his diplomatic messages. The secret code the president used for communications with diplomats abroad was not even known to Secretary of State Robert Lansing. Ambassadors were shocked by the knowledge Edith was privy to. She admitted to having known next to nothing about politics or government before she met Wilson, yet on her advice he rewrote a note to Germany on its sinking of the *Lusitania*.

Edith adapted her life to fit into her husband's in every way she could. He had always liked to bicycle, and in his younger days had made bicycling trips through England during his extensive vacations there. Edith got herself a bicycle and practiced riding it in the long ground-floor corridor of the White House, apparently with little success. She was not very athletic. She took golf lessons so she could accompany Wilson on his almost daily trips to the golf course. She absorbed all the diplomatic and political problems that he shared so freely with her, and her opinions seemed to merge with his, even on suffrage. Despite Wilson's liberal views and idealism, he was slow to accept the idea that women should be able to vote. Much to his embarrassment, women picketed the White House demanding suffrage. He invited them in for refreshments and was mystified when they refused. When they posted banners on the iron fence around the White House grounds, they were arrested and given harsh sentences in the workhouse, but Wilson, fearing they would become martyrs, pardoned them. Edith called them "disgusting creatures" and "detestable suffragettes."

After Wilson and Edith married, Edith felt their intimacy infringed upon by her husband's long-term relationship with Colonel House. Ellen had been willing to share her husband, but Edith was not and took an immediate dislike to House. Sensing a potential problem, House diplomatically praised Edith to Wilson, saying he "had not the words in which to express his admiration." Wilson told her, "I wish I could give you some impression of the way in which his face glowed when he spoke of you. . . . I love him more than ever."

House understood Wilson's insecurities and emotional needs, and knew what he wanted to hear. He said his policy was "to nearly always praise at first, in order to strengthen the President's confidence in himself which, strangely enough, is often lacking." Wilson said of his friend, "What I like about House is that he is the most self-effacing man that ever lived. All he wants to do is serve the common cause and to help me and others." But Colonel House—"Colonel" was an honorary title—had his own agenda, which he sought to further by being the power behind the throne. He was never on the public payroll, turning down all offers of official position, and he stayed in the background, avoiding reporters. He just wanted to guide affairs through Wilson. He was one of the rare men Wilson could relate to—nonmasculine, nonthreatening, and completely devoted.

When Wilson was president-elect and stayed with House in New York, House personally made his friend's doctor-ordered breakfast of cereal and two raw eggs mixed with orange juice. When he was lonely after Ellen's death, House sometimes invited Wilson to stay at his New York apartment. House would send his wife away—she didn't seem to matter. (In his *Reminiscences,* their thirty-seven-year marriage is covered in one sentence.) In the evening they would wander the streets of the city together. The president considered getting himself a fake beard. Once, they were recognized and ducked into a hotel, up an elevator, then down and out the other side of the building. When they stayed together in a rustic lodge just outside Washington, he got up first in order to give Wilson "uninterrupted use of our common bathroom." He told Wilson that he was "the bravest, wisest leader, the greatest and most gallant gentleman and the truest friend in all the world." Wilson believed in House so fully that during World War I he sent him to confer with the heads of the warring powers in Europe on his behalf without even written instructions. House had what he wanted. Of Wilson he said, "He signs letters, documents, and papers without question."

Wilson's other confidante was Dr. Cary Grayson, his personal physician. Grayson had served Taft, who recommended him to Wilson. He inherited a patient with a long history of medical problems. As a youth Wilson was sickly, suffering from indigestion, allergies, headaches, and poor eyesight. At college he had recurrent heartburn, nausea, and constipation. In 1895 a New York doctor diagnosed his stomach problems as the result of excess stomach acid and gave him a stomach pump, by which he could force water in through a long rubber tube. As president, Wilson also had hypertension, and suffered lingering effects of previous mild strokes, which affected his right hand and right eye. Dr. S. Weir Mitchell, an eminent neurologist, examined Wilson and predicted he would not live through his first term. Grayson got Wilson to give up the stomach pump and various powders he was using and put him on a diet that included raw eggs in the morning—Wilson said it was like eating an unborn thing. Grayson insisted the new president get nine hours' sleep, go motoring in the fresh air, and play a lot of golf. Wilson ordered that he never be wakened at night. White House chief usher Ike Hoover once did so at the urgent request of the secretary of the navy, and Wilson said he would answer in the morning, that no one could make an intelligent decision when awakened from a sound sleep.

He followed doctor's orders. Until his second term when World War I engulfed the United States, Wilson seldom spent more than four hours in his office. He had few appointments, and "always seemed to know beforehand what people wanted," Ike Hoover recalled. Grayson converted him into an ardent motorist, which was quite a transformation. When Wilson came into office, he sold off the auto-loving Taft's cars, and at his inauguration rode in a two-horse victoria. But then Congress bought the president a Pierce Arrow with right-hand drive, presidential seals on the doors, and a top that could be removed in good weather. Wilson personally mapped out routes into the surrounding countryside for his jaunts with Edith, which often lasted five or six hours. Sometimes Helen Bones joined them. Wilson insisted the chauffeur keep within the speed limit, generally twenty-two miles per hour, and he fumed when a speeder passed. He even wrote the attorney general to find out if, as president, he had the powers of a magistrate and could "hold up some scoffing automobilist and fine him about a thousand dollars." He was talked out of this approach. Once, his own car was stopped by a policeman on a bicycle. Wilson asked what the charge was, but the officer immediately realized who he'd stopped. The officer saluted and said, "It's all right, Mr. President. I didn't know it was you." "On the contrary," Wilson responded, "I of all people must observe the laws."

*Wilson liked to write his own memos and papers on a typewriter. When he was courting Edith Galt he wrote out long, passionate letters to her every day even though she was only blocks away.* (CORBIS)

He spent almost as much time golfing as motoring and may even have logged more hours on the course than Eisenhower, who became synonymous with the game. Dr. Grayson had recognized that much of the president's ill health was due to tension. He introduced him to golf, taught him some of the fundamentals, and frequently played with him. Wilson recognized the health value of fresh air and exercise but was not at all athletic and was never more than a golf hacker. Also, his physical impairments were a handicap. As he explained to a group of golfers: "My right eye is like a horse's. I can see straight out with it but not sideways. As a result I cannot take a full swing because my nose gets in the way and cuts off my view of the ball. This is the reason I use a short swing." He once took twenty-six strokes to make one hole. But he never cared about his score and didn't always bother to keep it. His favorite description of the game reflects his attitude toward it: "An ineffectual attempt to put an elusive ball into an obscure hole with implements ill-adapted for the purpose."

Wilson played at all hours, sometimes as early as five in the morning, and in all seasons. When there was snow on the ground he had the golf balls painted red. Once, in January, Wilson's fingers got too cold to unbutton his coat when he finished the game, and Agent Starling had to help him. He changed in and out of his golf clothes at the White House rather than use club facilities. He refused proffered memberships in elite clubs and was known as a "regular fellow." He never took advantage of his office to play through the group ahead, but the players would send him through as a courtesy by pretending to be looking for a lost ball. He always had a pleasant remark—almost always: Once, a player he called a "fool" drove a ball into them from the tee behind, hitting Grayson in the leg. Wilson was so angry that he went back to the tee and told the culprit off. It was after a golf game when he was vacationing at Pass Christian, Mississippi, before his marriage to Edith that he and Grayson once noticed smoke coming from the roof of a house. They ran to the door and banged on it. An excited lady greeted them with, "Oh, Mr. President, it is good of you to call on me," and offered them tea. Instead they organized a bucket brigade, and he and Grayson climbed to the attic and put out the fire. When the Secret Service heard about his adventure, all hell broke loose.

For all his playing, Wilson had only three other golf partners, all family: Edith, Ellen's brother Stockton Axson, and a cousin, T. E. Brown. Edith's score was almost beyond counting. She once asked a disgruntled caddy—in her "most beguiling way," she recalled—if he thought she could reach the green, which they were just short of, with a mid-iron. The caddy answered dourly, "Yes, if you hit it often enough." Agent Starling would retrieve balls she hit into the woods or, as he put it, "find" them on the edge of the fairway. But Edith didn't care about her score either. The couple were happy to be on the course together. As they walked, Wilson might tell one of his dialect stories or do an imitation. Once she playfully laid her club across his shoulders, and he immediately bent forward and changed stride to imitate a lumbering ape. He let the club roll over his head and caught it. They laughed. Typically, they played every day except Sunday, although generally only for an hour or two.

As the European war complicated affairs, Wilson and Edith arose at 5 A.M. in order to squeeze in their exercise on the golf course. Edith did not want to inconvenience the White House staff at that hour, so she asked them to prepare some food and leave it in the icebox. Naturally, the staff rose to serve them anyway. Generally they had only a snack and ate a regular breakfast at eight, after they returned from the golf course.

Wilson was never much interested in food anyway—chicken salad was his favorite. Traveling to the 1919 Paris Peace Conference by ship, he endured elaborate French cooking courtesy of the Hotel Belmont, which had, at their expense, provided him with their master chef. The rich sauces caused him indigestion, and he derided the lamb chops "done up in pajamas." On his next peace mission to Europe, he got rid of the chef. At the White House, his appetite was compromised by the huge animal heads of moose and elk Theodore Roosevelt had mounted in the State Dining Room. When he ate there, he turned his seat so his back was to them. In 1923 they were finally sent to the Smithsonian Institution.

In addition to impinging on his golf time, the European war restricted Wilson's movements as it became necessary to tighten the security around him. Instead of motoring into the countryside, he tried horseback riding in Rock Creek Park, but, as Starling said in his usual diplomatic way, the president "had rather a poor seat" and soon gave it up. Edith could not keep up with her husband in this activity. She rode sidesaddle, but mostly on the paths of the Ellipse behind the White House. Security was easier to maintain on the presidential yacht *Mayflower,* so the couple began using it more often. On one Sunday morning during the war, they disembarked on a small island in Chesapeake Bay where there were no automobiles or even horses. The fishermen who lived there thought the Germans were invading and hid in their houses. On another trip during the war years, Wilson and Dr. Grayson slipped away from the Secret Service guard, took a motor launch from the *Mayflower,* and landed at Yorktown, Virginia, where they walked idly through the streets without being noticed. Finally a little girl recognized Wilson and invited them to her house, where her mother served them cold tea on the porch. Farther downriver they left the yacht—guardless once again—to visit the site outside of Yorktown where the American Revolution ended with the British surrender. Not finding a landing spot, they removed their shoes and socks, rolled up their pants, and waded ashore, where they climbed a fence only to encounter a bull in a field. When the creature began snorting and bellowing, Grayson prudently suggested they beat a retreat.

Wilson often evaded his guards, or attempted to. When he received the news of the May 7, 1915, sinking of the *Lusitania* and the huge loss of life, he realized the implications and needed time to think. Impulsively he ducked out of the White House alone and headed down Pennsylvania Avenue, lost in his thoughts. It was evening and a light rain was falling. The newsboys shouted their "extras" about the sinking. He made a swing through the side streets and on returning to the White House went to his study without speaking to anyone. One warm July day passersby on Pennsylvania Avenue saw the president slip out the front door with a small bundle of papers under his arm. As he got to the street two Secret Service agents burst out of the White House in pursuit. The president darted around the crowd in the street but soon gave up. "I came very near to getting away that time," he said. He allowed the agents to accompany him to the bank. On another, somewhat more successful occasion, he had an old felt hat hidden inside his coat to put on as a disguise, forbidding the doorkeeper to give him away. The agents finally found him in a five-and-ten cent store buying penny candy for some local urchins.

In May 1918, at the height of the fighting in Europe, Wilson was staying at the Waldorf-Astoria in New York when he announced an urge "to take a little walk like an ordinary citizen." He told Starling he was tired of policemen and preparations and asked, "Can I sneak out the back way?" Starling took him out. They walked, talked, laughed. "He was like a kid," Starling recorded, "and he ran out in the middle of Madison Avenue ahead of a big dray, I right after him. An automobile was headed straight towards him. I grabbed his arm and jerked him back."

It was perhaps one of the few carefree moments of Wilson's second term. When he went to Congress to ask for a declaration of war against Germany, on April 6, 1917, he did so reluctantly. The Civil War and its devastation had influenced him a great deal. His earliest memories were of General Robert E. Lee coming through Augusta, Georgia, under Union guard and of wounded Confederate soldiers in his father's church. Congress greeted his speech with cheers, but Wilson returned to the White House deeply depressed. His secretary, Joe Tumulty, was amazed to see the president "let his head fall down on his big old oak desk" and "sob like a child."

Shortly thereafter the White House instituted an economy move. To save on manpower and upkeep of the lawns, Wilson purchased a flock of sheep. In her memoir Edith said, "Every tree and bush had been carefully protected beforehand, so that the sheep could not injure them, and they added a very picturesque touch to the grounds." The flock was fruitful and multiplied; the wool was sheared and sold as "White House wool," bringing in a hundred thousand dollars for the war effort. William Reeves, the gardener turned shepherd, claimed that mowing continued despite the sheep, who were more interested in munching on shrubberies and flowers than grass. In 1920 Wilson gave the sheep away.

Meantime the war worsened, and so did Wilson's health. His many physical problems, both as a young man and as president, seemed to be related to tension. Grayson noticed that the president got attacks of indigestion whenever his secretary, Joe Tumulty, brought up problems at mealtime. Grayson mentioned this to Colonel House, who put a stop to it by speaking to Tumulty. Early in his presidency, Grayson's regimen of plenty of sleep and exercise seemed to work well. Now, tension-producing crises were bigger and more frequent. Near the end of his first term, Wilson's kidneys were not functioning properly and at times his right arm, limp from an 1896 stroke, was so weak he could not write. Wilson would not admit the problem was serious, blaming "the rather hard game of golf I had." By the time the United States entered World War I in 1917, the president's hypertension, high blood pressure, and cerebral and arterial disease were such that Grayson did not believe he would live through his term, though the doctor did not inform Wilson of this.

At the 1919 Paris Peace Conference, Wilson worked almost eighteen hours a day in an environment of constant conflict. Finally, on August 3, he collapsed. He had fever, diarrhea, congestion in the lungs, and difficulty breathing. He evidently had another small stroke at this time, probably causing some brain damage. He became more irritable, suspicious, and impatient. Grayson gave him barbiturates for his insomnia. Wilson's frustrations compounded as the victorious Allies made a mockery of his dream of a peace without vengeance, and the U.S. Senate savaged his only remaining triumph, the League of Nations, which he dreamed would "ensure peace and justice throughout the world." A healthy Wilson might have saved the League of Nations, but the Wilson of 1919 could not. He decided to take the issue to the people in a whistle-stop tour across the country. "It may kill you," Grayson warned.

Wilson set out on September 3, making speech after speech on a tight schedule. On September 25, in Colorado, he suffered one of his blinding headaches. He could hardly see and was near collapse. At Grayson's urging, the private train was stopped outside of Pueblo so the president could stretch his legs. As Edith, Grayson, and Wilson were walking, an old farmer came by in an automobile. Wilson shook his hand, and the farmer presented him with a head of cabbage and some apples. Wilson then saw a sick soldier on a porch and climbed over a fence to go up to the house and shake his hand. After an hour they were back on the train. By the next morning Wilson was on the verge of a complete breakdown, but grimly resolved to push on. Grayson's warning became stern. He told Wilson he would fall in front of the next audience. "I suppose you are right," Wilson finally agreed, tears on his cheeks. "This is the greatest disappointment of my life."

The train sped back to Washington, and Grayson announced that the president had a "digestive upset." Wilson arrived at the White House early Sunday, and Grayson had to dissuade him from going to church. For the next three days he rested. Then he collapsed with a paralytic stroke from a clot in the brain artery. Just the night before he had played billiards and seemed cheerful. He was totally incapacitated for almost two months. Semiparalyzed, he could not even sign a document. His doctor, Hugh H. Young, told reporters, "You can say that the President is able-minded and able-bodied, and that he is giving splendid attention to the affairs of state." He grew a thin white beard and saw almost no one but his doctors and his wife, not even his longtime intimate and secretary Joe Tumulty or the members of his cabinet.

Gradually he improved sufficiently to receive a few visitors for short periods, but they were screened by Edith and the setting carefully staged. She said she was told by Grayson that each new anxiety would be like "turning a knife in an open wound," and that if Wilson resigned it would remove his greatest incentive for recovery. Dr. Young, in an interview with the *Baltimore Sun* on February 10, 1920, stated that the president's mental processes were unimpaired and that the "President walks sturdily now, without assistance and without fatigue. . . . I think in many ways the President is in better shape than before the illness came." Actually Wilson's left arm was useless, he could not get himself up out of a chair, and he could walk only a short distance and then only with the aid of a cane.

Wilson would never fully recover, although he did make progress during his last year in the White House. He shaved off the white beard, and Grayson had three wooden steps constructed in the basement that he practiced climbing over and over again. The rugs were taken up so that he would not trip over them with his cane. At times he was remarkably lucid and like his old self. At other times he would inexplicably sob or throw a temper tantrum, even against Dr. Grayson. A highlight of his life became the daily showing of a film. Ike Hoover ran out of films to get for him and ran old Signal Corps clips of the president's European triumphs. Grayson could never bring himself to tell his old friend the true nature of his condition, and Wilson never acknowledged it—he wanted to be nominated for a third term and would have run if he had gotten it.

Republican Warren Harding's election was a repudiation of all that Wilson stood for, including the League of Nations. At Wilson's last cabinet meeting, the president mustered one final flash of wit, saying of the man about to be inaugurated, "There will be one very difficult thing for me, however, to stand, and that is Mr. Harding's English." The poet e. e. cummings wrote that Harding was "the only man, woman, or child/who wrote a simple declarative sentence/with seven grammatical errors."

After the cabinet meeting, Wilson painfully made his way back to the White House elevator—170 steps that took seven minutes. On Inauguration Day, he insisted on riding to the Capitol with president-elect Harding. Grayson had determined that it would be impossible for Wilson to climb the long, steep set of steps to the inaugural platform. Wilson chatted pleasantly with Harding in the car, staying there while Harding mounted the steps, smiling and waving his hat to the cheers of the crowd. Wilson skipped the ceremony, signed some bills at the Capitol, and then left for his new home on S Street, purchased for him by friends.

Here he spent his last three years. For a while he showed slow improvement, but arteriosclerosis made a total recovery impossible. He liked the Pierce Arrow he had used as president so much that friends bought it from the government for him for $3,000. Edith had the flower vases removed from the car, as she thought they were too effeminate for him, and he had a push-button signal installed to communicate with the chauffeur—one to stop, two to go left, three to go right. He was allowed to park it along the right-field line at Griffith Stadium so he could watch the baseball games. Stadium owner Clark Griffith assigned a catcher to sit on the front fender to protect Wilson from line drives. In August 1923 Wilson attended Harding's funeral at the White House. Dressed in formal mourning attire, he stayed in his Pierce Arrow in the driveway, where old friends came to greet him. He was unwilling to go through the ordeal of climbing out of the car and up the White House steps in full public gaze.

Wilson died on February 3, 1924, and was buried in the new Washington Cathedral. He is the only president buried in Washington, D.C. Edith lived to publish her memoirs in 1938 and, just before she died, to attend John F. Kennedy's 1961 inaugural. She was buried beside her husband.

# 29

# Warren G. Harding

## 1921–1923

## *Playing the Part*

IF WARREN GAMALIEL HARDING had had his way, he probably wouldn't have been president. But then, he wasn't in the driver's seat.

A handsome charismatic man, Harding was born November 2, 1865, in Blooming Grove (now Corsica), Ohio. After graduating from Iberia College, he moved to Marion, Ohio, a growing manufacturing town, where he eventually became a newspaperman as the publisher of the *Marion Star*. In 1891, at the age of twenty-five, he succumbed to the pursuit of Florence Kling De Wolfe, a thirty-year-old divorcée with an eleven-year-old son. Her friends called her "Flossie"; Harding called her "the Duchess." As a young woman, she found herself pregnant by the boy next door, Simon De Wolfe, and married him. He drank and hardly worked, so she divorced him and allowed her parents to bring up the child. Once married to "Wurr'n," she set about organizing his life and pushing his career. As a *New York Times* article noted shortly after her husband's election to the presidency, "Even more than her husband, Mrs. Harding is a leader. She likes to sway the crowds." Flo put it more succinctly: "I know what's best for the president, I put him in the White House. He does well when he listens to me and poorly when he does not."

The other pusher in his life was Harry Daugherty, a small-town Ohio lawyer who thought Harding looked like a president from the first time he saw him. "I found him sunning himself like a turtle on a log, and I pushed him into the water," Daugherty liked to say. "Harry Daugherty is the best friend I have on earth," Harding said. "He can have anything he wants from me." When Harding became president, Harry Daugherty wanted to be the attorney general of the United States, and that's what he got.

Harding made his way to the Ohio state senate in 1901, and in 1914 Daugherty and the Duchess pushed him to run for the U.S. Senate. He did so, won, and found that he thoroughly enjoyed the job. The Senate was like a rich man's club—the responsibilities were light. Harding played poker and took care of his constituents, missing almost half the roll calls. When Daugherty began pushing him for the presidency in 1920, he was not enthusiastic. He understood that the job was probably more than he could handle. After the primary, it looked as if he wouldn't have to worry about it. He did so poorly that he told Flo he was quitting. But Flo had visited a Washington clairvoyant named Madame Marcia, who had predicted that Harding would become president, though she added, "He will not live through his term. It is written in the stars." Undeterred, Flo browbeat her husband into staying in the race. As first lady she occasionally slipped out of the White House for visits to Madame Marcia.

Though Harding's chances of getting the nomination seemed remote, Daugherty and Flo worked to keep him from quitting. Daugherty, a political pro, foresaw a possible convention deadlock and made this famous prediction to reporters: "I don't expect Senator Harding to be nominated on the first, second, or third ballot, but I think we can well afford to take chances that about eleven minutes after 2 o'clock on Friday morning at the Convention, when fifteen or twenty men, somewhat weary, are sitting around a table, some one of them will say, 'who can we nominate?' At that decisive time the friends of Senator Harding can suggest him and can afford to abide by the result." That was what happened, more or less. Harding was a good compromise candidate. Handsome, tall—a little over six feet—weighing 210 pounds, and square-jawed with silver hair and calm gray eyes, Warren Gamaliel Harding had the right looks. Perhaps more importantly, he was a kindly man who disliked argument and had a magnetic personality: he had few enemies.

On November 2, 1920, his fifty-fifth birthday, Harding was elected by the largest popular majority of any president up to that time. "Well, Warren Harding," Florence said to him after the election, pronouncing his name "Wurr'n." "I've got you the presidency; what are you going to do with it?" "May God help me, for I need it," the president-elect replied.

Unlike his predecessor, Woodrow Wilson, a noted scholar whose speeches were among the finest ever, Harding liked to "bloviate," as he called it. That is, he said almost nothing, but said it in a sonorous manner. Wilson commented privately that Harding was incapable of thought because he had "nothing to think with." Harding also opposed what Wilson held most dear: the League of Nations, formed after World War I in hopes of ensuring world peace. After winning the election, Harding bade an emotional farewell to his Senate friends and then, en route to the train station, dropped by the White House and left his card for Wilson. It was a token formal call—he didn't even get out of the car.

Edith steeled herself and invited Florence over for the customary preview. Recollecting the visit years later, Edith's contempt still came through: "She arrived on time, wearing a dark dress, a hat with blue feathers, and her cheeks highly rouged. Her manner was so effusive, so voluble, that after a half-hour over tea cups I could hardly stem the torrent of words to suggest I send for the housekeeper so she could talk over her desires as to the house."

Elizabeth Jaffray, the housekeeper, was called in and found both women standing. She recalled that the first lady said, "Mrs. Harding, this is Mrs. Jaffray," and without even a good-bye, turned and left. Edith fled the White House, and returned later to find Flo still chatting with the cook in the kitchen. Edith also invited the Hardings to tea the day before the inauguration. "As I recall," she said, "[Mrs. Harding] wore the same hat as before but another dress. We tried to make things go but they both seemed ill at ease and did not stay long. Mr. Harding sat in an armchair with one leg thrown over the arm."

Nevertheless, Edith also invited the Hardings to move some of their belongings to the mansion in advance. The Hardings were in the process of selling their house and most of their furniture, and on January 27, they sent a wagon load of items to the executive offices of the White House, including "an antique settee, several chairs, heirloom pictures, and some rare china," the *New York Times* reported on page one.

When the Hardings took over the White House in March 1921, they made few changes to the mansion, except to let the public back in. The White House had been closed to the public since the beginning of World War I—the war had required tightened security, and afterward the president had fallen gravely ill. Even before that, the Wilsons had closely guarded their privacy. But the Hardings were open people from small-town Ohio, and they stayed that way. On her arrival at the White House on inauguration day, the Duchess found the servants drawing the curtains on the windows to keep people from peering in. "Let 'em look in if they want to," she ordered. "It's their White House." The house was reopened, and visitors streamed in daily starting at nine to view not only the East Room but the state parlors and dining room, which had been closed to the public since 1902. The gates were left open all day, and tourists could walk up to the north portico and snap pictures of each other standing by the pillars. Flo sometimes even came downstairs, introduced herself to the visitors, and gave them a personal tour of the mansion.

Harding was also outgoing. He was a member of the Rotary Club, the Kiwanis Club, and the Aerie of Eagles in Marion. Part of his White House day was set aside for greeting people and shaking hands. "I love to meet people," he said. "It is the most pleasant thing I do; it is really the only fun I have." Generally he emerged from his office every day before lunch to shake hands with whoever was there. During his two and a half years in office he shook the hands of an estimated quarter of a million people, and, not for the first time, some questioned the handshaking tradition. On New Year's Day, 1922, the *New York Times* reported, "he accorded this form of greeting to some six or seven thousand of the men, women and children who flocked to the White House for the purpose of conveying to him their good wishes for 1922. Four-fifths of his visitors were without any official status, just merely the plain people, many of whom had come from afar." The writer continued worriedly, "It was something more than a tax upon his strength. It was a risk. For the National American Institute of Homeopathists . . . indicated some thirty or forty distinct diseases transmissible from one person to another by a handshake."

Given their sociability, the Hardings entertained a great deal at the White House. In fact, they persuaded Congress to allow them to use part of the regular $25,000 travel

*Harding and his wife Florence, shown on the South Portico, were small town Ohio and didn't mind tourists on the porch snapping pictures by the pillars or peeking in at the First Family. "It's their White House," Florence said. "Let them look in if they want to." (LIBRARY OF CONGRESS)*

allowance for official entertainments. Privately, they particularly liked to treat their friends to parties in the family quarters, with gatherings of six to fifteen guests taking place in the large central corridor or the Oval Room. For the public, they revived every abandoned White House tradition, including the New Year's reception, Easter-egg rolling, and May garden parties. Weekly public receptions were more democratic than they had ever been. The Hardings' state dinners usually filled the State Dining Room to its full capacity of 104. Preparations began thirty-two hours in advance. Among many other chores, servants replaced the usual mahogany dining table with a large pine horseshoe table made for Theodore Roosevelt, and century-old silver was released from lock and key and polished. As many as forty extra workers were called in the night of the event. During these formal dinners, the president and first lady sat across from each other at one end of the horseshoe, and dishes were served, never passed.

Harding pursued more personal pleasures as well. The sports pages of the newspaper were his favorite reading material. He followed boxing matches and baseball scores and liked going out to Washington's Griffith Park to see a game. The cavalry provided him with a horse named Arizona, but he never rode much, preferring to drive. He was the first president qualified to drive a car—his predecessors had chauffeurs. In the summer of 1922 he wanted to drive all the way home to Marion in a White House car. He did make the trip by car, but roads were not good in those days, and cars were unreliable, so the Secret Service talked him out of doing the driving. He received an Airedale puppy as a gift, and "Laddie Boy" became much photographed and reported on in the press. The dog was bathed daily by his caretaker, White House staffer Willy Jackson, and had his own chair at cabinet meetings. In the evening, Harding liked to go a burlesque show to see "the girls." The Gayety Burlesque had a special box for him where he couldn't be easily seen. He typically smoked two cigars a day, and also liked to chew tobacco. Thomas A. Edison commented, "Harding's all right. Any man who chews tobacco is all right." But Harding couldn't do it with the Duchess around. "She says cigars are all right," he explained, "but it's undignified to chew." Colonel Edmund Starling, a Secret Service agent, once saw Harding split open a cigarette and empty the tobacco into his mouth when he wanted a chew.

Gambling at cards was a favorite Harding pastime. He liked challenging someone to what he called a cold hand: each person cuts the deck, and the high card wins. He did this at a poker evening at the town house of the wealthy Louise Cromwell Brooks: "Just the two of us," he said, "winner names the stakes." She won and reportedly named as the stakes a barrel of the Harrisons' White House china, which Harding sent her. He wore a pearl in his tie valued at between $4,000 and $5,000. "Won it at a poker game Wednesday night," he once explained. He had bet he held the highest spade and won with a four. Harding may or may not have improved his odds with his good-luck

*Harding received an Airedale pup as a gift. Laddie Boy had his own valet and his own special chair at Cabinet meetings. Harding enjoyed shaking hands and accommodating photographers, as he did here by the South Portico.* (**LIBRARY OF CONGRESS**)

charm—a well-worn $10 gold piece. "I have carried it ever since the day I became owner of the *Marion Star*," he said. "I take it with me to every poker game."

What Harding called his "poker cabinet" met two evenings a week in the family quarters of the White House. Theodore Roosevelt's daughter, Alice, attended one evening with her poker-playing husband, Congressman Nicholas Longworth. "The study was filled with cronies," she said. "The air hung heavy with tobacco smoke, trays with bottles containing every imaginable brand of whisky stood about, cards and poker chips ready at hand—a general atmosphere of waistcoat unbuttoned, feet on the desk, and spittoons along side." The Duchess sat with them or hovered about mixing drinks for "the boys," but did not play.

The serving of alcohol at the White House became a moral dilemma for the president. As a senator, he had voted for the Eighteenth Amendment, which established Prohibition in 1919. Now, as president, he was sworn to uphold and defend the Constitution. The "Drys" were pressuring him to set a good example. Harding did ban liquor from White House dinners, but he was provided with illegal liquor through the efforts of Jesse Smith, a close friend of Harry Daugherty, now the attorney general. Smith was not a government employee, but he had an office next to Daugherty's in the Justice Department and could obtain liquor through special permits that allowed for its "medical" use. Harding had stomach problems and was allergic to alcohol except in small quantities, so he seldom took more than a couple of drinks, but for "the boys," drinking was a way of life.

Mark Sullivan, the author who chronicled the 1920s in *Our Times*, had a meeting with the president in the White House one hot summer night, and they had the urge for a drink. Harding said to Sullivan, "Oh, well, let's go upstairs and have a drink." Harding took Sullivan to his bedroom, and when Flo came in, he explained to her, "We both think we ought not to drink in the White House. But we feel that our bedrooms are our house, and we can do as we like here."

Harding took everything more seriously than the presidency, especially golf. One Sunday he tried skipping church to play golf, but it got into the papers, and the Duchess saw to it that it didn't happen again. On a golfing weekend in New Jersey in 1921, an aide arrived on July 2 with the joint resolution of Congress that made peace with Germany official for the president to sign. It took an hour and forty-three minutes to get him in from the course. He arrived in a Palm Beach suit, white shirt with gold studs, and a red-and-green bow tie. He read through the vellum document, signed it, and said, "That's all." He then returned to golf. He played at least twice a week and always took his clubs on vacations. He hit practice shots from an old carpet laid out on the south lawn. Though not a good golfer, he played each shot as if his life depended on it. He never took advantage of his office. "Forget that I am President of the United States," he said. "I'm Warren Harding playing with some friends and I'm going to beat the hell out of them." Those friends sometimes included Secretary of State Charles Evans Hughes, Speaker of the House Frederick Gillett, and Director of the Budget Charles Dawes. Harding carried his predilection for betting to his golf game. He made so many side bets that he needed his Secret Service guard, Colonel Edmund Starling, to keep track of them. Starling said the president made so many bets that sometimes he ended up betting against himself.

With his betting, tobacco chewing, spitting, and a habit of putting his feet up on the furniture, Harding was not as refined as some would have preferred. Alice Roosevelt unfairly encapsulated him in one of her famous epigrams: "Harding was not a bad man. He was just a slob." The housekeeper, Mrs. Jaffray, no doubt concurred. Harding liked stag dinners and pleaded with her, "Please, Mrs. Jaffray, could I have sauerkraut and wiener-wurst? You know how the men like that." Mrs. Jaffray gave in. But when the butler told her the president had ordered toothpicks for the dining room table, she drew the line. She told the butler he must have misunderstood and ignored the request. The next day, the butler again came to her and said the president had demanded toothpicks "real forceful like." This time, she relented.

While Harding had a good time as president, the job did have its downside. He did not like being guarded. He wrote to his mistress, Nan Britton, that he was a "prisoner." He particularly disliked having the Secret Service around when he was with his pals on the golf course. On a vacation to Florida the Secret Service insisted on caddying for his foursome, and the disgruntled Harding started deliberately hitting wild shots out into the mosquito-infested palmettos for the agents to retrieve. Harding once missed lunch before his game, and as he headed out to his tee with a sandwich in one hand and a bottle of mineral water in the other, he stopped and said to Starling, "Colonel, I'm afraid it wouldn't be dignified for me to walk out there in front of those people eating my lunch. Let's stand here until I finish." Then, "Damnit, Colonel, that's the trouble with being President. You can't do the things you want to, and what you can do you can't do your own way. It has to be done somebody else's way."

When it came to his presidency, Harding simply didn't know the way. Though he was conscientious and worked hard, he had little understanding of the job or how to do it, and he was quickly overwhelmed. Journalist William Allen White quoted a muddled president saying, "I don't know what to do or where to turn in this taxation matter. Somewhere there must be a book that tells me all about it, where I could go to straighten it out in my mind. But I don't know where the book is, and maybe I couldn't read it if I found it. . . . My God but this is a hell of a place for a man like me to be!" He was at his desk by 8 A.M. and gradually worked longer and longer hours until he rarely got to bed before midnight. "I never find myself with my work completed," he said. "I don't believe that there is a human being who can do all the work there is to be done in the President's office. It seems to me as though I have been President for twenty years." After only two years in office he was talking about returning to his hometown: "I would like nothing better than to be a Marionite again."

Harding appointed some distinguished and highly qualified people to important posts. But he also appointed others out of loyalty, because they were friends, or because he was urged to by Daugherty and the "Ohio Gang," as the media and others called his Ohio political friends. His personal secretary had no qualifications for the job except that he was a Marion friend. He didn't provide the guidance Harding needed or screen out the trivial and unnecessary. Mail poured into the White House from all sorts of people from eccentrics to well-wishers. Harding once hand-wrote a reply to a maker of bird houses who wanted to convert the White House grounds into a bird sanctuary. Nicholas Murray Butler, president of Columbia University, once found him trying to work his way through a large stack of letters. "Oh, come on, Mr. President, this is ridiculous," Butler told him. Harding's sad reply was, "I suppose so. I am not fit for this office and should never have been here."

He soon faced personal difficulties as well. In August 1922 Florence fell ill, and for two weeks her life hung in the balance. Seventeen years before she'd had one kidney removed, and she periodically suffered severe uremic problems. Dr. Charles Sawyer, a homeopath from Marion, cared for her. Harding had made him his personal physician, surgeon general, and a brigadier general. A little man with a pointed beard, he proudly rode around on the large cavalry horse that was one of his perks. When Flo's condition became critical, specialists were called in, and they unanimously agreed that immediate surgery was required. Sawyer disagreed. Flo supported him, and he turned out to be right—by mid-September she was out of danger, if not well. "This was a day of personal as well as traditional thanksgiving at the White House," the *New York Times* reported on November 30, 1922, "with Mrs. Harding having dinner in the dining rooms for the first time since she became critically ill. . . . Mrs. Harding's condition . . . had shown excellent progress. . . . She went to dinner today, however, in a wheelchair."

Despite their worry over her illness, few on the White House staff were fond of Flo. Mrs. Jaffray would recall that at times the first lady "had about as little self-control as any grown person I have ever met." Florence was aggressive and demanding, and sometimes exploded into screeching fits, as when she accused the servants of stealing a diamond sunburst pin Harding had given her as an inaugural present. It turned out she had mislaid it under a pile of letters. She checked all White House bills carefully, and once grilled Mrs. Jaffray about the amount of coffee she purchased, demanding to know how many cups she got from a pound. Mrs. Jaffray didn't know. "Well, I think you should know," Flo said, "and I can tell you: sixty cups." Mrs. Jaffray suggested the amount might vary with the strength of the coffee, but Flo, convinced they were using far too much, was undeterred. Florence was also easily offended. She had kept a written record of every social slight she had suffered while her husband was a senator, and as first lady she consulted it in making up her guest lists. There was no official provision for Secret Service protection for the first lady at this time, but Flo demanded her own agent, and Starling assigned one to her. Chief Usher Ike Hoover said the agent "acted as messenger, special watchman, general handyman, and at times almost as a lady's maid."

Florence continued to see fortune-tellers as first lady. One of the things she had been told was that her husband had many "clandestine affairs," which Flo already knew or suspected. Evidently she discovered Harding's long-standing affair with Carrie Phillips, an old friend of hers. Carrie and her husband had even gone on a European trip with Mr. and Mrs. Harding. Once, in Marion, Carrie stopped by to talk to Harding when he was sitting on the front porch, and Flo rushed out screaming and throwing whatever was handy at her, including a piano stool. When the leaders of the Republican party called Harding into that smoke-filled hotel room to tell him they would nominate him, they asked him if anything in his personal life might surface to hurt the party. He asked for time to think about it, went into another room, then came back and said no, there was nothing. But the party soon learned about Carrie and paid the Phillipses' way on a long, round-the-world tour.

Flo probably knew about Nan Britton also. As a schoolgirl Nan had become infatuated with Harding, then a newspaperman. Their relationship continued while he was a senator, and evidently her child, Elizabeth Ann, was his, although Harding believed he was sterile. The day after his election to the presidency they met in a house in Marion used by the Republican campaign staff while a Secret Service agent stood guard. "This is the best thing that happened to me lately, dearie," he told Nan and gave her several hundred dollars. Nan wrote her lover after he moved into the White House, marking the envelope "Personal," but Ira Smith in the mail office opened it. Harding, in an angry outburst rare for him, called Smith in. "I want you to understand something, Smith. I am President of the United States, but I also have a personal life. If you ever again open a letter of mine, you will be looking for another job." Smith managed to explain that hundreds of letters were marked personal. Harding learned to have Nan enclose her letters inside an envelope addressed to his valet, Arthur Brooks. Harding kept her letters in his desk drawer with instructions to secretary George Christian to burn them if anything happened to him.

Nan visited the president at the Oval Office several times. She would take a train to Washington, and a Secret Service agent would meet her at the station. Generally she was ushered in through the West Wing and waited for Harding in the Cabinet Room. Then she entered the Oval Office through an adjoining room. Harding showed her his desk and once had a Secret Service agent give her a White House tour. There was a guard at the door in the hall, but a second guard paced back and forth in front of the office window, and although he always looked straight ahead, he made Harding nervous. He took Nan into a closet, and there, as she recalled, "in the darkness of a space not more than five feet square the President of the United States and his adoring sweetheart made love."

The Duchess nearly caught them in the act once. Somehow she got wind of the situation. She evidently used her Secret Service agent as a "special watchman," according to Chief Usher Ike Hoover. Hot on the trail, Flo came charging over to the West Wing. The agent who had escorted Nan from the railroad station was at the interior door, and he refused to open it, "by order of the President." Flo got in through the secretary's office, but the agent had rapped on the door to warn Harding, and Christian was able to stall her long enough for the other agents to get Nan out. Florence was not taken in, and gave Harding quite a tongue-lashing. "She makes life hell for me," Harding wrote Nan.

Harding had an almost feverish need for companionship, and despite his poker and golf games, he became increasingly isolated and lonely. He wrote Nan, "I am in jail and I can't get out. I've got to stay." When Senator Frank Brandegee asked about the job, Harding couldn't contain himself: "Frank, it is hell! No other word can describe it." Sometimes he would flee to the estate of his friends the McLeans, or to the little house on Washington's K Street that Daugherty kept for the Ohio Gang.

Then, halfway through his term, Harding's health began to fail. Since young adulthood Harding had suffered bouts of depression and digestive disorders that affected his nerves. He went to Battle Creek Sanatorium five times between 1889 to 1901 for unspecified illnesses. After two years as president, he began having trouble finishing eighteen holes of golf. His blood pressure was up over 185, and he had to sleep propped up by pillows at night. He also began to have legitimate worries about the dealings of friends he had put in office. Charles Cramer, involved in corruption at the Veterans Administration, committed suicide although the scandal had yet to break. Jesse Smith, Attorney General Daugherty's friend, who shared an apartment with Daugherty, also shot himself. The day before, he and Harding had a long, emotional argument, the topic of which is unknown. He was found in his pajamas on the floor.

On June 20, 1923, Harding and his wife set off on a western trip that would include Alaska, perhaps to get away from the scandals that were brewing. Before he left he sold his prize possession, the *Marion Star,* and made out a new will. At Kansas City he met with the wife of Secretary of the Interior Albert Fall and doubtless heard something of the simmering Teapot Dome scandal. Fall had surreptitiously leased the naval oil reserves at Teapot Dome, Wyoming, and Elk Hills, California, without competitive bidding. An investigation revealed that both of the men to whom Fall gave the leases had "loaned" him large sums of money without interest. Harding had once said, "If Albert Fall isn't an honest man, I'm not fit to be the President of the United States." Albert Fall would become the first cabinet officer in American history to go to jail, but by then Harding would be dead. Once in Alaska, Harding received a long coded message and began muttering about his friends betraying him. Previously he had told William Allen White, the editor of the *Emporia Gazette* in Kansas, "My God, this is a hell of a job! I have no trouble with my enemies. I can take care of my enemies all right. But my damn friends, they're the ones that keep me walking the floor nights."

On July 28, Harding had stopped in Seattle to make a speech on his way home from Alaska when he was awakened by severe chest pain. He broke into a cold sweat, and his pulse rose to 120. Dr. Sawyer would report this as an "acute gastrointestinal attack," probably caused by bad crab meat. A navy doctor, Joel T. Boone, disagreed, diagnosing cardiac seizure, but Sawyer outranked him. Harding's speaking engagements were canceled, but as his train continued on to San Francisco he began feeling better. Sawyer told the press, "I may say he is out of danger, barring complications." At San Francisco Harding insisted on walking from the train to the car, and from the car to the elevator of the Palace Hotel, all of which probably aggravated his condition. The chest pains and the fever returned. Two leading San Francisco physicians were called in. With bed rest and heart stimulants, the president improved. Four days later, on the evening of August 2, 1923, Harding was still resting at the Palace Hotel when Flo read him a *Saturday Evening Post* article about himself entitled "A Calm View of a Calm Man." When she finished, he said, "That's good." Flo left him alone and went to her own room across the hall. Moments later Harding died.

Doctors wanted to perform an autopsy, but Flo refused permission. Back in Washington, she burned any of her husband's papers that she could find. His secretary, as instructed, burned the letters in his desk. This would later lead to rumors of poisoning and a cover-up as the public learned of the corruption Harding's so-called friends had been involved in. But the immediate reaction was sympathy and a huge outpouring of grief for the stricken president. As the funeral train headed toward Washington, great crowds gathered along the way. "The spectacle of the funeral train transversing the entire breadth of the United States, is not to be forgotten," observed the *Washington Post.* Forty thousand mourners were waiting in the rain at 2 A.M. in Omaha, and there were three hundred thousand in Chicago. "The solidarity of this nation," the *Post* said, "is a fact that stands out conspicuously upon such a melancholy occasion as the passing of a dead president's train, conveying him to the Capitol for a national funeral." An estimated thirty-five thousand filed past his bier in the Capitol. At his death, at least, Harding was the beloved president he had hoped to be.

# 30

# Calvin Coolidge

## 1923–1929

## *For the Roaring Twenties, a Man of Quiet*

"A MAN who lives in a two-family house? Never!" declared Henry Cabot Lodge when Calvin Coolidge ran for election in 1924.

Son of a Vermont farmer, Coolidge was a simple man. He spoke little and spent less. As both president and vice president under Warren Harding, he called home a $36-a-month white-porched two-family rental in Northampton, Massachusetts.

"Economy is idealism in its most practical form," Coolidge declared when he took office. He set about balancing the budget—not, he said, "because I wish to save money, but because I wish to save people." In July 1928, eight months before he left office, he announced a fiscal surplus of $398 million.

"There is no dignity quite so impressive, and no independence quite so important, as living within your means," Coolidge wrote when he was vice president. At the time he earned a salary of $12,000 (a move to raise it to $15,000 and provide a vice-presidential mansion had just been defeated in Congress). Twelve thousand dollars, he felt, could not cover the expenses of both his office and a suitable house. His friend and fellow Amherst alumnus, the wealthy Frank Stearns, offered to lease a proper home, but the vice president declined, choosing to board his family in an $8-a-day, two-bedroom suite at the Willard Hotel. His teenage sons, John and Calvin, Jr., seventeen and fifteen respectively, were sent to boarding school at Mercersburg Academy in Pennsylvania. When they came home, Grace Coolidge turned out chafing dish suppers.

"The cheap veep," Florence Harding called Coolidge. She felt that "a hotel apartment is plenty good enough for [him]!" and became apoplectic when Mrs. John B. Henderson, the wife of the former senator from Missouri, wanted to donate her Washington home as a vice-presidential mansion. "Not a bit of it, not a bit of it," Flo raged. "I am going to have that bill defeated. Do you think I am going to have those Coolidges living in a house like that?"

Within months, however, Warren G. Harding was dead and "those Coolidges" were ensconced in the White House.

The ensconcing was not immediate. Coolidge had been vacationing in Plymouth Notch, Vermont, in his unelectrified boyhood home, when word reached him that President Harding had died in California on August 2, 1923. It was 2 A.M. on August 3 by the time Coolidge's chauffeur drove up with the news. His lodgings were in the nearest town, Bridgewater, and he'd had been personally roused by the telegraph operator.

After some discussion it was decided that Coolidge's father, who happened to be a notary, could give the oath. Quickly Colonel John Coolidge shaved, swore in his son by kerosene lamp, and sent him back to bed. The next day the president and first lady began the journey back to Washington. At the Willard, Coolidge was quietly sworn in a second time by Justice A. A. Hoehiling of the Supreme Court.

The Coolidges gave Flo Harding time to gather her possessions. Their space at the Willard was expanded to accommodate a secretary, stenographer, and telephone operator. "The executive work of the government centered here for a time," Grace wrote. Secret Service agents shared the hall with newspaper reporters.

"Nobody ever notifies the White House of a new President's arrival," complained Irwin Hoover, a chief usher who worked at the White House for forty-two years. Through the newspapers, he and the staff learned that Coolidge had taken the oath in Vermont. And through the newspapers "word came . . . that the President and Mrs. Coolidge would move from the Willard Hotel to the White House at 3 P.M. on a certain day." The day was August 21, four days after Florence Harding had moved out.

The first morning in the White House, Coolidge rattled around like a traveler whose luggage had been lost. He summoned Frank Stearns to the Oval Office five times, but said not a word. Stearns, who later moved into the White House with his wife and sat in silence on the south porch while the president rocked for hours, could read his friend's moods. He answered Coolidge's repeated summonses, stayed a minute, and departed discreetly. "A dog would have done equally well," Stearns recalled. "The President was lonesome in his new quarters and just wanted somebody familiar around."

One can understand a president having time on his hands the first day in office. Coolidge, however, managed to have sizable quantities of time on his hands throughout his administration. "One rule of action more important than all others," he believed, "consists in never doing anything that someone else can do for you." Once Coolidge's secretary, Ted Clark, brought him a file from Labor Secretary James J. Davis, saying, "He would like to know if you agree with his decision." Coolidge brushed the papers aside. "I am not going to read them," he said. "You tell ol' man Davis I hired him as Secretary of Labor and if he can't do the job I'll get a new Secretary of Labor."

He refused to conduct business on the telephone and relegated the telephone to a booth in the hall outside his office. "The President should not talk on the telephone," he told a friend. "In the first place you can't be sure it's private and, besides, it isn't in keeping with the dignity of the office."

His view of the job was colored as much by his taciturn personality as by the Teapot Dome scandals, a firestorm left over from the Harding administration and which Coolidge deftly allowed to burn itself out. "The President shouldn't do too much. And he shouldn't know too much," Coolidge believed. "The President can't resign. If a member of the Cabinet makes a mistake and destroys his standing with the country, he can get out or the President can ask him to get out. But if he's involved with the President in the mistake, the President has to stay there to the end of his term, and to that extent the people's faith in their government is diminished."

With a clear conscience, Coolidge took an afternoon nap lasting two to four hours. He generally logged eleven hours of sleep a day. He turned in at 10 P.M., even if this meant leaving a White House function. In the wisecracking twenties Coolidge's straight-arrow farm boy habits were both a tonic and a national joke. When the president attended a performance of *Animal Crackers* in Washington, Groucho Marx stepped to the front of the stage, peered at the presidential box, and asked, "Isn't it past your bedtime, Calvin?"

Coolidge generally rose at six-fifteen. He took a morning walk and breakfasted at eight in his room. While he ate he liked to have his hair rubbed with Vaseline so it would stay slicked back. Sometimes he even had his hair cut at breakfast. He walked to the Oval Office and worked from nine-thirty to twelve-thirty, and then welcomed 400 tourists, 1,300 Boy Scouts, or other groups. If he was busy, he let them watch him at work or in conference. If he had time to spare, he shook their hands. "On one occasion I shook hands with nineteen hundred in thirty-four minutes," he recalled. Fifty-five hands per minute? Obviously there was little chatting with Silent Cal.

Coolidge's silences were notorious. He didn't believe in suffering fools. At his first White House diplomatic reception he didn't serve anything, not even water, though Mrs. William Vanderbilt did manage to procure a drink—a paper cup full of water from the usher's office.

At one of Grace's teas, a society matron rushed up and said, "Oh, Mrs. Coolidge, I'm so delighted. I am going to have the honor of sitting beside your husband at dinner tomorrow evening."

Grace replied, "I'm sorry for you. You'll have to do all the talking yourself."

When he was briefing his successor Herbert Hoover on the job, Coolidge said, "You have to [with]stand every day three or four hours of visitors. Nine-tenths of them want something they shouldn't have. If you keep dead still they will run down in three or four minutes. If you even cough or smile they will start up all over again."

Oddly enough the press considered Coolidge one of the most communicative presidents. He met with reporters twice weekly and once asked who they thought should be secretary of the navy. He spoke eloquently and at length, but he never allowed anyone to quote him directly (FDR was the first to condone such a practice). He forbid shorthand. "I don't object to you taking notes as to what I say," he once told a reporter, but having his words taken down as spoken "greatly interferes with my freedom of expression and my trying to disclose to the conference the things that I have in mind, which quite naturally, if they were to be used verbatim, I would want to give considerable thought to and perhaps throw into a little different form of language." Coolidge took only written questions. These he would read silently at his desk, cigar parked in an ashtray. If none interested him, he would announce "I have no questions today." And that was that—the press conference was over.

Coolidge's management style regarding governmental matters may have been hands off. But when it came to the domestic side of the White House, no detail was too small to catch his attention. When asked after his presidency what was his greatest disappointment, without hesitation he cited "the White House hams; they would always bring a big one to the table. Mrs. Coolidge would always have a slice and I would always have one. The butler would take it away and what happened to it afterward I never could find out."

It wasn't for lack of trying. The master of a grand house for the first time in his life, Coolidge was a kid in a candy shop. He insisted that his wife and sons dress in full evening attire, even when the family was dining alone. He called everything my—from "my Secretary of the Treasury" to "my lawn." He visited firemen in the basement, nosed about the kitchen, and on his way to the office, checked on the endless flow of gifts, which were spread out on the steward's table.

When Grace went to Northampton to visit her ailing mother, Coolidge liked to go down to the White House mail room and wait for the post to arrive. He'd sort through the letters himself until he spotted one with Grace's fine, flowing hand. Then he'd take his prize to a corner and read it immediately.

Once he showed up in the housekeeper's office, a tiny griddle cake in hand, complaining, "Why can't I have big ones like they have downstairs?" (The servants ate dinner-plate-sized pancakes, a time-saver for the cook.) Coolidge looked over menus (normally only the first lady passed muster on food) and even rearranged seating plans for dinner. He wrote out his own recipe for breakfast cereal—four pecks of whole wheat to one peck of whole rye.

"Never before has a President taken such a keen and active interest in small domestic affairs," exclaimed Elizabeth Jaffray, a housekeeper brought in by the Tafts who decided to retire in the spring of 1926. Grace was relieved. She complained that Mrs. Jaffray "had come to consider herself the permanent resident and the President and his family transients. For her to presume to tell how much a President saves from his salary is, of course, ridiculous."

Her successor was the able Ellen Riley, a friend of the Stearnses' who'd been running the cafeteria at the R. H. Stearns Company, a dry-goods store in Boston. With Miss Riley in place, the Coolidge household expenses averaged less than a thousand dollars a month, enabling the president to save more than any of his predecessors. Part of the reason for the success of his saving scheme was that in Harding's term a $25,000 traveling fund, first voted in under Taft, was diverted into an entertaining fund. It covered official events such as the congressional breakfasts that Coolidge hosted but sat through silently, often finishing in a half hour.

Coolidge liked his new housekeeper so much that he gave Miss Riley a raise and, risking the ire of longer-term servants, appointed her Custodian of The Plate, Furniture and Public Property of the Executive Mansion. With great delight he taught her the combination to the vault where the gold and silver services were kept. She promptly forgot it and had to have him show it to her again.

*Coolidge was very close to his family, shown here at the reflecting pool at the White House's east garden. When son Calvin, Jr., died as a result of an infected blister caused by playing tennis on the White House courts, Coolidge said, "the power and the glory of the Presidency went with him." (LIBRARY OF CONGRESS)*

Like Frank Stearns and his wife, Ellen Riley lived in the family quarters. "I had an office, large living-sleeping room, dressing room and bath," she wrote her mother. The Hardings hadn't let Miss Jaffray have guests, but Grace encouraged Ellen to invite friends to stay and even suggested she might want a double bed. When her mother was due, Ellen cautioned, "You may not see The P. at all. Or, perhaps he'll scare you to death looking into the room when you don't know he is there and he'll mumble something that you have no idea in the world what he says and look you all over as sharp as can be, and that will be all there is to it."

Ellen adored the Coolidges, her job, and the kitchen, calling it "about perfect, big, cool, white tiled, coal and gas ranges, ice-less refrigerator, etc." She went to market in a horse-drawn carriage driven by Daniel Webster, a coachman who wore a black silk hat. In the winter of 1927 Webster was converted to a chauffeur, and Ellen made her rounds by car.

Though she was a housekeeper, Ellen changed into fancy dresses and attended the musicales that followed large dinners. She joined the Coolidges for White House movies, the president with a cigar and collie Rob Roy at his side. When wild animals were on screen, Coolidge would try to get Rob Roy "to go for them," Riley wrote her mother. "The P. isn't nearly as solemn as he looks."

Indeed Coolidge had a wicked sense of humor, though it was hard to tell since he seldom cracked a smile. "His appetite for pranks was insatiable," his Secret Service agent Colonel Edmund Starling, head of the detail, recalled. "In the afternoon we sometimes left for our walk from the Executive Offices. If the mood suited him he would press the buzzer which notified everyone that he was on his way to the White House. Then, while ushers, policemen, doormen, and elevator operators were rushing about getting things ready and snapping to attention, we would stroll out West Executive Avenue and leave them."

Coolidge liked to take a morning walk and would sometimes try to elude Starling, who always waited outside the north entrance to accompany the president. "He would tell the elevator operator to take him to the basement," Starling recalled. "Then he would try to sneak out the East or the West entrance, just to fool me. Everyone on the staff cooperated with me and tipped me off, so I was always able to catch him. One day I turned the tables on him and hid in the police box on the East side. He came out of the engine room, up the East steps, and passed right by me. I fell into position behind him. When he reached the gate he turned around with a look of glee on his face, thinking he had at last eluded me.

"'Good morning, Mr. President,' I said.

"He turned and headed for F Street without a word."

Aside from Coolidge's walks, which were generally not very lengthy, at least compared to the five-mile hikes taken by his wife, he exercised little. Starling tried to interest him in fishing. Cabinet members bet the president would never get in a boat. But Starling collected when the Coolidges went to the Adirondacks in 1926. The president caught a four-pound pike and was so pleased that New York governor Al Smith had it stuffed. On subsequent vacations, Starling had rivers and lakes stocked. In 1928 at Cedar Island Lodge in Wisconsin a narrow channel was fitted with wire screens to keep in trout brought from a hatchery. The trout had been raised on chopped liver. When Coolidge took his first bite of his just-caught supper, he announced, "These damn fish taste like liver."

Starling got Coolidge to take up shooting—he became a fair shot—but his biggest success came when an admirer sent the president an electric horse. The chief electrician set it up in Coolidge's bedroom, and Starling imitated a cowboy on a bucking bronco. His boss "laughed so hard he had to sit down." The next morning, Coolidge secretly tried out the horse. That afternoon he brought Starling in to his room for a show. "He insisted on keeping his hat on," said Starling. "I told him to hold tight while I pressed some more of the buttons. I got a good grip on his coat and then pushed the buttons. The horse jumped, the President lost his hat, and almost lost his seat. I stopped the horse and he got off and spent about ten minutes trying to find out what made the thing jump. After that we rode every day, playing cowboy like a couple of kids."

Starling's most unusual detail involved rooming with John Coolidge at Amherst in the fall of 1925. Initially John spent his time studying dancing and Jazz Age amusements. To pull his marks up, the president sent Starling to school. "For my seminar work I undertook a complete study of the New England apple pie," the agent joked. John reformed, and by Christmas Starling was back at the White House.

Coolidge oversaw everything, including his wife's schedule. After being in the White House for two weeks Grace spoke up at breakfast, addressing her husband, hidden behind the morning newspaper. "Calvin, look at me," she said. "I find myself facing every day a large number of engagements about which I know nothing, and I wish you'd have your Secret Service prepare for me each day a list of engagements for the coming week, so that I can follow it."

"Grace," said the president, "we don't give out that information promiscuously." And indeed he never did.

He loved to have her at his beck and call, and cheerfully she waited for her marching orders, hat in hand. Once Ike Hoover asked if she were accompanying the president. "I do not know," she replied, "but I am ready."

Grace Coolidge was an exuberant, fun-loving woman who took her husband in stride. The first time she saw him was through an open window in Northampton where he was a lawyer and she was a teacher at the Clark School for the Deaf. Coolidge was shaving with his hat on (the better to keep his sandy-red hair in place). Grace laughed so hard that Calvin heard her, and asked his landlord to arrange a meeting.

The press was besotted with the enthusiastic first lady. "Washington likes Mrs. Coolidge and Mrs. Coolidge has made a success in Washington," the *New York Times Magazine* gushed on March 27, 1927. Grace joked that initially the press "expected me to hang my wash in the East Room." But she rose to the challenge of dinner parties and ball gowns, of entertaining kings and movie stars, all the while sticking strictly to the role of wife and mother and routinely declining requests for interviews. Once a group of newspaper women asked her to give a speech and she talked for five minutes in sign language.

She was wonderful at small talk. One assistant secretary in the administration recalled, "The memory she has for details about people! We'll be in a reception line, and Mrs. Coolidge will catch sight of us. 'How's the boy?' she will call to my wife. Now half of my friends don't know whether our baby is a boy or a girl, but Mrs. Coolidge knows and remembers."

Will Rogers, who wangled an invitation to stay at the White House in 1926 in order to meet the first lady, pronounced her "chuck plumb full of magnetism and you feel right at home from the minute you get near her. She has a great sense of humor, and is live and tight up and pleasant every minute, and Calvin is just setting there kinder sizing everything up." After dinner—the first meal Rogers "ever had on the government"—he and the Coolidges worked on a jigsaw puzzle (a puzzle craze had swept the nation) and talked until ten-thirty when the president shut down the party, asking, "Grace, where is Will going to sleep?"

Grace Coolidge's first visit to the White House came as a chaperone for a class trip from Northampton High School. In 1927 the *New York Times* recounted the trip, saying, "the tourist business was not so well organized in Washington then as it is now, when advertisements might read: 'See Washington and shake hands with the President'; but the East Room of the White House was open to visitors. In one corner of the white-walled room an elaborately carved and gilded piano stood out with all the prominence of a prize fighter's smile. Mrs. Coolidge spread her fingers above the keyboard. Before she could strike a chord a horrified White House guard ordered her to move either on or out."

In her new role as first lady, the President served as guard. He forbid her to dance in public, drive, fly (even with Charles Lindbergh), get her hair bobbed, or take advantage of the White House horses stabled at Fort Meyers. She surreptitiously took up horseback riding, but the press caught up with her the day of her first lesson. "I think you will find that you will get along at this job fully as well if you do not try anything new," Coolidge told her.

In the one area where she did need to concern herself with the new—fashion—he served as consultant. "I have never known any man more interested in his wife's clothes than Mr. Coolidge and the handsomer and more elaborate Mrs. Coolidge's dresses were the better he liked it," wrote Mary Randolph, Grace's secretary. The president never worried about the cost of gowns—a Boston paper reported Grace spent $1,000 in a day—and complained if she tried to wear a formal dress twice. He even nosed his way into fittings. Once Mary Randolph and the seamstress looked up in horror to find the president pacing a satin train.

On his walks around town, Coolidge would window-shop and look for things that would suit his wife. His taste was old-fashioned. "Where's the trimming?" he asked Grace when she came home with some of the new simple cloche hats.

"The trouble with him is," she said, "that he likes the hats in which he first remembers me—in the years when a hat was not a hat at all unless it had flowers and beads and feathers and bows all over it, weighed pounds, and was big as a cart wheel in the bargain."

Grace had her gowns made by name designers, but she either sewed her everyday wardrobe or bought outfits off the rack. Once at Garfinkel's, the department store, a saleswoman told her, "My, but you look like Mrs. Coolidge!"

Grace responded with a polite smile. The saleswoman tried again. "Did anyone ever tell you before that you look like Mrs. Coolidge."

"Yes," Grace replied and, still unsmiling, made her selection and left.

Grace's favorite hobby was needlework. Indeed, she stitched, knitted, and crocheted her way through the White House, making sweaters for the staff and presents for friends. "Many a time when I needed to hold myself firmly, I have taken my needle . . . as the needle of a compass, keeping me to the course," she wrote in her autobiography. Her mammoth two-year project was a crocheted coverlet for the Lincoln Bed. It bore her name across the top and the date of her residency—August 3, 1923, to March 4, 1929—across the side, even though she completed it nearly a year before leaving. She published the instructions in the *Herald Tribune*, calling her masterpiece "A Coverlet for the Ages," and explaining that she made it "with the hope that each mistress of the President's House will leave there some token which shall go down through the ages to serve as a definite and visible link connecting the present and the past."

Her wish was in vain. "I have a sad story to tell you about a coverlet," she wrote a friend after moving back to Northampton. "It is a secret of the first order and concerns the 'Coverlet for the Ages.' The morning of the fourth of March [1929] I spread it upon the heirloom bed over a blue silk foundation which I had made for it and with many a loving pat, I left it there. Alas, the bed was taken down and put in storage, not three days later. I had threatened to have it bolted to the floor and now wish I had." The Hoovers did not share the Coolidges' decorative tastes. Later they returned the Lincoln Bed from storage. Grace's coverlet, though not on view, remains in the White House collection today.

Grace's interest in handcrafts was part of a colonial revival movement that swept the country after World War I. When McKim remodeled the White House, tastes ran to the beaux arts. Now American antiques were collected, and the old and the pure and the handmade savored. In 1924 Grace attended the opening of the American Wing at the Metropolitan Museum in New York. "I had a strong desire to refurnish some of the rooms of the mansion with furniture of the period in which it was built," she wrote. "A joint resolution was passed by Congress at my request, authorizing the acceptance of such gifts as people might be induced to make towards this end. I thought I had but to make my wishes known, to have them come pouring in, that people who owned rare old pieces would prefer placing them in the White House to bequeathing them to a museum. They did not come quite so rapidly as I had anticipated, but a beginning was made."

Grace gathered a commission of experts to advise on appropriate furnishings. While she waited for antiques to appear, she set about redoing the family quarters, which were on the spare side since, in contrast to other presidents, the Coolidges brought no furniture with them to the White House. In 1925 she arranged for plastering and painting on the second floor, and word leaked out that McKim's interiors were being redone. A brouhaha erupted. One of Grace's committee men took it upon himself to visit the family quarters, pronouncing them "horrible and frightful."

Coolidge resolved the colonial versus beaux art matter simply: he put the kabash on any redecorating. But in 1928, after the roof was repaired and the third floor renovated, roughly $50,000 was left over in the allotted funds. Grace was able to buy new colonial-style furnishings from a firm in Grand Rapids, Michigan, for two third-floor guest rooms and redo the Green Room with colonial-style window treatments and a few antiques deemed appropriate.

Coolidge's personal contribution to the decor involved a portrait of John Adams. It hung in the Red Room but could be seen from the State Dining Room. The president summoned Irwin Hoover and said, "I am tired of looking at that old bald head. Will you put some hair on it?" Hoover obliged. "I got an artist and some turpentine was smeared on the head, taking off the shine and giving the appearance of a little hair. At the next meal the President thanked me and said he 'saw that Mr. Adams had grown some hair on the top of his head.' "

Often when she worked on her crochet and needlework, Grace listened to baseball games. She was passionate about the Washington Senators, kept score herself, and knew many of the players personally. The president sometimes came with her to games but left early.

Grace firmly refused to be "jailed" at the White House and headed out almost every day for at least an hour's walk. "The city . . . catches sight of her at her one form of exercise—walking—and it envies her easy, ground-covering stride," reported the *New York Times*. "Four miles an hour is a right-along pace for anyone and it is a gait that makes rangey James Haley, the quiet Secret Service man detailed to guard Mrs. Coolidge, stretch his long legs." He strode along with her, dressed in a coat and tie, she in stockings and three-inch heels, covering a minimum of four miles a day.

Haley, a handsome young man, got on the president's bad side when the family summered in the Badlands of South Dakota in 1927. He accompanied Grace for a walk and they got lost, returning several hours late to find the president spitting mad, worried about rattlesnake bites. Haley was sent away, and Colonel Starling assigned to cover both the president and first lady. Thus if Calvin went out, Grace had to stay in.

Grace loved the outdoors and though her husband didn't, she arranged her own life on the side. When she came home to Northampton, she and a group of friends picnicked by the stream, rain or shine, and the latter did not please her Secret Service agent. Grace described him as "a real 'dandy,' always immaculate with never a wrinkle in his carefully pressed clothes, his face gently patted and massaged, not a hair in his head astray." When she and her friends set forth in the rain, "his face took on an expression of woe and distress such as I never saw before but while he was eating, with the rain dripping from the ends of his ears and nose, he gurgled, 'Didn't know chicken and melted butter mixed with rain could taste so good!' Score one for the picnic artists."

In Northampton, the Coolidges hadn't had much room for pets, but the White House afforded them space for an extremely diverse menagerie. First came canaries, chosen for their suitability to life at the Willard Hotel. Before they'd arrived, the family had moved to Pennsylvania Avenue, affording them the ability to add to the flock. In addition to the canaries, the Coolidges had a trained troupial, who, Grace said, "liked nothing better than to sit on the shoulder of the unsuspecting and tweak the ear." Once the president was finishing a puzzle and determined a piece was missing. The troupial had deposited it on the top of a door frame.

From birds the Coolidges progressed to cats and dogs, a series of half a dozen that included Paul Pry, a half brother to Harding's Airedale, Laddie Boy (he was kenneled under the south portico). The president's favorite was Rob Roy, a white collie who followed him to press conferences. Grace's official portrait, paid for by her college sorority, shows her outside with Rob Roy. The artist, Howard Chandler Christy, protested the arrangement of a red dress, white dog, and blue sky. "She could still wear the dress and we'd dye the dog," the president, who liked the dress, told him.

The Coolidges' most famous pet was a raccoon, sent by an admirer for Thanksgiving dinner. Adopted rather than eaten, Rebecca lived in a tree house on the grounds and often visited the household, terrorizing the staff, snagging silk stockings, unscrewing lightbulbs, and unpotting palms. But the family loved her. Coolidge would drape her round his neck; Grace fed her shrimp and persimmons. Housekeeper Ellen Riley became her devoted patron, letting her splash in her tub with a cake of soap. She wrote her mother, "You should have seen the P. and Major Coupal and me in my bathroom watching Rebecca suck an egg." Rebecca acquired a mate, Reuben, who promptly ran away. She traveled with the family on vacation to South Dakota in the summer of 1927. But in 1928 when the Coolidges summered in Brule, Wisconsin, Rebecca was sent to a zoo, where she eventually got sick and died.

*A Thanksgiving gift from an admirer, Rebecca the raccoon arrived at the White House and was promptly turned into a pet. Grace Coolidge fed her shrimp and persimmon. The president took her on evening walks. But the staff detested Rebecca. She tore silk stockings, pecked holes in clothes, and terrified Grace's social secretary, Mary Randolph.* (LIBRARY OF CONGRESS)

**Crisis In Washington**

Mr. Coolidge refuses point blank to vacate the White House until his other rubber is found.

*It was the roaring twenties but somehow the press and the public took to the parsimonious, silent Yankee from Vermont. When asked what had worried him most during his Presidency, he said the White House hams: he and Grace would each have a slice and "what happened to it afterward I never could find out." But he did find his rubber, missing on his last day in office.* (LIBRARY OF CONGRESS)

The official duties of a First Lady held little allure for Grace. "I was more proficient in setting up and operating miniature tracks and trains on the dining-room floor than in receiving and entertaining guests in the drawing room," she wrote in her autobiography.

For the boys, the White House had many perks, including the tennis courts. Early in July 1924, sixteen-year-old Calvin Jr. went out to play even though he couldn't find his socks. He developed a blister and then blood poisoning. The boys' room, which had the Hardings' old twin beds, was turned into a hospital ward. Coolidge watched helplessly as the situation worsened. Starling found him out on the grounds catching one of the rabbits who frequented the planting. He took it upstairs to Calvin. "When he was suffering, he begged me to help him," the president wrote later. "I could not."

On July 6, Calvin was taken in an ambulance to Walter Reed Hospital. His parents held vigil. He imagined he was leading a charge of troops in battle. "He must have had some premonition, some intimation," his father wrote, "for suddenly his body seemed to relax and he murmured: 'We surrender.' " He lapsed into a coma and died the next day. The Democratic Convention was in full swing. Franklin Roosevelt read a resolution of sympathy.

"The power and the glory of the Presidency went with him," Coolidge wrote later.

And perhaps it did. Coolidge had worked very hard in his previous jobs, sitting at his desk from nine to five even when he was vice president, even when the Senate had adjourned for vacation. But the presidency never seemed to absorb his attention.

Three years after Calvin Jr.'s death the president and first lady set up a summer White House at a game lodge in the Black Hills of South Dakota. On August 2, 1927, Coolidge made one of his triweekly visits to his "office"—a high school thirty miles away in Rapid City. There he typed a ten-word sentence on a piece of paper over and over.

*As this 1927 air view of the White House shows, the third floor "attic" of the White House was dominated by a pitched roof that precluded comfortable living spaces. After Coolidge was told the attic floor was about to cave in, he reluctantly moved out and a new roof plus 18 rooms for guests and storage were added to the third floor.* (LIBRARY OF CONGRESS)

He cut it into strips, announced, "The line forms to the left," and handed his announcement out to reporters from his desk in a math classroom. It read, "I do not choose to run for president in 1928."

The press was stunned. "Isn't there something else to be said about this, Mr. President?" a reporter asked.

"No, that's all the news in the office this morning."

Coolidge came home and took a nap. Grace lunched with Senator Arthur Capper of Kansas. "That was quite a surprise the President gave us this morning," Capper said. Grace asked him what he was talking about. "I had no idea," she said laughing.

The Coolidges started packing well before their departure date. On February 12, 1929, the president allowed, "I am having rather more trouble in getting out of the White House than I had getting in. There is a very large accumulation of things that a President acquires while he is in the White House. . . . I think we have already reached something like over 150 boxes."

Coolidge retired to his two-family house at 21 Massassoit Street and attempted to sit on the porch and rock as always. But people flocked, stopping to stare or ask him to pose for a picture (generally he obliged). In 1930 he decided to break his lease and buy a shingled estate at the end of Monroe Street called The Beeches. Through close management of his household, he'd squirreled away most of his $50,000-a-year salary ("never has a President saved so much money," exclaimed housekeeper Jaffray). The cost of The Beeches and its eight wooded acres: $40,000. The fence that needed to be added was extra.

At his last news conference, Coolidge summed up his administration, saying that "perhaps one of the most important accomplishments of my administration has been minding my own business."

On Coolidge's last day as president, he deployed eight Secret Service men to hunt for one of his rubbers. Hoover's inauguration had arrived gray and damp. Coolidge refused to leave the White House until his rubber was found. It finally was, and the course of presidential history proceeded.

"We had not lived in the White House very long," Grace Coolidge wrote, "when we were told by the officer in charge of public building and parks that the roof over our heads was unsafe, that it had not been considered safe for several years, and that its condition was becoming serious." The year was 1923, and several factors had taken a toll on the historic building. In 1902 architect Charles McKim had removed a supporting brick wall in order to expand the State Dining Room on the first floor. The steel ceiling truss he'd used as a substitute was buckling, causing the roof to sag and the Monroe-era beams to splinter.

Coolidge's laconic response to the news that the roof was about to fall down on his head was that "there were plenty of others who would be willing to take the risk" if he wasn't. With only a month's residency in the White House and an election looming in 1924, Coolidge didn't feel it right to initiate a White House renovation estimated at half a million dollars. "If it is as bad as you say, why doesn't it fall down?" he asked.

Band-Aid attempts were made at repair, but the second-floor walls continued to crack. Drawings for an attic overhaul were made in 1925 by U. S. Grant III, the Army Corps of Engineers officer in charge of public buildings. Grace seized the opportunity to convert a largely idle attic into usable space.

The attic, untouched in the McKim renovation, had a slanting roof sheltering mostly unused space and a dormered area that served as storage and servants' rooms. Ellen Wilson had remodeled it, adding guest rooms and baths, but slanting ceilings were a decorating challenge.

By changing the pitch of the roof and lowering the floor to eliminate sixteen inches of wasted space between the attic and the second-floor ceilings, space was found for eighteen additional rooms. These included five bedrooms for servants, two guest rooms, and several new baths. Grace's pride and joy was the storage. The family quarters had acquired a few awkward closets in the McKim renovation, but hanging gowns and storing linens was still a major problem. At the first lady's direction, the renovated attic provided "a sewing room, a pressing room, a cedar room, a room with wardrobes, cupboards and drawers for out of season clothing, a storeroom for the President's personal effects, and three open storage rooms lighted by overhead windows over the north portico. There wasn't a blind corner anywhere in the whole place. Along one side of the wide corridor were shelves with mirrored doors for linen in daily use and other supplies."

Guests and family reached the third floor by a new mirrored electric elevator, servants by a back stair. A large skylight brought light into the central corridor.

Coolidge had resisted changes that required vacating the White House, but to accomplish the renovation, the roof and the ceiling above the second floor had to be removed. Congress voted $375,000 for the project in the spring of 1926. The following March, the Coolidges left the White House for a mansion at 15 DuPont Circle. "The moving was not so bad," reported housekeeper Ellen Riley, "for all we took from the White House was the linen, china, glass, silver, etc. No furniture." Nonetheless the move was national news. "I went to the movies yesterday," Ellen reported on May 15, 1927, "and saw myself on the screen—in the International News Reel—in connection with the P's moving day. It gave me a queer feeling—sort of ill."

All the furnishings on the top two floors were moved down to the state rooms and covered with canvas for protection from dust. Pictures and curtains were packed and sent to the basement, and ground floor walls shrouded in protective muslin.

A temporary wooden roof was built over the old slate roof, and in mid-March 1927 demolition began. Debris was lifted out with huge derricks or sent to the ground down covered chutes. One day Grace visited the site and delighted workers by donning a hard hat and climbing all the way up the temporary exterior stair to view the scene.

In July, while the Coolidges took an extended vacation in the Black Hills of South Dakota, a new steel framework was erected. In late August the newly enclosed second and third floors were plastered, and on September 11, 1927, the Coolidges moved back in. "Seems as though we had been on the move constantly for six months, between DuPont Circle, South Dakota and the overhauling of the White House," Ellen Riley wrote. "I move furniture and count trunks in my sleep."

The new third floor made White House living more enjoyable and efficient. But the rooms were not as desirable as those on the second floor because their view consisted of a large stone balustrade that ran around the whole top story. The solarium, however, was an exception. Grace had particularly wanted a sun room. Opening onto a small patio—the tiled roof over the south portico—it had glass on three sides and Venetian shades. "This I called my 'sky parlor,' " Grace wrote, "and it was understood that when there I was not to be disturbed unless for some urgent reason. A cot bed, a writing table, some porch furniture, a Victrola, and a portable radio provided comfort and entertainment."

Coolidge left office in 1929 convinced that the new third floor and the structural bolsterings had left the White House in "first-class condition—practically fireproof from top to bottom." Unfortunately the added 180 tons of weight from the concrete-and-steel third floor would take its toll on century-old brick supports, resulting in the total gutting and rebuilding of the Truman renovation.

# 31

# Herbert Hoover

## 1929–1933

## *And Then the Crash*

HERBERT HOOVER WALKED into the White House a charmed man. A millionaire many times over, he maintained, "If a man hasn't made a fortune by age forty, he isn't worth much." Like another millionaire president, John F. Kennedy, he donated his salary to charity and never had a cent in his pocket, borrowing from friends for emergencies and depending on his wife to slip him $5 to put in the plate at the Friends Meeting on Sunday.

A Stanford University engineer, Hoover had made his millions in mining—in Australia, in China as a consultant to the emperor, and in a dozen other countries. At the White House, he and his wife, Lou Henry Hoover, would occasionally talk in Chinese when they wanted to keep their conversation from guests or servants.

Wealth enabled Hoover to devote himself to public service. During World War I he volunteered to direct relief programs overseas and worked as Woodrow Wilson's wartime Food Administrator. He was widely admired by both Democrats and Republicans for his administrative ability, humanitarianism, and integrity. In 1920 even Democrat Franklin Delano Roosevelt, the man who would succeed him in 1933 following a bitter campaign, said, "He is certainly a wonder, and I wish we could make him President of the United States."

After working as secretary of commerce for both Harding and Coolidge, Hoover was the heir apparent. "The poorhouse is vanishing from among us," he said in his acceptance speech for the Republican nomination. His campaign slogan promised "a chicken in every pot and a car in every garage." In his inaugural speech he said, "I have no fear for the future of the country. It is bright with hope."

Lou Henry Hoover, also a Stanford graduate, shared her husband's talent for management. A professional volunteer, she'd worked ardently for everything from the National Women's Athletic Association to the National Women's Conference on Law Enforcement, which she founded. She was used to setting up house in foreign countries, and though she knew the White House extremely well—she'd been a frequent visitor during the last three administrations—she liked to be prepared. Even before March 4, she studied plans and contemplated changes.

The president likewise arrived with marching orders. The night of his inauguration he detailed plans to rearrange his study in the private quarters and remove the floor-to-ceiling bookcases installed by Coolidge. The work completed, he then shifted the location of his office to the one Lincoln had used. "The Hoovers came in and upset the whole private part of the White House," complained Chief Usher Ike Hoover. "Never was the place so changed, so torn up, so twisted around." The furniture would not stay stationary for four years.

When she arrived, Lou called the mansion "as bleak as a New England barn." Her solution was a lavish makeover of nearly every room, funded by her own money. She brought in furnishings from the family's Palo Alto, California, home and from the residence they'd used in Washington, a large house on S Street. For the presidential bedroom, she chose the room on the southwest corner of the second floor, converting the dressing room to a small office with a daybed for naps and a desk where she could work on her personal correspondence and the White House accounts. She worked long hours and had a staff of four, three of which she paid for personally. To keep the family quarters quiet, she situated her secretaries on the third floor.

The first lady's most dramatic change was the creation of an exotic palm court in the private quarters. She blocked off the west end of the upstairs hall, put down a green fiber rug, brought in bamboo furniture, painted the walls white, and filled the hall with palms, ferns, and tropical birds in cages. The curtains were removed from the great west lunette window to allow the light to stream down on this tropical setting. One secretary commented that Mrs. Hoover "had her own very definite ideas of interior decoration, and once she got things all together, it was very comfortable and lovely."

The Hoovers' son Allan, a Harvard student who came and went, thought otherwise. The White House, he said, gave him the "willies." Still, Allan, who liked pets, kept two alligators at the mansion, which were often allowed to wander about loose. His older brother, Herbert Hoover Jr., was off and married but in 1930 had to go to a sanatorium in Asheville, North Carolina, to be treated for tuberculosis. He sent his wife, Margaret, and their two young children, Peggy Ann and Herbert III, to live at the White House.

Lou also set about reorganizing the domestic staff. She oversaw fifty-eight White House employees, including thirty-two household servants. Lou developed a sign language to express her wishes. For the butlers, a hand to the hair meant dinner should be announced; a hand on the glass, clear the table. Secretaries and ushers sprang into action when she tossed her eyeglasses around her finger or dropped her handkerchief. All butlers and footmen had to be exactly the same height. The butlers were required to wear tuxedos with stiff white shirts and black ties during the day, and tails and white ties in the evening. Meals were served at precisely the same time each day. When the butlers were not serving, they had to stand at attention. Talking in the pantry was strictly forbidden; when they cleared away the dishes, the silverware must never clank against the plates.

The president had particular difficulty dealing with the servants. Typically he never looked at a servant or spoke to one, and he never wanted to meet one when he walked through the halls. The servants faced severe consequences if they were caught in the hall. A bell system warned them to take cover: three rings for the president, two for the first lady. Lillian Parks, an upstairs maid at the White House for thirty years, recalled dodging into closets when the bells sounded. "[There] was a closet near the elevator on the second floor that was used mostly for brooms and mops," she said. "But it was definitely for the help in an emergency, and butlers with trays would pop in and fall into a closetful of maids and housemen waiting for the coast to be clear." When the Roosevelts moved in and saw the servants "popping into closets," Lillian said, they told them to "just act natural." The gardeners could also stop hiding behind the bushes.

For seven months the Hoovers lived in impeccable elegance, and the twenties roared on. Then on October 29, 1929, the stock market crashed. Two months later, like an omen of political conflagrations to come, a fire broke out in the West Wing. It was Christmas Eve, and the Hoovers, complete with their children and grandchildren, were having dinner in the State Dining Room along with staff members and their families. Ike Hoover and the men rushed out. Lou tried to continue the festive spirit, drawing the curtains and gathering the children round the Christmas tree. She calmly told them stories and gave out presents. From the west terrace, the president, his sons, his secretaries, and his cabinet watched as flames consumed the West Wing. All but the president quickly joined the work of saving files from the offices. Allan, home from Harvard for Christmas, pulled the drawers out of his father's desk in the Oval Office. Ike Hoover threw a wet tarpaulin over the Cabinet Room table. More than a hundred men labored to douse the fire. There was a cold wind, and someone brought the president, still on the terrace, an overcoat. Then it started to snow. The fire was finally put out about one in the morning.

The next morning, the ruined West Wing offices were covered with snow and a thick layer of ice. On the north, only the brick walls remained; on the south, the framework stood but was severely damaged. The president's staff, seriously overcrowded, had hoped to move to the State, War, and Navy Building next door—they did so temporarily. Indeed, rebuilding the same cramped quarters was not the best alternative, but given the nationwide economic turmoil, Hoover was reluctant to make any major changes. The wing was rebuilt in 1930 so as to virtually duplicate what had burned.

Throughout the reconstruction men lined up for jobs, as they did all over the country. The Great Depression was on, and it was Hoover's problem, even though he had been one of the few within the Coolidge administration to deplore the speculation in the stock markets and the overextension of credit. Even before he took office he showed a sense of foreboding of what he might face: "My friends have made the American people think me a sort of superman, able to cope successfully with the most difficult and complicated problems. . . . They expect the impossible of me and should there arise conditions with which the political machinery is unable to cope, I will be the one to suffer."

Fundamentally, though, Hoover believed he was equal to the task. At first he felt that the economy would turn around by itself. When it didn't, he attacked the problem with his usual energy and efficiency. He created hundreds of commissions of business economists and every day had a dozen or more conferences on unemployment and other economic problems. He eventually persuaded Congress to pass laws that allowed government to help faltering businesses, and set up the RFC—Reconstruction Finance Corporation—to do this. It aided banks in danger of failing and supported conservation programs and public works projects like the Hoover Dam (then called the Boulder Dam).

Where Coolidge had one secretary, Hoover needed five. He drove himself, and he drove his assistants—employees were not expected to leave before the president did. He was at his desk at eight-thirty, had lunch with Lou and their invited guests at one o'clock, then went back to the office and did not leave before six-fifteen. He had a nap before dinner, and after dinner worked until about eleven. His lonely Quaker youth was reflected in his predilection for working by himself, studying charts and reports, looking for rational solutions. He was the first president to have a telephone on his desk—his predecessors thought it undignified to talk on the phone from the presidential desk and had used the telephones in an adjoining office.

The Hoovers felt they needed to keep up an appearance of optimism. Lou continued her redecorating and turned her organizational skills to the historic mansion itself. She paid the Signal Corps photographers to document every piece of furniture and had a friend begin compiling a catalog, creating for the first time a record of what the White House owned. Not until Jacqueline Kennedy became first lady in 1961 would so much time and energy be devoted to White House furnishings. She also tracked down some furniture used by James Monroe and donated by his descendants to a Fredricksburg museum. She had the pieces copied at her expense and installed them in an upstairs room east of the Oval Room that she called the "Monroe Room." She found the original furniture from Lincoln's study in a White House storage room and reconstructed the room from an old picture. She also discovered some chairs that were believed to be Dolley Madison's. When the president settled his husky, five-foot-eleven frame into one of them, it crashed to the floor. From flat on his back Hoover called to his wife, "Lou, didn't I tell you not to inflict Dolley's chairs on our guests?"

White House dinners continued to be as large and elaborate as ever. No expense was spared to bring in out-of-season foods. There was no alcohol even in private, as this was the era of Prohibition. Widespread evasion of the law led to gangsters supplying the liquor and to police corruption. Yet many people continued to support Prohibition, including Hoover, who was less than enthusiastic but said it was noble in motive. (For years previously he had enjoyed two martinis extra dry every day, and later, when he reached his eighties and his doctor urged him to cut back to one a day, Hoover amiably agreed and then ordered a double-size glass.) Lou said she would leave any party where illegal liquor was served. Hoover was a connoisseur of fine wine and at their Palo Alto home had had an expensive collection of port wines, which Lou insisted on emptying out when Prohibition took effect.

There were guests for lunch and dinner—almost always seven courses—virtually every day. The Hoovers dressed formally for dinner and ate in the State Dining Room instead of the family dining room. Chief Usher J. B. West said that during the first three years they ate alone only three times, on their wedding anniversary each February 10. Often there were last-minute guests, so Lou improvised by directing the servants to make what she called "White House Supreme"—croquettes of ham, beef, or anything else that was left in the refrigerator. At one party, some mix-up resulted in five hundred guests showing up when only two hundred were expected. Servants were sent to nearby shops for food, but there still wasn't enough. Lou, ever resourceful, had the servant break into picnic baskets packed with food for the Hoovers' trip to Virginia.

And then there was the occasional unwanted guest. In addition to the White House police force, Hoover had four Secret Service agents on the main floor plus two on each floor above, yet a strange man once walked right into the State Dining Room, where Hoover was seated with a dozen guests. When Hoover asked, "What do you want?" the man said, "I want to see you."

"I have no appointment with you," Hoover said.

"You better have an appointment with me!" the man shouted, advancing toward the president. A waiter intervened, and the Secret Service removed the intruder, who turned out to be harmless.

But most were welcome at the White House during the Hoovers' large and frequent receptions. Invitations to afternoon receptions were sent to anyone who left a calling card at the White House. Addressing, sorting, and hand-delivering the more than three thousand engraved invitations typical of a single reception took days. After each reception Lou held a conference with her housekeeper and her secretaries to discuss how the next could be improved. They spent hours planning changes that would make events run more smoothly. The daily public reception at twelve-thirty was drawing almost one thousand people, compared to three or four hundred during the Coolidge administration. The public reception on New Year's Day, 1930, drew nine thousand guests and left Hoover's right hand sore and bruised. By New Year's Day, 1933, Hoover, having lost the 1932 election, saw no point in facing the crowds on the first of the year. He fled to Florida, and so ended the tradition begun by Thomas Jefferson.

The first lady's entertaining included a series of teas for congressional wives. A problem arose when Oscar DePriest was elected to the House of Representatives, becoming the first black congressman since Reconstruction. Lou debated what to do. She wanted to invite his wife but feared the consequences. In her first social season she did not invite Mrs. DePriest. In the second, she invited her to a tea whose guests had been carefully screened to make sure there were no objections. The tea itself proved uneventful, but the subsequent firestorm reaction brought the first lady to tears. She was subjected to angry letters, violent attacks in southern newspapers, and official censure by the Texas legislature. Hoover tried to deflect some of the attention from her by inviting R. R. Morton, the head of the Tuskegee Institute in Alabama, to a White House dinner. Later, as Hoover's campaign for reelection neared, Lou made a trip through the South during which she carefully avoided meeting blacks for fear of bad publicity.

There was plenty of publicity to be had: Hoover was the first president of the media age. His inaugural was the first to be brought to the entire nation by radio and the first ever recorded in motion pictures with sound. Reporters liked him initially. He set up three types of news conferences: one at which he could be quoted directly, the first time a president had allowed this; one at which reporters could quote a "White House source"; and one for background information. Reporters commented on how well prepared he was. But the relationship quickly turned sour. Hoover was ill suited for politics. "I have never liked the clamor of crowds," he said early in his career. "I intensely dislike superficial social contacts." He never joked or engaged in pleasantries. He was also a poor public speaker, rarely lifting his eyes from his prepared text, which he wrote engineer-style in long sentences full of the statistics he was so fond of. He was the last president to write his own speeches. As an introvert, Hoover disliked any kind of personal exposure, and ultimately did not handle the press well. The press once reported that Hoover had caught eighteen fish during a thunderstorm, and Hoover, insisting that there had been no rain at all, railed about misrepresentation.

Lou also shunned reporters. She was abrupt, refused to discuss her personal life, and in fact preferred not to speak to journalists at all. Seemingly unconcerned with image, she was never a fashionable dresser and almost never wore jewelry or makeup. ("It isn't so important what others think of you as what you feel inside," she said.) One White House reporter, Bess Furman, found a unique way to get her story when Mrs. Hoover invited forty Girl Scouts to the White House on Christmas Eve, 1930, to sing carols to the president. Lou Hoover was a devoted supporter of the Girl Scouts and had been national president during the early 1920s. Her secretaries learned to keep the *Girl Scout Handbook* handy for ready reference. Furman got herself a Girl Scout uniform, scrubbed off her makeup, tucked her hair up under the brimmed Girl Scout hat, and walked into the White House with the girls. She was known personally to the chief usher and to Colonel Edmund Starling of the Secret Service, but as she said, "Nobody ever looks under the gray-green hat of a Girl Scout in a gray-green dress, holding high an English lantern and singing Christmas carols to her President, to see what kind of face she wears." She got ice cream, cookies, candy, and a great story. Lou even clipped it and wrote "very nice" in the margin, but she never found out how it was written.

As the Depression deepened, Hoover became vilified in the press. The shacks of the homeless poor were called "Hoovervilles," and the man in the White House came across as uncaring. No longer thought of as a humanitarian, he became the butt of jibes and jokes. In 1930 Babe Ruth made $80,000. When a reporter told him the president only made $75,000, the Babe replied, "I know, but I had a better year than Hoover." Criticism and jokes hurt Hoover deeply, but he rigidly adhered to what he believed. "This is not a showman's job," he said. "I will not step out of character."

And he didn't even when World War I veterans converged on the Capitol in the summer of 1932 to demand that Congress make an immediate payment on a war bonus that was due them in 1945. The so-called "Bonus Army," fifteen thousand strong, lived in shacks put up in temporary camps near the Ancostia River flats, just a few miles from the White House. Officials perceived them as a greater threat than they really were, and when the House passed the bonus and the Senate didn't, many feared the mob—rumored to be Communists—would take over the government. Secret Service agents were called in from around the country to guard the White House, which became a fortress. Hoover as a matter of principle refused to talk to the veterans, and eventually ordered the U.S. Army to clear out the camps. Hoover was concerned for the veterans' welfare and ordered the army to use humanitarian care, but that was not General Douglas MacArthur's style. His forces went in armed with bayonets and burned the veterans out. The resulting news stories and pictures all but sealed Franklin Roosevelt's election.

*Hoover's only relaxation was fishing. He was an expert but it was a lonely sport and his dress never got more informal than this. He said that fishing was a "chance to wash one's soul with pure air."* (LIBRARY OF CONGRESS)

Attempts by his staff to humanize Hoover failed miserably. Even now, he refused to publicize his generosity. Early in 1932 three children showed up on the White House doorstep seeking help. Their father had been searching for work and apparently resorted to stealing, ending up in jail. Hoover took them in, listened to their story, fed them, and then got the father out of jail and reunited him with his sons. It was a great human interest story and showed that Hoover did care. Theodore Joslin, his press secretary, asked if he could release the story. Hoover bristled: Absolutely not. Even praise for his humanitarian work during World War I caused Hoover to blush with embarrassment.

The Hoovers' private generosity was exceptional. When Lou found that a butler's $80 monthly pay wouldn't stretch far enough to buy milk or cream for his ulcer, she quietly arranged to have them delivered to his home. When the Depression set in, she assigned one secretary, Philippi Butler, to deal with letters from those in need. The first lady answered each one. If a relief agency couldn't handle the problem presented, Lou got out her checkbook. If they repaid her by check, she didn't cash it. But Hoover gifts were always anonymous—the president and first lady vehemently suppressed attempts by staff to publicize their generosity.

IN PURSUIT of good press, Hoover's staff finally persuaded him to let the press come on one of his fishing trips. Hoover, wearing hip boots and a tie with a buttoned collar, said little. The reporters tried to get him to open up by talking about his youth, but Hoover clammed up and said there was nothing unusual about it, although it certainly was unusual—he had played with Osage Indians and learned to hunt with a bow and arrow, for instance. Hoover was clearly irritated and humiliated by the episode and couldn't wait to get back to work.

Until he lost his bid for reelection, Hoover never missed a day of work or took a vacation. He even worked Sundays as the Depression wore on. But when he lost to Franklin Delano Roosevelt, he took to trout fishing on the weekends. The lonely sport was his only relaxation, and he was expert at it. He called fishing a chance "to wash one's soul with pure air." Lou's many hobbies included making home movies, which she liked to edit herself, but she also loved outdoor activities such as riding and camping. She urged her husband to buy a pristine 164-acre tract in the Virginia woods along the Rapidan River, 109 miles from Washington. The marines cut an access road through the woods, and Lou designed the layout of log cabins and a communal mess hall. Hoover paid for the whole thing, then gave the refuge to Shenandoah National Park when he left office. He fished in the Rapidan dressed in what was for him informal attire—white flannel trousers and a panama hat. When Lou learned that there was no school for the local children, she had a small one built and hired a teacher.

In addition to fishing, Hoover liked cigars—big, black Havana cigars—and smoked twenty a day. When he attended Howard Taft's funeral, he missed not having his usual cigar. In the car on the way back to the White House he said, "When they have my funeral, I want arrangements made so that everyone will have permission to smoke." The president also took time out to exercise, playing medicine ball in the morning with cabinet and other staff members. Even this was chosen on the basis of efficiency—he figured it was the most exercise he could get for the time spent. The group grunted and puffed for half an hour throwing the heavy ball over a net on the south lawn. They played in rain and snow. One of the rare times Hoover missed his game was when he had to get up at five-thirty to finish writing a message due for delivery to the Senate. After the game, if the weather was good, the men had grapefruit, toast, and coffee under a magnolia tree. Then Hoover went in for his usual breakfast with Lou at eight.

The magnitude of the Depression overwhelmed Hoover. Lou struggled as well, but tried to comfort her husband. She was often seen walking arm in arm with him to his office, brushing his hair back tenderly on leaving him. She kept up her large private gifts to charities and wore cotton clothing in promotion of American cotton growers. As the end of his term approached, the economy continued to worsen, and banks started failing. Hoover realized that for the first time in his life he faced defeat. He just worked harder. Once, when he was awakened at three in the morning by a mouse in his fireplace, he dressed and started working. At meals with guests in the State Dining Room he now often sat with his eyes cast down and was utterly silent through the entire meal. Sometimes he didn't even respond to his close associates. When he did, he had a tendency to mumble, head down—what Lou called "his awful habit."

During this period he was so anxious to get back to work that he hardly took time to eat. "All the servants and kitchen staff made bets on how long it would take him to eat," recalled Lillian Parks, who worked in the White House for thirty years as a maid. "He averaged around nine to ten minutes, and could eat a full-course dinner in eight minutes flat. They would come back saying, 'Nine minutes, fifteen seconds,' or whatever the time had been. For State dinners, though, he would slow down for the benefit of the guests." An aide suggested to Lou that her husband might be more comfortable eating without any guests present. No, Lou said, "he always wants to have people around him." Years later, after Lou died and he was living alone in the Waldorf-Astoria Hotel in New York, his eldest son would drive in from Connecticut to have dinner with him if he had no one else.

Lack of sleep and tension began to take a toll, though in four years Hoover missed no work due to illness. He lost thirty-five pounds during the course of his term, and by its end, his friends feared he would not survive the year. His face was lined and his hair white, and his hands shook when he tried to light his Cuban cigar or when he tried to bait a fish line. The expert fisherman caught his hooks in his trousers and his hat. He had pushed his aides as well, and their health also began to fail. "My men are dropping around me," he said. "Fighting this Depression is becoming more and more like waging a war." By the end of his term, he would say, "All the money in the world could not induce me to live over the last nine months. The conditions we have experienced make this office a compound hell."

The campaign of 1932, with Franklin D. Roosevelt as Hoover's opponent, was bitter and dirty. Hoover reluctantly decided that he had to go on the campaign trail and hit back. In St. Paul he was so weak he shook, and he lost his place in his speech. A Secret Service agent stood behind him with a chair in case he collapsed. To make matters worse, he was the first president to face boos and threatening crowds. In Detroit, mounted police had to charge the crowd and use armored cars. He had rotten eggs tossed at him; in Republican Kansas they threw tomatoes. "For the first time in my long experience on the Detail," wrote Secret Service agent Edmund Starling, "I heard the President of the United States booed." To Lou he said, "I can't go on with it any more." His swing across the country finally ended in Palo Alto, where the Hoovers had built a large, mission-style house on land leased to them by Stanford. There, Girl Scouts presented him with flowers, and Hoover's tension let go into tears. "Mommy," a twelve-year-old asked, "what do they do to a President to make a man look like Mr. Hoover does?" Unwilling to leave his command post in Washington, Hoover had not been home in four years. Now, on election night, he came downstairs to meet the friends and neighbors who had gathered in his house. The change in his appearance shocked them. His shoulders sagged, his hair had gone white, and his look was vacant. When the returns came in, there was little to lift his spirit. Hoover's defeat was overwhelming, with Roosevelt winning all but six states.

The first lady, Hoover's close adviser and supporter, may have been even more devastated by the results than he was. But she minded her manners and invited Eleanor Roosevelt to the White House to show her around. Everything went well until Eleanor asked to see the kitchens. There the interests of the two women parted. Lou said, "I'm sorry, but the housekeeper will have to show you the kitchen. I never go into the kitchens."

The day before Roosevelt's March 4, 1933, inauguration, Mr. and Mrs. Roosevelt and their son, Jimmy, made the customary courtesy call at the White House. Hoover kept them waiting and then showed up with Secretary of the Treasury Ogden Mills in another futile attempt to involve the incoming president in the financial crisis. As they parted, Roosevelt suggested that the president not wait, as with his braces and paralyzed legs it was "rather difficult" for him to move quickly. The scene replicated an earlier meeting when Roosevelt, not yet a candidate, was invited to the White House for a meeting of the governors. Hoover was again a half hour late. Protocol dictated that everyone remain standing for the president, and for Roosevelt, supported by a cane, his paralyzed legs in braces, it was agony. Now, being told by Roosevelt not to wait, Hoover gave him a look and said, "Mr. Roosevelt, after you have been President for a while, you will learn that the President of the United States waits for no one." Without another word he walked away, leaving Roosevelt fuming.

Roosevelt and Hoover rode to the inaugural together in an open car, the one smiling and the other dour. Hoover now considered Roosevelt nothing but "a gibbering idiot." He never changed his views. Eighteen years later he would say, "I am so immodest to believe that had we been continued in office we would have quickly overcome the depression"—without resorting to what he termed a "collective economy." He wrote books and articles and issued statements condemning Roosevelt's New Deal and, until Pearl Harbor, American involvement in another European war.

When Lou died on January 7, 1944, shortly after they moved to the Waldorf-Astoria Hotel in New York, Hoover decided to remain at the hotel permanently. Their Palo Alto home had been more Lou's than his—and for someone used to the presidency it was too far from the centers of power. Truman resurrected Hoover, who in 1946 once again coordinated food supplies to war-ravaged countries, and in 1947 headed up the Hoover Commission, which recommended administrative changes to the executive branch of government. He died October 20, 1964, at the age of ninety, second only to John Adams in presidential longevity.

During Hoover's last months in office, he had needed Roosevelt's support to take steps that would bolster the economy as more banks failed. Roosevelt refused any involvement, but when he took office, he did much of what Hoover had planned. "We didn't want to admit it at the time," a former Roosevelt adviser said in 1974, "but practically the whole New Deal was extrapolated from programs Hoover started."

# 32

# Franklin Delano Roosevelt

## 1933–1945

## *Full House*

FRANKLIN DELANO ROOSEVELT—FDR—liked to tell the story of his first day in the Oval Office. His valet, Irwin McDuffie, pushed the buzzer three times, the signal to the staff that the president was approaching. McDuffie pushed Roosevelt in a specially designed wheelchair—an armless kitchen chair on wheels. They entered the elevator, descended to the basement, and went outside along the white colonnade to the West Wing and the Oval Office. From his armless wheelchair Roosevelt slid easily into his desk chair without getting up. McDuffie then withdrew with the wheelchair.

It was March 1933, the midst of the Great Depression. One out of three American workers was unemployed; some were forced to live in shacks or sell apples on street corners. Roosevelt looked around. His desk was bare, the drawers empty. There were no papers awaiting him, no phone, no button to summon a secretary. Unable to get up, he was marooned in the Oval Office. Struck by the situation, Roosevelt sat still for a moment. Then he leaned back and shouted for help. His twelve hectic years had begun.

Roosevelt was no stranger to the White House. His first visit came when he was seven years old. Born in 1882 at his family's Hudson Valley estate in Hyde Park, he was a "Knickerbocker," one of the wealthy descendants of the Dutch-English families who had dominated New York society for two hundred years. In 1889 his father, a big contributor to the Democratic Party, paid Grover Cleveland a social call in Washington, bringing young Franklin along. Cleveland placed a large hand on the boy's head and said,

"My little man, I am going to make a strange wish for you. May you never be President of the United States." But Roosevelt was cut from different cloth than Cleveland. He loved the job. "Wouldn't you be President if you could?" he once said to a friend. "Wouldn't anybody?"

Eleanor Roosevelt, Franklin's distant cousin, knew the White House even better than her husband. She'd visited often at the invitation of her uncle, Theodore. First Lady Edith Roosevelt had offered to host a White House wedding, but Eleanor declined. Nonetheless the president gave the bride away. Afterward, he clapped the groom on the back and said, "Well, Franklin, it's nice to keep the name in the family." When Eleanor returned to the White House in 1933 as first lady, Chief Usher Ike Hoover, who worked there under Theodore Roosevelt, greeted her as "Miss Eleanor."

Franklin Roosevelt looked up to his new uncle, but following in his footsteps took every ounce of determination he had. In 1921, FDR's charmed career in politics nearly came to a halt when, at the age of thirty-nine, he was struck by poliomyelitis. He would never again walk or stand without help. Still, he became governor of New York in 1928, and he went on to head a nation—the first elected disabled leader in world history. Yet the public never understood exactly how disabled he was. Hundreds of canes were delivered to the White House as gifts from well-wishers who thought the president was just lame. Roosevelt could not walk, but wearing leg braces, he had learned a technique of swinging one leg in front of the other as he threw his upper body forward and thus progressing across a room. The Secret Service often built permanent ramps for Roosevelt at places he went to often, such as the Capitol or St. John's Episcopal Church in Washington. At the funeral of Senator William Bankhead, held in his home state of Alabama, they raised the level of the street so FDR could "walk" in to the services.

FDR hated his braces. Made of steel, with thick leather straps, they were heavy and pressed painfully into his body. They had to be locked when he stood up and unlocked when he sat down. They were also unreliable—they caused him to slip and fall in public at least three times, although the incidents were not photographed or reported. The cooperative news media never showed the president getting in or out of cars, in a wheelchair, or being carried—and FDR's devoted Secret Service agents didn't hesitate to knock a camera from the hand of anyone brash enough to try.

Roosevelt perfected his technique for getting from a wheelchair into a car. First he would turn his back to the vehicle, and Secret Service agent Mike Reilly, head of the detail, would lift him to a standing position. Roosevelt would stretch back, hold the door with both hands, then, Reilly said, "he'd actually surge out of your arms." He would vault into the jump seat, and then shift to the rear seat. "He did this with such speed and grace," said Reilly, "that literally thousands who saw him at ball games, rallies and inaugurations never suspected his condition." When he was not in public, two agents sometimes locked hands, scooped him up as one would a child, and carried him off. It was a sight that unsettled people who saw it.

Among the Secret Service agents, Gus Gennerich was special to FDR. A New York cop who had survived shoot-outs with gangsters, Gennerich became a guard to then-governor Roosevelt and was admitted to the Secret Service at the president's request. When there was no one else around, Gennerich got FDR into his big, seven-passenger open car by lifting him up, calling "alley-oop!" and tossing him into the backseat. Then, if the president could reach him, he would wrestle Gennerich into the car.

*This rare photograph of Roosevelt at Hyde Park shows the armless kitchen-like chair he used to wheel himself about. He maintained that he only used the chairs "to get about my room while dressing" and "solely for the purpose of saving time." Actually he was totally disabled, but the press never published pictures like this of the President posing with his dog Fala and admirer Ruthie Bie.* (FRANKLIN D. ROOSEVELT LIBRARY)

Fortunately, as president, the world came to Roosevelt. He wasn't expected to go to parties or restaurants. At small White House dinners guests would be escorted upstairs to the private quarters for drinks, where they would find FDR seated with a tray of drink mixes. Eleanor then led the guests down to dinner, taking time to tour the White House. FDR was pushed in his wheelchair to the dining room downstairs and would already be seated and calling a cheery greeting to the guests when they arrived. At receptions the gardeners would set up ferns and conceal a high seat, similar to a bicycle seat, in the greenery for FDR to rest on so he appeared to be standing.

Between his various tricks and his engaging personality, even those close to FDR could forget his incapacity. Chief Usher J. B. West had met Roosevelt several times, yet was shocked the first time he went to the private quarters and saw the president in a wheelchair. "Startled, I looked down at him," he said. "It was only then that I realized that Franklin D. Roosevelt was really paralyzed." Madame Chiang Kai-shek, wife of the Chinese leader, stayed at the White House several times during World War II and was aware of FDR's condition. Once, as she prepared to leave a conference in the Oval Office, she said, "Please don't get up." The president looked at her and said, "My dear child, I couldn't stand up if I had to."

The world not only came to the White House, but the Roosevelts put it up, often for extended periods. Eleanor invited everyone from political friends to servicemen she met on the street. The guests were left to their own devices, and at times she didn't know who was sleeping down the hall. The president's mother, Sara, looked in shocked dismay at the crowd Eleanor invited to Hyde Park. "*Where* does she get all these people?" Sara asked.

Eleanor's invitations sometimes exceeded capacity, for the White House had a large permanent cast. Eleanor selected the bedroom on the southwest corner as a workroom and put a narrow single bed for herself in the adjoining dressing room. Her husband took the bedroom adjacent to the Oval Room and used the Oval Room as an office and study. Lorena Hickok, an Associated Press reporter and good friend of Eleanor's, was given a bedroom on the northwest corner, across the hall from Eleanor's. Louis Howe, Roosevelt's political guru, and his wife were given a bedroom on the north front. Marguerite "Missy" LeHand, the president's secretary, moved into a small suite on the third floor.

The Roosevelts' twenty-seven-year-old daughter Anna Roosevelt Dahl, the eldest of their five children, lived in the White House for a time with her husband, Curtis, and their young children, Sistie and Buzz. But the Roosevelts' four boys were, for the most part, off living their adult lives and seriously embarrassing the president by drinking, womanizing, divorcing—highly stigmatized at the time—and entering into business deals that exploited them for the Roosevelt name. The youngest, John, was seventeen when Roosevelt took office. During his father's first term, John drove his old car up to the White House gates after midnight, and he wasn't allowed in. "No son of a President would be driving such a junk heap," he was told. When he was staying in the White House and tried to get a late-night snack from the kitchen refrigerator, he found it locked. Food loss was always a serious problem in the mansion due to the servants' pilfering. "What kind of joint is this?" John muttered.

It wasn't a joint presided over by a ladies-lunch first lady. When FDR was elected, Eleanor felt her career as a social activist was over, and she went to a corner and wept.

"I never wanted to be the President's wife," she said. Initially she tried to carry on as she'd always done. When outgoing first lady Lou Hoover invited Eleanor to tea and to inspect the White House, she declined a chauffeured car and instead walked by herself from the Mayflower Hotel to the White House to meet Mrs. Hoover.

In 1933, her first summer in the White House, Eleanor bought a light blue Buick convertible with a rumble seat and invited Lorena Hickok to accompany her on a trip through New England and part of Canada. The Secret Service was astonished, but at this time the law did not require that the first lady be protected. The two women stopped at tourist camps and small hotels. Few people recognized the first lady. In Quebec a priest saw her name and asked her, "Are you any relation to Theodore Roosevelt? I was a great admirer of his." Eleanor said proudly, "Yes, I am his niece." Later that year Eleanor and Lorena were together in San Francisco. They checked into a small hotel, ate at a small French restaurant, took the cable car up Russian Hill at night, and had ice cream sodas at a drugstore. It was late when they returned to their hotel, but the press had been tipped off about Eleanor, and the lobby was full of reporters. After meeting with reporters, Eleanor, embarrassed by the stir, went up to the room and told Lorena, "From now on I shall travel as I am supposed to travel, as the President's wife, and try to do what is expected of me."

Yet she did the unexpected again and again. She broke all precedent by being the first first lady to give regular press conferences, and held hundreds. Access was limited to women reporters, just as the president's press conferences were restricted to men. In the past, reporters had rarely had direct interviews with the president's wife, and Eleanor broke all precedent in allowing direct quotation from the opening bell. She held her first press conference in New York, before FDR's inauguration, and her first as first lady in the Red Room. Of it she wrote, "I could feel the disapproval of the ushers as I went in fear and trembling, trying to cover my uncertainty by passing around a large box of candy to fill in the first awkward moments." The conferences were somewhat informal, more akin to a social call, and the reporters were required to dress as such, in hats and gloves. Eleanor sometimes held them in her sitting room, and might even knit all the while. (She was a compulsive knitter—on airplanes, at parties, listening to speeches, even on a platform before her own speech. She gave the finished vests and sweaters to the White House staff.)

Eleanor generated her own news, writing a daily newspaper column called "My Day" throughout her husband's term, and got more press coverage than any first lady excepting perhaps Jacqueline Kennedy. Her mail reached three hundred thousand pieces in her first year, and she tried to read and answer all of it. She also wrote books and magazine articles, and went on a lecture tour. By 1938 her income had reached $100,000 a year—the president's salary never went over $75,000.

Eleanor loved being first lady, but even at the White House she struggled to maintain distance from her mother-in-law, Sara. "For the first year of my married life, I was completely taken care of," Eleanor said. "My mother-in-law did everything for me." That included providing a New York City town house for Eleanor and Franklin—and installing herself next door. The dining and drawing rooms on the upper floors connected, giving Sara easy access to her son's life. When Eleanor had children, Sara even told them, "Your mother only bore you. I am more your mother than your mother is." Hyde Park, where Franklin often brought his family, was Sara's home, and she ruled the roost. At family meals she sat at one end of the big dining table, her son at the other end, and Eleanor anywhere else. Now Eleanor was determined to be in charge of the White House. She fired all the white household servants and hired only blacks. "Mrs. Roosevelt and I agreed," wrote housekeeper Henrietta Nesbitt, "that a staff solid in any one color works in better understanding and maintains a smoother-running establishment." When Sara commented on the change, Eleanor told her, "Mother, you run your house. And I'll run mine."

Eleanor remained firmly in control of the White House household operations, the family quarters, the social secretary, the kitchens, and the ushers. She wanted a housekeeper who would be loyal to her and found one in Henrietta Nesbitt, a Hyde Park neighbor who had provided baking and cooking for the governor's mansion in Albany. She had no particular qualifications for running the White House other than an innate sense of frugality. "Mrs. Roosevelt and I had our economy program all mapped out," Nesbitt wrote in her memoir, "and we were going to stick to it. With so many Americans hungry, it was up to the head house of the nation to serve economy meals and act as an example. . . . And while there is nothing nicer than a good roast of lamb, still it isn't the most stylish dish one could set before a king—or the Polish Premier." Nesbitt shared her economy recipes with the women of America and proudly told reporters, "Yes, the Commander-in-Chief ate leftovers—hash and bread pudding. Relished them too."

Eleanor also hired two cooks she had used in the governor's mansion in Albany to work under Nesbitt. Always considerate, Eleanor created a job for Henrietta's out-of-work husband, knowing the two wouldn't be able to afford the move to Washington otherwise. Henrietta recorded how they arrived in 1933: "We just walked into the White House as if we belonged there. It was run informally in those days before the war, with no police at the gates, so it didn't seem at all formidable. The doorman took my coat with the big fur collar and hung it over a nail in the hall rack and the nail went right through the fur!"

Once settled, she discovered there were hardly enough utensils to cook a family meal. The range was ancient, cookbooks nonexistent. And the kitchen storage area, which had once been a dairy cooler, still had a cement trough that once ran with cool water in which to set the milk cans; now it ran with rats. "We were warring on rats day and night," Henrietta wrote in her memoir. The White House gardeners and government experts spent days studying the problem, but the rats prevailed. So did the ants. In the servants' dining room the table legs were set in cans of water to prevent ants from crawling up, but the insects dropped down from the ceiling. Eleanor liked to leave snacks out on the second floor for guests, which attracted ants and mice.

Eleanor had little interest in either the preparation or the taste of food. "She was too much interested in talk to care what she ate," said Mrs. Nesbitt. "She'd eat anything put before her. Only once did I hear her complain. This was after a wartime trip she made to England. 'Mrs. Nesbitt,' she said to me then, almost pathetically, 'please don't serve me any more Brussels sprouts or carrots.'"

Everyone else suffered. In 1937 Ernest Hemingway called the White House food "the worst I've ever eaten. We had rainwater soup followed by rubber squab, a nice wilted salad and a cake some admirer had sent in. An enthusiastic but unskilled admirer." The Roosevelt children groaned. The president said "the food around here would do justice to the Automat."

FDR was something of a gourmet. He liked exotic fish and game, which friends like Bernard Baruch—a wealthy financier with a big estate for hunting—sent to him. Mrs. Nesbitt ruined them. She maintained that a proper diet consisted of "plain foods plainly prepared." Two of FDR's favorite dishes were Brunswick stew and kedgeree, neither of which Mrs. Nesbitt cared to make. "Some of the dishes I served regularly were corned beef hash, poached eggs, and creamed chip beef," Mrs. Nesbitt recalled. FDR complained he had chicken six times in a week. Mrs. Nesbitt responded by substituting sweetbreads, and the president wrote Eleanor a memo saying he was becoming very "unsweet." He found White House coffee so bitter he got a percolator for his bedroom and made his own in the morning. At breakfast FDR exclaimed, "My God! Doesn't Mrs. Nesbitt know there are breakfast foods besides oatmeal? It's been served to me morning in and morning out for months now, and I'm sick and tired of it." Regular White House guests learned to predict what they would have for dinner just by noting the day of the week. As war rationing restricted items like butter, a January 1945 *New York Times* headline read, "Housekeeper Vetoes Roosevelt on Menu." FDR had announced there would be a luncheon of chicken à la king. Mrs. Nesbitt countered, "We aren't going to have it because you can't keep it hot for all those people." The menu, she decided, would be cold chicken salad, rolls but no butter, coffee, and unfrosted cake.

Eleanor tried, in her own way. She sent Henrietta to Schrafft's in New York to spend a few days in the kitchen. But Mrs. Nesbitt remained Mrs. Nesbitt. And backed by Eleanor, she seemed to take pleasure in frustrating the president. When told he didn't like broccoli, she said, "Fix it anyway. He *should* like it." She concluded, "Men just don't like vegetables. So one of the hardest jobs Mrs. Roosevelt and I shared was trying to coax vegetables down the President of the United States." When FDR was ill, Grace Tully, his secretary, visited his bedroom and asked if there was anything he wanted. "Yes," he said, "I'd love some of those big white asparagus that comes in cans." Grace asked him why he didn't ask Mrs. Nesbitt to get some. "I did ask her," he said, "but she said it is not to be found in Washington." Grace placed a phone call, and a grateful president got ten large cans of asparagus.

When his mother died in 1941, FDR brought her cook, Mary Campbell, to the White House, gave her a room on the third floor where a storage room had been converted to a kitchen in the 1935 renovation, and began ordering his meals from there. Mrs. Nesbitt tried to get the third-floor cook eliminated. She appealed to Chief Usher Howell Crim, who took her problem to the president. FDR said, "You tell Mrs. Roosevelt I'll get rid of Mary Campbell when she gets rid of old lady Nesbitt!"

Despite her methods, Mrs. Nesbitt had the president's interests at heart. His salary was $75,000 a year, and FDR had an independent income almost equal to that, but still he was unable to manage financially at the White House and had to depend on his mother to help out. Worried, he tried to cut expenses. He wrote Eleanor a memo—they communicated best in writing—that in view of the new income tax law, "we shall have to take some steps to reduce the White House food bill, to which I pay $2,000 a month or $24,000 a year. Next year the taxes on $75,000 will leave me about $30,000 net and SOMETHING HAS TO BE DONE!" He said he always got two eggs when he only needed one, although he had pleaded with the kitchen to send just one. He cut Eleanor's monthly allotment to $1,500 but raised it back to $1,800 when she wrote, "Franklin, I can't quite make it on this." Because of the depression, he also cut staff salaries 25 percent, and voluntarily reduced his own salary by 15 percent. Eleanor served more roast beef and potatoes at state dinners and trimmed the number of courses. The head butler, Alonzo Fields, was dismayed. So was FDR when, as an economy, he was served 19-cent lunches.

Reduced budgets never forced the Roosevelts to curtail their guest lists. As the war shattered Europe, they took in quite a few displaced royalty. Princess Martha of Norway stayed off and on with her children. When she developed an overly friendly relationship with FDR, Eleanor attempted to curtail her visits, but the first lady traveled so frequently that Martha came anyway. Soviet foreign minister V. M. Molotov was also a guest. The servant who unpacked his bags found black bread, a roll of sausage, and a pistol. Madame Chiang Kai-shek visited several times. She often napped in the afternoon, which kept the White House staff jumping as she demanded that the silk sheets she brought with her be washed and ironed after each use. Her entourage clapped sharply for service—not what the staff was used to.

The most distinguished live-in guest was Sir Winston Churchill, who always succeeded in exhausting everyone, even the president. His wartime visits, in which he and the president planned joint actions, began with a three-week stay in December 1941, and he visited several more times during the war. He wandered about in his Royal Air Force jumpsuit, changing things around as if he owned the house and demanding extensive personal service. He complained of the "oppressive heat" in late December. He kept odd hours, going down to the basement to the top secret map room late at night. A navy officer on guard duty, William C. Mott, would look up to see Churchill's cherubic face peeking at him from around the corner and asking, "How's Hitler? The ba-astard."

Butler Alonzo Fields told of a day during which Churchill was served a tumbler of sherry before breakfast, Scotch at lunch, and champagne at dinner, followed by ninety-year-old brandy until one-thirty in the morning. Fields wanted to go home and felt that Churchill couldn't possibly want anything more, but Churchill did—more brandy. Churchill said to Fields, "I am not too sure about you. I don't know whether you'll qualify or not. I need somebody I can depend upon."

Fields, puzzled, asked him, "Well, Mr. Prime Minister, what is it you want me to do?"

Churchill said, "If ever I am accused of being a teetotaler, I want you to come to my defense."

Fields assured him, "Mr. Prime Minister, I'll defend you to the last drop."

At a family dinner Roosevelt introduced one of his favorite foods to the British prime minister: sauerkraut with pigs' knuckles.

"What is this?" Churchill asked on being served.

"Sir, this is pigs' feet," the butler said.

"Pigs' feet," Churchill said. "I have never heard of them." After a taste, he issued his evaluation: "Very good, but sort of slimy."

The high point in royal visitations came in June 1939, just before World War II. King George VI and Queen Elizabeth of Great Britain arrived at Roosevelt's invitation, and stayed at the White House for one night. They were the first British rulers in history to come to America. Roosevelt was trying to rally American support for Britain in its stand against Hitler, and the royal visit was remarkably successful in doing this. The king and queen dominated the news for weeks, and the crowds were large and friendly.

The White House staff was not as pleased. Five months before the visit, Mrs. Nesbitt began a thorough cleaning and refurbishing. She even cut ten inches from the drapes in the Red Room to facilitate vacuuming—much to the horror of Mrs. Harriet Barnes Platt, a wealthy member of a committee that had raised money for an historically accurate refurbishing of the room. The royal entourage was exacting. The June heat was so oppressive the queen was barely able to touch her dinner. Fortunately it rained, and the royal couple were led to the south portico for some cooling breezes. Then their staff demanded that the White House supply them with blankets and hot water bottles. Maid Lizzie McDuffie was nearly fired when she forgot herself and asked for a royal autograph.

The king and queen got on well with the president and first lady, though, and traveled to visit Hyde Park. Sara, for once, was delighted. Roosevelt said to King George, "My mother thinks you should have a cup of tea—she doesn't approve of cocktails." King George thought for a moment, then replied, "Neither does my mother." Then they had martinis.

Sara had prepared for this great moment in her life, but things did not go as she planned. A serving table, made out of sawhorses, collapsed, sending family china crashing to the floor. Sara did not want the queen to know the dinnerware was borrowed, but the wealthy Helen Astor Roosevelt—widow of FDR's Uncle James—said, "I hope, Sally, that none of my dishes were broken." Then the butler tripped and fell with a tray of drinks right in front of the king and queen. To add to Sara's chagrin, Eleanor wrote the whole thing up in her newspaper column, "My Day."

Sara was a Delano, descended from the Pilgrims, and viewed the world of politics as she would a dead rat. When reporters asked her the usual mother-of-a-president question, she said, "Never, oh never! That was the last thing I should ever have imagined for him or that he should be in public life of any sort." When her only son contracted polio she fought with considerable logic for him to retreat to Hyde Park with her and become a country squire, as his father had been. She never got used to her son's associates, who crowded into her home. "Franklin should never have gone into politics," she said. "Look at these strange people around him all the time. Why, they look just like a lot of gangsters." When she found that aides were running up her phone bills at Hyde Park, she cut them off and had a pay phone put in the front hall.

But Sara was devoted to her son and always supported him, even when she didn't understand. Her sister, Mrs. Dora Forbes, was stranded in France in 1939 at the start of World War II. Sara insisted her son send a battleship over there for her and could not understand his refusal. "Well, Franklin," she said, "I don't see why not. What are you President for!" She never let the president leave the house on a rainy day without checking to see if he had his rubbers. During his second term she shouted to him, "Franklin, you'll catch your death of cold. Come in this instant and get a sweater." She once told the newsmen at Hyde Park, "I will not let Franklin go to church tomorrow because he is so far behind in his mail."

Roosevelt, generally in his mother's corner just as she was in his, usually did what she wanted. He was like her in many ways, sharing, among other things, a patrician streak. He called all the servants and reporters by their first names, but very few were privileged to call him Franklin. Butler Alonzo Fields recalled, "I could never go in and say, 'Mr. President, dinner is served.' I had to stand until he looked up. The first time I announced dinner to Truman, as soon as I walked into the room, he stood up."

Another person who was always in his corner was adviser Harry Hopkins, who ran some of the president's New Deal programs and became a close friend. In May 1940 FDR said to him, "Stay for dinner. I'm lonely." After dinner FDR told him, "Stay the night." Hopkins, a bachelor, borrowed pajamas and stayed almost four years. Eleanor wanted him out. He was rude to her, his diet required special foods at every meal, he was messy and dropped cigarette ashes around, and he was a rival for FDR's attention. In 1942 Hopkins married Louise Macy, and Eleanor thought that would be that. Instead he added his wife to the White House and took over a second bedroom—next to Roosevelt's. Eleanor was not pleased. The newlyweds drank excessively. "They really are quite *high* sometimes before they sit down to dinner," Eleanor said.

Hopkins was quite capable, but his biggest asset was total loyalty to his boss. "He agreed with the President regardless of his own opinion," Eleanor noted. Hopkins avoided confrontation with the president, but got him to change through indirect methods. FDR explained Hopkins to the 1940 Republican presidential candidate, Wendell Wilkie: "Someday you may well be sitting where I am now as President of the United States. And when you are, you'll be looking at that door over there and knowing that practically everybody who walks through it wants something out of you. You'll learn what a lonely job this is, and you'll discover the need for somebody like Harry Hopkins, who asks for nothing except to serve you."

Previously, the person closest and most loyal to FDR had been Missy LeHand. When she was disabled by a stroke in 1941, Hopkins became a sort of replacement. Missy had known FDR since 1922, when she was a secretary in his law office, and she became a sort of personal assistant. When he became president, she ran his White House office. The surest way to gain access to the president was through Missy LeHand. She never married and instead devoted herself to FDR. At the governor's mansion in Albany, she had lived in the room next to FDR's, and at the White House had a third-floor suite. She traveled with him, and at Warm Springs she was hostess when Eleanor wasn't there. She paid his personal bills, jumped into the pool with him, or sat around with him in the evenings listening to his stories or helping him with his stamps. Missy and "Effdee," as she called him, also loved to make small bets. Eleanor, on the other hand, disliked water, didn't have the patience to sit through FDR's stories, and refused to bet, even at cards.

Eleanor's relationship with Missy was pleasant. She would take her along on her early-morning horseback rides in Rock Creek Park—for which the first lady's horse was shipped in a van from the stables at Fort Meyer, in Virginia. And when she needed to get money out of her husband, she knew the best way was to go through Missy. She also knew that Missy was sometimes around FDR at night in the private quarters—in her nightgown and sometimes sitting in his lap. "Missy was young and pretty and loved a good time," Eleanor said in 1961, "and occasionally her social contacts got mixed up with her work and made it hard for her and others." In his will, FDR left money to pay Missy's medical bills. She died first, in 1944, but FDR never rewrote his will.

Missy was just one of many people FDR was dependent upon to help him perform normal daily functions. At the White House, a valet was on call to assist in dressing and personal care. The job was not difficult, but it required keeping the same hours as the president, seven days a week. Irwin McDuffie served faithfully at this for many years, and Roosevelt was fond of him. But he had a drinking habit. One night, FDR's son John found his father sitting in his wheelchair late at night. He couldn't get to bed by himself, and McDuffie had not responded to FDR's rings. Eleanor insisted he had to be fired. FDR reluctantly agreed, but gave Eleanor the unpleasant task of telling McDuffie, who was given another government job.

FDR always tried to avoid personal confrontations. Visitors came out of the Oval Office believing that FDR agreed with them because rather than say no, he resorted to dissembling, telling long stories, or subterfuge. Once Mariner Eccles, a governor of the Federal Reserve, had a short appointment scheduled with the president. The schedule was tight. FDR's Scottie dog, Fala, came into the office at the same time Eccles did. The president took a ball from his desk drawer. While the edgy Eccles tried to appear interested, FDR showed him some of Fala's tricks. Eccles had hardly begun his presentation when FDR roared, "Well, I'll be God-damned! Mariner, do you see what I see?" Fala had urinated on the carpet. By the time the mess was cleaned up, FDR's next appointment was announced.

Secretary Grace Tully, who replaced Missy, said the only time she ever heard her boss raise his voice to someone was over inviting bad luck by lighting three cigarettes on a match. (In the trenches of World War I, keeping a match lit that long invited a well-aimed bullet.) FDR was superstitious. Tully said she could never schedule his trips to start on Friday—he thought it unlucky—though his train could depart at 11:50 P.M. on Thursday or 12:10 A.M. Saturday. He would not sit down to a dinner set for thirteen. He was addicted to old hats or sweaters that he thought were lucky.

Perhaps it was the element of luck that drew FDR to poker. He was fond of the game and held frequent card sessions at the White House. In keeping with his personality, he was a bluffer and liked long shots. When he was dealing and entitled to name the game, he called for many wild cards. He rarely won, but he played for small stakes, and he enjoyed the camaraderie. As a child, he'd had few friends his own age to play with, and spent most of his time in the company of adults. He was not sent to school until he was fourteen, and after his polio attack, solitary ways were forced upon him. As president he still enjoyed playing solitaire, doing crossword puzzles, and watching movies, but did almost no serious reading.

FDR was an avid stamp collector from early childhood, and by his death had filled 150 albums. "I think it safe to say there was not a day, even during the war years, that he did not give half an hour to his stamps," said Admiral Ross McIntire, his personal physician. The president received the first sheet of new commemorative issues from the Postal Department, and he had the State Department on the lookout for unusual foreign stamps. During World War II he met with Walter Nash, Deputy Prime Minister of New Zealand, who wanted U.S. forces to occupy a small South Pacific island. FDR countered, "An island nearby called Mangareva would be better." Nash had never heard of it. "Oh, it's in the Tuamotu Archipelago in the postal administration of Tahiti," he explained. "I know the place because I'm a stamp collector."

Swimming was another pastime, one that developed as a way to exercise his paralyzed legs. In 1924, seeking a cure for his polio, he visited Warm Springs, Georgia, a resort whose springs came out of a mountain at 88 degrees and had buoyant qualities. After only a few days exercising in the Warm Springs pool, he discovered something marvelous—he could wiggle his toes! He bought Warm Springs and turned it into a rehabilitation facility for polio sufferers. He went back when he could. Soon after he took office, New York newspapers led a campaign to raise money to give him a pool in the White House. Congress then authorized a "swimming tank" in the West Wing. A flower room, laundry room, and black servants' dining room, all described in an official report as "dilapidated," were ripped out to make way for the pool.

Also to accommodate his disability, FDR kept an emergency canvas chute in his second-story bedroom that would allow him to escape in the event of a fire. He even brought his chute with him on trips. Roosevelt feared fire above all else. At the age two he must have heard about or may even have witnessed the hideous death of his aunt Laura, who ran shrieking out onto the lawn when her robe accidentally caught fire. He had also helped fight a fire in the stables at Groton, the Connecticut prep school he attended—"a horrible scene," he wrote. After he became incapacitated, he worried that he would be unable to escape a blaze. As president he never had a fire in fireplaces when he was alone in the room, and he insisted that the White House be inspected regularly for fire hazards. Mike Reilly of the Secret Service called the White House "the biggest firetrap in America, bar none." Not only was the building old, but the insulation around the electric wiring was worn, exits were lacking from the second and third floors, and during Theodore Roosevelt's breakneck reconstruction in 1902 combustibles had been left in the walls and floors. Yet when FDR discovered that the fireplace in the basement Diplomatic Reception Room where he gave his immensely popular fireside chats was a fake, he had the fake cut from the wall and the original fireplace behind it restored—even though the talks were radio broadcasts.

Roosevelt made many other changes to the White House during his dozen years there. The office staff had expanded exponentially over the years: by the end of 1933 Roosevelt's staff of over seventy was already twice the size of Herbert Hoover's. In 1934 the West Wing was remodeled in such a way as to double its square footage while altering its outward appearance and scale very little. This was accomplished in part with a subterranean wing. The Oval Office was shifted to the southeast corner, where it remains today. Roosevelt had taken care to prepare the public for the project. On June 28, 1934, he spoke of it reassuringly in one of his fireside chat radio broadcasts: "The structural lines of the old Executive Office Building will remain. The artistic lines of the White House buildings were the creation of master builders when our Republic was young. The simplicity and strength of the structure remain in the face of every modern test. But within this magnificent pattern, the necessities of modern government business require constant reorganization and rebuilding."

In 1935 the two White House kitchens, located in the basement, were modernized. Eleanor and her housekeeper had long wanted to eliminate the smoking ovens and paltry refrigerators. At the invitation of General Electric, Mrs. Nesbitt traveled to Cleveland, Ohio, to view its new electric kitchens. By June 6, 1935, plans were drawn up and excavation for new pipes started under the north portico driveway. But renovation involved shutting down the kitchen, and the president, though scheduled to depart, stayed for the better part of the summer. So did White House aide Louis Howe, who was too sick to move. Eleanor, away at Hyde Park and Campobello, Maine, had promised not to send house guests, but sent them anyway. The president's presence meant Nesbitt had to give various official dinners, trotting over boards laid across the tunnels. As construction hampered her resources, she resorted to serving the assorted White House residents picnic lunches with sausages, hot dogs, and cold cuts. In her *White House Diary*, Nesbitt wrote,

> All these hot months the blueprint of the kitchen was never far from my hands. I wore the edges thin, studying it. It was the last word in kitchen planning.
>
> The old kitchen was in the heart of a labyrinth, where passageways led to cupboards, refrigerators, locker rooms, storerooms, vaults, the package room, the canned-goods room, and the wine cellar.
>
> The new one was ample enough to provide a full course meal for a thousand people, with seven spacious windows, an electric fan to draw off the odors of cooking, rounded corners to prevent dust, stainless shining metal, electric ranges with red handles—the electric stove cost $5000 and was sixteen feet long—six electric roasting ovens—you could roast a dozen massive roasts at the same time or bake forty loaves of bread and two dozen pies, and a broiling oven that would hold a covey of quail, thermostat controlled. We had eight electric refrigerators and new dumb-waiters, electrically operated, instead of the old wooden one that went by a rope.
>
> Now we had . . . an electric meat grinder, all sorts of electric mixers, warming ovens, five dishwashers, waffle irons, an electric soup kettle, a thirty-gallon ice-cream pack, and an enormous oblong pancake griddle. Someone said we could bake enough cakes on it for the entire House of Representatives.
>
> . . . One of the innovations we liked best was the new electric wagon for the President's meals. It had three compartments, two for hot dishes and one for cold. It was tricked out with pilot lights and rheostats and thermostats and the President had as much fun with it as he did with one of his boats, and loved turning things on and off and seeing dishes come out smoking hot or dewy cold.

Mrs. Nesbitt was in heaven.

As part of the the basement overhaul a storage room was turned into a library. The second-floor Oval Room had been a library since the early 1850s, but other uses increasingly impinged on it until finally, in 1929, the books had been moved into the corridor. The Truman renovation in 1948 eliminated the Roosevelt library and created a proper one that remains today.

With the advent of World War II, many more people would be working at the White House as part of the war effort, so the East Wing, a social entrance with a porte cochere, guard stations, and cloakroom, was demolished in December 1941 to make way for a larger structure. The new building encompassed quarters for the White House police and, on the second floor, office space. The construction was complicated by the secret excavation of a bomb shelter in the subbasement of the new wing—the public would not learn of it until after the war, in 1945.

For all the energy he put into modernizing the White House, Roosevelt spent a fair amount of time away from it. He loved to travel, logging half a million miles during his twelve years in office. He even loved to campaign. He particularly liked traveling on trains and ships—he didn't care for planes, and the army always found itself at a disadvantage against the navy in vying for the commander-in-chief's favors. In 1940 he received as a gift from the railroads the *Ferdinand Magellan,* the first railroad car designed for a president. The 142-ton car had bedrooms with baths, a study, an oak-paneled dining room, and a cooling system that required six thousand pounds of ice. Because it was wartime, the car had no identification on the outside; it just said "Pullman." The windows were three-inch-thick bulletproof glass, and the body was armor-plated. There was a rear platform for speeches, and the Secret Service added a long, stationary ramp with sturdy handrails and a gentle slope so FDR could slowly walk on and off. The swaying of the train caused FDR problems—even just sitting in his seat he had to brace himself. So the train traveled at just thirty miles an hour in the daytime, and sped up at night. FDR always had maps and plotted his location. He loved taking in the passing scenery and waving to people. Once he said to William Simmons, a Secret Service agent who resembled him, "Bill, how would you like to be President for a while?" He positioned the agent by the window, gave him pince-nez glasses and a cigarette holder, and said, "Now every time we pass a town, sit there and wave. I'm going to take a nap."

The president was more difficult to guard when he traveled, and security was a genuine concern. Shortly before taking office, on February 14, 1933, FDR nearly lost his life during a trip to Miami. He was sitting in an open car next to Chicago mayor Anton Cermak when the deranged Giuseppe Zangara climbed on a chair and began firing shots at the president-elect. Cermak was killed; Roosevelt was unhurt. White House security was further tightened during World War II, when guards were stationed everywhere, yet Roosevelt's son Jimmy, home on leave from the army, witnessed what he called "the most incredible thing I ever saw happen at the White House." The family was watching a movie in the upstairs hall. At the end the lights went on, and to everyone's surprise, Jimmy said, "there was a neatly dressed young man—a complete stranger to all of us—standing near Father." The stranger asked for the president's autograph, which the astonished FDR gave him. Fortunately, the incident was just a lark. But Secretary of the Treasury Robert Morganthau was present and was particularly upset, since the Secret Service was a part of his department.

Like a number of presidents, FDR occasionally delighted in eluding his guards. "Nothing pleases my husband more," Eleanor said, "in Hyde Park or at Warm Springs, than to lose the Secret Service car which always follows him." The Secret Service were encumbered by big touring cars, whereas FDR had a Ford phaeton with hand controls, and he knew all the little roads in the woods around his Hyde Park estate. He loved to return to his mansion and in grave tones tell Colonel Edmund Starling, the head agent, "Ed, I have lost the Secret Service boys. I can't find them anywhere. Do you know where they are?"

Eleanor was not obliged to have Secret Service bodyguards and refused any, but she gave in to their request that she carry a gun. She went to the FBI firing range to practice shooting it. "I am a better shot each day," she wrote in a letter to reporter Bess Furman. But FBI Director J. Edgar Hoover told her husband, "If there is one person in the U.S. who should not carry a gun, it is your wife. She cannot hit a barn door." The effort was futile in any case, because, as Eleanor said later, "I would never have used it on a human being." When a local official learned that she was carrying a gun, he said it was illegal and threatened to arrest her, so the Secret Service gave her a Secret Service badge, which legally entitled her to carry a gun.

Security took on a whole new dimension on December 7, 1941. It was a Sunday, and about one-forty in the afternoon, Roosevelt got a call from Secretary of the Navy Frank Knox: the Japanese had attacked Pearl Harbor in Hawaii. Crowds began gathering outside the White House, just standing quietly. Immediately, army units were sent to the White House to guard the perimeter, and machine gunners were sent to the roof. The social season and tours were canceled, and access to the White House was severely limited. Life within changed dramatically. Blackout curtains went on all the windows, and each room was provided with a bucket of sand, a shovel, candles, matches, and gas masks. The corridors were patrolled, fire drills held, and a bomb shelter dug. The roof of the White House would have been painted black and its walls painted in Army camouflage, but FDR drew the line.

For the war effort, heat and electrical consumption were reduced. Mrs. Nesbitt carefully saved her food ration stamps, and the White House menu was further reduced to only three courses—soup, entrée, and dessert, and the entrée was always chicken or fish. Once the war started, food shopping was supervised by the Secret Service, which chose suppliers and picked up groceries.

FDR borrowed Churchill's idea of a top-secret war room and set one up in the basement next to the Diplomatic Reception Room. It contained maps with pins marking all the positions of all the Allied Forces, and had a twenty-four-hour military guard. Eleanor was not given access to the war room, but when she wanted to know the whereabouts of her sons, who were serving in the military, she burst past an astounded guard.

During the war years FDR became even more lonely. His four sons were away in the military. In his third term he lost his intimates—his mother; Missy LeHand; his appointments secretary, Edwin "Pa" Watson; and White House aide Louis Howe, his political mentor for decades. At the "Children's Hour"—his term for cocktail time—he would tell an usher, "See who's home and ask them to stop in." Often now he was told, "Sorry, Mr. President, there is no one home." FDR sat up working on his stamps by himself or after a solitary dinner went to bed early.

Eleanor, who traveled for much of her twelve years as first lady, more or less abandoned the White House during the war years, accepting speaking engagements and even going off to see the troops in the South Pacific. Excluded from war councils, unable to pursue her social programs because of international events, there was less and less of interest for her at the White House. Even when she did stay home, she rarely saw her husband. "We never saw Eleanor and Franklin in the same room alone together," Chief Usher West said. "They had the most separate relationship I have ever seen between man and wife." They joined forces for dinner on state occasions, but normally Eleanor ate with her guests in the State Dining Room—and she always had guests. (Among many others, she regularly invited black leaders to dine at the White House.) FDR found it easier to have his meals brought to his desk in the upstairs study.

Around this time he may have resumed an affair with Lucy Mercer, Eleanor's onetime social secretary. Years ago, when FDR was assistant secretary of the navy, Lucy had had a love affair with him. Eleanor found out after about a year, in the fall of 1918, which nearly resulted in the breakup of the Roosevelt marriage. Lucy subsequently married an older man, Winthrop Rutherfurd. But she and the president had not lost contact. Over the years, FDR sent a White House car to bring Lucy to his inaugurals. In 1939 Lucy's husband had a disabling stroke, and the calls between her and the president became more frequent. Then in 1944 Lucy's husband died, and, unbeknownst to Eleanor, she and FDR began seeing each other again.

The president's private train began stopping at Lucy's Aiken, South Carolina, estate on the way to Warm Springs. The train would pull off on a rusty spur near the estate, and the two would rendezvous. The Signal Corps laid special phone lines to Lucy's home so FDR could keep in touch with the White House, the Secret Service blocked off the road for privacy, and the pool reporters played cards and didn't ask questions. And when FDR traveled north from the White House to Hyde Park, the train would make an all-day stop in Allamuchy, New Jersey, where Lucy also had a home. Sometimes the Secret Service drove the president out to Rock Creek Park, where Lucy would be waiting in her car to join him in his for a few hours. She even came to the White House—with daughter Anna's approval in Eleanor's absence—to visit in his office or for private luncheons. "Never was there anything clandestine about these occasions," Anna wrote. She knew about the previous affair, but she felt the visits provided her father needed relaxation and relief from tension.

The president's loneliness was compounded by health problems, although he never spoke of them. Even before he took office there were persistent rumors of his poor health. At the urging of his advisers, he underwent a medical examination and released the information to the public. The report showed only slightly high blood pressure, and the rumors were quieted. But over the years his blood pressure kept rising: in 1935 it was 136/78; in 1937, 162/98; and in 1941, 188/105. His personal physician, Ross McIntire, was part of the problem. Traditionally, the president chooses a personal physician from the military. McIntire was a casual choice, an eye, nose, and throat specialist who FDR knew slightly and seemed suited to monitor the president's chronic sinus problems. As White House physician, McIntire was gradually promoted to vice admiral. He told his boss exactly what he wanted to hear—no bad news. He saw the president each morning and evening and treated his sinus problem, but never brought his black bag of medical instruments, as FDR didn't want to see it. McIntire made no physical contact: "A close but seemingly casual watch told me all I wanted to know."

Compounding matters, FDR had been taught from childhood to bear health problems stoically. When he was crippled by polio, or what was called infantile paralysis, he wrote, "I have renewed my youth in a rather unpleasant manner by contracting what was fortunately a rather mild case of infantile paralysis." His case was anything but mild, but he never discussed it or complained. If others tried to sympathize, he quickly turned them off with, "No sob sister stuff."

But FDR's physical deterioration was obvious. Eleanor, who was generally healthy, also minimized health problems, and did not seem concerned. Others close to FDR, especially his daughter Anna, became increasingly worried, but all they got from McIntire was that the president was "in better physical condition than the average man of his age." Finally Anna demanded a second opinion. McIntire was forced to arrange for a physical examination at Bethesda Naval Hospital. On March 27, 1944, a navy doctor, Howard Bruenn, examined FDR and found acute bronchitis, cardiac failure of the left ventricle, high blood pressure, and heart disease. Bruenn prescribed rest, a modified diet, abstinence from cigarettes and liquor, and digitalis, which was about all medical science knew to do for him at the time. Under those conditions, Bruenn thought FDR might live a year or so—he should not run for a fourth term in 1944. McIntire had told Bruenn, his subordinate, to report only to him and to tell the president nothing unless asked. FDR never asked. McIntire announced to the public that the check-up was satisfactory. "When we got through," he said, "we decided that for a man of sixty-two we have very little to argue about." FDR would not accept extended bed rest, but he wrote to Harry Hopkins, "I have cut my drinks down to one and a half cocktails per evening and nothing else—not one complimentary highball or nightcap. Also, I have cut my cigarettes down from twenty or thirty a day to five or six a day."

In the summer of 1944, on the day of his nomination for a fourth term, FDR, in his railroad car in San Diego, had a seizure, turned deathly pale, and said to his son, "Jimmy, I don't know if I can make it—I have horrible pains." Jimmy helped his father lie on the floor of the car, and for ten anxious minutes watched him until he recovered. A few months later, at Bremmerton Navy Yard near Seattle, FDR gave a speech from the foredeck of the *Cummings.* He suffered sharp chest pains, had to grasp the lectern with both hands, and collapsed after the speech in the captain's cabin. He had been some distance from his audience, and only a few people noticed anything unusual. There were rumors, however, so Admiral McIntire continued to announce, "The President's health is perfectly okay."

After FDR's election to a fourth term, McIntire told the press, "The President is in excellent health." Roosevelt's fourth inaugural consisted of a short ceremony on the south portico rather than the traditional trip to the Capitol, and when he went back inside the White House, he almost collapsed in his wheelchair. Jimmy rushed him to the Green Room and shut the door. Again there were chest pains. "Jimmy, I can't take this unless you get me a stiff drink," FDR said. After the pain subsided, he attended a tea and a family dinner. Two weeks later FDR called in Jimmy, took off a family ring and gave it to him, and explained the terms of his will.

"I want to be elected to a fourth term so I can fire Mrs. Nesbitt," FDR had said. But by his fourth term he had lost all interest in food. He began losing weight and looked gaunt. McIntire told him, "For heavens sake, get some new clothes. That old shirt is sizes too large, and the coat hangs on your shoulders like a bag." FDR just threw his head back and laughed. He could no longer shave or bathe himself. He dozed off over his mail and, as he put it, "drew a blank" in conversations and had to ask what was being talked about. His signature was a wobbly blur. Grace Tully was told to get him a double-size coffee cup because his hands shook so. After he was nominated for vice president, Truman had lunch with FDR for the first time. He told reporters, "The President looked fine and ate a bigger lunch than I did." Privately, he was appalled. Truman said to his friend Harry Vaughan, "His hands were shaking and he talks with considerable difficulty . . . physically he's just going to pieces."

On March 1, 1945, Roosevelt went to the Capitol to report to Congress on his grueling trip to Yalta, in the Crimea, for the meeting with Winston Churchill and Joseph Stalin that shaped the postwar globe. For the first time he mentioned the load of steel he was forced to wear. "I hope that you will pardon me," he said, "for the unusual posture of sitting down during the presentation . . . but I know you realize that it makes it a lot easier for me in not having to carry about ten pounds of steel around on the bottom of my legs, and also because of the fact that I have just completed a fourteen-thousand-mile trip."

In April Jimmy said to his father, "Old man, you look like hell." His father laughed. "Oh, I'm all right. I'm a little tired, that's all. A few days in Warm Springs will fix me right up." Jimmy, unconvinced, went to McIntire: "Mac, father looks awful. I'm worried about him." McIntire's reply was almost a repeat of the president's: "Gosh, no need to be, Jimmy. He's just a little tired. He's had a hard campaign. It's been a hard winter and he's working too hard. But a few days in Warm Springs will fix him up." Jimmy said it was as if the two had sat down and together written the script. McIntire decided that when FDR left for Warm Springs on March 29, 1945, he would not accompany him: "I don't think I'll be needed."

The president was joined, however, by Lucy Mercer. Lucy's painter friend, Madame Shoumatoff, wanted FDR to sit for a portrait, and Lucy got him to agree to do it at Warm Springs. The night before his death, FDR and Lucy had a long talk together. In contrast to Eleanor, she was a good listener, and she never tried to get him to do anything. She simply adored him. After his death she wrote, "The world has lost one of the greatest men that ever lived—to me, the greatest." She would always recall "his beloved presence . . . his ringing laugh . . . his extraordinarily beautiful head."

Around noon on April 12, 1945, FDR was signing papers and Madame Shoumatoff was painting when his head slumped forward. Daisy Suckly, a cousin also visiting Warm Springs, went to him and asked if he had dropped his glasses. He said, "I have a terrific pain in the back of my head." A Filipino mess boy and FDR's valet carried him to his bed. Dr. Bruenn arrived in about fifteen minutes and diagnosed a massive cerebral hemorrhage. He called McIntire at the White House, and the two agreed it was all over. Laura Delano, another cousin visiting Warm Springs, called Eleanor at the White House: "There is no cause for you to upset yourself but I think you should know that Franklin has had a fainting spell down here." McIntire had ordered a navy plane to take him to Warm Springs, but he told Eleanor she should go to her appointment at Washington's Sulgrave Club—a meeting of ladies in a fashionable charity—"since it would cause great comment" if she canceled at the last moment. But FDR died soon after the hemorrhage. Press secretary Steve Early called Eleanor out of her meeting to tell her the news. At a press conference at the White House that evening, Admiral McIntire said, "This came out of a clear sky."

By the time Eleanor arrived in Warm Springs, all traces of Lucy Mercer had been removed, and she had been omitted from the list of people present that had been issued to the press. The funeral train left Warm Springs the next morning, Friday the thirteenth—a day on which FDR would never have voluntarily started a trip. During the ride back to Washington, Laura Delano told Eleanor of Lucy's presence. Eleanor questioned Anna, and discovered that her husband had been seeing Lucy at the White House. If she had known, she later said, she would have left the marriage. Before the funeral service in the East Room, Eleanor ordered everyone out. She went in and visited with her husband for the last time—they were finally alone together. He was buried at his beloved Hyde Park estate.

Following FDR's death, Eleanor refused a reporter's interview by saying, "The story's over." Eleanor's story was not over, however. In December 1945 her husband's successor, Harry Truman, prevailed upon her to become the representative to the new United Nations, then forming in San Francisco. She so served until 1951. These were perhaps her golden years—she became first lady of the world. She died on November 7, 1962, and was buried next to her husband at Hyde Park.

# 33

# Harry S. Truman
## 1945–1953

## *What a Life!*

"I JUST DREAD moving over there," Bess Truman said of the White House in 1945 when she learned her husband would be president. She never did get used to the house or her role as first lady, and she spent a great deal of time back home in Independence, Missouri. When her White House years were through, Bess was asked what she missed most. "There's only one thing I miss. All that help," she said, referring to the servants. Truman appreciated the White House, even though he called it "the Great White Prison." But for four of Truman's nearly eight years as president, opinions about the White House were irrelevant. When it was discovered that the aging executive mansion was on the verge of collapse, the Trumans were forced to move across the street to Blair House while a total renovation took place. In 1952 they returned to a White House that was virtually new.

Truman's nomination as Franklin Roosevelt's running mate in 1944 came as something of a surprise—Truman himself had been against it. Bess certainly was. Her husband had risen from Jackson County judge in 1922 to senator in 1934, and she had found that being the wife of a little-known senator just suited her. Coming out of the Democratic Party nominating convention, Bess complained about the crowds that surged around them: "Are we going through this the rest of our lives?" Truman said nothing. "What would happen if he should die?" she said of Roosevelt. "You'd be President."

318

On his last day as vice president, April 12, 1945, Truman had slipped out of the Senate chamber to a lounge set up for select members of Congress. Speaker of the House Sam Rayburn got Truman a bourbon and water and mentioned that the president's press secretary, Steve Early, had called for him. Truman returned the call. Early, his voice strained, asked him to come to the White House as "quickly and quietly" as possible. "Jesus Christ and General Jackson," exclaimed Truman, who had witnessed FDR's ill health up close. He ran to his office, got his hat, and was driven to the White House. He met Mrs. Roosevelt in her sitting room, and she told him the president was dead.

"Is there anything I can do for you?" Truman asked.

"Is there anything *we* can do for you," Eleanor replied. "For you are the one in trouble now."

Truman said later, "I felt like the moon, the stars, and all the planets had fallen on me." After he was sworn in in the Cabinet Room, Secretary of War Henry Stimson took him aside and informed him of a secret weapon called an atom bomb—Truman would soon decide to use it against Japan, ending World War II. In addition, FDR had put a secret codicil to the Yalta peace agreement in a small safe and told no one where it was. Truman had to appeal to the British to find out what the United States was committed to. The safe was found only months later by Admiral William Leahy, chief of naval operations. Truman had had a poker date the night of Roosevelt's death with his World War I buddy Eddie McKim. He called him at the Statler Hotel, explained what had happened, and said regretfully, "I guess the party's off."

A couple of months before Roosevelt died, the Secret Service had assigned agents to Truman without bothering to tell him about it in advance. Now the Secret Service wanted him out of his $120-a-month, five-room Washington apartment immediately. Since it would be a few weeks before Eleanor could clear out the White House, the Trumans were moved to Blair House, a private home taken over by the government on Pennsylvania Avenue, directly across from the executive mansion.

Truman's friend Sam Rayburn called him a day or two later and said, "Now, Harry, a lot of people are going to tell you you are the smartest man in the country, but Harry, you and I know you ain't." But Rayburn called him up again the next Monday morning and said, "Mr. President, you are not 'Harry' to me any more." The transition from first name to "Mr. President" would naturally be difficult. That afternoon Truman addressed a joint session of Congress, and, in true Truman fashion, he just walked up to the big bank of microphones and started talking. Rayburn leaned forward, and in an aside broadcast coast-to-coast, said, "Just a minute, Harry, let me introduce you."

It was undeniably difficult for a relative unknown to replace a world figure such as Franklin Roosevelt, who had been president for an unprecedented twelve years. Roosevelt's funeral service was held in the East Room on April 14, 1945, and when the new president entered, no one thought to stand up. Two days into his term, he called an administrative official to notify him of an appointment to a position he was making, and the official asked him if the president had made it before he died. "No, he made it just now," Truman snapped. Weeks later, alone with his mother-in-law one morning, he phoned the White House pantry to order breakfast. "Breakfast for Mrs. Wallace and me." "Who is me?" he was asked. He answered that he was president of the United States. But after five months in office he confided to Eleanor Roosevelt, "I never think of anyone as President, but Mr. Roosevelt."

Indeed, he gave the public the impression of someone who had been unexpectedly thrown into a position of responsibility. To reporters he said, "Boys, if you ever pray, pray for me now." Yet Truman was always confident of his abilities and generally acted boldly and decisively. His first executive order as president was to name Eleanor Roosevelt the U.S. delegate to the United Nations Charter Conference in San Francisco, a position she held through 1951. But he made his first mistake when he appointed Eddie McKim, a poker buddy, his chief of staff—McKim got what Truman called "Potomac Fever." One day McKim investigated the first lady's domain in the East Wing and found two secretaries typing answers to sympathy letters written to Eleanor and mailed to the White House. He fired them both instantly. Bess had a talk with Harry, the secretaries were rehired, and Eddie McKim departed.

The Trumans were just moving into the White House when Germany surrendered on May 8, 1945—V-E Day. Much to Truman's surprise, Bess immediately fled to Independence. Despite living in Washington for the past decade, Bess suddenly claimed she was homesick, and would spend much of the next six months back in Missouri. Truman, struggling with his newfound responsibilities, had been unaware of the depth of her feelings. The Trumans were a compatible couple and had a solid marriage, but the stress of assuming the presidency created what daughter Margaret called an "emotional separation." After the Japanese surrendered on August 14, 1945—V-J Day—he wrote her that he now expected to get things organized, and "there will be no more to this job than there was to running Jackson County and not any more worry."

But crisis management at the White House proved to be far tougher than in Jackson County. As Christmas neared, Truman finally climbed into his plane, the *Sacred Cow*, and, in weather that grounded all commercial airliners, managed to get home for the holiday. "So you've finally arrived," Bess said. "I guess you couldn't think of any more reasons to stay away. As far as I'm concerned, you might as well have stayed in Washington." When he got back to the White House, Truman retorted in a scorching letter, special delivery. He thought about it during the night, and the next morning he called Margaret in Missouri and asked her to intercept the letter at the post office and burn it in the wire bin in the backyard.

Bess Wallace had known Harry Truman since childhood. "I had only one sweetheart from the time I was six," Truman said. Yet they didn't marry until he was thirty-five and she was thirty-four. They had one child, Margaret, and lived with Bess's mother in Bess's childhood home, a three-story, seventeen-room post–Civil War house at 219 North Delaware Street in Independence. It would always be home. Over the years, the house was outfitted with electricity and other modern conveniences, but otherwise changed little—except for the fence erected by the Secret Service to keep the souvenir hunters and voyeurs at a distance when Truman became president.

Before her husband took office, Bess was so little known that she could wander about Washington department stores doing her Christmas shopping without being bothered. She did not want to be recognized. Now she was first lady, and among other things, she feared increased scrutiny—the press might discover the story of her father's suicide and spread it across the front pages. It was a part of her family history that wasn't talked about. David Wallace, depressed over financial problems, had gone into the bathroom and shot himself when Bess was nineteen. Both she and her mother were devastated, and frightened at the thought of it becoming public. Bess also worried

*Truman, an admitted "architectural nut," disliked the sight of the dirty awnings on the South Portico and thought they "put the beautiful white columns out of proportion." The Commission of Fine Arts objected to a balcony. Truman said, "The hell with them. I'm going to do it anyway."* (LIBRARY OF CONGRESS)

about following Eleanor Roosevelt as first lady. Eleanor had revolutionized the role, and had been doing so for twelve years. "The country was used to Eleanor Roosevelt," Bess said. "I couldn't possibly be anything like her. I wasn't going down into any coal mines."

As soon as Bess became first lady, Eleanor offered to help her hold a press conference. Bess agreed, but then backed down. She never did hold a press conference. The women reporters who had thrived on reporting Eleanor's whirlwind activities now had no news. "I'm not the one elected. I have nothing to say to the public," she told them. They persisted. Bess consented to written questions. Asked in one what she was going to wear to tea that afternoon, she said to her secretary, Reathal Odum, "Tell 'em it's none of their damn business." Odum's more diplomatic answer was, "Mrs. Truman hasn't quite made up her mind yet."

Five foot four and stout, she continued to dress as she always had, in simple, matronly styles. She liked shoulder pads and square hats. *Time* magazine wrote that she would fit in perfectly well with the shoppers at the A&P. Her husband said she looked "exactly as a woman her age should look."

She kept up her interests. As a child she had been athletic—good at third base and the shot put—and as first lady she attended the Washington Senators' home baseball games whenever she had the chance and listened to their games on the radio. She drove her big Chrysler to shops and her bridge club until the Secret Service finally convinced her to stop.

Her first public appearance as first lady was an embarrassment. She tried to smash an unscored champagne bottle against a navy hospital plane at a dedication ceremony, and it wouldn't break. She swung and swung, and people laughed at the newsreels. Early on she also unwittingly became involved in an imbroglio with a black congressman from New York, Adam Clayton Powell. Quite casually Bess had accepted an invitation to tea from the Daughters of the American Revolution. African Americans were still barred from the DAR's Constitution Hall in Washington, and Powell verbally attacked the first lady. Bess regretted the situation, saying, "My acceptance of the hospitality is not related to the merits of the issue which has arisen." Now her stubborn streak showed, and she refused to withdraw her acceptance, as Powell demanded. "I was plenty burned up with the wire I had from that——in N.Y.," she wrote. Privately, Truman regretted his wife's decision.

The first lady's enthusiasm for White House life was not helped by the condition of her new living quarters. Daughter Margaret said her mother found them "far below the level of the furnished apartments" she had lived in during her years in Washington. Eleanor Roosevelt had not been much interested in furnishings or decor, and when the mansion was cleared of the clutter the Roosevelts liked, its deficiencies became glaring. Tracks were worn in the carpets around the pieces of furniture that had been there, and clean spots where picture frames had been showed just how dirty the walls were. When Chief Usher J. B. West first showed Bess around, even he was embarrassed. He said the place looked like an "abandoned hotel."

Margaret, twenty-one when her father took office, was more blunt. "The White House upstairs is a mess and looks awful. I was depressed when I saw it. The furniture is so old." She said "grubby" was the overall word that came to mind. She found the downstairs in better shape, but when she had a luncheon for a friend, she found the State Dining Room "freezing cold." And she discovered that the antique elevator "would only go down if you took the button off, stuck a pencil in the hole and gave it a twist." The president got stranded between floors and had to ring the gong that served as alarm. He finally got someone's attention, and then had to wait while workmen tinkered with the machinery.

Eleanor Roosevelt had warned Truman that the house was infested with rats. "[She] said that she was giving three high-hat women a luncheon on the south portico when a rat ran across the porch railing," the president wrote home to his mother. "She said each of them saw the rat but kept pretending that she didn't. But they all finally confessed that they'd seen it."

On top of it all, in the beginning Bess and Harry could not even sit down to a good stiff drink. The Trumans liked old-fashioneds, but not the White House variety. "They make the worst old-fashioneds here I've ever tasted," Bess complained. She kept asking for them a little drier. Finally, butler Alonzo Fields put two big splashes of bourbon and some ice in a chilled glass and left off the rest. The Trumans were at last pleased. "Now that's the way we like our old-fashioneds," Bess said. The Trumans complained about the coffee as well. Fields noticed that Bess always took some coffee in a spoon and looked at it before drinking. He began watching her closely, until he discovered the color that pleased her, and then matched it each day. His results pleased the Trumans so much that they sent him aboard the presidential yacht to instruct the crew in brewing coffee.

Many other White House inconveniences were less easily addressed. There were hardly any built-in closets when the Trumans arrived—the household was still dependent on wardrobes. Truman gave Eleanor Roosevelt a tour of the White House after the 1948 renovation, and she commented that having closets was "a great help"—her maid had constantly made trips to the third floor for clothing. The house was drafty, even after the renovation. Bess said that a northwest wind would come "whistling down the fireplace in the corner of my bedroom. To protect myself from the chilly blast, I had a bridge table leaning against the fireplace." During the night it fell over, and she woke the president to investigate the cause of the noise.

The first lady gradually overcame some of her initial frustrations and started spending more time in Washington, dealing with her mail, greeting visitors, and attending teas. She fixed up the living quarters, only to move to Blair House while the White House was renovated. By the time they returned to the White House three years later, she knew her husband would not run again. "I am only going to be around for a year," she said. "It would be unfair to the next first lady to impose too many of my ideas on the house." She had the B. Altman department store decorate with showroom reproductions.

Still, the first lady continued to spend a great deal of time in Independence, which left Truman alone a lot. His diary for New Year's in 1947 reads, "Never so lonesome in my life." But he was always glad to see Bess when she returned. After a summer away, a joyful president met her at the train station. The next morning Bess called in the White House usher.

"Mr. West, we have a little problem," she said.

"Yes." He waited.

Bess cleared her throat. "It's the President's bed. Do you think you can get it fixed today?"

"Why certainly," West assured her and asked what the problem was.

"Two of the slats broke during the night."

"I'll see that it has all new slats put in," West said.

Truman's devotion to Bess never wavered. "I saw her in Sunday school at the Presbyterian Church in Independence, when my mother took me there," Truman recalled in his diary on June 5, 1952. "She sat behind me in sixth, seventh, and high school grades, and I thought she was the most beautiful and the sweetest person on earth—and I am still of that opinion after twenty-six years of being married to her. I am old-fashioned, I guess." At the end of a postwar conference at Potsdam, Germany, with Churchill and Stalin, an army officer asked for a ride. Truman's driver overheard the young officer offer to get Truman "Anything, you know, like women." "Listen, son," Truman said, "I married my sweetheart. She doesn't run around on me, and I don't run around on her. I want that understood. Don't you ever mention that kind of thing to me again."

All during Truman's years as a senator, Bess had been his partner, his paid office assistant, and his adviser. She was a better judge of people than he. She also helped him write his speeches and make critical decisions. After a break during his vice presidency, she resumed this role in the White House. In the evening they would go into his study to work together. They didn't always agree, but Bess supported his decisions and didn't nag at him.

She was invaluable when his hair-trigger anger got him into trouble. When an ambassador canceled out on a diplomatic dinner at the last minute, Truman exploded, saying to Undersecretary of State Dean Acheson, "I wish to have that ambassador recalled at once." Acheson was trying to calm him down when a phone call from Bess interrupted them. She tried to calm her husband. Then she asked to speak with Acheson. Truman gave him the phone. "You must not let Harry do what he's going to do," Bess told Acheson. "Perhaps you can help me, Mrs. Truman," he said. As she remained silent, Acheson repeated for Truman's benefit: "The press will eat you up . . . you're acting too big for your britches . . . you don't need that kind of criticism right now." Truman took the phone back: "Well, if you two gang up on me, I'm just lost." The ambassador kept his job.

Truman was also impulsive, and when Bess wasn't around to reign him in, he would often regret it. Once, he impetuously directed the pilot of his presidential plane, a military DC-6 called the *Sacred Cow*, to buzz the White House while Bess and Margaret were on the roof. Pandemonium erupted among the security forces. The Secret Service was unaware that the president had left the White House and boarded his plane. Washington police, Air Force security units, and the Secret Service all scrambled, thinking that a maniac had commandeered the plane.

Bess accompanied her husband on his famous whistle-stop campaign in 1948. At the end of each stop he would introduce her as "The Boss," which delighted the crowd. Once he did it, and Bess—who could appear downright formidable with her square shoulders and no-nonsense stride—was picked up on a mike as she said, "You better believe that one."

We know so much about Truman's White House life because when Bess was away, he wrote to her faithfully—once, twenty-two letters in a month. Harry once found Bess burning his letters to her.

"You shouldn't be doing that," he said.

"Why not?" Bess wanted to know. "I've read them several times."

"But think of history," Harry argued.

"I have," Bess concluded.

But many of his letters survived, and they paint a vivid picture of the president's life at the White House. Here's how Truman described a lonely dinner at Blair House to "the madam," back in Independence:

> Had dinner by myself tonight. . . . A butler came in very formally and said, "Mr. President, dinner is served." . . . Barnett in tails and white tie pulls out my chair, pushes me up to the table. John in tails and white tie brings me a fruit cup, Barnett takes away the empty cup. John brings me a plate, Barnett brings me a tenderloin, John brings me asparagus, Barnett brings me carrots and beets. I have to eat alone and in silence in a candlelit room. I ring. Barnett takes the plates and the butter plates. John comes in with a napkin and silver crumb tray—there are no crumbs but John has to brush them off the table anyway. Barnett brings me a plate with a finger bowl and doily and John puts a glass saucer and a little bowl on the plate. Barnett brings me some chocolate custard. John brings me a demitasse (at home a little cup of coffee—about two good gulps) and my dinner is over. I take a hand bath in the finger bowl and go back to work. What a life!

The mansion was full of creaks and moans, and Truman said that when he was all alone at night on the second floor—no Secret Service agents or servants around—he heard ghosts. They "walk up and down the hallway, and even right into my study," he wrote Bess. "Night before last I went to bed at nine o'clock after shutting my doors. At four o'clock I was awakened by three distinct knocks on my bedroom. I jumped up and put on my bathrobe, opened the door, and no one there. Went out and looked up and down the hall, looked into your room and Margie's. Still no one. Went back to bed after locking the doors and there were footsteps in your room whose door I'd left open. Jumped up, and looked and no one there! Damn place is haunted sure as shootin'." Nevertheless, he once said, "I have no trouble sleeping. I read myself to sleep every night in the White House, reading biography or the troubles of some President in the past." The mansion's many clocks also emitted strange noises. Truman complained that the grandfather's clock in the upstairs hall had a high, squeaky voice "like fat tenors," and "the ship's clock in Mrs. Wallace's room bangs away in that crazy sailor count of bells."

Despite his grumbling, the president coped quite well. He wrote to Bess, "You know I have a valet, four ushers, five butlers, seven or eight secretaries, a dozen or so executive assistants, an assistant president—three of 'em in fact—and I can't open a door, get my hat, pull out my chair at the table, hang up my coat or do anything else for myself—even take a bath! I won't be worth a damn when I come out of here—if I ever do." He liked to do things for himself. His valet recalled finding him washing out his socks and underwear. Alone at night and awakened by a thunderstorm, he got up and, in his striped pajamas, went through the rooms checking the windows. He found water pouring in so he got some towels and went from room to room mopping up until an usher saw the lights and came to relieve him. Truman was accustomed to going to the bank to make regular payments on a loan, and initially continued to do so. On the due date, he called for his car and headed for Hamilton National Bank in the downtown district. It was the noon hour, and the streets were crowded. By the time Truman came out of the bank, smiling and waving but acutely embarrassed, traffic was backed up in four directions to catch a glimpse of the president.

The transition to the presidency was also difficult for twenty-one-year-old Margaret, who graduated from Georgetown University in 1945 and would spend a good deal of time at the White House, as well as with Bess in Independence. "Consider the effect of saying good night to a boy at the door of the White House in a blaze of floodlights, with a Secret Service man in attendance," she said. She was getting ready to go out on a date the night Roosevelt died. Her father had phoned with the news, her mother was crying, and the apartment doorbell rang. In her confusion, Margaret, who had been changing clothes, opened the door in her slip, only to find a woman who greeted her, "I'm from the Associated Press." Margaret slammed the door. Later she recalled the incident and said, "When I opened the door in my slip to that press girl, it was the last time I ever opened a door without finding out who was there. It was at that moment I ceased to be a free agent."

One day she went downtown to do some shopping for her mother and found she needed to call the White House. "I realized I didn't know my own phone number," she recalled. "It wasn't a phone number you just look up and I felt embarrassed to ask an operator for it, so I went home and found out what it was." But living in the White House had its benefits. She once invited two girlfriends from school over for a slumber party in the big Lincoln Bed. "I'm sure this was the only slumber party held in the Lincoln bed," she said, even though Theodore Roosevelt's children had beaten her to it. She found it "an overpowering old bed," the big, carved headboard dark and gloomy, and the mattress uncomfortable: "I'm here to tell you—lumpy." She and her friends giggled and talked more than they slept, anyway.

Margaret hoped to become a professional singer, and her father encouraged her. He himself had taken piano lessons at age thirteen and loved Chopin and Mozart. When the *Washington Post* music critic Paul Hume panned her—"She is flat a good deal of the time"—Truman's temper erupted and got him into another brouhaha. He wrote a scorching, 150-word letter to Hume, sealed it, addressed the envelope, and put on a three-cent stamp himself. He knew that if Bess or his press secretary, Charlie Ross, learned of it, they would never allow him to send it. He asked a White House messenger if, seeing that it was a pleasant day, he would like to take a stroll, and if, while strolling, he could drop a letter in a mailbox. Hume didn't reply, but the letter appeared on page one of the *Washington News*. Truman had called the thirty-four-year-old Hume "a frustrated old man" and told him that he hoped to meet him someday: "You'll need a new nose, a lot of beefsteak for black eyes, and perhaps a supporter below." Most of the country was outraged by the letter, and at first Margaret wouldn't even believe her father wrote it. It was the last thing she needed.

When they were all together at the White House, the Trumans did things as a family. Breakfast was at eight, and the president expected his wife and daughter there on time. In good weather, lunch was often on the south portico. Truman liked to feed the squirrels and crumbled crackers for them, but only after the meal was finished and Bess had gone—she didn't like the idea of squirrels crawling around under the table. Dinner was in the family dining room on the main floor. The waiters once made the mistake of serving watermelon for dessert. Margaret, Bess, and Harry started flipping watermelon seeds at each other, and even the waiters got bombarded.

Bess's mother, Madge Gates Wallace, lived at the White House off and on and had her own room there. Although they had all lived under the same roof in Independence for many years, Mrs. Wallace never did call her son-in-law anything less formal than "Mr. Truman." She never thought much of the Truman family. The Wallaces were among the elite of Independence; the Trumans were dirt farmers. At one White House dinner, Mrs. Wallace mentioned that Bess had married someone beneath her. And when Truman relieved General Douglas MacArthur from command in Korea, his mother-in-law asked Bess, "Why did your husband have to fire that nice man?"

Truman's mother, Martha, visited her son in the White House before her death in 1947. Born before the Civil War, her Missouri family had suffered at the hands of the Union forces. "Tonight, Mother," Truman teased, "we are going to give you a special treat, a chance to sleep in the famous room in the White House where Abraham Lincoln slept." After a pregnant silence, Martha turned to her daughter-in-law and announced: "Bess, if you will get my bags packed, I'll be going home this evening." She was given the bed in the Queen's Bedroom but found it too high and fussy, so she used a small one in the sitting room. She didn't care for Secret Service protection—"It isn't neighborly"— and thought the press and the photographers a nuisance. "Oh, fiddlesticks," she said. "If you're the President, Harry, why can't you shoo all these people away?" But she did consent to an interview. The Trumans were farm people, and her son had run a farm for eleven years. "Harry can milk with both hands," she proudly told the reporters.

The Trumans inherited Eleanor Roosevelt's formidable housekeeper, Henrietta Nesbitt. When the Trumans wanted hot biscuits, they were served dinner rolls. Alonzo Fields, the head butler, went to Mrs. Nesbitt and told her the Trumans had complained. "Hot bread doesn't mean warmed over bakery bread," he told her. But Mrs. Nesbitt was not one to change. She fended off Bess's criticisms by telling her, "Mrs.

Roosevelt never did things that way." Margaret was incensed. She said Mrs. Nesbitt served "hotel kitchen food" and "her attitude toward the Trumans was openly condescending." When Mrs. Nesbitt served brussels sprouts, Truman pushed them aside and made a face. Bess was away, so Margaret told Mrs. Nesbitt that the president disliked brussels sprouts and she should not serve them again. That didn't bother Mrs. Nesbitt. She served them again the next night. Again Margaret told her not to. "The next night we got them again!" she recalled. Margaret called her mother and threatened to leave the White House if Mrs. Nesbitt did not. Bess hesitated, recognizing the consequences of forcing out a disgruntled employee. But the last straw came when Bess tried to get Mrs. Nesbitt to give her a stick of butter to take to one of her women's meetings, and Mrs. Nesbitt refused, citing the need to save the White House supply, as it was wartime, and butter was rationed. Bess spoke to Chief Usher Howell Crim about the incident. He was shocked. Bess said that maybe it was time to get a new housekeeper. Shortly thereafter Mrs. Nesbitt retired to write a book about her White House experiences.

Truman had been told horror stories about Mrs. Nesbitt by the Roosevelt children on the way back from FDR's funeral at Hyde Park, but he didn't seemed to be bothered by her. He ate moderately. He was five feet seven and weighed 185 pounds at the beginning of his presidency, and 175 pounds at its end. "I eat no bread but one piece of toast, no butter, no sugar, no sweets," he said. "Usually have fruit, one egg, a strip of bacon and a half a glass of skimmed milk for breakfast; liver and bacon or sweetbreads or ham or fish and spinach and another nonfattening vegetable for lunch with fruit for dessert. For dinner I have a fruit cup, steak, a couple of nonfattening vegetables and an ice, orange, pineapple, or raspberry . . . So I maintain my waist line and can wear suits bought in 1935!"

Even the Roosevelts tried to cut the food and other bills. "Mrs. Truman was very conscious of economy in housekeeping," White House usher J. B. West recalled. "She kept her own books, went over the bills with a fine-tooth comb, and wrote every check herself." She even questioned West about a 25-cent item for dried ice. "How in the world could we have used so many dozens of eggs?" she asked. Unlike his wealthy predecessor, who could and did draw on family funds, Truman had only his salary as president. To cut costs, he "borrowed" Filipino kitchen workers from the navy—the navy paid their salaries. The presidential salary of $75,000 hadn't been increased since the time of Taft, and now almost half went to income taxes. Truman's finances improved during his second term, when Congress raised the president's salary to $100,000 and added a tax-free $50,000 expense account.

But even during his budget-conscious first term, Truman made doing away with a White House eyesore a priority. A self-described "architectural nut," he was offended by the unsightly appearance of the awnings affixed to the white columns of the south portico. They looked dirty and out of place and, he complained, "put the beautiful columns out of proportion." Soon after he took office, he did some investigating and found that he could replace the awnings with a balcony for $15,000—an amount he could get from available funds without having to go to Congress. He asked noted architect William Delano to design the balcony. However, Gilmore Clark, chairman of the White House Commission of Fine Arts, said the president could not make such a change to the historic building without the commission's approval. "The hell with them;

I'm going to do it anyway," Truman said. "All changes in the White House since Fillmore's time have faced resistance—like gaslights and cooking stoves. Mrs. Fillmore put in the first bathtubs and she was almost lynched for doing it." Truman got his balcony, but in the end the family used it very little because it was too public. They went back to eating underneath it on the south portico. Years later Truman had the satisfaction of hearing praise for his balcony, especially from first families who enjoyed the balcony despite its prominence. The Treasury Department was less enthusiastic. It had to redesign the twenty-dollar bill, which depicts the White House.

The issue of the balcony was dwarfed by the discovery that the White House was literally collapsing. There were plenty of signs that the house was in trouble. Truman noticed the big East Room chandelier swinging as the color guard marched across the floor, and he felt the floor shake when the "big fat butler brought me my breakfast." When Margaret's grand piano was hoisted up through a second-floor window into her sitting room, one of its legs sunk into the floor. In a letter to his mother Truman wrote that Chief Usher Crim and Secret Service agent Jim Rowley had informed him in the middle of an event in the East Room that the chain holding up the center chandelier was stretching. He said it made him "somewhat nervous," but "I let the show go on and ordered the thing down the next day. If it had fallen, I'd been in a real fix." When Truman's bathroom floor started to sink while he was in the tub, he had visions of himself ending up in the midst of a reception of Bess's ladies below, and he took action.

In the spring of 1948 he ordered a thorough investigation, which showed that the White House was on the verge of falling down. Truman got the news when he returned from a trip and was told that the safest place in the White House was his new balcony. "Doesn't that beat all," he commented. Steps were taken immediately. "The White House architect and engineer have moved me into the southeast or Lincoln Room—for safety—imagine that!" Truman wrote to Bess. A massive reconstruction effort began in late 1948, and the Trumans moved across the street to Blair House, where they were forced to stay for nearly four years.

Truman had not wanted to reveal the White House's structural problem to the public before his 1948 reelection campaign. As daughter Margaret wrote, "The whole mess would have been blamed on Harry Truman." And that, he did not need. A week before he hit the campaign trail, Elmo Roper of the famous Roper Poll announced that his organization would stop sampling voters. "My whole inclination is to predict the election of Thomas E. Dewey by a heavy margin and devote my time and effort to other things," Roper said. No reporter, columnist, radio commentator, or expert predicted a Truman victory. The only one who called it right was Harry himself.

Truman set off on his campaign trip on September 17, 1948, in a seventeen-car private train with the presidential car *Ferdinand Magellan* attached to the rear. A pilot locomotive with one car raced ahead to "absorb" any explosive devices that might be on the tracks, and all switches ahead were spiked to prevent sabotage. Crowds were large right from the beginning. Truman's prepared speeches before large audiences tended to be given in flat tones. But in his stump speeches from the rear platform of the train, he was at his combative best. Someone from the crowd would yell, "Give 'em hell, Harry!" After the campaign Truman said, "I never gave anybody hell. I just told the truth and they thought it was hell."

On election night a crowd gathered in front of the Wallace home in Independence,

*When the engineers told Truman the White House could collapse at any time, he moved out to Blair House and the building was gutted. But when they asked Truman's permission to break through a wall to get a bulldozer inside, Truman refused. The bulldozer was disassembled and then re-assembled inside.* (**WHITE HOUSE HISTORICAL ASSOCIATION**)

but the president was not there. Margaret came out on the porch of her home and told the crowd and waiting reporters, "Dad isn't here. I don't know where he is." He had slipped out the back door, and Secret Service agents had driven him to a hotel in the little town of Excelsior Springs. Truman had not packed a bag, and he borrowed a bathrobe and slippers from the hotel manager when he went to the steam room. He went to bed around nine and told the Secret Service to wake him if anything important happened. Meanwhile James Maloney, head of the Secret Service detail, was supervising a crew in New York that was guarding the man they were sure would be the next president, Thomas Dewey. Around midnight Truman awoke, switched on the radio, and heard the distinctive voice of H. V. Kaltenborn, the famous radio commentator, say that Truman was ahead by 1,200,000 in the popular vote but was "undoubtedly beaten." At about 4 A.M. the agents woke Truman, saying, "We've won!" His victory and modest manner made him a folk hero.

Though living at Blair House for most of his second term, the president still went to work in the White House's West Wing—already modernized and expanded during the Roosevelt administration. He walked across busy Pennsylvania Avenue, stopping traffic, four times a day—in the morning, going to and from lunch, and returning home in the evening. Truman complained that he was having trouble with "the boys in the

Secret Service; they wanted to drive me from Blair House to the White House in one of those damn limousines. Can you imagine being *driven* across the street?" Once, however, he was nearly run down by a driver who was not expecting to be stopped in the middle of the block. The driver screeched to a stop, saw the president, and pressed both hands to his head. Truman and his Secret Service agents walked right on.

Truman finally yielded to be being driven across the street after two Puerto Rican men tried to shoot their way into Blair House and assassinate him on November 1, 1950. The would be assassins, Oscar Collazo and Girsel Torresola, did not hate Truman—perhaps no other president has been so favorably disposed toward Puerto Rico, and he was well liked there. But Torresola and Collazo were part of an independence movement that wanted to make a statement, and they were willing to die to do it. They were hardly seasoned killers. They actually had to have a taxi driver point out Blair House. If they'd read the papers, they would have learned there was no need to force their way in—Truman was scheduled for a speech at Arlington Cemetery, Virginia, that afternoon and in a short while would have walked right out.

It was an exceptionally warm day in Washington, and the front door of Blair House was open, with only a locked screen door blocking the way. The Secret Service agents, posted outside and in, wanted to at least rope off the area in front of the house, but Truman demurred. "Nobody wants to shoot me," he said. The president was taking his afternoon nap in his undershorts when, at 2:19, the shots erupted on his front steps. The assassins never made it through the door. Torresola was killed and Collazo was wounded, but in stopping them Private Leslie Coffelt of the White House police force was killed, and Private Donald Birdzell was wounded. Truman awoke at the sound of the shots and stuck his head out the bedroom window to see what was happening. The guards had to yell at him, "Get back! Get back!"

Truman kept his afternoon speaking engagement, and the next day told reporters, "A President has to expect these things." Truman's courage was undeniable—he had risked his life many times with Battery D in World War I. But he did not want to risk the lives of others. Coffelt's death and Birdzell's injury affected him keenly. He was always concerned about the people around him, talking to them, asking about their families. "He would treat us almost like sons. He talked nearly the whole time as we walked," said Rex Scouten, then a Secret Service agent and later chief usher and then curator at the White House.

The president began taking the limousine across the street to his office. "Since the assault on the police and the Secret Service," he wrote to Bess, "I ride across the street in a car the roof of which will turn a grenade, the windows and sides will turn a bullet and the floor will stop a land mine! Behind me in an open car ride six or seven men with automatics and machine guns. The uniformed police stop traffic in every direction— and I cross the street in state and wonder why anyone would want to live like that." His morning walks on the streets of Washington were over. The Secret Service drove him to secure outlying locations for his walks.

Truman enjoyed walking. As an adult it was his main form of exercise, for he had never played sports. When he was five in Lamar, Missouri, where he was born in 1884, his mother noticed he ignored the Fourth of July fireworks bursting in the sky. The next day he got quarter-inch thick glasses, and his world became very different—he could see it now, but he had to be very careful in it. The doctor warned him to avoid "rough and tumble play" with friends, or his eyes might get "knocked out." Once, after he left office, he was accused of knocking a bystander on the head with a golf ball. "I never played golf in my life," he answered, "never had a golf club in my hands." He was forty before he learned to swim, but as president he used the indoor pool that had been put in for Franklin Roosevelt. He called it his "swimming hole." He did a choppy, unorthodox side-stroke, keeping his head out of the water so his glasses would stay dry. He also had a horseshoe pit installed on the south grounds. But mainly he walked. Each morning he got up at five-thirty, dressed—he was a natty dresser with tailored suits, sharply creased pants, and neatly folded handkerchiefs in his pocket—and by six he was charging through two miles at 120 paces to the minute. The Secret Service agents had to scurry to keep up.

Truman loved being around people, and his pre-assassination-attempt walks gave him a chance to mix. Heading down K Street in Washington, he tipped his hat to passersby and occasionally joined a line of people waiting for a bus. Some looked up from their papers, some didn't. He would give them a pleasant "good morning" and move on. One morning he started across Memorial Bridge. Near the middle he saw a door and iron steps. On impulse he decided to investigate and came upon Charles Barnhill, the bridge tender, who was about to eat his meal. He was not at all surprised to see the president of the United States. "You know, Mr. President," he said, "I was just thinking about you." Truman loved the story and enjoyed telling it.

It was Truman's friendly, down-to-earth ways that endeared him to so many people. Truman was often very open. Other presidents, including his predecessor, liked to play poker and drink, but the public didn't hear about it—reporters would not even have asked these questions. But Truman had a different public image. When he mentioned a poker game to reporters, they asked him what he'd had to drink. "Kentucky bourbon," he answered. He was known for his swearing, but other presidents swore more egregiously and more often than Truman—just not in public.

Truman liked to take poker cruises with his friends on the presidential yacht *Williamsburg*. George Allen, a Truman intimate, said the president would start a game in the morning that would last until late at night. One of Truman's favorite poker stories involved chief justice of the Supreme Court Fred Vinson. The two old friends were contending for a pot that had risen to $3,000. Truman was dealing, and Vinson was ready to take the pot—he simply needed any card except an ace, king, or queen to win.

"OK, Mr. President, hit me," Vinson said.

The card was a queen. Vinson had lost.

"You son of a bitch," Vinson burst out. Amidst shocked silence Vinson stammered, "Oh, Mr. President, Mr. President . . ."

Truman loved it. He often got adviser Clark Clifford, who was present, to tell the story, "leaving nothing out."

When Winston Churchill, no longer prime minister, came to visit Truman in March 1946, they traveled together by train to Fulton, Missouri, where Churchill made his famous Iron Curtain speech. On the way they played poker.

"Mr. President, I think that when we are playing poker I will call you Harry," Churchill said.

"All right, Winston," Truman replied.

In March 1952 the first family finally returned to a much safer White House for Truman's last year in office. The receptions were huge. The official guest list was up to two

*Truman celebrated this birthday at Blair House where he spent almost four years of his presidency. He called this picture "Just one more," because the White House photographer, as usual, wanted just one more picture.* (TRUMAN LIBRARY)

thousand, forcing two sessions to be planned for each event. Bess, speaking of an especially busy period of entertaining in the spring of 1952, wrote Margaret, "These two weeks are really going to be a handshaking two weeks—conservative estimate forty-one hundred." Her arm was "a wreck" afterward, and her glove size went from six to six and a half. Truman had to show her how to grasp a hand without getting hurt.

Truman thought about running again in 1952. The term-limit amendment just passed by Congress exempted him, and legally he could have. But the political trials of his second term—accusations of cronyism and the country's rocky adjustment to a peacetime economy, including strikes and inflation—had eroded his popularity to one of the lowest for a departing president. Bess was also influential in persuading him to retire. She wanted to go home.

Truman respected General Dwight D. Eisenhower, who he appointed supreme commander of the North Atlantic Treaty Organization forces in 1950, and had wanted him to run for president as a Democrat. But Eisenhower ultimately declared himself a Republican, and the relationship became strained. "He'll sit right here and he'll say,

'Do this! Do that!' And nothing will happen," Truman predicted after Eisenhower was elected. "Poor Ike—it won't be a bit like the Army. He'll find it very frustrating."

As the inauguration approached, the Republican committee informed Truman that on his way to the ceremony he should pick up Eisenhower at the Statler Hotel. Truman was outraged. He felt propriety dictated that the incoming president call at the White House. "If he doesn't pick me up, then we'll go in separate cars," Truman said. Eisenhower agreed to pick him up, even though he said he didn't know if he could manage to "sit next to that guy." Then there was a crisis over hats. Eisenhower unilaterally announced a change in the traditional inaugural attire: he would wear a homburg, not a top hat. Truman was angry at the treatment but gave in, saying that he didn't want his last fight to be over a hat. On the day of his inauguration, Ike was driven to the White House, but he refused to go in. Truman at first refused to go out unless Eisenhower had the courtesy to call on him. Bess broke the impasse by calming her husband down and convincing him they should get the ceremony over with. It was a chilly ride to the Capitol.

During his last weeks in office, Truman had been forced to take out a loan to tide him over. At this time ex-presidents received no Social Security, no pension, no Secret Service protection, and no secretarial help, as they do now. Truman had only his army pension of $112.66 a month—and he continued to receive thousands of letters. He refused a variety of lucrative offers, as he felt they would demean the presidency. He had to be persuaded that writing his memoirs was acceptable. *Years of Decisions,* published in 1955, and *Years of Trial and Hope,* published in 1956, brought him substantial sums. He and Bess returned to Independence and the white Victorian house that had always been their home. He worked on his writing and on setting up the Truman Library. He said, "I wasn't one of the great presidents but I had a good time trying to become one, I can tell you that."

As the years passed, and the White House seemed engulfed in political doublespeak, Truman was remembered not for his shortcomings but for his blunt, no-nonsense manner. His popularity and reputation greatly increased, until many historians were calling him one of the greatest U.S. presidents. By the time he died on December 20, 1972, his estate was valued at $600,000. He was buried in the courtyard of his library in Independence. Bess died at ninety-seven on October 18, 1982, having lived longer than any other first lady.

# 34

# Dwight D. Eisenhower
## 1953–1961

## *TV Dinners*

BY THE TIME General Dwight Eisenhower reached the White House in 1953, he and his wife, Mamie, had averaged a move a year thanks to his long and varied military career. "Ike" was sixty-two, Mamie, fifty-six, and it would be the first time they were together in one place for any extended period. "At last I have a job where I can stay home nights, and, by golly, I'm going to stay home," Ike said. For Mamie, it was a dream come true. "I've got my man right here, where I want him," she said.

The move into the White House was not a particularly smooth one, however. Eisenhower and his predecessor, Democrat Harry Truman, were not on good terms. When Ike decided to run as a Republican, Truman campaigned for his Democrat opponent, Adlai Stevenson. Hurtful things were said on both sides, and General Eisenhower was not accustomed to criticism. As soon as he took over the White House, he removed all reminders of Truman, even hanging a picture over a marble plaque commemorating Truman's massive renovation of the White House. He also dismissed all the Secret Service agents who had been close to Truman.

On the night of his inauguration, there were twin inaugural balls. Mamie spent three of her first hours in the White House getting ready for the evening. She wore a gown with two thousand pink rhinestones, plus pink gloves and pink high heels. She carried a pink purse encrusted with 3,450 pink pearls and beads. Ike, on the other hand, had his dinner undressed and then yelled, "Hey, Mamie, where the hell is my monkey suit!" His evening attire—tails, boiled shirt, and white tie—was nowhere to be seen, and a search of the closets and luggage did not uncover it. Ike sat on the bed in his undershorts while the Secret Service pursued the matter. Ike growled that he was already facing the first crisis of his administration. Finally his valet, Sergeant John Moaney, and a Secret Service agent found the bag. It had been left behind at the train station.

Because of his aversion to Truman, Ike had yet to tour the White House and didn't know his way around. The next day, he got up at 7 A.M. as usual and went downstairs with Secret Service agent Rufus Youngblood. "Would you show me where my office is?" Eisenhower asked. "I want to get an early start." He was led to the west wing. After viewing the Oval Office, he pointed to another door.

"What's in there?"

"That's the Cabinet Room, sir," Youngblood told him.

"What's the room across the hall?" Ike then asked.

"That's the Fish Room," said Youngblood (it is now the Roosevelt Room), who later wrote that he was beginning to feel like a White House tour guide.

Ike walked over and opened the door. The Fish Room was full of women, who stared at him. He quickly closed the door.

"Who the devil are all those women?" he demanded of Youngblood.

"That's your secretarial pool, sir," Youngblood explained. "I doubt that they expected to see you this early."

He was soon rising even earlier. The new president found that he had no trouble getting to sleep at 11 P.M., but after five hours he tended to wake up. "I find that when I have weighty matters on my mind I wake up extremely early," he said, "apparently because a rested mind is anxious to begin grappling with knotty questions." He also found that the White House kitchen was not prepared to serve such an early riser, so he brewed coffee for himself in an electric percolator in his bedroom. Later, when the kitchen staff was ready, he had his usual breakfast of four ounces of rare steak, orange juice, toast, and coffee. Eventually he had a small kitchen built in the second-floor family area. He had the counters installed higher than usual to suit his five-foot-eleven height—which would later be a problem for five-foot-tall Tricia Nixon.

Ike left his bedroom quietly each morning so he would not disturb Mamie, who sometimes stayed in bed all day. "I believe that every woman over fifty should stay in bed until noon," she said. Chief Usher Howell Crim and Assistant Chief Usher J. B. West were astonished to find the first lady in bed for their first meeting. "I'd like to make some changes right away," she informed them. West would later comment that Mamie "could give orders, staccato crisp, detailed and final, as if it were she who had been a five-star general." "First of all," Mamie said, "I'm not going to sleep in this little room. This is a dressing room and I want to make it into *my* dressing room. The big room will be *our* bedroom." The bedroom question was always a delicate one for the White House staff—one bed or two. Franklin and Eleanor Roosevelt had separate rooms, and Bess Truman had preferred to put the marital bed in the dressing room and to use the big bedroom for other purposes. Mamie needed the space—she ordered a king-size bed shipped in. The morning after it arrived, she said, "I've just had the first good sleep I've had since we've been in the White House. And now," she said, "I can reach over and pat Ike on his old bald head anytime I want to."

One night her pattings left their mark. Mamie had a cold and mistook an ink bottle for a jar of Vicks in the middle of the night. Her nose was stopped up, and she didn't want to wake Ike, so she didn't turn on the light. She applied the ink to her nostrils. "It seemed to just get drier, instead of moister, so I kept applying more and more," she said. In the morning she found that she was "black and blue all over—and the President, too."

The White House staff restored the room to its proper color: pink. Mamie decorated the presidential bedroom in pink from the pincushioned headboard to the sheets, from the bedcovers to the slip-covered upholstery. All of which went with her pink satin breakfast jacket, her pink nightgown, the pink bow in her hair (done with bangs, which she refused to give up), and the monogrammed pink wastebasket. When she joined Ike at the Denver hospital where he was recovering from a heart attack in 1955, she lived in a suite adjoining his and had a pink toilet seat flown out to her. "Mamie pink" became a signature color of the 1950s.

Ike met Mamie Doud while stationed in Fort Sam Houston in Texas in 1916, and they married on July 1 of that year, the same day Ike was made first lieutenant. Ike had been graduated from West Point the year before. Mamie was just nineteen and came from a wealthy Colorado family; she even had her own maid. When she married, her father helped out by giving her $100 a month, but she still had to adjust to army quarters—two small, insect-infested rooms, gas lighting, a two-burner range, and no electricity. Ike's young wife knew how to make mayonnaise and fudge and little else. "I was never permitted in the kitchen when I was a young girl," she said. Ike did the cooking and let out her dresses when she became pregnant.

Mamie never did learn to cook. Still, she was every bit the housewife—the "best career that life has to offer a woman," she said—and at the White House her concerns were almost entirely domestic. She once said to a White House reporter, "I never knew what a woman would want to be liberated from." She let Ike run his shop, visiting the Oval Office just four times in eight years, and ran her side of the house determinedly. Early on Mamie noticed that much of the bed linen in the White House was patched and mended, and she told the maid in charge, Miss Walker, "Please see that the best linens are used all the time. I don't want to see mended linens again." In her second week as first lady she spotted a menu that Ike had approved for a luncheon for his male friends. "What's this?" Mamie demanded of one of the staff. "I didn't approve this menu!" The explanation didn't wash with her: "I run everything in my house. In the future all menus are to be approved by me and not by anybody else!"

Ike should have known better. Failing to touch base with his wife had gotten him into hot water before. When Truman appointed him supreme commander of the NATO forces in Europe, the French had offered Ike the former home of Marie Antoinette, the Villa Trianon, as a residence. Mamie made French headlines by vetoing the whole idea. Straight-backed Louis XIV chairs were not for her. Instead, the Eisenhowers accepted a two-story chateau where Mamie could have the sort of furniture she wanted and could call in the Army Corps of Engineers to redecorate to her taste.

For Mamie, running the White House meant keeping tabs on everything, even leftovers. "I don't want a morsel wasted around here," she told the housekeeper. In the morning she checked the previous night's leftovers, instructing, "Three people turned down second servings of Cornish hen last night. Please use it in the chicken salad

*Grandson David Eisenhower became quite familiar with the White House as a child. When he returned with his new in-laws, the Nixons, he showed them around parts of the private quarters that Eisenhower's Vice-President had never been privileged to visit.* (CORBIS)

today." She read the food advertisements in the local papers, and when there was a special on something she wanted, she had a staff member go out and get it. And when White House staff used the swimming pool, she complained, "Do you know that all these people come over here and swim and they use my towels, and I have to pay for having them laundered out of my allowance." She lost her temper if there were footprints on "my rug"—referring to the state room carpets—when guests were expected. Nobody could walk across the rug once it was vacuumed. Heidi, Ike's weimaraner, once left more than paw prints on the Aubusson rug in the Diplomatic Reception Room. The costly rug was custom-woven, with the state seals on the borders. Mamie was so distressed that she got down on her hands and knees along with the housekeeper to try to get the stain out. Ike heard more about it than he wanted to hear, and finally said, "Mamie, I've got a few other things more important than that to worry about."

The president did find the elevator important enough to worry about. Doorman Preston Bruce always escorted Ike to and from the elevator and ran it for him. When Bruce got to the second-floor living quarters, he would leave the elevator on hold so no one would call it to another floor while he went down the hall to get the president. But putting it on hold made it stick. Bruce reported the problem to the electricians, but it had not been fixed. So the next time he went down the hall to get Ike, he didn't put the elevator on hold, and while he was gone the elevator was called down. Bruce stood in the hall with an impatient president and waited for the slow-moving elevator to return. Ike started tapping his foot, and after five minutes he was boiling. The two watched the dial as it indicated the elevator was going to the basement. Ike was never a minute late—and he had an explosive temper. Bruce was told, "Tell Mr. West that if he can't get this elevator fixed, take the damn thing out and put in a new one." Mamie also encountered a problem with the elevator. Once she was waiting to use the elevator, and houseman George Thompson glided right by her on it. She was furious. "Never use my elevator again!" she told Thompson.

The Eisenhower household also included their only child John, his wife, Barbara, and their four children. The president's favorite grandson, David, called his grandmother "Mimi." The first time he saw the White House, he asked her, "Mimi, why did you build yourself such a big house?" Mamie's answer may have been somewhat confusing to a five-year-old: "This isn't my house. It belongs to Uncle Sam." By now, Secret Service protection had been expanded to presidents' families, which led agents into unusual duty. When Ike's granddaughter, Barbara Ann, was sent to an all-girls camp, two agents accompanied her. The men slept in tents, danced around the ritual fires, were privy to the secrets of the Tentling code, and joined in the sing-alongs. The campers were delighted, and one agent, Max Phillips, claimed it was "one of the finest times I've ever had."

Although pleased to have Ike with her under the same roof, Mamie also wanted a home of her own, in part for her grandchildren. For the first time in their lives, the Eisenhowers purchased a house, on a 190-acre farm near Gettysburg, Pennsylvania. The farmhouse proved to be beyond remodeling and had to be torn down and rebuilt. Mamie designed the new house with four guest bedrooms, eight bathrooms, and a separate room just for Ike's afternoon naps. It cost hundreds of thousands of dollars, but the president's wealthy friends helped him pay the bill.

Ike was never reluctant to accept gifts. As president he would not take cash, but he did accept some $300,000 worth of gifts for the Gettysburg farm, including prize cattle, a tractor, and a putting green. The house was furnished almost entirely with gifts, as observed by friend Ellis "Slats" Slater when Mamie gave him and his wife a tour: "[We] toured every room in the house, looking at every piece of furniture and knickknack, this one came from here, that one from there—so and so gave us this, the president of Korea gave this coffee table, Freeman and Jan Gosden these chairs—and so on, right through the house." Yet in 1958 Ike's chief of staff, Sherman Adams, ultimately lost his job when he accepted a $700 vicuna coat, among other gifts, from industrialist Bernard Goldfine. Ike defended him at first, saying a gift was "not necessarily a bribe" but just "a tangible expression of friendship." But public pressure ultimately forced Adams's resignation.

Ike expected and even sought out special treatment. He used White House servants at Gettysburg, and the White House discreetly accepted confiscated liquor from the General Services Administration, a government supply bureau. Once he even asked Secretary of State John Foster Dulles if he could arrange with the U.S. ambassador to France to import cases of wine "without the need for paying the usual duty." He thought it could be done "quietly" but admitted that if it became known he would be "horribly embarrassed."

When Eisenhower went to New York City's famous Tiffany jewelry store to buy a gift for Mamie, William Hoving, the board chairman, personally took care of him. Ike asked Hoving if Tiffany gave discounts to presidents of the United States. A startled Hoving checked with the store president, William Lusk, who considered the question for a moment, then said, "Well, we didn't give a discount to Lincoln." Lincoln had bought a pearl necklace for his wife, Mary. Ike too paid full price.

When Mamie shopped for herself, she bought costume jewelry and patronized cheap variety stores in Gettysburg and other places she stayed often, like Augusta, Georgia, where Ike frequently played golf. She liked to go to department stores for off-the-rack clothing, but the Secret Service discouraged this, so she read through the ads and sent a maid to pick up the items. The White House now had built-in closets, but Mamie complained they still were not sufficient, and she had to use additional closets on the third floor.

With her lack of pretension and warm, breezy manner, Mamie became immensely popular, and Ike realized that in her he had a political asset. When Ike had his heart attack in 1955, Mamie personally received over ten thousand get-well notes. In marked contrast to Bess Truman, Mamie loved her role. At their Gettysburg home her chair

*The Rose Room, occupied by Queen Elizabeth II in 1957, shows the lingering effects of the Truman redecorating: department store carpets and an assortment of reproduction furniture. Prince Philip stayed across the hall in the Lincoln Bedroom. In 1939 the Rose Room, now called the "Queen's Room," was also used by Queen Elizabeth's mother when she visited Franklin Roosevelt.* (AP/WORLD WIDE PHOTOS)

was clearly marked "FIRST LADY." While she eschewed press conferences—she held one and decided they weren't for her—she stood in reception lines for hours, enjoying the chitchat with women about clothing or children. She received several thousand letters a year and tried to answer each one "in a personal way." She even sent the White House staff cakes on their birthdays, and at Christmas personally wrapped presents for each of them.

Mamie's cheeriness belied her many health problems—one reason she stayed in bed so much, and occasionally delegated her first lady responsibilities to daughter-in-law Barbara, or to Patricia Nixon, the vice president's wife. Mamie suffered from asthma and from a heart condition that produced scary flutters if she was fatigued or upset. She had a very low tolerance for heat or cold. She disliked going outdoors or engaging in any kind of physical exercise—instead she had a masseuse come in three days a week. Her activities were further limited by claustrophobia, fear of flying, and a distaste for foreign travel and the seashore. In addition, the press continually printed stories that she had been drunk. Many army wives who endured long periods of loneliness at remote bases indulged in alcohol, and Mamie may have done so, but at the White House her drinking was moderate. In fact, she had an inner ear disorder called Ménière's disease, which affected her balance and gave the appearance of drunkenness. "I never know when it's going to hit me," she said. "Doctors tell me there's no assurance that an operation would do any good. I'll probably walk down this hall and hit the wall. I'm black and blue from walking around the house."

Eisenhower drank moderately as well, though later in his presidency, after his heart attack, he tended to drink a little more. If he ordered a second Scotch, his personal physician, Major General Howard Snyder, would warn him to stick to one. "Thank you, Howard, you've done your duty," Ike said, and, to the butler, "Bring me a second Scotch." On a trip to Mexico near the end of Ike's second term Snyder noted, "The old boy was feeling no pain."

The Eisenhowers enjoyed their before-dinner drinks, although Ike had to learn to do it the White House way. Once he and Mamie were sitting with old friends, and as the butler entered the room with their drinks, Ike said, "Watch this." The butler served Ike, then Mamie, then their guests, with the wife first. After the butler left, Ike said, "The first night we were in the White House this happened and I told the boy, 'Look, in my house the ladies are served first.' The next day and the day after that they sent in a different waiter each time we were served, and I had to give them the same directions. Finally, I sent for the head man and explained the new procedure for what I thought would be the final time. When the traditional procedure continued, it finally dawned on me. These boys are teaching me how to be President." A half-century earlier, William McKinley had learned a similar lesson.

The Eisenhowers' formal dinners consisted of five or six courses with twenty-one dishes and four wines, followed by music by groups such as Fred Waring and His Pennsylvanians. After Ike's chef resigned in 1957, he was replaced by Pedro Udo, a Filipino with twenty-eight years' experience cooking in the navy. Mamie liked him because of his ability to do fancy cake decorations. Mary Thayer, on a reconnaissance of the White House for incoming Jacqueline Kennedy, realizing that the White House kitchen was in the basement and the family lived on the second and third floors, reported that the food "must be plenty cold when it reaches them since it is prepared 2 floors below in another part of the house." She described the cuisine at state dinners as "nothing short of *awful*."

When the Eisenhowers dined alone, they often ate on trays in front of the television. When Jackie Kennedy moved into the White House, she saw two holes in a wall in the living quarters and asked, "What are those portholes for?" The usher explained that they had housed his-and-hers TV sets for Ike and Mamie, who watched different shows at the same time. Ike enjoyed westerns, Mamie soap operas and the situation comedies. Mamie's favorite program was *As the World Turns,* and the staff quickly learned not to bother her when it was on. She also liked *Talent Scouts* and *You Bet Your Life,* and especially *I Love Lucy.* In November 1953 she invited the stars of the show, Lucille Ball, Desi Arnaz, Vivian Vance, and William Frawley, to a White House reception.

Ike sometimes watched his westerns in the White House movie theater. Chief Usher West searched newspaper advertisements and the Library of Congress film collection to find films Ike hadn't seen. Ike also read western novels at night. He said they relaxed him and helped him get to sleep. In early 1959 Prime Minister Harold Macmillan of Britain was a guest at the White House, and Ike treated him to a showing of *The Big*

*Country.* Ike had already seen it three times before; Macmillan thought it "inconceivably banal."

"The folks' tastes are strictly cornball," the Eisenhowers' son John said. When Howard Mitchell, conductor of the National Symphony Orchestra, asked, "Mr. President, what kind of music do you like?" Eisenhower replied, "Do you have anything by Lawrence Welk?"

Ike's other interests included fishing, landscape painting, and bridge. During his army career Ike had played a good deal of poker and won so consistently he could supplement his pay with it. But by the time he took office he had given it up and replaced it with bridge and canasta. Mamie also played bridge, but was partial to canasta and bolivia. But Ike's real passion was golf. He took up golfing seriously only a few years before becoming president but became an avid, intense player—not surprising considering his earlier athleticism. As a boy, Ike said, "I wanted more than anything else in the whole world to be a ballplayer, a good baseball player, a real professional." At West Point, he was praised by the *New York Times* as "one of the most promising backs in Eastern football." A knee injury ended his football days, but as president, he, along with television, helped popularize the sport of golf in the 1950s. A publicity release for the Professional Golf Association quoted Ike as saying that golf was a sport for the "whole American family," and that it offered "healthy respite from daily toil, refreshment of body and mind."

It could also be preoccupying. When Secret Service head U. E. Baugham met with Eisenhower in New York before his inauguration to discuss security procedures, there was a lapse in the conversation in which Baugham later said he thought Ike "seemed to be staring dreamily into space." Abruptly, the president-elect asked, "What is the distance from the South Portico of the White House to the fence that surrounds the grounds?" Baugham calculated it at about two hundred yards. "Great. It'll be just perfect for a nine iron. And maybe I'll be able to get a little sand in there and if I can I'll be able to practice my wedge shots too."

Practicing his irons on the south lawn created problems Ike had not anticipated. One day he was chipping to an imaginary green, and spectators and newsmen started gathering along the fence to watch. Motorists stopped their cars and got out to look. Soon there was a big crowd and a traffic jam. Ike was highly irritated. "You know," he said, "once in a while I get to the point, with everybody staring at me, when I want to go way back indoors and pull down the curtain."

The American Public Golf Association offered to build the president a putting green at the White House. Ike was immensely pleased. He had it located in a more secluded place hidden by shrubs. Now he could practice chip shots and putting on his way to and from his West Wing office. He even swung a club as he walked through the halls of the White House. He ordered the gardeners to flick off the morning dew off his putting green with fishing poles. The squirrels that dug up his green, however, would not take orders. They were numerous and not intimidated by presidents because Ike's predecessor, Harry Truman, had fed them. Ike, furious, ordered Moaney: "The next time you see one of these squirrels go near my putting green, take a gun and shoot." The Secret Service didn't want any shooting, so the maintenance crew was put to work setting traps. The trapped squirrels were sent to outlying areas such as Rock Creek Park. The newspapers got hold of the story, and soon Ike had to contend with an angry citizen who captured squirrels, brought them to the iron fence of the White House in a bag, and released them onto the grounds.

Ike liked to bang out iron shots to the far reaches of the grounds, taking the necessary divot out of the lawn each time, which kept the gardeners busy resodding. After his practice sessions, the plumber, Howard Arrington, donned waders and, with the aid of Ike's ball retriever (a long pole with a collapsible cup), fished the balls out of the fountains. Moaney recovered the rest. Sometimes Ike would say, "I got that one," which was followed by the shattering of glass as the ball caught a streetlight. The grounds crews would then go out to replace the lamps. Eventually, the lamps were equipped with plastic protectors.

Ike never played golf for big stakes. One Saturday he spent the morning with Secretary of the Treasury George Humphrey deciding whether to lend Brazil $100 million or up to $300 million. As they parted, Ike said, "George, do you realize that after kicking all this money around, and signing it away like that, I'll be out at the first tee in about thirty minutes at Burning Tree, fighting over handicap strokes on a one-dollar Nassau?" The ante was small, but that did not mean that Ike was not deadly serious about the game. When he was winning, he liked to joke and banter; when he was losing and playing poorly, he swore and banged his clubs into the turf. Most of all he didn't like the game interrupted—as in September 1957, when Ike was on a golfing vacation in Newport, Rhode Island, and racial violence broke out during the integration struggle in Little Rock, Arkansas. Pressure built for him to return to Washington to deal with the crisis, and finally he did, but it made him furious. Referring to Governor Orval Faubus of Arkansas, Ike complained to Vice President Richard Nixon that he couldn't play golf "because of the stupidity and duplicity of one called Faubus."

Ike played so much golf that he was attacked for it in Congress and in the media. Reporters added up 150 days on the golf course in one year. Ike's personal physician, Dr. Howard Snyder, a loyal friend of many years, tried to mute the criticism: "Golf is fine for him, so I say he should play whenever he gets a chance. Sometimes I actually have to urge him to go to the course. He doesn't get away from the office nearly as much as I'd like him to. . . . We want the President to have all the rest and relaxation he can."

Golf didn't always provide the cure. The president's public image was one of smiling geniality, but he had an explosive temper, even in childhood. As president he could erupt over something as small as not finding salt on his meal tray—and certainly over a bad putt. During one golf game, Ike threw his sand iron at Snyder, hitting him in the shin. Snyder said if the head of the club had hit him, he would have had a fractured leg.

Nevertheless, Ike was never without golf or bridge partners. As the Republican nominee in 1952, he was backed by a small group of top corporate executives who helped pay his campaign expenses and then, when he took office, made themselves available to him at anytime for anything. If Ike needed a fourth for golf or bridge, one of them would drop everything and show up. John F. Kennedy, during his campaign to succeed Eisenhower, was critical of these friends, implying that they were just rich men who latched on to the president. "I could understand it if he played golf all the time with old Army friends," he said, but "all his golfing pals are rich men he has met since 1945." Eisenhower, who needed the companionship, felt differently, and later said, "It is almost impossible for me to describe how valuable their friendship was to me."

Ellis Slater, president of Frankfort Distilleries, was part of this group and recounted receiving a call from Ike one morning to go to Key West to play bridge. Ike sent his presidential plane, the *Columbine,* for Slater. "A White House car picked me up at 8:20 and drove me to the Military Air Transport Hangar where I went on board." He stayed in an officer's house on the base at Key West. After playing bridge in the afternoon, Eisenhower and Slater had cocktails with the commandant of the base, then dinner, more bridge, and a movie. On another occasion, Thursday morning, March 7, 1953, Slater arrived at the White House for a date with Ike and found him on the south grounds hitting golf balls. Slater joined him, then the two showered, and then they had lunch together. The bridge game started at 2 P.M. and ran until 6 P.M. After dinner, the game continued "until after midnight," Slater said.

Mamie fit easily into this routine. The men played bridge in the Monroe Room (now the Treaty Room, upstairs next to the Oval Room), while she and the other wives played canasta or bolivia in the sun parlor. Slater's wife, Priscilla, described a visit to the Eisenhowers' Gettysburg home when Ike and the husbands were off to Camp David: "Cards that afternoon and an outdoor movie that night. Sunday Mamie stayed in her negligee until dinnertime, and we played bolivia all day long and well into the night. Monday the same." By Eisenhower's second term, Mamie was asking Pat Nixon, as wife of the vice president, to cover more of her first lady duties, especially overseas. But when somebody suggested that Mamie invite Pat and her husband to Gettysburg, Mamie—who once invited the White House staff to a barbecue there—flatly refused: "What on earth would we talk about? We don't have anything in common! She doesn't play bridge!"

When Ike's "gang" came to visit the White House, Ike generally did the cooking, often grilling steaks on the White House roof outside the sun parlor. He was known for his vegetable soup, which called for a heavy beef stock and took two days to make. After all the gang had a couple of helpings, Ike told them, "Put what's left in the ice box."

One reason Ike had so much time for golf and bridge was that he was well organized and, when he had a specific job to do, a hard worker. In 1926 he was first in his class at the army's Command and General Staff School in Fort Leavenworth, Kansas. "I was, when working, driven by the need to go at top speed, day after day, starting early and continuing past midnight," he said. He smoked four packs of cigarettes a day at this time, quitting smoking shortly before becoming president.

Come World War II, Ike's hard work paid off. He had spent years as a major in the shrunken peacetime army, but during the war he rose rapidly through the ranks, leaping over other high-ranking officers. In 1942 he was made commander of the U.S. forces in Europe, and in 1943, of the Allied Expeditionary Force. The D-Day invasion on June 6, 1944, was the largest in history, and Ike worked eighteen-hour days to make it successful. Clearly, he was ambitious. A month into his marriage he had to leave for the Mexican border, and when Mamie protested, he said, "Mamie, there's one thing you must always understand. My country comes first and always will. You come second." When he was with the army in the Philippines, where the army sent him as an aide to General Douglas MacArthur in 1935, a noted gypsy fortune-teller in Manila had actually predicted he would "be President" someday. But then in 1909 his Abilene, Kansas, high school yearbook cast his brother, Edgar, as chief executive of the nation. Following the war, Ike claimed he was putting higher ambitions on hold, but in truth, he had his eye on the presidency.

Ike attributed his success in part to his mother, Ida. "I think my mother was the finest person I have ever known," he said. She and his father were members of a fundamentalist Christian sect called the River Brethren. She taught him to be self-disciplined and to do the right thing, not for fear of punishment but from a sense of duty. She was also a pacifist, and taught him that hatred was futile. When her son went off to West Point in 1911, Ida went to her bedroom and wept. While Ike didn't share all of his mother's beliefs, in 1948 he said, "I am the most intensely religious man I know." Yet he was not baptized until 1953, in the National Presbyterian Church in Washington. And it was at the urging of Agriculture Secretary Ezra Taft Benson, a Mormon, that Ike opened cabinet meetings with a silent prayer. Once, when Ike forgot, a clerk passed him a note reminding him. Ike said, "Oh goddamnit, we forgot the silent prayer." He called for a national day of prayer on July 4, 1953, and spent the day fishing in the morning, golfing in the afternoon, and playing bridge in the evening.

Once Ike was practicing golf shots on the south lawn and talking with Secretary of State Dulles when he saw his chief of staff, Sherman Adams, approaching with a stack of papers. He turned to Dulles and said, "Look, Foster, here comes my conscience." Ike, a self-styled Mr. Nice Guy with a winning grin, needed someone like Adams. Adams, a hard-driving, imperious former governor of New Hampshire, hung up the phone without saying good-bye and left secretaries in tears. He did not allow turf fights or other arguments get as far as Ike, telling disputants to make up their minds or he would do it for them. Another person who took care of Ike was his valet, John Moaney. As a sergeant, Moaney had taken care of the general in the army and was devoted to him. When Ike left the army and became president of Columbia University in 1948, Moaney followed him. As valet to the president, the former sergeant laid out Ike's suits. New York clothing makers kept the president so well supplied with suits that often he only wore a suit once or twice. Moaney helped Ike put on socks, shoes, pants, jacket and tie. He even held out the president's undershorts so he could step into them. As Ike came out of the bedroom properly attired, he held out his arm, and Moaney slid his watch on for him. Moaney had a drinking habit, and there were times when Ike had to do the caretaking, but when the president retired to his Gettysburg farm, Moaney and his wife followed them there and lived on the farm.

Ike ran his life and his presidency efficiently, but the one thing he couldn't control was his health. On September 24, 1955, he suffered a massive heart attack. The day began on the Cherry Hills golf course at Denver—one of his favorite courses. The president was staying at Byer's Peak Ranch, about 7,700 feet above sea level. After breakfast he was driven to a lower elevation and by midmorning was on the first tee. He was well into the game when he was notified of an important call from Secretary of State Dulles in Washington. Ike returned to the clubhouse only to be told that Dulles had not been able to wait any longer but would call back in an hour. Ike's infamous temper began to fray. When he was called off the course a second time, the phone connection was lost. After the third interruption to his game, he at last talked with Dulles, and his foursome decided to break for lunch. Ike had a double hamburger with slices of raw Bermuda onion. Again in the afternoon Ike was pulled off the course for a phone call. This time it turned out to be a mistake. "At this point his anger became so real that the veins stood out on his forehead like whipcords," Snyder said later. Ike began to have symptoms of indigestion. He told the club pro, Rip Arnold, "Boy, those raw onions are sure backing up on me." Cardiologists later would say these were heart attack symptoms.

That evening, Ike had dinner at Mamie's family home in Denver, played billiards, and went to bed. Around two-thirty in the morning, Mamie became aware that her husband was tossing around. He said he had stomach pains, and she knew he had complained of indigestion earlier, so she gave him milk of magnesia. She called Dr. Snyder, who arrived quickly and immediately diagnosed a heart attack. He injected morphine to relieve the pain. Ike's blood pressure collapsed, his pulse rate shot up, and he went into shock. Dr. Snyder admitted to being "alarmed" and "shaken." Snyder asked Mamie to get into bed with Ike and wrap herself around him. She did, and Ike became calm and fell asleep.

Around noon the next day, Snyder took Ike to Fitzsimons Army Hospital. Snyder told the press that the president had a "digestive upset" and that it was not serious. A press aide said it was "the kind of twenty-four-hour stuff that many people have had." Later it became a "mild coronary thrombosis," and then the "mild" was eliminated. On Monday the stock market lost a record $14 billion in value. Dr. Snyder was later severely criticized for, among other things, helping Ike get up to go to the bathroom during that first night, then allowing him to walk down the stairs and to sit upright in his car on the way to the hospital—all of which put stress on his heart at a critical time. At one point the seventy-four-year-old Snyder was in tears.

A top heart specialist, Dr. Paul Dudly White, flew out from Boston. Aware of the press hostility to Dr. Snyder, White explained how he would deflate it: "I shall give the press and the nation a course on myocardial infarction. They will get so interested, the press will not raise the issue of management before hospitalization, especially if in the morning he continues to be doing satisfactorily." After the press conference an elated White said, "It worked." White later got carried away with his star media role. Press Secretary James Haggerty had opened Ike's oxygen tent to ask him how much to tell the public. "Tell them everything," Ike said and went back to sleep. Ike later suffered "acute embarrassment" when he learned that Dr. White had told the press that the president had "a successful bowel movement."

Ike flew back to the White House on November 11, then retreated to Gettysburg, where he became depressed and sat passively for long stretches. There had been some debate concerning whether Ike should seek another term in 1956. Cardiologist Thomas Mattingly believed that Ike had actually suffered two heart attacks, one prior to taking office, in 1949, that Snyder had described to the press as indigestion, and the recent massive one. Not only should Ike decline to run in 1956, Mattingly said, but he should not have run the first time. Dr. White advised Ike not to run: "His heart would stand the strain, I told him, but I felt the inevitable political maneuvering might endanger his peace-making role." Dr. White added that he had "learned a lot about politics by this time." Ike, thoroughly annoyed by the doctor, privately called him "a publicity seeker," but he knew that if White said publicly that Ike was a poor risk to last four years, he would not be running for a second term. However, White, a Republican, said at a press conference, "The President should be able to carry on an active life satisfactorily for another five to ten years." Even Mamie wanted him to run, seeing how frustrated and irritable he was sitting around their Gettysburg home with little to do.

Ike returned to the White House the week before Christmas. The doctors warned him of the danger of tensions to his body. "How the hell can anyone carry the load of the presidency without permitting the tensions to affect his physical self?" Ike said. Six days after that warning, on November 25, 1957, Eisenhower was at his desk when he felt dizzy. He dropped his pen but couldn't pick it up. He rang for Ann Whitman, his secretary. "Words—but not the one I wanted—came to my tongue," Ike recalled. "It was impossible for me to express any coherent thought whatsoever." He refused to acknowledge his condition and refused to leave the Oval Office. He could not even focus his eyes on his appointment secretary, Robert Gray, and called him by the wrong name. Dr. Snyder arrived. Ike was thoroughly irritated and had to be coaxed to return to his bedroom.

That night Ike had been scheduled to attend a state dinner. Vice President Nixon was called to substitute for him, and a press release stated, "The President suffered a chill and the doctors have ordered him to bed." That evening Ike came out of his bedroom dressed in a bathrobe and slippers. An astonished Mamie asked, "What are you doing up, Ike?" Speaking slowly, he answered, "Why shouldn't I be up? I have a dinner to go to." Ike's words were jumbled, but he refused to acknowledge the seriousness of his condition. "I am perfectly all right." He became so frustrated at not being able to produce the words he wanted that he beat the bedcovers with his fists. The next day, a press release announced a "cerebral occlusion." Within a few days, Ike's speech was back to normal.

The doctors recommended sixty days of complete rest. Ike tried, but even if the pressures of office had allowed it, his temperament made it impossible. He compounded his problems by refusing to change his eating habits. He continued to wolf down food. Shortly after Ike's Denver stroke, Snyder saw him eat a breakfast of ten cornmeal griddle cakes covered with syrup, plus large amounts of sausage. Ike had suffered undiagnosed stomach pains for decades. On the night he was nominated for his first term, the pains were so severe he didn't know if he would be able to make his acceptance speech. As the 1956 campaign approached, an exam finally revealed ileitis, a restriction of the intestine. Nonetheless, the press was told, "Barium studies showed a normal functioning digestive tract." Ike was warned to stick to a bland diet.

At a White House dinner on June 7, 1956, Ike ate a Waldorf salad. Undigested pieces of celery lodged in the constricted intestine, and later he suffered cramps, vomiting, and increasingly severe pain. Because he was the president, the medical decision became complex. The doctors did not want to operate unless all agreed that it was a necessity, and not all did. As the hours passed, Snyder feared that the delay was endangering Ike's life. When the doctors at last agreed, Mamie refused to sign the consent papers, and son John had to. Because the reelection campaign would soon begin, the doctors opted for the simplest procedure with the best chance for a quick recovery. Ike would need a second operation later. At 7 A.M. the morning following the operation, Dr. Snyder announced to the press that Ike had an "upset stomach."

Eisenhower made it through his campaign, and won a second term. But during the latter half of his term, he was beset by physical ills and became increasingly worried about his health, particularly his cholesterol levels. Yet he continued to eat steaks marbled with fat. He asked his cardiologist, Dr. Thomas Mattingly, if it was all right for him to fly to Denver to play Cherry Hills Golf Club again. Without hesitating, Dr. Mattingly told him not to. With Dr. Snyder right there, Ike told Mattingly, "Tom, I will not go. You are the only one around here who has the guts to tell me something which you know I will not like."

Over the winter of 1957–58, Ike became noticeably more irritable. His temper flared over little things, or when Mamie tried to boss him. He complained more, particularly about his job. He coped by getting away from the White House, sometimes going on extended trips, including a 1959 goodwill tour to twenty countries. He also worried about Mamie and wanted her to give up handshaking at White House receptions. "[She] insists on talking to everyone. It's a strain on her," he said.

Ike said he was looking forward to leaving the presidency, but he wasn't pleased when young John Kennedy won the Democratic nomination. "I will do anything to avoid turning my chair and country to Kennedy," he said. But "anything" did not include active, wholehearted support for Republican nominee Richard Nixon, Ike's vice president and Kennedy's opponent. Though Nixon was always loyal to Ike, particularly when Ike was incapacitated, Ike disliked him. Ike had wanted to dump him from the ticket in 1952, but Nixon's emotional "Checkers" speech, to which Americans responded so favorably, made that difficult. In 1956 he tried to entice Nixon out of the vice presidency, but Nixon wouldn't bite. Nixon felt the rebuff. "General Eisenhower never asked me to see the upstairs at the White House where he lived," he said. "It was years before he asked me inside the house at Gettysburg."

Kennedy did win, and Ike took it well enough to invite his successor to the White House. When Ike showed Kennedy around the Oval Office, he said to him, "Watch this!" He stepped to his desk, picked up a phone, and said, "Opal Drill Three!" They stood together looking out the window behind the desk. In three minutes the Marine One presidential helicopter set down on the south lawn.

As he left office and entered retirement, Eisenhower found that his many years at the top—in the army, in NATO, and as president—had insulated him from the nitty-gritty of everyday life. The only time in many years he had been in a retail store was in 1958, when he had taken his grandson David to a sporting goods shop to buy him fishing equipment. He walked out with no thought of paying. A reporter, Merriman Smith, reassured the shop owner by telling him that Ike never carried money, but if he sent the bill to the White House, it would get paid. Ike did not know what to do at automatic toll lanes on the highway, had never adjusted a TV set, and couldn't place a telephone call. After he left office, he tried to call son John from Gettysburg. He expected to be able to give a number to an operator, but only got a buzzing sound. He tried clicking the button and turning the rotary dial as one would a safe dial. Irritated, he slammed the receiver down and yelled for Secret Service agent James Flohr: "Come show me how you work this goddamned thing." When he was shown how, he was delighted and fascinated by the phone.

Historians have never given Eisenhower very high ratings, but he remained popular with the public—he had the highest approval rating of any president over an eight-year span. After he left office Congress restored his lifetime rank as a five-star general with full pay and allowances. His estate would be valued at $3 million. He had several more heart attacks, but managed to play plenty of golf. Shortly before he died on March 28, 1968, he had the "thrill of a lifetime," a hole in one. Mamie died November 11, 1979, following a stroke. Both were buried in Abilene.

# John F. Kennedy

## 1961–1963

## *Style*

"KEN, LOOK AT THIS," John F. Kennedy called to John Kenneth Galbraith, the economist. The president had just moved into the White House, and he'd dropped to the floor to inspect a dresser. Kennedy, who had a passing knowledge of antiques, looked up and gave his verdict: "It's not even authentic. It's not even a good reproduction."

In 1961 the same was true of 75 percent of the White House furnishings, most of it bought at B. Altman, the New York department store, after the Truman renovation. Jacqueline Bouvier Kennedy had a much stronger reaction to what she called "the dreary Maison Blanche." "Oh, God. It's the worst place in the world," she sobbed. "I hate it, I hate it, I hate it." Thirty-one, the mother of an infant, John Jr., and a three-year-old, Caroline, she had barely survived her traditional preinauguration tour with Mamie Eisenhower. "I came straight from the hospital," Jackie said later. "I had only walked about in my room and a little bit down the hall since I had had John. I really shouldn't have gone. But what can you do?" Mamie actually had a wheelchair ready for the hour-long tour, but Jackie didn't use it, saying later that she was too embarrassed.

Now she faced private quarters bare of the Eisenhower furniture. Her own had not yet arrived. She had inherited spotted carpets, peeling wallpaper, and tattered drapes. One toilet wouldn't flush. The White House furnishings looked to Jackie like they'd come from "discount stores." Downstairs she pronounced the East Room "a roller skating rink" and the rest of the house "a dentist's office bomb shelter" and "a dungeon like the Lubianka."

Jackie later wrote, "I felt like a moth banging on the window pane when I first moved into this place. It was terrible. You can't even open the windows in the rooms, because they hadn't been opened for years. . . . When we tried the fireplaces, they smoked because they hadn't ever been used. Sometimes I wondered, 'How are we going to live as a family in this enormous place?' I'm afraid it will always be a little impossible for people who live there. It's an office building."

In January, just before Kennedy's inauguration, Letitia "Tish" Baldridge, Jackie's newly appointed social secretary, went to the White House to meet with Mary Jane McCaffree, Mamie Eisenhower's social secretary. Tish wrote in a memo to Jackie, who was at Palm Beach, that she was shocked to find there was no budget for "proper flowers, proper linens," and a host of other things. She listed some of the pluses: "swimming pool, nice little movie theatre. . . . Even a tennis court. 2nd floor, a tiny, sunny room off the elevator where Ike painted. . . . There is a dental chair tucked away in a cranny in the White House. A top Walter Reed [Army Hospital] dentist will always come to the White House."

Tish also outlined some of the enduring difficulties of not being able to move into the White House until twelve noon of inauguration day—a day on which the first family is expected to participate in social and ceremonial functions from the time they walk in the door until late that night. Tish wrote that she had asked Mrs. McCaffree "if we couldn't smuggle a lot of stuff over without the E's knowing and she said yes, the head Usher could store cartons, suitcases, etc., out of sight and then whisk them into sight on the stroke of 12 noon. Isn't that marvelous??? Right out of Alfred Hitchcock."

Even with Tish's reconnaisance, it took the first family time to get oriented. At the president's first state luncheon, Kennedy entertained the prime minister of Denmark and selected guests upstairs in the private quarters beforehand. Then he escorted them to the elevator and down to the main floor, heading, he thought, to meet the other guests in the Blue Room. But he took a wrong turn and ended up in the pantry. After that the chief usher assigned an aide to wait by the elevator. At the end of the first state dinner, Kennedy and three male guests went searching for a men's room. They didn't want to ask a butler for directions and felt there must be one somewhere nearby. However, there were no facilities for either sex on the main floor (there still aren't).

Jackie, meanwhile, had appointed a new housekeeper, Anne Lincoln, who set about investigating her new domain. She found "towels with pulled places," and "sheets mended to a fare-you-well." Food had to be purchased only from vendors with FBI clearance, and then could not be delivered but had to be picked up by the Secret Service and delivered by them to the kitchen. Wine had to be bought for each occasion, rather than in bulk, as Thomas Jefferson's wine cellar had long since disappeared.

Both Jack and Jackie brought their own servants to the White House and put them on the government payroll. Kennedy brought George Thomas, his valet, and John "Muggsy" O'Leary, who had been with him for years. O'Leary ran errands, but he was put on the Secret Service payroll, so he carried a badge. Jackie brought her maid, Providencia Paredes, plus her secretary and a masseuse. Since the government only authorized a certain size of staff, layoffs were necessary to accommodate the Kennedy hirees.

(The domestic help were covered by Civil Service but were unclassified, which meant that they need not take an exam to be hired—but they could be fired.) When Chief Usher J. B. West suggested to Jackie that instead of dismissing people she might want to absorb some of these costs, she replied, "We don't have that kind of money. My husband is a federal employee, just like the rest of the White House staff."

Well, not quite like the rest of the staff. At forty-three, JFK was not only the youngest president ever elected but the wealthiest. His father had given him a million dollars when he turned twenty-one to encourage him to go into public service. He grew up in a twenty-room redbrick colonial in Bronxville, a wealthy suburb of New York City. His family wintered in Palm Beach, Florida, and summered at Hyannis Port on Cape Cod, Massachusetts. Kennedy's family also had fashionable lodgings on Rodeo Drive in Hollywood. Like Herbert Hoover, JFK donated his $100,000-a-year salary to charity. Jackie was annoyed when she found out. She wanted to use the money for Glen Ora, the new home she was having built in Virginia. Jackie had a talent for spending large sums. Kennedy once received a statement from the family accountant in New York with a line item, "Department Stores . . . $40,000."

"What the hell does this mean?" he demanded of his wife.

"Oh, heck, I don't remember," Jackie said in her low whisper.

On another occasion when he questioned her expenses, she framed one of young John's finger paintings and sent it over to the Oval Office with a note asking if it was okay to buy the painting for $9,000.

Sporadically Kennedy became very economy-minded. He had the White House grocery account changed from a fancy French market in Georgetown to a local wholesaler. He drank Dom Pérignon champagne but wanted to know why guests were also being served French champagne. "Isn't New York champagne good enough?" he asked. After a dinner-dance he found half-full champagne bottles and glasses. He issued orders not to refill any glass until it was empty and not to let any waiter have a new bottle of champagne until he turned in an empty one.

Jackie's spending was a recurring theme. She spent money wildly on her personal wardrobe—$121,000 in 1962 alone. JFK avoided direct confrontation with Jackie on these issues if he could. When he found that the cutbacks he wanted her to make amounted to mere hundreds of dollars, he got Mary Gallagher, Jackie's secretary, to send her a memo: "The President feels that these accounts are still too high, and would like you to go over them again. He says we need to do better than only $700 a month." He urged Gallagher to show Jackie the figures, cautiously adding, "And Mary, you sign the memo."

Jackie had her moments when she attempted to toe the line. "Well, just remember this," she said to Chief Usher J. B. West, "I want you to run this place just like you'd run it for the chinchiest President who ever got elected!" Then she gave him one of her dramatic whispers: "We don't have nearly as much money as you read in the papers!" She told Gallagher, "Oh, Mary, do you know what I just learned from Anne Lincoln? You know all the food we buy here at the White House? Well, she told me with the stamps the stores give us, we can trade them in for these marvelous gifts!"

Green stamps or no, plenty of gifts came the first family's way from organizations, well-wishers, and promoters. When Jackie accepted some expensive gifts from foreign heads of state—including some fine horses from the king of Saudi Arabia and the prime minister of Ireland—Kennedy became concerned. He asked Angier Biddle Duke, chief of protocol, to convince Jackie that this was inappropriate.

"I understand what you're saying, Angie," Jackie said. "But there's a problem."

"What's that?" Duke asked.

"I want the horses," Jackie replied.

She got them.

At first JFK and his aides considered Jackie a liability. Prior to his election, she'd had been criticized for her clothes—even her mother said, "Why can't you look more like Muriel Humphrey or Pat Nixon?"—and as president JFK was not pleased when she was honored as the "First Lady of Fashion." "The New Frontier is going to be sabotaged by a bunch of goddamned French couturiers," he moaned. On a trip to India in March 1962, she was criticized for wearing high fashion in a poor third-world country. Jackie was unfazed. She told her press attaché, "If you say anything, tell them it's second hand and that I bought everything at the Ritz Thrift Shop." She liked exclusivity. She told her favorite designer, Oleg Cassini, that she didn't want "any little fat women hopping around in the same dress." When the tide turned and the women of America—fat and thin—began to idolize her, Jackie commented, "I am absolutely the same now as I was before. Before they hated it and now they love it." On another occasion, she said, "People told me ninety-nine things that I had to do as First Lady, and I haven't done one of them."

Almost. When Jackie was about to enter the White House, a friend reminded her that she'd have to make concessions. "I will," she said. "I'll wear hats." Her husband was not so accommodating. He carried a hat for the inaugural, but spoke bareheaded. Later he went so far as to be photographed, hat in hand. "I've got to carry one for a while," he told reporters. "They tell me I'm killing the industry." Indeed, industry representative Al Webb came to the White House to tempt JFK and friend Paul B. "Red" Fay Jr. with the latest headgear. "You both look great," Webb told them as they modeled their hats. Fay and Kennedy took one look at each other and started laughing. "Al," asked the president, "are you willing to destroy the beloved image of our country's leader just to save the hat industry?"

Jackie, on the other hand, was good for the hat industry. Fashion interested her. Being first lady did not. She said the very title sounded like a saddle horse. "I'm a mother. I'm a wife," she complained to Angier Duke. "I'm not a public official." Her theory was, "Why should I traipse around to hospitals playing Lady Bountiful when I have so much to do around here?" referring to the White House. She favored what she called the "PBO"—polite brush-off—and would skip appointments in favor of a walk, saying, "I can't stand these silly women." Sometimes she simply said, "Give them to Lady Bird," referring to Claudia Johnson, the vice president's wife. Tish Baldrige later recalled, "Whenever Jackie had to do all the woman things, like teas, she would get sudden stomach distress and have to go ride horses. Lady Bird would always come and fill in. She was so much brighter and smoother and diplomatic than LBJ. The Kennedys got along with them better than is portrayed in the books."

Once Jackie refused to come downstairs to meet a delegation of Girl Scouts in the Rose Garden. Presidential press secretary Pierre Salinger went to Kennedy.

"Just give me a minute," JFK said as he headed upstairs. "I'll straighten this right out."

Fifteen minutes later he returned and announced that Jackie would do it. "It cost me. Bet you won't guess what it is."

"A new dress," Salinger guessed.

"No, worse than that," Kennedy said. "Two symphonies."

Jackie once said that the only music her husband really appreciated was "Hail to the Chief." One of his favorite songs was "Bill Bailey Won't You Please Come Home." Symphonies put him to sleep.

Jackie was not entirely remiss as first lady. Even before her husband took office, she announced her intention to make the White House "a showcase of American arts and history." She said she was "warned, begged, and practically threatened" not to take on the project. Her husband was one of those most strongly opposed, fearing that redecorating the venerable White House meant crossing a minefield. But Jackie never called her project "redecorating." Like McKim in 1902, she relied on the word *restoration,* evoking disinterested authenticity. "Mrs. Kennedy made the nation aware that the time had come to stop treating the White House like a stepchild," said Clement Conger, a Nixon-appointed curator who added, "like everything else about the Kennedy administration this was over publicized."

Jackie institutionalized the idea of the White House as a living history museum. In her first month as first lady Jackie formed the White House Fine Arts Committee, chaired by Henry F. Du Pont, founder of the Winterthur Museum in Delaware. The task of its twelve distinguished members was to locate historic furniture and works of art and to procure tax-deductible donations of both money and furnishings. She herself trekked to a huge government warehouse in Fort Washington, on the Maryland side of the Potomac, to rescue valuable White House antiques stored there. "I had a backache every day for three months," she said. She set up the Office of the Curator in 1961 and had twenty-six-year-old Lorraine W. Pearce inventory all the White House furnishings. A catalog was published in 1964. In 1962 Pearce was succeeded by William V. Elder III and then in 1963 James Ketchum, who stayed as curator until 1970. The establishment of the Office of the Curator meant that for the first time professional standards were applied to the care and acquisition of art and furnishings. The transition from home to museum was helped by the establishment of the White House Historical Association in 1961, an organization that has proved essential in raising money for the refurbishment of the White House. Jackie's other lasting legacy was her role in stimulating legislation that made presidential furnishings the inalienable property of the White House.

In truth, Jackie Kennedy's interests were more French than American, as reflected by her choice of decorators, Parisian Stéphane Boudin. Boudin swept through the state rooms creating grand stage sets and using antiques in a witty French way. He covered the walls with silks, as had Charles McKim, even though wallpaper was de rigeur for early nineteenth-century rooms. He broke with tradition, using cream-striped silk for the Blue Room and relegating tradition's color to accents. But there was a deep appreciation of history. Antiques with a White House provenance were solicited from collectors, including a fourth chair from Monroe's Bellangé suite, acquired in 1963. James Ketchum, curator during the Kennedy and Johnson years, recalled, "We'd say our morning and evening prayers that a loan would be turned into a gift." In asking for donations for the White House, he said it helped that "a very gracious and interested student of White House history"—i.e. Mrs. Kennedy—"was putting forth the questions."

In February 1962 Jackie did a televised tour of the White House that reached 42 million Americans, made the White House the top tourist attraction in Washington, and increased the first lady's popularity enormously. Sales of a White House guide book, published in 1962 by the White House Historical Association, topped 2 million copies in two years. Wealthy patrons funded the acquisition of some 1,100 antiques and works of art.

For the second-floor family quarters Jackie called in one of the country's most esteemed decorators, Sister Parish, from New York, and told her, "Let's have lots of chintz and gay up this old dump." Throughout the mansion, she brought in paintings borrowed from the Smithsonian Institution and removed furnishings she deemed inappropriate. "If there is anything I can't stand," she said, "it's Victorian mirrors—they're hideous. Off to the dungeons with them." Jackie dismantled the second-floor presidential study. Once the Lincoln Cabinet Room it had been known as the Monroe Room since Lou Henry Hoover had made it a showplace of Monroe-era furniture and reproductions, Jackie renamed it the Treaty Room in recognition of the fact that the Spanish-American War peace treaty had been signed there. Kennedy used this room to sign the United States instrument of ratification of the Treaty for a Partial Nuclear Test Ban on October 7, 1963.

Jackie also made some changes to the living quarters. Having young children made eating in the family dining room on the main floor inconvenient, so Jackie turned Truman's daughter's bedroom into a family dining room. When it was used for the first time, Larry O'Brien, an assistant to the president, sat in one of the antique chairs and it collapsed, leaving him on the floor. The president's chair also crumbled. For the Diplomatic Reception Room, Jackie rescued wallpaper from a historic house in Maryland that was about to be torn down. She paid to have it steamed off the walls and installed in the White House. "I saw the paper going up," recalled Clement Conger, curator of the State Department who was appointed White House curator by Richard Nixon. "It took two weeks. The paper had hundreds of holes. Artists had to be employed to paint them in." Since the Diplomatic Reception Room is near the principal door used by visitors, it is blasted with hot air in summer. When the air meets the air conditioning, condensation forms on the historic wallpaper. "Every two to three years artists have to be brought back to repaint it," said Conger. The paper is an 1834 Zuber print called "Wonders of America" made by a factory in the Aix-le-Rixgion region of France. Jackie Kennedy installed a later version of the same paper in a bedroom she converted into a dining room. When Kennedy discovered that the same wallpaper was readily available commercially, Jackie defended herself by claiming the original wallpaper had better colors, a view supported by the antiques world. "I don't give a damn," Kennedy said. "Twelve thousand dollars is entirely too much money for wallpaper." Not that he was paying. In two weeks, Jackie went through a $50,000 decorating appropriation meant to last four years. She relied on donors to finance major acquisitions.

The addition of a second floor dining room made family meals and small parties more convenient, but the main kitchen was still on the basement level. Jackie found she "had to wait an hour for a pat of butter" or else take the elevator down to get it. She added a small kitchen adjacent to the new dining room. She also found that the pantry on the main floor, which served the State Dining Room, was not only too small but was linked to the downstairs kitchens only by a narrow staircase. "The first meals we had in the State Dining Room were so full of delays that I decided to cut the number of courses," she said. "For that reason we never had soup because it could not be served hot."

Another problem was the heating system. In a note to Chief Usher J. B. West, Jackie complained that when the heat was not "suffocating," there were "great gusts of cold air" blowing in through the air conditioners. She asked that the heat not be regulated by turning on the air conditioners, "as everyone gets a crick in the neck—[the] greatest brains at Army Engineering Corps can figure out how to have this heated like a normal, rattletrap house." It was, however, a condition that defied correction.

Jackie had a penchant for painting and repainting. As a senator, Kennedy once returned to their Georgetown home from a trip and said, "Damnit, Jackie, why can't I come home to the same house I left?" For her bedroom in the White House she wanted the walls pale green and the door and moldings white. It had to be done over a single weekend when she was away, so an extra White House crew was pressed into duty. On her return Jackie looked at the result and said, "Oh, gosh! I'm not sure I like the room this way." One of the painters told Jackie's secretary, "You know, it's not that we mind the work so much—after all, it's all in a day's work. But, tell me, Mrs. Gallagher, you've been with Mrs. Kennedy now longer than any of us here—does she always go around changing her mind like this?"

She was set, at least, on having a French chef. Eisenhower's chef, Pedro Udo, a Filipino, had been a navy cook and was not what Jackie had in mind for the White House. She tried for the chef of the French embassy in London but couldn't get him. Jackie had a close relationship with her father-in-law, Joseph P. Kennedy, and could count on him for help. He secured René Verdon, former chef for the posh Carlyle Hotel in New York. JFK ordered the Secret Service to speed up citizenship papers for Verdon and his French assistant, Julius Spessot, since he didn't want the press reporting that the White House was hiring foreigners. Jackie said Verdon had absolutely no temperament, which is "divine in a Frenchman," but the chef would depart the White House in a huff in 1965, during the Johnson administration. Once installed in the White House, he chattered away in French with his assistant but found the Filipino kitchen help "impossible."

Maude Shaw, who cared for young Caroline and John, asked the chefs if she could prepare three weeks of menus that would give the children something different every day. The chefs offered to see to it themselves. The children got liver three days out of four. Caroline exclaimed, "Liver! Miss Shaw, why do we have to have liver again!" Her father wasn't much happier. His tastes leaned to hot dogs topped with chili, and tomato soup laced with whipped cream. Verdon proposed trout with wine and meringue shells filled with raspberries. JFK—who sometimes carried a thermos full of New England clam chowder with him—said he preferred fish chowder and chocolate ice cream. "He told me you had to be from New England to make fish chowder," Verdon said, "and I believe him."

The president had little taste for high culture, either. Pablo Casals, the famous cellist, was persuaded to visit. He had played in the White House for Theodore Roosevelt a half century earlier. Kennedy confided to a friend, "Pablo Casals? I didn't know what

*Jackie was very protective of her children and kept them away from reporters and photographers whenever possible. Kennedy felt that press pictures of his children were good public relations and liked to play with them even though his bad back meant he couldn't pick them up.* (JOHN F. KENNEDY LIBRARY)

the hell he played—someone had to tell me." As for ballet, he found it boring. After a performance of the Bolshoi, he said, "I don't want my picture taken with all those Russian fairies." During music programs in the East Room, the president tended to clap at the wrong time or get up before the program was finished. So Tish Baldridge would signal the end by opening the center door about two inches.

What Kennedy cared about was the White House lawn. He had a running feud with the White House gardener about it. Viewing the lawn from the Oval Office window and from his helicopter as it set down, he saw that it was covered with weeds, crabgrass, and huge brown patches. Jackie wrote to West: "It is driving the President crazy—and I agree with him. In Glen Ora, where we have one man who cuts the lawn every two weeks, it looks like green velvet—and this place looks as well as corn fields in Virginia." Experts from far and wide analyzed the problem. The National Park Service spent some $200,000 digging, steaming, fertilizing, and seeding. "Isn't that damn lawn ever going to grow?" Kennedy asked. When he was expecting important guests, he had the brown patches spray-painted green.

JFK's schedule gave him time to ponder the lawn. He was awakened between 7:30 and 8:00 A.M. by his longtime valet, George Thomas, and took a hot bath, which helped ease the back pain that stemmed from his war injuries. He shaved while in the tub, which had a board across it for reading and viewing memos. Then he dressed, immaculately. JFK changed suits two to three times during the day. When Jackie first met him, he was sloppy in his dress and personal habits. When Kennedy was campaigning, adviser Ted Sorenson had to tell him, "Presidential candidates do not chew gum."

The president worked in the Oval Office from about 9 A.M. until around 1:30 P.M., when he went to the White House pool for a half-hour swim. He always swam nude, and for the sake of his back the water was kept at ninety degrees. Dave Powers, a friend and aide, said there was one rule for swimming with JFK: "All you've got to do is keep your head above water so you can talk." In the spring of 1961 Joe Kennedy paid to have the pool area redecorated. The wall with high windows was covered over with a mural of a sunset at St. Croix, and a private passageway was constructed from the pool area to the elevator, as JFK always left the room wearing nothing but a towel wrapped around his middle.

He took the elevator to the living area, and Jackie joined him in his bedroom, where they were served lunch in bed—for JFK, a hamburger would do. Then the doors were closed, and Kennedy napped. The rule was absolutely no interruptions until three-thirty. George Thomas usually woke the president, but if he was not going to be available, he asked Preston Bruce, a doorman, to do it. Bruce was initially startled at the assignment and wanted to know just how he was supposed to wake up the president. "Oh, just tickle his toes, Bruce," Thomas told him. Bruce was incredulous, but he tiptoed into the bedroom and found JFK and Jackie sleeping. He jiggled the president's toe. Kennedy opened his eyes and said, "Hello, Bruce." As doorman, Bruce kept extra rubbers and raincoats for Kennedy at the first floor entrance, but sometimes Kennedy refused them. "He was like a little schoolboy," Bruce said. JFK would ask to borrow a comb from Bruce, run it through his hair, then slip it in his pocket. Later, Bruce would get his combs back from George Thomas.

His nap over, Kennedy showered, dressed in a fresh suit, and was back in the Oval Office a little after three-thirty. After finishing his business day, he had another swim and dressed for dinner, again in a fresh suit. He seldom worked in the evening. He liked to have his head massaged, and often watched the *Huntley-Brinkley Report* news show on television. He loved gossip, especially about Hollywood stars, and was an avid reader of *Variety*. He screened films at the White House theater, where he had a reclining chair for his back that allowed him to be almost horizontal. He often ate dinner late, telling Bruce to send the butlers home and leave his meal in a warming oven so he could help himself.

Jackie frequently left her husband on his own. He lived and breathed politics, while she found it boring and intrusive. When Adlai Stevenson's call from the United Nations during the October 1962 Cuban missile crisis interrupted the Kennedys' evening at home, Jackie turned up the volume on her record player. She took to spending three- or four-day weekends with the children in Virginia at Glen Ora. Jackie liked Glen Ora in part because she could go horseback riding, but JFK disliked it as there was no water for sailing. But going separate ways was not unusual for their social set. "Their nomadic lives, their separateness—a phenomenon of great wealth—was not fully understood by the public," said friend Hugh Sidey, White House correspondent for *Time*.

When Jackie and JFK were both home in the White House, Bruce had to contend with a small problem. It was his job to secure the upstairs family quarters for the night—turn off lights and lock the doors to the stairwell. He could count on the Eisenhowers to be in bed and asleep by about ten, but the Kennedys were always up late. Bruce sometimes came across one or the other, skimpily attired, going from one bedroom to another—they had separate bedrooms. His presence didn't seem to bother the first couple, but Bruce was embarrassed. He asked Chief Usher West what to do, but West just gazed off into space. Bruce got up the nerve to approach the Kennedys. JFK told him not to worry about coming into the private quarters: "Sure, come right ahead." Jackie added with a little smile, "Don't worry, Bruce. We know you're married too."

On weekends, Kennedy seldom stayed in the White House, usually leaving Friday afternoon for Palm Beach or Hyannis Port. He liked sailing, swimming, and golf. From the first time he picked up a golf club at prep school, he had a fluid, naturally graceful swing. He played on the golf team at Harvard, and as president his score was still excellent—in the seventies—though he played only fifteen to twenty times a year. He once called Cecil Stoughton, the White House photographer, to Hyannis Port to take slow-motion pictures of his swing so he could analyze it later.

Golf, however, invited unwanted comparisons with Eisenhower, who had been roundly criticized for his frequent play. During his run for the presidency, Kennedy sneaked away with buddy Red Fay for a round of golf in Monterey, California. On a par-three hole, Kennedy's first shot hit the green and began rolling toward the cup—it looked like he was about to get a hole in one.

"Go! Go, baby!" Red yelled.

"No! No!" yelled Kennedy.

"If that ball had gone into the hole," JFK later explained, "it would be all over the country . . . another golfer trying to get into the White House."

Speechwriter Dick Goodwin once entered the Oval Office and found the president standing by the glass doors that open onto the south grounds. Kennedy pointed to the indentations in the floor. "It's from Ike's golf shoes," he explained. "He put them on at his desk, then walked out here to practice his putting." Smiling, he added, "Maybe we ought to put a rope around this piece of floor and leave it as an Eisenhower memorial." Kennedy joked about it, but he was acutely conscious of avoiding the Eisenhower golf image. He tried to keep the press away when he did play. Ike's putting green was too public, and Kennedy never used it, but he didn't have it taken out.

Another problem with golf was that a full swing aggravated his back. JFK's back problems began when he was a scrawny, sickly child and were aggravated by his wartime injury. In 1944, while still in the navy, he had his first back surgery, to insert a metal plate. The procedure was unsuccessful, and from then on he lived with varying degrees of back pain. By 1954 he was back on crutches and could hardly walk. Doctors at the Lahey Clinic in Boston refused to perform a spinal operation because by then Kennedy had been diagnosed as having Addison's disease—an adrenal insufficiency that makes one more susceptible to infection. Doctors at the New York Hospital for Special Surgery, however, did agree to do the operation. Kennedy's personal physician at the time, Dr. Sara Jordan, opposed the operation because of the risk of postoperative infection, but Kennedy told Jackie, "I'd rather be dead than spend the rest of my life on crutches." The graft was done, and as feared, infection set in. Kennedy was in critical condition for three weeks and received the last rites of the Catholic Church. He improved, but two months later he required further surgery to remove the metal plate and again nearly died. During the long, painful recovery period, he wrote a best-selling book, *Profiles in Courage.*

In the early months of his presidency, on a visit to Canada, Kennedy tried to lift a silver shovel of dirt at a tree-planting ceremony and reinjured his back. By the time he got back to Air Force One he could hardly move. His personal physician, Dr. Janet Travell, prescribed a back brace and exercises, and injected procaine when the pain was severe. From then on, Kennedy always used crutches when he was out of sight of the public. His secretary, Evelyn Lincoln, said, "He would hide his crutches and canes around the office. It was hard for him to use them even in front of me. He used them mostly when he was alone. He was a very proud man. But I used to buy those athletic rubber supports for his back."

*Kennedy was the first President to have live televised press conferences. He enjoyed repartee with the press and liked to say, "I am now ready for the questions to my answers."* (JOHN F. KENNEDY LIBRARY)

Admiral George Burkley, a navy doctor, noticed toward the end of 1961 that Kennedy's back problem was getting worse. His body was getting soft, and he had increasing difficulty getting out of chairs. Dr. Travell was relieving the pain with injections several times a day, but specialists disagreed with this treatment, arguing that the shots were of decreasing effectiveness as the body adapted to them and that the muscles meanwhile were atrophying from lack of exercise. Burkley insisted that Dr. Travell bring in Dr. Hans Kraus, a New York orthopedic surgeon. Kraus told Kennedy, "You are going to be a cripple if you do not exercise." Kennedy rejected the suggested three-hour physical therapy sessions because he knew the press would find out. "It's your decision," Dr. Kraus said. "But you will only get worse. What will they write then?" Kennedy began a conditioning program in October 1961, in a new gym adjacent to the White House pool. His abdominal and back muscles rapidly increased in strength by 50 percent.

Kennedy returned from his 1961 meeting with Khrushchev in Vienna in severe pain and went to Palm Beach to recuperate. Returning to Washington, he had to be lifted onto Air Force One with an airport cherry picker. Back at the White House, he worked out of his bedroom. At this time he also suffered one of his periodic bouts of debilitating fever—related to Addison's—his worst as president. Dr. Travell gave him large doses of penicillin, and the fever came down to 101 degrees. She told the press about the 101-degree fever, but skipped mentioning that it had soared to 105 degrees during the night.

It was in the late 1940s that Kennedy developed symptoms of Addison's disease. In addition to susceptibility to infection, Addison's can cause weakness, weight loss, and low blood pressure. When the issue of Kennedy's health came up during the 1960 campaign, Dr. Travell gave a statement to the press that covered the situation without specifically denying that JFK had Addison's disease. She said he had "tremendous physical stamina" and "above average resistance to infections, such as influenza." His bouts of fever were generally attributed to exposure to malaria during the war. In the 1920s, 90 percent of Addison's sufferers died within five years, but by 1939 treatment was available to control it. JFK went to the Mayo Clinic for an experimental procedure that involved implanting pellets of drugs in his thighs every three months. Stress and exertion had to be avoided. In the 1950s he began taking cortisone—he was one of the first Addison sufferers to be treated this way. Some common side effects of cortisone treatment are tan skin, thick hair, puffy face, an enhanced sense of confidence, and increased sex drive.

For his back pain, JFK was also taking a drug-laced concoction developed by Max Jacobson, a New York doctor, who visited the mansion at least thirty-four times during 1961 and 1962, according to White House logs. Jacobson—known as "Dr. Feelgood"— had many famous clients, most of them in show business. He injected Kennedy with his own unspecified mix of multivitamins, hormones, steroids, enzymes, and animal organ cells, all laced with amphetamines, which can produce addiction, hyperactivity, impaired judgment, and hypertension. Robert Kennedy had the mixture analyzed and tried to warn his brother of the hazards. "I don't care if it's horse piss. It works," Kennedy said. Jacobson also injected Jackie with his mixture. "They never could have made it without me," the doctor claimed.

Kennedy first met Jacobson during his election campaign. He was tense and run down, and he arranged an office visit. After the injection, Jacobson noted that JFK felt "calm and very alert. I gave him a bottle of vitamin drops to be taken orally, after which he left." Jacobson treated Kennedy regularly, including at many critical times: just before the first televised presidential debate with Nixon in 1960, before his radio address during the integration crisis at the University of Mississippi in September 1962, and during the Cuban missile crisis in October 1962. In June 1961 Kennedy asked Jacobson to accompany him to Paris, where he was meeting with French president Charles de Gaulle. He didn't want the press to see the doctor boarding Air Force One, so Jacobson and his wife, Nina, flew on a chartered Air France plane, the only passengers on board. But when Kennedy went on from Paris to Vienna to meet Khrushchev, he did take Jacobson along on Air Force One. The doctor's last visit with Kennedy was at Palm Beach in November 1963, as JFK was getting ready for his fatal Texas trip. In 1975 Dr. Jacobson lost his medical license for manufacturing "adulterated drugs consisting of filthy, putrid and/or decomposed substances."

While Kennedy was busy heading off publicity about his various ailments, Jackie, the most photographed first lady in history, was trying to avoid publicity, period. She held no press conferences, avoided interviews, and was particularly protective of her children. Instead of sending Caroline off to school, she hosted kindergarten and then first grade in the third-floor solarium. Children of friends and administrative staff shared the cost of a teacher. Jackie set up a sandbox filled with sand ordered from the national parks. On the south lawn, she designed a play yard complete with a rabbit hutch, barrel tunnel, leather swing, and slide. Lamb pens were added, and a stable for ponies Macaroni and Tex, along with dog houses and guinea pig cages. Kennedy could watch the hubbub from the Oval Office and so could tourists, who lined up at the fence. Tourist buses began stopping and unloading passengers who wanted a look. "I'm sick and tired of starring in everybody's home movies," Jackie said, and ordered a thick row of rhododendrons planted along the fence. She told her press secretary, Pamela Turnure, that her job was not to get the family in the papers, but to keep them out. She wanted to be just a family. Once, on Cape Cod, Caroline showed her cousin, Maria Shriver, a postcard with a picture of JFK on it. "That's the President," Maria said. "No, no, it is not. That's my Daddy," Caroline insisted.

Jackie had reason to be concerned about the intrusions of reporters. When she gave birth to John, a photographer came out of hiding and snapped a flash picture of her as she was being wheeled unconscious from the delivery room. Attempts were even made to get a picture of John in the nursery, despite the fact that the exploding flashbulbs used at that time were dangerous in a hospital where oxygen was in use.

Jackie was devoted to the care of John and Caroline. "If you bungle raising your children, I don't think whatever else you do well matters very much," she maintained. Among other things, she provided them with plenty of pets. There were at least fifteen pets of different types at the White House at any one time, and their upkeep ran to $1,500 a month. There was Zsa Zsa, a beer-drinking rabbit that could play the trumpet; a canary named Robin; lovebirds Maybell and Bluebell; Tom Kitten; and two ponies, Leprechaun and Macaroni. She also got ducks for them—"I wanted something the children would love on the White House lawn." The experiment was short-lived because the ducks destroyed the tulip beds around the south pool. Jackie turned down gifts of an Indian tiger cub and an Indian elephant but wanted to keep the Irish deer from the president of Ireland, Eamon de Valera. Warned that the deer were dangerous,

Jackie reluctantly released them to the zoo. A few weeks later she asked the chief usher, "Mr. West—will you see about getting a pair of peacocks." West came back with, "The zoo says peacocks are dangerous and unpredictable." He was lying, but enough was enough, he thought. There were hamsters all over the White House. One day, secretary Mary Gallagher entered her office, turned on the light, and a hamster ran out at her. She screamed. Then one drowned in the president's bathtub. Press secretary Salinger was wakened at 3 A.M. by a call from a reporter, Helen Thomas: "I wouldn't call you at an ungodly hour like this, Pierre, if it weren't important. But we have a report that one of Caroline's hamsters has died. Would you check it out for me?" Dogs included Charlie, a Welsh terrier that chased the ducks; Clipper, a police dog; an Irish wolfhound; a cocker spaniel; and Pushinka, a gift from Nikita Khrushchev.

Pushinka was the offspring of Strelka, a dog the Soviets sent up in space, who had just had puppies when Jackie met Khrushchev in Vienna in 1961. Jackie, who captivated Khrushchev, said, "Why don't you send me one?" The Soviet leader's meetings with Kennedy were antagonistic, but he sent Jackie liqueurs, a picture album of Moscow, a gold tea set, nine bottles of perfume—and Pushinka. The Secret Service had to check the gifts, including the dog, for bugs. Though there were no secret listening devices, the dog proved problematic for JFK. Pushinka, like all dogs, caused problems with JFK's allergies. His eyes would tear and his face swell to the point that he had trouble breathing.

Kennedy tolerated the pets for the sake of his children. He was an indulgent parent and liked to play with his kids, even though he couldn't lift them because of his back. He loved it when Caroline told reporters that her father was "upstairs with his shoes and socks off, doing nothing." And he let her steal the show at a press conference when she wandered in among the wires and lights wearing pajamas and a robe and flopping about in her mother's shoes. Young John played in the Oval Office and discovered a panel in the front of the Resolute desk used by his father. It allowed him to surprise visitors. Jackie, as always, objected to the public exposure of the children and often frustrated JFK when he wanted them around for publicity shots.

His children saved his life on December 11, 1960. President-elect JFK and his family were staying in Palm Beach, and Jackie and Caroline and several nieces and nephews came out of the house to JFK's car to see him off to church. Richard K. Pavlick was watching from a parked car with seven sticks of dynamite that could be exploded by pressing a switch. He was moved by the scene: "I did not want to harm her or the children. I decided to get him at church or someplace later." Later never came. The Secret Service had received reports from police in Belmont, New York, that a man, probably insane, had uttered threats against JFK and was headed to Palm Beach. A massive hunt located him.

As president, when asked about the danger of assassination, Kennedy answered, "I guess there is always the possibility, but that is what the Secret Service is for. I guess that is one of the less desirable aspects of the job." Like most modern presidents, he worried less about attempts on his life than about the restrictions of White House life. Friend Charlie Spaulding recalled parting from Kennedy, distraught after the Bay of Pigs fiasco: "[He] walked down with me to the gate, to that big fence on Pennsylvania Avenue where I was getting a cab. He actually came out on the street with me, with Secret Service men scrambling all over the place, and he said to me, 'Charlie, what's out

there? What's out there?' and I said, 'There's people out there. People and places to go.'
And he said, 'Tell me, am I missing something? What am I missing?'"

The president once slipped out of New York's Hotel Carlyle, where he had a duplex
penthouse, without the Secret Service knowing it. When they couldn't find him, they
were angry; they locked all but the main entrance. He returned after midnight, and
asked breezily, "Is there anything you'd like to talk about?" On another occasion the
Secret Service helped him escape reporters camped out in the lobby. They took him
out a hidden exit, accessed by underground tunnels that led to neighboring apartment
buildings. "It was kind of a weird sight," recalled Spaulding. "Jack and I and two Secret
Service men walking in these huge tunnels underneath the city streets alongside those
enormous pipes, each of us carrying a flashlight. One of the Secret Service men also
had this underground map, and every once in a while he would say, 'We turn this way,
Mr. President.' " Kennedy came to appreciate and cooperate with the Secret Service.
Working late in the Oval Office on a cold night, he told the agent outside the French
doors, "I don't want you out there in this terrible cold." The agent wouldn't leave his
post, so JFK got him a fleece-lined coat, brought out two hot chocolates, and sat outside
drinking with him for a while.

For whatever security imperatives denied him of the outside world, JFK, as all presidents, also had access to the world in ways ordinary citizens do not. To make calls outside the White House, the president had only to pick up the phone and say, "Get
me. . ." The White House operators were known for being able to find anyone, anywhere. On a social evening with their friends Toni and Ben Bradlee, White House correspondent for *Newsweek,* the Kennedys were discussing the operators' fame and
decided to put them to the test. Jackie suggested calling Truman Capote, as she knew
he had an unlisted phone number in New York. Kennedy picked up the phone and
asked for Truman Capote. A half hour later, Capote was on the phone from another
unlisted number in California.

Getting mistresses was almost as easy, thanks to the Secret Service. According to
Secret Service agent Marty Venker, "The agent was supposed to set up dates for the
President. If he was new to the job and wasn't aware of this fact, Kennedy let him know
pretty quickly. He'd say something to the effect of 'You've been here two weeks already
and still don't have any broads lined up for me? You guys get all the broads you want.
How about doing something for your Commander-in-Chief?' " The Secret Service did
its duty, although they required some "broads," such as airline stewardesses, to go
through a full security investigation.

A variety of friends also procured women for the president. "Jack was something like
a Roto-Rooter," commented George Smathers, a Florida senator. JFK's friend and
adviser Kenny O'Donnell escorted female guests into the White House through a back
door to avoid official log entries. His brother-in-law, Peter Lawford, the movie star,
found Leslie Devereaux, a New York call girl. "I visited him twice at the White House,"
Devereaux recalled, "the first time for only 15 minutes in a small room off the Oval
Office. His secretaries didn't so much as blink when they saw me. They showed me in
and out as they would the Secretary of State." On the second visit, a Secret Service
agent escorted her to the Lincoln Bedroom. "That's Abraham Lincoln's bed," the agent
told her. "You mean I'm to lie down on that, on Abraham Lincoln's bed?" she asked.

"Lady, it's the best we've got," the agent replied. JFK first met Marilyn Monroe at Peter Lawford's home, and their affair was widely talked about, with rumors appearing in gossip columns and even *Variety*. Frank Sinatra passed along his former mistress, Judith Campbell Exner, who at the time was also intimate with Sam Giancana, a Chicago Mafia boss. She made some twenty visits to the White House, and the White House logs show many phone calls from her, but she and Kennedy usually met in hotels around the country. When Kennedy arrived at the Conrad Hilton Hotel in Chicago, he was able to slip out to Judy's hotel, the Ambassador East, for twenty minutes. The White House press office covered, announcing that the president "remained in his suite until 7 P.M."

His approach to sex was open and casual—he startled one ambassador, a bachelor, on a receiving line by asking, "Are you getting any lately?"—and Jackie was not ignorant of her husband's extracurricular activities. Her maid gave her a pair of silk panties she had found. Jackie handed them to Kennedy: "Here, would you find out who these belong to? They're not my size." She was aware that her press secretary, Pamela Turnure, was having an affair with JFK, yet the two women remained friends for many years, even after JFK's death. But Jackie knew, as Peter Lawford put it, that Kennedy was not "the type to confuse sex with love, not even when it involved somebody as glamorous and famous as Marilyn Monroe."

Lawford also introduced JFK to cocaine and hashish, and JFK sometimes took drugs with another of his lovers, Mary Meyer. Meyer had been a friend of JFK's since his prep school days at Choate, and was also Jackie's friend and walking companion. Her husband was a CIA agent. According to her confidant, James Angleton, director of covert operations for the CIA, Mary brought "a small box with six joints" to the White House in July of 1963. "They shared one," said Angleton, "and Kennedy laughingly told her they were having a White House conference on narcotics in a couple of weeks. They smoked two more joints and Kennedy drew back his head and closed his eyes. He refused a fourth joint. 'Suppose the Russians drop a bomb,' he said." Mary and the president met in the White House thirty to forty times. On another occasion they made love and tripped on LSD.

The Russians didn't drop the bomb, but there were other crises to contend with. On April 7, 1961, guerrillas backed by the United States invaded Cuba at the Bay of Pigs in hope of ousting Communist leader Fidel Castro. The mission, already in the advanced planning stages when Kennedy took office, turned into a fiasco. "I must have been out of my goddamn mind to listen to those people," Kennedy said. "How could I have been so far off base? All my life I've known better than to depend on experts. How could I have been so stupid to let them go ahead?" He suffered severe stress. He was going over options with aides in the Oval Office at 4 A.M. when he suddenly left in the middle of a sentence and walked out on the south lawn. The next morning he was crying in his bedroom. After the Bay of Pigs invasion was behind him, he said to adviser Clark Clifford, "Let me tell you something. I have had two full days of hell—I haven't slept—this has been the most excruciating period of my life."

The Kennedys' marriage showed signs of strain as well. In the summer of 1962, when Marilyn Monroe died and rumors circulated regarding Kennedy's relationship with her, Jackie took Caroline and left for a vacation on the Amalfi coast of Italy. Weeks went by with no sign of her return, but she got plenty of press coverage: Jackie at parties, Jackie doing the Twist, Jackie swimming with Italian billionaire Gianni Agnelli off his yacht. JFK sent messages urging her to return, and she did around Labor Day.

In 1963 Jackie became pregnant again but on August 6 had to be rushed to a Cape Cod hospital, where a son, Patrick Bouvier Kennedy, was born five weeks prematurely. JFK came to her side immediately, but the infant lived for only three days. It was the second child she had lost. Her first, an unnamed girl, was stillborn in 1954. The couple reached out to each other. Jackie sobbed, "Oh, Jack. Oh, Jack. There's only one thing I could not bear now—if I ever lost you." Friends noticed how much closer they became. "At long last, they were truly coming closer together," reporter Theodore White said.

Jackie had distanced herself from JFK's first presidential campaign. Now he was planning reelection strategy and wanted Jackie to join him on a trip to Texas, where he hoped to unite two warring Democratic factions. Jackie said, "If Jack wants me, I'll go anywhere." Kennedy was elated.

"Dallas is a very dangerous place," Senator William Fulbright warned Kennedy. "I wouldn't go there. Don't you go." Texas wasn't Kennedy country. It was right wing, conservative, dangerous for a liberal proponent of civil rights. But it was Democratic, and the president needed to hold the party together for the 1964 election. Throughout his term JFK had speculated about assassination, and even about being shot while riding in an open car. His feeling about the Dallas trip was, "If they are going to get me, they will get me even in church." The Secret Service wanted him to use the bulletproof bubble top on his car, a big Lincoln that traveled wherever he did, but Kennedy overruled them. Initially it seemed like the right decision. The president and first lady, traveling with Lyndon and Lady Bird Johnson, were received with warm enthusiasm in San Antonio, Houston, and Fort Worth. Jackie was overwhelmingly popular. At Dallas airport it was the same.

On November 22, 1963, JFK's motorcade was winding its way to the Dallas Trade Mart, where the president would make a speech. Kennedy, riding in the open car, was shot and killed by Lee Harvey Oswald. The car sped to Parkland Hospital in Dallas, Jackie cradling her dying husband in her arms. A stunned country saw her bloodstained clothes, shared her grief, and admired her courage and dignity throughout the ordeal of the funeral back in Washington.

Jackie was devastated, and in private gave way to days of sobbing. "My mommy cries all day," Caroline said. She didn't understand.

She asked Jackie, "Mommy, did they love Daddy?"

"Oh, yes, they loved Daddy," her mother said.

But Caroline shook her head. She didn't believe it. "They didn't, or they wouldn't have done that to him."

Maude Shaw, the children's nanny, had to tell three-year-old John his father had gone to heaven.

"Did Daddy take his big plane with him?" he asked. Miss Shaw told him he did.

"I wonder when he's coming back," John said.

Before she left the White House, Jackie ordered a bronze plaque placed over the mantel in the president's bedroom: "In this room lived John Fitzgerald Kennedy with his wife Jacqueline—during the two years, ten months and two days he was President of the United States—January 20, 1961–November 22, 1963."

"I'm a living wound," Jackie said. "My life is over." She asked Lyndon Johnson if Caroline's school could continue at the White House, and it did for six months. But she herself resisted all his entreaties to come back to the White House. On October 20, 1968, she married Greek shipping magnate Aristotle Onassis. She died May 19, 1994, and was buried in Arlington National Cemetery beside President Kennedy, her son Patrick Bouvier Kennedy, and her stillborn daughter.

In 1961 Congress passed a law decreeing that White House objects were "considered to be inalienable and property of the White House." It was a new concept. Prior to that presidents had given away china in poker bets, handed it out as souvenirs, and sold it off at lawn sales, routinely held in the nineteenth century as a means of disposing of "decayed furnishings." Much has been lost to history—or breakage.

Thousands of dollars of china were lost in the melee following Andrew Jackson's inauguration. The Lincolns ordered purple-rimmed china in their first term (amid accusations of pretensions to royalty), but quickly needed a second service. Mourners and curiousity seekers so ravaged the White House after the death of their son Willie that new china was necessary. Mary Todd Lincoln chose the simplest pattern she could find, white with a buff border and tiny lines of gold. As was customary, it even decorated the presidential chamber pot.

The history of the White House china collection dates back to Caroline Harrison, who discovered odds and ends during her top-to-bottom cleaning of the old mansion. She planned to display her finds, but ill health intervened. Her project was continued by Ida Saxon McKinley, who invited Abby Gunn Baker to spend the summer of 1901 studying china at the White House. She discovered that not more than seven administrations were represented and wrote articles pleading for gifts or loans from collectors or former presidents. Edith Roosevelt made the first attempt at a proper china display after the 1902 renovation, setting up shelves in the basement that held twenty or thirty pieces. She put an end to the custom of selling or giving away chipped or broken china, keeping it in a tub in the basement and then having it dumped in the Potomac. In 1917 Edith Wilson set aside the present China Room.

Not all presidents have commissioned a china service, preferring to use their congressional appropriations decorating or on general repair. But when the opportunity has arisen, many have relied on patriotic motifs to decorate the centers of plates. Eagles, clutching the olive branch of peace and the arrows of war, have been the most consistent theme. Harry Truman discovered when it came time to order his china that sometimes the eagle's beak on his predecessor's plates faced the arrows, sometimes, the olive branches. He had a law passed mandating a peaceful orientation.

The rims of plates have varied more widely over the years. Caroline Harrison, a china painter, designed ears of corn and goldenrod, appropriately American themes. These were sketched in gold and overlaid on blue. Other borders have ranged from red, Nancy Reagan's signature color, to the brilliant yellow of the Grant china. Harry Truman had the simplest of design methods. He said, "Just have it match the State Dining Room walls." They were celadon, and so was the border on his china. When the Eisenhowers came into office, they couldn't rationalize a complete new service, so Mamie ordered service plates with an ornate gold band to set beneath Truman's celadon-edged dinnerware. Hillary Clinton did something no other first lady had done. Instead of designing her own plates, she asked Lenox to reissue service plates from the Woodrow Wilson dinnerware and dinner plates from the Franklin Roosevelt china.

The most striking of all the White House plates were ordered by Lucy Webb Hayes. She'd signed a contract to purchase plates with fern motifs from Haviland in France when artist Theodore Davis persauded her to abandon her plans and let him paint wildlife scenes for each plate. Thus the turkey platter features a fowl on a snowy landscape, a crab crawls to the center of a soup bowl, a snowshoe marks an ice cream dish, and the ever-popular Victorian oyster plate displays half-opened shells. The results were not entirely successful. Guests complained that they didn't want to see the animal they just ate in its original habitat.

Lucy Hayes tried to have her china made in the United States, but France still held the monopoly on quality. Even the British firm Wedgwood didn't successfully produce and market bone china until 1878. This did not please Theodore Roosevelt. He thundered, "Is it possible? Is it possible that we are dependent on foreign factories for the very dishes upon which the Chief Executives of the United States must eat?" Woodrow Wilson was the first president able to order from Lenox in Trenton, New Jersey.

Flowers were the features of several presidential services. Polk had a wonderful spray of roses on his dessert plates, typically the most elaborate of nineteenth-century tableware. Grant's dinnerware featured American flowers, but nobody made native blooms as important as the Lyndon Johnsons, who used wildflowers on the dinner plate borders and on the dessert plates, individual blooms representing all fifty states and the District of Columbia.

"When I look back at these china plates, I look back with satisfaction," recalled Lady Bird Johnson in a recent interview. "I'm so pleased that I chose wildflowers. The pattern is simple and restrained. So many people who came to the White House when we were there—and have come since—tell me how they look for their state flower. The china is so varied that you can come to the White House every day and not get the same place setting. That's what wildflowers are like."

When Tiffany & Company designed the china, every detail was meticulously accounted for. Artist André Piette even came down to Washington to observe the effects of candlelight in the White House dining room. After each gold-dotted piece was finished, it was sent to Lady Bird for approval—with one exception. In Tiffany's haste to complete the service before the Johnsons left office, only one dessert plate was shown to the first lady. Since each featured a different flower, that proved to be a grave mistake. Tiffany chairman Walter Hoving arrived for the china's unveiling only to insist that the dessert service be redone.

The imperfect plates were taken "down to the White House bomb shelter," recalled Bess Able, Lady Bird's social secretary. She, curator James Ketchum, and others "threw the plates at a wall. We just had a marvelous time."

# 36

# Lyndon B. Johnson

## 1963–1969

## *Power*

On December 22, 1963, exactly one month after the assassination of John F. Kennedy, President Lyndon Johnson ordered that the black netting shrouding all of the White House chandeliers in mourning of Kennedy be taken down. The Johnson family then put up Christmas decorations. "I walked the well-lit hall for the first time with a sense that life was going to go on, that we as a country were going to begin again," Claudia "Lady Bird" Johnson recalled.

On the day of the assassination, Johnson was riding in an open limousine two cars behind President Kennedy when shots rang out. Secret Service agent Rufus Youngblood pushed then vice president Johnson down to the floor of the car and jumped on top of him. Johnson was crushed between the hump in the floor and the weight of the man on top of him. He was not sure what had happened, and Youngblood, listening and talking on his miniature radio, told him nothing as the limousine roared off at eighty miles an hour.

Then he told Johnson, "We are going into the hospital and we aren't going to stop for anything or anybody. Do you understand? We will separate from the other party the moment we stop!"

"Okay pardner, I understand," Johnson replied in a rare moment of meekness.

Just how rare a moment it was for the new president Youngblood would find out that evening at the airport in Washington.

"Rufus," said Johnson, "where's my hat?"

"Your hat, sir?" Rufus asked.

"It was in the car during the motorcade."

"Then that's where it probably still is, sir. I didn't get it."

"Well, get the damn thing! Call Dallas and have one of your men get it!" LBJ demanded.

"I'll see to the hat, sir," Rufus said.

Suddenly, Lyndon Johnson was president. He had always planned to be. At the age of twelve LBJ told a classmate, "Someday, I'm going to be President of the United States." That hardly seemed realistic. Born August 27, 1908, near Stonewall, Texas, he grew up poor, driven, and insecure. When the wealthy banker father of Lyndon's college sweetheart, Carol Davis, told his daughter not to have anything to do with those worthless Johnsons, LBJ was enraged. "I wouldn't marry you or anyone in your whole damned family," he said, and repeated his childhood declaration," and you can tell your daddy that someday I'll be President of this country." He was elected to Congress in 1937, and to the Senate in 1948. In 1954 he became the Democratic majority leader. He was chosen as Kennedy's running mate in 1960. And in November 1963 he made good on his promise, if by unexpected and tragic means.

Thrust into the presidency, Johnson was also thrust into a new home, the White House. He came to it from The Elms, the mansion he had recently purchased from Perle Mesta, the famous Washington hostess. Over the years Johnson had become not only powerful, but rich, with holdings of real estate, banks, and radio and TV stations worth $15 million. ("I do not have any interest in government regulated industries of any kind and never have had," he told reporters in 1964. The Austin TV station was in his wife's name, and when he took office, his other interests were put in a blind trust.) Now he was less than satisfied with the White House, and the staff, like Agent Youngblood, was about to get a taste of Johnson's demanding personality.

In particular, the new president found the shower in his bathroom entirely unacceptable. He wanted a shower like the one he had at home, one that sprayed from every direction, including from the floor, "to hit him up in his rear" according to White House plumber Howard "Red" Arrington. "Mr. West," LBJ said to the chief usher, "if you can't get that shower of mine fixed, I'm going to move back to The Elms."

West went over to Johnson's home with the plumbers and the White House engineer to study the shower he had there. Back at the mansion, with some help from the shower manufacturer's engineers, they tried five different versions of the shower LBJ had at The Elms. "We ended up with four pumps," Red Arrington said, "then we had to increase the size of the water lines because the other parts of the house were being sucked dry. One day the head usher tried the shower. It pinned him right up against the wall." When Johnson gave his successor, Richard Nixon, a tour of the White House, he proudly showed him the shower. The first time Nixon tried it, the blast almost knocked him out of the bathroom. "Please have the shower heads all changed to normal pressure," he wrote to the chief usher.

Johnson never was completely satisfied with the shower. But then LBJ was also unhappy with his shower at his Texas ranch. "Goddamnit," he said, "I want a shower here at the ranch just like I have at the White House." When LBJ was told that this would require laying new pipe and installing a booster pump, he said, "Then do it." Then he added, "I want the military to handle this. And since this is a military operation, you can pay for it." The new water pump cost $125,000 and had to be covered with classified funds intended for security measures.

Despite such excesses, Johnson could also be exceedingly cost-conscious. He was particularly concerned about the White House electric bill. All unused lights were to be off at night, including the exterior lights, and the president roamed the mansion at night turning them off. Isaac Avery, a carpenter, was working in his basement shop when suddenly he was plunged into darkness.

"Goddamnit, who turned off that light?" Avery shouted.

"I did," the president said, and admitted, "I didn't realize you fellows worked so late."

Daughter Lynda always carried a flashlight in her bathrobe pocket because the upstairs corridors were pitch-black at night. "It was important to have a flashlight around during the Johnson administration," said Traphes Bryant, an electrician. "The President was forever turning the lights off on me. He never looked around to see who needed light."

Johnson was finally in power, and he didn't want anyone to forget it. When he didn't like the way a steward mixed his drink—a simple Cutty Sark and soda—he threw it on the floor. "Get somebody who knows how to make a drink for me." When he wanted to show singer Dinah Shore his dogs, he dialed the wrong extension and instead of the dog handler got Bill Ruback, the White House gardener. Ruback told LBJ he had dialed the wrong number. "You're fired!" LBJ roared. Ruback made himself scarce until LBJ forgot about the incident.

Perhaps the most frequent recipient of the president's abuse was Jack Valenti, the forty-seven-year-old former advertising executive Johnson appointed chief of staff but treated more like a butler: "Jack! What time's that damn plane leave? And why are we always running out of Fresca?"

Later, Fresca didn't satisfy. On Air Force One, Master Sergeant Joe Ayres served LBJ one root beer after another, with the president belching loudly between servings. He called for another.

"I'm sorry, Mr. President, but we don't have any more diet root beer. I can offer diet Fresca, diet Pepsi, diet orange, or diet ginger ale."

Johnson shouted, "Sergeant, how many times do I have to tell you I want diet root beer on this plane at all times! It is not a very difficult transaction. You can get the fuckin' stuff anywhere. Sergeant, I want an order sent out to all Air Force bases: stock root beer!"

"Yes, sir," replied Sergeant Ayres.

When Air Force One landed, Ayres turned in a request for a new assignment.

During another trip on Air Force One, reporter Frank Cormier was startled to see Sergeant Paul Glynn, LBJ's valet, approach the president and, "kneeling before him without saying a word," remove the shoe and sock from one foot, bathe the naked foot, then put on a fresh sock and replace the shoe. "Talking all the while, Johnson paid no heed except to cross his legs in the opposite direction when it was time for Glynn to attend to the other foot. After seeing this, I was not surprised to be told that the sergeant also clipped the President's toenails."

Secret Service received similar treatment from Johnson. As vice president he once insisted that Secret Service agent Jerry Kivett help him dress for a formal party. When LBJ criticized his technique, Kivett replied, "Well, sir, you have to consider that this is the first time in my life I ever dressed another full-grown man!" At Johnson's ranch, just west of Austin, Texas, agents consented to clean out his pool, but when he asked them to wash his car, they refused. He ordered the Secret Service to install and pay for a car-washing machine on the premises. And when nature called, the agents were ordered to gather around the president to shield him from view. Once, an agent named Henderson felt the warm stream on his pants leg. When he protested, Johnson told him that it was all right—"That's my prerogative."

The ranch was a status symbol—it was a working ranch, but not really profitable. LBJ much preferred it to the White House. "It's not a home," he said of the executive mansion. "It's someplace you go when you finish work." During the five years he served as president, he spent a total of about a year at the ranch. When he bought the place in the 1940s, it was a run-down wreck of a house that cost just $20,000. "It reminded me of the Addams cartoons," Lady Bird said. There were bats under the chimney. She wailed, "How could you *possibly* do this to me?" By the time Johnson was president, the ranch had expanded to 4,400 acres, the straggly stream called the Pedernales had been dammed to make a small lake, and there was a 6,300-foot landing strip.

The president liked showing his ranch off to guests, touring it in his big white Lincoln Continental convertible with the Secret Service eating dust behind him in their station wagon. He was known for driving at high speeds with one hand on the wheel and a foam cup of Cutty Sark and soda in the other. When he wanted a refill, he slowed down, stuck out his left arm, and shook the ice in the cup. On that signal, an agent had to run up to his car, take the cup, and run back to the station wagon, where another agent would refill the cup, then run back to Johnson's car to hand it to him. Throughout the procedure, Johnson never stopped the Lincoln.

He also had an amphibious vehicle that looked like a car, and liked to scare guests by driving it into the water. Political adviser Clark Clifford recounted how one day when he and his wife, Mary, were riding in it LBJ accelerated down the hill to the lake. "The brakes have failed," he shouted. Clifford and his wife scrambled to the backseat as the vehicle hit the water and were about to jump out when LBJ pushed a button and the amphibian moved through the water. Johnson enjoyed teasing the guests he subjected to this stunt, and naming people who had jumped out.

LBJ also liked to race around the ranch in an old fire engine, a gift from a small town. It had a bell, which he clanged as he drove. Once, as he drove by White House reporter Marianne Means, he shouted, "This is why Barry Goldwater wanted to be President." Johnson had no qualms about accepting gifts. When he received an expensive grandfather's clock, he was reminded by Jack Valenti, "Sir, there's a rule we can't accept anything over fifty dollars." "I wouldn't pay fifty dollars for that thing," LBJ said, and put it in his library at the ranch.

On a helicopter flight in Texas, the pilot, Marine Colonel Walt Sienko, banked away from a thunderhead. LBJ told Secret Service agent Rufus Youngblood to find out why the pilot was turning. When informed of the storm, LBJ ordered the agent to go back and tell the pilot to keep a straight course. After the third set of instructions from the

*Lyndon Johnson loved telephones, especially ones with lots of buttons. He had them everywhere, even in the bathroom, and demanded that his aides do the same. He had direct lines installed to them with a red button on them marked POTUS— President of the United States.* (LYNDON BAINES JOHNSON LIBRARY)

president via Youngblood, Colonel Sienko poked his finger in Youngblood's chest: "Look, Rufe, you go back there and deliver a message for me! You tell him I'm flying this damn thing!"

"Well, what did he say?" LBJ asked.

"Mr. President, he said for me to tell you he was flying this damn thing, sir."

LBJ thought for a moment, then nodded.

"Good man," he said. "We need more like him."

Few were able to stand up to LBJ. One who did was Bill Moyers, his aide and speechwriter, also trained as a Baptist minister. At one White House dinner, LBJ had him say grace, but Moyers spoke in such a low voice it was difficult to hear him. "Speak up, Bill," LBJ commanded. "I wasn't addressing you, Mr. President," was Moyers's soft reply.

LBJ's top aides had direct-line phones to the president marked POTUS—President of the United States—all of which had a constant, rather than an intermittent, ring that did not stop until the phone was picked up. Later when Luci's son Lyndon Nugent came to the White House, staffers would pick up their phones and hear breathing, baby mumbles, and LBJ telling his grandson not to press the direct dial buttons.

Those who worked for LBJ had to be available to him at all times and places. He didn't want his cabinet to leave Washington for any reason, even for vacations. Even in the bathroom they were not safe from his calls, as Joseph Califano, LBJ's assistant for domestic affairs, found out. Califano's secretary tried to explain obliquely that he was not available, but that never worked with Johnson. "Where the hell is he?" Johnson demanded. When he found out, he ordered Califano to put a phone in the bathroom. Califano felt that was unnecessary, so he didn't do it. So LBJ ordered two Army Signal Corps technicians over to install the phone.

On another occasion LBJ couldn't reach Califano because he was at a Sunday mass. Radio car phones were still rare, so LBJ told Califano to take a White House limousine equipped with a radio phone when he went to church, then sit in the back. "If your President ever needs you," he said, "the driver can go in and quietly get you so you can talk on the phone."

The president, in turn, was always accessible—also when he was in the bathroom. LBJ exposed his body without inhibition, and at times quite deliberately. On one occasion he brought National Security Adviser McGeorge Bundy—whom he called "one of those delicate Kennedyites"—right into the bathroom with him. "[He] found it utterly impossible to look at me while I sat on the toilet," Johnson related. "You'd think he'd never seen those parts of the body before. For there he was, standing as far away from me as he possibly could, keeping his back toward me the whole time, trying to carry on a conversation. I could barely hear a word he said. I kept straining my ears and finally I asked him to come a little closer to me. Then began the most ludicrous scene I have ever witnessed. Instead of turning around and walking over to me, he kept his face away from me and walked backwards, one rickety step at a time. For a moment I thought he was going to fall into my lap. It certainly made me wonder how that man made it so far in the world."

Given his availability, Johnson expected to be consulted on every move. George Ball, undersecretary of state, was harshly reprimanded for approving an action in Brazil without LBJ's prior approval. "I don't give a damn if you're right or wrong," Johnson told Ball, or whether it was "three in the morning. I want to know what's being done whatever time of night it is." During the Vietnam War he picked out the targets himself. "They can't hit an outhouse without my permission," he said, and ordered that he be wakened at 3 A.M. for the strike reports.

Thanks to advances in communications and electronics, Johnson could know what was going on at all times. In the Oval Office, the Associated Press and United Press news tickers clattered endlessly, printing the latest news on long rolls of paper. In the Oval Office, three TV sets ran continuously so Johnson could see all three major networks simultaneously. He could regulate the sound with a remote control. "He had little television sets in the bathroom and he had one in the sitting room, the anteroom off the Oval Office, and three in his bedroom," Richard Nixon said. "I took them all out." Johnson also liked electronics for their own sake. He had a remote control button for opening and closing his bedroom window. Nixon removed that as well—he said he was afraid that if he pushed the button, he'd "blow up the world." When Gerald Ford became president he noticed there were ten electric outlets over his bathroom sink— when an outlet didn't work, LBJ ordered ten installed to replace it.

Communication by phone was particularly easy for the president—he needed only to pick up the phone and demand of a White House operator to speak to whomever he wanted. Johnson once barked, "Get me Tic Forrester. I want to talk to him. Now you find him." Helpfully, LBJ added, "Little biddy fellow—no bigger than a tic." The White House operators kept files, and they knew that Elijah Forrester was a congressman from Georgia. His office said he had started home by car for the Christmas holidays. The White House operator got a description of the car, license plate number, and approximate location based on his time of departure. They contacted the head of the Georgia State Highway Patrol, Major L. E. Floyd, who sent out police helicopters to look for the car. Fifteen minutes later he reported: "Our helicopter has intercepted the congressman and we have him on it. The helicopter has a two-way radio and we can patch that into your telephone." Major Floyd added, "You can tell the President of the United States, suh, that the Georgia State Patrol stands behind him to a man."

Johnson liked desperately to be in touch and felt the isolation of the White House keenly. "It's so different now," he said. "There's a wall around me that nobody gets through—people I've known for years, worked with side by side; like Jim Eastland or Allen Ellender—they come in here and they don't see me, they see the President. I'm now 'Mr. President' to my oldest friends."

His sense of isolation was no doubt compounded by his staff, which he carried over from the Kennedy administration. They were part of the eastern establishment that Johnson, who often said he came from "the wrong side of the country," feared and hated. He felt that he would never receive credit for anything he did in foreign affairs because he "didn't go to Harvard." As vice president to Kennedy, Johnson had always been loyal, and publicly, Kennedy had gone out of his way to treat him with respect. But the relationship was strained. "Every time I came into John Kennedy's presence, I felt like a goddamned raven hovering over his shoulder," Johnson said. Still, he said while working with Kennedy, "He's done much better by me than I would have done by him under the same circumstances." But others in the Kennedy administration were not so kind, including some of those Johnson kept on. Though as president LBJ carried out many of the programs begun by his predecessor, some of the Kennedy staff considered him an uneducated boor from southwest Texas and privately despised and ridiculed him.

One person whose support LBJ could virtually always count on was his wife, who described her husband as "a warm and mellow man in so many ways, gentle, extremely loving." Lady Bird understood that he could be deep hearted enough to sob seeing *The Grapes of Wrath* in the White House theater and vain enough to forbid photographers to take pictures from his right profile or while he was wearing glasses. Johnson asked Lady Bird Taylor to marry him on the first date. She was twenty-one. "I was so surprised I couldn't believe it. I thought it was some kind of joke." But they married in 1934, and she would learn that this was Lyndon's way. He was "always in a rush," she said.

When she moved into the White House, Lady Bird was in awe at first. She found herself tiptoeing around. She told a friend, "I feel as if I am suddenly on stage for a part I never rehearsed." It was not easy, either, to follow the tremendously popular Jackie Kennedy. The fifty-one-year-old Texan certainly didn't try to compete with Jackie's style. Unlike her high-fashion predecessor, Lady Bird was price conscious. Faced with an official event, she often shopped the sales racks in Garfinckel's, a Washington department store, at the last minute. When the Smithsonian Institute asked to display one of her dresses for the First Ladies Hall, she sent this reply: "I'd better wait a while unless I can work out an arrangement to borrow the dress back after the museum's closing hour."

But also unlike her predecessor, Lady Bird, who had degrees in history and journalism, savored politics. She followed political machinations closely and wrote down her observations for LBJ. She reviewed drafts of his speeches. When the president of Italy visited, she asked for briefings on the economy of Italy and the political situation. In a first for a first lady, Lady Bird even campaigned for her husband in the South in the 1964 election. She had a campaign train—the eighteen-car "Lady Bird Special"—with 250 reporters on board. White southerners were antagonistic to LBJ because of his strong civil rights stand, but Lady Bird used her charm and emphasized her southern roots, and the trip was a remarkable success.

Lady Bird had a strong work ethic. She had breakfast in bed with Lyndon at about seven-thirty, then she dressed and went to her office. She tried to find an hour a day to dictate her diary. She gave special attention to her mail. She wanted her letters of response to "glow." She said, "I want them to be ones I'm proud of." As a personal project, the first lady launched a national campaign to beautify America. She started locally with the nation's capital, she later said, "with the hope it would have a ripple effect out across the land. Everybody who did it loves his hometown. You just say hometown and you get a smile, at least from a whole lot of Americans. That's where you start with any hoped-for environmental programs." She was able to lure some big names to help her—Mary Lasker, Laurence Rockefeller, Brooke Astor—and they raised $2 million. She also rallied the cooperation of government agencies, foremost the National Park Service, and reached out to the poor in the black community. Many garden clubs participated. LBJ complained that his naps were interrupted by Lady Bird in the next room, "with Laurence Rockefeller and eighty ladies talking about the daffodils on Pennsylvania Avenue." In the course of four years, Lady Bird directed the planting of 2 million daffodil bulbs around the capital city.

Moving to the national level, she sponsored a law to control billboards and junkyards along highways. She traveled two hundred thousand miles making speeches and gathering support. The result was the Highway Beautification Act of 1965. After the White House years she would continue her beautification work, and in 1983 she founded the National Wildflower Research Center in Austin, now the Lady Bird Johnson Wildflower Center.

None of this came easily to Lady Bird, who was naturally quiet and diffident. To make matters worse, she aroused the ire of many politicians and special interest groups, who plastered billboards with IMPEACH LADY BIRD signs. One of her more difficult moments occurred on January 18, 1968, when Eartha Kitt, the African-American actress and dancer, attended a White House luncheon in the State Dining Room on "What Citizens Can Do to Help Insure Safe Streets" and took the opportunity to direct a furious antiwar statement at Lady Bird. Kitt said young blacks would sooner choose crime and drugs than fight. "Boys I know across the nation feel it doesn't pay to be a good guy," she said. "They figure with a record they don't have to go off to Vietnam." Lady Bird retained her composure as best she could and expressed regret that "the shrill voice of anger and discord" had disrupted the proceedings,

The shy first lady also had to contend with the lack of privacy inherent in living in a largely public building. Conscientiously trying to turn off the hall lights late after a party one night, Lady Bird accidentally locked herself out of the family quarters in her bathrobe and slippers. It was one-thirty in the morning. She could get back in via the family elevator, but to access it she had to go downstairs, where she might encounter lingering guests in the main entrance hall. She recalled, "I thought about all those funny ads—'I went to the opera in my Maidenform Bra.'" Fortunately she was only caught in her nightclothes by "two or three of the departing musicians and staff members. I smiled as if the whole thing were a matter of course, caught the elevator back up to my own floor, and so to bed."

The usual lack of privacy at the White House was compounded by Johnson's inclination to be constantly surrounded by people from the moment he woke up each morning until the time he went to bed. His aides gathered at his bedside each morning, and sometimes Lady Bird was still in bed. "Now you boys look the other way," she would say as she made her exit. Johnson would invite reporters to lunch, then take them up to his bedroom and continue talking while he changed his clothes for his afternoon nap. When he fell asleep, the interview was over. Once, after midnight, Lady Bird came into the bedroom and found ten or twelve men, including actors Gregory Peck and Hugh O'Brien. They surrounded LBJ, who was on a table getting a rubdown. She shrieked and backed out. "What a household!" she said. "And what a moral to always have your hair combed and give that comfortable old bathrobe to the Goodwill charity organization."

Lady Bird complained that she and her husband spent less and less time together. She tried, usually unsuccessfully, to make "dates" with him. Eventually, the Johnsons established separate bedrooms at the White House. Johnson pursued other women, developing what he termed a "harem." Starting in 1965, the White House logs show multiple private meetings in the Oval Office between the president and a half-dozen women. Lady Bird remained loyal. She also developed a tendency to befriend her husband's mistresses. "It was very odd," said one longtime staff member. "Johnson would add someone new to what he called his 'harem,' and the next thing we knew Lady Bird was inviting them to dinner, taking them to the ranch, and treating that woman like her best friend."

The Johnsons' two daughters, Luci, sixteen, and Lynda, seventeen, also found the White House experience a difficult one. "You feel so alone," Luci said, "the ceilings are so high. It's kind of morbid walking down the halls and never meeting anyone." For both girls the house was less of a problem than dating in the public eye. "I'd just gotten a driver's license," recalled Luci, "and then I got the answer to every teenager's nightmare and every mother's prayer: a 24 hour chaperone. I wanted to feel like I belonged and suddenly I was different." She was a student at National Cathedral, an Episcopal school, but in 1966 she converted to Catholicism and changed her name from Lucy to Luci. At White House parties, she liked dancing the frug or the Watusi, and the press nicknamed her "Watusi Luci." In the campaign of 1964, Johnson used both daughters to make speeches and act as his eyes and ears. "I was in high school and got the best grades I'd ever gotten," recalled Luci. "I had to be organized." Luci got what she called "two free term papers" by writing reports on the White House and brought all sixty-two members of her class for a White House tour.

"Lynda Bird," the quiet one, was unhappy with media comparisons with her partying sister. She was a sophomore at the University of Texas, but when her father took office, Lady Bird insisted she transfer to George Washington University. She commuted there from the White House. Johnson sent her to represent the United States at the wedding of Princess Anne Marie of Greece. Columnist Drew Pearson wondered why Lynda was wearing a "silk coverall that looked like an old-fashioned dust protector." What was she trying to hide? Her father read the column and exploded: "Christ, is he trying to say my daughter is pregnant? Why doesn't the bastard attack me? Why my daughter? He's lower than a lizard's belly, and I'd like to nail his hide to a barn door."

LBJ's brother, Sam Houston, a bachelor, also lived at the White House. Sam Houston was the black sheep of the Johnson family. Lyndon feared his brother would embarrass him, and liked to have him at the White House so he could keep an eye on him. "It seemed, in fact, as if Sam Houston was under some sort of house arrest," Usher J. B. West said. In his will, LBJ would leave Sam Houston a token $5,000 out of an approximately $25 million estate. Once the president got drunk and called his brother: "I want you to take a damned good look at me, Sam Houston. Open your eyes and look at me. 'Cause I'm drunk, and I want you to see how you look to me, Sam Houston, when you come home drunk." LBJ "had episodes of getting drunk," according to press secretary George Reedy. "There were times when he would drink day after day. You would think this guy is an alcoholic. Then all of a sudden, it would stop. He pretended to drink American bourbon but Scotch and soda was his drink."

Also living in the White House were a number of dogs. Luci came across a lonesome stray dog at a gas station in Texas, named the dog Yuki, and brought it back to the White House, where it was given free run of the place. Yuki lounged in the Oval Office and under the table at cabinet meetings. Johnson also let his own dogs—he always had several—run where they wished, which distressed Traphes Bryant, who cared for the dogs of several presidents. He told LBJ the dogs would damage the rugs, but the president didn't care. "He did it anyway, so they did it anyway," Bryant said. "What a mess!" When Lady Bird later gave Pat an orientation tour of the White House, Julie Nixon recalled, she apologized for "the numerous dog spots on the once-white carpeting in the family quarters." LBJ had a favorite beagle, called "Him," which he once picked up by the ears in front of the usual swarm of reporters and photographers. Him yelped. Johnson claimed it was good for Him. The story went global. The chairman of the Canine Defense League in London defended the president, but most others criticized him.

The Johnsons also had plenty of guests—Watusi Luci wasn't the only one who enjoyed a good party. Chief Usher J. B. West called them "the dancingest First Family" he had ever known. In their five years the Johnsons had two hundred thousand guests at the White House. LBJ liked to dance with every woman in the room so each one could tell her friends, "I danced with the President." One party ran on until 3 A.M. before Lady Bird finally asked the band to play "Goodnight, Sweetheart." LBJ stopped in the middle of the dance floor and, glaring at the band, stuck out his tongue. But the band listened to the first lady.

One performer invited to entertain White House guests was African American singer Sarah Vaughan. Lady Bird's social secretary found her afterward in the dressing room sobbing. "Nothing's the matter," she said. "It's just that twenty years ago when I came to Washington, I couldn't even get a hotel room, and tonight I sang for the President of the United States in the White House—and he asked me to dance. It's more than I can stand."

Johnson's abrupt style meant entertaining could be last-minute. "Bird," LBJ shouted to his wife one night, "let's have Congress over tonight." That meant a potential guest list of more than a thousand, counting representatives and their wives. It was two days before Christmas 1964. Johnson was maneuvering the Civil Rights Act through Congress—he would be successful—and he wanted to offer a perk for the legislators. The butlers hurriedly made tubs of punch and bourbon-laced eggnog, and the servants cleaned the local stores out of cookies.

The Johnsons' guests must have appreciated René Verdon, the world-class chef the first family inherited from Jackie Kennedy, who assured Lady Bird he was "divine." LBJ, however, was no gourmet. He ate very rapidly, and only liked food he could eat quickly. He scarcely noticed the food he ate at banquets or state dinners. He might grab chicken legs from a buffet table, wolf down the meat while continuing to talk, and then stuff the bones in his pocket. His preferences were for the very basic. As one reporter said, "His knowledge of sauces stopped at catsup." Verdon bristled when he saw what he was up against. "These things you just don't do to a respectable chef," he said. "You don't ask a chef to serve red snapper with the skin still on it, beets with cream all over them. Look, I have a master pastry chef who has been doing yule logs for forty years. You don't just open the Gourmet Cookbook to page forty and stick it under his eyes. I've tried to cooperate. I've tried to get along. But I've reached the end of the line." Particularly distasteful to Verdon was Johnson's favorite dish, chili con queso. Verdon called the hot, gooey cheese concoction "chili con-crete."

So for family meals LBJ brought in a different cook, Zephyr Wright from Marshall, Texas. She had cooked for him in Washington for twenty years and knew how to make another Johnson favorite, tapioca pudding. "Tapioca has less calories than any other dessert that you can get," LBJ explained, "and it has great advantages when it is made with skim milk and sucaryl. It's easy to make, and it's satisfying and it's filling. Zephyr makes it in big batches and puts it up in containers, so I can have some when I want it." The ultimate insult to Verdon was when Johnson sent back the tapioca pudding he'd made and suggested he go upstairs and take lessons from Zephyr. Verdon was fuming: "The President eats so much tapioca pudding that Zephyr doesn't even cook it herself. She has the pot washer do it." Verdon resigned and went on to better things.

Verdon was replaced by Henry Haller, who knew what was expected of him and accepted it. "To stay in his good graces, I always served the President the foods he likes," Haller said. But remaining in LBJ's good graces was difficult even for the amenable Haller. The first time Haller made a crabmeat salad ring, LBJ pushed it aside and told him, "Take the rest of this home to your wife." At a state luncheon the president thought the meat was spoiled. He announced loudly, "Don't anybody eat it. It's spoiled." Panic ensued in the kitchen and among Lady Bird's staff. Haller tasted the meat and pronounced it perfect: "It's supposed to taste like that." It was Tornedos Rossini—fillet of beef stuffed with fois gras. "Don't ever serve that stuff again in this house," LBJ said. Henry Haller survived it all in good humor. He even wrote a White House cookbook in which he described chili con queso as "a great dish . . . smooth and tasty when prepared properly."

The president periodically tried to lose weight. Wright once sent him a memo: "Mr. President, you have been my boss for a number of years and you always tell me you want to lose weight and yet you never do very much to help yourself. Now I'm going to be your boss for a change. Eat what I put in front of you and don't ask for any more and don't complain." (Wright enjoyed the White House food—she gained eighty pounds in five years.) One night, late, the president got up and went to the family kitchen, where he took a bowl of tapioca from the refrigerator and started eating. Lady Bird followed the sound of the metal spoon scraping the bowl and took the tapioca away. The next morning, LBJ ordered an assistant press secretary to buy him a wooden spoon.

Lady Bird was not merely worried. By 1965 LBJ's weight had climbed to 226—more than when he nearly died from a heart attack ten years before, on July 2, 1955. He had been a three-pack-a-day cigarette smoker at the time, and he quit. The doctors ordered him to take naps and swim for exercise. As president, Johnson used the White House pool—he always swam naked, and demanded that aides who swam with him do the same. He also had an exercise bike in the White House and one bolted to the floor of Air Force One. But sports were not a part of his life. He never skied or played tennis, and baseball bored him. He tried golf, but that bored him, too. In any case, according to a fellow player, he hit the ball "like he was killing a rattlesnake." Hunting was a southwest Texas sport but LBJ did it his way: from his air-conditioned Lincoln Continental, or from a Volkswagen bus with a sunroof, accompanied by a white-coated attendant with an ice chest and drinks.

Three days after his inauguration in January 1965, Johnson was rushed to the hospital with chest pains, which proved to be caused by a respiratory infection. His temperature reached 104.4 degrees. Later that year he had surgery to remove his gall bladder and a kidney stone. As the stress of office wore him down, he feared a disabling illness, and thought of Woodrow Wilson, who had collapsed from a paralytic stroke near the end of his second term. As LBJ's own term ground on, he later recalled, "When I walked through the Red Room and saw the portrait of Woodrow Wilson hanging there,

I thought of him stretched out upstairs at the White House, powerless to move, with the machinery of American government in disarray around him. I frankly did not believe in 1968 that I could survive another four years of long hours and unremitting tensions I had just gone through."

Indeed, it was a tumultuous time for the country. On June 29, 1966, Luci came home from a date and found her father pacing the floor. He had just ordered bomb raids around the Communist North Vietnam capital of Hanoi. "Your daddy may have started World War III," he said, obviously worried. "Would you like to go to see my little monks, Daddy?" Luci asked. She often went to visit the Benedictines at St. Dominic's Roman Catholic Church in downtown Washington. They went there and prayed together. Johnson would sometimes appear in his wife's adjoining bedroom late at night to agonize over the war. "We can't get out," he said, "and we can't finish it." These were some of the few hours they spent alone together in the White House. At breakfast in his bedroom, with LBJ surrounded by military advisers and cabinet members, the first lady, in her dressing gown and often with her hair in rollers, listened to every word as she drank her coffee.

Although the majority of the American public supported bombing North Vietnam, an increasingly vocal opposition made LBJ's life miserable. As the war escalated, protests grew so frequent and vehement that LBJ could no longer travel freely about the country. His trips were confined to secure areas such as military bases. He received over ten thousand threatening letters, and there were increased security violations and arrests around the White House. In time it became difficult even to physically leave the White House. All of this hurt LBJ, who thrived on popular acclaim. When he ran for his first full term in 1964, he had shown reporters his swollen and bleeding right hand. "Have you ever seen anything like that?" he said. "The folks like me." Now, he lay in bed in the morning reluctant to get up and face the day. "I can't read the *Washington Post* this morning," he would say. His sleep became more disturbed. He had dreams in which he was being "chased on all sides by a giant stampede . . . forced over the edge by rioting blacks, demonstrating students, marching welfare mothers, squawking professors, and hysterical reporters."

Lady Bird wrote, "I wish I could do something about these sleepless nights. Lyndon said he slept from 12:30 to 2:30 and then turned and tossed the rest of the night. And yet he gets up and puts in a full day's work." She worried that her husband's nocturnal habits were inconveniencing the servants. She suggested that, rather than linger to serve him a late dinner, they just go home when they were supposed to, at 8 P.M., and leave something she could warm up. John Ficklin, the butler, was indignant. "We've served the Presidents and First Ladies every meal in formal service as long as I can remember. Even if it's a cheese sandwich and a bowl of chili or a boiled egg. That's tradition. Let's just work it in shifts."

In the midst of these upheavals, both Johnson daughters left the nest. In 1966, at nineteen, Luci married Patrick Nugent in the first White House wedding in fifty-two years, the last being Eleanor Wilson in 1914. She had met him on a blind date at Marquette University in Milwaukee, during which she had slipped away from reporters by wearing a blond wig and using a false name. Her parents had some reservations about the marriage, and it did end in divorce in 1979. In December 1967 Lynda married a

Marine captain, Charles Robb, in a White House ceremony. At her wedding, crowds could be heard outside the White House chanting the words that haunted her father: "Hey! Hey! LBJ! How many kids did you kill today?"

Lady Bird was strongly against her husband running again in 1968. She too feared he would suffer Woodrow Wilson's fate. "A physical or mental incapacitation would be unbearably painful for him to recognize, and for me to watch," she said. LBJ tentatively agreed not to seek reelection but kept postponing any announcement. Then, in January 1968, the North Vietnamese launched the Tet offensive. Johnson got almost no sleep for days. His brother, Sam, remembered him shuffling down the hall in bathrobe and slippers toward the elevator for the 3 A.M. briefing: "He looked tired and lonely as he pushed the down button." With his old friend Richard Russell, LBJ cried uncontrollably. Although the Tet offensive failed, the American public had been misled for so long that the war was being won that now they didn't believe it. They had had enough of war. Johnson's approval rating was down to 36 percent, the lowest since he took office in 1963.

On March 16, 1968, Robert Kennedy declared that he would challenge Johnson in the 1968 primary. "The thing I feared from the first day of my Presidency was actually coming true," LBJ said. "Robert Kennedy had openly announced his intention to reclaim the throne in the memory of his brother and the American people, swayed by the magic of his name, were dancing in the streets." Kennedy, however, would be shot and killed on June 5 in Los Angeles as he celebrated his victory in the California primary.

Meanwhile, the situation only got worse, for LBJ and the country. On April 4, 1968, Martin Luther King Jr. was shot and killed in Memphis, Tennessee. There were riots and demonstrations in every major city in the country, including the capital, where within a few days seven had been killed and three hundred wounded. There were riots and fires just four blocks from the White House. Lady Bird recalled, "I thought, and maybe everybody else did, that we had been pummeled by such an avalanche of emotions that we couldn't feel anymore, and here we are, poised on the edge of another abyss, the bottom of which we could in no way see."

On March 31, 1968, Johnson was scheduled to give one of his many speeches about Vietnam. That morning, at 7 A.M., Lynda returned to the White House after dropping off her husband of four months at Camp Pendleton, from which he would leave for a thirteen-month tour of duty in Vietnam. By now, she was pregnant. Luci's husband had already gone off to Vietnam, and she had come back to live at the White House with her son, Lyndon. Lynda had taken a sedative on the plane, and when she arrived, she looked "like a wraith from another world," her mother recalled. Lynda looked at her father and asked, "Daddy, why do they have to go to Vietnam?"

Johnson was deeply affected, and his decision not to seek reelection was sealed. He went to work on the draft of his speech for that night and by afternoon was reading the final version—with the announcement that he would not run—to Lady Bird, Luci, and several friends. Luci was in tears. Lady Bird was afraid he would change his mind. He didn't. "I shall not seek, and I will not accept, the nomination of my party for another term as your President," he read that night. As soon as the decision was final, LBJ seemed happier. A weight had lifted. His popularity rating went up.

As his term drew to a close, LBJ continued to manage the war, and peace continued to elude him. When he left office in January 1969, he returned to his Texas ranch, taking with him all the presidential trappings he could. He stripped Air Force One of china, silverware, blankets, towels, even toilet tissue. He had his swivel chair unbolted and removed.

On retirement, Johnson worked on the plans for his library in Austin, which was dedicated in May 1971, and wrote his memoirs, published in 1972. He went back to chain-smoking, drinking, and ignoring his diet. "I don't want to linger the way Eisenhower did," he said. "When I go, I want to go fast." He did, of a heart attack as he napped, on January 22, 1973. The next day, the Paris peace accords were initialed, ending the tragedy of Vietnam.

# 37

# Richard M. Nixon

## 1969–1974

## *Caught*

IN JANUARY 1969 Richard Nixon entered a house still shadowed by Lyndon Johnson. "Dick, let's turn on all the lights on the White House and make it cheery," Pat said. "It's done," Nixon said. On came the hall lights and the outdoor flood lights that Johnson had turned off in an economy move. The staff no longer had to grope their way through the halls. "I hardly needed a flashlight anymore," one servant remarked. But no amount of lighting could banish the shadow of the Vietnam War.

"It was the faculty leaders and professional agitators and the pampered kids on campus who were out screaming, protesting, crowding around the White House," complained the president. "Sometimes it was so loud you couldn't even go to sleep at night."

"It was like living in a bunker in the White House," remembered special counsel Charles Colson. "I mean, you'd look out on the streets and you'd see thousands of people protesting. You were literally afraid for your life. There are times when I can remember saying, 'I can't believe this is the United States of America, a free country,' and here we are in the White House with barricades up and buses around the White House and tear gas going off and thousands, hundreds of thousands of protestors out on the streets and troops sitting here."

Pat Nixon said simply, "We are shut up in this house."

Part of the sense of being in a bunker was a normal response to suddenly living in the continual presence of the Secret Service and attentive servants. Nixon echoed the thoughts of a number of presidents when he said, "The biggest surprise . . . was that we had not been prepared for the paradoxical combination of loss of privacy and sense of isolation that we experienced in the White House." His daughter Julie, twenty when her father was elected, complained about the "pressure box atmosphere" at the White House. "If we could live anywhere else, it would be just great," she said. "I guess it's because the phones are always ringing. People are always around. It's not really a home." Tricia, twenty-two, took to her room for the first months after the move to Pennsylvania Avenue.

But the Nixons were isolated of necessity. Though the president had been elected by what he called the "Silent Majority," he was savagely disliked by a vocal minority. At a conference in Williamsburg, Virginia, he had just entered a hall to make a speech when a protester confronted him. "A little girl, I don't think she was more than sixteen," he recalled, "sort of broke through the line of people there, and, ah, she spat in my face, just covered my face with spit, and she said, 'You are a murderer.' Of course, I wiped the spit off, went in and made the speech. As I was walking in, I was thinking, she was such a pretty girl, but at that moment, she was so ugly, and the war made her so." Anti-war hecklers jeered at Pat, even showering her with confetti and yelling, "If this was napalm, you would be dead." During the antiwar demonstrations that took place outside the White House, Pat, Julie, Tricia, and Mamie Eisenhower were eating lunch one day when a guard outside an open window accidentally dropped a container of tear gas, forcing them to flee the room.

Nixon recorded in his diary that during crises his pulse raced and his stomach churned. Julie was once asked how her father dealt with pressure. One way was to sit down at the piano and play soft, melodic tunes, she said: "Sometimes all alone at night, you'll hear this music in the hallways."

Nixon once said, "A major public figure is a lonely man. . . . [Y]ou can't enjoy the *luxury* of the intimate personal friendships. You can't confide absolutely in anyone. You can't talk too much about your plans, your personal feelings."

But the job suited him in many ways. "I'm an introvert in an extrovert's profession," he admitted. Nixon disliked glad-handing and socializing. "I never wanted to be buddy-buddy. . . . Even with close friends," he said. Charles "Bebe" Rebozo, one of his best friends, would sit with Nixon for hours exchanging hardly a word. Rebozo listened, or they sat in silence. Even he always called Nixon "Mr. President."

"I can't really let my hair down with anyone . . . not even with my own family," Nixon once admitted. His family felt the same way. Tricia kept her engagement to Edward Cox a secret for two years before deciding to broach the marriage question with her father in 1971. "Eddie was white as a sheet when he went in to see the President," she said. "We had been watching *The Greatest Show on Earth* and we got so nervous that we had to go out and take a walk around the grounds. Then he talked to my father." Nixon "was speechless for a moment, but you know how fathers are."

Before the presidency, Julie had ventured into her father's office to announce her engagement to David Eisenhower, the grandson of Nixon's 1952 running mate. Nixon had responded to the news with nothing more than a nod. Julie fled in tears. However that night on her pillow she found a note of congratulations.

Nixon communicated with the family by memo. "It occurs to me that from time to time you may be asked for anecdotes," he wrote Tricia and Julie on July 24, 1972, during his reelection campaign. "On a personal side, you might mention some of our Christmas parties where I played the piano for group singing, etc., always by ear. . . . Another personal note that could be made is that when I come in to dinner at the White House—before dinner I will often make phone calls [to] people who may be sick, who have had hard luck like losing an election or not getting a promotion. . . . These calls never, of course, are publicized because they are personal in nature." He signed the memo "the President."

He also memoed Pat, discussing even small matters like bedroom furniture:

To: Mrs. Nixon
From: The President

In talking with GSA Director with regard to RN's room, what would be most desirable is an end table like the one on the right side of the bed. . . .

Jan 25, 1969

Nixon was mortified by public affection and often embarrassed Pat by ignoring her, or worse: "I have a wonderful family and a pretty good wife," he once said to a group of congressmen. In a 1990 television interview he recalled that his mother, Hannah, "never said 'I love you' because she considered that to be very private and sacred. And I feel the same way. . . . That's just the way I was raised." When he ran for president in 1968 and announced a "New Nixon," his mother told the press that no, she didn't think there was anything new about him. "I never knew anyone to change so little," she said.

As president Nixon counted on two aides so loyal and protective the press called them the "German shepherds." He installed H. R. Haldeman, the former ad agency executive who had been his campaign manager, as his chief of staff. John Ehrlichmann became Nixon's chief aide for domestic affairs. With both he could talk and ramble. Ehrlichmann described how Nixon thought through a problem: "Richard Nixon was like a cow. . . . He would chew his cud over and over on a subject and turn it over and chew it some more. . . . Probably you'd grunt at the right times or make some comment or other."

With Haldeman and Ehrlichmann Nixon felt free to do more than ponder. He swore, vented his paranoia, and expressed things that, as the Watergate tapes later revealed, a president would never want to publicly express. "They're not like us," he said of Italians. "They smell different, they look different, they act different. The trouble is you can't find one that's honest."

"Listen to what these sons of bitches are saying," exclaimed Peter Rodino, chairman of the House Judiciary Committee, as he reviewed the tapes.

Of the two German shepherds, Haldeman was ostensibly closest to Nixon. For a decade before and during Nixon's presidency, the two were invariably together, even on vacations. Yet Haldeman once said, "To this day he doesn't know how many children I have or anything else about my private life. He never asked."

As chief of staff, Haldeman served as keeper of the gate. In the beginning he restricted access to the president so severely that Rose Mary Woods, Nixon's secretary and longtime friend, virtually a family member, had a hard time getting into the Oval Office. When she tried to see her boss, Secret Service agents obeying Haldeman's orders tried to stop her. A heated argument ensued. Finally Woods said, "Go ahead and shoot, but I'm going in there."

With access limited, Haldeman was the primary recipient of the president's orders, which were occasionally imperatives issued in the heat of the moment. Nixon would explode: "All press is barred from Air Force One," or, "Put a 24 hour surveillance on that bastard." Haldeman would dutifully make a note. He considered "the staff officer's duty to ignore any clearly inappropriate demand." He wrote in his diary that sometimes he decided not to obey a direct order "on the basis that it was not an order that was really intended to be carried out, but rather a letting off of steam, or that it was clearly not in the P's interest that it be carried out." This was clearly true when Nixon, furious at the low turnout to greet him at airport stops, shouted: "There will be no more landing at airports!" Once Nixon got angry at Hugh Sidey, an influential *Time* magazine reporter, and ordered him banned from Air Force One. Haldeman nodded. Later, Nixon said, "What have you done about Sidey?" Haldeman replied, "I'm working on it." He continued to delay until Nixon said, "I guess you never took action on that, did you? Well, I guess that's the best thing." Nixon once ordered Haldeman to have the tennis court on the south grounds removed. He did not play tennis, and he was angry with his cabinet members and sought to deprive them of this perk. Haldeman thought it was "a spiteful way to take a jab at the Cabinet" and dragged his feet as usual. After a while, Nixon said, "I realized that the only way to get rid of it would be if I rented a bulldozer one night and did it myself."

In a conversation with Haldeman in June 1969, Nixon said, "I have an uneasy feeling that many of the items I send out for action are disregarded when any staff member just reaches the conclusion that it is unreasonable or unattainable. . . . I respect this kind of judgment."

Nixon once said he had no interest in the trappings of the presidency. "If I never had to review an honor guard, I'd have been delighted," he said. But Haldeman's diary entry regarding a January 31, 1969, ceremony contradicts this: "P like a little kid, or a wooden soldier, arms stiff, trying not to look as tickled as he obviously was. Stands behind colors in the Cross Hall, is announced, 'Hail to the Chief,' follows colors into and through East Room to Green Room, where he receives. P really ate it up, as at all ceremonies. He loves being P!"

Nixon liked things to look presidential. When he first came to the White House, he was upset by "the slovenly White House police." He had Ehrlichmann design new uniforms—white tunic, lots of gold braid, and pillbox hats. The uniforms were greeted with so much laughter and ridicule that Nixon soon gave them up.

He loved the presidential seal and had it emblazoned on everthing from his golf bag and balls to his windbreaker. He delighted in handing out small gifts—ballpoint pens, ash trays, and paper weights, all with the presidential seal—though his lack of coordination made the actual process difficult. At San Clemente, California, after leaving office, he apologized for his fumbling, saying, "I used to have an aide who'd stand by and hand me these."

Nixon had been angling for the presidency most of his adult life. Born in Yorba Linda, California, in 1913, he grew up in a hardworking Quaker family and believed in doggedly pursuing his goals. He scrimped and managed to graduate from Duke University Law School. As a navy officer during World War II, he won enough money playing poker to help finance his early political campaigns. His star rose quickly. In eight years, 1946 to 1952, he went from congressman to senator to vice president. In 1960 he fully expected to succeed Dwight Eisenhower, but in a grueling campaign he lost narrowly to John F. Kennedy. Undeterred, Nixon ran for governor of California, only to take another trouncing. Defeated, he railed against the press, "You won't have Dick Nixon to kick around any more."

His wife dearly hoped he meant it. After each campaign she tried to get her husband to promise to give up politics. He always agreed and then reneged. After he lost to Kennedy, she made him put the promise in writing. When he decided to run for governor, she burst into tears. In 1968 he didn't even tell Pat he was once again seeking the presidency. When she found out, she tumbled into a depression. A reporter once asked her if he tried his speeches out on her. She answered, "He never tries anything out on me."

Pat met Nixon at a Yorba Linda theater group, and he proposed to her the same day. "I thought he was nuts or something," she said. With characteristic tenacity, Nixon pursued Pat for two years, even driving her to her other dates. Finally they were married June 21, 1940.

At the White House, the couple had separate bedrooms. Pat explained it this way: "Nobody could sleep with Dick. He wakes up during the night, switches on the light, speaks into his tape recorder or takes notes—it's impossible." Pat redecorated her husband's and Tricia's rooms, but kept her own just as Lady Bird Johnson left it. Julie had a room on the third floor, but she was recently married and seldom stayed at the White House.

On December 22, 1968, just before her father took office, she had married Dwight Eisenhower's grandson David. Nixon had never been a favorite of Eisenhower. When asked for Nixon's major contributions to his administration, Eisenhower had said, "If you give me a week, I might think of one." The general never even invited his vice president into the family quarters, Nixon said. David, on the other hand, had grown up visiting the White House and knew all about the place. When the Nixons returned from the 1969 inaugural ball, it was David who led the way to the second-floor family quarters and then showed them a little-known stairway to the third floor hidden behind a wall panel in the main hall. Upstairs, he lifted up a rug and pulled out a note he had hidden there eight years earlier that said, "I will return."

Pat took Lady Bird's advice to set up her own office in a small dressing room off her bedroom. There she spent countless hours answering her mail. She received over one thousand letters a month and tried to answer each one, personally signing them all. Occasionally, when someone wrote of a personal problem, she took the time to help the writer. Rather than take on a specific cause as first lady, she emphasized "volunteerism." In four years she visited thirty-nine states supporting voluntary groups. She herself served on the Commission on the Status of Women.

Pat also traveled all over the world organizing relief efforts and making goodwill visits. She traveled to Vietnam with her husband in 1969 and became the first first lady to enter a combat zone. There, she insisted on meeting wounded soldiers, whose names she took down so she could contact their families. For Nixon's historic February 1972

China trip that restored U.S. relations with Communist China, she studied Chinese culture and political structure, learned basic phrases, and familiarized herself with Mao's writings. In May 1972 she became the first first lady to visit the Soviet Union. With Victoria Brezhnev she toured the Moscow subway and a school. Altogether she visited thirty-one nations as first lady. During Nixon's first term she shook hands with almost 750,000 people, mostly in groups visiting the White House.

Despite Pat's training as an actress, being a public persona was a strain for her. She loathed political campaigning and being onstage before thousands of people, and tended to freeze up and just smile—the press labeled her shy, and worse, "Plastic Pat." Her husband was little help. Haldeman routinely ignored requests from her office. Pat's press secretary, Helen Smith, wrote Ron Ziegler, Nixon's press secretary at the time, "I cannot stress too emphatically that closer cooperation between the President's and Mrs. Nixon's press offices will benefit all." Ziegler turned a deaf ear.

The first lady perservered on her own, quietly as always. Though Jacqueline Kennedy had gone on television and charmed America into regarding the White House as a national treasure, it was Pat Nixon who oversaw the actual transformation of a house full of second-rate reproductions into a period museum reflecting the decorative arts of the White House's heyday, the first quarter of the nineteenth century. She studied fabrics, colors, and furnishings, and enlisted Clement Conger, curator of the State Department's diplomatic rooms, as White House curator. On a quiet Sunday afternoon the two spent three hours going through every room in the mansion, from attic to basement. Pat had no notes with her, Conger recalled. "It was all in her head. Mrs. Nixon told me what needed to be done." With Conger's help, Pat raised funds to acquire more than five hundred pieces of eighteenth- and nineteenth-century furnishings, increasing the number of antique furnishing in the White House from one-third to two-thirds. But she never wanted any publicity for it—in particular, she didn't want her efforts to be compared to Jackie Kennedy's.

As for the mansion's art collection, Pat removed the fierce-looking oil paintings of the Catlin Indians that Jackie had borrowed from the Smithsonian Institution. "I felt like I was about to be scalped every time I walked down the hall," Tricia recalled. Conger was able to acquire a Gilbert Stuart portrait of Dolley Madison. Dolley had saved it, along with Stuart's portrait of George Washington, when the British burned the White House during the War of 1812. It was rehung in the Red Room, whose walls were covered in red twill satin that matched the red velvet drapes in the painting. Pat replaced unexceptional art with newly acquired portraits of first families.

Aaron Shikler's portraits of Jacqueline and John Kennedy were completed and hung in the White House in early 1971, and Pat invited Jackie to come to view them. Jackie couldn't face a public ceremony but came privately with her two children, thirteen-year-old Caroline and ten-year-old John. She was apprehensive about their reactions to the White House and to their dead father's portrait. But Caroline and John accepted their father's portrait matter-of-factly, and the Nixon daughters, Julie and Tricia, showed them around the White House, since they remembered very little. Pat took Jackie through the refurbished parlors on the first floor, which garnered some praise from the former first lady.

Pat found it difficult to get away from her public life. Since the grounds were too public for a walk, she would go to Roosevelt Island, in the Potomac. But the park was not easy to access, and it closed at dusk. Sometimes she put on sunglasses and a scarf and went out after dark with Julie and the requisite Secret Service agents. They walked the streets around the White House, even though the area was, as Pat said, "a favorite spot for muggers." Once on the spur of the moment Pat, Julie, and Tricia informed the Secret Service that they wanted to walk across Lafayette Park to Trader Vic's in the Statler Hilton Hotel. They ate like ordinary citizens and simply walked out. They forgot entirely about one little detail: the check. After some deliberation, the manager decided to send the bill to the White House.

The Nixons' tastes were not particularly fancy. One night Tricia asked for a hot dog. Chef Henry Haller didn't have any in the house. Suddenly he remembered that the vending machines used by the office workers in the West Wing dispensed fast food. Using change from his pocket, he bought a hog dog, brought it to the kitchen, reheated it, and presented it to Tricia, who pronounced it the best she'd ever had.

Pat flummoxed him with her dinner request on inauguration night. "For two weeks we've laid in supplies in the kitchen. I think we could open a grocery store in the pantry. We've tried to find out everything they like," said Haller. The president ordered steaks for the family—Tricia, Julie, and her husband David Eisenhower—but Pat thought she'd just have a bowl of cottage cheese. There was not, recalled Haller, "a spoonful of cottage cheese in the house. And what in the world would be open this time of night—and Inauguration night to boot?" A limousine was summoned, and a butler dispatched in search of an open deli. Cottage cheese was located—and served in due course. Five feet six inches tall and just 110 pounds, Pat was thin and frail looking. Nixon forbade pictures of her in a bathing suit. Chief Usher J. B. West said, "I'd worried that Mrs. Nixon was so thin. Now I realized, she intended to stay that way."

After inaugural night Haller learned that Pat Nixon wasn't the only one who liked cottage cheese. "I eat cottage cheese until it runs out of my ears," said Nixon, who often ordered it for lunch with fruit or catsup. "Catsup," he said, "disguises almost anything."

Nixon was not one for lingering over a meal. "Unless I have a guest," he said, "I eat breakfast alone in five minutes, never have guests for lunch—I do that in five minutes, too." When he ate with Pat or his daughters in the evening, there was so little conversation the waiters had to rush the courses.

Despite his utilitarian approach to eating, Nixon took an interest in White House entertaining. After his first formal state dinner, he analyzed everything "as if it had been a major military battle," observed Haldeman. The president announced, "We've got to speed up these dinners. They take forever. So why don't we just leave out the soup course? . . . Men don't really like soup." Sensing that there was more to the story, Haldeman asked Nixon's valet Manolo Sanchez, "Was there anything wrong with the president's suit after that dinner last night?"

"Yes," he said. "He spilled the soup down his vest." Never again was soup served at a Nixon state dinner.

Nixon was not much for hard liquor. Ehrlichmann said that one drink could knock the president "galley west" if he was tired. "Even if he is not tired, about two and a half drinks will do it." He believed Nixon was "much more susceptible" than most to the effects of alcohol. Chief of Staff Alexander Haig, who replaced Haldeman after Watergate broke, claimed he had to act as president when Nixon was drunk, but Haig had delusions of grandeur. He once berated his staff for not informing him that Senate majority leader Mike Mansfield had called Nixon. "What did you say?" he exclaimed. "I run this White House and don't you ever forget it."

If Nixon drank, it was usually late in the evening, though he did like wine with dinner and was something of a connoisseur. His favorite was Chateau Margaux, which cost $30 a bottle, and he was not inclined to share it with congressmen. For run-of-the-mill guests, he ordered a six-dollar wine and had his Chateau Margaux served to him in a plain carafe or a bottle wrapped in a towel.

Nixon never dined at the White House without a jacket and tie, even if he ate alone. "A President cannot be one of a crowd," Nixon said. "He must maintain a certain figure. People want him to be that way. Now I wear a coat and tie all the time. It isn't a case of trying to be formal, but I'm more comfortable that way." Even late at night in the family quarters, he refused to shed his white shirt and tie. At the White House, he started wearing a flag pin on his lapel. He borrowed the idea from Haldeman, who in turn lifted it from the movie *The Candidate*.

The 1960s and early 1970s were an unstarched era, and one of the few who managed to update Nixon's image was White House barber Milton Pitts, who operated out of the basement. He charged $7.50 a cut—by the time Clinton fired him and closed the barbershop, rates were up to $25. "When I first met Nixon," Pitts said, "he was wearing Brylcreem and Wildroot cream oil. He would use one or the other. It makes wavy hair curl more." Pitts got him to give up the slick look.

Nixon's staff wanted to soften his image further by setting up an informal "photo op." They chose the beach at the president's California home, San Clemente, and invited some news photographers to shoot from an overlooking cliff. As the president followed orders and strolled down the beach, one said in disgust, "Good Christ, he's wearing shoes!" Not just street shoes, but dress trousers, too.

Nixon got a made-in-heaven publicity opportunity when Elvis Presley drove up to the White House gate early on the morning of December 21, 1970, and left a letter with the Marine Guard. He wanted to meet the president. Presley, who was armed at all times, collected sheriff's badges, but someone had told him that the president was the only one who could give him a federal narcotics agent's badge. Aide Dwight Chapin quickly sent Haldeman a two-page memo outlining his suggestions for handling the meeting. On the margin of the memo Haldeman wrote, "You must be kidding."

He wasn't. That same day Nixon welcomed Presley to the Oval Office. "I'm on your side," Presley said. He showed the president all his badges and then unveiled a gift of a gold-plated .45-caliber pistol and bullets, which he'd somehow managed to bring into the White House. They are now on display at the Nixon Library. Elvis looped his arm around Nixon, gave him a hug, and posed for a picture that is the most requested White House photograph at the National Archives. Presley, a major substance abuser, got his federal drug agent's badge.

Hobnobbing with Elvis aside, Nixon did loosen up, but in his own way. He had a single-lane bowling alley built under the White House driveway and liked to bowl game after solitary game late at night. At Camp David, he also bowled, again usually alone, rousing the staff at odd hours. When a bowler entered the alley, a warning light came on in the barracks—Camp David is run by the navy—alerting the person on duty to take his shift at the lanes. There the bowling alley had automatic pin setters, but enlisted personnel were assigned to monitor it round the clock in case something went wrong.

Nixon found Camp David an essential respite. In 1969 he spent almost as many days away from the White House as in it, most of them at Camp David. When the press was critical, Haldeman explained, "The man knows the value of contrasts, and he's entitled to be wherever he chooses. Besides, he likes to be left alone, and getting out of Washington is the only way he can be alone, really alone."

Not that he didn't bring guests. When Soviet leader Leonid Brezhnev visited the United States, Nixon invited him to Camp David and presented him with a dark blue Lincoln Continental, donated by the manufacturer. "Brezhnev, a collector of luxury cars . . . got behind the wheel and enthusiastically motioned me into the passenger's seat," Nixon recalled. "The head of the Secret Service detail went pale." Speeding over "the narrow roads that run around the perimeter of Camp David," they came to "a very steep slope with a sign at the top reading, 'Slow, dangerous curve.' Even driving a golf cart down it, I had to use the brakes in order to avoid going off the road at the sharp turn at the bottom. Brezhnev was driving more than fifty miles an hour." Despite Nixon's pleading, Brezhnev didn't slow down. Afterward he pronounced, "This is a very fine automobile. It holds the road very well."

When Nixon drove a golf cart at Camp David, it was just a way to get around. Camp David only has a few short holes, and Nixon wasn't one to practice there. He played golf only about two or three times a year. Eisenhower's putting green on the south grounds sat idle, and Nixon had it removed in 1971 because it was difficult and expensive to maintain.

Nixon was not coordinated enough for most sports. He had trouble with simple tasks and never did master the controls of the elaborate presidential chair on Air Force One. The crew would watch him struggling and joke about how soon he would call for help. When he was vice president, Eisenhower tried, unsuccessfully, to teach him how to cast for trout. Nixon recorded, "After hooking a limb the first three times, I caught his shirt on my fourth try. The lesson ended abruptly." But Nixon liked football—as a spectator. When an Ohio State-Michigan game conflicted with a dental appointment, he had a TV set up in the dental office in the White House basement.

Lack of exercise contributed to a continuing problem with phlebitis, an inflammation of the veins. On a trip to Austria and the Middle East in June 1974, Nixon's condition flared up, and his left leg swelled to twice its normal size. General Walter Tkach, his personal physician, warned him of the potentially fatal consequences should a clot break loose and lodge in the heart or lungs. He wanted Nixon hospitalized. Another doctor, William Lukash, examined him and felt that the risk of continuing the trip was not unreasonable. But once he was in the Middle East, the various activities and ceremonies scheduled would leave the president little chance to rest with the leg elevated. "The purpose of this trip is more important than my life," Nixon said. "I know it is a calculated risk."

With Watergate consuming the national news, Nixon was determined to act the part of the international statesman. But even before his presidency began to spiral downward, he had trouble sleeping, disturbed by war worries. "I never tired of walking around late at night," Nixon said. His nighttime worrying led to a bizarre episode, what

*Nixon was a loner and, as he said, "an introvert in an extrovert's profession." He had a single lane bowling alley installed underneath the White House driveway and bowled game after game by himself in the wee hours of the morning. Notice his foot is over the line.* (CORBIS)

biographer Tom Wicker, a journalist with the *New York Times,* called "one of the strangest in the modern Presidential history." After four students were shot on the campus of Kent State University on May 4, 1971, a National Day of Protest was called for Saturday, May 9, in Washington. In anticipation, the White House was surrounded by helmeted police and army troops, and ringed by military buses parked bumper to bumper. National Guard troops were held in reserve in the Executive Office Building.

The evening before the day of protest, Nixon held a White House press conference, in which he was conciliatory and spoke of how he too wanted to end the war. He was agitated afterward, too keyed up to go to bed. He made a series of phone calls to friends and advisers. He finally got to bed about two-thirty in the morning, but in an hour he was up again. He put a Rachmaninoff record on the stereo set in the Lincoln Sitting Room and stood by the window watching small groups of students gathering near the Washington Monument. His valet, Manolo Sanchez, who lived at the White House, woke up and came in to see if Nixon needed anything.

Nixon asked him, "Have you ever been to the Lincoln Memorial at night?"

Sanchez gave the expected answer, no.

Nixon said, "Get your clothes on; we'll go!"

Nixon said the Secret Service was "petrified with apprehension" when he told them what he was going to do, and directed them not to notify any staff members.

At 4:30 A.M. Egil "Bud" Krogh, a Nixon aide in charge of security, was listening in on the Secret Service frequency when he heard the code word for Nixon: "Searchlight is on the lawn." Then, moments later, "Searchlight has asked for a car."

Once at the Lincoln Memorial, Sanchez and the president walked up the stone steps with the agents. Nixon revered Lincoln, and knew most of the words on the curved wall that he was pointing out to Sanchez by heart. Then he left Sanchez and began speaking in low tones to a group of students. Bud Krogh recalled: "It was very quiet, even hushed, and the President was speaking in a very low, conversational tone to the students, really in with them, not out in front talking to them." They talked about Vietnam. Nixon said, "I know that probably most of you think I am an S.O.B., but I want you to know that I understand just how you feel."

Sanchez went back to the car, then came up the steps again and tried to get Nixon to the car by telling him he had a phone call. Finally Nixon shook hands and walked back down the steps to his limousine. On the way, a student described by Krogh as having "wild, shaggy hair and a red beard" ran down the steps taking pictures. Nixon called the student over and had him give the camera to Dr. Walter Tkach, Nixon's personal physician, who had also arrived on the scene. The doctor took a picture of them together.

Nixon finally got in the car, and as it started to move away, another bearded student came up to the window and made an obscene gesture right in the president's face. They were eyeball to eyeball. Nixon, amused, gave it right back to him. He told Sanchez, "That S.O.B. will go through the rest of his life telling everybody that the President of the United States gave him the finger. And nobody will believe him!"

Nixon did not want to go back to the White House. He asked Sanchez if he had ever visited the Capitol. No, he hadn't. They were driven over and tried to enter the Senate chamber, but it was locked. They walked through the rotunda to the House side, where they met a custodian who got the keys and opened the House chamber. Nixon took Sanchez up to the dais, had him sit in the speaker's chair, and then went down to a front-row seat. He urged Sanchez to make a speech, and Sanchez spoke about his pride in being an American citizen. Nixon, his entourage, and the cleaning lady applauded.

On the way out he met another cleaning lady, Mrs. Carrie Moore, who brought out her Bible and asked Nixon to sign it. As he signed, Nixon commented, "Most of us don't read it enough."

"Mr. President, I read it all the time," she told him.

He held her hand, paused, then told her, "You know, my mother was a saint. She died two years ago. You be a saint, too."

"I'll try, Mr. President," she told him.

It was now dawn, and still Nixon did not want to return to the White House. He said he wanted to eat breakfast in a restaurant. He hadn't been in a restaurant since he became president. Haldeman, Press Secretary Ziegler, and other staff had caught up with him by now. They all went to the Rib Room of the Mayflower Hotel. Nixon had corned beef hash with a poached egg on it. "The last time I had this was on a train," he said. Haldeman—who would note the day in his diary as "the weirdest day so far"—had caught up with Nixon at the Capitol and was with him in the restaurant. He described the president as "completely beat and just rambling on, but obviously too tired to go to sleep."

After breakfast the president was still rebelling. He insisted on walking back to the White House. That would mean crossing Lafayette Park, where all the demonstrators were camped. His entourage tried to dissuade him, but he headed down Connecticut Avenue. Bud Krogh related: "So I finally went up and took him by the arm real solid and said, 'We can't walk back. We've got to ride back.' " At last Nixon got in the car and was headed toward the White House. He would note that the Mayflower waitresses "all stood at the door, outside on the street, and waved good-bye." At 7:30 A.M. he was back in the White House. He tried to go to bed but tossed and turned and finally got up again.

Nixon had asked his wife and daughters to go to Camp David for the duration of the protest, and at this point they were just waking up. Pat decided that she should return to the White House to be with her husband during the demonstration. The Secret Service did not like the risks, but Pat was determined. They secured an ambulance as a lead vehicle so they could get through blocked intersections, and used a big, black limousine as a decoy vehicle. Then they put Pat, Tricia, and Julie and her husband in a plain sedan. They put Pat's maid, Fina Sanchez—Manolo's wife—and the dog in the decoy limousine.

The streets were flooded with hundreds of demonstrators, some carrying Vietcong flags. Agents were out ahead at street corners to try to prevent blockages. Helmet police and soldiers guarded the White House gate. Julie wrote that the ride was "like a play, removed from reality," and she had a "sick, hollow feeling" in her stomach. She described the White House as "a tomb." All the shades were drawn, and all the lights turned off. The chants of the protesters were constant. She and Tricia watched the demonstrators on television and twice peeked out through the sheer lace curtains in the window of Tricia's bedroom closet. By nightfall, Julie said, "we inside the White House felt the numbness that comes after an intense assault on the senses."

Nixon viewed politics as war. "I often think of myself as leading an occupation force in the nation's capital," he said. From the beginning of his presidency he kept an "enemies list," and those on it were subject to investigation, phone tapping and harrassment by the FBI, the CIA, the Internal Revenue Service, or the Secret Service.

In September 1973 the *Washington Post* revealed that Nixon even had the Secret Service tap the phone of his brother, Donald. His "poor damn, dumb brother," as Nixon so fondly called him on the Watergate tapes, had long been something of an embarrassment. In his memoirs the president wrote almost nothing about the man who, when Nixon was vice president, opened a string of restaurants selling "Nixonburgers," financed with a $205,000 loan from Howard Hughes. The venture went bankrupt—and caused Nixon heckling in his 1962 bid for California's governorship. His opponent, Pat Brown, asked whether it was "proper for a governor, morally or ethically, to permit his family to receive a secret loan from a major defense contractor in the United States." When Nixon became president, he took no chances. He told Ehrlichmann, "You've got to do something about Don. . . . He's getting himself in some more business deals. People keep coming to him with their great ideas. Now it involves a lot of foreign governments. . . . Look, I want a complete surveillance on Don. Keep tabs on him and all the contacts he makes. I don't want people taking advantage of him."

An incredulous Ehrlichmann asked, "You mean like the FBI or something?"

"I don't care how you do it—just keep him covered," Nixon said.

Nixon's "dirty tricks" got more adventurous. The day after Tricia's 1971 wedding, he picked up the *New York Times.* On the front page, next to an account of the wedding, was a story about a series of classified National Security Council documents on the Vietnam War that a psychiatrist on the council, Daniel Ellsburg, had released to the press. They came to be called the Pentagon Papers. Nixon showed little concern, but Secretary of State Henry Kissinger called Ellsburg "the most dangerous man in America" and prodded the president to take action. When the FBI would not go after Ellsburg, Nixon called in Erhlichmann and told him, "If we can't get anyone in this damn government" to do something about leaks, "then, by God, we'll do it ourselves. I want you to set up a little group right here in the White House. Have them get off their tails and find out what's going on and figure out how to stop it."

The "little group" became known as "the Plumbers," and included Gordon Liddy, who had been discharged from the FBI, and Howard Hunt, a CIA specialist in covert operations. The two broke into Ellsburg's office, and when they didn't find any evidence that Ellsburg had leaked the Pentagon Papers, they trashed the office to cover their tracks. "This is far beyond anything I ever authorized," Ehrlichmann said.

For reasons that aren't clear, Liddy then devised a plan to break into Democratic National Headquarters, in the Watergate Hotel complex, to tap lines and copy documents. The line of approval went all the way up to Attorney General John Mitchell. On June 17, 1972, the "Plumbers" were discovered and arrested. Whatever information they might have obtained was of minimal use. That fall Nixon defeated George McGovern by a landslide. But even as his popularity crested, his doom was sealed.

Before Nixon took office, he was notified by aide Robert Finch that Lyndon Johnson had a taping system in places like the Oval Office and the Cabinet Room. "Get rid of it. I don't want anything like that," Nixon said. But in early 1971 he changed his mind and had voice-activated microphones installed in the Oval Office, the Cabinet Room, and his office in the Executive Office Building. In addition, the phones in the Lincoln Sitting Room and other places were tapped. Nixon never told Pat about the taping, which inevitably included some family conversations. When Watergate broke, she urged him to burn the tapes. Nixon later agreed that he should have, but he had been in the hospital at the time. "I was recovering from pneumonia when I made the decision not to burn the tapes," he said, and "You don't make good decisions when you are sick."

When a Senate committee began investigating the Watergate break-in, the odds of them finding out about a presidential taping system were remote. But Haldeman aide Alexander Butterfield, the man who had installed the system, happened to be called to testify in 1973. "It was just one of those pro forma interviews," recalled Republican counsel Fred Thompson. Out of the blue "one of our guys . . . on the minority staff said, 'By the way [John] Dean had said something about the President walking to the corner of the office or something and saying something in an almost inaudible tone. Is there any reason to believe there is an electronic eavesdropping device in the Oval Office?' "

Butterfield replied, "I'm sorry you asked that question. Yes, there was."

The Senate hearings were televised. The nation watched as day by day a new Nixon emerged. The tapes, sprinkled with deleted expletives, documented a web of lies covering up presidential involvement in the Watergate break-in and validating the president's privately held belief that "if you can't lie, you'll never go anywhere." Both Haldeman and Ehrlichmann would go to jail for their role in the Watergate cover-up.

Nixon's family urged him to stand and fight. Pat said, "Dick has done so much for the country. Why is this happening?" But Nixon could only endure so much. On April 17, 1973, the president gave a televised address, then "walked only a few feet—just far enough to be out of sight of the office—when he abruptly stopped, leaned against one of the columns, and began to cry. I felt completely helpless," recalled Secret Service Agent Dennis McCarthy.

As the scandal was unraveling Nixon told Haldeman, "You know, Bob, there's something I've never told anybody before, not even you. Every night since I've been president, every single night before I've gone to bed, I've knelt down on my knees beside my bed and prayed to God for guidance and help in this job. Last night before I went to bed, I knelt down and this time I prayed that I wouldn't wake up in the morning. I just couldn't face going on."

On July 27, 1974, Nixon returned from a swim in the Pacific near his San Clemente home. He was getting dressed in his beach trailer when the phone rang. His press secretary told him that the House Judiciary Committee had voted 27 to 11 in favor of an article of impeachment charging that Nixon had engaged in a "course of conduct" designed to obstruct the investigation of the Watergate case. "That was how I learned I was the first president in one hundred and six years to be recommended for impeachment," Nixon recalled, "standing in a beach trailer, barefoot, wearing old trousers, a Banlon shirt, and a blue windbreaker emblazoned with the Presidential Seal."

Reporters peppered the first lady with questions about Watergate. "I just pretend I don't hear them," she told Helene Drown, a close friend visiting the White House from California. "The next I know there will be a report that I am getting deaf." Helene went to Pat's study to say good-bye. She found the first lady "more worn and fragile than I have ever seen her, as if a little puff of wind could have blown her away. . . . She had always been a doer and now there was nothing she could do."

Julie visited her father at the Executive Office Building, where he also had an office, on the morning of August 2, and he told her he had reached the end—he had decided to resign. She returned to her third-floor bedroom in the White House and, crying, called her husband, who was in class at law school. David left for the White House. Julie then went down to the second floor and told her mother. "I could hardly bear to tell her the fight was over, just as my father could not."

"But why?" Pat asked, with tears in her eyes.

Julie said, "For me, those tears that were shed so briefly were perhaps the saddest moment of the last days in the White House."

On Monday, August 5, 1974, Nixon admitted that he had ordered the FBI to cease its investigation of the Watergate break-in. That day he invited the whole family to dine on the presidential yacht *Sequoia*. Reporters and photographers hung off the bridges and pursued in press boats. "We were the subject of a death watch," Julie wrote.

The next day, Press Secretary Ron Ziegler and Chief of Staff Alexander Haig came to the Executive Office Building to tell the president that he had no support in the Senate—they would vote to convict. Nixon stood by the window that looked out on the White House. He said, perhaps to himself, "Well, I screwed it up good, real good, didn't I?"

The Nixons had their last White House meal together as a family on August 7, in the third-floor solarium, on trays—they didn't want servants around. Nixon told them, "No man who ever lived had a more wonderful family than I have." They ordered their dogs brought up to help lighten the atmosphere. Then Ollie Atkins, the White House photographer, showed up with his camera. Pat told him they weren't in the mood to pose, but Nixon had requested a picture "for history." They stood and linked arms for a final photo. Pat never liked the picture: "Our hearts were breaking and there we are smiling." The following evening, August 8, 1974, Nixon went on television to tell the nation of his decision. He became the first president to resign. He couldn't bear to have his family with him. They watched the TV from the upper floor of the White House.

The next morning, Friday, August 9, the Nixons shook hands with the White House staff in the upper hall, then descended in the elevator to the East Room for Nixon's good-bye speech to staff and friends. It was in the elevator that Pat learned the TV networks would be there. "Oh, Dick," she said, "you can't have it televised." The East Room was jammed with people, many already teary-eyed. Nixon's speech was rambling. He mentioned his mother but didn't trust himself to talk about Pat because she was standing right there. Gerald Ford, appointed vice president following Spiro Agnew's resignation, and his wife, Betty, friends of many years, were waiting for them in the Diplomatic Reception Room below. Together they walked to the big Marine One helicopter. To make conversation, Betty commented on how long the red carpet seemed. Pat said, "You'll see so many of these, you'll get to hate them." Nixon was the last one in the copter. He turned at the door and gave a final, sweeping wave. His resignation was effective at noon. Air Force One, carrying the Nixons back to San Clemente, was over Missouri at the time. Its call sign was changed to the number on the tail of the plane—it had become just another airplane. The Nixon presidency was officially over.

Ford unconditionally pardoned Nixon on September 8, 1974, blocking all further prosecution. But Nixon already had some twenty lawsuits and twelve judicial procedures pending against him. His legal bills were huge. His papers and tapes had been seized. He hesitated to accept the pardon, calling it "the most humiliating day of my life." Then, a few months after his resignation, his phlebitis flared up again. This time, a clot did reach the lung, and he was hospitalized. Then, while he was in the hospital, another clot developed in the leg, and surgery was required. Nixon went into shock and nearly died. He convalesced for a year.

The ex–first lady was relieved to have no more press interviews. She had enjoyed coming to San Clemente during the presidency. "It's the only place in the world where we can sit unguarded," she said. "There may be a few people outside, but we don't see them." Now she loved digging in the garden, and she read several books a week. She continued to refuse interviews, and the media termed her a recluse. On July 7, 1976, she suffered a stroke and worked long and hard to fully recover.

Not long after he left office, Nixon agreed to do a TV interview with David Frost to help pay his legal expenses. Barred from practicing law, he wrote his memoirs, which were very profitable. He raised money for his presidential library in Yorba Linda and helped design it around his modest childhood home. He became an elder statesman and traveled widely, meeting world leaders and greatly restoring his reputation. In 1980, the Nixons decided California was too far from their children and grandchildren and moved to New York City to a four-story town house. In 1981 they moved to Saddle River, New Jersey, to a luxurious home with a garden and lots of trees. Pat died in 1993, and Nixon on April 22, 1994.

## THE NIXON REFURBISHMENT: A CURATOR'S VIEW

In the fall of 1969 the man whose decorating decisions would shape the White House from the 1970s right through the 1990s was deputy of protocol at the State Department and part-time curator of the department's antiques-filled Diplomatic Rooms. Clement Conger had known Richard Nixon for years. During a government conference at the State Department, the president whispered, "Clem, will you take Pat upstairs to see the Diplomatic Rooms—they look better than the White House." Pat Nixon evidently agreed, because in short order Conger had a new job. He resigned his job as deputy of protocol and worked as State Department curator in the morning, White House curator in the afternoon.

Pat took him through all the executive mansion's rooms and assorted nooks and crannies in the living area and state rooms. "Two-thirds of the furniture was department store reproductions," recalled Conger. "The curtains were in threads, the wallpaper worn right through to the plaster. No one ordered any extra materials—the chairs were simply retired to the warehouse when the fabrics wore out. In my opinion it was a disgrace second only to the burning of the White House in 1814."

Conger set about acquiring private funds. "I was raising an average of two to three million a year at the state department and here I was trying to do this at the White House, too," he said. But his mission was clear—a refurbishment more ambitious than the Kennedys undertook, a complete rethinking of the rooms to re-create what Conger calls "the glory days of the first quarter of the nineteenth century." What exactly did that constitute? "There were not really any good records until Mrs. Hoover," he said. "We did have some photographs from earlier eras, basically we had to start from scratch."

He brought in Edward Vason Jones, a Georgia restoration architect and authority on color and fabric who worked for experience, never a fee. What Conger called the triumvirate—Jones, Pat Nixon, and himself—started on the Green Room, which had green moire fabric by Schumacher from the Kennedy era. Though Conger considered it "a depressing color at night," new lengths were ordered and the walls redone as they were. "We lightened the room with curtains of beige, green, and coral satin, and added beautiful valances from a document of the period," said Conger. "It was all quite correct." He raised money to purchase Duncan Phyfe side tables and a settee and pieces by other New York cabinetmakers. Finding a suitable rug took some doing. "Green is the color of Mohammed's turban, and Moslem countries consider it irreverant to walk on green," he explained. But in the Turkish town of Hereke weavers were taught to make rugs with a French accent. Conger found one that included green in its elaborate patterning. It lasted until the Bush era, when it was reproduced. "The rugs are rolled up when the tourists go through," said Conger, "But the guards walk back and forth and ruin it."

For the Blue Room, Jones found a historic wallpaper fragment with a light-beige-patterned background and Directoire borders at the top and bottom that contained a certain amount of blue. Conger located the French company that made it and had two sets produced. He even purchased the silk screens so that it could be remade at a later date. But when the second set wore out during the Clinton administration, a new pattern was chosen to replace it. A blue and cream oval rug—not a shape made in the Islamic world—was turned up in France. President Monroe's Bellangé suite of chairs was filled out with reproductions. In 1976 a matching sofa was returned to the White House. It had been found in a storage room at the Henry Ford Museum in Dearborn, Michigan. Henry Ford had bought it from a family that had purchased it at an 1860 White House auction.

To match the period furnishings, Conger had the Blue Room's architectural detailing redone. "The Truman renovation was a very second rate job," he maintained. "The plaster ornament in the Blue Room ceiling was one you could buy at a store, the woodwork could be made in any mill shop." With Pat Nixon and Edward Jones, he visited historic houses close by in Virginia on the theory that they might find work done by the original craftsmen used at the White House. They adapted an oval plaster ceiling ornament from the Custis House and had moldings carved with acanthus leaves that echoed the border of the wallpaper. An acanthus-leaf chandelier from another part of the White House was moved to the Blue Room, creating in Conger's view a perfect representation of a fifteen-year, early nineteenth-century decorative arts period.

The Red Room, which needed the least refurbishing, continued the American Empire decor chosen by the Kennedys. Since the silk on the walls was worn, a new red silk was chosen after being carefully tested to look cheerful in both day and candlelight.

Throughout the house Conger and the Nixons created an impressive collection of American antiques and arts. Pat Nixon's special project was to acquire paintings of the first ladies. When one of the Adams descendants agreed to donate a portrait of John Quincy and Louisa Adams, the president was so thrilled he invited every known Adams descendant in America for a presentation ceremony. About a hundred came.

In his sixteen years at the White House—he was asked to retire in 1986 by Nancy Reagan—Conger made a record 1875 major aquisitions, most of them in the Nixon years. In the Kennedy administration some 1,100 major pieces were acquired. Harry Truman, who believed only in the sturdiness of new furniture, would have been horrified. After all the White House accommodates an annual influx of roughly 1.25 million tourists and 60 to 70,000 invited guests.

"The wear and tear on the upholstery is severe," said Conger. "Even if you've washed your hands three seconds before you touch fabric, you leave a little film of oil. Imagine what happens after 70,000 people touch that same fabric. There's an instinct in many people—they can't resist touching a curtain. Once we put up a sign, but it had the reverse effect." His pet peeve was the way furniture was shifted for media events. "These rooms are small," he pointed out. "Moving something out to the hall is just as dangerous as moving it from here to Baltimore." Nonetheless Conger maintained that antiques were practical. "If you keep eighteenth and early nineteenth century furniture well glued and nailed, it's as safe or safer than new furniture and certainly better built," he said. The curatorial staff looked at everything an average of once a week, as it does today. The maids and the housemen who dust are trained to look for loose legs and nicks. Working at the White House is considered a career position—normally people are expected to stay twenty-five years. There's a carpenter on staff for minor repairs and a conservator on call for major problems. "It's a constant restoration project that costs thousands and thousands of dollars," said Conger. "But it's the president's home and it has to be treated like a house."

The Nixon imprint on the White House continued until the Clinton administration, when the state rooms were again in need of refurbishment. By then views on what was historically correct had changed, and the Blue Room in particular was rethought. But back in 1972, as Conger said, "We felt for an hour of time all the rooms were perfect."

# 38

# Gerald R. Ford

## 1974–1977

## *The Unelected President*

ON THE STROKE of noon on August 9, 1974, Gerald Ford Jr., was sworn in as the thirty-eighth president of the United States in the East Room of the White House. One minute earlier, Richard Nixon, airborne for California, had been president. The White House is used to such split-second changes, but normally the transition of power and possessions takes place on inauguration day and packing is carefully planned. Since Nixon's Watergate-induced resignation was sudden, the staff had only time to send him off with essentials. Ford, likewise, hadn't had time to pack, so on his first day as president he left the White House and went home to his four-bedroom, split-level ranch house at 514 Crown View in Alexandria, Virginia. He celebrated with a lasagna party with friends. The next morning he was out on the front porch retrieving his daily newspaper in what First Lady Betty Ford described as his "baby-blue short pajamas." He came back in and, as usual, fixed his orange juice and English muffin.

Ten days later, his family's possessions crated and boxed, he and Betty were scheduled to take up residency at the White House. But rather than going straight to Pennsylvania Avenue with their household goods, they boarded Air Force One for Chicago, where Ford was scheduled to make a speech. When they returned to Washington that night, the Marine One helicopter took them to the White House. "That night we came back to new living quarters in perfect order," Betty said, "our clothes, our knickknacks, everything just where I've said we'll want it."

But not all the Nixon possessions had been removed. Betty found a box marked "Tapes: Don't Touch." She was afraid to open it, thinking it held secret Watergate conversations. But curiosity prevailed. The box, it turned out, contained Nixon's collection of Montovoni recordings.

Betty was unintimidated by being first lady. "I'm just going to be Betty Bloomer Ford and might as well have a good time doing it," she said. Her Secret Service code name was Pinafore, but when Betty talked to truckers on her CB radio, her handle was "First Mama." She was open and frank with the press, even responding to questions about White House sleeping arrangements. Betty told journalist Myra MacPherson that in her first weeks as first lady reporters had "asked me everything but how often I sleep with my husband and if they'd asked me that, I would have told them." Hardly able to pass up an opening like that, MacPherson asked how often that was. "As often as possible," Betty replied.

The Fords actually used twin beds that attached side by side to a common headboard. "We can't share a double bed," she said, "because when Jerry rolls over, everything goes with him; I'd never have a blanket." Sleeping in separate rooms, she said, was "just too far to go." She chose Pat Nixon's bedroom for the marital bed and turned Richard Nixon's room into a family sitting room. Other first families had created a living room out of the huge west hall by the lunette window, but Betty said she wasn't going "to sit out in some dumb hall." She wanted the privacy of a closed door. In the presidential sitting room she put familiar furniture—Jerry's blue leather chair and footstool, his pipes in his pipe rack, and their old TV set. Family pictures were all around.

Ford liked the White House, saying, "It is the best public housing I've ever seen." But he hadn't expected to live there. When he was sworn in, he asked the Marine Band to refrain from playing "Hail to the Chief." Throughout his two-and-a-half-year term the tune would embarrass him. Ford is the only president who ascended to the highest office in the land without getting a single electoral vote.

A longtime Republican congressman from Michigan, Ford was the House minority leader when Nixon's vice president, Spiro Agnew, resigned in 1973 amid charges of graft. Ford's ambition in life was to be Speaker of the House, but that required being a member of the majority party, and a change seemed unlikely. "I'm never going to be speaker, it would be a nice cap for my career," he said of the vice presidency. Democrats in Congress warned Nixon that they would not confirm any Republican who might be a serious contender to succeed him in 1976. Nixon had known Ford since the two men were freshmen in Congress in 1949, and certainly didn't think him presidential material. "Can you imagine Jerry Ford sitting in this chair?" he once said incredulously. Ford

On Nixon's last day in office, Gerald and Betty Ford waited downstairs away from the TV cameras while Nixon said goodbye in the East Room. Then the two families walked together to the waiting helicopter, the picture of harmony. On the way back to the White House to be sworn in, Ford confidently told Betty, "We can do it." (CORBIS)

seemed to agree. He assured Nixon, "I made a firm commitment to Betty to be out of politics come January nineteen hundred and seventy-seven."

Ford's appointment to the vice presidency was confirmed on December 6, 1973. The next spring, he talked of retiring after his term was up in January 1977, living on his modest investment income and pension and spending his days playing golf. But on August 8, 1974, Betty and Jerry Ford sat at home watching Nixon give his televised resignation speech. They were joined by daughter Susan, seventeen, a student at a Bethesda, Maryland, high school, and Steven, eighteen, who had just graduated from high school. Two other sons, Michael, twenty-four, and Jack, twenty-two, no longer lived at home. "The night of August eighth, in our house, was surprisingly uneventful," the vice president said. "We retired early. Before sleeping we held hands and offered my prayer from Proverbs—'Trust in the Lord with all thine heart.'" In the morning, Ford said, "I had slept well and this reflected my confidence that I was prepared to do the job." The next day, after escorting the departing Nixons to the Marine One helicopter and retirement, he said to Betty on the way back inside the White House, "We can do it."

Ford thoroughly enjoyed his new job, getting up at 5:15 A.M. each day raring to go. But matters of foreign and domestic policy waited until the president finished his exercise routine. At sixty-two, Ford was perhaps the most physically active and well-conditioned president ever. Back in his college days at the University of Michigan, he had been a star football player (he played sports right-handed but ate and wrote left-handed). He was even a male model for a time, and in 1942 appeared on the cover of *Cosmopolitan* magazine. Football left him with bad knees, so he started his morning workout with leg lifts, strapping a forty-pound weight to his left leg and a twenty-five-pound weight to his right. Then he did a mile on a stationary bicycle, twenty push-ups and twenty sit-ups, and later in the day swam laps. He was an avid swimmer and missed the pool in the backyard of his Alexandria home. Because of his interest, an outdoor pool was donated to the White House in 1975. Installed sixty feet south of the Oval Office in the West Wing, the pool could be reached via an underground tunnel that let out at the pool's edge. It was heated and had a cover that could be peeled back enough for a single lane, allowing the president to swim outdoors in the winter. Nixon had turned Franklin Roosevelt's indoor pool into a press room.

After his workout, Ford read his briefing papers and the *New York Times*, showered, dressed, and at seven-thirty was at his desk ready to go. Sometimes he set aside an hour to just smoke his pipe and think. He enjoyed the view from the Oval Office—roses, azaleas, forsythia, and his dog, Liberty, being run about by a gardener—especially in the spring, which he found "gorgeous" in the capital. At night, he would occasionally slip into the Lincoln Cabinet Room, which Jackie Kennedy had made the Treaty Room, on the second floor to reflect. "Lincoln used to hold his cabinet meetings there, and history permeates the room," Ford recalled. "I would sit alone and gaze at the paintings and photographs of another time, and I could almost hear the voices of 110 years before. When I left the room, I always felt revived." In the evening, he sometimes worked in the family room in front of the television with Betty. "After dinner, when Jerry was home and we were alone, we'd get up from the table and go straight in there," Betty said. "He'd work and I'd watch television. He had a fantastic ability to study, to look up once in a while, see what Kojak is doing, then go back to his papers." When people asked Ford about the pressures of the presidency, he said, "I never felt better physically. I never had a clearer mind. I never enjoyed an experience more. The truth is I couldn't wait to start the day."

The perks of the job appealed to him as well. He had a personal valet, a masseur, a tailor, and a doctor in residence. He rode in a limousine instead of the beat-up family station wagon he'd driven for years. The Air Force One crew made sure to have a bowl of strawberries—a favorite—ready for him. They also made sure his tobacco tin was filled. Ford smoked about eight bowls of Sir Walter Raleigh tobacco a day. There was a barbershop in the basement, and the barber, Milton Pitts, would come to him whenever he wanted—no waiting.

"I need a little trim," Ford told Pitts on his first visit. "You see my hair is thinning and light and if you cut my sideburns too thin, it looks like I have none. I'm using Vitalis."

"I know, Mr. President," said Pitts, who had considerable experience cutting the hair of chief executives, "everything you're doing is wrong."

David Kennerly, a young friend of the Fords, was there, and he laughed. Pitts realized the implications of what he had just said and hastened to add, "Excuse me, Mr. President, I'm talking about your hair."

Pitts later described his corrective strategy: "I took the Vitalis out and razor cut his hair, left his sideburns fuller, left hair lower on the back, and by [blow] drying it, I fluffed that light hair up."

Another benefit of the job was the attractive reporters, with whom Ford liked to flirt. A former Miss America, Phyllis George, was working for CBS, and while dancing with the president, she got him to agree to a filmed interview talking about football. When Ford told Ron Nessen, his press secretary, to set it up, Nessen couldn't believe he meant it, so he didn't do it. But Ford didn't forget about it. "She's awfully attractive," he told Nessen. So Nessen not only set up the TV interview but arranged for Ford and Phyllis George to talk privately in the president's study off the Oval Office. "Thank God Betty didn't find out about it," Nessen commented.

The White House press corps treated him less graciously. Prior to his first press conference, the new president spent hours reviewing a wide range of issues, but at the conference the reporters peppered him with questions about Watergate and a possible pardon for Nixon. At his confirmation hearing for vice president, Ford was asked if he thought he would have the power to pardon Nixon should Nixon resign, and Ford answered, "I do not think the American people would stand for it." Now, without consulting party leaders, Congress, or the public, he decided to pardon Nixon, and the act would cloud his entire presidency.

Just thirty days into his term, on Sunday, September 8, 1974, Ford went to an early communion at St. John's Episcopal Church, across Lafayette Park from the White House, then returned to the Oval Office to face a TV camera from behind his desk. In nine minutes he explained his reasons for granting Nixon a "full, free, and absolute" pardon. Convinced he had done the right thing, he then left for a round of golf at Burning Tree, an exclusive golf club in suburban Washington. He was on the golf course when his statement was aired. The firestorm of disapproval that ensued bewildered him. His 71 percent approval rate plummeted. In October he would voluntarily testify before the House Judiciary Committee to try to calm the protests. "There was no deal," he declared. He viewed his action as a means to put the Watergate scandal behind both himself and the country, and as a humanitarian gesture.

Jerry Ford had always been known as a nice guy. He was born July 14, 1913, in Omaha, Nebraska, and named Leslie Lynch King Jr. Three years later his mother divorced King and married Gerald R. Ford. She changed her son's name, and when he was about twelve, she told him about his real father. As a young man he was an Eagle Scout and worked in Yellowstone National Park as a ranger. At Yale Law School he was in the top quarter of his class. During World War II he served as a navy officer. Even after he entered politics, he liked to say he had many rivals but no enemies. Once, at the ski lodge he owned in Vail, Colorado, his dog messed on the floor. The White House steward who had accompanied the president on the trip moved to clean it up. Ford got up from the table, took the cloth from the steward, and cleaned it up himself. "No man should have to clean up after another man's dog," he said. At the White House he even insisted on walking his pregnant dog, Liberty, in the middle of the night. She'd been trained to lick his face when she needed to go out, and Ford responded to her cue. He put on his slippers and went out to the south grounds. When he tried to get back in, the elevator to the family quarters wouldn't work. Ford and Liberty, who was barely able to waddle, padded upstairs but found the stairwell doors on the second and third floor locked. As Betty Ford recounted in her memoir, "there they were in the wee small hours of the morning, not able to get back to bed." Finally the Secret Service agents, who normally pay attention to their closed-circuit TV monitors, noticed something was amiss and came to the duo's rescue.

Initially the press was taken with Ford's unassuming manner. "The story had gotten out that the President made his own breakfast, didn't require a Navy steward to fix his muffins for him," recalled press secretary Jerald terHorst. "And so I said, 'Well, we'll send a [press] pool up there. And it certainly seemed to work." The honeymoon didn't last. Ford had a talent for bloopers. "If Lincoln were alive today, he'd roll over in his grave," he announced at a Lincoln's Birthday party. In an October 6, 1976, debate with Jimmy Carter he declared, "There is no Soviet domination in Eastern Europe, and there never will be during a Ford administration." Every president has slip-ups, but Ford's got reported vigorously. On a May 1975 trip to Austria for a conference with Egypt's Anwar Sadat, Ford stopped for a short visit in Madrid. The Spanish gave him a huge bedroom but a short, hard bed with a hard round pillow. He tossed and turned and got little sleep. His knees were stiff the next day as he walked down a rickety metal ramp in the rain in Salzburg, Austria. Ford took an umbrella from an aide, held it over Betty, and took her arm. "Betty and I were descending the steps," he said. "I had my right arm around her, and I was carrying the umbrella in my left hand. Two or three steps from the bottom of the ramp, the heel of my shoe caught on something. I had no free hand to grab the rail, so I took a tumble to the tarmac below." Ford immediately jumped to his feet and thought no more about it.

The media, however, had a field day. One network news program played his fall eleven times in one newscast, including once in slow motion. Press Secretary Ron Nessen tried to attribute the fall to the sleepless night in Madrid, to no avail. Ford quickly acquired an indelible image as a klutz. Late-night television comedians exploited the incident with gusto. "The news coverage was harmful," Ford later wrote, "but even more damaging was the fact that Johnny Carson and Chevy Chase used my missteps for their jokes. Their antics—and I'll admit that I laughed at them myself—helped create a public perception of me as a stumbler. And that wasn't funny."

Future mishaps were reported and exaggerated, or even made up. The president became a popular subject of cartoonists. When he went skiing at Vail on a Christmas holiday, his aides warned him that if he fell, the media would jump on it. "I told them their concerns were ridiculous," Ford said. "I had skied for most of my life, and I wasn't about to stop doing something I loved just because reporters and photographers might be there. *Every* skier falls, I said. Surely, the press would understand that." The fit president was rated an advanced intermediate skier, but inevitably he did fall, and it made the TV news and page one of some papers. As vice president, Ford had hit a spectator on the head with a stray golf ball during a charity golf tournament in Minneapolis. As president, he had several wild shots that hit spectators or were near misses. He was in fact a good golfer—he had a handicap of eighteen—but comedian Bob Hope was led to quip, "It's not hard to find Jerry Ford on a golf course, you just have to follow the wounded."

Ford told reporters that their jests didn't bother him, but he complained bitterly to Nessen that the reporters half his age who wrote such jibes couldn't get down a beginner's slope on skis. Eventually he admitted to reporters, "It kind of hurts your pride a little bit because you know it isn't true. You have to be a little thick-skinned." Nessen later observed that Ford, unlike other presidents, was routinely described as "acting presidential," rather than as "the president."

Being first lady was "no breeze," either, as Betty put it. "You have no private life, the demands on your time are constant, you are under terrific pressure." Born Elizabeth Bloomer, she married William Warren in 1942 and divorced him in 1947. She and Jerry were married on October 15, 1948. When they moved from their modest Alexandria home to the White House, she initially felt ill at ease. She greeted the White House guards in her cheery manner, but they never answered. She said to Chief Usher Rex Scouten, "I feel terribly uncomfortable here when I speak to one of the guards or the White House police; they never answer me, just sort of back off." Scouten explained that Nixon had a rule that they were not allowed to speak to him or the first lady.

"This house has been like a grave," Betty said. "I want it to sing." She changed the annual Senate Wives Lunch to a brown-paper-bag picnic on the south lawn and did away with protocol. Everyone was seated by picking a number. She found the family dining room "depressing." The Zuber print installed by the Kennedys, "Wonders of America," showed Niagara Falls and Boston harbor. But it also depicted Revolutionary War scenes, and Betty said, "I couldn't stand to look at soldiers fainting and dying while I was eating my soup." She had the paper removed and the walls painted "a bright sunny yellow." Clement Conger, the White House curator who had worked so closely with Pat Nixon, quickly realized that he and Betty Ford were not on the same wavelength. He told her that he had arranged for a new bed for the Queen's Bedroom. "It's more beautiful than the bed that's there now," he told Betty. "It's in Charleston, waiting for us to move it in." Betty informed him that the new bed would be staying in Charleston: "It's not the bed that five queens have slept in." Betty did not share Conger's love for antiques. She called the furniture that Conger and Pat Nixon had installed in the upstairs Oval Room "stark, stiff, formal furniture, all stripes and arms and legs. The maids could tell you how many legs—something like 127—because they had to dust them." She kept it anyway. Betty occasionally checked to see if the maids had cleaned thoroughly by leaving a cigarette between the hands of some angels that decorated one of the flower vases.

Though the family room stayed in the so-called president's bedroom, Betty came to enjoy sitting on the sofa by the big lunette window in the upstairs hall. "I like it because I can see the Oval Office. It reminds me that my husband is close by," she said. She could also see reporters coming and going from the press room, and people walking by on the street. "You can't imagine how isolated the White House feels at times. It's a luxury to be able to see people, to see without being seen," she said. "But there is no privacy out there. There are always people at the fence with binoculars trying to catch a glimpse. That is what is so confining."

As president, Jerry was home more than ever before in their married life, and Betty appreciated that. As a congressman, he had been on the road more than two hundred nights a year making paid appearances to supplement his modest income. But now their life was much more public. Betty sometimes managed to slip out of the White House—with the Secret Service, of course—to go to MacDonald's for a hamburger or to stores to shop. But going places with the president was more difficult. In 1976 Betty tried to take her husband out for a quiet lunch on his birthday, July 14. She wanted it to be private—"Just the two of us"—at Sans Souci in Washington. But her reservation included one table for the Secret Service and another for the press pool. She went to the Oval Office, surprised Jerry with a happy birthday greeting, and said "Come on, dear, I'm treating." They entered the restaurant to clicking cameras and a standing ovation from the other diners. Flashes popped when they clinked glasses, and as they left they were filmed by the TV cameras.

Being a public figure also meant being on time—a first for Betty, who had been chronically late for appointments all her life. But her staff helped keep her on schedule. For starters, she was a late riser. She didn't even like to talk before ten and ate breakfast alone in her sitting room. When her husband left early for a trip, Betty always came out on the balcony to wave to him as he boarded the helicopter. But at that hour she was rarely dressed, so she would take off her robe, put on shoes and a coat, tuck her nightgown up under the coat, and go out to the balcony to see him off. When she was ready to dress, she turned to four closets full of clothes and accessories—one for her formal gowns, one for long dresses, one for shoes and pocketbooks, and one for day clothes. Her scarves were arranged by color in a separate bureau. Her daily routine included reading her Bible and the Saint Francis prayer that hung in her bathroom. Once in her office, Betty read her mail, but found it "almost a waste of time" because her writers' questions were uninteresting to her. On spring and fall weekends her office work was interrupted by the noise of tourists tramping through the house and grounds on special garden tours, accompanied by military bands playing. "You could practically go out of your mind, hearing their martial music when you're trying to work."

Betty also watched the family budget. She served only domestic wines, economized on foods, and like Lyndon Johnson turned off lights. When she discovered that the Ford family all had to pay first-class air fares to fly on Air Force One with Jerry when they were going on a ski vacation, she decided they would go tourist class on a commercial airliner. But that complicated security so much that she gave up the idea. On official trips she was not charged airfare, but when she brought her hairdresser, Jim Merson, along, Ford had to pay first-class fare for him. It also fell to Betty to oversee the gifts that came to the White House for the first family. A special gift unit logged, filed, and acknowledged the packages. The Secret Service destroyed any food that was sent in. Betty let the gifts pile up unopened in an empty bedroom, and when the room was full she declared what she called "gift day," and they were all opened.

The first lady's real interests were political. Betty regularly read her husband's briefing papers. She was one of the few people Ford consulted before he pardoned Nixon—she had urged him to do it. She considered Pat Nixon her friend and spoke admiringly of her predecessor, making sure to send her birthday cards. Betty supported rights for lesbians, the Equal Rights Amendment (she wore an oversize ERA button), and abortion rights. To influence Ford to support her causes, she said she used "pillow talk," especially in prodding him to appoint women to high positions. She was influential in getting Carla Hills appointed as secretary of housing and urban development, for example. As a result of her public stands, she became the first first lady to have her own protesters outside the White House gate.

The media and the public found her candor refreshing. But an August 1975 interview with Morley Safer on the *60 Minutes* television show taught her that she could be too candid. She would later say that Safer's questions caught her "off balance."

"What if Susan Ford came to you and said, 'Mother, I'm having an affair?' " Safer asked.

"Well," Betty said, "I wouldn't be surprised. I think she is a perfectly normal human being like all young girls. I would certainly counsel her and advise her on the subject, and I'd want to know pretty much about the young man—whether it was a worthwhile encounter or whether it was going to be one of those—"

Here she stopped, perhaps realizing she might be going in the wrong direction. She backtracked, saying, "She's pretty young to have affairs."

"Nevertheless old enough?" Safer asked.

"Oh, yes," Betty agreed. "She's a big girl."

The show was taped, and when it aired Ford was in Vail. He had just announced he would run in 1976. "You just cost me ten million votes," he exclaimed. Susan watched the show in Kansas, then called Betty and asked, "Mother, what is an affair?" Susan would later say, "It put me in a tight spot as far as dating guys. They thought, 'She's easy, her mother'll let her have affairs.' "

Not that dating was especially easy with Secret Service protection. As Susan's older brother Steven explained, "When you're eighteen, ten Secret Service guys is not really the group you want to hang out with. First dates were always bizarre. . . . I'd call for a reservation and say, 'I'd like a table for two, and I'd also like another table for two—but way across the room, please.' " On the other hand, he said, "I always had enough guys for a card game."

Betty also told Safer that the Supreme Court's controversial ruling that a woman had a right to an abortion was "a great, great decision." An avalanche of mail poured into the White House, most of it critical. Betty also allowed that she might well have tried marijuana had it been available to her when she was growing up. Then Safer asked her if she thought her children had tried marijuana, and she answered, "Probably," which upset her children because they hadn't.

The first lady's popularity rating plummeted after the *60 Minutes* interview. Ford always supported her, but Betty heard from Ron Nessen, who was highly critical, that her husband was "very upset." Her popularity recovered, but she admitted she regretted the interview.

It was no doubt neither the first nor the last time the Ford children were subjected to unwanted publicity. Their eldest son, Michael, was a student at Cornwall Theological Seminary in Essex, Massachusetts. He took pains to avoid publicity, even taking a job under an assumed name. Jack had a summer job as a forest ranger but was at an unsettled stage of his life. He caused his father some loss of sleep, something even the presidency couldn't do. He had a so-called hippie lifestyle, and tended to be sloppy and to say things to the press that embarrassed his father. He disliked the Secret Service agents assigned to him, and they disliked him.

Steve was a recent high school graduate when his father took office, and he occasionally stayed at the White House. In December 1976 he picked up a date while visiting the Georgetown nightspots and brought her back to the White House—and the Queen's Bedroom. In the morning, he heard noises in the hall, peeked out, and saw television crews setting up for Betty's White House tour with Barbara Walters. He called a White House limousine for his overnight friend, instructed her on how to make her exit downstairs, and then walked out into the hall to distract the set-up crew while she made her escape.

Susan, the youngest, was just seventeen when her father was elected and was most affected by the move to the White House. She entered Mount Vernon College, Virginia, in the fall of 1975 to study photography, commuting there from the White House. She would later marry Secret Service agent Charles Vane. Betty's assistant Nancy Howe told Susan she should give up wearing blue jeans, and Susan rebelled. "I will always wear jeans," she said. But when Betty was in the hospital for a mastectomy in September 1974, Susan helped out as White House hostess. She also went with her mother and father when they visited China. Susan had a good relationship with her mother and resented Nancy Howe's attempts to keep her from visiting Betty in her office. "My mother keeps me in stitches," Susan said. "I'll come home from school in the worst mood, and she'll cheer me up. . . . She's a nut. I don't know what I'd do without her." She called her mother a real ham.

Betty agreed. "Yes, I am a ham," she said. "I think all theatrical people are. We absolutely love an audience." Betty had longed for a career in dance and had been in the famous Martha Graham dance group. She said of Graham, "More than anyone else, she shaped my life." At the annual "roast" of the president at the Gridiron Club, on March 31, 1976, Betty performed some soft-shoe numbers. In preparation, she rehearsed with a professional dance coach, a cellist, a drummer, and a pianist in the upstairs hall of the White House. She and dance coach Vic Daumit also did the Hustle up and down the hall. The first lady even appeared on television, on the *Mary Tyler Moore* comedy show.

When the star of the television show *Mission Impossible*, Peter Graves, was invited to a White House reception, he called from Dulles Airport to say that the airline had lost all his luggage, so he and his wife couldn't make it that evening. Betty told him to rent formal clothes and come anyway, and she set out several formal dresses for his wife to choose from. Jerry danced with Mrs. Graves that night and, unawares, complimented her on her dress.

Ford also liked to dance. At a party for Foreign Minister Cosgrave of Ireland, the Marine Band played music that was fashionable, but not to Ford's taste. He was even less pleased when they played an Irish jig. He called for his military aide, Robert Barrett. "If they won't play some music I can dance to," he told Barrett, "I'm just not gonna come to these things anymore." Barrett told the leader of the Marine Band to play "Star Dust" or "Bad Boy Leroy Brown." The band leader was nonplussed: "I've been playing at the White House for twelve years and I just don't understand." Things finally changed when Barrett told the band leader that if he kept it up, he'd be playing out on the street. Ford was smiling when he said good night to his guests, but as soon as he was in the elevator, he said, "Now, listen, Barrett, I'm President of the United States, and I should be able to have some music I can dance to."

Ford had another problem with the band on July 8, 1976, when Queen Elizabeth II of Great Britain visited. Ford escorted her royal majesty with her tiara and medals out onto the dance floor, and the band struck up "The Lady is a Tramp."

What Ford called the "lowest and loneliest moment" of his presidency came on September 26, 1974. Betty had a routine medical examination. That evening the White House doctor called to tell her there was a lump on her breast, and a biopsy was necessary to determine if it was malignant. The Fords told no one. The next day Betty went through her normal schedule and then left for Bethesda Naval Hospital. Ford was in the Oval Office when he learned that the lump was malignant and that an immediate radical mastectomy was necessary. To his top aide, Robert Hartmann, he said, "Bob, I just don't know what I'd do without her. I just don't know what I'd do." They both cried. It was two weeks before Betty was able to return to the White House, and then she needed chemotherapy treatments for a year, and she was on anticancer drugs that made her weak. Although Betty was uncomfortable with the publicity around her illness, she was frank as always, and helped raise awareness of the value of early detection.

Betty's health was complicated by her addictions. She suffered from an inoperable pinched nerve in her neck, which was aggravated by the pressures of her life. She turned to painkillers, tranquilizers, and alcohol for relief from pain, as well as from loneliness. Her drinking had begun years ago. With Ford away so much as a congressman, Betty had raised four children virtually alone, and it took a heavy toll on her. In 1970 she had sought psychiatric help for eighteen months. "The loneliness, the being left to yourself at night, is what makes marriages crack, makes liquor more attractive," she said, "but who am I to criticize? . . . During the time when Jerry was gone so much I developed a problem." In his eight months as vice president, Ford still traveled 118,000 miles for speaking engagements with some five hundred groups in forty states. During this time, Betty admitted, she took a Valium tablet a day to stay calm. The pressures of being first lady only exacerbated her problems. Curator Clement Conger would recall, "Betty Ford was not well from medications. She would receive me in her bedroom with her secretary and we'd take notes."

On March 12, 1976, during the reelection campaign, Betty made a speech in which she sounded tired. She slurred and mispronounced some words. "What's the matter with her?" a reporter whispered to Betty's secretary, Sheila Weidenfeld. The first lady sounded drunk, although she'd only had her usual vodka tonic on the plane. Later, she was fine. On subsequent occasions she exhibited similar problems. She once referred to Ford's rival primary candidate, Ronald Reagan, as "President Reagan." Finally, she admitted to Weidenfeld that she wasn't well, that she had been "uncomfortable the whole trip." Her mixing of sedatives, painkillers, and alcohol had finally caught up with her. "I've lived with it for twelve years. I've learned to hide it," the first lady finally admitted. Both of her parents had been alcoholics. Fifteen months after leaving the White House, she entered an alcohol and drug rehabilitation center. After her recovery she would speak freely of her struggle and would found the Betty Ford Clinic to help others.

Her husband was in good health during his presidency, but his life was seriously threatened twice. The first time was in Sacramento, where he had addressed a joint session of the California legislature on the subject of crime. The next morning, September 5, 1975, he had an appointment to see Governor Jerry Brown. Ford decided to walk the short distance from his hotel across the street to the Capitol. Outside the hotel, he noticed a small crowd of people behind a rope to his left. He later recalled, "They were applauding and saying nice things; I was in a good mood, so I started shaking hands. That's when I spotted a woman wearing a bright red dress. She was in the second or third row, moving right along with me as if she wanted to shake my hand. When I slowed down I noticed immediately that she thrust her hand under the arms of other spectators. I reached down to shake it and looked into the barrel of a .45 caliber pistol pointed directly at me." Ford ducked, and Secret Service agent Larry Buendorf lunged for her hand, wrestling Lynette "Squeaky" Fromme to the ground. She explained herself this way: "Well, you know when people treat you like a child and pay no attention to the things you say, you have to do something." The Secret Service hustled Ford into the Capitol, and he met with Governor Brown without mentioning the incident. He did not walk back to the hotel, however. The Secret Service brought a car into the basement of the Capitol and drove him back.

Ford thought Squeaky Fromme was "an aberration." He had been getting about one hundred threats a month, but that was not particularly unusual for a president. So he was not especially concerned for his safety when he returned to California on September 10. As he was readying to leave San Francisco's St. Francis Hotel on September 22, 1975, the Secret Service agents warned him not to shake hands with the crowd gathered at the entrance but to go directly to his limousine. As an agent reached to open the rear car door, there was a loud pop. "Bang! I recognized the sound of a shot, and I froze," Ford said. "There was a hushed silence for a split second. Then pandemonium broke out." Agents shoved Ford into the car and piled on top of him. The bullet fired by Sara Jane Moore hit the hotel wall, then the curb to Ford's left, then bounced up and hit a taxi driver. Moore said, "I did not want to kill somebody, but there comes a point when the only way you can make a statement is to pick up a gun." The president's limousine roared off toward the safety of Air Force One. "You guys sure are heavy," the president complained. "Can we turn on the air conditioning. It's getting stuffy in here."

Back on Air Force One, Ford dropped into his big swivel lounge chair and accepted a cold martini. Betty had just arrived.

"How did they treat you in San Francisco, dear?" she bubbled.

After Squeaky Fromme's assassination attempt, Betty said, "It's something I have to live with, I suppose. I've got to get myself squared away." After Sara Jane Moore's attempt, she said, "Thank God she was a poor shot."

Following these assassination attempts, the Secret Service began requiring all presidents to wear bulletproof vests when greeting crowds. Ford's first vest was bulky and heavy and made him sweat so much he became dehydrated. Then he got a vest that was almost like an undershirt. Bulletproof linings were sewn into the vests of his three-piece suits.

The next year, Chester M. Plummer climbed the eight-foot-high White House fence one summer night. Seismic detectors went off, and the lawn was flooded with light. A guard called for him to halt, but he kept coming, a long pipe raised above his head. The guard shot him dead. Ford was inside, reading.

Despite these experiences—and despite stating unequivocally when he was appointed vice president that he would not run for president in 1976—Ford decided to seek a second, full term. Betty agreed. She had become one of the world's most popular women, and as she later said, "I loved it." She told White House reporter Helen Thomas, "I want him to run. He couldn't be running unless I wanted him to." Ford had done well in the presidency, with the salary now at $200,000 a year and most expenses paid except food for his family. A February 12, 1976, report showed that since 1973, Ford's net worth had increased from $256,378 to $323,000.

But he had limited appeal as a candidate. His greatest asset was his honesty and openness. It wasn't enough. He lacked showmanship and communication skills. Even son Jack said his speeches were "boring." During the campaign, Ford attempted to polish his appearance and speaking style. A Georgia haberdasher recommended by his aides outfitted him in what Ford called a "more relaxed and modern style." But Ford could not change his image, nor was he truly cognizant of its importance. In early 1975, when the Vietnam War was at its height and the carnage of the American evacuation of Saigon was broadcast daily on television, Ford went to Palm Springs to play golf. He received word of the fall of Danang en route there. Clips of Ford on the golf course and of the horrors of war were televised back to back. Afterward, Ron Nessen dreaded facing reporters.

Ford's 1976 loss to Democrat Jimmy Carter devastated him, so much so that the Secret Service feared the even-tempered president might become suicidal. He admitted to being "terribly hurt. . . . I was crestfallen. Betty and I had worked very hard to win." The couple retired to a gated community in Rancho Mirage, California, near Palm Springs. They built a huge, rambling house with enough bedrooms for the entire family, plus a pool and a tennis court, along the thirteenth fairway of the community's exclusive golf course. Ford wrote his memoirs, joined boards of large corporations, worked on the Ford Library in Ann Arbor, Michigan, received handsome consulting fees, and gave speeches at up to $15,000 a clip. Now he could play golf and ski to his heart's content.

# 39

# Jimmy Carter
## 1977–1981

## *Down Home*

THE FIRST TIME Rosalynn Carter picked up the White House telephone and asked to speak to "Jimmy," the operator, more accustomed to requests for "the president," asked "Jimmy who?" inadvertently echoing a familiar line. Carter had met with the same question so many times during his campaign that he used *Jimmy Who?* as the title of a campaign autobiography. A decidedly dark-horse candidate, he was so little known nationally that in 1975, a year before the election, he went on the television game show *What's My Line?* and his identity almost stumped the panel. When he told his mother, Lillian, that he was considering running for president the following year, she asked, "Of what?"

A prosperous peanut farmer from rural Plains, Georgia, Carter's un-Washingtonness appealed in the post-Watergate era. As president-elect he played up his small-town roots, organizing his new administration from his one-story, four-bedroom brick house—a mansion by Plains standards. Rosalynn, who had never had a cook, served the stream of visitors herself, although helpful neighbors sent in food. Henry Kissinger visited and drank iced tea from a Tweety-Bird jelly glass. The down-home tone the Carters would bring to the White House had begun.

For the inaugural ceremony Carter wore a three-piece suit he had bought in Americus, the nearest large town to Plains, for $175. Afterward he shattered all recent precedent and defied the Secret Service by walking down Pennsylvania Avenue from the

Capitol to the White House hand in hand with Rosalynn. At each inaugural ball that night, the new president called out, "How many of you like my wife's old blue dress? She made it herself six years ago." In addition to the evening's traditional waltzes and fox trots, he introduced square dancing.

In a Jeffersonian move, the new president and first lady spent their first two White House days receiving people who had lined up to greet them. "My hand throbbed, my feet hurt," Rosalynn said. She had carefully matched her shoes to her dress for her first White House appearance. When her feet started to ache, she changed to an old, stretched pair of shoes. Finally, she slipped those off as the crowds kept coming. "I would go upstairs to our bedroom," she said, "and sprawl across the bed for a few minutes until it was time to get up and do it all over again."

Exhausted as they were, "the luxury of the White House was wonderful," Rosalynn said. "It was a pleasure to have someone shop and cook and serve, but a shock when we got our food bill for the last ten days of January and it was over $600!" She discovered that the White House had an executive chef plus four additional chefs, one of whom was assigned to the family kitchen on the second floor. All five chefs were government employees, but the president had to pay for all the food served to the family, and the Carters had a lot of family who visited. As Chief Usher Rex Scouten informed the first lady, "Mrs. Carter, it's not cheap to live in the White House."

Miss Lillian recalled that her son was "tight with money, all right." But Carter was affluent enough to devote himself to public service. As president he took to frugality on principle. During his first fireside chat he declared, "I am reducing the size of the White Staff by one-third," a promise that was virtually impossible to meet. He wouldn't even prove successful in reducing the size of the crew on board Air Force One.

Carter maintained that "the pomp and ceremony of office does not appeal to me. . . . I'm no better than anyone else, and . . . I don't think we need to put on the trappings of a monarchy in a nation like our own." He immediately limited the use of "Hail to the Chief," traditionally played by the Marine Band to announce the president's entrance, but later admitted he enjoyed it. He got rid of the presidential yacht *Sequoia*. At his first cabinet meeting Carter announced the elimination of chauffeur services for White House aides, even though this meant getting to work was much more difficult, since parking at the White House was virtually nonexistent.

Carter ordered a survey that revealed the presence of 325 television sets and 220 radios in the White House proper and its West Wing offices. He had most of them removed. When he learned that the bill for magazines and newspapers for the staff in the executive offices was $85,000 a year, he ordered it reduced. He told the Secret Service to have the presidential automobiles trucked instead of flown to his destination when he was traveling, but this was quietly discontinued when it proved to be too awkward and actually more expensive.

Initially he tried billing congressmen for their occasional White House breakfasts despite a $50,000 annual allotment for entertaining. (One year, he spent only $1,372 of his entertaining budget.) Forced to change course, Carter finally treated congressional leaders to breakfast in the Cabinet Room. The proffered fare: juice, coffee, and a roll. "I guess you'd call it a continental breakfast. It must be that economy wave that's hit the White House," said House Speaker Tip O'Neill, who weighed in at 265 pounds. The president did not endear himself further to Congress when he sent mimeographed invitations to a White House picnic—he'd cut the traditional staff of calligraphers in half—and asked Rosalynn's former music teacher to provide the entertainment.

A number of his austerity measures involved saving energy. On February 2, 1977, Carter made his first televised address to the country. He called it a "fireside chat." Carter sat by a blazing fire built with special paper logs that didn't roar, so as not to interfere with the sound track. He wore a warm sweater that symbolized the new casualness at the White House and set an example of dressing warmly to save heat. The president urged all Americans to follow the White House's example and lower their home and office temperatures to 65 degrees during the day and 55 at night. The Arab oil cartel was raising fuel prices and restricting output. Later the country would suffer from severe gasoline shortages. "I couldn't believe it," Rosalynn said. "I had been freezing ever since we moved in." The first lady wore long underwear and slacks and pleaded with her husband to change his mind. "My staff was typing with gloves on," she said. Carter admitted that Rosalynn "shed a few tears," but he kept the thermometer down. "I've got on heavy underwear," he said. He also had solar panels installed on the White House roof, but they were a costly fiasco and abandoned.

The president's personal life replicated his politics. He washed his own socks, sewed buttons back on his jacket, and sewed up rips in his pants. He told Barbara Walters in an interview that blue jeans were "normal attire" for him. He carried his own bags when traveling. "[I] didn't want to lose them, in the first place, and it's just part of my nature to do my own physical work," he said. According to Air Force One steward Charles Palmer, Carter gave up his role as porter after a while, though others pointed out that he resumed it when photographers were present.

Determined to live as if he were in Plains, he sent his shy nine-year-old daughter Amy to public school, something that hadn't happened since Theodore Roosevelt resided at the White House. The Carters had three grown sons—the eldest, Jack, was thirty and a lawyer; James, or "Chip," moved into the White House with his wife and children and worked for the Democratic National Committee; Jeffrey was a consultant. Miss Lillian visited frequently, even though she complained, "It's so boring. . . . I just feel like I'm waiting for Amy to come home from school." After the inauguration, Amy went off to fourth grade with her book bag, Secret Service agent Dennis McCarthy, and a mass of TV newsmen, newspaper reporters, and curious onlookers. At first her presence caused so much commotion that her teacher didn't let Amy go out to play with her classmates, insisting she stay in the classroom with McCarthy, who accompanied Amy everywhere.

Rosalynn could be just as thrifty as her husband. She requested the cheapest brands of foods and made suggestions for using leftovers. She made her own clothes, sometimes from fabrics from Washington's G Street Remnant Shop. On the other hand, she increased her staff to an all-time high of twenty-one. "With more staff I could have done so much more," she later said. For the first time, the "Office of the First Lady," as it was now officially called, had a chief of staff, Kit Dobelle. Her salary was $56,000 a year, the same as the president's chief of staff. She ran the office, and she was included in the daily briefings of the president's senior staff.

In commuting to her East Wing office where her staff was located, Rosalynn had to pass through a corridor that was often filled with tourists in the morning. She decided to bypass them by taking an outdoor route. A doorman who saw her bundled up against the cold and rain showed her an alternate route through the basement. It passed the laundry, machine shop, and bomb shelter, but Rosalynn didn't mind because there were steam pipes running along the hall ceiling—she'd found the one warm place in the White House.

Among her duties was, as always, the family bookkeeping and check writing. However, people tended to keep checks signed by the first lady as souvenirs, so she put the account in the name of her correspondence supervisor, Madeline MacBean. Rosalynn found the task of answering mail and autographing photographs "endless." She resorted to using the autopen (a device that can replicate a signature) and responded to general questions by enclosing a preprinted card about the White House. She gave personal friends a three-number code to write on the envelope—part of the phone number she had "when Jimmy and I were courting"—so her staff knew to send their letters directly to her. Then there was the usual problem of what to do with the hundreds of gifts the Carters received at the White House each week. At first, they returned them unopened—it was the cheapest thing to do. Rosalynn soon realized how much the donors were hurt by this policy and had the correspondence unit open them and send out thank-you notes. Then the gifts were donated to charity.

Since the Nixon redecoration was still in its prime, Rosalynn made few changes in the decor of the White House, traditionally the domain of the first lady. But when guests complained that the Lincoln Bed was too hard, she checked and found there was a board under it. Removing it did not quell grumbling. The Queen's Bed was also deemed uncomfortable, but Rosalynn declined to purchase new mattresses. "We thought the mattresses would give the people who spent the night something to talk about," she said.

To give the house a touch of Plains, she brought rocking chairs from Georgia and put them on the Truman balcony and used barnwood from a peanut farm in Georgia to panel a small bedroom on the third floor. "We were a little surprised when it came," recalled curator Clement Conger. "There wasn't enough wood to cover all the walls so the others had red fabric, silk or damask I believe. It was interesting."

Rosalynn's major change was the resurrection of Jackie Kennedy's historic "Wonders of America" wallpaper that Betty Ford had removed from the family dining room. According to Conger, the impetus for its restoration occurred when "Mrs. Carter gave a nice lady's lunch to which Lady Bird Johnson was invited. Lady Bird came in and gasped and said, 'What happened to the wallpaper?' Mrs. Carter picked up the phone right after lunch. She wanted to know if I had any pictures of the room as it had been. I sent for books of pictures. 'Can I keep them overnight?' she asked. 'I'd like to show them to Jimmy.' The next morning she called and said, 'Jimmy and I think we'd like the wallpaper back up.'"

The Carters and Conger got on well because they shared an interest in art. "One of the things Mrs. Carter and the president were most proud of was that they'd added American impressionists to the White House collection," recalled Conger. The Carters established a White House trust fund to purchase a permanent collection of American art and eliminate the necessity of borrowing from museums. But in the meantime, they faced bare nail heads where some of the paintings loaned to the Fords had hung. Conger set about borrowing prime examples of American impressionists' work from museums and private collections, a process that took five weeks. "The president didn't seem

*Willie Nelson sang for Carter at the White House, but what Carter didn't know was that later that night Nelson lolled on the roof smoking "a fat Austin torpedo." He said the White House roof was "the safest place I can think of to smoke dope."*

to care," said Conger. When the paintings were finally amassed, he spent a day positioning them around the mansion. "At half past four or five in the afternoon, I was up on the second floor putting things around," he recalled. "I didn't hear the elevator open and close, but I sensed someone was there. It was Mrs. Carter. She gasped, 'This is just like Christmas. Jimmy will be thrilled when he sees all these pictures. Living down in Plains, Jimmy and I were a long way from art galleries.'"

The president decorated his study with Childe Hassam's *Avenue in the Rain.* It had hung in the East Lobby. On Carter's first day, Conger transferred it as soon as the tours stopped. For a desk in the Oval Office, Carter picked the Resolute desk used by Kennedy. "The Carters really were surprisingly interested in American art and antiques," Conger recalled in 1993. "They'd bought a lot of books in Atlanta and studied them. They were better informed than any president and first lady I've known in this half century."

Though Rosalynn, like her husband, had a regard for the history and grandeur of the White House, she had little interest in the everyday details of running a complicated establishment. "My social secretary would bring me menus and suggestions for entertainment. I would choose one. I was through," she said. She helped share cultural interests by organizing a series of classical music concerts in the East Room that were aired on public television. She took on a cause, as is traditional for first ladies; dedicating herself to mental health, she served as honorary chairperson of the President's Commission on Mental Health. In her first year in office she logged 250 hours in support of this heartfelt cause, holding public hearings, organizing twenty-four task panels, and compiling what she called on September 15, 1988, "thousands and thousands of pages of data that add up to what I can only describe as a compelling mandate for change." Though she was unable to drum up much enthusiasm in the press, she persisted. The first lady also worked to promote volunteering and bring recognition to the plight of the elderly and underprivileged. She tried to rally support for the Equal Rights Amendment and termed the amendment's failure her "greatest disappointment."

Rosalynn admitted that she held "very strong opinions about almost everything." She had spent eighteen months on the campaign trail helping her husband get elected, and now she took a speed-reading course so she could quickly study government documents after dinner. "There's very seldom a decision that I make that I don't discuss with her," the president said. He scheduled a working lunch with her every Wednesday in the little study off the Oval Office. To the displeasure of many, he invited her to attend cabinet meetings. Rosalynn sat quietly, taking notes. "It was helpful to the people in the country," she explained, "because I could go out there and let people know in an intelligent way what was happening with the administration. I think that's important."

Soon after her husband's inauguration she undertook a goodwill tour of South America as the president's official representative. She said she was "determined to be taken seriously," knowing that she was stepping outside the traditional role of a first lady. She spent 210 hours taking Spanish lessons and immersed herself in the affairs of the countries she intended to visit. Members of Congress and the State Department were not thrilled, but Rosalynn persisted. "I knew the issues," she later wrote. "Every one of the leaders wanted to talk to the President of the United States. And who is closer to the President, who better has his ear than his wife?" Once there, she drafted detailed memos of her meetings, which she sent back to the president and to the State Department. In her first year as first lady Rosalynn traveled to sixteen foreign countries and twenty-one U.S. cities. In addition she spent seventy-one hours being briefed, held twenty-one press conferences, and welcomed nineteen heads of state at White House ceremonies. She oversaw thirty-nine receptions, twenty congressional breakfasts, and eight state dinners, in addition to her own projects as first lady. *U.S. News and World Report* said that she had a "workload and status approaching that of a head of state." Rosalynn said, "I've always worked and helped with the business. It never occurred to me to do anything else."

Her role as a polished representative of the administration involved seven years of determination. Until Carter ran for reelection to the Georgia State House in 1970, Rosalynn had refused to speak in public. Even then, she recalled, "it was torture for me. I never knew when I opened my mouth whether any words would come out or not." One problem she had to overcome was her vision. She needed glasses or contacts to see her speech, but when she looked up the audience was a blur. She came up with a unique solution: she wore two different contacts, one for looking at her notes, one for distance. That way, she said, she could "read with one eye, and look out at the audience with the other."

In her free time, Rosalynn liked to do things with her husband—swim, play tennis, bowl, or jog. She kept her late afternoons free so she could join the president in some activity. They had known each other since childhood, and married on July 7, 1946. Carter said she was the only woman he had ever loved. At Camp David, the helicopter landing pad was a mile away from Aspen, the presidential lodge, and Rosalynn and Jimmy liked to walk the narrow road to the lodge hand in hand, with the limousines and the Secret Service slowly following behind them. "We have been ridiculed at times for allowing our love to be apparent to others," Carter said. "It was not an affectation, but as natural as breathing."

They also shared a religious life. Depressed following his first, unsuccessful run for governor in 1966, Carter turned to religion and became "born again." "I formed a very close, intimate relationship to God, through Christ," he said. In his presidential campaign he promised voters a moral regeneration. As president he taught a Bible class at the First Baptist Church in Washington. The Secret Service code-named the president "Deacon." Jimmy and Rosalynn prayed together several times a day, and in the evening took turns reading the Bible to each other. Rosalynn said, "I do what I think is right, and if I have prayed about it first, I can be sure it will be right."

All of the Carters were readers, including Amy. It was the family custom to silently read a book while at lunch or dinner, so when Amy's father invited her to attend a state dinner, she brought a book with her to ward off the boredom of adult conversation. A New York socialite, who had bought a designer gown and hired a limousine especially for the occasion, found herself sitting next to a nine-year-old girl reading a book. Rosalynn's response to the subsequent criticism: "Amy attends some state dinners because we like her to be with us."

Amy adjusted well to both school and the White House. She brought her new classmates for sleepovers in the hard Lincoln Bed, where they listened for ghosts. She liked to roller-skate around the big white pillars of the north portico, and Carter had a tree house built for her in a tree on the south lawn. When she held sleepovers there, Secret Service agents stood guard under the tree. Amy also had a large library at her disposal. The halls on the second and third floor of the White House are lined with shelves of books, and the American Booksellers Association gives every new president 250 books. But evidently these were not help enough for one of Amy's book reports. Rosalynn called a government agency for help and, much to her embarrassment, received a huge load of statistics that government employees had worked overtime to produce. The family talked about issues concerning the presidency, and during Carter's 1980 campaign for reelection he quoted Amy's opinion in a televised debate with Ronald Reagan, saying she thought that "the atomic bomb is the most important issue." He was ridiculed in the media, and later admitted it was a mistake.

Amy was a serious child and seemed mature for her age. One night when the family was watching a movie in the White House theater, she said, "I'm going upstairs to do my homework, Dad, because I don't think I'm supposed to be seeing this." The Carters watched about two movies a week, ordering free films from catalogs provided to the White House by the film industry. The theater seated about fifty people—the front row had lounge chairs and ottomans—so they often invited staff members to join them, ordering popcorn, wine, or hors d'oeuvres from the kitchen.

As a governor's wife Rosalynn had not served hard liquor, nor did she at White House state dinners, where she allowed only wine. Liquor was not ruled out at other times or in the private quarters. Some of the press mocked her as "Rosé Rosalynn," but she was steadfast. "They make me sound like a real prude," she said. "I'm not a prude!" She noted that liquor was unnecessary, and justified it by saying, "I'm saving money."

However, there was marijuana in the White House on at least one occasion. Carter liked classical music and had it piped into the Oval Office, but he also liked contemporary musicians such as Bob Dylan, Paul Simon, and Willie Nelson. Nelson once performed at the White House and stayed over as a guest. Late at night he went out to one of the wide, flat spaces on the White House roof outside the third-floor solarium. (The Carters' son Chip and his wife Caron put their baby's playpen there.) Nelson recalled that he and a friend sat out there "with a beer in one hand and a fat Austin torpedo in the other." His friend noted the points of interest they could see. "It was a good way to soak up a geography lesson, laid back on the roof of the White House. Nobody from the Secret Service was watching us," Nelson said. He concluded, "The roof of the White House is the safest place I can think of to smoke dope."

The White House was indeed secure—perhaps too secure for the Carters' tastes. The Secret Service had installed panic buttons in strategic places around the White House, including the bathroom off the Oval Office. If the president needed emergency help, all he had to do was to press the button and an agent would appear—without knocking, gun drawn. Agent Marty Venker recalled, "So one day I heard the alarm go off in the bathroom near the Oval Office. Hand on my gun, I rushed to the bathroom door, practically knocking it down. Inside I found Carter zipping up his pants. Apparently he'd pressed the panic button, thinking that it flushed the toilet. Carter was pretty chilly to me after that." Carter was even less happy with Venker when the agent asked him to move in off the Truman Balcony because demonstrators had taken over the top of the Washington Monument. There was danger of sniper fire, Venker explained to the president. "He said, 'Whaaaat!' I said, 'They're right over there.' He looked up at the Monument and he came inside. But he was steamed."

Carter also objected to having the hall doors to the living quarters locked all the time, which forced the family to use the elevator rather than the stairs. The Secret Service agreed to unlock the doors to the hall as long as there were no public tours going on.

Secret Service protection began the moment any family member left the private quarters, even if it was just to walk to the Oval Office. Travel involved motorcades as long as forty cars. When they got into their bulletproof limousine, Rosalynn would say, "Just don't look back, Jimmy. Don't look back." Rosalynn handled the security intrusions better than her husband. She always did what the agents told her to do. "After a while I didn't even notice them; they were just there," she said.

Once, however, she slipped away from the Secret Service and everyone else for a shopping trip to New York City with Madeline MacBean, her correspondence supervisor. She told no one, not even her press secretary, Mary Hoyt, where she was going. Still, the New York press caught up with the first lady. Then the Washington press got wind of the adventure and rushed to Mary Hoyt, who told them the first lady hadn't even left the White House. Rosalynn took a commercial flight home, and when the passengers discovered her presence, a woman with a package said she had a bomb and was arrested. Her explosive device turned out to be a vase. Then the press got on the case and published a list of all Rosalynn's clothes purchases. In addition, Mary Hoyt was cha-grined and upset to find her own credibility damaged. The first lady summed it up: "My quiet little shopping trip had turned into a fiasco."

Carter had less time for his family as his term went on. When he first took office, he was up at 6 A.M. The stewards left him two glasses of orange juice. He drank one while he dressed and left the other on the bedside table for Rosalynn. He did some light exer-cises before breakfast. He was on his way to the Oval Office by six-thirty. Soon he began getting up at five-thirty. He had anticipated working fifty-five hours a week, but he was soon up to seventy or eighty. He often left official dinners early to get back to work.

Part of the problem was his tendency to micromanage and concern himself with unnecessary, even inappropriate, details. Washington insider Clark Clifford once called on Carter at the Oval Office, and the president noticed him eyeing a large stack of papers on the corner of the desk. It was a military budget. "I have read every page," Carter said proudly. Clifford thought to himself that Carter should have assigned that job to someone else, but said nothing. He held marathon meetings, leading Vice Presi-dent Walter Mondale to complain that his boss had "a bladder the size of a football." He once issued a White House memo on the misuse of the pronoun "I." He chastised Housing and Urban Development employees who were "living in sin," urging them to get married. Carter required White House staff to get his personal permission before using the tennis courts. The same applied to the pool. One aide said, "He spends hours on stuff like that."

When Carter first took office, his staff drew up a list of all the campaign promises he made so he could be sure he never went back on them. The document was 112 pages long. To Carter's chagrin, the press got hold of it, and for the next four years they kept track of all the president wasn't able to do. As his term ended in 1981, two journalists wrote, "Today much of the president's official list of promises reads like a page out of an H. G. Wells science fiction novel."

One issue that required his talent for detail was the Oval Office mice. Carter called a meeting with the General Services Administration (GSA) and White House aides to discuss the problem. The White House had a long history of rodent infestation, but a GSA manager, Lucille Price, said rats and mice were everywhere because they'd been disturbed by the construction of the Washington subway. The GSA put out poison for the mice, and some died in the walls, as evidenced by the smell. Carter called the GSA back, but they claimed their jurisdiction only extended to the interior wall—the exte-rior was the responsibility of the National Parks Service. But the Park Service insisted its jurisdiction only extended to the exterior wall. Carter had to bang a few heads before he got the situation resolved. Later, an Olympic team waiting to see Carter encoun-tered a rat on the south lawn; the Park Service had put out pellets that caused the rats to stagger around looking for water.

Carter was an avid jogger—on rainy days he jogged up and down the White House stairs from the basement to the third floor—and on one hot, muggy day he ran a marathon, overdid it, and passed out. "We thought it was all over," Secret Service agent Marty Venker said. They laid him out in the backseat of the car, and his doctor gave him oxygen. Later Carter would boast, "They had to drag me off. . . . I didn't want to stop." He did not accept criticism well. When he was confronted on an issue, his eyes and face froze, and veins on his face throbbed. At times he was moody and sarcastic, and aides feared to approach him. He didn't like criticism, and neither did Rosalynn, who was hurt when the press dubbed her "the steel magnolia." As her husband's administration wore on, she found it difficult to read through the morning papers. Son Jack said, "Mom [has] always taken every affront to Dad personally. She's a lot worse now."

Although Carter claimed he didn't care for pomp or ceremony, he loved adulation. Of a visit to a New Hampshire school he said, "They just mobbed me. They ran up and grabbed my legs, my hands—they wanted to touch me. It really makes me feel good." He was often described as an enigma, but his mother, Lillian, said, "Jimmy isn't mysterious. I would say he is original and stubborn."

Carter stayed close to White House during the 1980 campaign for reelection, feeling unable to leave because Americans were being held hostage in Iran, a crisis he tried to resolve through both diplomacy and a failed military rescue mission. Rosalynn went on the campaign trail, visiting 166 cities in thirty-nine states, but it was a losing cause.

Rosalynn did not accept defeat easily. When a reporter said, "Mr. President, you're a great example. You don't seem bitter at all," Rosalynn said, "I'm bitter enough for both of us." Looking back she said, "People want a country to be tough. If we had bombed Teheran, I think Jimmy would have been reelected, even though the hostages would have died." Her husband said, "There's no doubt about it. I have never had any questions about it at all. Had the hostages been released before November the fourth, I would've been reelected without any problems. In fact, even a week before the elections, Reagan and I were neck-and-neck." When Reagan was sworn in, Iran immediately released the hostages.

But Carter went on to became one of the most respected of former presidents, using his position and principles to serve humanitarian causes. As "one of the youngest survivors of the office," he said he "didn't want to just build a library or go back to farming." He founded the Carter Center in Atlanta and 1989 helped negotiate peace in the Ethiopian civil war. In 1991 he founded the International Negotiation Network Council, and President Clinton sent him as an emissary to broker a peace deal in Haiti. Both he and Rosalynn became prolific authors and ardent workers for causes ranging from Habitat for Humanity to mental health. "To me this is part of my duty as a human being," Carter said. "It is part of my duty to capitalize on my reputation and fame and influence as a former President of a great nation. And it's exciting. It's unpredictable. It's gratifying. It's adventurous. I just enjoy it."

The Carters were especially proud of their daughter, who as a nineteen-year-old Brown University sophomore participated in a protest against the CIA and was arrested and acquitted of charges of disorderly conduct. "Amy's been arrested four times, three for protesting apartheid and this last time for what she considers, and I consider, illegal activity of the CIA in Nicaragua," said Carter, who declared himself "a very proud father."

# 40

# Ronald Reagan

## 1981–1989

## *Perfectly Cast*

RONALD AND Nancy Davis Reagan, both Hollywood actors, knew instinctively what was required of the presidency: a grand sense of ceremony and plenty of rehearsal. Before she gave her first party, Nancy was tutored for six weeks by Letitia Baldridge, etiquette maven and former social secretary to Jacqueline Kennedy. Before any dinner was approved, she had the White House chefs send Polaroid snapshots of the dishes so she could be sure the meal held no surprises.

As president, Ronald Reagan told Attorney General Ed Meese, an old friend, "Ed, I don't know I could do this job if I were not an actor." He became known as "the great communicator," skilled at acting the part. Handsome with hardly a gray hair despite his seventy years, he still retained his star aura. At the White House he was careful not to deviate from character. One day in the Oval Office Michael K. Deaver, longtime associate and aide, noticed the president perspiring and suggested he remove his jacket, as he used to do as governor of California. "Oh, no," Reagan replied, "I could never take my coat off in this office."

Accustomed to being in front of the camera, he brought in aides who made the most of the White House's visual possibilities. For press conferences, Reagan would stride down the red carpet of the cross hall, enter the East Room, and talk in front of the open doors. When George Bush became president and changed the setup, choosing a more casual stance when encountering the press, Deaver explained, "The open doors with the light coming across the hall make a much better picture. And television is, after all, a visual medium."

Before a press conference, Reagan would rehearse for two days in the White House movie theater, with aides posing sample questions. Even so, recalled Patrick J. Buchanan, Reagan's communications director, "We'd always be in the East Room sitting on the edge of our chairs. At his first press conference, he just came crashing through and began talking about how the Soviets reserved to themselves the right to lie, cheat and steal.' . . . [Y]ou were never sure exactly what would come out. It was exciting."

The country greeted Reagan with enthusiasm, breathing a sigh of relief after the austerity of the Carters. Magazines heralded the return of style and applauded Nancy's desire to add more "pomp" to the White House. "I believe the White House is a special place and should have the best of everything," she said. "I think people want it that way."

She set her entertaining tone immediately, hosting a surprise birthday party for Reagan, who had turned seventy just a few weeks after taking office in January 1981. Nancy got her husband to dress up in black tie formal wear for what he thought would be a dinner for twenty. On the morning of February 6, they heard Tom Brokaw say on the *Today* show that there would be one hundred guests for dinner at the White House that night. Reagan said to Nancy, "My, that Tom Brokaw exaggerates—where in the world did he ever come up with that figure?" As the couple descended the stairs that evening, Reagan heard the voices below and said, "It certainly sounds like more than twenty people." "Well, you know how marble makes noise reverberate," Nancy explained. Reagan professed to be surprised when it turned out Tom Brokaw had not exaggerated the head count. A hundred people sitting at ten tables were served ten vanilla sponge cakes each topped with raspberry brandy and a white horse. Nancy had gotten together the old gang from California—a set of wealthy socialites—and a few of them chipped in for the party's six-figure cost.

Clearly, Jimmy Carter's austerity and informality were now a thing of the past. "We do not wear pants. We do not wear clogs. We represent our country," Mabel "Muffie" Brandon, Nancy's social secretary, told a magazine reporter. Society orchestra leader Howard Devron observed, "I don't see spangled jeans anymore."

Though the Reagans' expensive lifestyle brought a new formality to the White House, the president's personal and work style was relaxed. He described his approach to his job this way: "Surround yourself with the best people you can find, delegate authority, and don't interfere." He was neither interested in nor informed on the details of government. He didn't even know where his top aides' offices were. It didn't matter—everyone had to come to him. He didn't know *who* some of his top aides were. At a conference of mayors, he once greeted Samuel Pierce Jr., his secretary of housing and urban development and the only African American in his cabinet, with "How are you, Mr. Mayor? How are things in your city?" The day before the 1983 economic summit at Colonial Williamsburg, Reagan's chief of staff, James Baker, dropped off a thick briefing book. The next day he was astonished to find that Reagan hadn't opened it. "Why, Jim," the president said, "*The Sound of Music* was on last night."

He successfully deflected criticism about his easygoing manner with humor. He liked to say, "It's true hard work never killed anybody, but I figure, why take the chance?" When the navy shot down two military jet aircraft in a confrontation with Libya, aide

Ed Meese did not wake Reagan to tell him. "If our planes were shot down, yes, they'd wake me up right away," Reagan explained. "If the other fellows were shot down, why wake me up?" During his 1980 election campaign Reagan had complained that he was being roused too early in the morning. His aide, Stu Spencer, told him, "You better get used to it, Governor. When you're President, that fellow from the National Security Council will be there to brief you at seven-thirty every morning." "Well," Reagan said, with his characteristic pause, "he's going to have a helluva long wait." As president, he received the National Security Council briefing at nine-thirty.

Reagan's aides protected and covered for him. "We had a rule," said Press Secretary Larry Speakes, "that the President is aware of everything. We would be asked by the press, 'Is the President aware of Congressman So and So?' and the answer was always 'Well, yes, he is.' "After he left his post to write a memoir, Speakes admitted to manufacturing quotes for the president, something done by other aides for other presidents, but not talked about. "It was just a way to save the President time," he later said, "and I always told him later what quote I attributed to him. I would never have quoted him on substantive matters."

The president tried to avoid conflict and face-to-face confrontations. He allowed his aides to fight out an issue and then accepted their verdict. He hated to fire anyone. A White House personnel director said that Reagan had no trouble making decisions on policy, but that it was "very hard for him to make a decision on people." He did, however, fire his chief of staff and close adviser, Donald Regan, in 1987, partly at Nancy's instigation. She felt he pushed her husband too hard and assumed too much power. "[Reagan] dislikes confrontations more than any other man I have ever known," Regan said.

Reagan had a lifelong habit of ignoring bad news. The son of an alcoholic, he maintained an idyllic view of his upbringing, even though when he was eleven, his father passed out on the front porch, and Reagan had to haul him inside and put him to bed. When the future president graduated from Dixon High School, he wrote in his yearbook: "Life is just one grand, sweet song, so start the music." In his first job, as a radio sports broadcaster, he conjured the substance and drama of a major league baseball game from terse telegraphic messages such as "strike two." He became a film star in Hollywood and spent World War II as an army officer. Newsreels and film magazines portrayed him as a war veteran. "By the time I got out of the Army Air Corps," Reagan said, "all I wanted to do—in common with several million other veterans—was to rest up awhile, make love to my wife, and come up refreshed to do a better job in an ideal world." In fact, he spent the war years making films in nearby Burbank.

At times Reagan seemed to confuse film and reality. After his swearing in at his 1981 inauguration, he went to the office of House Speaker Tip O'Neill to change clothes. He made an admiring remark about O'Neill's ornate oak desk. O'Neill was proud of the huge desk and told Reagan that Grover Cleveland had used it as president. "That's very interesting," the new president said. "You know, I played Grover Cleveland in the movies." O'Neill responded, "No, Mr. President, you're thinking of Grover Cleveland Alexander, the ball player." Reagan had played the part of the famous baseball pitcher in a film called *The Winning Season*. At the time of Reagan's inaugural his old films were being rerun on television, and O'Neill had recently seen it.

*The Reagans were happiest when alone together eating off trays or watching a movie. Although they totally renovated the White House guest rooms, fitting them out with individual bathrooms and hotel amenities like bathrobes, they actually had few guests. Family visited rarely.* (REAGAN LIBRARY)

In any case, the modern presidency is far removed from real life. Reagan acknowledged that security needs made it a prison. "In a way," he said, "you're a bird in a gilded cage." After he left office, he would recall standing at a window, "looking out across the big lawn of the White House, through its black iron fence at the people strolling along Pennsylvania Avenue, and . . . envying their freedom." Only a few weeks after taking office, Reagan tried to do what he would usually do in February—buy Nancy a valentine. He asked the Secret Service to take him to a nearby gift shop. "It caused such a commotion," Reagan said, "that I never wanted to do that to a shopkeeper again." He found that he lost his bearings from being driven around so much. "It's the funniest thing, but when you're in this job, you forget where things are," he told a reporter. "When I used to be able to drive my own car, I'd have some sense of where things are geographically located. And when I've driven in this town, before I was President, I knew where the hotels and monuments and such are. But now, being driven everywhere in the backseat of the car and not navigating—it's the oddest thing, but you lose track of where these things are." Reagan also noted that as president he rarely saw the fronts of buildings such as hotels: "Your limo comes in the back where they stack the green plastic bags." He described the experience, as he often did, in movie terms: "What was that line from *Kitty Foyle?* She used to describe coming into Chicago on the train. 'It's like seeing civilization with its pants down.'"

Reagan retained his love of Hollywood and designated Friday and Saturday nights movie nights at Camp David. (The Reagans often escaped there, taking Pat Nixon's advice, "Without Camp David, you'll go stir crazy.") "We usually all got together to watch a movie with big baskets of popcorn in front of us," Reagan said. He and Nancy went through all the new releases, then Reagan insisted on the oldies, including his best film, *King's Row*. When actress Jane Wyman was married to Reagan, she said she "couldn't stand to watch that damn *King's Row* one more time." Reagan made use of the White House movie theater for special screenings and caught whatever films were on TV, watching the set in the family quarters upstairs or his hotel when he was when traveling. In July 1985, after Lebanon released thirty-nine hostages, Reagan joked, "Boy, I saw *Rambo* last night. Now I know what to do the next time this happens." Once at a White House briefing on MX missiles, he interrupted to recount the plot from the movie *War Games*.

Another source of relaxation was Rancho del Cielo, near the California coast in the Santa Ynez mountains, where he spent 345 days of his eight-year presidency. Two years before becoming president, Reagan purchased the 688-acre ranch with its small stucco house for $527,000. Thanks to a loophole in the tax code, the property qualified as an agricultural preserve, so the taxes were $862 a year instead of $40,000. His land holdings would appreciate tremendously, bringing him more wealth than films, television, and political office combined. Mike Deaver tried to persuade Reagan to shorten his visits to blunt media criticism. "Look, Mike," Reagan said, "you can tell me to do a lot of things but you're not going to tell me when to go to the ranch. I'm seventy years old and I figure that ranch is going to add some years onto my life, and I'm going to enjoy it."

It was hard to argue with Reagan, president or no. He was easygoing, genial, sincere, and a great storyteller. Almost everybody who had any personal contact with him liked him, even if they disagreed with his policies. Democrat Tip O'Neill, the powerful Speaker of the House, got along much better with Reagan than he had with Carter, a fellow Democrat. Although most liked Ronald Reagan, almost no one really got close to him. "You could walk away from a dinner with Ronald Reagan believing he was your new friend for life, and you'd never hear from him again," said Ed Rollins, a political consultant. He chatted easily with the White House police and heads of state alike.

A particular friend was Prime Minister Margaret Thatcher of Great Britain—Reagan referred to her as "the other woman in my life." The Reagans' first state dinner, on February 26, 1981, honored Thatcher. Nancy said she planned the menu down to the smallest detail. "We even had a dress rehearsal. Several days in advance the chef prepared every dish on the menu and I had a tasting." Nancy liked nouvelle cuisine, and the menu included supreme of pompano with a champagne sauce, rack of lamb, Grand Marnier soufflé, and vegetables, tiny potatoes and mushrooms.

The president also got on well with Mikhail Gorbachev of the Soviet Union. When Reagan first met Yasuhiro Nakasone, prime minister of Japan, he must have thoroughly startled him when he asked, "What does your wife call you at home?" He learned it was Yasu. "Well, Yasu," Reagan said, "my name is Ron." Nakasone would come to regard Reagan as a "special friend."

Both Reagans liked Prince Charles. Nancy flew to London, accompanied by her hairdresser, maid, nurse, photographer, four of her staff, and ten Secret Service agents, to attend his wedding to Lady Diana Spencer. When the prince visited in the Oval Office,

Reagan offered him tea. "After a few minutes," Reagan recalled, "I noticed the prince was staring rather quizzically down into his cup, and I thought he seemed a little troubled." Charles never did have any tea and later explained to Reagan, "I just didn't know what to do with the little bag."

Reagan even won the grudging respect of French premier François Mitterrand, despite an entertaining snafu. At a White House dinner in Mitterand's honor, the guests were lining up to march into the State Dining Room. The premier escorted the first lady, and the president was to follow with Danielle Mitterrand on his arm. But she just stood stock-still and wouldn't move. Reagan whispered, "We're supposed to go over there to the other side." She replied in a low voice in French. Reagan did not understand. An interpreter ran up. "She's telling you that you're standing on her gown."

Reagan was less successful in charming the dour Soviet ambassador, Andrei Gromyko. As they were about to leave the Oval Office for lunch one day, Reagan asked:

"Would you like to wash your hands?"

"No."

"Would you like to use the facilities?"

"No."

"What I mean is, would you like to go to the toilet?"

"Oh, da, all right."

Though his job cast him among world leaders, Reagan paid attention to the little people, just as he had to the members of the Ronald Reagan fan club when he was a young star. Of the sometimes 8 million letters he received annually, he answered about fifty a week, by hand, sometimes writing on sheets from crude yellow notepads sent by an admirer and stamped FROM THE DESK OF PRESIDENT REAGAN. He invited some of his correspondents to visit him in the White House, including the Rossow family from Connecticut, who arrived with fourteen children, mostly handicapped or adopted. He kept up with Miss Jane and Miss Sally, who ran a roadside stand in Sacramento and sent him homemade leather articles as gifts. He'd met them many years earlier when he was governor. Reagan also took the time to write in his diary each evening, filling five leather-bound volumes in eight years.

For all his popularity, Reagan had virtually no close friends. Nancy provided the social contacts, invariably rich and influential. At the ranch Reagan was happy to be alone chopping wood. An aide said, "I've never known him to need people." Except, of course, for Nancy. "Of all the ways God blessed me, giving her to me was the greatest," Reagan said. He seemed happiest when he was alone with "Mommy," as he called her in private. They often ate dinner alone together on trays in the family quarters. Reagan "never came in without kissing her hello, and he never left for the office in the morning without kissing her good-bye," said Elaine Crispen, Nancy's personal secretary. Nancy returned his regard: "When I say my life began with Ronnie, well, it's true." Often as Reagan gave a speech, Nancy would sit in the first row of the audience fixing an adoring look on him. It became known as "The Gaze." Nancy didn't mind talk of hero worship. "But he is my hero," she said simply, explaining at another point, "Some people think I overdo it, but I love to look at Ronnie."

Nancy was not Reagan's first love. In 1940 he'd married actress Jane Wyman. In 1941 they had a daughter, Maureen, and in 1945 adopted a son, Michael. To Reagan's shock and dismay, Wyman divorced him in 1948. But in 1952 he married another actress, Nancy Davis. The same year, they had a daughter, Patti, followed in 1958 by a son, Ronald, but parenting didn't really interest the Reagans. "I never knew who he was," Patti said of her father. "I could never get through to him." It wasn't for lack of trying. Patti rebelled publicly, but the Reagans never seemed to take much notice. At age twenty-two she legally changed her name from Reagan to Davis. Seven years later she agreed to go to the 1981 inaugural ball, even though, as she wrote in her book, *The Way I See It,* she felt, "Oh, God, isn't there an island I can escape to, to wait out the next four years." Jeans were Patti's usual attire, but for the ball she let her mother talk her into a red ruffled Adolfo gown. Patti promptly put her foot through the dress, tearing it so that the hem had to be taped at the last minute.

"I hated the White House," she reported. "It's like this tiny claustrophobic town. There are eyes and ears everywhere." She visited her parents four times in eight years, and they communicated mostly through the media, as Patti wrote about herself, in fiction and nonfiction, letting it be known that she liked cocaine and gardened in the nude. For her father's second inauguration, she brought an overnight bag but left after the ceremony. "I didn't have the balls to vote against my father, but I couldn't vote for him either," she said in her outspoken way. "Still I was horrified when my father got re-elected. From the homelessness to the environmental neglect to the rise in racism—if you have an elitist atmosphere, you have a racist atmosphere—I couldn't believe what was going on."

The other Reagans had less stormy but by no means idyllic relationships with their parents. "He doesn't like to open himself up, even with us," Maureen said. Maureen became a Republican party worker in California and announced that she would run for the Senate in 1982. When a reporter asked for his reaction, Reagan commented, "I hope not."

Reagan's adopted son Michael joined the family cottage industry and wrote a book about his parents with the telling title *On the Outside Looking In.* Michael said he felt insulted when he read about Nancy saying how wonderful it was to be a grandparent. Michael and his family lived in Los Angeles, a city the Reagans often visited. "She never came to see her own grandchildren," Michael commented.

The youngest son, Ron, was twenty-two when his father became president. Speaking of his father with a reporter, he said, "You get just so far and then the curtain drops." He left Yale to become a ballet dancer—a decision his parents tried to talk him out of. In October 1982 he was between engagements when a reporter found him standing in a line for unemployment compensation.

But with the exception of Patti, when the Reagan children did visit the White House, they were impressed. Michael recounted how his family were sitting in the third-floor solarium when a waiter came in and asked their son, Cameron, what he wanted for dinner. "A McDonald's cheeseburger, strawberry shake, and a large order of fries," Cameron stated unhesitatingly. "Just bring him a hot dog," his father said. Half an hour later the waiter reappeared with a serving tray covered by a large silver dome. The waiter lifted it with a flourish: underneath was Cameron's McDonald's feast.

Maureen and her husband, Dennis Revell, came and stayed in the Lincoln Bedroom. The next morning they insisted they had seen Lincoln's ghost. It appeared as an "aura" that was sometimes red, sometimes orange. "I'm not kidding," Maureen said. "We've really seen it." Winston Churchill and Princess Juliana of the Netherlands had also noted strange sightings in the room. Reagan's dog, Rex, would not go into the Lincoln Bedroom, and he barked as he passed. Other times he circled the presidential study on his hind legs, peering at the ceiling. The president wondered if the dog was picking up electronic signals sent by the Soviets and had the Secret Service bring in communications experts. No mysterious vibrations were detected.

Maureen had a kid-in-the-candy-shop reaction to being at the White House. As if she were at a hotel, she rounded up matchbooks that said "President's House," in deference to the White House's original name. "I needed about twenty of them to send home," she said. "Finally I looked around the West Hall, where we were staying, and the tables really looked bare . . . and so I said to Dennis, 'Well, maybe if I just take them all, they'll think they didn't put any out.' "

According to Maureen, her father loved the White House: "He loved the mansion's charming, unpretentious architectural style, its warmth and elegant staff, its spacious rooms and historical furnishings. He even loved the squirrels." Eisenhower had hated the squirrels and tried to have them removed because they damaged his putting green, but Reagan fed them. In the fall, he would return from his weekends at Camp David with a large plastic bag full of acorns and each day throw some out on the lawn. He watched from his Oval Office desk as the squirrels retrieved them. "He used to say that by Friday the squirrels would practically nose up to the windows and give him a sad, pleading look, reminding him to bring back some more goodies after the weekend," Maureen said. At his ranch in California, though, Reagan shot ground squirrels with a pistol because they were disease carriers. He also killed rattlesnakes with big rocks. Yet he would rather sidestep a bug than step on it.

When Reagan moved into the White House and heard the sounds of tourists shuffling through the state rooms below, he said to Nancy, "Honey, I'm still living above the store." Other presidents had used the phrase—Lyndon Johnson in reference to an Austin, Texas, home above the family's broadcast holdings. But Reagan had actually lived over a proper store, a five-room rented flat above a bakery on Main Street, Tampico, Illinois, where he was born on February 6, 1911. He didn't mind the lack of privacy or the design of the family rooms, but Nancy was not one for public housing. When Reagan was governor of California, she'd declined to live in the governor's mansion in Sacramento and rented a twelve-room Tudor-style mansion for $1,250 a month.

Before the Reagans moved into the White House, the Carters had given them a tour of the state rooms. "We expected the Carters to give us a tour of the family quarters," Reagan said, "but they made a quick exit and turned us over to the White House staff." The family quarters were Nancy's primary concern, and she immediately asked Los Angeles decorator Ted Graber to redo the second and third floors, much to the disgruntlement of curator Clement Conger. "In my opinion," Conger said, "Mrs. Reagan made the same mistake that other first ladies, including Mrs. Clinton, made. They immediately brought their decorators. It's a shame. They should live with the place a while." Conger, a classicist, looked on in horror as Graber replaced oriental rugs with white or coral carpeting and brought in family furniture from California. "He knew nothing about American classical decorating," complained Conger, who was further bothered by the fact that "Mrs. Reagan had no interest in improvements to the White House collections though I would try to suggest certain acquisitions. She worked through the office of the chief usher instead of the office of the curator." In 1986 Nancy asked Conger to retire and made Chief Usher Rex Scouten curator. His role as chief usher was filled by Gary Walters, who went on to serve Bush and Clinton.

Nancy did like some things as she found them. She thought the family kitchen and dining area "the best thing that has happened to the White House in years." She found the dining room's "Wonders of America" wallpaper—hung by Jackie Kennedy, removed by Betty Ford, and rehung by Rosalynn Carter—"fascinating." But elsewhere, she said, "There was a great deal to be done . . . a real need for upgrading, restoring, and repainting." Some of the existing drapes and carpeting had seen twenty years of wear.

The frugal Carters had not spent much of their $50,000 congressional allowance for refurbishing. Nancy returned her $50,000 to Congress and instead began seeking private funding. The work she had in mind—mostly for the family quarters—would cost more like $1,000,000. Even when Reagan ran for governor of California, he hadn't lacked for ardent wealthy supporters. Now money poured in, much of it from rich oil men—Reagan had lifted oil price controls right after taking office. Their donations were, of course, tax deductible. Oklahoma oilman Jack L. Hughes gave $50,000, which, he said, "wouldn't even buy throw rugs in my house."

Decorator Ted Graber, who was featured in the book *Decorating for Celebrities,* was accustomed to spending $50,000 on a single room in a private home. He and Nancy went through the government warehouses in which White House articles were stored, found "beautiful antiques," and had them brought to the White House. Nancy admitted to being a "frustrated decorator" and enjoyed rearranging a room "a half dozen times." Graber redecorated the living area in cheerful California colors—pink, salmon, and yellow. In the upstairs Oval Room he added yellow sofas and marble-topped tables. Four antique chairs that had been regilded were worth an estimated $40,000 to $50,000 each. The walls of the presidential bedroom were covered in eighteenth-century hand-painted Chinese paper in a salmon color with a pattern of swirling birds. Twenty-one other rooms were repainted, and 150 pieces of furniture were refurbished. Nancy also replaced eighteen carpets, drapes and curtains for twenty-six windows, and shades for seventy-two lamps. Plumbing was also upgraded in eight bathrooms. "The plumbing was obsolete," commented Scouten. "Some of the bathrooms dated to 1850. Most of the money the Reagans spent went into nuts and bolts." The remodeled bathrooms were fitted out with bathrobes and toothbrushes so the White House would be as comfortable as a hotel. In the West Wing, the Cabinet Room was restored to the time of Franklin Roosevelt's administration.

The most costly individual item Nancy purchased, and the one that garnered the most criticism, was her 1982 purchase of a new set of chinaware for $209,508. The 4,372-piece set of Lennox china, made in the United States, was red-rimmed with a gold border. The White House announced that new china was a necessity for proper entertaining. Indeed, there was no one set with enough unbroken pieces to serve a large dinner. Compounding matters, entertaining had increased under the Reagans—75,761 guests in four years as compared to 47,797 during Carter's term. Over eight years they were host to seven kings, three queens, seventy-seven prime ministers, forty-five foreign ministers, a sheik, and thirteen princes. Nancy increased the number of state dinners, although she cut their size from 130 to 96 guests. Largely lost on the public was the fact that the china had been purchased with private funds. "I tried again and again to get someone to explain that the Knapp Foundation was donating the china,"

Nancy complained. In her book *My Turn*, she wrote: "The timing was unfortunate. The new White House china was announced on the same day that the Department of Agriculture mistakenly declared ketchup to be acceptable as a vegetable for school lunches. As you can imagine, the columnists and cartoonists had a field day with that one."

She was also criticized for her wardrobe. The estimated cost of her inaugural outfit was $25,000, which included a $10,000 Maximillian mink coat, a gift from Reagan. The media made invidious comparisons, such as the fact that her handbag cost more than the annual allotment of food stamps for a family of four. Nancy continued to dress fashionably, accepting "loans" of designer gowns. Galanos, Bill Blass, and Adolfo sent her evening gowns, dresses, and accessories; all were ostensibly borrowed, but most found a permanent home in Nancy's closet. Bill Blass sent her videos from which she picked what she wanted. The total value of this wardrobe was over a million dollars, and it never appeared on the Reagan tax return. "I don't know that I did anything wrong," Nancy said when the press caught wind of her wardrobe arrangements. Her office learned not to release information on her gowns. The first lady reflected, "One thing most people don't realize—and I certainly didn't realize it until I'd gotten a few bumps and scrapes—is this: You just don't just move into the White House, you must learn how to live there. Life in that mansion is different."

Criticism of the first lady was fierce and unrelenting. Nancy felt that as long as "no money came from the taxpayers," there was nothing wrong with how much she spent. But under the Reagans, the National Park Service budget for maintaining and operating the White House—which has a swimming pool, a bowling lane, a large medical facility in the basement, a beauty salon, a tennis court, a barbershop, and a library—rose 29 percent, to $3.8 million. This included eighty-six full-time employees plus many part-timers. Among the White House staff were the chief usher, who ran the mansion, three other ushers, an administrative assistant, an accountant, seven maids, nine housemen, one maitre d', six butlers, three chefs, three cooks, a laundress, an executive housekeeper, plus plumbers, engineers, painters, doormen, four calligraphers, four florists, and a five-person curatorial staff. Seventeen gardeners tended the eighteen-acre grounds. In other expenses, the president's travel allowance was $100,000 a year, but in reality it ran to $185 million when all costs were included. Eighteen jet aircraft plus Marine helicopters were assigned to the White House. Air Force One had a crew of seventeen and operating costs of $5,200 an hour.

However, from the opening bell of the $16 million inaugural party—the most expensive on record—charges of extravagance were leveled primarily at Nancy. "You can only be yourself," she said. "If you try to be anything else, it's phony." But the outcry was so great she even had to stop redecorating. One poll showed that 62 percent of Americans felt she put "too much emphasis on style and elegance." At one point she had the lowest approval rating of any first lady since such statistics had been kept. Of her critics she said, "Ronnie says I should just forget them but I can't." So she called San Francisco astrologer Joan Quigley, who she'd begun consulting after Reagan's near-assassination in March 1981, and said, "I'm getting a terrible press. It's so unfair. I'm really a very nice person. Can you tell me what to do?"

Nancy heeded the advice of Joan Quigley and a select group of White House staff on how to change her image. She also changed her staff, which now had sixteen people and a budget of $650,000. In eight years she would go through three speechwriters, three social secretaries, three press secretaries, and five chiefs of staff. Part of Nancy's image problem was that she had no identifiable cause as first lady, aside from bringing "the best of everything" to the White House. She was advised to adopt a cause that the media would like, and she chose an antidrug program—"Just Say No to Drugs." She was sincere about the cause and had been involved with it previously, if in a small way. "The first time I received a letter saying that I had saved a person's life, I wept," she said. "I never dreamed I had the ability to do that—to influence people unknown to me." In 1984 she attended over one hundred antidrug events and gave fourteen speeches. Nancy also began minimizing her contacts with her glitzy friends.

Within a short time, she achieved a spectacular reversal. The turning point was the Gridiron Club dinner of March 1992. Nancy's press secretary, Sheila Tate, queried the press club as to whether a personal appearance by the first lady would be welcome at the dinner—an annual "roast" of the president. It would. Someone suggested to Nancy that she make fun of the press. Nancy recalled, "I said, 'No, uh, no. I'm not going to do that. If I'm going to do it, then I'm going to make fun of myself.'" She had already tried this approach with some success. The press had taken to referring to her as "Queen Nancy," and at a dinner in New York she said, "Now that's silly because I'd never wear a crown. It messes up your hair." So for the Gridiron dinner, a White House speechwriter, Landon Parvin, wrote a song to the tune "Secondhand Rose" that he called "Secondhand Clothes." Nancy secretly rehearsed it at the White House. At the dinner, after her husband had been roasted, she slipped away from the table and appeared onstage dressed in what she called a "crazy bag lady's outfit" and wowed the Washington press corps. She got a standing ovation—something she'd never gotten as a stage actress. "I was relieved when they applauded at the end," she said. Her popularity in the polls climbed until she was even more popular than her husband. She had become a political asset rather than a political liability. "Everybody likes to be liked," she said.

While her public popularity went up and down, Nancy never faltered in her private role as the power behind the throne. According to Richard Burt, an assistant to Secretary of State George Schultz, "Nancy Reagan was the most powerful First Lady of the last 35 or 40 years. And she went about it in the right way, the appropriate way—entirely behind the scenes." Nancy followed the TV news and talk shows, read the papers, and networked on the phone. She tried to protect her husband's health, preventing aides from overscheduling him. He was, after all, in his seventies, and in 1984, at the age of seventy-three, became the oldest president ever elected. "I protect Ronnie from himself," she said. "You know he has a big Irish heart. He trusts everybody, and doesn't see when he's being blindsided, or when people are acting out of motives that are less than noble. And he never acts upon it once he does. I do." Many agreed with her. Nancy viewed the secretary of health and human resources, Margaret Heckler, as inept and wanted her husband to fire her. Chief of staff Donald Regan agreed. Nancy told Regan, "We've got to get rid of her. You know Ronnie will never fire her—he can't even talk to a woman in a stern voice. She'll just twist him around her little finger." In the end, Heckler was removed via an ambassadorship to Ireland. Reagan's secretary, Helene von Damm, said of Nancy, "No matter how much she denied it, the role of 'power behind the throne' suited her to perfection."

Reagan, meanwhile, typically began his day at seven-thirty, when he was awakened by a steward after the eight hours' sleep he needed. He watched the morning news programs and skimmed the front pages of the papers before going on to the sports and comics pages. "I read every comic strip in the paper," he said. He did little other reading. Breakfast was light—juice, toast, cereal or soft boiled eggs, decaffeinated coffee—and he always had it with Nancy.

His workday in the Oval Office began precisely at nine, and he did not return to the living quarters until he cleared his desk around five. For lunch he had fruit and a bowl of soup. He snacked on jelly beans, which he had begun popping when he gave up smoking in 1969. He said, "You can tell a lot about a man's character by whether he picks out all of one color or just grabs a handful." He worked methodically. Reagan "paced himself in a very disciplined way. He was incredibly organized," domestic aide Martin Anderson said. He had a list of scheduled appointments on his desk each day, on a pad with the presidential seal at the top. As each appointment ended, he checked it off and moved down to the next one. "I cannot remember a single case in which he changed a time or canceled an appointment or even complained about an item on his schedule," said Chief of Staff Donald Regan.

Reagan occasionally suffered gaffes and memory lapses, or dozed off at meetings, and the press poked fun at him for it. In addition to perhaps being in the early stages of Alzheimer's disease, which he was diagnosed with in 1993, part of the problem may have been hearing loss. He'd suffered hearing problems ever since an actor fired a pis-

*Our oldest President, Reagan sometimes nodded off at meetings but he worked a full day from nine to five without any naps and only a brief, light lunch.* (REAGAN LIBRARY)

tol near his head during the making of a film, and only in 1985 did he finally begin wearing hearing aids. Prior to that, the stories and jokes that sometimes constituted his response to a briefing or a caller may have obscured the fact that he hadn't heard all of what was said. He was also nearsighted and had worn contact lenses for thirty years. But by all accounts Reagan worked full nine-to-five days—no napping, unlike Kennedy or Johnson—and he only dozed off when his aides overscheduled him. When he napped at a meeting at the Vatican, White House physician from 1981 to 1985 Dr. Daniel Ruge maintained that Reagan had been up late at Versailles the night before, and added that the pope had also fallen asleep.

Reagan responded to this and other criticisms with good-natured humor. When a reporter reminded him, "You said that you'd resign if ever your memory started to go," Reagan came back with, "When did I say that?" Even ABC White House correspondent Sam Donaldson, one of Reagan's loudest hecklers, later said, "I didn't think I would say this, but I miss him. There is no one like him on the scene today."

After leaving the Oval Office at about 5 P.M., Reagan worked out for thirty to forty-five minutes in a bedroom outfitted with gymnastic equipment. He rarely missed his workout, taking portable equipment with him when he traveled, and successfully built up his body strength, particularly in his chest muscles following the 1981 assassination attempt that put a bullet in his chest. His physical fitness program, plus physical work around his ranch, gave him a trim, sturdy body—at six feet one inch tall, he weighed 185 pounds. He didn't like the bulletproof vest the Secret Service gave him to wear. "Everybody will think I'm getting fat," he complained.

Unless there was a formal occasion, he and Nancy ate dinner together from folding tables in front of the television. Reagan's tastes ran to meat loaf and mashed potatoes, Nancy's to nouvelle cuisine—small portions, light meat entrées, sorbets, all attractively arranged. A Reagan favorite was macaroni and cheese, but if Nancy was there, she'd say, "You're not eating that." Reagan didn't mind. He said, your wife will tell you "things no one else will, sometimes things you don't want to hear, but isn't that how it should be?" Reagan watched the evening news on three television sets, taking in all three network channels. Later, Nancy would watch romantic comedies. Reagan preferred war movies. Often in the evening Reagan had a vodka and tonic. He also liked wine. At his ranch he devoted a small building, custom-built and climate-controlled, to storing his wines, yet he usually drank no more than one glass in an evening.

Reagan needed his sturdy body, good health, and positive outlook on Monday, March 30, 1981. Nancy subsequently referred to the event only as "March 30th." It was the seventy-year-old president's seventieth day in office. At 2 P.M. he gave a short speech to an AFL-CIO meeting at the Washington Hilton Hotel. Afterward, the Secret Service led him through a VIP corridor toward his limousine. The car was only a few feet from the door of the Hilton. He did not wear his bulletproof vest because he was not supposed to shake hands or greet the public. Just outside the door, to Reagan's left, John Hinckley Jr. had positioned himself at the front of the press area. He later said he wanted to assassinate the president to impress Jodie Foster, a movie actress and Yale student he didn't even know. During his forced stay in a mental hospital, he would write Reagan, "I'm very sorry. . . . I thank God no one died." Hinckley used "devastator-type" bullets—six shots went off within three seconds, the sound like a string of firecrackers. One bullet hit the armor plate of the presidential limousine, flattened out to about the size of a dime, then ricocheted into Reagan's seventh rib and into his lung. Press Secretary Jim Brady was hit in the head and would be permanently disabled. Secret Service agent Tim McCarthy and patrolman Thomas Delahanty were also hit, though not severely injured.

Agent Jerry Paar shoved Reagan into the car, pushed him to the floor, and jumped on top of him. "Take off. Just take off," Paar ordered. Reagan did not realize that he had been hit. Although he felt "the most paralyzing pain, as if someone hit me with a hammer," he blamed it on Paar throwing him across the hump in the floor of the car. "You son of a bitch," he said to Paar. "You broke my ribs." Paar ran his hands over Reagan's chest and back but found no wound. He ordered the car to head for the White House. "Rawhide not hurt, repeat not hurt," he radioed. Reagan, now in his seat, dabbed his mouth with a Hilton napkin that was in his pocket. It came away red with blood. "Rawhide is heading for George Washington," Paar now radioed. "We're just going to check you out at GW," Paar told Reagan.

The decision to change course and to take Reagan to George Washington Hospital turned out to be crucial. One of the chief surgical residents, Dr. David Gens, later commented, "It doesn't happen often that a patient like that coughs up blood. Thank God he did, because if they had continued to the White House, he probably would have died." Right after walking from the car through the double doors of the hospital, Reagan collapsed. "I feel like I can't breathe," he said.

At the time of the shooting, Nancy was at a luncheon with Barbara Bush, wife of the vice president, in the Georgetown home of the president of the National Trust for Historic Preservation, Michael Ainslie. She had a strange feeling and suddenly announced, "For some reason I think I'd better get back to the White House." Once she was there, a Secret Service agent told her, "There's been a shooting at the hotel. Your husband was not shot. Your husband wasn't hurt, but he's at the hospital." That was all Nancy had to hear. She left immediately.

At the hospital there was now pandemonium. Doctors, nurses, Secret Service, police, reporters—all rushed about amid shouting and confusion. Nancy learned that Ron had been shot and was told it wasn't serious, but she couldn't see him. She had to wait in what she called "that awful little room." Herman Goodyear, the emergency room secretary, said she was "so white and tense" she looked like she was "made out of plastic." Nancy gave verbal permission for the doctors to operate and remove the bullet. When she finally got to see her husband, he spoke to her through an oxygen mask: "Honey, I forgot to duck." This and other Reagan quips led the public to believe that the president's condition was far less serious than it actually was. The first photo of Reagan to be released after the shooting showed him smiling with Nancy on his right. The nurse and the tubes to his chest had been retouched out of the photo. Alone at the White House, Nancy slept on Ronnie's side of the bed in search of comfort. Much later she would admit, "There was a kind of unspoken agreement that none of us would let the public know how serious it was and how close we came to losing him."

"The 25th Amendment should have been invoked, no doubt about it, because Mr. Reagan could not communicate with the people a President is supposed to communicate with. . . . This was not a cold or diarrhea," said Dr. Daniel Ruge. He was speaking about the transfer of power from the president to the vice president, authorized if the president is in any way disabled. Fred F. Fielding, counsel to the president, brought up the issue at the time. "To be very frank with you, when I mentioned the 25th Amendment [after Reagan was shot] I could see eyes glazing over in some parts of the Cabinet. They didn't even know about the 25th Amendment." Later when Reagan underwent surgery in 1985 for colon cancer, he did sign a letter authorizing Bush to assume power.

But in 1981 Reagan, having had a very close brush with death, remained his irrepressible self through all the pain and discomfort. In the recovery room about 4:30 A.M., the lights were dimmed and a nurse put a gauze pad over Reagan's eyes so he could sleep, but he kept pushing the pad off to talk to her. The nurse, Joanne Bell, said, "Mr. President, in the most polite way I can tell you, when I put this over your eyes, that means I want you to shut up." Reagan looked at her, winked, and shut up. When he was mobile again, he saw a few carefully screened visitors. Vice President George Bush found the president on his hands and knees in the bathroom mopping up water from the floor. The doctors had forbidden him to take a shower, and he had tried to sponge himself off. He didn't want the nurse to be blamed for the resulting mess.

Reagan had always held the Secret Service in high regard, even more so now. In 1976, he had seen some agents practicing on a pistol range. He noticed they did not use a marksman's crouch when they fired and asked why. He was told, "When we're firing, we're standing between you and the assassin." Reagan said, "I've loved them ever since. When I saw the film of March thirtieth, Tim McCarthy was standing up [to shield me]. You wonder where they find men like that."

The Secret Service responded to the assassination attempt with even more strict security measures. A car filled with agents armed with machine guns was added to every motorcade. In the week following the shooting, the usual threats against Reagan more than doubled. Even as he was recovering from Hinckley's bullet, there were protesters outside the White House. Unemployment was high at the time. The homeless gathered on park benches on Pennsylvania Avenue across from the White House, but Reagan was unsympathetic. He counted the number of pages of job ads and said he found "twenty-four full pages of classified ads of employers looking for employees." One of his first moves on taking office had been to submit budget cuts to Congress that included school lunch programs, welfare ($41 billion in cuts), and antidrug programs.

A homeless man tried to get over the fence. In 1984 the Secret Service shot and wounded a man carrying a sawed-off shotgun on the sidewalk behind the White House. In 1987 the Secret Service made 374 arrests. While Reagan was playing golf at Augusta National Golf Club in 1983, a group of agents suddenly swooped down on his foursome and herded everyone into limousines. An armed man had smashed a pickup truck through a golf course gate and taken hostages in the pro shop. He threatened to kill his hostages unless Reagan met with him. After some tense moments the intruder was talked into giving up.

Reagan was able to put March thirtieth out of his mind, as he did all unpleasantness. He repeatedly said, "I don't remember being shot." When reminded of the shooting, he could pass it off lightly. He returned to the Hilton the next year to speak to the same group. A reporter asked if he were afraid. "No," Reagan said, "but I'm wearing my oldest suit." Later, in 1985, he would shrug off a cancer scare with similar ease. When a routine examination at Bethesda Naval Hospital revealed that he had cancer of the colon. Nancy, calling herself a doctor's daughter (her stepfather was a physician), told the doctors, "I want you to tell me everything." Then she went to her husband and, without mentioning cancer, told him, "You've got something that needs surgery. What do you want to do?" Reagan followed her advice without even a question. A two-foot section of his upper intestine was removed. Reagan would later say, "I didn't have cancer. I had something inside of me that had cancer in it and it was removed."

Nancy could not shake off March thirtieth so easily. At any mention of the shooting, her eyes filled with tears. She had difficulty sleeping and lost weight. Already thin, she dropped ten pounds in weight to around one hundred, and her dress size went from six to four. It was at this point, on the suggestion of friend Merv Griffin, that Nancy first began consulting astrologer Joan Quigley. Though Nancy had used astrologers before, Quigley would come to assume far greater importance than the others. Both Reagans were superstitious. Reagan knocked on wood and carried a good-luck coin, and believed his presidency had been prophesied by one of his college teachers. Nancy believed it was bad luck to put shoes under a bed or a hat on the bed. Both had gone to clairvoyants in the past. Joan Quigley told Nancy that she could have foreseen that March thirtieth was extremely dangerous for Reagan from his astrological charts. Nancy asked Quigley for detailed daily predictions and began planning the president's schedule based on them. "I advised them when to be careful," Quigley said. "I don't make decisions for them."

Nancy feared the curse of the White House, and was trying to thwart it: since Lincoln, elected in 1860, every president elected at a twenty-year interval had died in office; the historical odds were seemingly against Reagan, elected in 1980. Nancy usually talked to Quigley by phone on weekends at Camp David. If Quigley placed a collect call to the White House, Nancy would move to a private room to talk to her. Once, she was simultaneously talking to Quigley on one phone and arranging her husband's schedule on another. When Donald Regan became chief of staff, it took him a while to figure out that he had to adjust his plans according to the advice of the woman in San Francisco Nancy referred to only as "my friend." Aide Mike Deaver advised Regan, "Humor her. At least this astrologer is not as kooky as the last one." Nancy had used astrologers before, but never to this extent. Regan set up colored scheduling charts—green for positive days, yellow for uncertain days, and red for negative days. Public appearances and Air Force One takeoffs were timed, sometimes to the second, by Quigley. For example, when Reagan wanted to appoint Anthony M. Kennedy to the Supreme Court, the announcement was scheduled for 11:32:25 A.M. Reagan had failed to get approval for Robert Bork and Douglas Ginsburg, and for the third try Nancy brought in Quigley. The astrologer wrote in her memoir, "I knew, of course, from his horoscope that Kennedy would be confirmed, but the mood on Capitol Hill was not favorable for any nominee to the Supreme Court proposed by Reagan. Nancy felt it wise to have me pick the time of the announcement." Finessing the announcement down to the precise second took careful engineering. "Nancy arranged to start a little early and stall until the person chosen to man the stopwatch gave the signal for the President to make the announcement." Kennedy was confirmed by a vote of 97–0 on February 3, 1988.

Quigley's relationship with the first lady did not end well. By 1988 word was out about the presidential astrologer, and Quigley called to ask, "What will I do if someone asks about a sensitive matter?" Nancy had told her, "Lie if you have to." It was their last conversation. "After seven years of constantly being in touch," Quigley wrote, "the last word Nancy ever said to me was, 'Lie!' "

Once the first lady was asked if Joan Quigley's predictions were a reason why there were no more assassination attempts. Nancy replied, "I don't really believe it was, but I don't believe it wasn't. But I do know that it didn't hurt and I'm not sorry I did it."

Nancy started looking for a retirement home soon after Reagan was reelected in 1984. She selected a three-bedroom, six-bath house in the beautiful Los Angeles suburb of Bel-Air. The address, 666 St. Cloud Road, was a number with satanic associations for the superstitious Reagans, and they had it changed to 668. The house had sweeping views of the Los Angeles basin, a half an acre of grounds, and a pool. Rich friends bought the $2.5 million home for the Reagans, and then offered it to them on generous terms. Reagan left office seemingly unaged, and as good-natured as when he entered. "Stick around," he quipped on his last day. "We're having a tag sale upstairs and everything has to go."

For many recent presidents, post–White House life was far more lucrative than government service. On one two-week trip to Japan in 1989 to make appearances and speeches, Reagan received $2,000,000. He answered criticism by saying, "I could have made a lot more money if I'd gone back to my original career making movies." Indeed, while he was making $200,000 a year as president, ex-wife Jane Wyman went back to acting at age sixty-seven and made more than three times that. Reagan's presidential library, a project that again attracted support from his rich friends, was built in nearby Simi Valley. All five living presidents—Reagan, Bush, Carter, Ford, and Nixon—attended the dedication in the fall of 1991.

Two years later, at his annual physical examination at the Mayo Clinic in Rochester, Minnesota, Reagan was diagnosed as having Alzheimer's disease. He withdrew totally from public life, and sold Rancho del Cielo to a nonprofit youth-outreach group. Reagan made his illness public in November 1994 by releasing a handwritten letter that read in part, "Let me thank you, the American people, for giving me the great honor of allowing me to serve as your President. When the Lord calls me home, whenever that may be, I will leave with the greatest love for this country of ours and eternal optimism for its future. I now begin the journey that will lead me into the sunset of my life. I know that for America there will always be a bright dawn ahead."

# 41

# George Herbert Walker Bush

## 1989–1993

## *Stepping Up to the Plate*

"I COULDN'T HELP but think that old Martin Van Buren was up there giving me the high-five sign," George Bush announced when he was elected president. The first vice president to succeed his boss since 1837, Bush was the quintessential Washington insider: Congressman from Texas, ambassador to the United Nations, chief U.S. liaison in China, director of the Central Intelligence Agency, and chairman of the Republican Party. Bush had been a frequent guest at the White House, but the 33-room vice presidential mansion, set on the grounds of the U.S. Naval Observatory, actually offered more spacious accommodations than the 132-room White House, which is mostly office and public space and has only nine bedrooms. On inauguration night, some twenty visiting Bushes filled every one.

As vice president, Bush was used to taking off for a midday jog and running two or three miles. His first week in office, he attempted to keep up his routine. He summoned a driver and the requisite two-block motorcade to go to Fort McNair Army Base, where there was a track. The whole process was so cumbersome and time-consuming he didn't go back. Saying that he couldn't very well run around the White House grounds for fear of "what it would do to traffic," he took to exercising on an indoor treadmill and a stationary bike out by the pool.

The Bushes presided over a large and active family that included five grown children—George Walker Jr., John E. "Jeb," Neil, Marvin, and Dorothy—and thirteen grandchildren. But president and first lady felt they could no longer go visiting. "We barely get to go to our children's homes. . . . We don't feel we can cause that kind of problem for our children," Barbara said, citing security risks. She continued, "I've never been to a grandchild's school play or an athletic event. I mean, I would go to every one that I was available for, but I just can't do that, . . . It would risk our grand-children and I'm just not going to do that."

Instead, children, grandchildren, and the world came to the Bushes. "Not in recent history had so many people been entertained at the White House," commented presi-dential decorator Mark Hampton. The president kept a canvas bin of battered toys in the Oval Office, the upstairs family room was populated by stuffed animals, the Lin-coln Bedroom was constantly booked, and the rest of the guest rooms were generally occupied.

Barbara called her husband "Perle Mesta Bush" after the legendary Washington hostess. They had frequent casual dinners, private formal dinners, and movie nights for friends. The president was prone to inviting Oval Office visitors upstairs for "burgers and bloodies." Once, when Barbara was away at their home in Kennebunkport, Maine, for five nights, he asked friends to the White House for tennis, took other friends to a Mexican restaurant in Bethesda, Maryland, invited another group to the White House for drinks and dinner, went to a congressional barbecue, and took more friends to a baseball game.

The Bushes' biggest fete, of course, was the inaugural ball, or more precisely balls. The 1989 celebration, which cost even more than Ronald Reagan's record-breaking $16 million inaugural bash, included ten luncheons, thirty-three dinners, six worship ser-vices, twenty-three receptions, and an open house at the White House. George and Barbara danced their way through only a smattering of the balls, the president foxtrot-ting "no matter what the tune," according to his wife. It was 1 A.M. before the Bushes returned to their new home. The new president said he had "that almost so tired you couldn't sleep feeling," but at 8 A.M. he was playing the good host again.

The day's open house began with the president escorting fifteen of the tourists and party faithful who'd spent the night on line on a special tour of the state rooms. Thou-sands more waited for a chance to see the new president, and by the time the White House doors were closed at 11 A.M., 4,002 people had gotten in.

Ronald and Nancy Reagan had been gone roughly twenty-four hours, but the White House retained their imprint, as it would for the next four years. Barbara delighted in saying that for the first time in twenty-eight moves she didn't have to do a thing. The state rooms were still in good shape from the Nixon refurbishment—the Green Room's Turkish rug was showing signs of wear, and the Bushes had it copied—and the family quarters had just undergone an extensive redecorating under the Reagans. The house had "never been in better shape," said Chief Usher Gary Walters. "Nancy Reagan deserves great credit for making the place so sparkling," Barbara said. "I don't have to think about decorating or improvements."

But Barbara was quick to add her personal touch. She eliminated the Reagans' pri-vate gym, turning it into a guest room for grandchildren, and banished the beauty salon, making it a scrapbook storage room and later a puppy whelping station when the Bushes' famous dog Millie birthed her litter. Barbara called upon the services of New York dec-orator Mark Hampton, who had redone the vice president's mansion. He tackled the too-dark Treaty Room, which he said "hadn't been touched in twenty-five years," the solarium, which was "falling apart," and the guest rooms, "which had been used as offices during the Reagan administration." In the family room next to the presidential bedroom Barbara installed a needlepoint rug that had taken her eight years to complete. The Reagans' California furniture was replaced with family pieces Barbara described as in "classic American taste with a strong strain of New England Colonial." "Everything was very light, airy, with lots of blue, which was the Bushes' favorite color," Hampton said. "It was a very traditional Yankee look—chintz and glazed walls and lots of American and English furniture—but not opulent at all."

The Treaty Room required the most work. Hampton told Barbara that the president "would *never* be happy working in a room with walls that are almost black. He suggested white walls, but Barbara thought white "too cold." They compromised on pale, faded green, and Hampton selected brown-striped chintz curtains, three antique mahogany chairs that had been made for James Monroe, and an oriental rug in yellows, greens, and blues. In the Oval Office Bush rejected the Resolute desk that had been used by Reagan and Carter and brought in a walnut partner's desk and a chair from his old vice president's office.

Though opulence was not the Bush style, they had led privileged lives. Both grew up in an affluent East Coast family. They met at a country club dance when he was seventeen, she sixteen. "I married the first man I ever kissed. When I tell this to my children, they just about throw up," Barbara said. She waited out World War II while Bush served overseas for three years. The two were married on January 6, 1945, and soon headed west for a cramped duplex on East Seventh Street in dusty Odessa, Texas. Bush was determined to make his fortune in oil, but while he was getting his start, the newlyweds shared a bathroom with a mother-daughter prostitute team.

Both of the Bushes played down their elite roots. While campaigning, Bush drank beer, not his usual vodka martini on the rocks. He talked about country music and stopped wearing his preppy striped shirts with the white collars and cuffs after Roger Ailes, his image adviser, termed them "elitist." On the other hand, the president's food preferences were inherently lowbrow. Former speechwriter Peggy Noonan said Bush ate "like a big teen-age boy, unembarrassed by hunger." Maureen Dowd of the *New York Times* wrote,

> The sort of food the President loves can be procured at baseball games, fast-food joints or 7-Elevens: beef jerky, nachos, tacos, guacamole, chile, refried beans, hamburgers, hot dogs, barbecued ribs, candy, popcorn, ice cream and cake. Even when he eats yogurt or oat bran, he likes to spice it up with Butterfingers or something else to give it a little zip. Ordinarily the President, who jogs regularly, can eat "like a horse," as [former aide Pete] Teeley puts it, without it affecting his weight, 190 pounds, or his cholesterol level. But occasionally he eats so much he gets a little queasy. At other times it's his guests who get queasy. The president had breakfast one Monday with John Elway, Denver Broncos quarterback, who proceeded to miss that night's game. Coach Dan Reeves complained that Bush had fed Denver's star player "the worst-looking thing you can imagine: creamed chip beef."

Bush made headlines when he banned broccoli, saying "I hadn't liked it since I was a little kid and my mother made me eat it. And I'm President of the United States and I'm not going to eat any more broccoli." Barbara joked that she'd countermand him by ordering an all-broccoli dinner and "finish it with a little broccoli ice cream." But Bush maintained, "Just as Poland had a rebellion against totalitarianism, I am rebelling against broccoli, and I refuse to give ground."

Green vegetables aside, Bush was naturally soft-spoken, courteous, and considerate. During his first weeks in the White House he continued to personally greet tourists, even taking them upstairs—an exceedingly rare privilege—and taking pictures of them sitting on the Lincoln Bed. He became famous for his thank-you notes. The first left-handed president since James Garfield, Bush probably signed more personal mail than any other president. He sometimes wrote thirty to forty personal notes in an evening. He even penned an expression of sympathy to a Washington woman whose husband, a pizza delivery man, was shot while working. In 1990, courtesy of the autopen, he sent out over three-quarters of a million birthday and anniversary cards. He received forty to fifty thousand letters a week, which were handled by the correspondence unit on the ground floor of the Executive Office Building. Some 350 volunteers helped the 158-member correspondence unit with the workload.

Bush's oral communications were less impressive, and he became infamous for his truncated Bushspeak. "Poor George is hopelessly inarticulate," said his sister, Nancy Ellis. "He never finishes a sentence or puts in a verb." In 1992 Bush's doctor, Burton J. Lee 3rd, explained, "He's had a problem with syntax when he's tired, stressed out and hassled that goes back decades, and he's aware of that." So was the press, which delighted in reporting Bush comments like, "So, I'm glad you asked it because then I vented a spleen here." Once asked what a summit with Soviet leader Mikhail Gorbachev would mean for the world, he offered, "Grandkids. All of that. Very important." Running for reelection in 1992, he declared he had "New Hampshire values" and explained them with: "Remember Lincoln, going down on his knees in times of trial and the Civil War and all that stuff."

His most famous elocution was "the vision thing," his term for the big picture, and "thing" shorthand punctuated his presidency. "But let me tell you this gender thing is history," he declared. "You're looking at a guy who sat down with Margaret Thatcher across the table and talked about serious issues." His worst public relations bout involved the "stomach thing." On a trip to Tokyo, Bush became violently ill during a dinner and vomited onto the pants of his host, Japanese prime minister Kiichi Miyazawa. "I could see it coming 40 seconds before it happened," said his doctor, Burton Lee. "I saw his face go absolutely white. He looked like a curtain coming down! I was out of my chair and trying to get to him before he went, but I did not get there in time."

Bush had enough of the "vision thing" to determine to join the computer age. Paul Batemen, director of the Office of Administration, provided him with some one-on-one training and said the president took to it "like a duck to water." Once computer literate, Bush gave up typing memos on index cards and started producing computer documents. Computers were now in widespread use in the White House. In 1989 there were ten separate electronic mail systems with 175 users, according to Batemen, but the White House updated to a single system accessible to most of the seventeen hundred people employed by the executive office of the president. Barbara also took to computers. She said in 1989 that she found that she wasn't reading books as much. "I learned the computer this summer and, as George will tell you, I married the computer. I'm loving my little friend," she said. She was counseled in her new marriage by a White House usher whom she later called for help after leaving office. The incident provoked the wrath of Hillary Clinton and led to the usher's firing, the first in the 107 years since the ushers were established.

Barbara also spent three hours a day answering her mail, which at nearly eight thousand letters a month attested to the fact that she was more popular than her husband, especially as recession gripped the country toward the end of his term. She devoted personal attention to what she called "my homework"—a sampling of the letters screened by the White House Correspondence Unit—because "I'm disciplined."

She decided to make literacy her cause as first lady. When son Neil was in school, he faked his way to an A in reading, with the other kids whispering the words to him, until it was discovered that he had dyslexia. However, Barbara said, "I didn't choose literacy because of Neil Bush. I thought about all the things that seemed important to me, and I realized everything I worry about would be better if more people could read, write, and comprehend."

She took a relaxed approach to the traditional role of hostess. Regarding menus, flowers, and the countless decisions involved in official dinners, she told the staff, "Ditto—just do what she did," accepting Nancy Reagan's precedents. Instead of fretting about the fine print of protocol, she said, "What difference does it matter as long as people have a good time?"

She immediately set herself apart from her designer-dress predecessor by accepting the fact that she looked like a grandmother, gray-haired in a size fourteen dress. At a preinauguration Kennedy Center gala, she said, "Please notice—hairdo, makeup, designer dress. Look at me good this week. You may never see it again." She loved pearls but only wore fakes. When asked why, she said, "Because I don't have real ones." When Bush questioned whether she ought to have dessert, she quipped, "I have to eat it, George, for my fans." She suggested that her official portrait include her dog, Millie, or a hat as a prop, saying, "I'll do anything I can to take the picture off my face." Her down-to-earth humor—"I mean, nobody likes me because of my great beauty, anyway"—deflected attention. When a reporter asked how much she weighed, she could get away with answering, "Come on! Even my husband doesn't know that!"

But for all her self-effacement, she played the part of first lady with class. She selected designs by New York's Arnold Scaasi, and when questioned on her wardrobe, brought the press up short by saying, "One of the myths is that I don't dress well. I dress very well—I just don't look so good."

Barbara tried to keep to a diet and to swim a mile in the White House pool every day. But getting to the pool on the south lawn meant going near the Oval Office and her gregarious husband. She told a reporter, "I looked so ghastly and George is so bad about saying, 'Come in and say hello.' He caught me the other day in my pre-swimming clothes, and there was a new ambassador from a foreign country. There we were, eyeball to eyeball. I don't trust George anymore."

*George Bush liked to walk his dogs on the south lawn, even when Millie produced a menagerie.*
*After his defeat in 1992, one of his last acts as President was to take a nostalgic walk with his dogs.*
(CORBIS)

Swimming was occasionally an adventure because of the White House rats. Once a reporter asked Bush about whether First Dog Millie hunted rats and squirrels, and his cryptic reply was, "She's doing her part." Questioned further, the president finally said, "Our dog is a fearless hunter, and what she does on her own time, that's her business." The reporter persisted: "What does that tell us—that there are rats in the White House yard here?" A harassed president answered, "Look, I just want to keep them out of the swimming pool. When my wife—one jumped in there when Barbara was swimming. And we're relying heavily on Millie to cut that down."

Bush, in his unique speaking style, was referring to a rat that Barbara encountered in the White House pool. "I swim with a mask," she explained. "It went by right in front of me—I mean, it was enormous." She screamed and got out of the pool. Bush caught the rat in a pool-cleaning scoop. "Fortunately George Bush was there and drowned the beast. It was horrible," Barbara said. From then on she had the guards check the pool before she swam.

Millie, given to Barbara by a relative, was a thirty-one-pound English springer spaniel. Barbara could be seen walking Millie on Pennsylvania Avenue, on the south grounds of the White House, or outside the Bush home in Kennebunkport, Maine. When reporters spotted her in Kennebunkport walking Millie while wearing her bathrobe and slippers, she called to them, "Haven't you seen an old lady walking a dog before?" Bush in his bantering way kidded Barbara about Millie: "That dog literally comes between us at night. She wedges right up between our heads, and Bar likes it. She's failing with the discipline. She was better with the kids." The birth of Millie's puppies—five females and a male—in March 1989 became a page-one story. Barbara assisted in the birth and later published *Millie's Book,* as dictated to Barbara Bush. The book earned $885,176 in royalties, which the first lady donated to charity. (Her husband's campaign book, *Looking Forward,* earned $2,718.)

Having her husband around more was a big plus for Barbara. She said, "I considered the South Lawn my front yard, and I consider this my home. I love the fact that I don't think I've ever been closer to George. He calls much more on the phone than he used to. He'll call and say, 'Look out the window, there's a friend of yours.' And I can look right out here and see who is in his office, and we'll wave hankies back and forth. I've never had that opportunity before, and I love that."

Barbara, who gallantly waved to tourists as well, stood for the kinds of family values she had experienced—children, home, caregiving. But she did not want to be pigeonholed into the homemaker role. When Raisa Gorbachev, wife of the Soviet leader, came with her husband, she spent the day with Barbara and tried to make conversation by offering to share a recipe for her favorite blueberry dessert. Barbara, sensing instantly that Gorbachev had been told the first lady was a housewife, bristled and said, "Raisa, do you cook at home?" She answered, "Well, sometimes." Barbara responded, "Well, I never cook at home, so let's talk about something else." They started up on education.

When the first lady was selected as commencement speaker at Wellesley College, feminists protested, saying her prominence in life was due entirely to the man she dropped out of Smith College to marry. Barbara defended her "family-oriented" role, saying she was "very George Bush oriented." She won over the graduates, bringing Raisa Gorbachev along as a cospeaker and telling them, "At the end of your life, you will never regret not having passed one more test, not winning one more verdict or not closing one more deal. You will regret time not spent with a husband, a child, a friend or a parent." She continued, "Who knows? Somewhere out in this audience may even be someone who will one day follow in my footsteps and preside over the White House as the President's spouse. And I wish him well."

The Secret Service code name for Barbara was "Tranquility." But son George W. called her "the Enforcer," and as a mother and first lady she was a force to be reckoned with, though usually behind the scenes. She'd say "I am going to tell George Bush how I feel upstairs." However, in 1980, during Bush's first vice presidential campaign, she was not so circumspect. There was a stir over the income tax returns of Geraldine Ferraro, the opposing vice presidential candidate. Barbara impulsively remarked that Ferraro was not only rich but something that rhymed with rich. The incident left Barbara in tears; she told a relative she cried all day until she finally called Ferraro and apologized.

Barbara's political savvy was acquired the hard way. As a young mother she had found it difficult to address even the Houston Garden Club: "I'd get sort of sweaty and headachy and teary and I'd say, 'I think we ought to put more trees in South Park.'" But she gradually gained confidence and as first lady was comfortable making speeches. In

one year she made public appearances in twenty-eight cities and thirteen foreign countries. She was surprised by how much she loved being first lady. "I can hardly wait to get
up every morning," she said. Generally she was up with Bush at six. The two would eat
breakfast, watch the TV news, read the papers, and discuss the issues of the day. "Very
rarely do I disagree with him," Barbara said. "We've been married so long, and we've
really grown up together. We've had the same experiences, we've met the same people;
he's just better briefed than I am." But one issue on which she and her husband agreed
to disagree was abortion. He took a prolife stance and she was privately prochoice. She
described the issue as "one of those things, along with that unmentionable gun control,
that we have had a gentle past argument about it. We stopped discussing both these
things about fifteen, twenty years ago, thirty years."

Bush was an avid sportsman and loved hunting. Though he gave up his World War
II–issue .38 automatic from his navy days at Barbara's urging, at the White House he
kept "a couple of shotguns and a rifle," he said. "I skeet shoot up at Camp David almost
every time I'm up there, and I like quail hunting, and I am going to do it again this year.
I'm not a pistol guy."

The Secret Service nickname for Bush was "the Mexican Jumping Bean." He valued
speed, racing from his office to a ceremony, from a tennis match to dinner. He even
watched TV with gusto, surrounding a big-screen TV with four smaller sets in a large
wooden cabinet in his upstairs study. Each set had its own videocassette recorder. Bush
controlled the whole thing with a clipboard-size remote control panel. He was somewhat embarrassed to describe it. "I don't like to tell you this," he said in his own unique
way, "because you'll think I'm into some weird TV freak here."

Like Theodore Roosevelt, Bush instituted a tennis cabinet—men who could match
his pace. Press secretary Marlin Fitzwater explained, "Subconsciously, at least, he
judges people by their competitive attitude on the courts." He'd call aides, ostensibly
for business reasons, and then go over who won and lost at the White House or Camp
David. Those with the skill to bounce balls—and ideas—across the net found little
need for memo writing. Bush often played with Secretary of State James A. Baker, with
whom he'd formed a friendship after being invited by President Gerald Ford to be
partners at a White House tennis game. "I'm a great believer that sports can do wonders for friendships and establishing common ground," Bush said. "Have always felt
that way. Still feel that way."

In addition to tennis, Bush played horseshoes and had pits installed on the White
House grounds and at Camp David, as well as at his family retreat on the coast at Kennebunkport, Maine. When he was vice president in 1987, he built a twenty-six room
house on six acres of waterfront property that he purchased for $800,000 from his aunt,
Mary Walker. There at remote Walker's Point he fished from his boat, although he
didn't care much for seafood and generally threw his catch back or gave it to the Secret
Service agents.

His favorite "leisure" pursuit was golf, which he claimed "clears the mind," but to
Bush the sport was one practiced at a manic pace. When his staff asked him if he broke
90 on a round of golf, they meant minutes, not strokes. Bush played what he called
"aerobic golf" or "electric polo." He raced through the course at the Cape Arundel Golf
Club, near Kennebunkport, in less than two hours. In 1981 he did eighteen holes in an

hour and eighteen minutes and proudly announced it was his "all-time record." He liked to say, "We're not good but we're fast." He explained, "I don't concentrate too much out there. I'm in it for the competition, the camaraderie."

Bush's golf game reflected his personality—classic Type A. It led him to success, but not without side effects. While struggling to succeed in the Texas oil business, he developed a bleeding intestinal ulcer. He was warned to slow down and stop worrying about things he had no control over. While in office, Bush felt the usual pressures and was aware of how they can age a president. He told a reporter, "There's just an accumulation of problems. You might start in and there's two or three. A month later, there's six or seven." When he went to the barbershop in the White House basement, he joked about passing "the Milton Pitts test," in which the longtime White House barber assessed how much hair the president was losing. Every night Bush said a prayer "about trying to get the job done."

The greatest stress in Bush's presidency came when Iraq invaded Kuwait, and the United States, in January 1991, led a coalition of nations in a massive air war that became known as Operation Desert Storm. The sixty-seven-year-old president's tension led to pains and headaches. He visited his old friend and personal physician, Dr. Burton Lee, at the doctor's White House office. Lee said his patient was "a workaholic, really, and never paid any attention to me." After signing the order to strike the Iraqi force, Bush wrote in his diary, "Oh, God, give me the strength to do what is right." The next day, with the air strikes ready to start within twelve hours, he thought about what other presidents had gone through. Like Lyndon Johnson and Richard Nixon he faced antiwar protesters across the street in Lafayette Park and complained, "Those damn drums are keeping me up all night." He went down to Dr. Lee's office on the ground floor near the entrance to the south portico. He had arthritis pain and tightness in his shoulders. One of the young nurses on duty gave him a rubdown. "She's very nice and caring," Bush said. "All the people in the medical unit simply remind me of how spoiled I am."

When Bush faced the media at 9 A.M., he was visibly tired and admitted he "screwed up a couple of times" in his speech. During the military buildup in Saudi Arabia he had visited the troops. "Bar," as he called his wife, came along and dressed in camouflage fatigues and her fake pearls. The commander-in-chief had a Thanksgiving meal with the marines. "As I ate lunch with the troops," he said, "I kept thinking to myself, 'How young they all are.' " A half century earlier, Bush had been the youngest combat pilot in the U.S. Navy. He flew fifty-eight combat missions and was honored with the Distinguished Flying Cross. He was the last of the World War II presidents.

On March 1, 1991, the Iraqi forces began to crumble. "It's a proud day for America, and by God we've kicked the Vietnam syndrome once and for all," Bush said. Bush had often been referred to as a wimp, and Barbara particularly resented the term. "Nobody could be married to me and be a wimp," she stated. There was a surge of patriotic feeling at the end of the war, and Bush's approval rating shot up. On March 10, Saturday, Bush went to Ford's Theater for a country music show. Actor Morgan Freeman faced the box where Abraham Lincoln had sat when he was shot and thanked Lincoln for saving the Union. Then he turned to Bush and saluted him with a second thank-you. Bush said that on his return to the White House, he cried.

But after the Gulf War, Bush's popularity was eroded by a serious economic recession that he underestimated. Campaigning for reelection in 1992, he said, "I probably have made mistakes in assessing the fact that the economy would recover. . . . I think I've known, look, this economy is in freefall. I hope I've known it. Maybe I haven't conveyed it as well as I should have, but I do understand it. I don't know what I have to do to convince people here that I really care about this; I do." He felt he was misrepresented and expressed frustration with the press for what he called "sniping, carping, bitching, predictable editorial complaints, the newsboys of the world." All his public life he had disliked the press, although the press tended to like him. "He held a deep animosity that he doesn't try to hide," Press Secretary Marlin Fitzwater said.

But the president's problems weren't the press and politics alone. "For some reason," he complained, "my whole body is dragging and I'm tired. I don't understand it." At another point he said, "I don't seem to have the drive." He began losing weight, and Dr. Lee noticed that his sleep was even more erratic. He seemed to be indifferent to running for reelection. On May 4, 1991, at Camp David, he developed shortness of breath and atrial fibrillation. He was taken to Bethesda Naval Hospital, where he was diagnosed as having Graves' disease, a common form of hyperthyroidism—the same thing Barbara had. His thyroid gland was neutralized, and he was put on hormones. "I must admit I'm glad to be out of the hospital," Bush said. "It's a little unsettling to turn on the news and see Peter Jennings pointing to a diagram of a heart with your name on it."

In 1992 Bush lost his reelection bid to Democrat Bill Clinton. To General Colin Powell he admitted, "It hurts. It really hurts to be rejected." Barbara agreed. "The last campaign just killed me," she said. "It was so painful. And you have to be careful that you don't sound bitter, because I'm not." The Bushes said their good-byes to the White House staff on the morning of Clinton's January 20, 1993, inauguration. Bush took a final walk around the south grounds with his dogs, and from a White House window had a long last look at the Washington Monument. When Bush first took office, he found a note of encouragement left to him by Ronald Reagan in the Oval Office desk drawer. It read, "Don't let the turkeys get you down." Now Bush left a similar note for Clinton.

As he left office, Bush claimed he still felt "the same sense of wonder and majesty" about being president that he had four years before. "I've tried to serve here with no taint of dishonor; no conflict of interest; nothing to sully this beautiful place and this job I've been privileged to hold."

As a former president, Bush received 71.5 percent of his pay, or $153,269 a year. The federal government also provided free office space, salaries for staff, and $1.5 million in transition expenses. The Bushes built a home in Houston—they hadn't had a residence in Texas during their time in Washington—but were forced to erect a six-foot high wall around it to thwart the curious. "The worst shock I had was the fact that I couldn't just meld into real life," Barbara said. She had to learn to drive her own car again after having been chauffeured for twelve years as wife of the vice president and president.

When the Bushes left the White House, Barbara recalled, "We had a household staff of 93. Next morning we woke up and it was George, me and two dogs—and that's not all that bad!"

Her husband offered a similar sentiment: "I make the coffee. Barbara makes the beds, and we're right back to square one where we got married when we were twenty years old."

Would John Adams recognize the White House? The house has been tinkered with over the years—porticos, balconies, and a third floor have been added—but the basic silhouette would be recognizable. What would probably astonish Adams the most is how the eighty-two acres set aside by Congress in 1791 for a President's Park have changed. The perimeter remains the same—the park runs from H Street to Constitution Avenue between Fifteenth and Seventeenth Streets—and the green areas that remain within it look nothing like the "barren expanse" Adams described. In 1800, the seventeen acres that compose the immediate grounds of the White House had no trees, nor any landscaping, only gullies, piles of construction materials, and shacks for the workers. The rest was pasture and forest. Pennsylvania Avenue wasn't cut through until 1822, so initially Lafayette Park was simply an extension of the White House's north grounds.

Today the President's Park is home to five hundred trees, four thousand shrubs, and twelve acres of lawn, all maintained by the National Park Service. But in addition to plants, the land has acquired large buildings, namely the Treasury Building to the east of the White House and the huge French Empire–style Old Executive Office Building west. Lafayette Park is also flanked by buildings, including Blair House and the New Executive Office Building on the west.

The first architectural intrusions, the Treasury and an office building housing various goverment departments, were sanctioned by George Washington. They were built of brick, as was most of the city except for the White House and the Capitol, and far smaller than the buildings that occupy the same sites today.

Other additions to the grounds came in Thomas Jefferson's term. He turned the shacks that had housed construction workers into sheds for sheep, cows, horses, and chickens and also built an exterior wine vault and added wings that contained a coal house, meat house, and milk house. He enclosed about six acres around the house with fencing and installed an entrance gate on the east, where Pennsylvania Avenue came to an end at the President's Park. Within the fenced area Jefferson planted trees, built paths, and put in a vegetable garden—a necessity in those days. Throughout the nineteenth century the White House cooks were charged with preserving fruits and vegetables grown on the property. The north side beyond the fence—currently the location of Lafayette Park—was designated for public use and became known as a common. The south side, overlooking the Potomac, was considered private. There Jefferson built a stone wall to separate the south grounds from the malarial tidal flats. Some of the outlying land was used for grazing, with local farmers charged by the day for its use. For all Jefferson's improvements, in 1806 an English gentleman who visited him wrote, "In a dark night instead of finding your way to your house you may perchance fall into a pit or stumble over a heap of rubbish." Much of Jefferson's work was destroyed during the War of

1812, with the British capture and burning of the White House and other parts of the federal city in 1814.

John Quincy Adams, elected in 1825, was an experienced gardener who had studied European gardening. He hired John Ousley to work on the grounds and dug at his side, planting hundreds of seedlings, some transplanted from his woodland walks, others sent by overseas consulates. Ousley was kept on and labored over the grounds for almost thirty years. He helped Adams's successor, Andrew Jackson, plant magnolia saplings in memory of his beloved wife, Rachel. In 1877 Rutherford Hayes began the tradition of planting a tree on the grounds, and it has been followed through up to the present day. Most recently, in 1993, Bill Clinton planted an American elm eight feet in diameter that required a huge mechanical spade to set in place. It is the largest tree ever planted on the White House grounds.

Living heirlooms, White House trees have been cared for scrupulously. During the heavy construction that took place under Harry Truman from 1948 to 1952, Andrew Jackson's magnolias were frozen while dormant, moved to a safe area, and put back four years later. Today every tree is given a feeding of special nutrients every three years, and many are protected from lightning by copper cables.

For much of the nineteenth century, the south grounds were open to the public and served as a park. People picnicked there, and on warm nights the Marine Band held free concerts. Midcentury, Zachary Taylor was one of several presidents who liked to stroll with the public among the trees. When baseball became popular in the 1870s, government employees played the game in the park during their lunch breaks. In the late 1800s both Ulysses Grant and Grover Cleveland closed the south grounds to the public to protect the privacy of their young children.

In time the swamps near the tidal basin were drained and the river pushed back a quarter mile. In 1872 the canal to the south—basically an open sewer—was covered over to form Constitution Avenue. Grant added a fountain powered by a steam engine to the south lawn. Hayes laid out the Ellipse, and each year more fill dirt was brought in until the ground had been raised almost ten feet. East Executive Avenue was added in 1866 and West Executive Avenue in 1871, flanking the White House on both sides.

Chickens were still running loose on the grounds in the 1870s. And when Ike Hoover, a longtime White House usher, first came to the mansion in 1891 to help wire it for electricity, he was surprised to find that a wine vault, meat house, and smokehouse were still out back. But by the turn of the century the park's pastoral origins were quickly disappearing. The last White House cow, Pauline, went out with William Howard Taft in 1913, though sheep appeared in Woodrow Wilson's term, part of the effort to reduce manpower during World War I. Ellen Wilson planted a rose garden in 1913, which was redesigned by Rachel Lambert Mellon at the request of John F. Kennedy. Adjacent to the Oval Office, the now-famous Rose Garden can accommodate one thousand guests for outdoor ceremonies. Before Ellen died, she commissioned the well-known designer Beatrice Farrand to plan a companion garden on the east. Lady Bird Johnson completed it and named it the Jacqueline Kennedy Garden. Its reflecting pool, flowers, and trellis are what the 1.2 million tourists who visit the White House every year see as they file into the mansion. In 1969 Lady Bird also added a secluded Children's Garden, adjacent to the tennis court, that includes a goldfish pond. When Richard Nixon took office in 1969, he removed Dwight Eisenhower's putting green, which Clinton reinstalled. Gerald Ford built an outdoor pool in 1975.

Security concerns have led to ever-increasing restrictions on public access to the President's Park. Franklin Roosevelt closed West Executive Avenue in 1941. The south grounds have been closed to the public since World War II, although garden parties for as many as two thousand invited guests are often held in the spring. East Executive Avenue was closed to vehicular traffic in 1987. In 1995 Clinton even closed Pennsylvania Avenue in front of the White House to vehicular traffic after a gunman shot at the mansion from the sidewalk. Today, planners are considering pushing the security perimeter back on the north side to the original boundary on H Street to include all of Lafayette Park.

A proposed thirty-year plan for meeting the long-term needs of the park includes a two-story parking garage to be built under Pennsylvania Avenue for White House personnel, and an 850-car garage under the Ellipse. An enlarged visitor center in the nearby Commerce Building would include a White House museum, four video theaters, and a moving sidewalk under Fifteenth and E Streets that would take tourists to the White House fence.

# 42

# William Jefferson Clinton

## 1993–2001

## *Peephole on the Presidency*

IN 1993 William Jefferson Clinton came into office a man of the people. He didn't make as much of a statement about it as rabble-friendly Andrew Jackson or cardigan-sweatered Jimmy Carter, but in a close election, he played his small-town roots—he was born in improbably named Hope, Arkansas—against George Bush's patrician upbringing. His tastes ran to McDonald's and Dunkin' Donuts. He shared the baby boomers' affinity for rock and roll and took a turn playing the saxophone at his inaugural ball. But as president, Bill Clinton became a very different man of the people than his predecessors. He became someone the Americans knew more about than most people on their block.

No other president's private life has been subjected to the scrutiny that afflicted Bill Clinton. His finances were raked through by an independent counsel, Kenneth Starr, in search of impropriety in a money-losing investment in an Arkansas resort called White-water. Diagrams of the White House family quarters appeared in magazines and newspapers when a subpoenaed file thought to have been in the office of Vincent Foster, a lawyer who committed suicide, mysteriously traveled from the third-floor Book Room to the office of Hillary's aide, Carolyn Huber. The biggest window on the White House came, of course, in 1998 when the whole nation watched over the shoulder of former White House intern Monica Lewinsky as she detailed her Oval Office affair to Ken Starr's grand jury.

Clinton's public exposure stemmed from flawed damage control as much as from character flaws. His behavior hadn't been much different as governor of Arkansas; in the White House, however, there was no room to hide.

Clinton's whereabouts, along with those of the vice president and first lady, were tracked by a Secret Service computer system. One quick look at a computer terminal or a supplementary locator board revealed whether Clinton was upstairs in the family quarters or in his private study off the Oval Office. Matching his movements with the dates Monica Lewinsky visited the White House after her transfer to the Pentagon—often weekends when Hillary was traveling—easily sealed his fate.

Just as the Secret Service perfected its technology in Clinton's term, so did the media. The president had the misfortune to preside over a media revolution that included twenty-four-hour television news coverage and the instant dissemination of information—and rumor—on the Internet. Hillary Rodham Clinton's social secretary, Capricial Penavic Marshall, compared the administration's social events with those held by the Kennedys. Thirty years ago, she said, "it was more elitist. At a state dinner only 130 people got to see it. Now, my mom calls after the dinner's been on C-Span and says, 'You looked great, honey.'"

Other entertaining events were videotaped by a special Pentagon-trained crew, supposedly for archival purposes. However, congressional investigators looking for campaign finance abuse were able to view the tapes and track White House courting of deep-pocket donors. Clinton's 1996 reelection team was so effective at raising money, offering coffees with the president and nights in the Lincoln Bedroom in exchange for big-ticket donations, that the White House earned the sobriquet Motel 1600.

Clinton felt hounded from the start, maintaining that no other president had been subjected to the same level of personal attacks. In 1996 he exploded, "The hammering, the pounding, the garbage, the lies, the dirt, the innuendo, the stuff they make up and they throw at me, at my wife, at my friends, at my staff—you can't tell me that's having no effect. You can't tell me that!" Throughout 1998, the year of the Monica Lewinsky scandal, so many television reporters set up permanent broadcast spots on the north lawn that at night the klieg lights were so bright the family could make handshadows in their private quarters.

Adultery aside, Clinton made his marriage fair game by giving his wife quasi-governmental responsibilities. In the campaign of 1992 he'd joked that he and Hillary were a deal—"buy one get one free." From the start he treated his wife as his unelected equal.

Considered the brainier half of the equation, Hillary had met Clinton, a tall southerner with unruly hair, when they both attended Yale University Law School. After they had watched each other for weeks, she approached her classmate and said, "If you're going to keep looking at me, and I'm going to keep looking back, we at least ought to know each other." Later she recalled, "On our first date—which was not really a date—we stood in line to register for classes, and after we finished we went out for a Coke. We started talking, went for a long walk—and we ended up in front of the Yale University Art Gallery. It was closed. But my husband had been there a week or two before and he wanted to show me the Mark Rothko exhibition. . . . . He found a worker, who said it was closed because of a labor dispute. And so my husband said, 'Well, if we pick up the garbage, will you let us in?' " They got to see the exhibit, and the marriage of intellects proceeded.

Hillary followed Clinton to Arkansas, participating in his campaigns and advising him as governor. But his salary never topped $35,000, so she took up corporate law, becoming the family breadwinner. Initially, she kept her maiden name, but when polls showed that voters in Arkansas were displeased, she consented to become plain old Mrs. Clinton, a role she maintained during the 1992 campaign. Immediately after the inauguration ceremonies, however, she reasserted her identity. Her first announcement was that her title was First Lady Hillary Rodham Clinton. "That's the way I want to be addressed from here on," she said.

Having given up a good job to move to Washington, Hillary wanted more than a name change. She broke precedent and took a small office in the West Wing—in addition to the traditional first lady's suite in the East Wing—so that she could be near the Oval Office. She began interviewing candidates for government jobs, attending the president's staff meetings, and overseeing the president's schedule. Clinton's first chief of staff, Thomas McLarty, accepted her position of power and made no moves contrary to Hillary's wishes.

Initially Hillary explored the possibility of a cabinet post but realized it was off limits due to a post-Kennedy law on nepotism. Then Hillary made inquiries about becoming chief of staff. She was dissuaded from the idea, since the president has to be able to fire the chief of staff when problems arise. Just days after becoming first lady, her job situation was firmed up. On January 25, 1993, President Clinton appointed his wife head of the National Task Force on Health Care Reform. In the campaign, he'd made health care a major issue and pledged that it would be a top priority for legislation. "I'm grateful that Hillary has agreed to chair this task force," he said when he made his announcement.

Rewriting the role of first lady, Hillary proceeded to form committees, lead discussions, and address over 1,100 groups around the country. She recruited six cabinet members, a slew of White House aides, and more than 500 outside experts to help. She told a group in Williamsburg, Virginia, "there has been nothing like this effort since the planning of the invasion of Normandy." The task force met behind closed doors, rushing to fulfill Clinton's mandate to come up with a report within 100 days. But health care was a complex issue, and many powerful, conflicting interest groups were intent on sabotaging any sweeping change. Even Congress was uninterested, and when Democrats finally produced a 1,364-page bill in January, 1994, support was so low that the bill was retracted. Later the president said of his wife, "I may have asked her to do more than anybody should ever have been asked to do when I asked her to undertake the health care effort."

Complicating Hillary's life at this time were two other major eruptions. One became known as Travelgate. In the campaign Clinton had promised to reduce staff by 25 percent. Mostly this was accomplished by changing accounting methods and adding volunteer workers like Monica Lewinsky. But the White House travel office was a different story. Clinton partisans felt the office was badly run and suspected the holdover employees might be receiving kickbacks. Hillary got involved, telling David Watkins, a West Wing staffer, "We need to get these people out. We need our people in." Watkins would later say of Hillary: "She's a good screamer. She can cut someone to ribbons and make them feel like an idiot. It was a lot easier to do what she wanted." The entire travel office staff of seven—all career employees—was fired and given ninety minutes to clear out its desks. The office head, Billy Dale, who'd put in thirty-two years of service and was months shy of retirement, left under a cloud of suspicion, and Worldwide Travel, run by the Clintons' friend Harry Thomason, took over. The firings made headlines, partly because Dale had been responsible for taking care of the reporters on charter flights and making special arrangements such as getting technical equipment into foreign countries. The brouhaha forced the Clintons to backtrack and rehire all the staff except for Dale, who was brought to trial and later cleared of charges of financial impropriety. Watkins and deputy attorney Vincent Foster tried to minimize Hillary's role in the affair, but she still had to suffer through a lot of criticism.

Her troubles had only just begun. On July 29, 1993, Hillary was in her mother's condo in Little Rock when she received a message that Foster, who had known the president since kindergarten, had been found dead in Fort Marcy Park across the Potomac River from Washington, an apparent suicide. Like Hillary he had been a partner in the Rose Law Firm in Little Rock. Though they were both married—Foster had a wife and two children—Hillary and Foster never hid their closeness. Foster had not adjusted well to Washington, bringing with him a case of depression that was being treated by medication. It was not helped by the twelve-hour days he put in at the office or the fact that, knowing he had lied to cover up Hillary's role in the Travelgate fiasco, he would have to testify under oath in a congressional investigation of the affair.

When Foster took his life, Hillary faced not only a shocking personal loss but the potential for a public relations disaster. Foster also had been handling her personal business and had files on her involvement in Whitewater as well as a failed bank—Madison Savings and Loan—both of which were under investigation for possible criminal prosecution. As soon as she heard about Foster's death, Hillary called her chief of staff, Maggie Williams. Secret Service agent Henry P. O'Neill, who was escorting cleaning ladies about 11 P.M., said he saw Williams and her assistant Evelyn Lieberman coming out of Foster's office carrying a stack of file folders. Williams denied taking anything. Foster's office should have been sealed immediately after the news of his suicide but was not cordoned off until 10 A.M. the next morning. When a Senate special committee investigated, Maggie Williams said she couldn't remember exactly what had happened.

With bad press issuing forth from nearly every front, Hillary Clinton's first two years, which began with so much promise, turned her into one of the most unpopular first ladies in memory. The president's strategist, Dick Morris, said, "It is hard to overstate the emotional beating Hillary took." A nether point came in July 1994, when she went to Seattle for a health care rally. The Secret Service warned her the crowd was hostile and put agents on a special alert. The police confiscated two guns from one man and a knife from another. When she got up to speak, she faced boos and jeers so loud that even with a public address system on full blast, the first lady had difficulty making herself heard. Hillary-bashing proliferated on talk radio and on the Internet. The personal attacks were so devastating that in late 1994 she retreated from both the West Wing and her public role, secluding herself in the friendly environment of Hillaryland, as some called her East Wing offices staffed by longtime loyalists. She began work on a safer, but still passionate concern, writing a book, *It Takes a Village And Other Lessons Children Teach Us.* She gave interviews on food and decorating, but these were not sudden

*Among those watching the Super-bowl at the White House theater were Clinton guests Texas Governor Ann Richards, left, and New York Governor Mario Cuomo, right. Chelsea Clinton brought Socks to the White House as a companion. One of the President's perks is that he can also order any movie, from the newest to the oldest, for private viewing here.* (CORBIS)

interests. Even before she moved into the White House, Hillary had initiated plans for change.

"The Bushes allowed me to come and study the rooms when they were away on weekends," says Little Rock decorator Kaki Hockersmith, whom the Clintons asked to work on the White House. "All the plans were made before inauguration day. The execution took some time." The Clintons had relied on public housing most of their married life and didn't purchase a home while at the White House until 1999, when they needed to establish residency in New York in order for Hillary to make a bid for the senate. In Arkansas, at the Governor's Mansion, "their quarters were small," said Hockersmith, who gave the rooms an English country look. "All the Clintons really brought with them were personal mementos—things of sentimental value. There was so much available in the White House permanent collection that it really wasn't necessary for them to bring much else."

What the Clintons did bring, Hockersmith was charged with arranging in the rooms just vacated by the Bushes. As soon as Clinton took the oath of office, the decorator was whisked to the White House in a Secret Service van and given till 6 P.M. to make the family quarters and the Oval Office look like home.

Over the following months, she turned her attention to redecorating. "As fairytale as this project sounds, there are tremendous limitations on budget," Hockersmith explained. "If the yellow paint in the West Sitting Hall is in good condition, you work with it, whether you like yellow or not." The Clintons came into the White House at a moment when both the family quarters, last revamped in the Reagan years, and the state rooms, virtually unchanged since Nixon's time, needed work.

For the $396,429.46 privately funded makeover of the family quarters, Hockersmith relied on pastels. "They love yellow and beautiful colors. Their taste is English country, certainly not Victorian," said Hockersmith. Chelsea's bedroom, which overlooked the north portico, was redone in blue and white. A butler's pantry that had been a serving and warming station was turned into an eat-in kitchen, covered in fruit-patterned wallpaper. The Clintons wanted an alternative to the family dining room with its Revolutionary War paper so they could sit en famille, and could make toast and coffee. The converted butler's pantry offered just enough room for three. On the third floor, Hockersmith undid the Plains, Georgia, barnwood installed by the Carters. Some timber was removed and put in storage, the rest hidden behind paneled mirrors that "make the room look larger," she explained. To give the Clintons a place to work out, Hockersmith opened up a few walls and created an exercise room complete with a treadmill. Both husband and wife regularly took advantage of the perk.

In the Treaty Room, the president's second-floor office and sitting room, Hockersmith paid tribute to the Victorian era, reviving an idea from the Kennedy administration when the decor reflected Ulysses Grant's Cabinet Room. "I worked closely with the curators," said Hockersmith. "We discovered all kinds of historical objects associated with that area of the White House during Lincoln and Grant's time." The room suited the president, a great admirer of Lincoln's and also a voracious reader. Hockersmith added bookshelves—Hillary's comment during the tour with Barbara Bush had been, "There aren't enough bookshelves"—and covered the walls with paper that looks like red leather book binding. The red-and-blue curtains were elaborately swagged, and the president's desk was a conference table from a nineteenth-century Cabinet Room.

Keeping to the Victorian theme, Hockersmith redid the Lincoln Sitting Room, adjacent to the Lincoln Bedroom, with a whirl of pattern. She papered the ceiling with burgundy-and-cream wallpaper that simulates architectural relief and covered the floor in thirty-six-inch strips of floral medallion carpeting, made as it was in Victorian times.

The Treaty Room and the Lincoln Sitting Room were widely photographed, and the reviews were not always positive, partly because Hockersmith was not considered part of the decorating cognoscenti like Mark Hampton or Ted Graber, whom the Bushes and the Reagans used. "There are only two Victorian rooms in the entire White House and it's been widely reported that the entire house is Victorian," said Hockersmith. "That's been a real frustration. The Lincoln Sitting Room, a tiny room which connects a bedroom and bath, has been Victorian for 105 years and really shouldn't be anything else. There's an amazing load of misinformation."

In the Oval Office, traditionally accented in blue, Hockersmith traded Bush's muted palette for a brilliant rug and curtains in strong blues and golds. The president wanted the room "to be more dynamic, to show more energy," she said. To set off the blues she chose upholstery striped in burgundy and gold, causing *Time* magazine to report that a Washington insider had dubbed the Oval Office "the Redskin Room," since burgundy and gold were the NFL team's colors.

The refurbishing of the Blue Room, a $358,000 project paid for by the White House endowment fund, fared better with the critics. Richard Nixon's cream wallpaper with blue-patterned acanthus leaf borders had finally worn out (ten years is the normal life expectancy of a state room decorating; since curator Clement Conger had ordered double lengths of wallpaper, the Nixon imprint was prolonged). The Nixon blue was more aqua than indigo, and Hillary said, "My one hope was that we would create a more blue feeling in the room, but not make it so blue that it would be dark and would shrink the room, especially at night." She worked with the Committee for the Preservation of the White House, of which Hockersmith was a member and the leading decorating consultant. Working primarily in January 1995, when the crush of Christmas tourists had passed, Hockersmith papered the walls with a historic chamois-colored pattern and trimmed them with a faux-swag border in sapphire and gold. The room won accolades.

*House Beautiful* called it "grand but unpompous, venerable and yet fresh . . . an interior that shows off America at its best."

In the Red and Green Rooms, the Clintons made only minor changes, reproducing a red rug used by the Kennedys and, in the Green Room, hanging a painting by Georgia O'Keeffe and Henry Tanner, respectively the first woman and the first African American to be represented on the state floor. The State Dining Room needed more attention. "More than in any other room, the architectural details from the McKim renovation were intact," said Hockersmith. "We wanted to maintain that Colonial Revival style but we also had to consider the way the room is used today, a hundred years later." Rather than strip off all the paint and restore the dark oak paneling that Theodore Roosevelt preferred, she kept the walls painted, choosing flattering tones of cream and biscuit. Three pedestal console tables that the Kennedys had painted were returned to their original mahogany. "The Kennedys painted a lot of things," Hockersmith explained, pointing out that the State Dining Room baseboards were faux marbled. The paint was removed to reveal "beautiful granite."

The Cross Hall also needed redoing, and the Clintons chose Empire furnishings as a tribute to James Monroe. New carpeting was needed for the Grand Staircase and the Cross Hall. Traditionally it had been colored red, but Hockersmith had to work to find a red that looked well on television. With receiving lines and processions into the State Dining Room, "this is probably the most photographed space in the White House," she explained.

The Clintons were very involved in the decorating process. Always the student, Hillary Clinton read forty books on White House history to make sure the changes suited the house. Even the president looked at fabric swatches. They also studied up on art. "When we first got here, my husband and I looked through the book on the collection," said Hillary, referring to William Kloss's *Nation's Pride: Art in the White House,* "and tried to find everything in it. What we couldn't find on the walls we brought in [to the Map Room] to study. I think we've pulled out every painting that's been in storage. We've tried to find a place for everything but the only one I despair of is Whistler's Nocturne. There doesn't seem to be a wall where it gets enough light." One of the Clintons' goals was to display contemporary American art, and they arranged for a loan of a painting by Willem de Kooning. His work could not be represented in the 450-piece art collection, since White House rules require that the artist be dead for twenty years.

For the most part the Clintons liked living in the White House. They explored it from top to bottom and liked to recount the history of the house and its artifacts for guests. Hillary was entranced by the view at night: "Looking out at the Washington Monument and the Jefferson Memorial across the fountain, there is a sense of magic and beauty unmatched." They cultivated the friendship of Hollywood stars—Barbra Streisand stayed so frequently and provoked so much gossip she eventually had to be banned—and invited the likes of Paul Newman and Tom Hanks to see their movies in the White House's sixty-seat theater, outfitted with its own popcorn machine. The Clintons bowled in their own private alley, took nighttime swims in the heated outdoor pool put in by Gerald Ford, and had a seven-seater hot tub installed on the lawn. Private donors anted up for a $30,000 padded jogging track, though the president seldom used it because he found the south grounds too public. An avid golfer, Clinton brought back the White House putting green. The first had been installed by Eisenhower, only to be

*Head Chef Roland Meisner spent 150 hours creating this gingerbread model of the White House. It was called the House of Socks after Chelsea's cat who appears in 21 miniatures made of marzipan.* (CORBIS)

removed by Nixon in 1971. Not one for horseshoes, he removed Bush's pits and also did away with the basement barbershop, which became a coveted office occupied by aide Sidney Blumenthal. Clinton's naturally curly hair was something of a problem, and in an effort to tame it, he called Hollywood hair stylist Christophe to Air Force One while it was on the tarmac at Los Angeles International Airport in May 1993. When it was reported—falsely, some said—that Clinton had delayed air traffic because of a haircut, the press had a heyday.

One thing the Clintons did not like about the White House was the lack of privacy. Early on a steward surprised them in bed, and they restricted staff access to the family quarters, even though this made completing tasks difficult, and some servants were forced to work overtime. The staff was further stressed since the Clintons rarely left for Camp David, where trees plagued the president's allergies. Domestic staff overtime ran to $600,000 in 1995, as opposed to $388,472 during Bush's last year.

The Clintons also resented Secret Service supervision. When they found agents stationed near the second-floor living area, they reduced the size of the detail and had the Secret Service station moved farther away from the living quarters. But the president's ability to be alone ceased the minute he left the family quarters. Agents accompanied him everywhere, even downstairs in the small elevator or along the exterior corridor to the Oval Office.

In the Oval Office especially, privacy was at a premium. The room had elaborately curtained windows, but they were never drawn. Staff members wondering if a meeting had broken up could check through two peepholes—one in a door by the desk of Clinton's secretary, Betty Currie, the other in a door leading to a hall outside his private study. A third door, which had no peephole, was guarded by a Secret Service agent. The office opened onto a private dining room, staffed by the two naval aides, who, as Clinton testified during the Monica Lewinsky turmoil, "have total unrestricted access to my dining room, to that hallway, to coming into the Oval Office." Off his dining room was a patio sheltered by trees and shrubs. This location was overseen by a Secret Service agent posted at a modest distance.

The president's only real chance for working privacy was in a small study adjacent to the Oval Office. It was decorated with a portrait of his wife, a copy of Rodin's *The Thinker,* a globe, and a rocking chair. Its accoutrements included golf putters and a computer connected to the Internet. Generally Clinton liked to work in the Oval Office, often sipping Diet Coke or chewing on an unlit cigar. He used his study for reading and napping.

Recent presidents such as Bush and Reagan had gotten along well with the Secret Service. The agents had undoubtedly saved Reagan's life by rushing him to the hospital when he was shot, and Bush made a point of spending Christmas at the White House instead of Camp David so the agents could be with their families. From the first day Clinton complained the Secret Service didn't like him. Clinton's avoidance of serving in the Vietnam War and his relaxed, informal lifestyle were said to bother the agents. Hillary also sensed their hostility—she referred to them as "trained pigs" and insisted they stay ten yards away at all times.

Clinton was used to being guarded by Arkansas state troopers, who readily engaged in small talk or helped carry luggage or even recruited female companionship for the governor. The Secret Service did not engage in any unneeded conversation, an annoyance to the gregarious Clinton—he didn't like sitting in a limousine with two men who wouldn't talk to him. The Secret Service did not feel it should open doors, hold purses, or carry luggage. At one point Hillary told an agent, "If you want to remain on this detail, get your fucking ass over here and grab those bags."

After some time in office Clinton came to have more appreciation for the Secret Service and developed a working relationship with them. His security was indisputably at risk. Late at night on September 12, 1994, a depressed veteran pilot dove his small plane through a holly hedge, damaging a magnolia tree, smacking into the house two floors below Clinton's bedroom, and killing himself. Clinton was not in the White House at the time. In December 1995 a former pizza delivery man was tackled and shot by the Secret Service when he climbed the fence. He had an unloaded pistol. "Just another day at the White House," Clinton quipped. To keep it from being just that, the Secret Service was careful not to reveal information that would facilitate copycat intrusions.

Both the president and first lady were used to doing things spontaneously, and constant surveillance made this virtually impossible. To go anywhere they needed at least thirty minutes' lead time to form up the Secret Service motorcade. The destination had to be checked out and agents stationed along the route. This is not to say that the Clintons didn't get out; they attended art museums, including a Willem de Kooning exhibit at the National Gallery of Art, but they generally went after hours. They went to trendy

restaurants, but the Secret Service brought bottled water and watched food being prepared. Once Clinton asked for decaf coffee while paying a visit to Capitol Hill. The
Secret Service went back and got it from the White House. When his staff ordered out
from Domino's late at night—Clinton's meetings were known to go on and on—the
president wasn't allowed to partake unless the Secret Service supervised the pizza making. For a White House Super Bowl party in 1998 twenty-nine large pies with the works
and one large cheese pie were ordered. The Secret Service oversaw the preparation
and took care of delivery. Normally all food used by the White House chef, whether for
family or official dinners, is ordered from approved suppliers and transported to the
White House in secure trucks.

Clinton frustrated both the Secret Service and staff by his habit of being chronically
late. He would continue a conversation long past the time when he should have left for
the next appointment. In his 1992 campaign aides wore badges reading HE'S RUNNING
A FEW MINUTES LATE, and when he became president the aides referred to being on
"Clinton Standard Time." On inauguration day the Clintons, who stayed at Blair House
right across the street from the White House, kept the Bushes waiting twenty-seven
minutes for the customary courtesy call. When Clinton came to see Chief Justice
William Rehnquist at the Supreme Court, he was forty-five minutes late. The king of
Spain, Juan Carlos, was forced to cool his heels for seven minutes at the White House
before Clinton showed up to greet him.

Clinton's mode of operation was free-form and somewhat haphazard. He tempo-
rized or delayed decisions or appointments, and missed deadlines. When his chief of
staff, Thomas McLarty, said, "I told the President the other day, only half-jokingly, 'I'm
convinced more than ever of your goodness. But what I'll never understand is how a
man with such a genius for organizing his thoughts and articulating them could be so
disorganized in managing himself.' " On February 17, 1993, the ceremonies for his first
speech to Congress, an address on his economic legislative proposals were scheduled to
begin at 9 A.M. Clinton, caught up in last-minute revisions, didn't leave the White House
until 8:40. He was still working on his speech in the car and even in the Speaker's office
at the Capitol. While Clinton stood at the podium acknowledging the applause of congressmen and senators, a frantic TelePrompTer operator was struggling to get the latest
revision up on the screen. The following September, the frenzy was even worse. Clinton, scheduled to address a joint session on health care, again spent his limo ride to the
Capitol making last minute changes in his speech. George Stephanopoulos, a top aide
in Clinton's first term, rushed the final version to the TelePrompTer operator, who
loaded it incorrectly. Clinton got up to speak and realized something was amiss. He
whispered to Vice President Gore, who was alongside him, "The speech, check the
speech. It's the wrong one." Gore summoned Stephanopoulos, who frantically raced to
the TelePrompTer operator and managed to get it straightened out. Meanwhile Clinton, a master at speechmaking, never seemed to falter or look at his much-corrected
script. For seven minutes he talked and looked the television cameras in the eye while
the right speech was loaded on the TelePrompTer and the words scrolled down to catch
up with Clinton.

With his casual approach to the presidency, Clinton changed the hierarchical tone of
the Reagan-Bush White House. Gone were the Wall Street suits and ties. In came

T-shirts, jeans, and earrings for men, and pants, bare midriff blouses, and miniskirts for women. The Clintons dressed formally, but Hillary was fundamentally indifferent to fashion. She bought a wedding dress the day before her marriage and settled on an inaugural ball gown only when close friend Susan Thomas chided her, "Hillary, treat it like a piece of history. What dress do you want to wear in the Smithsonian?" With every crisis she faced as first lady, she allowed friends and consultants to make her over, giving rise to websites that tracked her ever-changing hairdos.

With a baby boomer as president and a baby-faced staff, White House and executive offices became known as "the campus." Workers brought in radios and coffee makers and lounged about. George Stephanopoulos chewed bubble gum at his first press conference. Hillary Clinton insisted on using the regular West Wing ladies' room, startling staffers. Security clearances, routine in the previous years, were resisted and resented, particularly questions dealing with the present or past use of drugs.

Clinton did away with the White House operators, famed for being able to find anyone anywhere. Previous presidents had just picked up a phone and said, "Get me . . ." Concerned about confidentiality, Clinton wanted to dial numbers for himself. A new $27 million phone system was installed for the entire White House staff that allowed for direct dialing and voice mail.

*Working in the Oval Office, Bill Clinton had little privacy. Aides could check to see what he was doing through a peephole in the door. Secret Service agents were stationed beyond the full-length windows whose curtains were not meant to be drawn.* (LIBRARY OF CONGRESS)

At first Clinton did not see any need to look or act presidential. He tried to prevent his staff from standing up when he entered a meeting, instead waving them down. His military salute was sheepish, given with the head slightly bowed. It was commented on so much that National Security Adviser Tony Lake finally got up the nerve to talk to Clinton about it and got him so he could snap off a proud salute. He liked to go jogging and bring the press along, causing late-night show hosts to ridicule his chunky legs.

Clinton had a perpetual weight problem—he was so plump in kindergarten that he broke a leg skipping rope—and counted on jogging to control his paunch. He was generally up at around 6 A.M., awakened by a call from a steward. He seemed to survive well on only about six hours sleep. Since he didn't like the White House track, he was driven to an isolated park along the Potomac River, where he jogged three to five days a week. Usually he jogged about three eight-minute miles. His conveyance back and forth from the White House was a ten-car motorcade that often included motorcycle police, police cars, a Secret Service SWAT team vehicle, a communications truck, an ambulance, a press van, and cars for guests, including a van to pick up those who thought they could keep up with the president but were unable to. "Jogging with the President is bigger than an audience in the Oval," one White House aide said. George Stephanopoulos thought that Clinton was addicted to running and that missing it two days in a row made him irritable. Before his jog Clinton would have fruit and a cup of coffee; afterward he'd shower and around 8 A.M. head to the Oval Office.

Clinton's routine was permanently upset in the fall of 1997 when he fell down the stairs at the home of golf pro Greg Norman and injured his knee. Wheelchair-bound, he couldn't leave the family quarters for two weeks. For the next three or four months, he was dependent on braces, crutches, and canes. He was still on crutches when he met Monica Lewinsky, one of the volunteers who kept working when government shut down in November 1997 and federal employees were sent home due to a congressional impasse on the budget. When Clinton recovered, he took to exercising in the private quarters gym and playing golf, a favorite sport.

Hillary had a plan to help maintain her husband's weight, and it involved switching from the French cuisine practiced by Pierre Chambrin, a famous chef who was a holdover from the Bush administration. Hillary sent down thirty cookbooks featuring low-fat nouvelle American cuisine, not a move that endeared her to Chambrin. She was interested in regional American foods and American wines. She wanted to put an end to menus written in French. Chambrin agreed, but even in English, his style remained haute cuisine.

The situation was not helped when Hillary brought in Dr. Dean Ornish, a low-fat diet advocate, to provide lessons in nutrition. The Clintons also had a habit of inviting up to fifty for dinner on short notice, sometimes just two hours. As if this weren't enough, the president was allergic to dairy and chocolate, and chronically late for White House dinners. Chambrin responded by holding up meals. He was quoted as saying, "They'll have to learn to wait." Chambrin may have won a battle or two, but ultimately he lost the war. After only a year with the new administration, he was forced to resign. When asked to comment on his departure, the president hewed to tradition and avoided East Wing problems: "I read about it in the paper. That's one place where I'm afraid I'm a traditional and limited male. It's not my deal." Chambrin received a $37,026 settlement that included a promise not to discuss the Clintons or his dismissal.

In his place Hillary brought in Walter Scheib, a graduate of the Culinary Institute of America in Hyde Park, New York, and the chef at the Greenbrier Resort, a spa in West Virginia. Beginning in March 1994 Scheib presided over a staff that included two assistant chefs, a kitchen steward, and two assistant stewards. For the large state dinners, chefs from local restaurants were brought in to help. For special occasions chef Scheib made up several menus and forwarded them to Hillary for suggestions. "She's very interested," he said, "and a woman on her staff used to be a chef, so it's great. We use a very seasonal menu, the newest baby vegetables in spring, heavier in winter, sometimes game at a fall luncheon—venison, rabbit." Scheib explained that he got "the gratuitous fat out by using vegetable or fruit purees, by using big and fresh flavors instead of just adding butter and slapping on a piece of fois gras." He said he searched the country for the best ingredients—from Michigan blueberries to buffalo milk mozzarella from upstate New York. Meats in rich sauces were replaced by fish and steamed vegetables. Cooking oil in spray bottles replaced the traditional vegetable oils that were poured in pans. Scheib claimed that his low-calorie dishes were "almost like normal food." Although Scheib often worked twelve-hour days, he said he loved the job—"People will have to pry me out of here with a crowbar."

The Clintons did keep the Bushes' pastry chef, Roland Mesnier, and his assistant, Franette McCulloch, who worked in a separate kitchen hidden halfway between the first floor and the family quarters on one of the White House's elevator-accessed mezzanines. For a luncheon for President Hosni Mubarak of Egypt Mesnier created a pyramid of pistachio mousse with edible palm trees and a marzipan camel. For Chelsea's sixteenth birthday he frosted a replica of her new driver's license, including her photo ID in color and a chocolate car with the license plate "Sweet 16."

For parties and state events Clinton did manage to go off a spa diet. For his fiftieth birthday party at the Sheraton Hotel in New York he received a huge buttercream-frosted pound cake valued at $4,000 and contributed by the employees of a local bakery. When dining at Boris Yeltsin's dacha in Moscow he was served a Russian delicacy—moose lips. But en route he didn't get to munch on the traditional boxes of presidential M&Ms. These were removed from his area of Air Force One in an effort to help keep his weight down. Similarly, candy dishes were barred from the Oval Office, replaced instead by fruit baskets.

In addition to instituting healthy American fare, Hillary shortened the time for state dinners to just four courses—appetizer, main course, salad and cheese, and dessert. Time was also saved by introducing restaurant-style "plate service"—instead of having each dish served from the left by a waiter from a platter, servers now come with the complete main course on a plate, allowing the chef to create attractively composed combinations.

The Clintons were also innovative in other ways. At a 1998 dinner for Prime Minister Romano Prodi of Italy, Hillary arranged for entertainment during the meal rather than in another room afterward. Thirty-two American singers performed an Italian opera during the meal. Her social secretary, Capricia Penavic Marshall, said, "I was so worried that it wouldn't work until I saw Prime Minister Prodi start singing the opera to Mrs. Clinton."

Hillary tried using several rooms for dinners. For Christmas 1996 guests drew place cards from a large vermeil bowl to determine the room they would be eating in—this way there could be no group considered more select than another. In addition to the State Dining Room, the Diplomatic Reception Room, the Red Room, and the Map Room were used. Afterward all met together in the East Room for a Christmas ball. Another time the Truman Balcony was the scene for a dinner for sixty with buffet tables set up in the adjoining Yellow Oval Room. The guests sat down to dine on the balcony as the evening sun lit up the Washington Monument and the Jefferson Memorial. For Clinton's twenty-fifth reunion at Georgetown University, the president invited all 600 members of the class of 1968 and their guests to a dinner at the White House. Most of the state rooms were used, and a special dance floor was set up on the south lawn.

Planning for state dinners began as much as two months ahead, leaving nothing to chance. Diplomatic and military protocol were researched, and for something big like a peace signing, everything was scripted and an advance team walked through the ceremony. State dinners came out of the State Department budget. In his first term President Clinton spent about $3.6 million on entertaining at the White House. The total figure, about half of which was later reimbursed by corporate donors or the Democratic National Committee, was between two to three times the costs of the last two years of the Bush administration. There were at least seventy-three receptions or dinners for party donors in the first term alone. The Clintons also hosted 938 overnight guests in the first term, including close Hollywood friends Harry Thomason and Linda Bloodworth-Thomason, who were invited to spend inauguration night in the Lincoln Bedroom. They in turn invited fellow guests Markie Post and her husband into the room, and Markie jumped up and down on the Lincoln Bed shouting, "We won! We won!" Thomason took pictures that eventually turned up being printed in the *National Enquirer.*

The Clintons instituted a blanket ban against all smoking in the White House and began a project called "the Greening of the White House" which involved replacing older lighting fixtures with more energy-efficient models, installing water conservation devices in the faucets and lawn sprinklers, and placing recycling bins around, even in the family quarters. The aim of the project was to decrease energy use by 30 percent by 2005 without seeking additional congressional appropriations.

Hillary said her greatest surprise in the job of being first lady was to discover that she had to start planning for Christmas in the spring. "I've never been anyone who planned for Christmas much before mid-December, and my husband and I would race around." She couldn't have imagined that her White House Christmas would involve twenty-two separate trees with 27,000 lights, 7,500 ornaments, and over 100,000 visitors. For the first White House Christmas in 1993 pastry chef Roland Mesnier spent 150 hours constructing an enormous model of the White House made out of gingerbread. Named for Chelsea's cat Socks, it was called the House of Socks. Architecturally accurate, it included chocolate trees and twenty-one renditions of Socks in marzipan. Hillary instituted the tradition of asking American artists and designers to craft Christmas ornaments, not anticipating that the art students who responded to her 1994 call would send in R-rated gingerbread men. Volunteers apparently broke some of the more lewd creations.

Christmas cards were a massive production. In 1993 some 200,000 were sent out—in typical Clinton fashion, just barely in time to beat the December 25 deadline. After much debate the family settled on a photo of the president and first lady but omitted thirteen-year-old Chelsea. Fiercely protective of a daughter who had to go through pimples and braces in the most public house in the country, the Clintons did everything within their power to shelter their precious eighth-grader. Instead of sending her to public school like Amy Carter, the Clintons, longtime supporters of public education, opted for the cloistered environment of Sidwell Friends School, run by Quakers and costing $14,000 annually. In a radio interview Hillary defended the decision, saying, "We wanted to be able to tell the press and the public that they could not be allowed on the property."

Though she was first lady, Hillary continued to try to be a regular mother. Shortly after moving into the White House, Chelsea got sick during the night and asked Hillary to make her an omelet. The first lady padded down the hall to the second-floor kitchen, got eggs out of the refrigerator, and began cracking them into a bowl when a steward appeared and offered to whip them up. On another occasion, she recalled, "Chelsea wasn't feeling well and I went down to make her some applesauce. The call went out. 'She's in the kitchen! She's got out the pots!' They all came and hovered. It just kind of spoiled it, so I left."

For Chelsea's initiation into White House life, Hillary organized an inauguration night scavenger hunt. "While Bill and I attended thirteen inaugural balls, Chelsea's friends roamed all over the house finding items of historical significance like the Gettysburg Address, as well as the hidden staircase between the second and third floors," Hillary recalled. In the first four years, Chelsea had seventy-two sleepover guests.

Hillary arranged her schedule so she could be upstairs when Chelsea came home from school. She made a point of attending her daughter's dance performances at the Washington School of Ballet. In *The Nutcracker*, Chelsea, at thirteen, danced the role of Favorite Aunt. When given instructions on care of her costume, she told her teacher, "The problem is I don't do my own laundry." Chelsea sometimes did her homework in the president's study off the Oval Office—his job was to help with math. When she got sick at school and needed aspirin, she told the nurse, "Call my dad, my mom's too busy."

But having a working mother and father with home offices meant the family was able to spend more time together than in the past. They tried to meet regularly for dinner at seven-thirty. Hillary said, "We watch movies together in the theater, play cards (usually pinochle or spades), and take walks or bike rides together. Occasionally Chelsea and I sneak out for a meal at a local restaurant or go to the mall to do some shopping. Some of the best times with Chelsea come when we're just sitting around talking, usually after school or when she comes home from ballet classes, while we get ready for dinner." Chelsea was also active in a church group and volunteered to serve meals to Washington's homeless.

Chelsea and the president liked to watch action movies that didn't interest Hillary. C-Span would be on in the family quarters at night, though the president might be talking on the phone, doing the crossword puzzle (he works in pen and is by all accounts a whiz), or reading at the same time. Clinton liked to get his information firsthand. Briefing books, fifteen pages during the Bush administration, expanded to a hundred pages. In addition to his "homework," Clinton read as many as four books a week, usually starting several at once and proceeding in fits and starts. His tastes ranged from the latest works on politics to mysteries. Able to read German since he was an undergraduate at Georgetown University, he also perused foreign periodicals.

On June 7, 1997, Chelsea graduated from high school. Her dad spoke at the ceremony, the first president to do so since Theodore Roosevelt. "Dad, I want you to be wise, briefly," Chelsea told her father, who restricted his remarks to fourteen minutes. He said of his daughter, "a part of us longs to hold you once more as we did when you could barely walk, to read to you just one more time, *Good Night Moon.*" In September Chelsea went off to Stanford University with her parents and 200 reporters. Her mother learned how to send e-mail in order to keep up with her. To reach her parents, Chelsea could send regular mail to the president's private zip code or fax a note to the Oval Office's exclusive number.

In November 2000 the Clintons presided over the two-hundredth anniversary of John Adams's arrival at the White House. The house envisioned by George Washington now had 132 rooms, uncounted nooks and crannies, and a new coat of paint, applied after forty coats were removed and fire-blackened stone was exposed. Clinton had called the White House "the crown jewel of the penal system," but he'd lived out his childhood dream. He'd become a resident of the house he visited as a seventeen-year-old representative of the American Legion Boys Nation in 1963. John F. Kennedy was president, and Clinton recalled, "I remember very distinctly where I was standing and what I did. The fellow we elected president of Boys Nation gave him a T-shirt and something else, and Kennedy gave his little talk. Then he came down in the crowd and started shaking hands, and I was afraid he would just shake one or two hands and quit. I was at the head of the alphabet anyway, and I was bigger than anybody around me, so I just made sure I was there so I got to shake hands with him."

# Acknowledgments

This book would not have been possible without the research assistance of Claudia Condruz, the editorial skills of Laura J. MacKay, who wrote the second draft of the book, the persistence of our remarkable agent, Barbara Hogenson, and of course the dedication of our editor, Paula Kakalecik. We would also like to thank our families, all three generations, who loyally took a backseat to a love of history.

# Notes

**Chapter 1. Washington**

**"drawn into precedent"** Graff, Henry F., ed., *The Presidents: A Reference History*. New York. Charles Scribner's Sons, 1997, p. 5.
**"invitations to entertainments"** Seale, William, *The President's House: A History, Volume I*. Washington, D.C.: White House Historical Association, 1986, p. 5.
**"impertinent applications"** Seale, *The President's House, Volume I*, pp. 5–6.

**Chapter 2. John Adams**

**"bake oven"** Editors of American Heritage. *The American Heritage Pictorial History of the Presidents of the United States, Volume I*. New York: Simon and Schuster, 1968, p. 72.
**"of rooms"** Ibid. p. 63.
**"for your company"** Levin, Phyllis, *Abigail Adams*. New York: St. Martin's Press, 1987, p. 387.
**"idea of it"** Ibid., p 387.
**"under this roof"** Editors of American Heritage, *The American Heritage Pictorial History of the Presidents of the United States, Volume I*, p. 72.
**"unseen abode"** Levin, *Abigail Adams*, p. 388.
**"only in name"** Hurd, Charles, *The White House Story*. New York: Hawthorne Books, 1966, p. 30.
**"were broken"** Singleton, Esther, *The Story of the White House*. New York: Benjamin Blom, 1907, p. 13.
**"and cart it"** Ibid., p. 12.
**"a new country"** Ibid.
**"audience-room"** Ibid.
**"want of punctuality"** Smith, Page, *John Adams, Volume II*. Garden City, NY: Doubleday, 1962, p. 1050.
**"have been removed"** Levin, *Abigail Adams*, p. 389.
**"I ever saw"** Means, Marianne, *The Woman in the White House*. New York: Random House, 1963, p. 48.
**"and discretion"** Truman, Margaret, *First Ladies*. New York: Random House, 1995, p. 90.
**"ages to come"** Singleton, *The Story of the White House*, p. 11.
**"situation is beautiful"** Truman, *First Ladies*, p. 96.
**"three months"** Singleton, *The Story of the White House*, p. 12.
**"toothless Adams"** Means, *The Woman in the White House*, p. 46.
**"vain, conceited"** Editors of American Heritage, *The American Heritage Pictorial History of the Presidents of the United States, Volume I*, p. 63.
**"me in buckets"** Levin, *Abigail Adams*, p. 391.
**"a glass bubble"** DeGregorio, William, *The Complete Book of United States Presidents*. New York: Barricade Books, 1993, p. 19.

**"years and strength"**    DeGregorio, *The Complete Book of United States Presidents*, p. 19.
**"of my days"**    Smith, Page, *John Adams*, Volume II, p. 1055.
**"their company"**    DeGregorio, *The Complete Book of United States Presidents*, p. 19.
**"his grandpapa"**    Cavanah, Frances, *They Lived in the White House*. Philadelphia: Macrae Smith, 1961, p. 21.
**"Giddap"**    Reit, Seymour, *Growing Up in the White House*. New York: Crowell-Collier, 1968, p. 12.
**"wilderness"**    Levin, *Abigail Adams*, p. 390.
**"difficulties alone"**    Ibid.


**Chapter 3.    Thomas Jefferson**

**"handsome house"**    Smith, Margaret Bayard, *The First Forty Years of Washington Society*. New York: Frederick Ungar, 1965, p. 19.
**"out of courtesy"**    Smith, *The First Forty Years of Washington Society*, p. 32.
**"for the cheese"**    Singleton, *The Story of the White House*, p. 41.
**"all the citizens"**    Smith, *The First Forty Years of Washington Society*, p. 30.
**"dined alone"**    Thomas, Helen, *Dateline: White House*. New York: Macmillan, 1957, p. 15.
**"and left them"**    Singleton, *The Story of the White House*, p. 43–44.
**"beginning to end"**    Smith, *The First Forty Years of Washington Society*, p. 29.
**"like a turnstile"**    Singleton, *The Story of the White House*, p. 40.
**"blessed interim"**    Malone, Dumas, *Jefferson the President: Second Term, 1805–1809*. Boston: Little, Brown, 1974, p. 18.
**"me to do it"**    Randall, Willard, *Thomas Jefferson: A Life*. New York: Holt, 1993, p. 553.
**"in her breast"**    Brodie, Fawn, *Thomas Jefferson: An Intimate History*. New York: Norton, 1975, p. 379.
**"morning visits"**    Malone, *Jefferson the President: Second Term, 1805–1809*, p. 65.
**"close built town"**    Brodie, *Thomas Jefferson: An Intimate History*, p. 336.
**"escaped his notice"**    Brodie, *Thomas Jefferson: An Intimate History*, pp. 568–69.
**"of those gardens"**    Smith, *The First Forty Years of Washington Society*, p. 402.
**"native victuals"**    Jeffries, Ona, *In and Out of the White House*. New York: Wilfred Funk, 1960, p. 46.
**"in fifty years"**    Adler, Bill, ed., *Presidential Wit*. New York: Trident Presss, 1966, p. 22.
**"name is SALLY"**    Brodie, *Thomas Jefferson: An Intimate History*, p. 349.
**"upon this point"**    Ibid.
**"of his history tracts"**    Ibid., p. 319.
**"or trust him"**    Ibid. pp. 321–23.
**"of Callender"**    Ibid., p. 326.
**"its correctness"**    Randall, *Thomas Jefferson: A Life*, p. 559.
**"parts of Spain"**    Jensen, Amy, *The White House and Its Thirty-four Families*. New York: McGraw-Hill, 1965, p. 17.
**"to back out"**    Ibid., p. 18.
**"morning-attire"**    Malone, *Jefferson the President: Second Term, 1805–1809*, p. 378.
**"sovereign I represented"**    Singleton, *The Story of the White House*, p. 34.
**"omission of all distinction"**    Malone, *Jefferson the President: Second Term, 1805–1809*. pp. 378–79.
**"such a place"**    Singleton, *The Story of the White House*, p. 37.
**"out of office"**    Randall, *Thomas Jefferson: A Life*, p. 554.
**"white silk hose"**    Singleton, *The Story of the White House*, p. 28.
**"and powdered"**    Brodie, *Thomas Jefferson: An Intimate History*, p. 364.
**"and revilers"**    Malone, *Jefferson the President: Second Term, 1805–1809*, p. 394.
**"in that office"**    Ambrose, Stephen, *Undaunted Courage*. New York: Simon and Schuster, 1996, p. 59.
**"main avenue"**    Aikman, Lonelle, *The Living White House*. Washington, D.C.: White House Historical Association, 1982, p. 123.
**"until it cracked"**    Whitney, David C., *The American Presidents*. New York: Prentice-Hall, 1990, p. 27.
**"forwarded by Lewis"**    Ambrose, *Undaunted Courage*, p. 340.
**"or ornaments"**    Smith, *The First Forty Years of Washington Society*, p. 402.
**"believe anything"**    Ibid. p. 403.
**"femail"**    Terrell, John, *Zebulon Pike: The Life and Times of a Great Adventurer*. New York: Weybright and Talley, 1968, pp. 175–76.
**"Docile"**    Ibid., pp. 224–25.
**"to humor him"**    Seale, *The President's House, Volume I*, p. 115.
**"of my life"**    Brodie, *Thomas Jefferson: An Intimate History*, p. 424.
**"loss of friends"**    Editors of American Heritage, *The American Heritage Pictorial History of the Presidents of the United States, Volume I*, p. 103.
**"political passions"**    Singleton, *The Story of the White House*, p. 53.


**Chapter 4.    James Madison**

**"his friends"**    Seale, *The President's House, Volume I*, p. 25.
**"wall remained"**    Smith, *The First Forty Years of Washington Society*, p. 109.
**"affability"**    Ibid., p. 58.
**"to a ball"**    Ibid., p. 412.
**"loves Mr. Madison"**    Ibid., p. 63.
**"entertainment bad"**    Dean, Elizabeth, *Dolley Madison: The Nation's Hostess*. Boston: Lothrop, Lee & Shepard, 1928, p. 115.
**"become oppressive"**    Smith, *The First Forty Years of Washington Society*, p. 61.
**"brilliant will they be"**    Moore, Virginia, *The Madisons*. New York: McGraw-Hill, 1979, p. 227.
**"this evening"**    Blodgett, Bonnie, and D. J. Tice, *At Home with the Presidents*. Woodstock, N.Y.: Overlook Press, p. 41.
**"of my life"**    Ibid., p. 44.
**"polish of fashion"**    Smith, *The First Forty Years of Washington Society*, p. 82.
**"native character"**    Ibid.
**"for everybody"**    Jensen, *The White House and Its Thirty-four Families*, p. 23.
**"care about people"**    Truman, *First Ladies*, p. 23.
**"my polisher"**    Hay, Peter, *All the Presidents' Ladies*. New York: Viking 1988, pp. 51–52.
**"which to charm"**    Singleton, *The Story of the White House*, p. 71.
**"indeed are beautiful"**    Moore, *The Madisons*, p. 264.
**"were enchanting"**    Ibid.
**"to a funeral"**    Truman, *First Ladies*, p. 21.
**"apple-John"**    Jensen, *The White House and Its Thirty-four Families*, p. 23.
**"nest of traitors"**    Blodgett, *At Home with the Presidents*, p. 44.
**"with my husband"**    Truman, Margaret, *Women of Courage: From Revolutionary Times to the Present*. New York: Morrow, 1976, p. 49.
**"are all gone"**    Moore, *The Madisons*, p. 312.

"at a moment's warning"  Ibid., p. 309.
"must be sacrificed"  Ibid., p. 310.
"may not be taken"  Dean, *Dolley Madison: The Nation's Hostess*, p. 140.
"a retreat"  Seale, *The President's House, Volume I*, p. 133.
"directed to take"  Dean, *Dolley Madison: The Nation's Hostess*, p. 141.
"with the blaze"  Smith, *The First Forty Years of Washington Society*, p. 111.
"never saw again"  Moore, *The Madisons*, p. 322.
"yet smoking"  Smith, *The First Forty Years of Washington Society*, p. 109.
"without tears"  Ibid., p. 110.
"spies and traitor"  Singleton, *The Story of the White House*, p. 78.
"in Paradise"  Blodgett, *At Home with the Presidents*, p. 45.
"take it to her"  Gerson, Noel, *The Velvet Glove A Life of Dolley Madison*. Nashville, Tenn: Thomas Nelson, 1975, p. 386.

**Chapter 5.  James Monroe**

"a blemish"  Blodgett, *At Home With the Presidents*, p. 47.
"single day"  Seale, *The President's House, Volume I*, p. 146.
"Era of Good Feeling"  Editors of American Heritage, *The American Heritage Pictorial History of the Presidents of the United States, Volume I*, p. 153.
"a short time"  Morgan, George, *The Life of James Monroe*. Boston: Small, Maynard, 1921, p. 372.
"series of service"  Ibid., p. 412.
"gentlemen's house"  Wilmerding, Lucius, Jr., "James Monroe and the Furniture Fund." *The New-York Historical Society Quarterly*, vol. XLIV, no. 2 (April 19, 1960): 138.
"nudities"  Ibid.
"5,000 francs"  Jensen, *The White House and Its Thirty-four Families*, p. 34.
"highest finish"  Ibid.
"residence"  Ibid., p. 33.
"were foreigners"  Ibid., p. 32.
"stiff as pasteboard"  Ibid., pp. 37–38.
"little firebrand"  Jensen, *The White House and Its Thirty-four Families*, p. 36.
"before nine"  Morgan, *The Life of James Monroe*, p. 415.
"hastily left"  Steinberg, Alfred, *The First Ten*. Garden City, N.Y.: Doubleday, 1967, p. 244.
"a public spectacle"  Morgan, *The Life of Monroe*, p. 387.
"wonted tranquility"  Ibid.
"European powers"  Jensen, *The White House and Its Thirty-four Families*, p. 38.
"before a multitude"  Wilmerding, "James Monroe and the Furniture Fund," p. 148.
"ever meeting again"  Blodgett, *At Home with the Presidents*, p. 50.
"well express"  Ibid.

**Chapter 6.  John Quincy Adams**

"Alms House"  Hecht, Marie, *John Quincy Adams*. New York: Macmillan, 1972, p. 414.
"great palace"  Nagel, Paul, *John Quincy Adams*. New York: Knopf, 1997, p. 3.
"till bed time"  Butterfield, L. H. "Tending a Dragon-Killer: Notes for the Biographer of Mrs. John Quincy Adams." *Proceedings of the American Philosophical Society*, vol. 118, no. 2 (April, 1974): 171.
"president of us"  Nagel, *John Quincy Adams*, p. 171.
"going to decline"  Smith, *The First Forty Years of Washington Society*, p. 186.
"majority of the people"  Jensen, *The White House and Its Thirty-four Families*, p. 41.
"ninetieth year"  Nagel, Paul, *John Quincy Adams*. New York: Knopf, 1997, p. 296.
"my own partisans"  Shepherd, Jack, *The Adams Chronicles*. Boston: Little, Brown, 1975, p. 286.
"entirely hopeless"  Nagel, *John Quincy Adams*, pp. 301–02.
"a solitary"  Graff, *The Presidents: A Reference History*, p. 118.
"of the nation"  Wolfe, Perry, *A Tour of the White House with Mrs. John F. Kennedy*. Garden City, N.Y.: Doubleday, 1962, p. 68.
"gambling furniture"  Jensen, *The White House and Its Thirty-four Families*, p. 43.
"forbidding manners"  Hargreaves, Mary W., *The Presidency of John Quincy Adams*. Lawrence: University of Kansas Press, 1985, p. 23.
"correct judgment"  Nagel, *John Quincy Adams*, p. 297.
"without its trials"  DeGregorio, *The Complete Book of United States Presidents*, p. 94.
"peremptory"  Shepherd, Jack, *Cannibals of the Heart*. New York: McGraw-Hill, 1980, p. 256.
"utterly astonished"  Blodgett, *At Home With the Presidents*, p. 27.
"Never"  Truman, *First Ladies*, p. 279.
"and better world"  Bemis, Samuel Flagg, *John Quincy Adams and the Union*. New York: Knopf, 1956, pp. 112–13.
"everybody else"  Shepherd, *Cannibals of the Heart*, p. 262.
"too much at dinner"  Ibid., p. 256.
"tone and manners"  Ibid.
"in your presence"  Gwynne-Thomas, E. H. *The Presidential Families*. New York: Hippocrene Books, 1989, pp. 88–89.
"him and his suite"  Nagel. Paul C., *The Adams Women*. New York: Oxford University Press, 1987, p. 216.
"of existence"  Jensen, *The White House and Its Thirty-four Families*, p. 41.
"an Irishman"  Nagel, *John Quincy Adams*, p. 307.
"tooth drawn"  Ibid., p. 307.
"Inflexible determination"  Steinberg, *First Ten*, p. 260.
"until nine"  Singleton, *The Story of the White House*, p. 166.
"of my shirt"  Bemis, *John Quincy Adams and the Union*, p. 121.
"on the bank"  Nagel, *John Quincy Adams*, pp. 216–17.
"altogether ridiculous"  Nagel, *The Adams Women*, pp. 216–17.
"an irresistible impulse"  Falkner, Leonard, *The President Who Wouldn't Retire*. New York: Coward-McCann, 1987, p. 299.
"of the garden"  Singleton, *The Story of the White House*, p. 299.
"his own residence"  Jensen, *The White House and Its Thirty-four Families*, p. 43.
"one thousand"  Seale, *The President's House, Volume I*, p. 169.
"and wormwood"  Singleton, *The Story of the White House*, p. 170.
"becoming ripe"  Seale, *The President's House, Volume I*, p. 169.
"many disappointments"  Shepherd, *Cannbials of the Heart*, p. 301.
"in my children"  Bemis, *John Quincy Adams and the Union*, p. 118.

**"weakness and languor"**    Nagel, *John Quincy Adams*, p. 305.
**"were terminated"**    Shepherd, *Adams Chronciles*, p. 305.
**"honors of war"**    Smith, *The First Forty Years of Washington Society*, p. 248.
**"begins in gloom"**    Editors of American Heritage, *The American Heritage Pictorial History of the Presidents of the United States, Volume I*, p. 175.
**"billiard table"**    Hecht, *John Quincy Adams*, p. 490.
**"health and happiness"**    Jensen, *The White House and Its Thirty-four Families*, p. 45.
**"specially be preserved"**    Ibid.
**"wanting to live"**    Whitney, *The American Presidents*, p. 61.
**"I am content"**    DeGregorio, *The Complete Book of United States Presidents*, p. 100.

### Chapter 7.   Andrew Jackson

**"dreadful danger"**    Editors of American Heritage. *The American Heritage Pictorial History of the Presidents of the United States, Volume I*, p. 197.
**"in my ears"**    Seale, *The President's House, Volume I*, p. 178.
**"with living matter"**    Smith, *The First Forty Years of Washington Society*, p. 57.
**"a regular Saturnalia"**    Editors of American Heritage. *The American Heritage Pictorial History of the Presidents of the United States, Volume I*, p. 198.
**"as soon as possible"**    Smith, *The First Forty Years of Washington Society*, p. 56.
**"People would rule"**    Ibid.
**"some measure misapplied"**    Ibid.
**"an eel skin"**    Editors of American Heritage, *The American Heritage Pictorial History of the Presidents of the United States, Volume I*, p. 200.
**"in the nation"**    Blodgett, *At Home with the Presidents*, p. 57.
**"to be President"**    Editors of American Heritage. *The American Heritage Pictorial History of the Presidents of the United States, Volume I*, p. 203.
**"Very Remarkable"**    Blodgett, *At Home with the Presidents*, p. 57.
**"profligate woman"**    Truman, *First Ladies*, p. 262.
**"of his bosom"**    Ibid., p. 260.
**"them at me"**    Miller, Hope, *Scandals in the Highest Office*. New York: Random House, 1973, pp. 116–17.
**"in Washington"**    Boller, Paul, *Presidential Wives*. New York: Oxford University Press, 1988, p. 65.
**"to God for mercy"**    DeGregorio, *The Complete Book of United States Presidents*, p. 108.
**"black and gold slab"**    Singleton, *The Story of the White House*, p. 223.
**"comfortless"**    Cross, Wilbur, and Ann Novotny, *White House Weddings*. New York: David McKay, 1967, p. 52.
**"warm that corner"**    Aikman, *The Living White House*, p. 115.
**"desolate"**    Wilbur and Novotny, *White House Weddings*, p. 52.
**"drawing room"**    James, Marquis, *Andrew Jackson: Portrait of a President*. New York: Grosset & Dunlap, 1937, pp. 372–74.
**"new man"**    Graff, *The Presidents: A Reference History*, p. 146.
**"other is tobacco"**    Remini, Robert V., *Andrew Jackson and the Course of American Democracy, Volume 3*. New York: Harper & Row, 1984, p. 70.
**"and best pipe"**    James, *Andrew Jackson: Portrait of a President*, p. 311.
**"at any moment"**    Davis, Burke, *Old Hickory: A Life of Andrew Jackson*. New York: Dial Press, 1977, p. 345.
**"quantities of slime"**    Moss, John R., and Wilbur, Cross, *Presidential Courage*. New York: Norton, 1980, p. 41.
**"then who didn't"**    Blodgett, *At Home with the Presidents*, p. 54.
**"peaceable possession"**    Davis, *Old Hickory*, p. 304.
**"spell his own name"**    Ibid., p. 331.
**"last ten days"**    Remini, *Andrew Jackson and the Course of American Democracy, Volume 3*, p. 105.
**"American home"**    Seale, *The President's House, Volume I*, p. 181.
**"with their advice"**    James, *Andrew Jackson: Portrait of a President*, p. 241.
**"in the East Room"**    Sadler, Christine, *Children in the White House*. New York: Putnam, 1987, p. 87.
**"does not suit me."**    Blodgett, *At Home with the Presidents*, p. 53.
**"simple operations"**    James, *Andrew Jackson: Portrait of a President*, p. 227.
**"Peggy's good name"**    Boller, Paul F., *Presidential Anecdotes*. New York: Oxford University Press, 1981, pp. 80–81.
**"virtuous womanhood"**    Miller, *Scandals in the Highest Office*, pp. 119–21.
**"sooner abandon life"**    James, *Andrew Jackson: Portrait of a President*, p. 227.
**"Mrs. Eaton"**    Jensen, Amy, *The White House and Its Thirty-Three Families*. New York: McGraw-Hill, 1962, pp. 52–54.
**"as a virgin"**    Ibid., pp. 53–54.
**"Man loves me"**    Remini, *Andrew Jackson and the Course of American Democracy, Volume 3*, p. 60.
**"than it did"**    Ibid.
**"such a thing again"**    Ibid.
**"of insanity"**    Ibid., p. 229.
**"of the city"**    Singleton, *The Story of the White House*, p. 216.
**"emaciated"**    Ibid.
**"nearly exhausted"**    Remini, *Andrew Jackson and the Course of American Democracy, Volume 3*, p. 237.
**"24 hours"**    Ibid., p. 40.
**"without a passage"**    Ibid., p. 238.
**"of blood"**    Ibid., pp. 369–70.
**"black and white"**    Whitney, *The American Presidents*, p. 76.

### Chapter 8.   Martin Van Buren

**"Asiatic mansion"**    Jensen, *The White House and Its Thirty-four Families*, p. 58.
**"finger cups"**    Seale, *The President's House, Volume I*, p. 222.
**"mons sens"**    Jensen, *The White House and Its Thirty-four Families*, p. 59.
**"hominy"**    Ibid. p. 59.
**"Republican self"**    Editors of American Heritage. *The American Heritage Pictorial History of the Presidents of the United States, Volume I*, p. 246.
**"five dollars"**    Steinberg, *First Ten*, p. 374.
**"considerable"**    Ibid., p. 346.
**"all the world"**    Blodgett, *At Home with the Presidents*, p. 62.
**"much larger sum"**    Jensen, *The White House and Its Thirty-four Families*, p. 56.
**"living picture"**    Seale, *The President's House, Volume I*, p. 213.
**"dining-room"**    Ibid., p. 219.
**"as other people do"**    Ibid.
**"I derive from it"**    Blodgett, *At Home with the Presidents*, p. 67.
**"political plans"**    Ibid.

**Chapter 9.   William Henry Harrison**

**"in retirement"**   Boller, *Presidential Wives*, p. 75.
**"elastic step"**   Seale, *The President's House, Volume I*, p. 229.
**"a new bonnet"**   Steinberg, *First Ten*, p. 401.
**"moral philosophy"**   Blodgett, *At Home with the Presidents*, p. 65.
**"common arrangements"**   Singleton, *The Story of the White House*, p. 270.
**"robbing commenced"**   Cleaves, Freeman, *Old Tippecannoe*. Newton, Conn.: APB Press, 1939, p. 333.
**"one of them"**   Steinberg, *First Ten*, p. 401.
**"Clodhopper"**   Ibid., p. 378.
**"positively rabid"**   Ibid., p. 379.
**"I am president"**   Ibid., p. 400.
**"too impetuous"**   Whitney, *The American Presidents*, p. 88.
**"governor of Iowa"**   Steinberg, *First Ten*, pp. 404–05.
**"drive me mad"**   Seale, *The President's House, Volume I*, p. 231.
**"functions of nature"**   Butterfield, Roger, *American Past: A History of the United States from Concord to Hiroshima*. New York: Simon and Schuster, 1947, p. 106.
**"on his steward"**   Singleton, *The Story of the White House*, p. 272.
**"become a pleasure"**   Cleaves, *Old Tippecanoe*, p. 332.
**"across the table"**   Seale, *The President's House, Volume I*, p. 232.
**"palace about it"**   Ibid.
**"a little more"**   Ibid.
**"bilious pleurisy"**   Steinberg, *First Ten*, p. 410.
**"never cease"**   Cleaves, *Old Tippecanoe*, p. 342.
**"they think me"**   DeGregorio, *The Complete Book of United States Presidents*, p. 145.
**"every tongue"**   Seale, *The President's House, Volume I*, p. 236


**Chapter 10.   John Tyler**

**"wholly unquestioned"**   Seager, Robert, *And Tyler Too*. New York: McGraw-Hill, 1963, p. 127.
**"inferior consideration"**   Blodgett, *At Home with the Presidents*, p. 68.
**"Vice-President"**   Seager, *And Tyler Too*, p. 148.
**"flash in the pan"**   Ibid., p. 150.
**"unknown"**   Tally, Steve, *Bland Ambition*. New York: Harcourt Brace Jovanovich, 1992, p. 81.
**"By all means"**   Jeffries, *In and Out of the White House*, p. 115.
**"magnificent distances"**   Ibid.
**"by the English"**   Seager, *And Tyler Too*, p. 173.
**"poor little hand"**   Ibid., p. 176.
**"dried and brushed"**   Ibid., pp. 174–75.
**"new Whigs"**   Ibid., p. 149.
**"adamantine cheek"**   Steinberg, *First Ten*, p. 414.
**"for my administration"**   Ibid.
**"him before me"**   Seager, *And Tyler Too*, p. 53.
**"I shall think proper"**   Ibid., p. 154.
**"courageous action"**   Ibid., p. 156.
**"the Bank Bill"**   Seale, *The President's House, Volume I*, p. 240.
**"caricatured"**   Ibid., pp. 240–41.
**"out of a brothel"**   Seager, *And Tyler Too*, p. 177.
**"on the carpet"**   Jensen, *The White House and Its Thirty-four Families*, pp. 63–64.
**"of the President"**   Seale, *The President's House, Volume I*, p. 244.
**"flock"**   Seager, *And Tyler Too*, p. 208.
**"principal treasure"**   Blodgett, *At Home with the Presidents*, p. 70.
**"prices for everything"**   Seager, *And Tyler Too*, p. 177.
**"echoing with sighs"**   Blodgett, *At Home with the Presidents*, p. 70.
**"thousand compliments"**   Seager, *And Tyler Too*, p. 35.
**"perfect amazement"**   Ibid.
**"of his conversation"**   Ibid.
**"Interestingly sentimental"**   Ibid., p. 192.
**"siege to my heart"**   Ibid.
**"quite a flirtation"**   Ibid., p. 194.
**"truly amazing"**   Steinberg, *First Ten*, p. 71.
**"for a while"**   Seager, *And Tyler Too*, p. 195.
**"brushed his face"**   Smith, Marie, *White House Brides*. Washington, D.C.: Acropolis Books, 1966, p. 71.
**"ransacked every room"**   Seager, *And Tyler Too*, p. 197.
**"proposing point"**   Ibid., p. 196.
**"woman of the age"**   Ibid., p. 7.
**"in my prime"**   Boller, *Presidential Wives*, p. 82.
**"toward the President"**   Seager, *And Tyler Too*, p. 207.
**"position in society"**   Smith, *White House Brides*, p. 73.
**"elegancies of life"**   Seager, *And Tyler Too*, p. 2.
**"repose"**   Ibid., p. 6.
**"any interest to you"**   Ibid., p. 7.
**"President's bride"**   Ibid., p. 8.
**"my heart's content"**   Ibid., p. 8.
**"time kissing"**   Ibid., pp. 9–10.
**"laughed at"**   Ibid., p. 9.
**"in Washington"**   Ibid., p. 10.
**"with me every day"**   Ibid., p. 11.
**"like her looks"**   Ibid.
**"Presidential mansion"**   Healy, Diana Dixon, *America's First Ladies*. New York: Atheneum, 1988, p. 53.
**"talk of Washington"**   Boller, *Presidential Wives*, p. 83.

**"rather vulgar"**    Seager, *And Tyler Too*, p. 107.
**"to see the show"**    Boller, *Presidential Wives*, p. 83.
**"Admiring faces"**    Seager, *And Tyler Too*, p. 260.
**"repeating verses"**    Ibid., p. 246.
**"Already forgotten"**    Seale, *The President's House, Volume I*, p. 236.
**"my public life"**    Seager, *And Tyler Too*, p. 247.
**"sheep in a pen"**    Ibid., p. 261.
**"set of diamonds"**    Ibid., p. 259.
**"without a party"**    Ibid., p. 207.
**"my annexation bill"**    Truman, *First Ladies*, pp. 295–96.


Chapter 11.    James K. Polk

**"any leisure"**    Furman, Bess, *White House Profile.* Indianapolis, Ind.: Bobbs-Merrill, 1951, p. 142.
**"converse about"**    Haynes, Sam W., *James K. Polk.* New York: Longman, 1996, p. 76.
**"who is James K. Polk?"**    Whitney, *American Presidents*, p. 96.
**"fine looking"**    Seale, *The President's House*, p. 250.
**"handsome"**    Ibid., p. 250.
**"but unaffected"**    Singleton, *The Story of the White House*, p. 305.
**"won me entirely"**    Haynes, *James K. Polk*, p. 76.
**"with Mr. Polk"**    Boller, *Presidential Wives*, p. 88.
**"make butter"**    Anthony, Carl Sferrazza. *First Ladies, 1789–1961.* New York: Morrow, 1990, p. 141.
**"of the gospel"**    Boller, *Presidential Wives*, pp. 89–90.
**"select company"**    Furman, *White House Profile*, p. 137.
**"unprofitably spent"**    Ibid., p. 137.
**"Hail to the Chief"**    Seale, *The President's House*, p. 267.
**"boiled ham"**    Furman, *White House Profile*, p. 145.
**"my gravity"**    Bergeron, Paul, *The Presidency of James K. Polk.* Lawrence: University of Kansas Press, 1987, p. 218.
**"grip on me"**    Ibid., p. 226.
**"greatly delighted"**    Ibid., p. 222.
**"than the stars"**    Ibid., p. 223.
**"well pleased"**    Ibid.
**"has visited me"**    Ibid.
**"in this country"**    McCoy, Charles, *Polk and the Presidency.* Austin: University of Texas Press, 1960, p. 73.
**"to subordinates"**    Furman, *White House Profile*, p. 142.
**"my cabinet"**    Ibid., pp. 141–42.
**"of government"**    Bergeron, *The Presidency of James K. Polk*, p. 140.
**"office seekers"**    Ibid., p. 140.
**"should die"**    McCoy, *Polk and the Presidency*, p. 193.
**"nature to be"**    Haynes, *James K. Polk*, p. 77.
**"in great distress"**    Ibid., p. 77.
**"at the house"**    Seale, *The President's House, Volume I*, p. 264.
**"I ever felt"**    Sellers, Charles, *James K. Polk, Continentalist: 1843–1846.* Princeton, N.J.: Princeton University Press, 1966, p. 485.
**"excessive heat"**    Ibid.
**"in order"**    Ibid., p. 309.
**"the great event"**    Hoyt, Edwin P., *James K. Polk.* Chicago: Reilly & Lee, 1965, p. 147.
**"near its close"**    Ibid., p. 1.
**"for my successor"**    Haynes, *James K. Polk*, p. 189.


Chapter 12.    Zachary Taylor

**"public affairs"**    Furman, *White House Profile*, p. 145.
**"and manner"**    Hamilton, Holman, *Zachary Taylor: Soldier in the White House.* Indianapolis, Ind.: Bobs-Merrill, 1951, p. 159.
**"in front of him"**    Ibid.
**"grand affair"**    Ibid.
**"and soul together"**    Ibid., p. 160.
**"stately"**    Ibid., p. 24.
**"and responsibility"**    Holloway, Laura C., *The Ladies of the White House.* Philadelphia: Bradley, 1881, p. 445.
**"any sane person"**    Blodgett, *At Home with the Presidents*, p. 79.
**"about the office"**    Hamilton, *Soldier in the White House*, p. 42.
**"if elected"**    Ibid., p. 51.
**"to go with him"**    Adler, *Presidential Wit*, p. 40.
**"gayest attire"**    Hamilton, *Soldier in the White House*, p. 242.
**"in jeopardy"**    Holland, Barbara, *Hail to the Chiefs.* New York: Ballantine Books, 1990, p. 87.
**"the people"**    Hamilton, *Soldier in the White House*, p. 219.
**"for office"**    Ibid., p. 220.
**"have been outraged"**    McKinley, Silas Bent, and Silas Bent, *Old Rough and Ready: The Life and Times.* New York: Vanguard Press, 1946, p. 286.
**"seriously ill"**    Hamilton, *Soldier in the White House*, p. 388.
**"survive the day"**    Hoyt, *Zachary Taylor*, p. 150
**"leave my friends"**    Seale, *The President's House*, Volume I, p. 288.
**"ZACHARY TAYLOR"**    Hamilton, *Soldier in the White House, Volume 1.* p. 396.


Chapter 13.    Millard Fillmore

**"of the White House"**    Furman, *White House Profile*, p. 155.
**"endure it"**    Blodgett, *At Home with the Presidents*, p. 83.
**"eglantine"**    Hurd, *The White House Story*, p. 133.
**"at a word"**    Blodgett, *At Home with the Presidents*, p. 82.
**"pints of champagne"**    Smith, Elbert B., *The Presidencies of Zachary Taylor and Millard Fillmore.* Lawrence: University of Kansas, 1988, p. 198.
**"of a volcano"**    Blodgett, *At Home with the Presidents*, p. 84.
**"charming society"**    Ibid.

**Chapter 14.    Franklin Pierce**

**"would not either"**    Gara, Larry, *The Presidency of Franklin Pierce.* Lawrence: University of Kansas Press, 1991, p. 33.
**"suitable for others"**    Graff, *The Presidents: A Reference History,* p. 228.
**"anybody but Pierce"**    Blodgett, *At Home with the Presidents,* p. 87.
**"in the evening"**    Minor, Michael, and Larry F. Yrzzalik, "A Study in Tragedy: Jane Means Pierce First Lady (1853–1857) Manuscripts, vol. XL, no. 3, Summer (1988): 182–83.
**"impressed"**    Ibid., p. 183.
**"place of entertainment"**    Seale, *The President's House, Volume I,* p. 315.
**"lace-paper"**    Ibid., p. 312.
**"walk of life"**    Ibid., p. 319.
**"more happiness"**    Boller, *Presidential Wives,* p. 103.
**"if you wish"**    Seale, *The President's House, Volume I,* p. 320.
**"his complaint"**    Nichols, Roy Franklin, *Franklin Pierce: Young Hickory of the Granite Hills.* Philadelphia: University of Pennsylvania Press, 1969, p. 356.
**"ground for him"**    Seale, *The President's House, Volume I,* p. 330.
**"leaving a trace"**    Blodgett, *At Home with the Presidents,* p. 87.


**Chapter 15.    James Buchanan**

**"in the country"**    Boller, *Presidential Anecdotes,* p. 127.
**"small quantities"**    Klein, Philip, *President James Buchanan.* University Park: Pennsylvania State University Press, 1962, p. 275.
**"Majesty"**    Jensen, *The White House and Its Thirty-four Families,* p. 70.
**"in the White House"**    Klein, *President James Buchanan,* p. 350.
**"an hour's walk"**    Seale, *The President's House, Volume I,* p. 335.
**"National Hotel disease."**    Klein, *President James Buchanan,* p. 268.
**"to Providence"**    Seale, *The President's House,* p. 358.
**"as a president"**    Klein, President James Buchanan, p. 340.
**"there before"**    Seale, *The President's House, Volume I,* p. 359.
**"putridity"**    Blodgett, *At Home with the Presidents,* p. 88.


**Chapter 16.    Abraham Lincoln**

**"& unrefined"**    Seale, *The President's House, Volume I,* p. 363.
**"brands recollected"**    Graff, *The Presidents: A Reference History,* p. 35.
**"for looks"**    Ibid., p. 35.
**"magnificent President"**    Means, *The Woman in White House,* p. 114.
**"exceedingly becoming"**    Illinois State Historical Society, Springfield: 1939 Papers in Illinois History (1938): 68.
**"any other occasion"**    Ibid., pp. 69–70.
**"mauling rails"**    *Lincoln Herald,* February 1945, p. 14.
**"on exhibition"**    Boller, *Presidential Wives,* pp. 110–11.
**"Mrs. D.?"**    Keckley, Elizabeth, *Behind the Scenes.* Salem, N.H.: Ayer, 1868, pp. 124–25.
**"from school"**    Ibid., pp. 124–25.
**"don't you?"**    Means, *The Woman in the White House,* p. 106.
**"to the roots"**    Blodgett, *At Home with the Presidents,* p. 100.
**"at your feet"**    *Lincoln Herald,* February 1945, pp. 17–18.
**"cannot have blankets"**    Seale, *The President's House, Volume I,* p. 390.
**"critical curiosity"**    Anthony, *First Ladies, 1789–1961,* p. 174.
**"rich & full"**    Ross, Ishbel, *The President's Wife: Mary Todd Lincoln.* New York: Putnam, 1973, p. 194.
**"long tail tonight"**    Seale, *The President's House,* p. 382.
**"if he is defeated"**    Means, *The Woman in the White House,* p. 105.
**"favor to me"**    Baker, Jean. *Mary Todd Lincoln.* New York: Norton, 1987, p. 194.
**"awful dark"**    Randall, Ruth Painter. *Lincoln's Sons.* Boston: Little, Brown, 1955, p. 96.
**"send you there"**    Means, *The Woman in the White House,* p. 104.
**"this gives me"**    Baker, *Mary Todd Lincoln,* p. 333.
**"curing rock"**    Luthin, Reinhard. *The Real Abraham Lincoln.* Englewood Cliffs, N.J.: Prentice-Hall, 1960, p. 116.
**"of great importance"**    Ross, *The President's Wife: Mary Todd Lincoln,* p. 185.
**"Let him run"**    Randall, *Lincoln's Sons,* pp. 122–23.
**"Sanitary Fund"**    Brooks, Noah. *Washington, D.C. in Lincoln's Time.* Chicago: Quadrangle Books, 1971, pp. 24–28.
**"on the code"**    Kunhardt, Dorothy. *Twenty Days.* New York: Harper & Row, 1965, p. 75.
**"a wildcat"**    Cavanah, *They Lived in the White House,* p. 67.
**"poor Nanny"**    Truman, Margaret. *White House Pets.* New York: David McKay, 1969, p. 61.
**"sent me in any"**    Brooks, *Washington, D.C. in Lincoln's Time,* p. 246.
**"one up this way"**    Ibid., p. 245.
**"entering a cafe"**    Baker, *Mary Todd Lincoln,* p. 199.
**"Send her to me"**    Seale, *The President's House, Volume I,* pp. 409–10.
**"a barn floor"**    Furman, *White House Profile,* p. 176.
**"a man's life"**    *Journal of the Illinois State Historical Society* (1927): 71.
**"woman came in"**    Cottrell, John, *Anatomy of an Assassination.* New York: Funk & Wagnalls, 1966, p. 94.
**"to say 'No.'"**    Ibid., p. 41.
**"unlikely to live"**    Moss, *Presidential Courage,* p. 89.
**"better employed"**    Kunhardt, Philip B. Jr., Philip B. Kunhardt III, and Peter W. Kunhardt, *Lincoln An Illustrated Biography.* New York: Knopf, 1992, p. 278.
**"bristles tonight"**    Keckley, *Behind the Scenes,* pp. 202–03.
**"almost paralyzed"**    Boller, *Presidential Anecdotes,* p. 143.
**"signing this paper"**    Seale, *The President's House, Volume I,* p. 406.
**"plug-hat"**    Cottrell, *Anatomy of an Assassination,* pp. 36–37.
**"able-bodied womam"**    Leech, Margaret, *Reveille in Washington.* New York: Harper, 1941, p. 359.
**"How can they?"**    *Harper's Weekly* (January 1908), p. 12.
**"while they could"**    Ibid., p. 12.
**"will ever make"**    Seale, *The President's House, Volume I,* p. 416.
**"great cheerfulness"**    Ibid., p. 417.

**"very miserable"**    Ibid.
**"over with me"**    Keckley, *Behind the Scenes*, pp. 199–200.
**"waiting for it"**    Cottrell, *Anatomy of an Assassination*, p. 128.
**"place for him"**    Ibid., p. 131.
**"broke my heart"**    Seale, *The President's House, Volume I*, p. xix.


**Chapter 17.    Andrew Johnson**

**"scarce recovered"**    Seale, *The President's House, Volume I*, p. 424.
**"badly used"**    Ibid.
**"called hunger"**    Thomas, Lately, *The First President Johnson*. New York: Morrow, 1968, p. 11.
**"southern traitor"**    Hoyt, Edwin P., *Andrew Johnson*. Chicago: Reilly and Lee, 1965, p. 39.
**"man of the age"**    Blodgett, *At Home with the Presidents*, p. 108.
**"ever known"**    Severn, Bill, *In Lincoln's Footsteps*. New York: Ives Washburn, 1966, p. 133.
**"public life at all"**    Jensen, *The White House and Its Thirty-four Families*, p. 97.
**"their confidence"**    Truman, *White House Pets*, p. 4.
**"clayey soil"**    Seale, *The President's House, Volume I*, p. 427.
**"no drunkard"**    Whitney, *The American Presidents*, p. 145.
**"and a cracker"**    Severn, *In Lincoln's Footsteps*, p. 125.
**"legally President"**    Editors of American Heritage. *The American Heritage Pictorial History of the Presidents of the United States, Volume I*, p. 434.
**"my own grave"**    Ibid., p. 449.
**"children thought"**    Seale, *The President's House, Volume I*, pp. 444–45.
**"air of Tennessee"**    Ibid., p. 447.


**Chapter 18.    Ulysses Grant**

**"I won't go"**    Editors of American Heritage, *The American Heritage Pictorial History of the Presidents of the United States, Volume I*, p. 456.
**"battle did come"**    Blodgett, *At Home with the Presidents*, p. 112.
**"storm a fort"**    Jeffries, *In and Out of the White House*, p. 206.
**"dear old house"**    Seale, *The President's House, Volume I*, p. 455.
**"fellow myself"**    Moss, *Presidential Courage*, p. 70.
**"look at them"**    Grant, Julia Dent, *The Personal Memoirs of Julia Dent Grant*. New York: Putnam, 1975, p. 174.
**"same person"**    Seale, *The President's House, Volume I*, p. 455.
**"on two legs"**    DeGregorio, *The Complete Book of United States Presidents*, p. 259.
**"right at once"**    Reit, *Growing Up in the White House*, pp. 45–46.
**"your daughter"**    Ross, Ishbel, *The General's Wife*. New York: Dodd, Mead, 1956, p. 236.
**"at the floor"**    Butterfield, *American Past: A History of the United States from Concord to Hiroshima*, p. 196.
**"honest fisherman"**    Seale, *The President's House, Volume I*, p. 474.
**"but pleasant"**    Grant, *The Personal Memoirs of Julia Dent Grant*, p. 174.
**"was it then"**    Boller, *Presidential Wives*, p. 143.
**"smooth road"**    Crook, Colonel W. H., *Memories of the White House*. Boston: Little, Brown, 1911, pp. 91–92.
**"do your duty"**    Butterfield, *American Past: A History of the United States from Concord to Hiroshima*, p. 196.
**"and combinations"**    Seale, *The President's House, Volume I*, p. 464.
**"political training"**    Whitney, *The American Presidents*, p. 155.
**"not paralleled"**    Blodgett, *At Home with the Presidents*, p. 110.
**"great efficiency"**    Medved, Michael, *The Shadow Presidents*. New York: Times Books, 1979, p. 50.
**"of the presidency"**    Ross, *The General's Wife*, p. 247.
**"immeasurably happy"**    *The White House: An Historic Guide*. Washington, D.C.: White House Historical Association, 1964, p. 42.
**"deeply injured"**    Boller, *Presidential Wives*, p. 137.
**"Wide commons"**    Ibid.
**"Know where"**    Blodgett, *At Home with the Presidents*, p. 114.


**Chapter 19.    Rutherford B. Hayes**

**"Hold your state"**    Hoogenboom, Ari, *Rutherford B. Hayes: Warrior and President*. Lawrence: University Press of Kansas, 1995, p. 274.
**"similar circumstances"**    Davidson, Kenneth, *The Presidency of Rutherford B. Hayes*. Westport, Conn.: Greenwood Press, 1972, p. 45.
**"Rutherfraud B. Hayes"**    Barnard, Harry, *Rutherford B. Hayes and His America*. Indianapolis, Ind.: Bobs-Merrill, 1954, p. 401.
**"I acquiesced"**    Ibid., p. 404.
**"always calm"**    Davidson, *The Presidency of Rutherford B. Hayes*, p. 70.
**"went to sleep"**    "The Age of Innocence in the White House" *Literary Digest* (February 5, 1927): 27–29.
**"state paper"**    Sadler, *Children in the White House*, p. 185.
**"deal of trouble"**    Geer, Emily Apt, *First Lady Lucy Hayes*. Kent, Ohio: Kent State University Press, 1984, p. 170.
**"young brave"**    Geer, *First Lady Lucy Hayes*, p. 170.
**"first lady"**    Ibid., p. 138.
**"merry as a girl"**    Hoogenboom, *Rutherford B. Hayes: Warrior and President*, p. 347.
**"crepe lisse"**    Ibid.
**"their bonnets"**    Ibid., p. 348.
**"giant among nations"**    "The Age of Innocence in the White House" *Literary Digest* (February 5, 1927): 27–29.
**"like champagne"**    Boller, *Presidential Anecdotes*, p. 286.
**"not an affront"**    Barnard, *Rutherford B. Hayes and His America*, p. 480.
**"painful for me"**    Geer, *First Lady Lucy Hayes*, p. 222.
**"friction as possible"**    Hoogenboom, *Rutherford B. Hayes: Warrior and President*, p. 458.
**"perfectly splendid"**    Ibid., p. 460.
**"pleasing to them"**    Ibid., p. 363.
**"trade generally"**    Davidson, *The Presidency of Rutherford B. Hayes*, p. 212.
**"in the lan'"**    Ibid., p. 80.
**"away next month"**    Williams, T. Harry, ed., *Hayes: The Diary of a President*. New York: David McKay, 1964, p. 243.
**"way of life"**    Ibid., p. 129.
**"Rutherford the Rover"**    Hoogenboom, *Rutherford B. Hayes: Warrior and President*, p. 487.
**"scenery mad"**    Davidson, *The Presidency of Rutherford B. Hayes*, p. 20.
**"or a journey"**    Hoogenboom, *Rutherford B. Hayes: Warrior and President*, p. 346.

**"and toil"**   Boller, *Presidential Anecdotes*, p. 166.
**"than I have had"**   Geer, *First Lady Lucy Hayes*, p. 231.
**"at the door"**   Williams, *Hayes: The Diary of a President*, p. 262.
**"in Spiegel Grove"**   Blodgett, *At Home with the Presidents*, p. 122.

### Chapter 20.   James Garfield

**"in this house"**   Seale, *The President's House, Volume I*, p. 516.
**"like a Greek"**   Caldwell, Robert, *James A. Garfield: Party Chieftan*. Hamden, Conn.: Archon Books, 1965, p. 339.
**"in great force"**   Ibid.
**"without mercy"**   Jensen, *The White House and Its Thirty-four Families*, p. 120.
**"to get into it"**   Boller, *Presidential Anecdotes*, p. 166.
**"sixty minutes"**   Peskin, Allen, *Garfield*. Kent, Ohio: Kent State University Press, 1978, p. 547.
**"he could find"**   Aikman, *The Living White House*, p. 93.
**"delerium of passion"**   Blodgett, *At Home with the Presidents*, p. 123.
**"living"**   Leech, Margaret, and T. Harry Brown, *The Garfield Orbit*. New York: Harper and Row, 1978, p. 585.
**"fire upon him"**   Anthony, *First Ladies, 1789–1961*, pp. 241–42.
**"General at Paris"**   Leech, *The Garfield Orbit*, pp. 240–41.
**"long as you live"**   Peskin, *Garfield*, p. 590.
**"the President was"**   Crook, *Memories of the White House*, p. 152.
**"about either"**   Peskin, *Garfield*, p. 593.
**"act of God"**   Baughman, U. E., *Secret Service Chief*. New York: Harper, 17 1961, p. 61.
**"would go well"**   Donovan, Robert J., *The Assassins*. New York: Harper, 1955, p. 38.
**"removing him"**   Ibid., p. 42.
**"What is this?"**   Peskin, *Garfield*, p. 596.
**"of the U.S."**   Ibid.
**"in this town"**   Ibid.
**"a dead man"**   Ibid.
**"fatal wound"**   Ogilvie, J. S., *History of the Attempted Assassination of James A. Garfield*. New York: J. S. Ogilvie, 1881, p. 57.
**"out of my hands"**   Moss, *Presidential Courage*, p. 113.
**"all reasonable doubt"**   Rosenberg, Charles E., *The Trial of the Assassin Guiteau: Psychiatry and the Law in the Gilded Age*. Chicago: University of Chicago Press, 1968, p. 9.
**"serious complications"**   Smith, T. Burton, *White House Doctor*. Lanham, Md.: Madison Books, 1992, p. 63.
**"probes and catheters"**   Brooks, Stewart M., *Our Assassinated Presidents: The True Medical Stories*. [no city] Bell, 1966, p. 113.
**"shot at him"**   Peskin, *Garfield*, p. 603.
**"only an hour"**   Smith, Theodore Clark, *The Life and Letters of James Abram Garfield, Volume Two: 1877–1882*. Hamden, Conn.: Archon Books, 1968, p. 1172.
**"swam together"**   Graff, *The Presidents: A Reference History*, p. 325.

### Chapter 21.   Chester A. Arthur

**"considered eligible"**   Blodgett, *At Home with the Presidents*, p. 127.
**"Good God!"**   Whitney, *The American Presidents*, p. 171.
**"disturb him"**   Reeves, Thomas, *Gentleman Boss: The Life of Chester Alan Arthur*. New York: Knopf, 1975, p. 247.
**"the nation"**   Seale, *The President's House, Volume I*, p. 544.
**"kept barracks"**   Jeffries, *In and Out of then White House*, p. 227.
**"house like this"**   Furman, *White House Profile*, p. 231.
**"foul matters"**   Seale, *The President's House, Volume I*, pp. 536–37.
**"and formalities"**   Reeves, *Gentleman Boss: The Life of Chester Alan Arthur*, pp. 268–69.
**"might have been"**   Ibid.
**"in the best manner"**   Furman, *White House Profile*, p. 235.
**"dresses fashionably"**   Ibid., p. 235.
**"and worse"**   Reeves, *Gentleman Boss: The Life of Chester Alan Arthur*, p. 271.
**"damned business"**   Anthony, *First Ladies, 1789–1961*, p. 248.
**"where you work"**   Reeves, *Gentleman Boss: The Life of Chester Alan Arthur*, p. 274.
**"snivel service"**   Editors of American Heritage, *The American Heritage Pictorial History of the Presidents of the United States, Volume II*, p. 143.
**"or even Hayes"**   Blodgett, *At Home with the Presidents*, p. 129.
**"the President himself"**   Reeves, *Gentleman Boss: The Life of Chester Alan Arthur*, p. 317.
**"not sick at all"**   Ibid., p. 359.
**"raise big pumpkins"**   Ibid., p. 412.
**"deplorable"**   Ibid., p. 417.
**"as good as new"**   Ibid.

### Chapter 22.   Grover Cleveland

**"all a dream"**   Seale, *The President's House, Volume I*, p. 556.
**"no home at home"**   Blodgett, *At Home with the Presidents*, p. 133.
**"Tell the truth"**   Ibid.
**"their dinner to me"**   Lynch, Dennis, *Grover Cleveland: A Man Four-Square*. New York: Liveright, 1932, p. 321.
**"had in months"**   Ibid.
**"do it well"**   Whitney, *The American Presidents*, p. 175.
**"surrounds me"**   Ibid., p. 180.
**"things in life"**   Durant, John, *The Sports of Our Presidents*. New York: Hastings House, 1964, p. 65.
**"and shameless"**   Ibid., p. 66.
**"of their pursuit"**   Ibid., p. 59.
**"constant grind"**   Seale, *The President's House, Volume I*, p. 561.
**"to be let alone"**   Nevins, Alan, *Grover Cleveland: A Study in Courage*. New York: Dodd, Mead, 1933, p. 308.
**"in the East Room"**   Seale, *The President's House, Volume I*, p. 560.
**"old ladies all the while"**   Butterfield, *American Past: A History of the United States from Concord to Hiroshima*, p. 242.
**"during the day"**   Seale, *The President's House, Volume I*, p. 561.
**"PROVE TRUE"**   Anthony, *First Ladies 1789–1961*, p. 250.
**"Yum-Yum"**   Seale, *The President's House, Volume I*, p. 564.

**"colossal impertinence"**    Cross, *White House Weddings*, p. 131.
**"try anything new"**    Anthony, *First Ladies 1789–1961*, p. 258.
**"and remained such"**    Seale, *The President's House, Volume I*, p. 564.
**"She'll do"**    Ibid., p. 565.
**"at an auction"**    Wolfe, *A Tour of the White House with Mrs. John F. Kennedy*, p. 110.
**"drinking glass"**    Carpenter, Frank C., *Carp's Washington*. New York: McGraw-Hill, 1960, p. 56.
**"unmentiomable garments"**    Wolfe, *A Tour of the White House with Mrs. John F. Kennedy*, p. 110.
**"overturned ashcans"**    Furman, *White House Profile*, p. 243.
**"my daily work"**    Ibid., p. 243.
**"as affectionate as mine"**    Seale, *The President's House, Volume I*, p. 570.
**"right to come in"**    Sadler, *Children in White House*, p. 204.
**"years from today"**    Blodgett, *At Home with the Presidents*, p. 134.
**"more safe in bed"**    Ferrell, Robert, *Ill-Advised Presidential Health and Public Trust*. Columbia: University of Missouri Press, 1992, p. 7.
**"they nearly killed me"**    Ibid., p. 9.
**"entirely to resting"**    Furman, *White House Profile*, p. 257.
**"have more sense"**    Seale, *The President's House, Volume II*, p. 606.
**"from his teeth"**    Ferrell, *Ill-Advised Presidential Health and Public Trust*, p. 8.
**"my life put together"**    Moss, *Presidential Courage*, p. 26.
**"enemies he has made"**    Blodgett, *At Home with the Presidents*, p. 133.
**"rest I crave"**    Ibid., p. 135.
**"above all others"**    Ibid., p. 133.
**"so hard to do right"**    Ibid., p. 137.

### Chapter 23.   Benjamin Harrison

**"public arena"**    Graff, *The Presidents: A Reference History*, p. 296.
**"given us the victory"**    Ibid., p. 299.
**"to do with it"**    Ibid., p. 299.
**"a human iceberg"**    Blodgett, *At Home with the Presidents*, p. 138.
**"a hitching post"**    Sievers, Harry J., *Benjamin Harrison: Hoosier President*. Indianapolis: Bobbs-Merrill, 1968, p. 43.
**"obstinate"**    Blodgett, *At Home with the Presidents*, p. 141.
**"a drudge"**    Ibid., p. 138.
**"lack of accomodations"**    Frank, Sid, and Arden Davis Melick, *The Presidents: Tidbits and Trivia*. New York: Greenwich House, 1984, p. 39.
**"and winter gardens"**    Jensen, *The White House and Its Thirty-four Families*, p. 39.
**"the same way"**    Ibid., p. 139.
**"himself every day"**    Sievers, *Benjamin Harrison: Hoosier President*, p. 207.
**"of the White House"**    Seale, *The President's House, Volume II*, p. 578.
**"in my old age"**    Colman, Edna M., *White House Gossip from Andrew Johnson to Calvin Coolidge*. Garden City, N.Y.: Doubleday Page, 1927, p. 200.
**"any further experience"**    Seale, *The President's House, Volume II*, p. 582.
**"proof against criticism"**    Ibid., p. 599.
**"laid him out"**    Sievers, *Benjamin Harrison: Hoosier President*, p. 54.
**"scampered away"**    Seale, *The President's House, Volume II*, p. 592.
**"I am still alive"**    Ibid., p. 590.
**"we had hoped"**    Sievers, *Benjamin Harrison: Hoosier President*, p. 218.
**"would have bought"**    Ibid., p. 250.

### Chapter 24.   William McKinley

**"than a bishopric"**    Morgan, H. Wayne, *William McKinley and His America*. Syracuse, N.Y.: Syracuse University Press. 1963, pp. 269–70.
**"a saint"**    Blodgett, *At Home with the Presidents*, p. 144.
**"always your lover"**    Leech, Margaret, *In the Days of McKinley*. New York: Harper, 1959, p  28.
**"fainting spells"**    Ibid., p. 433.
**"only in tradition"**    Seale, *The President's House, Volume II*, p. 618.
**"major"**    Leech, *In the Days of McKinley*, p. 28.
**"I want to go too"**    Morgan, *William McKinley and His America*, pp. 524–25.
**"boy of thirteen"**    Kohlsaat, H. H., *From McKinley to Harding*. New York: Scribner, 1923, p. 67.
**"and it worked"**    Ibid., p. 67.
**"hissing sound"**    Boller, *Presidential Wives*, p. 188.
**"after the contact"**    Morgan, *William McKinley and His America*, p. 318.
**"for generations"**    Kohlsaat, *From McKinley to Harding*, p. 63.
**"done about this"**    Morgan, *William McKinley and His America*, pp. 307–08.
**"scum of the city"**    Leech, *In the Days of McKinley*, pp. 129–31.
**"unbonnetted head"**    Ibid., p. 470.
**"a presidential levee"**    Ibid., p. 470.
**"but a fool"**    Ibid., p. 470.
**"over thirty years"**    Kohlsaat, *From McKinley to Harding*, p. 63.
**"out the window"**    Leech, *In the Days of McKinley*, pp. 124–25.
**"see the President smoking"**    Hadley, Arthur T., *Power's Human Face*. New York: Morrow, 1965, p. 128.
**"to see one another"**    Seale, *The President's House, Volume II*, p. 622.
**"chocolate eclair"**    Hadley, *Power's Human Face*, p. 129.
**"other side of the world"**    Leech, *In the Days of McKinley*, p. 345.
**"slept soundly"**    Ibid., p. 345.
**"revolver in his pants"**    Morgan, *William McKinley and His America*, p. 318.
**"Why should I fear?"**    Leech, *In the Days of McKinley*, p. 584.
**"wish to hurt me"**    Ibid., p. 584.
**"know I tried"**    Morgan, *William McKinley and His America*, p. 520.
**"ride, good-bye"**    Leech, *In the Days of McKinley*, p. 590.
**"with the President"**    Donovan, *The Assassins*, p. 104.
**"oh, be careful"**    Boller, *Presidential Wives*, p. 190.
**"I am not sorry"**    Nash, Jay Robert, *Bloodletters and Bad Men*. New York: M. Evans, 1973, pp. 142–43.
**"a deep hole"**    Brooks, *Our Assassinated Presidents*, p. 153.

"monster of death"   Moss, *Presidential Courage,* p. 126.
"not quite so good"   Brooks, *Our Assassinated Presidents,* p. 160.
"to have a prayer"   Morgan, *William McKinley and His America,* pp. 524–25.

**Chapter 25.   Theodore Roosevelt**

"I have enjoyed myself"   Graff, *The Presidents: A Reference History,* p. 386.
"Theodore Roosevelt"   Morris, Edmund, *The Rise of Theodore Roosevelt.* New York: Coward, McCann & Geoghegan, 1979, p. 23.
"make my body"   Ibid., p. 60.
"nothing in the fray"   *The Letters of Archie Butt.* Garden City, N.Y.: Doubleday, Page, 1924, pp. 27–28.
"we will go"   Wagenknecht, Edward, *The Seven Worlds of Theodore Roosevelt.* New York: Longmans, Green, 1950, p. 14.
"of the way back"   Ibid., p. 14.
"we should meet ladies"   Miller, Nathan, *The Roosevelt Chronicle.* Garden City, N.Y.: Doubleday, 1979, p. 259.
"hurt at all"   Collier, Peter, *The Roosevelts.* New York: Simon and Schuster, 1994, p. 128.
"fine little bad boy"   Truman, *First Ladies,* pp. 310–11.
"can't do anything here"   Morris, Sylvia Jukes, *Edith Kermit Roosevelt: Portrait of a First Lady.* New York: Coward, McCann & Geoghegan, 1980, pp. 318–19.
"their own inclinations"   Morris, *Edith Kermit Roosevelt: Portrait of a First Lady,* p. 268.
"whip him"   Ibid., pp. 5–6.
"am dispensing justice"   Looker, Earle, *The White House Gang.* New York: Fleming H. Reeves, 1929, pp. 16–17.
"Bring them to me"   Ibid., pp. 208–210.
"he never bites faces"   Morris, *Edith Kermit Roosevelt: Portrait of a First Lady,* p. 268.
"cannot possibly do both"   Boller, *Presidential Anecdotes,* p. 206.
"Out of my life forever"   Whitney, *The American Presidents,* p. 207.
"to buy readymade"   Felsenthal, Carol, *Alice Roosevelt Longworth.* New York: Putnam, 1988, p. 3.
"under my roof"   Teichmann, Howard. *The Life and Times of Alice Roosevelt Longworth.* Englewood Cliffs, N.J.: Prentice-Hall, 1979, p. 56.
"in great disgrace"   Brough, James, *Princess Alice.* Boston: Little, Brown, 1975, p. 162.
"grounds for divorce"   Felsenthal, *Alice Roosevelt Longworth,* p. 59.
"underbelly of a fish"   Ibid., p. 60.
"anything but trouble"   Ibid.
"I regret it"   Ibid.
"until it was all over"   *Taft and Roosevelt: The Intimate Letters of Archie Butt, Volume I.* Garden City, N.Y.: Doubleday, Doran, 1930, p. 122.
"slops, etc"   Harbaugh, William H., *Pine Knot 1905–1908: The Theodore Roosevelt Retreat in Southern Albemarle.* Theodore Roosevelt Association Manuscript (May 13, 1993): 11.
"as daylight lasted"   Ibid., p. 170.
"quickly as I did"   Morris, *Edith Kermit Roosevelt: Portrait of a First Lady,* pp. 292–94.
"so declare it"   Harbaugh, *Pine Knot 1905–1908: The Theodore Roosevelt Retreat in Southern Albemarle,* p. 28.
"marriage license"   Morris, *The Rise of Theodore Roosevelt,* p. 11.
"making it this time"   Wilson, Dorothy Clark, *Alice and Edith: The Two Wives of Theodore Roosevelt.* Garden City, N.Y.: Doubleday, 1989, p. 312.
"two dinner plates"   Wagenknecht, *The Seven Worlds of Theodore Roosevelt,* pp. 28–29.
"the front wheel"   Ibid., p. 380.
"damaged the bone"   Morris, *Edith Kermit Roosevelt: Portrait of a First Lady,* pp. 224–5.
"valiant trencherman"   Miller, *The Roosevelt Chronicle,* p. 26.
"nature of a bathtub"   Wagenknecht, *The Seven Worlds of Theodore Roosevelt,* p. 26.
"in the White House"   Morris, *Edith Kermit Roosevelt: Portrait of a First Lady,* pp. 264–65.
"shock the multitude"   Ibid., p. 245.
"over the store"   Ibid., p. 222.
"at Oyster Bay"   Ibid., p. 277.
"Only killed two"   Russell, Thomas H., *Life and Work of Theodore Roosevelt.* New York: The Free Press, 1919, pp. 224–05.
"through the windows"   Morris, *The Rise of Theodore Roosevelt,* p. 181.
"drop on me"   Morris, *Edith Kermit Roosevelt: Portrait of a First Lady,* pp. 292–94.
"lawless mind"   Wagenknecht, *The Seven Worlds of Theodore Roosevelt,* p. 10.
"toward church"   Letter to Ethel, June 24, 1906. John F. Kennedy Library Lectures, Boston (August 1998).
"terror-stricken panic"   Morris, *Edith Kermit Roosevelt: Portrait of a First Lady,* p. 294.
"irritate him"   Ibid., p. 294.

**Chapter 26.   William Howard Taft**

"at the White House"   Anthony, *First Ladies 1789–1961,* p. 227.
"president of the United States"   Anderson, Judith, *William Howard Taft: An Intimate History.* New York: Norton, 1981, pp. 48–49.
"make it the presidency"   Gardner, Joseph L., *Departing Glory Theodore Roosevelt as ex-President.* New York: Scribner, 1973, pp. 88–89.
"convention-going type"   Blodgett, *At Home with the Presidents,* p. 158.
"he loves the law"   Whitney, *The American Presidents,* p. 221.
"inexpressibly happy"   Means, *The Woman in the White House,* p. 118.
"President of the United States"   Anderson, *William Howard Taft: An Intimate History,* p. 120.
"being kicked around"   Brinkley, David, *Washington Goes to War.* New York: Knopf, 1988, p. 41.
"of his entire life"   Anderson, *William Howard Taft: An Intimate History,* p. 255.
"that table over there"   Anthony, *First Ladies 1789–1961,* p. 306.
"at the White House door"   Anderson, *William Howard Taft: An Intimate History,* p. 156.
"exactly as she pleases"   Anthony, *First Ladies 1789–1961,* p. 314.
"Japaneses art"   Busby, Katherine Graves, "Mrs. Taft's Home-Making" Good Housekeeping (June 1913): pp. 347–49.
"built-for-comfort home"   Ibid.
"dictating to you"   Ibid.
"than one imagines"   Anderson, *William Howard Taft: An Intimate History,* p. 26.
"expecting to see Roosevelt"   Seale, *The President's House, Volume II,* p. 739.
"as anything else"   *Taft and Roosevelt: The Intimate Letters of Archie Butt, Volume I,* p. 14.
"even talk about it"   Seale, *The President's House, Volume II,* p. 739.
"of anything else"   *Taft and Roosevelt: The Intimate Letters of Archie Butt, Volume II,* p. 350.
"act the gentleman"   *Taft and Roosevelt: The Intimate Letters of Archie Butt, Volume I,* p. 92.
"off for golf"   Anderson, *William Howard Taft: An Intimate History,* p. 120.
"get in a game"   *Taft and Roosevelt: The Intimate Letters of Archie Butt, Volume II,* p. 731.
"to see this fellow"   *Taft and Roosevelt: The Intimate Letters of Archie Butt, Volume I,* p. 460.

**"a boy of ten"**    *Taft and Roosevelt: The Intimate Letters of Archie Butt, Volume II*, p. 731.

**"get another opportunity"**    Anderson, *William Howard Taft: An Intimate History*, pp. 33–34.

**"at the head of it"**    Ibid., pp. 33–34.

**"no business while away"**    *Taft and Roosevelt: The Intimate Letters of Archie Butt, Volume I*, p. 54.

**"periodic sprees"**    Ibid., pp. 240–43.

**"the machine sing"**    Ibid., p. 721.

**"standpatters"**    *Taft and Roosevelt: The Intimate Letters of Archie Butt, Volume II*, p. 702.

**"a diner on it"**    Smith, Ira R. T., *Dear Mr. President: The Story of Fifty Years in the White House Mail Room.* New York: Messner, 1949, p. 68.

**"cream and sugar"**    Jaffray, Elizabeth, *Secrets of the White House.* New York: Cosmopolitan Book, 1927, p. 31.

**"imposed on me"**    Ibid., p. 31.

**"everybody around him"**    Anderson, Donald F. *William Howard Taft: A Conservative's Conception of the Presidency.* Ithaca, N.Y.: Cornell University Press, 1973, p. 126.

**"attack of illness"**    Anthony, *First Ladies 1789–1961*, p. 324.

**"entirely from the press"**    *Taft and Roosevelt: The Intimate Letters of Archie Butt, Volume I*, p. 92.

**"stole these for you"**    Means, *The Woman in the White House*, p. 130.

**"under my orders"**    *Taft and Roosevelt: The Intimate Letters of Archie Butt, Volume I*, pp. 97–98.

**"take a try at it"**    Ibid., pp. 220–21.

**"where I live"**    Ibid., pp. 240–43.

**"all outdoors"**    Anderson, *William Howard Taft: A Conservative's Conception of the Presidency*, pp. 159–61.

**"such profligacy"**    Manners, William. *TR and Will.* New York: Harcourt, Brace and World, 1969, pp. 197–98.

**"buried in silver"**    Ibid., pp. 197–98.

**"Scandinavia"**    Jeffries, *In and Out of the White House*, p. 292.

**"next four years"**    *Taft and Roosevelt: The Intimate Letters of Archie Butt, Volume I*, p. 161.

**"corner will fight"**    Anderson, *William Howard Taft: A Conservative's Conception of the Presidency*, p. 232.

**"hope Wilson will"**    Ibid., p. 258.

**"did not believe me"**    Anthony, *First Ladies 1789–1961*, p. 333.

**"place in the world"**    Walworth, Arthur, *Woodrow Wilson.* New York: Norton, 1978, p. 283.

## Chapter 27.   Woodrow Wilson

**"to the White House today"**    Walworth, Arthur, *Woodrow Wilson.* New York: Norton, 1978, p. 262.

**"President of the United States"**    Boller, *Presidential Anecdotes*, p. 217.

**"power of religion"**    Whitney, *The American Presidents*, p. 227.

**"Jesus Christ"**    Koenig, Louis W., *The Invisible Presidency.* New York: Rhinehart, 1960, pp. 214–15.

**"impassive and lifeless"**    Smith, Page, *America Enters the World: A People's History of the Progressive Era and World War I.* New York: McGraw-Hill, 1985, p. 312.

**"being amused"**    Walworth, *Woodrow Wilson*, p. 312.

**"good-looking ladies"**    Starling, Colonel Edmund W. *Starling of the White House.* New York: Simon and Schuster, 1936, pp. 104–05.

**"my chief pleasure"**    Tribble, Edwin, ed., *A President in Love: The Courtship Letters of Woodrow Wilson and Edith Bolling Galt.* Boston: Houghton Mifflin, 1981, p. xvii.

**"admiring females"**    Miller, *Scandals in the Highest Office*, p. 193.

**"will be assailed"**    Anthony, *First Ladies 1789–1961*, p. 344.

**"in the nose"**    Bell, Jack. *The Splendid Misery.* Garden City, N.Y.: Doubleday, 1950, p. 299.

**"but man to man"**    Gwynne-Thomas, *The Presidential Families*, p. 293.

**"Secretary of the Treasury"**    Ibid., p. 291.

**"no heart"**    Anthony, *First Ladies 1789–1961*, p. 350.

**"meet your fate"**    Ross, Ishbel, *Power with Grace.* New York: Putnam, 1975, p. 34.

**"About ten minutes"**    Seale, *The President's House, Volume II*, pp. 794–95.

**"carries with her"**    Weinstein, Edwin A. *Woodrow Wilson: A Medical and Psychological Biography.* Princeton, N.J.: Princeton University Press, 1981, p. 282.

**"as soon as can be"**    Hatch, Alden, *Woodrow Wilson: A Life.* New York: Henry Holt, 1947, pp. 164–67.

**"live without you"**    Starling, Colonel Edmund W., *Starling of the White House*, p. 56.

**"beautiful doll"**    Ibid., pp. 61–62.

**"into the Blue Room"**    Wilson, Edith Bolling. *My Memoir.* Indianapolis: Bobbs-Merrill, 1939, p. 92.

**"what I have written"**    Ibid., pp. 91–92.

**"detestable suffragettes"**    Means, *The Woman in the White House*, p. 154.

**"express his admiration"**    Weinstein, *Woodrow Wilson: A Medical and Psychological Biography*, p. 294.

**"more than ever"**    Ibid., p. 294.

**"is often lacking"**    Medved, *The Shadow Presidents*, p. 142.

**"help me and others"**    Koenig, *The Invisible Presidency*, pp. 214–15.

**"common bathroom"**    Medved, *The Shadow Presidency*, p. 148.

**"friend in all the world"**    Ibid., p. 137.

**"papers without question"**    Ibid., p. 147.

**"what people wanted"**    Hoover, Irwin, *Forty-Two Years in the White House.* Boston: Houghton Mifflin, 1934, p. 267.

**"a thousand dollars"**    Weinstein, *Woodrow Wilson: A Medical and Psychological Biography*, p. 372.

**"must observe the laws"**    Grayson, Cary, *Woodrow Wilson: An Intimate Memoir.* Washington, D.C.: Potomac Books, 1947, p. 48.

**"use a short swing"**    Doran, George H., *The True Story of Woodrow Wilson.* New York: George H. Doran, 1924, p. 247.

**"ill-adapted for the purpose"**    Tribble, *A President in Love: The Courtship Letters of Woodrow Wilson and Edith Bolling Galt*, pp. 112–13.

**"you to call on me"**    Schachtman, Tom, *Edith & Woodrow.* New York: Putnam, 1981, p. 104.

**"hit it often enough"**    Wilson, *My Memoir*, p. 108.

**"done up in pajamas"**    Ross, *Power with Grace*, p. 128.

**"rather a poor seat"**    Starling, *Starling of the White House*, pp. 89–91.

**"getting away that time"**    Smith, Merriman, *The Good New Days.* Indianapolis: Bobbs-Merrill, 1962, pp. 52–54.

**"ordinary citizen"**    Starling, *Starling of the White House*, p. 110.

**"sneak out the back way"**    Ibid.

**"jerked him back"**    Ibid.

**"game of golf I had"**    Weinstein, *Woodrow Wilson: A Medical and Psychological Biography*, p. 295

**"It may kill you"**    Means, *The Woman in the White House*, p. 161.

**"digestive upset"**    Ibid., p. 162.

**"the affairs of state"**    Crispell, Kenneth R., and Carlos Gomez, *Hidden Illnesses in the White House.* Durham, N.C.: Duke University Press, 1988, pp. 73–74.

**"an open wound"**    Means, *The Woman in the White House*, p. 136.

**"before the illness came"**    Crispell, *Hidden Illnesses in the White House*, pp. 73–74.

**"Mr. Harding's English"**  Smith, *America Enters the World: A People's History of the Progressive Era and World War I*, p. 805.
**"seven gramatical errors"**  Shenkman, Richard, and Kurt Reiger, *One Night Stands with American History.* New York: Morrow, 1980, p. 216.


## Chapter 28.   Warren G. Harding

**"into the water"**  Lee, Charles L., Jr., *The Ohio Gang: The World of Warren G. Harding.* New York: M. Evans, 1981, p. 79.
**"anything he wants from me"**  Miller, *Scandals in the Highest Office*, p. 210.
**"written in the stars"**  Russell, Francis, *The Shadow of Blooming Grove.* New York: McGraw-Hill, 1968, p. 259.
**"abide by the result"**  Graff, *The Presidents: A Reference History*, p. 392.
**"to do with it"**  Means, *The Woman in the White House*, p. 166.
**"nothing to think with"**  Heckscher, August, *Woodrow Wilson.* New York: Macmillan, 1981, p. 668.
**"as to the house"**  Wilson, *My Memoir*, p. 316.
**"this is Mrs, Jaffray"**  Jaffray, *Secrets of the White House*, p. 78.
**"thrown over the arm"**  Wilson, *My Memoir*, p. 316.
**"it's their White House"**  Russell, *The Shadow of Blooming Grove*, p. 437.
**"only fun I have"**  Ibid. pp. 437–38.
**"tobacco is all right"**  Graff, *The Presidents: A Reference History*, p. 394.
**"undignified to chew"**  Russell, *The Shadow of Blooming Grove*, p. 52.
**"names the stakes"**  Ibid., p. 435.
**"Wednesday night"**  Adams, Samuel Hopkins, *Incredible Era: The Life and Times of Warren Gamaliel Harding.* Boston: Houghton Mifflin, 1939, p. 214.
**"every poker game"**  Starling, *Starling of the White House*, p. 188.
**"spittoons along side"**  Lee, *The Ohio Gang: The World of Warren G. Harding*, p. 108.
**"have a drink"**  Adams, *Incredible Era: The Life and Times of Warren Gamaliel Harding*, p. 192.
**"as we like it here"**  Ibid.
**"That's all"**  Russell, *The Shadow of Blooming Grove*, p. 461.
**"hell out of them"**  Starling, *Starling of the White House*, p. xviii.
**"just a slob"**  Ross, Ishbel, *Grace Coolidge and Her Era.* New York: Dodd, Mead, 1962, p. 90.
**"men like that"**  Jaffray, *Secrets of the White House*, p. 81.
**"real forceful like"**  Russell, *The Shadow of Blooming Grove*, p. 438.
**"somebody else's way"**  Starling, *Starling of the White House*, p. 191.
**"for twenty years"**  Graff, *The Presidents: A Reference History*, p. 197.
**"Marionite again"**  Ibid.
**"never have been here"**  Russell, *The Shadow of Blooming Grove*, p. 453.
**"I have ever met"**  Adams, *Incredible Era: The Life and Times of Warren Gamaliel Harding*, p. 215.
**"sixty cups"**  Jaffray, *Secrets of the White House*, pp. 88–89.
**"lady's maid"**  Hoover, *Forty-two Years in the White House*, p. 235.
**"lately, dearie"**  Hunt, Irma, *Dearest Madame: The President's Mistresses.* New York: McGraw-Hill, 1978, p. 137.
**"another job"**  Smith, *Dear Mr. President: The Story of Fifty Years in the White House Mail Room*, p. 111.
**"sweetheart made love"**  Russell, *The Shadow of Blooming Grove*, pp. 465–67.
**"special watchman"**  Hoover, *Forty-two Years in the White House*, p. 235.
**"of the President"**  Truman, *First Ladies*, p. 40.
**"life hell for me"**  Ibid.
**"got to stay"**  Russell, *The Shadow of Blooming Grove*, p. 185.
**"can describe it"**  Ibid.
**"President of the United States"**  Mitchell, Jack, *Executive Privilege.* New York: Hippocene, 1992, p. 156.
**"walking the floor nights"**  Sinclair, Andrew, *The Available Man: Warren Gamaliel Harding.* New York: Macmillan, 1965, p. 83.
**"gastrointestinal attack"**  Murray, Robert K., *The Harding Era.* Minneapolis: University of Minnesota Press, 1969, pp. 448–49.
**"barring complications"**  Marx, Rudolph, M.D., *The Health of Presidents.* New York: Putnam, 1960, p. 25.
**"That's good"**  Russell, *The Shadow of Blooming Grove*, p. 385.


## Chapter 29.   Calvin Coolidge

**"its most practical form"**  Quint, Howard H., and Robert H. Perrell, eds., *The Talkative President: Calvin Coolidge.* Amherst: University of Massachusetts Press, 1964, p. 102.
**"within your means"**  Fuess, Claude Moore, *Calvin Coolidge, The Man from Vermont.* Boston: Little, Brown, 1948, p. 267.
**"cheep veep"**  Anthony, *First Ladies 1789–1961*, p. 388.
**"plenty good enough for"**  Ross, Ishbel, *Sons of Adam, Daughters of Eve.* New York: Harper & Row, 1969, pp. 72–73.
**"in a home like that"**  Ibid.
**"centered here for a time"**  Wikander, Lawrence E. and Robert H. Ferrell, eds., *Grace Coolidge, An Autobiography.* Worland, Wyo.: High Plains Publishing, 1992, The Calvin Coolidge Memorial Foundation, pp. 60–61.
**"a new President's arrival"**  Hoover, *Forty-two Years in the White House*, pp. 245–46.
**"somebody familiar around"**  Fuess, *Calvin Coolidge: The Man from Vermont*, p. 323.
**"else can do for you"**  Hunt, *Dearest Madame: The President's Mistresses*, p. 147.
**"New Secretary of Labor"**  Starling, *Starling of the White House*, p. 209.
**"know too much"**  Barton, Bruce, "The Real Calvin Coolidge," magazine clipping c. 1933, Forbes Library, Northampton, Mass.
**"government is diminished"**  Ibid.
**"your bedtime, Calvin?"**  Ross, Ishbel, *Grace Coolidge and Her Era.* New York: Dodd, Mead, 1962, p. 65.
**"he shook their hands"**  Coolidge, Calvin, *The Autobiography of Calvin Coolidge.* New York: Cosmopolitan Book Company, 1931, pp. 201–02.
**"all the talking yourself"**  Ross, *Grace Coolidge and Her Era*, p. 108.
**"no questions today"**  Quint, Howard H., and Robert H. Ferrell, eds., *The Talkative President: Calvin Coolidge.* Amherst: University of Massachusetts Press, 1964, p. 26.
**"I could never find out"**  White, William Allen, *A Puritan in Babylon: The Story of Calvin Coolidge.* Macmillan, 1938, p. 416.
**"like they have downstairs"**  Ross, *Grace Coolidge and Her Era*, p. 104.
**"small domestic affairs"**  Furman, *White House Profile*, p. 306.
**"of course, ridiculous"**  Ibid.
**"dressing room and bath"**  Ellen Riley correspondence, collection of the Vermont Division for Historic Preservation, President Calvin Coolidge State Historic Site.
**"all there is to it"**  Ibid.
**"ice-less refrigeration"**  Ibid.
**"as solemn as he looks"**  Ibid.
**"and leave them"**  Latham, Edward, ed., *Meet Calvin Coolidge.* Brattleboro, Vt.: Stephen Greene Press, 1960, p. 76.

**"without a word"**  Starling, *Starling of the White House*, p. 208.
**"taste like liver"**  Lindup, Edmund, and Joseph Jares, *White House Sportsmen*. Boston: Houghton Mifflin, 1964, p. 72.
**"he had to sit down"**  Starling, *Starling of the White House*, pp. 237–38.
**"a couple of kids"**  Ibid.
**"New England apple pie"**  Ibid., pp. 243–45.
**"information promiscuously"**  Waldrop, Carole, *Presidents' Wives*, Jefferson, N.C.: McFarland, 1989, p. 266.
**"but I am ready"**  Ross, *Grace Coolidge and Her Era*, p. 99.
**"success in Washington"**  Ibid.
**"in the East Room"**  Letter to Mrs. Adams, August 24, 1923, collection of Forbes Library, Northampton, Mass.
**"knows and remembers"**  New York Times Magazine, March 27, 1927.
**"sizing everything up"**  Ross, *Grace Coolidge and Her Era*, p. 194.
**"will going to sleep"**  Ibid.
**"more either on or out"**  Ibid.
**"try anything new"**  Boller, *Presidential Wives*, p. 261.
**"the better he liked it"**  Ross, *Grace Coolidge and Her Era*, pp. 144–45.
**"Where's the trimmings"**  Ibid.
**"cart wheel in the bargain"**  Ibid.
**"Yes"**  Ibid., p. 68.
**"keeping me to course"**  Ibid., p. 58.
**"present and the past"**  "Mrs. Calvin Coolidge, A Coverlet for the Ages," *New York Herald Tribune*, February 12, 1928.
**"and now wish I had"**  Ibid.
**"a beginning was made"**  Ibid.
**"horrible and frightful"**  Ibid.
**"the top of his head"**  Letter to Mrs. Carl Medinus, July 5, 1929, collection, Forbes Library, Northampton, Mass.
**"stretch his long legs"**  Ibid.
**"in his head astray"**  Ibid.
**"score one for the panic artists"**  Ibid.
**"tweak the ear"**  Mrs. Calvin Coolidge, "Our Family Pets," *The American Magazine*, December 1929, p. 146.
**"we'd dye the dog"**  Ross, *Grace Coolidge and Her Era*, p. 152.
**"suck an egg"**  Riley correspondence.
**"in the drawing room"**  Ross, *Grace Coolidge and Her Era*, p. 56.
**"I could not"**  White, *A Puritan in Babylon*, p. 308.
**"we surrender"**  Ross, *Grace Coolidge and Her Era*, p. 120.
**"went with him"**  White, *A Puritan in Babylon*, p. 308.
**"line forms to the left"**  McCoy, Donald, *Calvin Coolidge: The Quiet President*. New York: Macmillan, 1967, p. 384.
**"for President in nineteen . . ."**  Ibid.
**"in the office this morning"**  Ross, *Grace Coolidge and Her Era*, p. 223.
**"I had no idea"**  Boller, *Presidential Wives*, p. 262.
**"over 150 boxes"**  Quint, *The Talkative President: Calvin Coolidge*, p. 18.
**"saved so much money"**  Furman, *White House Profile*, p. 306.
**"minding my own business"**  Quint, *The Talkative President: Calvin Coolidge*, p. 19.


**Chapter 30.   Herbert Hoover**

**"he isn't worth much"**  Graff, *The Presidents: A Reference History*, p. 415.
**"of the United States"**  Editors of American Heritage, *The American Heritage Pictorial History of the Presidents of the United States*, Volume II, p. 767.
**"from among us"**  DeGregorio, *The Complete Book of United States Presidents*, p. 468.
**"car in every garage"**  Ibid., p. 470.
**"bright with hope"**  Smith, Richard Norton, *An Uncommon Man: The Triumph of Herbert Hoover*. New York: Simon and Schuster, 1986, p. 107.
**"New England barn"**  Blodgett, *At Home with the Presidents*, p. 266.
**"willies"**  Seale, *The President's House*, Volume II, p. 905.
**"coast to be clear"**  Parks, Lillian, *My Thirty Years Backstairs at the White House*. New York: Fleet Publishing, 1961, p. 43.
**"just act natural"**  Ibid., p. 44.
**"be the one to suffer"**  Smith, *An Uncommon Man: The Triumph of Herbert Hoover*, p. 103.
**"on our guests"**  Ibid., p. 110.
**"an appointment with me"**  Hoover, *Forty-two Years in the White House*, p. 315.
**"social contacts"**  Lyons, Eugene, *Our Unknown Ex-President: A Portrait of Herbert Hoover*. Garden City, N.Y.: 1948, p. 23.
**"what you feel inside"**  Anthony, *First Ladies 1789–1961*, p. 442.
**"face she wears"**  Furman, *White House Profile*, pp. 57–60.
**"than Hoover"**  Mead, William, and Paul Dickson, *Baseball: The President's Game*. Washington, D.C.: Farragut, 1993, p. 59.
**"step out of character"**  Barber, James David, *The Presidential Character: Predicting Performance at the White House*. Englewood Cliffs, N.J.: Prentice-Hall, 1972, p. 69.
**"pure air"**  Lindup, *White House Sportsmen*, p. 70.
**"permission to smoke"**  Smith, *An Uncommon Man: The Triumph of Herbert Hoover*, p. 55.
**"his awful habit"**  Barber, *The Presidential Character: Predicting Performance at the White House*, p. 98.
**"benefit of the guests"**  Parks, *My Thirty Years Backstairs at the White House*, p. 221.
**"have people around him"**  Smith, *An Uncommon Man: The Triumph of Herbert Hoover*, p. 34.
**"like waging a war"**  Smith, Gene, *The Shattered Dream*. New York: Morrow, 1970, p. 102.
**"a compound hell"**  Smith, *An Uncommon Man: The Triumph of Herbert Hoover*, p. 132.
**"with it anymore"**  Truman, *First Ladies*, p. 272.
**"like Mr. Hoover does?"**  Barber, *The Presidential Character: Predicting Performance at the White House*, p. 49.
**"into the kitchens"**  Boller, *Presidential Wives*, p. 49.
**"rather difficult"**  Roosevelt, James, and Sidney Shalett, *Affectionately, FDR*. New York: Harcourt, Brace, 1959, p. 252.
**"waits for no one"**  Ibid.
**"gibbering idiot"**  Smith, *An Uncommon Man: The Triumph of Herbert Hoover*, p. 52.
**"overcome the depression"**  Whitney, *The American Presidents*, p. 259.


**Chapter 31.   Franklin D. Roosevelt**

**"United States"**  Morgan, Ted, *FDR: A Biography*. New York: Simon and Schuster, 1985, p. 43.
**"wouldn't anybody?"**  Goodwin, Doris Kearns, "The Home Front," *The New Yorker* (August 15, 1994): 38–61.

**"name in the family"**   Cooke, Blanche Weisen, *Eleanor Roosevelt, Volume I 1884–1933.* New York: Viking, 1992, p. 166.
**"Miss Eleanor"**   Seale, *The President's House, Volume II*, p. 915.
**"out of your arms"**   Lippman, Theo, Jr. *The Squire of Warm Springs.* Chicago: Playboy Press, 1977, p. 63.
**"suspected his condition"**   Ibid.
**"was really paralyzed"**   Gilbert, Robert E., *The Mortal Presidency.* New York: Basic Books, 1992, p. 49.
**"stand up if I had to"**   Roosevelt, *Affectionately, FDR*, p. 155.
**"get all these people"**   Miller, Nathan, *FDR: An Intimate History.* Garden City, N.Y.: Doubleday, 1948, p. 358.
**"a junk heap"**   Ibid., p. 265.
**"kind of a joint is this?"**   Ibid.
**"the President's wife"**   Miller, *FDR: An Intimate History*, p. 358.
**"I am his niece"**   Roosevelt, Eleanor, *This I Remember.* New York: Harper, 1949, p. 121.
**"do what is expected of me"**   Hickok, Lorena, *Eleanor Roosevelt: Reluctant First Lady.* New York: Dodd, Mead, 1962, p. 176.
**"first awkward moments"**   Seale, *The President's House, Volume II*, p. 936.
**"did everything for me"**   Miller, *The Roosevelt Chronicle*, p. 268.
**"than your mother is"**   Ibid., p. 270.
**"running establishment"**   Seale, *The President's House, Volume II*, 930.
**"I'll run mine"**   Anthony, *First Ladies 1789–1961*, p. 471.
**"Relished them, too"**   Nesbitt, Henrietta, *White House Diary.* Garden City, N.Y.: Doubleday, 1948, p. 62.
**"through the fur"**   Ibid., p. 22.
**"rats day and night"**   Ibid., p. 83.
**"sprouts or carrots"**   Ibid., p. 62.
**"unskilled admirer"**   Miller, *FDR: An Intimate History*, p. 356.
**"Automat"**   West, J. B., *Upstairs at the White House.* New York: Coward, McCann and Geoghegan, 1973, p. 28.
**"foods plainly prepared"**   Goodwin, Doris Kearns, "The Home Front," *The New Yorker* (August 15, 1994): 38–61.
**"creamed chipped beef"**   Nesbitt, *White House Diary*, p. 66.
**"unsweet"**   Parks, *My Thirty Years Backstairs at the White House*, p. 244.
**"tired of it"**   Tully, Grace, *F.D.R. My Boss.* New York: Scribners, 1949, p. 116.
**"for all those people"**   Goodwin, Doris Kearns, *No Ordinary Time.* New York: Simon and Schuster, 1994, p. 572.
**"should like it"**   Ibid., p. 199.
**"United States"**   Nesbitt, *White House Diary*, p. 63.
**"not to be found in Washington"**   Tully, *F.D.R. My Boss*, pp. 115–16.
**"old lady Nesbitt"**   West, *Upstairs at the White House*, p. 28.
**"HAS TO BE DONE"**   Harrity, Richard, and Ralph G. Martin, *The Human Side of FDR.* New York: Duell, Sloan and Pearce, 1960, p. 192.
**"quite make it on this"**   Tully, *F.D.R. My Boss*, p. 114.
**"sort of slimy"**   Fields, Alonzo, *My 21 Years in the White House.* New York: Coward-McCann, 1961, p. 58.
**"does my mother"**   Roosevelt, *Affectionately, FDR*, p. 323.
**"dishes were broken"**   Ibid.
**"life of any sort"**   Friedel, Frank, *Franklin D. Roosevelt: The Apprenticeship.* Boston: Little, Brown, 1952, p. 3.
**"a lot of gangsters"**   Reilly, Michael, *Reilly of the White House.* New York: Simon and Schuster, 1947, p. 82.
**"President for?"**   Ibid., p. 83–84.
**"get a sweater"**   Bishop, Jim, *FDR's Last Year.* New York: Morrow, 1974, p. 43.
**"behind in his mail"**   Gunther, John, *Roosevelt in Retrospect.* New York: Harper, 1950, p. 165.
**"he stood up"**   "The White House," *Life* (October 30, 1992): 76.
**"I'm lonely"**   Goodwin, *No Ordinary Time*, p. 37.
**"Stay the night"**   Ibid.
**"down to dinner"**   Medved, *The Shadow Presidents*, p. 212–13.
**"his own opinion"**   Ibid., p. 198.
**"except to serve you"**   Ibid.
**"for her and others"**   Roosevelt, Elliott, and James Brough, *A Rendezvous with Destiny: The Roosevelts of the White House.* New York: Putnam, 1975, pp. 45–46.
**"see what I see?"**   Morgan, *FDR: A Biography*, p. 549.
**"to his stamps"**   McIntire, Vice-Admiral Ross T., *White House Physician.* New York: Putnam, 1946, pp. 78–79.
**"would be better"**   Miller, *FDR: An Intimate History*, p. 357.
**"a stamp collector"**   Ibid., p. 78–79.
**"dilapidated"**   Seale, *The President's House, Volume II*, p. 924.
**"horrible scene"**   Ward, Geoffrey, *Closest Companion.* Boston: Houghton Mifflin, 1995, p. 629.
**"bar none"**   Reilly, *Reilly of the White House*, p. 16.
**"rebuilding"**   Seale, *The President's House, Volume II*, p. 945.
**"to take a nap"**   Gallagher, Hugh Gregory, *FDR's Splendid Deception.* New York: Dodd, Mead, 1985, p. 89.
**"at the White House"**   Roosevelt, *Affectionately, FDR*, p. 346.
**"standing near Father"**   Ibid., p. 346.
**"always follows him"**   Leuchtanburg, William, ed. *Franklin D. Roosevelt: A Profile.* New York: Hill and Wang, 1967, pp. 52–53.
**"where they are?"**   Starling, *Starling of the White House*, p. 311.
**"shot each day"**   Anthony, *First Ladies 1789–1961*, p. 465.
**"cannot hit a barn door."**   Parks, Lillian Rogers, *The Roosevelts—A Family in Turmoil.* Englewood Cliffs, N.J. Prentice-Hall, [no date], p. 225.
**"ask them to stop in"**   Miller, *An Intimate History*, p. 493.
**"no one home"**   Ibid.
**"between man and wife"**   West, J. B., *Upstairs at the White House.* p. 23.
**"about these occasions"**   Miller, *An Intimate History*, p. 494.
**"all I wanted to know"**   McIntire, *White House Physician*, pp. 63–64.
**"infantile paralysis"**   Marx, *The Health of Presidents*, p. 360.
**"man of his age"**   McIntire, *White House Physician*, p. 17.
**"little to argue about"**   Gilbert, *The Mortal Presidency*, p. 55.
**"five or six a day"**   Morgan, *FDR: A Biography*, p. 711.
**"horrible pains"**   McCullough, David, *Truman.* New York: Simon and Schuster, 1992, pp. 323–24.
**"is perfectly OK"**   Bishop, *FDR's Last Year*, p. 145.
**"excellent health"**   Ibid., p. 185.
**"a stiff drink"**   Roosevelt, *Affectionately, FDR*, p. 355.
**"fire Mrs. Nesbitt"**   Tully, *F.D.R. My Boss*, pp. 115–16.
**"shoulders like a bag"**   McIntire, *White House Physician*, p. 194.
**"drew a blank"**   Bishop, *FDR's Last Year*, p. 243.
**"going to pieces"**   McCullough, *Truman*, p. 327.

**"fix me right up"**    Roosevelt, James, *My Parents: A Differing View.* Chicago: Playboy Press, 1976, p. 281.
**"fix him up"**    Ibid.
**"I'll be needed"**    Fields, *My 21 Years in the White House,* p. 114.
**"the greatest"**    Miller, *The Roosevelt Chronicle,* p. 337.
**"of my head"**    Ward, *Closest Companion,* p. 417.
**"spell down here"**    Roosevelt, Elliot, and James Brough, *Mother R.* New York: Putnam, 1977, p. 23.
**"cause great comment"**    Ibid.
**"of a clear sky"**    Bishop, *FDR's Last Year,* p. 551.


Chapter 32.    Harry Truman

**"moving over there"**    Anthony, *First Ladies: 1789–1961,* p. 517.
**"All that help"**    Truman, Margaret, *Harry S. Truman.* New York: Morrow, 1973, p. 246.
**"You'd be President"**    Editors of American Heritage, *The American Heritage Pictorial History of the Presidents of the United States, Volume II,* p. 869.
**"General Jackson"**    McCullough, *Truman,* p. 341.
**"had fallen on me"**    Editors of American Heritage, *The American Heritage Pictorial History of the Presidents of the United States, Volume II,* p. 869.
**"the party's off"**    McCullough, *Truman,* p. 348.
**"know you ain't"**    Ibid., p. 357.
**"to me any more"**    Ibid., p. 359.
**"introduce you"**    Ibid.
**"he made it just now"**    Editors of American Heritage, *The American Heritage Pictorial History of the Presidents of the United States, Volume II,* p. 852.
**"Who is me?"**    Parks, *The Roosevelts—A Family in Turmoil,* p. 285.
**"but Mr.Roosevelt"**    Steinberg, Alfred. *The Man from Missouri.* New York: Putnam, 1952, pp. 242–43.
**"pray for me"**    Editors of American Heritage, *The American Heritage Pictorial History of the Presidents of the United States, Volume II,* p. 852.
**"emotional separation"**    DeGregorio, *The Complete Book of United States Presidents,* p. 510.
**"not any more worry"**    Seale, *The President's House, Volume II,* p. 1006.
**"stayed in Washington"**    Anthony, *First Ladies 1789–1961,* p. 528.
**"I was six"**    Hillman, William, *Mr. President.* New York: Farrar, Strauss and Young, 1952, p. 121.
**"into any coal mines"**    Anthony, *First Ladies 1789–1961,* p. 517.
**"say to the public"**    Ibid., p. 527.
**"damn business"**    Boller, *Presidential Wives,* p. 312.
**"made up her mind yet"**    Anderson, Alice, and Hadley Baxendale, *Behind Every Successful President.* New York: S.P.I. Books, 1952, p. 242.
**"her age should look"**    West, *Upstairs at the White House,* p. 59.
**"which has arisen"**    Anthony, *First Ladies 1789–1961,* p. 527.
**"-NY"**    Ibid., p. 528.
**"furnished apartments"**    Truman, Margaret, *Bess W. Truman.* New York: Macmillan, 1986, p. 260.
**"abandoned hotel"**    Seale, *The President's House, Volume II,* p. 1005.
**"is so old"**    Truman, Margaret, *Souvenir.* New York: McGraw-Hill, p. 96.
**"freezing cold"**    Ibid., p. 131.
**"gave it a twist"**    Truman, *Bess W. Truman,* p. 329.
**"that they'd seen it"**    Truman, *Harry S. Truman,* p. 241.
**"I've ever tasted"**    Boller, *Presidential Anecdotes,* p. 286.
**"old fashioneds"**    Ibid.
**"a great help"**    West, *Upstairs at the White House,* p. 123.
**"against the fireplace"**    Truman, *Harry S. Truman,* p. 554.
**"ideas on the house"**    Anthony, *First Ladies 1789–1961,* p. 544.
**"lonesome in my life"**    Jenkins, Roy, *Truman.* New York: Harper & Row, 1986, p. 95.
**"new slats put in"**    West, *Upstairs at the White House,* p. 212.
**"old-fashioned, I guess"**    Hillman, *Mr. President,* p. 121.
**"to me again"**    McCullough, *Truman,* p. 435.
**"recalled at once"**    West, *Upstairs at the White House,* p. 94.
**"I'm just lost"**    Ibid.
**"better believe that one"**    Anthony, *First Ladies 1789–1961,* p. 535.
**"I have"**    Seale, *The President's House, Volume II,* p. 1004.
**"What a life!"**    Hadley, *Power's Human Face,* p. 197.
**"sure as shootin'"**    McCullough, *Truman,* pp. 512–13.
**"count of bells"**    Steinberg, Alfred, *The Life and Times of Harry S. Truman.* New York: Putnam, 1962, p. 249.
**"if I ever do"**    Ferrell, Robert H., ed., *Off the Record: The Private Papers of Harry S. Truman.* New York: Harper & Row, 1980, p. 198.
**"man in attendance"**    Truman, *Souvenir,* p. 95.
**"to be a free agent"**    Ibid., p. 85.
**"what it was"**    Ibid., pp. 103–04.
**"lumpy"**    Ibid., p. 108.
**"supporter below"**    Steinberg, *The Life and Times of Harry S. Truman,* pp. 394–95.
**"that nice man"**    Anthony, *First Ladies 1789–1961,* p. 539.
**"home this evening"**    Clifford, Clark, *Counsel to the President.* New York: Random House, 1991, p. 73.
**"these people away"**    Steinberg, *The Life and Times of Harry S. Truman,* p. 251.
**"with both hands"**    Ibid., p. 247.
**"over bakery bread"**    Fields, *My 21 Years in the White House,* p. 123.
**"did things that way"**    Truman, *Harry S. Truman,* p. 246.
**"openly condescending"**    Ibid.
**"we got them again"**    Ibid.
**"bought in 1935"**    McCullough, *Truman,* p. 857.
**"every check herself"**    Seale, *The President's House Volume II,* p. 1021.
**"dozens of eggs"**    West, *Upstairs at the White House,* p. 85.
**"out of proportion"**    McCullough, *Truman,* p. 594.
**"to do it anyway"**    Goodwin, Doris Kearns, "The Home Front" *The New Yorker* (August 15, 1994): 38–61.
**"lynched for doing it"**    Steinberg, *The Life and Times of Harry S. Truman,* p. 303.
**"me my breakfast"**    Steinberg, *The Life and Times of Harry S. Truman,* p. 235.
**"in a real fix"**    McCullough, *Truman,* pp. 536–37.
**"that beat all"**    Ibid., p. 725.
**"effort to other things"**    McCullough, *Truman,* p.657.

**"it was hell"**　Kenin, Richard, and Justin Wintle, *Dictionary of American Biographical Quotation.* New York: Knopf, 1978, p. 743.
**"across the street"**　Miller, Merle, *Plain Speaking: An Oral Biography of Harry S. Truman.* New York: Putnam, 1973, p. 213.
**"wants to shoot me"**　Parks, *My Thirty Years Backstairs at the White House,* p. 305.
**"Get back!"**　McCullough, *Truman,* p. 811.
**"expect these things"**　Ibid., p. 812.
**"as we walked"**　Ibid., p. 805.
**"want to live like that"**　Ferrell, Robert H., ed., *Off the Record: The Private Papers of Harry S. Truman.* New York: Harper & Row, 1980, pp. 239–40.
**"knocked out"**　Blodgett, *At Home with the Presidents,* p. 197.
**"club in my hands"**　Steinberg, *The Life and Times of Harry S. Truman,* p. 263.
**"just thinking about you"**　McCullough, *Truman,* p. 623.
**"Kentucky bourbon"**　Clifford, *Counsel to the President,* p. 69.
**"leave nothing out"**　Ibid., p. 72.
**"All right, Winston"**　McCullough, *Truman,* p. 487.
**"forty-one hundred"**　Truman, *First Ladies,* p. 85.
**"very frustrating"**　Steinberg, *The Life and Times of Harry S. Truman,* p. 417.
**"in separate cars"**　Ibid., pp. 418–19.
**"next to that guy"**　Brenden, Piers, *Ike: His Life and Times* (audio tape).
**"I can tell you that"**　Whitney, *The American Presidents,* p. 280.

### Chapter 33.　Dwight Eisenhower

**"going to stay home"**　Jensen, *The White House and Its Thirty-four Families,* p. 92.
**"where I want him"**　Anthony, *First Ladies 1789–1961,* p. 559.
**"my monkey suit"**　David, Lester, and Irene David, *Ike and Mamie.* New York: Putnam, 1981, p. 192.
**"get an early start"**　Ibid., p. 193.
**"see you this early"**　Youngblood, Rufus, *20 Years in the Secret Service.* New York: Simon and Schuster, 1973, pp. 37–38.
**"with knotty questions"**　Ambrose, Stephen, *Eisenhower Volume II The President.* Simon and Schuster, 1984, p. 290–91.
**"in bed until noon"**　West, *Upstairs at the White House,* p. 178.
**"changes right away"**　Ibid., p. 129.
**"a five-star general"**　Anthony, *First Ladies 1789–1961,* p. 552.
**"our bedroom"**　West, *Upstairs at the White House,* p. 129.
**"anytime I want to"**　Ibid.
**"and the President, too"**　Ibid., p. 142.
**"was a young girl"**　Ambrose, *Eisenhower, Volume II: The President,* pp. 213–14.
**"has to offer a woman"**　Anthony, *First Ladies 1789–1961,* p. 565.
**"to be liberated from"**　Boller, *Presidential Wives,* p. 347.
**"mended linens again"**　West, *Upstairs at the White House,* p. 155.
**"not by anybody else"**　Hay, Peter, *All the Presidents' Ladies.* New York: Viking, 1988, p. 186.
**"wasted around here"**　West, *Upstairs at the White House,* p. 146.
**"chicken salad today"**　Ibid.
**"out of my allowance"**　David, *Ike and Mamie,* pp. 213–14.
**"to worry about"**　Ibid., p. 201.
**"put in a new one"**　Bruce, Preston, *From the Door of the White House,* New York: Lathrop, Lee and Shepard, 1984, p. 44–46.
**"my elevator again"**　West, *Upstairs at the White House,* p. 133.
**"to Uncle Sam"**　David, *Ike and Mamie,* p. 197.
**"times I've ever had"**　Baughman, *Secret Service Chief,* p. 192.
**"right through the house"**　Slater, Ellis, *The Ike I Knew.* [no publisher] 1980, p. 114.
**"expression of friendship"**　Woodward, C. Vann, *Responses of Presidents to Charges of Misconduct.* New York: Delacorte, 1974, p. 21.
**"horribly embarrassed"**　Ambrose, *Eisenhower, Volume II: The President,* pp. 198–99.
**"a discount to Lincoln"**　David, *Ike and Mamie,* p. 237.
**"in a personal way"**　Anthony, *First Ladies 1789–1961,* p. 556.
**"around the house"**　Ibid., p. 523.
**"a second scotch"**　Gray, Robert Keith, *Eighteen Acres under Glass.* Garden City, N.Y.: Doubleday, 1962, p. 111.
**"feeling no pain"**　Ferrell, *Ill-Advised Presidential Health and Public Trust,* pp. 144–45.
**"how to be President"**　Gray, *Eighteen Acres under Glass,* p. 155.
**"another part of the house"**　Thayer, Mary Van Rennsselaer, *Jacqueline Kennedy The White House Years.* Boston: Little, Brown, 1971, p. 18.
**"short of awful"**　Ibid.
**"those portholes for?"**　Heymann. C. David, *A Woman Named Jackie.* New York: Lyle Stuart, 1989, p. 263.
**"inconceivably banal"**　Brendon, Piers, *Ike: His Life and Time* (audio tape).
**"strictly cornball"**　Ibid.
**"Lawrence Welk"**　David, *Ike and Mamie,* p. 267.
**"a real professional"**　Lindop, *White House Sportsmen,* p. 21.
**"in Eastern football"**　Ibid., p. 17.
**"of body and mind"**　Smith, Merriman, *Meet Mr. Eisenhower.* New York: Harper, 1955, pp. 162–63.
**"wedge shots too"**　Baughman, *Secret Service Chief,* pp. 166–67.
**"pull down the curtain"**　Lindop, *White House Sportsmen,* pp. 97–98.
**"take a gun and shoot"**　West, *Upstairs at the White House,* p. 162.
**"I got that one"**　Bryant, Traphes, *Dog Days at the White House.* New York: Macmillan, 1975, p. 33.
**"one-dollar Nassau"**　Brendon, Piers, *Ike: His Life and Times* (audio tape).
**"called Faubus"**　Brendon, Piers, *Ike: His Life and Times.* New York: Harper & Row, 1984, p. 346.
**"relaxation he can"**　Smith, *Meet Mr. Eisenhower,* p. 172.
**"met since 1945"**　Wicker, Tom, *One of Us: Richard Nixon and the American Dream.* New York: Random House, 1981, p. 199.
**"friendship was to me"**　Ambrose, *Eisenhower, Volume II: The President,* p. 70.
**"I went aboard"**　Slater, *The Ike I Knew,* p. 119.
**"until after midnight"**　Ibid., pp. 39–40.
**"Monday the same"**　Ibid., p. 75.
**"doesn't play bridge"**　Anthony, *First Ladies 1789–1961,* p. 583.
**"in the ice box"**　Slater, *The Ike I Knew,* p. 38.
**"past midnight"**　Gilbert, *The Mortal Presidency,* p. 79.
**"be President"**　Anthony, *First Ladies 1789–1961,* p. 457.
**"I have ever known"**　Gilbert, *The Mortal Preesidency,* p. 76.

**"silent prayer"** Medved, *The Shadow Presidents*, p. 247.
**"comes my conscience"** Ibid., pp. 246–47.
**"like whipcords"** Gilbert, *The Mortal Presidency*, pp. 86–87.
**"backing up on me"** Ferrell, *Ill-Advised Presidential Health and Public Trust*, p. 75.
**"Shaken"** Gilbert, *The Mortal Presidency*, p. 88.
**"digestive upset"** Brendon, *Ike: His Life and Times*, p. 313.
**"people have had"** Gilbert, *The Mortal Presidency*, p. 89.
**"was eliminated"** Ibid.
**"doing satisfactorily"** Ferrell, *Ill-Advised Presidential Health and Public Trust*, p. 80.
**"It worked"** Ibid., p. 87.
**"Tell them everything"** White, Paul Dudley, *My Life and Medicine*. Boston: Gambit, 1971, p. 179.
**"bowel movement"** Gilbert, *The Mortal Presidency*, p. 92.
**"peace-keeping role"** White, *My Life and Medicine*, pp. 188–89.
**"politics by this time"** Ibid.
**"publicity seeker"** Gilbert, *The Mortal Presidency*, p. 97.
**"five to ten years"** Ferrell, *Ill-Advised Presidential Health and Public Trust*, p. 110.
**"affect his physical self"** Ibid., p. 128.
**"thought whatsoever"** Gilbert, *The Mortal Presidency*, p. 107.
**"ordered him to bed"** Ferrell, *Ill-Advised Presidential Health and Public Trust*, p. 130.
**"perfectly all right"** Ambrose, *Eisenhower Volume II The President*, pp. 436–37.
**"cerebral occlusion"** Ferrell, *Ill-Advised Presidential Health and Public Trust*, p. 130.
**"digestive tract"** Ibid., p. 118.
**"upset stomach"** Ibid., p. 119.
**"I will not like"** Ibid., p. 125.
**"strain on her"** Anthony, *First Ladies, 1789–1961*, p. 582.
**"country to Kennedy"** Manchester, William, *One Brief Shining Moment Remembering Kennedy*. Boston: Little, Brown, 1983, p. 420.
**"Opal Drill Three"** Reeves, Richard, *President Kennedy*. New York: Simon and Schuster, 1993, p. 30.
**"goddamned thing"** Ambrose, *Eisenhower, Volume II: The President*, pp. 616–17.
**"thrill of a lifetime"** Ibid., p. 655.

## Chapter 34.  John F. Kennedy

**"not a good reproduction"** Collier, Peter, and David Horowitz, *The Kennedys: An American Dream*. New York: Summit Books, 1984, p. 263.
**"Maison Blanche"** Ibid., p. 282.
**"I hate it"** Kelley, Kitty, *Jackie Oh!* Secaucus, N.J.: Lyle Stuart, 1978, p. 100.
**"what can you do?"** Thayer, Mary Van Rensselaer, *Jacqueline Kennedy: The White House Years*. Boston: Little, Brown, 1971, p. 8.
**"discount stores"** Martin, Ralph, *A Hero for Our Time*. New York: Fawcett Crest, 1983, p. 234.
**"Lubianka"** Kelley, *Jackie Oh!*, p. 100.
**"office building"** Martin, *A Hero for Our Time*, p. 63.
**"proper linens"** Thayer, *Jacqueline Kennedy: The White House Years*, p. 18.
**"the White House"** Ibid., p. 19.
**"Alfred Hitchcock"** Ibid.
**"fare-you-well"** Ibid., p. 159.
**"White House staff"** Heymann, C. David, *A Woman Named Jackie*. New York: Lyle Stuart, 1989, p. 268.
**"I don't remember"** Martin, *A Hero for Our Time*, p. 353.
**"champagne good enough"** Reeves, Thomas C., *A Question of Character: A Life of John F. Kennedy*. New York: Macmillan, 1991, p. 313.
**"you sign the memo"** Gallagher, Mary, *My Life with Jacqueline Kennedy*. New York: David McKay, 1969, p. 271.
**"read in the papers"** West, *Upstairs at the White House*, p. 209.
**"marvelous gifts"** Gallagher, *My Life With Jacqueline Kennedy*, p. 223.
**"I want the horses"** Reeves, *A Question of Character: A Life of John F. Kennedy*, p. 255.
**"French couturiers"** Blodgett, *At Home with the Presidents*, p. 217.
**"Ritz Thrift Shop"** Heymann, *A Woman Named Jackie*, p. 351.
**"in the same dress"** Truman, *First Ladies*, p. 33.
**"now they love it"** Leigh, Wendy, *Prince Charming: The John F. Kennedy, Jr. Story*. New York: Dutton, p. 24.
**"done one of them"** Gallagher, *My Life With Jacqueline Kennedy*, p. 159.
**"I'll wear hats"** *Vanity Fair*, January 1989 p. 94.
**"killing the industry"** Manchester, *One Brief Shining Moment: Remembering Kennedy*, p. 135.
**"save the hat industry"** Ibid., p. 135.
**"not a public official"** Reeves, *A Question of Character: A Life of John F. Kennedy*, p. 154.
**"to do around here"** Heymann, *A Woman Named Jackie*, p. 333.
**"these silly women"** Truman, *First Ladies*, p. 39.
**"to Lady Bird"** Ibid.
**"Two symphonies"** Reeves, *A Question of Character: A Life of John F. Kennedy*, p. 476.
**"arts and history"** Caroli, Betty, *Inside the White House*. New York: Canopy Books, 1992, p. 127.
**"practically threatened"** Ibid., pp. 127–29.
**"for three months"** Reeves, *A Question of Character: A Life of John F. Kennedy*, p.43.
**"this old dump"** Blodgett, *At Home with the Presidents*, p. 217.
**"dungeons with them"** West, *Upstairs at the White House*, p. 198.
**"money for wallpaper"** Kelley, *Jackie Oh!*, p. 137.
**"pat of butter"** Sidey, Hugh, *John F. Kennedy, President*. New York: Atheneum, 1963, pp. 280–81.
**"not be served hot"** Thayer, *Jacqueline Kennedy: The White House Years*, p. 150.
**"rattletrap house"** Ibid., p. 131.
**"same house I left"** Truman, *First Ladies*, p. 38.
**"like the room this way"** Gallagher, *My Life With Jacqueline Kennedy*, p. 115–16.
**"her mind like this"** Ibid., p. 115–16.
**"divine in a Frenchman"** Johnson, Lady Bird, *A White House Diary*. New York: Holt, Rhinehart and Winston, 1970, p. 12.
**"liver again"** Hay, *All the Presidents' Ladies*, p. 92–3.
**"I believe him"** Martin, *A Hero for Our Time*, p. 270.
**"had to tell me"** Reeves, *A Question of Character: A Life of John F. Kennedy*, p. 316.
**"cornfields in Virginia"** Thayer, *Jacqueline Kennedy: The White House Years*, p. 143.
**"ever going to grow"** Salinger, Pierre, *With Kennedy*. Garden City, N.Y.: Doubleday, 1966, p. 75.

**"do not chew gum"**   Mclendon, Winzola and Smith, Scottie, *Don't Quote Me.* New York: Dutton, 1970, p. 25.
**"so you can talk"**   Lindop, *White House Sportsmen,* p. 137.
**"tickle his toes, Bruce"**   Bruce, *From the Door of the White House,* pp. 84–85.
**"Hello Bruce"**   Ibid., pp. 84–85.
**"a little schoolboy"**   Ibid., p. 77.
**"understood by the public"**   Anthony, *First Ladies 1789–1961,* p. 51.
**"married too"**   Bruce, *From the Door of the White House,* p. 78–80.
**"the White House"**   Reeves, *A Question of Character: A Life of John F. Kennedy,* p. 90.
**"an Eisenhower memorial"**   Goodwin, Richard, *Remembering America: A Voice from the Sixties.* Boston: Little, Brown, 1988, p. 146.
**"life on crutches"**   Heymann, *A Woman Named Jackie,* p. 170.
**"supports for his back"**   Martin, *A Hero for Our Time,* p. 370.
**"do not exercise"**   Reeves, *A Question of Character: A Life of John F. Kennedy,* pp. 242–43.
**"they write then"**   Ibid.
**"such as influenza"**   Crispell, *Hidden Illnesses in the White House,* p. 195.
**"It works"**   Reeves, *A Question of Character: A Life of John F. Kennedy,* p. 297.
**"it without me"**   Seaman, Barbara, *Lovely Me: The Life of Jacqueline Susann.* New York: Morrow, 1987, p. 388.
**"after which he left"**   Heyman, *A Woman Named Jackie,* p. 298.
**"decomposed substances"**   Ferrell, *Ill-Advised Presidential Health and Public Trust,* p. 156.
**"home movies"**   West, *Upstairs at the White House,* p. 229.
**"That's my Daddy"**   Bergquist, Laura, *A Very Special President.* New York: McGraw-Hill, 1965, p. 82.
**"matters very much"**   Anthony, *First Ladies 1789–1961,* p. 46.
**"White House lawn"**   Thayer, *Jacqueline Kennedy: The White House Years,* p. 242.
**"unpredictable"**   West, *Upstairs at the White House,* p. 218.
**"check it out for me"**   Salinger, *With Kennedy,* p. 315.
**"send me one"**   Anthony, *First Ladies 1789–1961,* p. 42.
**"doing nothing"**   Giglio, James N., *The Presidency of John F. Kennedy.* Lawrence: University Press of Kansas, 1991, p. 258.
**"or someplace later"**   Baughman, *Secret Service Chief,* pp. 9–11.
**"what am I missing"**   Martin, *A Hero for Our Time,* p. 314.
**"like to talk about"**   Reeves, *A Question of Character: A Life of John F. Kennedy,* p. 292.
**"terrible cold"**   Giglio, *The Presidency of John F. Kennedy,* p. 257.
**"Commander-in-Chief"**   Sullivan, Michael, *Presidential Passions.* New York: Shapotsky Publishers, 1991, p. 65.
**"Roto-Rooter"**   Reeves, *A Question of Character: A Life of John F. Kennedy,* p. 242.
**"Secretary of State"**   Heymann, *A Woman Named Jackie,* pp. 284–85.
**"the best we've got"**   Ibid.
**"7 P.M."**   Reeves, *A Question of Character: A Life of John F. Kennedy,* p. 110.
**"getting any lately?"**   Dickerson, Nancy, *Among Those Present.* New York: Random House, 1976, p. 67.
**"not my size"**   Collier, *The Kennedys: An American Drama,* p. 283.
**"Marilyn Monroe"**   Heymann, *A Woman Named Jackie,* p. 233.
**"'a bomb' he said"**   Ibid., p. 375.
**"let them go ahead"**   Martin, *A Hero for Our Time,* p. 308.
**"period of my life"**   Clifford, *Counsel to the President,* p. 349.
**"ever lost you"**   Anderson, Christopher, *Jack and Jackie.* New York: Morrow, 1996, p. 353.
**"closer together"**   Ibid., p. 354.
**"I'll go anywhere"**   Ibid., p. 360.
**"Don't you go"**   Clarke, James, *American Assassins.* Princeton, N.J.: Princeton University Press, 1982, pp. 107–09.
**"done that to him"**   Andersen, *Jack and Jackie,* p. 367.
**"he's coming back"**   Ibid., p. 366.
**"Nov 22, 1963"**   Ibid., p. 369.
**"My life is over"**   Ibid.

## Chapter 35.   Lyndon Johnson

**"I understand"**   Youngblood, *20 Years in the Secret Service,* p. 114.
**"to the hat, sir"**   Ibid., pp. 133–34.
**"of the United States"**   Moody, Booth, *LBJ: An Irreverent Chronicle.* New York: Crowell, 1976, p. 279.
**"President of this country"**   Blodgett, *At Home with the Presidents,* p. 218.
**"never have had"**   Bailey, Thomas A., *Presidential Saints and Sinners.* New York: The Free Press, pp. 256–57.
**"up his rear"**   *Life,* "The White House" (October 30, 1992): 76.
**"The Elms"**   West, *Upstairs at the White House,* pp. 290–91.
**"against the wall"**   *Life,* " The White House" (October 30, 1992):76.
**"to normal pressure"**   West, *Upstairs at the White House,* p. 357.
**"at the White House"**   Gulley, Bill, *Breaking Cover.* New York: Simon and Schuster, 1980, p. 55.
**"Then do it"**   Ibid.
**"pay for it"**   Ibid.
**"worked so late"**   West, *Upstairs at the White House,* p. 292.
**"who needed light"**   Bryant, *Dog Days at the White House,* p. 16.
**"a drink for me"**   Kessler, Ronald, *Inside the White House.* New York: Pocket Books, 1995, p. 31.
**"You're fired"**   *New York Times Magazine* (April 17, 1994): 42.
**"Yes, sir"**   Cormier, Frank, *LBJ The Way He Was.* Garden City, N.Y.: Doubleday, 1977, p. 217.
**"President's toenails"**   Ibid., p. 135.
**"full-grown man"**   Ibid.
**"my prerogitive"**   Higgins, George V., *The Friends of Richard Nixon.* Boston: Little, Brown, 1975, p. 177.
**"do this to me"**   Blodgett, *At Home with the Presidents,* p. 222.
**"brakes have failed"**   Clifford, *Counsel to the President,* p. 393.
**"to be President"**   McLendon, *Don't Quote Me,* p. 28.
**"for that thing"**   Kessler, *Inside the White House,* p. 20.
**"we need more like him"**   Youngblood, *20 Years in the Secret Service,* pp. 217–18.
**"you, Mr. President"**   Thomas, *Dateline: White House,* p. 74.
**"where the hell is he?"**   Califano, Joseph, *Triumph and Tragedy of Lyndon Johnson.* New York: Simon and Schuster, 1991, pp. 25–26.
**"on the phone"**   Ibid., p. 26.
**"delicate Kennedyites"**   Goodwin, *Remembering America: A Voice from the Sixties,* pp. 258–59.

**"so far in the world"**    Ibid., pp. 258–59.
**"night it is"**    Reston, James, *Deadline*. New York: Random House, 1991, p. 305.
**"without my permission"**    Thomas, *Dateline: White House*, p. 291.
**"took them all out"**    Green, Bob, *Cheeseburgers: The Best of Bob Greene*. New York: Atheneum, 1985, p. 154.
**"blow up the world"**    Ambrose, Stephen, *Nixon, Volume II: The Triumph of a Politician 1962–1972*. New York: Simon and Schuster, 1989, p. 248.
**"no bigger than a tic"**    Goldman, Eric, *The Tragedy of Lyndon Johnson*. New York: Knopf, 1969, p. 32.
**"behind him to a man"**    Ibid.
**"my oldest friends"**    West, *Upstairs at the White House*, p. 320.
**"side of the country"**    Graff, *The Presidents: A Reference History*, p. 504.
**"didn't go to Harvard"**    Thomas, *Dateline: White House*, p. 118.
**"over his shoulder"**    Schlesinger, Arthur M., Jr., *Robert Kennedy and His Times*. Boston: Houghton Mifflin, 1978, p. 649.
**"same circumstances"**    Ibid.
**"extremely loving"**    DeGregorio, *The Complete Book of United States Presidents*, p. 563.
**"some kind of joke"**    Dugger, Ronnie, *The Life and Times of Lyndon Johnson*. New York: Norton, 1980, p. 177.
**"always in a rush"**    DeGregorio, *The Complete Book of United States Presidents*, p. 563.
**"I never rehearsed"**    Boller, *Presidential Wives*, p. 387.
**"museum's closing hour"**    Russell, Jan Jaroboe, *Lady Bird: A Biography of Mrs. Johnson*. New York: Scribner, 1999, p. 274.
**"I'm proud of"**    Anthony, *First Ladies 1789–1961*, p. 113.
**"on Pennsylvania Avenue"**    Sidey, Hugh. *A Very Personal Presidency Lyndon Johnson in the White House*. New York: Atheneum, 1968, p. 47.
**"off to Vietnam"**    Russell, *Lady Bird: A Biography of Mrs. Johnson*, p. 197.
**"anger and discord"**    Ibid., pp. 151–52.
**"Maidenform Bra"**    Johnson, *Lady Bird. A White House Diary*. New York: Holt, Rinehart and Winston, 1970, pp. 161–62.
**"and so to bed"**    Ibid.
**"the other way"**    Califano, *Triumph and Tragedy of Lyndon Johnson*, pp. 27–28.
**"charity organization"**    Johnson, *A White House Diary*, p. 325.
**"never meeting anyone"**    Smith, *White House Brides*, p. 183.
**"I was different"**    (author interview).
**"had to be organized"**    (author interview).
**"to a barn door"**    Bryant, p. 114.
**"sort of house arrest"**    Kellerman, Barbara, *All the President's Kin*. New York: The Free Press, 1981, p. 215.
**"came home drunk"**    Ibid., p. 216.
**"getting drunk"**    Kessler, *Inside the White House*, p. 31.
**"they did it anyway"**    Bryant, *Dog Days at the White House*, p. 173.
**"what a mess"**    Ibid.
**"dancingest First Family"**    Boller, *Presidential Wives*, p. 388.
**"with the President"**    Thomas, *Dateline: White House*, p. 83.
**"more than I can stand"**    Carpenter, Liz, *Ruffles and Flourishes*. Garden City, N.Y.: Doubleday, 1970, p. 209.
**"Congress over tonight"**    Whalen, Charles, and Barbara Whalen, *The Longest Debate: A Legislative History of the 1964 Civil Rights Act*. New York: Mentor, 1985, p. 90.
**"stopped at catsup"**    Smith, Merriman, *Merriman Smith's Book of the Presidents*. Norton, 1972, p. 42.
**"chili con-crete"**    West, *Upstairs at the White House*, p. 326.
**"when I want it"**    Cormier, *LBJ The Way He Was*, p. 204.
**"pot washer to do it"**    West, *Upstairs at the White House*, p. 326.
**"the foods he likes"**    Haller, Henry, *The White House Family Cook Book*. New York: Random House, 1987, p. 23.
**"home to your wife"**    Ibid., p. 45.
**"It's spoiled"**    West, *Upstairs at the White House*, pp. 336–37.
**"to taste like that"**    Ibid.
**"again in this house"**    Ibid.
**"when prepared properly"**    Haller, *The White House Family Cook Book*, p. 37.
**"don't complain"**    Ibid., p. 24.
**"killing a rattlesnake"**    Barber, *The Presidential Character: Predicting Performance at the White House*, p. 52.
**"just gone through"**    Connally, John, *In History's Shadows*. New York: Hyperion, 1993, p. 4.
**"my little monks, Daddy"**    Califano, *Triumph and Tragedy of Lyndon Johnson*, pp. 334–35.
**"we can't finish it"**    Russell, *Lady Bird: A Biography of Mrs. Johnson*, p. 282.
**"folks like me"**    Moody, *LBJ: An Irreverent Chronicle*, p. 160.
**"this morning"**    Truman, *First Ladies*, p. 184.
**"hysterical reporters"**    Fay, Paul, *The Pleasure of His Company*. New York: Harper & Row, 1966, p. 905.
**"a full day's work"**    Johnson, *A White House Diary*, p. 347.
**"work it in shifts"**    West, *Upstairs at the White House*, p. 293.
**"for me to watch"**    Dallek, Robert, *Flawed Giant: Lyndon Johnson and His Times*. New York: Oxford, 1998, p. 524.
**"the down button"**    Ibid., p. 526.
**"dancing in the streets"**    Fay, *The Pleasure of His Company*, p. 905.
**"in no way see"**    Russell, *Lady Bird: A Biography of Mrs. Johnson*, p. 302.
**"to go to Vietnam?"**    Anthony, *First Ladies 1789–1961*, p. 153.
**"as your President"**    Dallek, *Flawed Giant Lyndon Johnson and His Times*, p. 526.
**"to go fast"**    Bornet, Vaughn Davis, *The Presidency of Lyndon B. Johnson* Lawrence: University of Kansas, 1983, p. 296.

## Chapter 36.    Richard Nixon

**"It's done"**    Ambrose, Stephen, *Nixon, Volume II: The Triumph of a Politician 1962–1972*. New York: Simon and Schuster, 1989, p. 245.
**"flashlight anymore"**    Bryant, *Dog Days at the White House*, p. 16.
**"shut up in this house"**    Thomas, *Dateline: White House*, p. 173.
**"not really a home"**    Ambrose, Stephen, *Nixon, Volume III: Ruin and Recovery 1973–1990*. New York: Simon and Schuster, 1991, p. 265.
**"you would be dead"**    Anthony, *First Ladies 1789–1961*, p. 177.
**"music in the hallways"**    Ambrose, *Nixon, Volume III: Ruin and Recovery 1973–1990*. New York: p. 265.
**"extrovert's profession"**    Mazlish, *In Search of Nixon*. New York: Basic Books, 1971, p. 33.
**"Even with close friends"**    Greene, *Cheeseburgers: The Best of Bob Greene*, p. 149.
**"with my own family"**    Rogin, Michael Paul, *Ronald Reagan The Movie*. Berkeley: University of California, 1987, p. 108.
**"1969"**    Colson, Charles, *Born Again*. Old Tappan, N.J.: Chossen Books, 1976, p. 179.
**"a pretty good wife"**    Brodie, Fawn, *Richard Nixon*. New York: Norton, 1981, p. 143.
**"way I was raised"**    Greene, *Cheeseburgers: The Best of Bob Greene*, p. 651.

"some comment or other"   Aitken, Jonathan, *Nixon: A Life.* Washington, D.C.: Regnery, 1993, p. 383.
"He never asked"   Medved, *The Shadow Presidents*, p. 316.
"going in there"   Aitken, *Nixon: A Life*, p. 382.
"Air Force One"   Medved, *The Shadow Presidents*, p. 320.
"surveillance on that bastard"   Ibid.
"inappropriate demand"   Morris, Roger, *Haig: The General's Progress.* Chicago: Playboy Press, 1982, p. 109.
"be carried out"   Haldeman, H. R., *The Haldeman Diaries.* New York: Putnam, 1994, p. 63.
"landing at airports"   Medved, *The Shadow Presidents*, p. 320.
"that's the best thing"   Ibid.
"and did it myself"   Nixon, Richard, *In the Arena.* New York: Simon and Schuster, 1990, p. 205.
"this kind of judgment"   Aitken, *Nixon A Life*, p. 414.
"have been delighted"   Haldeman, *The Haldeman Diaries*, p. 211.
"Loves being P"   Ibid., p. 25.
"White House police"   Ambrose, *Nixon Volume Two The Triumph of a Politician 1962–1972*, p. 325.
"hand me these"   Hartman, Robert T., *Palace Politics An Inside Account of the Ford Years.* New York: McGraw-Hill, 1980, p. 263.
"nuts or something"   Degregorio, *The Complete Book of United States Presidents*, p. 584.
"it's impossible"   David, Lester, *The Lonely Lady of San Clemente: The Story of Pat Nixon.* New York: Crowell, 1978, p. 133.
"I will return"   Ambrose, *Nixon, Volume II: The Triumph of a Politician 1962–1972*, p. 245.
"will benefit all"   Anthony, *First Ladies 1789–1961*, p. 211.
"needed to be done"   Eisenhower, Julie Nixon, *Pat Nixon.* New York: Simon and Schuster, 1986, p. 263.
"walked down the hall"   West, *Upstairs at the White House*, p. 355.
"spot for muggers"   Eisenhower, *Pat Nixon*, p. 391.
"everything they like"   Boller, *Presidential Wives*, p. 415.
"night to boot"   Ibid.
"stay that way"   Ibid.
"out of my ears"   Haller, *The White House Family Cook Book*, p. 82.
"disguises almost anything"   Ibid.
"in five minutes, too"   Sidey, Hugh, *A Very Personal Presidency: Lyndon Johnson in the White House*, p. 127.
"drinks will do it"   Wicker, *One of Us: Richard Nixon and the American Dream*, p. 393.
"more susceptible"   Ibid.
"comfortable that way"   Greene, *Cheeseburgers: The Best of Bob Greene*, p. 144.
"hair curl more"   Kessler, *Inside the White House*, p. 58.
"dress trousers too"   Rather, Dan, and Gary Paul Gates, *The Palace Guard.* New York: Harper & Row, 1974, p. 244.
"must be kidding"   Bailey, Thomas, *The Pugnacious Presidents.* New York: Macmillan, 1980, p. 65.
"I'm on your side"   Ibid.
"is not illegal"   Haldeman, *The Haldeman Diaries*, p. 183.
"lesson ended abruptly"   Nixon, *In the Arena*, p. 163.
"calculated risk"   Woodward and Bernstein, *The Final Days.* New York: Simon and Schuster, 1976, p. 213.
"late at night"   Greene, *Cheeseburgers: The Best of Bob Greene*, p. 148.
"presidential history"   Wicker, *One of Us: Richard Nixon and the American Dream*, pp. 634–35.
"we'll go"   Safire, William, *Before the Fall: An Inside View of the Pre-Watergate White House*, Garden City, N.Y.: Doubleday, 1975, pp. 205–11.
"with apprehension"   Aitken, *Nixon A Life*, p. 406.
"asked for a car"   Safire, *Before the Fall: An Inside View of the Pre-Watergate White House*, pp. 205–11.
"front talking to them"   Ibid.
"just how you feel"   Ibid.
"and a red beard"   Ibid.
"will believe him"   Wicker, *One of Us: Richard Nixon and the American Dream*, pp. 634–35.
"try, Mr. President"   Safire, *Before the Fall: An Inside View of the Pre-Watergate White House*, pp. 205–11.
"was on a train"   Ibid.
"weirdest day so far"   Haldeman, *The Haldeman Diaries*, p. 163.
"tired to go to sleep"   Ibid.
"got to ride back"   Permet, Herbert S., *Richard Nixon and His America.* Boston: Little, Brown, 1990, p. 13.
"waved good-bye"   Safire, *Before the Fall: An Inside View of the Pre-Watergate White House*, pp. 205–11.
"a bomb"   Eisenhower, *Pat Nixon*, pp. 289–90.
"assault on the senses"   Ibid.
"nation's capital"   John F. Kennedy Library Lectures, Boston (August 1998).
"keep him covered"   Haldeman, H. R., with Joseph DiMona, *The Ends of Power.* New York: New York Times Books, 1978, p. 36.
"man in America"   Aitken, *Nixon: A Life*, pp. 421–22.
"how to stop it"   Ibid.
"I ever authorized"   Ibid.
"anything like that"   Wicker, *One of Us: Richard Nixon and the American Dream*, p. 446.
"when you are sick"   Nofziger, Lyn, *Nofziger.* Washington, D.C.: Regnery Gateway, 1992, p. 229.
"never go anywhere"   Brodie, *Richard Nixon*, p. 504.
"why is this happening"   Eisenhower, *Pat Nixon*, p. 416.
"I am getting deaf"   Ibid.
"nothing she could do"   Ibid., p. 417.
"in the White House"   Ibid., p. 418.
"death watch"   Ambrose, *Nixon, Volume III: Ruin and Recovery 1973–1990*, p. 416.
"real good, didn't I?"   Eisenhower, *Pat Nixon*, p. 420.
"family than I have"   Ibid., p. 424.
"there we are smiling"   Anthony, *First Ladies 1789–1961*, p. 217.
"have it televised"   Ibid.
"day of my life"   Eisenhower, *Pat Nixon*, p. 433.
"we don't see them"   Ibid., p. 512.

## Chapter 37.   Gerald Ford

"short pajamas"   Ford, Betty, *The Times of My Life.* New York: Harper & Row, 1978, p. 162.
"we'll want it"   Ibid., p. 165.
"Don't Touch"   Ibid., p. 397.
"time doing it"   Anthony, *First Ladies 1789–1961*, p. 222.

**"often as possible"**    Ibid., p. 227.

**"have a blanket"**    Ford, *The Times of My Life*, p. 157.

**"too far to go"**    Anthony, *First Ladies 1789–1961*, p. 227.

**"some dumb hall"**    Ford, *The Times of My Life*, p. 165.

**"I've ever seen"**    Ibid.

**"cap for my career"**    Cannon, James, *Time and Chance*. New York: HarperCollins, 1994, pp. 206–07.

**"sitting in this chair"**    Reeves, Richard, *I'm a Ford, Not a Lincoln*. New York: Harcourt Brace Jovanovich, 1975, p. 42.

**"seventy-seven"**    Cannon, *Time and Chance*, p. 211.

**"all thine heart"**    Ibid., p. 340.

**"to do the job"**    Ibid., p. 342.

**"we can do it"**    Ibid., p. 347.

**"always felt revived"**    Ford, Gerald, *A Time to Heal*. New York: Harper & Row, 1979, p. 206.

**"back to his papers"**    Ford, *The Times of My Life*, p. 175.

**"start the day"**    Ford, *A Time to Heal*, p. 205.

**"about your hair"**    Kessler, *Inside the White House*, p. 81.

**"awfully attractive"**    Nessen, Ron, *It Sure Looks Different from the Inside*. Chicago: Playboy Press, 1978, p. 25.

**"find out about it"**    Ibid.

**"would stand for it"**    Whitney, *The American Presidents*, p. 375.

**"was no deal"**    Ibid.

**"another man's dog"**    Nessen, *It Sure Looks Different from the Inside*, p. xiv.

**"a Ford administration"**    Ford, *A Time to Heal*, pp. 422–24.

**"the tarmac below"**    Ibid., p. 289.

**"that wasn't funny"**    Anthony, *First Ladies 1789–1961*, p. 231.

**"would understand that"**    Ford, *A Time to Heal*, pp. 343–44.

**"follow the wounded"**    Hope, Bob, *Confessions of a Hooker*. Garden City, N.Y.: Doubleday, 1985, Foreword.

**"thick-skinned"**    Nessen, *It Sure Looks Different from the Inside*, p. 169.

**"the president"**    Graff, *The Presidents: A Reference History*, p. 536.

**"sort of back off"**    Ford, *The Times of My Life*, p. 16.

**"I want it to sing"**    Anthony, *First Ladies 1789–1961*, p. 223.

**"eating my soup"**    Ford, *The Times of My Life*, p. 174.

**"sunny yellow"**    Weidenfeld, Sheila, *First Lady's Lady*. New York: Putnam, 1979, p. 36.

**"have slept in"**    Ford, *The Times of My Life*, p. 174.

**"to dust them"**    Ibid., p. 175.

**"husband is close by"**    Weidenfeld, *First Lady's Lady*, p. 37.

**"without being seen"**    Ibid.

**"is so confining"**    Ibid.

**"the two of us"**    Ibid.

**"I'm treating"**    Ibid.

**"waste of time"**    terHorst, J. T., *Gerald Ford and the Future of the Presidency*. New York: The Third Press, 1974, p. 201.

**"trying to work"**    Ford, *The Times of My Life*, p. 222.

**"off balance"**    Anthony, *First Ladies 1789–1961*, p. 299.

**"be one of those"**    Ford, *A Time to Heal*, p. 306.

**"a big girl"**    Ibid., p. 307.

**"ten million votes"**    Truman, *First Ladies*, p. 138.

**"what is an affair"**    Weidenfeld, *First Lady's Lady*, pp. 173–74.

**"let her have affairs"**    Thomas, *The Presidential Families*, p. 412.

**"the room, please"**    *People Weekly*, August 31, 1992, p. 108.

**"a card game"**    Ibid.

**"a great decision"**    Anthony, *First Ladies 1789–1961*, p. 299.

**"Probably"**    Ford, *A Time to Heal*, p. 307.

**"very upset"**    Truman, *First Ladies*, p. 139.

**"blue jeans"**    terHorst, *Gerald Ford and the Future of the Presidency*, p. 209.

**"without her"**    Weidenfeld, *First Lady's Lady*, p. 241.

**"love an audience"**    Anthony, *First Ladies 1789–1961*, p. 223.

**"shaped my life"**    Ibid., p. 243.

**"things anymore"**    Ford, *The Times of My Life*, pp. 229–30.

**"don't understand"**    Ibid.

**"I can dance to"**    Ibid.

**"loneliest moment"**    Anthony, *First Ladies 1789–1961*, p. 228.

**"what I'd do"**    Hartman, *Palace Politics: An Inside Account of the Ford Years*, p. 294.

**"developed a problem"**    Ford, *The Times of My Life*, p. 122.

**"the matter with her"**    Weidenfeld, *First Lady's Lady*, pp. 272–73.

**"the whole trip"**    Ibid., p. 371.

**"to hide it"**    Ibid.

**"directly at me"**    Ford, *A Time to Heal*, p. 309.

**"to do something"**    Clarke, *American Assassins*, p. 165.

**"an aberration"**    Ford, *A Time to Heal*, p. 309.

**"pandemonium broke out"**    Ibid., p. 311.

**"pick up a gun"**    Clarke, *American Assassins*, p. 165.

**"stuffy in here"**    Nessen, *It Sure Looks Different from the Inside*, p. 186.

**"San Francisco, dear"**    Clarke, *American Assassins*, pp. 186–7.

**"a poor shot"**    Weidenfeld, *First Lady's Lady*, p. 193.

**"I loved it"**    Ford, *The Times of My Life*, p. 211.

**"boring"**    Feldman, Trude B., "Our Private Life at the White House," *Ladies Home Journal*, October 1976; p. 86.

**"modern style"**    Ford, *A Time to Heal*, p. 376.

**"very hard to win"**    Cannon, *Time and Chance*, p. 409.

## Chapter 38.    Jimmy Carter

**"Jimmy who?"**    Aikman, *The Living White House*, p. 18.

**"Of what?"**    Bauer, Stephen M., with Frances Spatz Leighton, *At Ease in the White House*. New York: Birch Lane Press, 1991, p. 216.

**"six years ago"**  Leighton, Frances, *The Search for the Real Ronald Reagan*. New York: Macmillan, 1987, p. 193.
**"all over again"**  Carter, Rosalynn, *First Lady from Plains*. Boston: Houghton Mifflin, 1984, p. 149.
**"$600"**  Carter, *First Lady from Plains*, p. 152.
**"in the White House"**  Ibid.
**"with money all right"**  Blodgett, *At Home with the Presidents*, p. 246.
**"by one-third"**  Kaufman, Burton, *The Presidency of James Earl Carter*. Lawrence: University of Kansas Press, 1993, p. 412.
**"hit the White House"**  Shogan, Robert, *Promises to Keep: Carter's First Hundred Days*. New York: Crowell, 1977, p. 124.
**"we moved in"**  Carter, *First Lady from Plains*, p. 157.
**"with gloves on"**  Ibid., p. 106.
**"shed a few tears"**  Shogan, *Promises to Keep*, p. 115.
**"normal attire"**  Lasky, Victor, *Jimmy Carter: The Man and the Myth*. New York: Richard Marek, 1979, p. 313.
**"own physical work"**  Ibid.
**"so much more"**  Anthony, *First Ladies 1789–1961*, p. 284.
**"endless"**  Carter, *First Lady from Plains*, p. 170.
**"I were courting"**  Ibid.
**"to talk about"**  Ibid., p. 158.
**"It was interesting"**  (author interview).
**"wallpaper back up"**  (author interview).
**"to the White House collection"**  (author interview).
**"didn't seem to care"**  (author interview).
**"from art galleries"**  (author interview).
**"this half century"**  (author interview).
**"I was through"**  Anthony, *First Ladies 1789–1961*, p. 280.
**"about almost everything"**  Anthony, *First Ladies 1789–1961*, p. 296.
**"discuss with her"**  Ibid., p. 276.
**"that's important"**  Ibid., p. 296.
**"be taken seriously"**  Ibid., p. 273.
**"with the other"**  Anthony, *First Ladies 1789–1961*, p. 278.
**"as breathing"**  Ibid., p. 274.
**"through Christ"**  DeGregorio, *The Complete Book of United States Presidents*, p. 620.
**"it will be right"**  Anthony, *First Ladies 1789–1961*, p. 278.
**"to be with us"**  Ibid.
**"most important issue"**  Carter, Jimmy, *Keeping Faith*. New York: Bantam Books, 1982, pp. 29–30.
**"to be seeing this"**  Carter, *First Lady from Plains*, p. 250.
**"not a prude"**  Anthony, *First Ladies 1789–1961*, p. 280.
**"saving money"**  Ibid.
**"to smoke dope"**  Nelson, Willie, with Bud Shrake, *Willie: An Autobiography*. New York: Simon and Schuster, pp. 195–96.
**"to me after that"**  Rush, George, *Confessions of an Ex-Secret Service Agent: The Marty Venker Story*. New York: Donald I. Fine, 1988, p. 124.
**"he was steamed"**  Ibid., p. 147.
**"Don't look back"**  Carter, *First Lady from Plains*, p. 178.
**"they were just there"**  Ibid.
**"into a fiasco"**  Ibid., p. 181.
**"read every page"**  John F. Kennedy Library Lectures, Boston (August 1998).
**"living in sin"**  Shogan, *Promises to Keep*, p. 135.
**"on stuff like that"**  Miller, William, *Yankee from Georgia: The Emergence of Jimmy Carter*. New York: Times Books, 1978, p. 136.
**"it was all over"**  Rush, *Confessions of an Ex-Secret Service Agent: The Marty Venker Story*, p. 127.
**"want to stop"**  Kaufman, *The Presidency of James Earl Carter*, p. 501.
**"steel magnolia"**  Truman, *First Ladies*, p. 146.
**"a lot worse now"**  Ibid., p. 151.
**"me feel good"**  Glad, Betty, *Jimmy Carter: In Search of the Great White House*. New York: Norton, 1980, p. 62.
**"and stubborn"**  Blodgett, *At Home with the Presidents*, p. 242.
**"for both of us"**  Boller, *Presidential Wives*, p. 444.

## Chapter 39.  Ronald Reagan

**"were not an actor"**  D'Souza, Dinesh, *Ronald Reagan*. New York: The Free Press, 1997, p. 44.
**"in this office"**  Ibid., p. 201.
**"want it that way"**  Boller, *Presidential Wives*, p. 450.
**"with that figure"**  Reagan, Nancy, *Nancy*. New York: Berkeley Books, 1980, p. 223.
**"noise reverberates"**  Ibid.
**"represent our country"**  McLellan, Diana, *Ear on Washington*. New York: Arbor House, 1982, p. 225.
**"jeans anymore"**  Boller, *Presidential Wives*, p. 450.
**"don't interfere"**  Anthony, *First Ladies 1789–1961*, p. 350.
**"things in your city"**  Dugger, Ronnie, *On Reagan*. New York: McGraw-Hill, 1983, p. 30.
**"was on last night"**  Cannon, Lou, *President Reagan: The Role of a Lifetime*. New York: Simon and Schuster, 1991, pp. 56–57.
**"take the chance"**  Ibid., p. 120.
**"why wake me up?"**  Slansky, Paul, *The Clothes Have No Emperor*. New York: Simon and Schuster, 1989, pp. 28–29.
**"helluva long wait"**  Cannon, *President Reagan: The Role of a Lifetime*, p. 144.
**"yes he is"**  Schieffer, Bob, and Gary Paul Gates, *The Acting President*. New York: Dutton, 1989, p. 93.
**"substantive matters"**  Ibid., p. 92.
**"decision on people"**  *Vanity Fair*, July 1998, p. 174.
**"I have ever known"**  *Time*, May 16, 1988, p. 33.
**"start the music"**  Graff, *The Presidents: A Reference History*. p. 570.
**"in an ideal world"**  Wills, Gary, *Reagan's America: Innocents at Home*. Garden City, N.Y.: Doubleday, 1987, p. 168.
**"the ball player"**  Schieffer, *The Acting President*, pp. 167–68.
**"a gilded cage"**  *Parade*, August 12, 1990, p. 5.
**"their freedom"**  Reagan, Ronald, *An American Life*. New York: Simon and Schuster, 1990, p. 395.
**"a shopkeeper again"**  Ibid.
**"these things are"**  Noonan, Peggy, *What I Saw at the Revolution*. New York: Random House, 1990, p. 181.
**"its pants down"**  Ibid., p. 181.
**"go stir crazy"**  Reagan, *An American Life*, pp. 396–97.

**"in front of us"**   Ibid., pp. 296–97.
**"one more time"**   Rogin, Paul, *Ronald Reagan: The Movie.* Berkeley: University of California, p. 26.
**"time this happens"**   Ibid., p. 7.
**"to enjoy it"**   Cannon, *President Reagan: The Role of a Lifetime,* p. 528.
**"from him again"**   D'Souza, *Ronald Reagan,* p. 218.
**"I had a tasting"**   Reagan, *Nancy,* p. 226.
**"my name's Ron"**   D'Souza, *Ronald Reagan,* p. 215.
**"special friend"**   Ibid.
**"the little bag"**   Reagan, *An American Life,* p. 274.
**"on her gown"**   Ibid., pp. 390–1.
**"da, all right"**   Noonan, *What I Saw at the Revolution,* p. 115.
**"DESK OF PRESIDENT REAGAN"**   Ibid., p. 173.
**"to need people"**   Blodgett, *At Home with the Presidents,* p. 253.
**"was the greatest"**   Truman, *First Ladies,* p. 162.
**"her good-bye"**   *Vanity Fair,* July 1998 p. 170.
**"well, it's true"**   *Vanity Fair,* July 1998 p. 84.
**"he is my hero"**   *Newsweek,* October 23, 1989 p. 55.
**"look at Ronnie"**   *Newsweek,* October 23, 1989 p. 55.
**"through to him"**   D'Souza, *Ronald Reagan,* p. 8.
**"the next four years"**   Davis, Patti, *The Way I See It.* New York: Putnam, 1992, p. 247.
**"ears everywhere"**   *Vanity Fair,* July 1991 p. 132.
**"what was going on"**   *Vanity Fair,* July 1991 p. 91.
**"even with us"**   D'Souza, *Ronald Reagan,* p. 8.
**"I hope not"**   *New York Times Book Review,* March 26, 1989, p. 8.
**"her own grandchildren"**   Anthony, *First Ladies 1789–1961,* p. 379.
**"the curtain drops"**   D'Souza, *Ronald Reagan,* p. 8.
**"him a hot-dog"**   Reagan, Michael, with Joe Hyams, *On the Outside Looking In.* New York: Zebra Books, 1988, pp. 249–50.
**"didn't put any out"**   Reagan, Maureen, *First Daughter.* Boston: Little, Brown, 1989, p. 323.
**"loved the squirrels"**   Ibid., pp. 325–26.
**"after the weekend"**   Ibid.
**"above the store"**   Reagan, *An American Life,* p. 201.
**"to the White House staff"**   Ibid., p. 225.
**"place a while"**   (author interview).
**"classical decorating"**   (author interview).
**"of the curator"**   (author interview).
**"the White House in years"**   Reagan, *Nancy,* p. 220.
**"fascinating"**   Ibid.
**"and repainting"**   Ibid.
**"rugs in my house"**   Dugger, *On Reagan,* p. 122.
**"beautiful antiques"**   Reagan, *Nancy,* p. 221.
**"half dozen times"**   Ibid.
**"donating the china"**   Truman, *First Ladies,* p. 157.
**"with that one"**   *Vanity Fair,* July 1998, p. 170.
**"did anything wrong"**   Anthony, *First Ladies 1789–1961,* p. 413.
**"mansion is different"**   Grimes, Ann, *Running Mates: The Making of a First Lady.* New York: Morrow, 1990, p. 22.
**"it's phony"**   Truman, *First Ladies,* p. 156.
**"style and elegance"**   Ibid., p. 157.
**"but I can't"**   Ibid.
**"what to do"**   Anthony, *First Ladies 1789–1961,* p. 344.
**"best of everything"**   Truman, *First Ladies,* p. 155.
**"unknown to me"**   Anthony, *First Ladies 1789–1961,* p. 364.
**"make fun of myself"**   *New Republic,* September 16–23, 1985, p. 21.
**"messes up your hair"**   Ibid.
**"lady's outfit"**   Ibid.
**"at the end"**   Ibid.
**"likes to be liked"**   Ibid., p. 21.
**"behind the scenes"**   *Vanity Fair,* July 1998, p. 115.
**"I do"**   *Vanity Fair,* July 1998, 175.
**"her little finger"**   Regan, Donald, *For the Record.* New York: Harcourt Brace Jovanovich, 1988, p. 291.
**"to perfection"**   Anthony, *First Ladies 1789–1961,* p. 370.
**"in the paper"**   Slansky, *The Clothes Have No Emperor,* p. 116.
**"grabs a handful"**   D'Souza, *Ronald Reagan,* p. 203.
**"incredibly organized"**   Ibid., p. 205.
**"on his schedule"**   Ibid., pp. 203–04.
**"did I say that"**   Ibid., p. 237.
**"the scene today"**   Ibid., p. 239.
**"getting fat"**   Ibid., p. 219.
**"not eating that"**   Kessler, *Inside the White House,* p. 111.
**"how it should be"**   Truman, *First Ladies,* p. 164.
**"no one died"**   Rush, *Confessions of an Ex-Secret Service Agent: The Marty Venker Story,* p. 280.
**"Just take off"**   Leamer, Laurence, *Make Believe: The Story of Nancy and Ronald Reagan.* New York: Harper & Row, 1983, p. 308.
**"with a hammer"**   *Congressional Quarterly,* "Reagan's First Year," Washington, D.C. (1982): 4.
**"broke my ribs"**   Leamer, *Make Believe: The Story of Nancy and Ronald Reagan,* p. 308.
**"repeat not hurt"**   Ibid., p. 308.
**"out at GW"**   Ibid.
**"would have died"**   Ibid., p. 320.
**"can't breathe"**   Ibid., p. 308.
**"at the hospital"**   Ibid., p. 312.
**"awful little room"**   Ibid.
**"made out of plastic"**   Ibid., p. 313.
**"forgot to duck"**   Ibid., p. 314.

**"to losing him"**   Abrams, Herbert L., *The President's Been Shot.* New York: Norton, 1992, p. 152.
**"you to shut up"**   Leamer, *Make Believe: The Story of Nancy and Ronald Reagan,* p. 320.
**"and the assassin"**   Rush, *Confessions of an Ex-Secret Service Agent: The Marty Venker Story,* p. 42.
**"for employees"**   Gwynne-Thomas, *The Presidential Families,* p. 442.
**"remember being shot"**   Smith, *White House Doctor,* p. 158.
**"oldest suit"**   D'Souza, *Ronald Reagan,* p. 206.
**"tell me everything"**   Anthony, *First Ladies 1789–1961,* p. 384.
**"want to do?"**   Ibid., p. 484.
**"it was removed"**   Gilbert, *The Mortal Presidency,* p. 226.
**"decisions for them"**   *Time,* May 16, 1988, p. 41.
**"my friend"**   Anthony, *First Ladies 1789–1961,* p. 384.
**"as the last one"**   Regan, *For the Record,* p. 74.
**"of the announcement"**   Quigley, Joan, *"What Does Joan Say?."* New York: Birch Lane Press, 1990, pp. 170–71.
**"the announcement"**   Ibid., pp. 270–71.
**"not sorry I did it"**   Cannon, *President Reagan: The Role of a Lifetime,* pp. 583–84.
**"career making movies"**   *20/20,* ABC, November 17, 1989.
**"bright dawn ahead"**   *New York Times,* November 6, 1994, p. 1.

## Chapter 40.   George Bush

**"high-five sign"**   *New York Times Magazine,* December 18, 1988, p. 18.
**"do to traffic"**   *New York Times,* January 25, 1988, p. A16.
**"going to do that"**   David Frost interview, PBS, January 3, 1992.
**"at the White House"**   (author interview).
**"bloodies"**   *People Weekly,* May 16, 1990, p. 32.
**"what the tune"**   *New York Times,* October 27, 1988, p. B15.
**"sleep feeling"**   Parmet, Herbert, *George Bush.* New York: Simon and Schuster, 1997 p. 364.
**"better shape"**   *Time,* December 5, 1989 p. 24.
**"Reagan administration"**   (author interview).
**"New England colonial"**   Anthony, *First Ladies 1789–1961,* p. 424.
**"opulent at all"**   (author interview).
**"are almost black"**   *People,* May 17, 1990 p. 7.
**"too cold"**   *People,* May 17, 1990, p. 9.
**"about throw up"**   *Time,* January 23, 1989, p. 25.
**"elitist"**   Duffy, Michael, and Don Goodgame, *Marching in Place: The Staus Quo Presidency of George Bush.* New York: Simon and Schuster, 1992, p. 208.
**"by hunger"**   *New York Times,* March 23, 1990, p. A14.
**"chip beef"**   Ibid.
**"more broccoli"**   DeGregorio, *The Complete Book of United States Presidents,* p. 669.
**"ice cream"**   *New York Times,* March 23, 1990, p. A14.
**"to give ground"**   Ibid.
**"puts in a verb"**   *Spy,* August 1988, p. 100.
**"a spleen here"**   *New York Times Magazine,* July 29, 1990, p. 48.
**"Very important"**   *New York Times,* March 9, 1990, p. A14.
**"all that stuff"**   *New York Times,* January 17, 1992, p. A14.
**"serious issues"**   *Spy,* August 1988, p. 102.
**"there in time"**   *New York Times,* February 18, 1992, p. C3.
**"duck to water"**   *Home Office Computing,* February 1992, p. 44.
**"my little friend"**   *People Weekly,* December 25, 1989, p. 42.
**"disciplined"**   *Vogue,* August 1989, p. 316.
**"and comprehend"**   *Ladies Home Journal,* March 1990, p. 231.
**"what she did"**   *New York Times,* September 11, 1997, p. A1.
**"a good time"**   Ibid.
**"see them again"**   *People Weekly,* Spring 1990, p. 32.
**"have real ones"**   Blue, Rose, and Corinne Nadey, *Barbara Bush: First Lady.* Hillside, N.J.: Enslow, 1991, p. 19.
**"for my fans"**   *New York Times,* January 20, 1989, p. A10.
**"off my face"**   *Vogue,* August 1989, p. 314.
**"beauty, anyway"**   *Ladies Home Journal,* March 1990, p. 231.
**"doesn't know that"**   *Ladies Home Journal,* March 1990, p. 159.
**"look so good"**   *Ladies Home Journal,* March 1989, p. 231.
**"George anymore"**   *Ladies Home Journal,* March 1989, p. 230.
**"to cut down on that"**   *Millie's Book as Dictated to Barbara Bush.* New York: Morrow, 1990, p. 18.
**"it was horrible"**   Ibid., p. 174.
**"dog before"**   Truman, *First Ladies,* p. 317.
**"with the kids"**   *Reader's Digest,* April 1989, p. 84.
**"I love that"**   *Ladies Home Journal,* March 1990, p. 229
**"George Bush oriented"**   Parmet, *George Bush,* p. 426.
**"I wish him well"**   *New York Times,* June 2, 1990, p. A1.
**"I feel upstairs"**   Blue, *Barbara Bush: First Lady,*, p. 19.
**"in South Park"**   *Ladies Home Journal,* November 1989, p. 232.
**"morning"**   *Good Housekeeping,* November 1989, p. 255.
**"briefed than I am"**   *Newsweek,* January 23, 1989, p. 25.
**"thirty years"**   Parmet, *George Bush,,* p. 426.
**"a pistol guy"**   *People Weekly,* December 25, 1989, p. 46.
**"TV freak here"**   Duffy, *Marching in Place: The Staus Quo Presidency of George Bush,* p. 44.
**"on the courts"**   *New York Times,* July 5, 1990, p. A14.
**"feel that way"**   Ibid.
**"clears the mind"**   *Sports Illustrated,* August 19, 1991, p. 33.
**"electric polo"**   *Vanity Fair,* August 1992, p. 124.
**"but we're fast"**   Bauer, *At Ease in the White House,* p. 300.
**"camaraderie"**   *Sports Illustrated,* August 19, 1991, pp. 33–34.
**"six or seven"**   Parmet, *George Bush,* p. 391.

"attention to me"  Ibid., p. 461.
"what is right"  Ibid., p. 475.
"up all night"  *New York Times*, January 29, 1991, p. A13.
"spoiled I am"  Parmet, *George Bush*, p. 462.
"couple of times"  Ibid., p. 463.
"they all are"  Ibid., p. 472.
"and for all"  *ABC News*, March 1, 1991.
"be a wimp"  Anthony, *First Ladies 1789–1961*, p. 426.
"of the world"  Parmet, *George Bush*, p. 488.
"try to hide"  Ibid., p. 420.
"don't understand it"  Ibid., p. 469.
"have the drive"  Ibid., p. 488.
"name on it"  *New York Times*, May 8, 1991, p. A21.
"be rejected"  Parmet, *George Bush*, p. 508.
"because I'm not"  *People Weekly*, October 3, 1994, p. 144.
"get you down"  Parmet, *George Bush*, p. 366.
"wonder and majesty"  Ibid., p. 510.
"privileged to hold"  Ibid.
"into real life"  *People Weekly*, October 3, 1994, p. 144.
"not all that bad"  *New York Times*, October 18, 1993, p. A14.
"twenty years old"  *People Weekly*, July 19, 1993, p. 6.

## Chapter 41.   Bill Clinton

"looked great, honey"  *New York Times*, May 24, 1998.
"tell me that"  Morris, Dick, *Behind the Oval Office*. New York: Random House, 1998.
"will you let us in?"  *Art News*, September 1994, p. 141.
"from here on"  Carpozi, George, *Clinton Confidential*. Del Mar, Calif.: Emery Dalton, 1995, p. 455.
"this task force"  Brock, David, *The Seduction of Hillary Rodham Clinton*. New York: Free Press, 1996, p. 326.
"invasion of Normandy"  Walker, Martin, *The President We Deserve*. New York: Crown, 1996, p. 218.
"health care effort"  Brock, *The Seduction of Hillary Rodham Clinton*, p. 326.
"need our people in"  Milton, Joyce, *The First Partner*. New York: Morrow, 1999, p. 289.
"what she wanted"  Brock, *The Seduction of Hillary Rodham Clinton*, p. 383.
"beating Hillary took"  Morris, *Behind the Oval Office*, p. 287.
"took some time"  (author interview).
"quarters were small"  (author interview).
"bring much else"  (author interview).
"yellow or not"  (author interview).
"not Victorian"  (author interview).
"room look larger"  (author interview).
"and Grant's time"  (author interview).
"enough bookshelves"  (author interview).
"load of misinformation"  (author interview).
"show more energy"  (author interview).
"the Redskins Room"  (author interview).
"especially at night"  (author interview).
"America at its best"  (author interview).
"hundred years later"  (author interview).
"beautiful granite"  (author interview).
"in the White House"  (author interview).
"gets enough light"  *Art News*, September 1994, p. 138.
"beauty unmatched"  *People Weekly*, March 6, 1995.
"into the Oval Office"  *New York Times*, September 11, 1997.
"trained pigs"  Aldrich, Gary, *Unltmited Access*. Washington, D.C.: Regnery, 1996, p. 90.
"grab those bags"  Milton, *The First Partner*, p. 249.
"day at the White House"  *Newsweek*, December 25, 1995, p. 50.
"MINUTES LATE"  *Newsweek*, May 31, 1993, p. 4.
"STANDARD TIME"  *Newsweek*, May 31, 1993, p. 4.
"managing himself"  Brummett, John, *High Wire*. New York: Hyperion, p. 44.
"the wrong one"  Stephanopoulos, George, *All Too Human*. Boston: Little, Brown, 1991, p. 201.
"to the Smithsonian"  *Esquire*, August 1993, p. 86.
"the campus"  Milton, *The First Partner*, p. 263.
"in the Oval"  *New York Times*, July 26, 1993, p. A1.
"learn to wait"  Kessler, *Inside the White House*, p. 224.
"not my deal"  *New York Times*, March 5, 1994.
"venison, rabbit"  *The Washingtonian*, July 1997, p. 53.
"fois gras"  *New York Times*, February 11, 1998.
"like normal food"  Milton, *The First Partner*, p. 338.
"with a crowbar"  *New York Times*, February 11, 1998.
"to Mrs. Clinton"  *New York Times*, May 24, 1998.
"We won"  Milton, *The First Partner*, p. 263.
"I would race around"  Ibid., p. 339.
"on the property"  *New York Times*, June 7, 1997.
"and third floors"  *Parade*, July 4, 1995, p. 4.
"do my own laundry"  *People Weekly*, November 29, 1993, p. 70.
"mom's too busy"  Walker, *The President We Deserve*, pp. 198–99.
"wise, briefly"  *New York Times*, June 7, 1997, p. 56.
"*Good Night, Moon*"  *New York Times*, June 7, 1997, p. 57.
"penal system"  Kessler, *Inside the White House*, p. 243.

# Index